Microsoft®
Office 2000

Introductory Course™

William R. Pasewark, Sr., Ph.D.
Professor Emeritus, Texas Tech University
Office Management Consultant

William R. Pasewark, Jr., Ph.D., C.P.A.
University of Houston

VISIT US ON THE INTERNET
www.swep.com

South-Western Educational Publishing
an International Thomson Publishing company I(T)P®
www.thomson.com

Cincinnati • Albany, NY • Belmont, CA • Bonn • Boston • Detroit • Johannesburg • London • Madrid
Melbourne • Mexico City • New York • Paris • Singapore • Tokyo • Toronto • Washington

Library of Congress Cataloging-in-Publication Data

Pasewark, William Robert.
   Microsoft Office 2000 introductory course / William R.
Pasewark, Sr., William R. Pasewark, Jr.
   p. cm.
  Includes index.
  ISBN 0-538-68824-6 (sprial bound)
  ISBN 0-538-68846-7 (softcover)
  ISBN 0-538-68825-4 (perfect bound)
  1. Microsoft Office. 2. Business—Computer programs. I. Pasewark,
William R., 1956- II. Title.
  HF5548.4.M525 P376 1999
  005.369—dc21

99-23219
CIP

Team Leader: Karen Schmohe
Managing Editor: Carol Volz
Project Manager: Dave Lafferty
Production Coordinator: Angela McDonald

Art Coordinator: Mike Broussard
Consulting Editor: Custom Editorial Productions, Inc.
Marketing Manager: Larry Qualls
Production: Custom Editorial Productions, Inc.

Copyright © 2000

By SOUTH-WESTERN EDUCATIONAL PUBLISHING/ITP
Cincinnati, Ohio

ISBN: 0-538-68824-6, Spiral Cover Text
ISBN: 0-538-68846-7, Soft Cover Text
ISBN: 0-538-68825-4, Soft Cover Text/Data CD Package

1 2 3 4 5 6 DR 03 02 01 00 99

Printed in the United States of America

I(T)P®

International Thomson Publishing

South-Western Educational Publishing is a division of International Thomson Publishing, Inc. The ITP® registered trademark is used under license.

Microsoft® is a registered trademark of Microsoft Corporation.

The names of these and all commercially available software mentioned herein are used for identification purposes only and may be trademarks or registered trademarks of their respective owners. South-Western Educational Publishing disclaims any affiliation, association, connection with, sponsorship, or endorsement by such owners.

WARNING: Reproducing the pages of this book by any means may be a violation of applicable copyright laws. Illegal copying robs authors and publishers of their proper revenues and makes educational materials expensive for everyone. South-Western Educational Publishing is interested in knowing about violations of copyright laws. If you know of materials being illegally copied and distributed, please contact us.

Microsoft and the Office logo are either registered trademarks or trademarks of the Microsoft Corporation in the United States and/or other countries. South-Western Educational Publishing is an independent entity from Microsoft Corporation and not affiliated with Microsoft Corporation in any manner. This text may be used in assisting students to prepare for a Microsoft Office User Specialist exam (MOUS). Neither Microsoft Corporation, its designated review company, nor South-Western Educational Publishing warrants that use of this publication will ensure passing the relevant MOUS exam.

Open a Window to the Future!
With these (exciting new products)
from South-Western!

Our exciting new **Microsoft Office 2000** books will provide
everything needed to master this software. Other books include:

 NEW! Microsoft® Office 2000 for Windows® Introductory Course by Pasewark & Pasewark
75+ hours of instruction for beginning through intermediate features

0-538-68824-6	Text, Hard Spiral Bound
0-538-68825-4	Text, Perfect Bound, packaged with Data CD-ROM
0-538-68826-2	Activities Workbook
0-538-68827-0	Electronic Instructor Package (Manual and CD-ROM)
0-538-68934-X	Testing CD-ROM Package

 NEW! Microsoft® Office 2000 for Windows® Advanced Course by Cable, Morrison, & Skintik
75+ hours of instruction for intermediate through advanced features

0-538-68828-9	Text, Hard Spiral Bound
0-538-68829-7	Text, Perfect Bound, packaged with Data CD-ROM
0-538-68830-0	Activities Workbook
0-538-68831-9	Electronic Instructor Package (Manual and CD-ROM)
0-538-68934-X	Testing CD-ROM Package

 NEW! Microsoft® Word 2000 for Windows® Complete Tutorial by Morrison & Pasewark
75+ hours of beginning through advanced features

0-538-68832-7	Text, Hard Spiral Bound
0-538-68833-5	Text, Perfect Bound, packaged with Data CD-ROM
0-538-68834-3	Activities Workbook
0-538-68835-1	Electronic Instructor Package (Manual and CD-ROM)
0-538-68934-X	Testing CD-ROM Package

 NEW! Microsoft® Excel 2000 for Windows® Complete Tutorial by Cable & Pasewark
35+ hours of beginning through advanced features

0-538-68836-X	Text, Soft, Spiral Bound
0-538-68837-8	Text, Perfect Bound, packaged with Data CD-ROM
0-538-68838-6	Activities Workbook
0-538-68839-4	Electronic Instructor Package (Manual and CD-ROM)
0-538-68934-X	Testing CD-ROM Package

 NEW! Microsoft® Access 2000 for Windows® Complete Tutorial by Cable & Pasewark
35+ hours of beginning through advanced features

0-538-68841-6	Text, Soft, Spiral Bound
0-538-68842-4	Text, Perfect Bound, packaged with Data CD-ROM
0-538-68843-2	Activities Workbook
0-538-68844-0	Electronic Instructor Package (Manual and CD-ROM)
0-538-68934-X	Testing CD-ROM Package

A new feature available for these products is the **Electronic Instructor**,
which includes a printed Instructor's manual and a CD-ROM.
The CD-ROM contains tests, lesson plans, all data and solutions files,
SCANS correlations, portfolio analysis, scheduling, and more!

South-Western
Educational Publishing

PREFACE

You will find much helpful material in this introductory section. The *How to Use This Book* pages give you a visual summary of the kinds of information you will find in the text. The *What's New* section summarizes features new in this version of Microsoft Office. Be sure to review *Guide for Using This Book* to learn about the terminology and conventions used in preparing the pages and to find out what supporting materials are available for use with this book. If you are interested in pursuing certification as a Microsoft Office User Specialist (MOUS), read the information on *The Microsoft Office User Specialist Program.*

An Ideal Book for Anyone

Because computers are such an important subject for all learners, instructors need the support of a well-designed, educationally sound textbook that is supported by strong ancillary instructional materials. *Microsoft Office 2000: Introductory Course* is just such a book.

The textbook includes features that *make learning easy and enjoyable*—yet challenging—for learners. It is also designed with many features that *make teaching easy and enjoyable* for you. Comprehensive, yet flexible, *Microsoft Office 2000: Introductory Course* is adaptable for a wide variety of class-time schedules.

The text includes a wide range of learning experiences from activities with one or two commands to simulations and case studies that challenge and sharpen learners' problem-solving skills. This book is ideal for computer courses with learners who have varying abilities and previous computer experiences. A companion text, *Microsoft Office 2000: Advanced Course*, is available for a second course.

The lessons in this course contain the following features designed to promote learning:

- Objectives that specify goals students should achieve by the end of each lesson.

- Concept text that explores in detail each new feature.

- Screen captures that help to illustrate the concept text.

- Step-by-Step exercises that allow students to practice the features just introduced.

- Summaries that review the concepts in the lesson.

- Review Questions that test students on the concepts covered in the lesson.

- Projects that provide an opportunity for students to apply concepts they have learned in the lesson.

- Critical Thinking Activities that encourage students to use knowledge gained in the lesson or from PowerPoint's Help system to solve specific problems.

Each unit also contains a unit review with the following features:

- A Command Summary that reviews menu commands and toolbar shortcuts introduced in the unit.

- Review Questions covering material from all lessons in the unit.

- Applications that give students a chance to apply many of the skills learned in the unit.

- An On-the-Job Simulation that proposes real-world jobs a student can complete using the skills learned in the unit.

Acknowledgments

For committing themselves to produce a quality book that will help learners understand computers and for working effectively with each other, the authors gratefully thank the following colleagues for their fine work:

Laura Melton for her significant experience as a writer and editor.

Rhonda Davis for applying her recent computer business experiences to producing this book.

Scott Pasewark for his computer technology abilities.

Carolyn Denny, Jan Stogner, and Beth Wadsworth for completing a variety of tasks.

Billie Conley, computer instructor at Lubbock High School, for updating the Computer Concepts appendix.

Many professional South-Western sales representatives make educationally sound presentations to instructors about our books. We appreciate their valuable work as "bridges" between the authors and instructors.

Authors' Commitment

In writing *Microsoft Office 2000: Introductory Course,* the authors dedicated themselves to creating a comprehensive and appealing instructional package to make teaching and learning an interesting, rewarding, and challenging experience.

With these instructional materials, instructors can create learning experiences so learners can successfully master concepts, knowledge, and skills that will help them live better lives—now and in the future.

About the Authors

William R. Pasewark, Jr., Ph. D., CPA, teaches accounting at the University of Houston and computer courses for United States and foreign business executives. He has worked for a bank and an oil company.

William R. Pasewark, Sr., Ph. D., has authored more than 90 books, including Canadian adaptations and Spanish and Danish translations. He is a management consultant and was the 1972 Texas Business Teacher of the Year.

The Pasewarks won the Textbook and Academic Authors Association *Texty Award* for the best computer book in 1994.

How to Use This Book

What makes a good computer instructional text? Sound pedagogy and the most current, complete materials. That is what you will find in *Microsoft Office 2000: Introductory Course*. Not only will you find an inviting layout, but also many features to enhance learning.

Objectives—Objectives are listed at the beginning of each lesson, along with a suggested time for completion of the lesson. This allows you to look ahead to what you will be learning and to pace your work.

SCANS (Secretary's Commission on Achieving Necessary Skills)—The U.S. Department of Labor has identified the school-to-careers competencies. The eight workplace competencies and foundation skills are identified in exercises where they apply. More information on SCANS can be found on the Electronic Instructor.

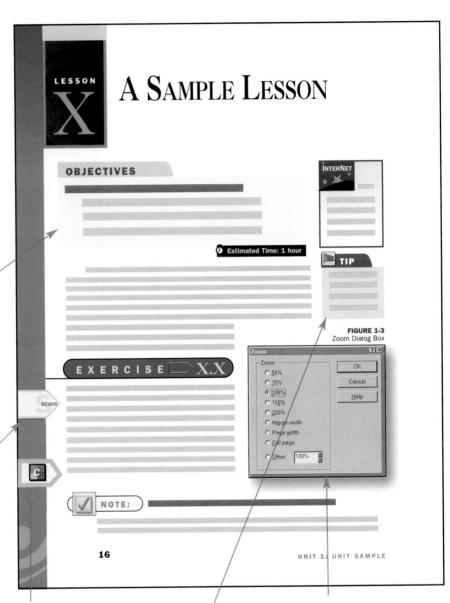

FIGURE 1-3
Zoom Dialog Box

Certification Icon—This icon is shown wherever a criteria for Microsoft Office User Specialist (MOUS) certification is covered in the lesson. A correlation table with page numbers is provided elsewhere in this book and on the Electronic Instructor.

Marginal Boxes—These boxes provide additional information for Hot Tips, fun facts (Did You Know?), Concept Builders, Internet Web Sites, Extra Challenges activities, and Teamwork ideas.

Enhanced Screen Shots—Screen shots now come to life on each page with color and depth.

How to Use This Book

Summary—At the end of each lesson, you will find a summary to prepare you to complete the end-of-lesson activities.

Review Questions—Review material at the end of each lesson and each unit enables you to prepare for assessment of the content presented.

Lesson Projects—End-of-lesson hands-on application of what has been learned in the lesson allows you to actually apply the techniques covered.

Critical Thinking Activities—Each lesson gives you an opportunity to apply creative analysis and use the Help system to solve problems.

Command Summary—At the end of each unit, a command summary is provided for quick reference.

End-of-Unit Applications—End-of-unit hands-on application of concepts learned in the unit provides opportunity for a comprehensive review.

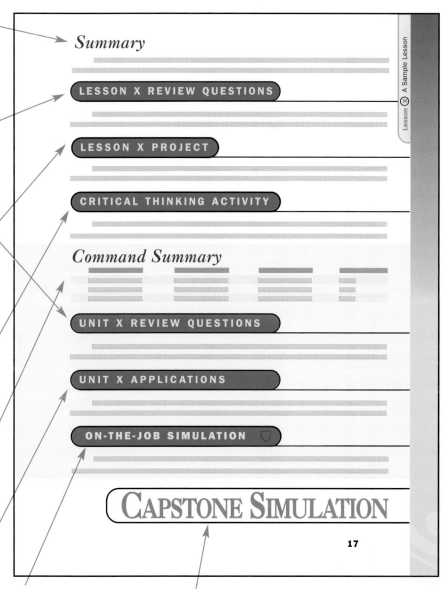

Summary

LESSON X REVIEW QUESTIONS

LESSON X PROJECT

CRITICAL THINKING ACTIVITY

Command Summary

UNIT X REVIEW QUESTIONS

UNIT X APPLICATIONS

ON-THE-JOB SIMULATION

CAPSTONE SIMULATION

17

Lesson ⊗ A Sample Lesson

On-the-Job Simulation—A realistic simulation runs throughout the text at the end of each unit, reinforcing the material covered in the unit.

Capstone Simulation—Another simulation appears at the end of the text, to be completed after all the lessons have been covered, to give you an opportunity to apply all of the skills you have learned and see them come together in one application.

Appendices—Appendices include Microsoft Office User Specialist Program, Windows 98, and Computer Concepts.

WHAT'S NEW

Microsoft Office 2000 has many features that help you to be more productive and to enjoy using your computer. Some of the new features covered in this Introductory Course are listed below. Other features are identified and taught in the companion book, *Microsoft Office 2000: Advanced Course.*

- New programs include Publisher and FrontPage.
- Software is easier to install, use, and manage.
- Office 2000 identifies and corrects installation and operating errors.
- All Office files can be saved directly to the Web.
- Office 2000 is designed to allow multiple user collaboration on intranets and the Web.
- Tables are easily placed within a document and text can be wrapped around them.
- Office 2000 detects a document's language and automatically initiates proofing tools specific to that language.
- The Slide, Outline, and Notes views in PowerPoint are combined into a single screen.
- In Outlook, the Outlook Today screen summarizes information about today's activities from Calendar, Tasks, and Mail.
- You can e-mail directly from each program.

START-UP CHECKLIST

HARDWARE

Minimum Configuration

- ✓ PC with Pentium processor
- ✓ 32 Mb RAM
- ✓ Hard disk with 200 Mb free for typical installation
- ✓ CD-ROM drive
- ✓ VGA monitor with video adapter
- ✓ Microsoft Mouse, IntelliMouse, or compatible pointing device
- ✓ 9600 or higher baud modem
- ✓ Printer

Recommended Configuration

- ✓ Pentium PC with greater than 32 Mb RAM
- ✓ Super VGA 256-color monitor
- ✓ 28,800 baud modem
- ✓ Multimedia capability
- ✓ For e-mail, Microsoft Mail, Internet SMTP/POP3, or other MAPI-compliant messaging software

SOFTWARE

- ✓ Windows 95, 98, or NT Workstation 4.0 with Service Pack 3.0 installed
- ✓ For Web collaboration and Help files, Internet Explorer 5 browser or Windows 98

JOIN US ON THE INTERNET

WWW: **http://www.thomson.com**
E-MAIL: **findit@kiosk.thomson.com**

South-Western Educational Publishing is a partner in *thomson.com,* an on-line portal for the products, services, and resources available from International Thomson Publishing (ITP). Through our site, users can search catalogs, examine subject-specific resource centers, and subscribe to electronic discussion lists.

South-Western Educational Publishing is also a reseller of commercial software products. See our printed catalog or view this page at:

http://www.swep.com/swep/comp_ed/com_sft.html

For information on our products visit our World Wide Web site at:

http://www.swep.com

To join the South-Western Computer Education discussion list, send an e-mail message to: **majordomo@list.thomson.com.** Leave the subject field blank, and in the body of your message key: SUBSCRIBE SOUTH-WESTERN-COMPUTER-EDUCATION <your e-mail address>.

A service of I(T)P®

GUIDE FOR USING THIS BOOK

Please read this Guide before starting work. The time you spend now will save you much more time later and will make your learning faster, easier, and more pleasant.

Terminology

This text uses the term *keying* to mean entering text into a computer using the keyboard. *Keying* is the same as "keyboarding" or "typing."

Text means words, numbers, and symbols that are printed.

Conventions

The different type styles used in this book have special meanings. They will save you time because you will soon automatically recognize from the type style the nature of the text you are reading and what you will do.

WHAT YOU WILL DO	TYPE STYLE	EXAMPLE
Text you will key	**Bold**	Key **Don't litter** rapidly.
Individual keys you will press	**Bold**	Press **Enter** to insert a blank line.

WHAT YOU WILL SEE	TYPE STYLE	EXAMPLE
Filenames in book	**Bold upper and lowercase**	Open **IW Step2-1** from the student data files.
Glossary terms in book	***Bold and italics***	The ***menu bar*** contains menu titles.
Words on screen	*Italics*	Highlight the word *pencil* on the screen.
Menus and commands	**Bold**	Choose **Open** from the **File** menu.
Options and areas in dialog boxes	*Italics*	Key a new name in the *File name* box.

Data CD-ROM

All data files necessary for the Step-by-Step exercises, end-of-lesson Projects, end-of-unit Applications and Jobs, and Capstone Simulation exercises for this book are located on the Data CD-ROM supplied with this text. Data files for the *Activities Workbook* are also stored on the Data CD-ROM.

Data files are named according to the first exercise in which they are used and the unit of this textbook in which they are used. A data file for a Step-by-Step exercise in the Introduction to Microsoft Word unit would have a filename such as **IW Step1-1**. This particular filename identifies a data file used in the first Step-by-Step exercise in Lesson 1. Other data files have the following formats:

- End-of-lesson projects: **IW Project1-1**
- End-of-unit applications: **IW App2**
- On-the-Job Simulation jobs: **IW Job3**

Electronic Instructor® CD-ROM

The *Electronic Instructor* contains a wealth of instructional material you can use to prepare for teaching Office 2000. The CD-ROM stores the following information:

- Both the data and solution files for this course.

- Quizzes for each lesson and unit, and answers to the quizzes, lesson and unit review questions, and activities workbook.

- Copies of the lesson plans that appear in the instructor's manual, as well as student lesson plans that can help to guide students through the lesson text and exercises.

- Copies of the figures that appear in the student text, which can be used to prepare transparencies.

- Grids that show skills required for Microsoft Office User Specialist (MOUS) certification and the SCANS workplace competencies and skills.

- Suggested schedules for teaching the lessons in this course.

- Additional instructional information about individual learning strategies, portfolios, and career planning, and a sample Internet contract.

- PowerPoint presentations showing Office 2000 features for Word, Excel, Access, and PowerPoint.

Additional Activities and Questions

An *Activities Workbook* is available to supply additional paper-and-pencil exercises and hands-on computer applications for each unit of this book. In addition, testing software is available separately with a customizable test bank specific for this text.

SCANS

The Secretary's Commission on Achieving Necessary Skills (SCANS) from the U.S. Department of Labor was asked to examine the demands of the workplace and whether new learners are capable of meeting those demands. Specifically, the Commission was directed to advise the Secretary on the level of skills required to enter employment.

SCANS workplace competencies and foundation skills have been integrated into *Microsoft Office 2000: Introductory Course*. The workplace competencies are identified as 1) ability to use *resources*, 2) *interpersonal* skills, 3) ability to work with *information*, 4) understanding of *systems*, and 5) knowledge and understanding of *technology*. The foundation skills are identified as 1) basic communication skills, 2) thinking skills, and 3) personal qualities.

Exercises in which learners must use a number of these SCANS competencies and foundation skills are marked in the text with the SCANS icon.

THE MICROSOFT OFFICE USER SPECIALIST PROGRAM

APPROVED COURSEWARE

What Is Certification?

The logo on the cover of this book indicates that the book is officially certified by Microsoft Corporation at the **Core** user skill level for Office 2000 in Word, Excel, Access, and PowerPoint. This certification is part of the **Microsoft Office User Specialist (MOUS)** program that validates your skills as knowledgeable of Microsoft Office.

Why Is Getting Certified Important?

Upon completing the lessons in this book, you will be prepared to take a test that could qualify you as a **Core** user of Microsoft Office in Word, Excel, Access, and PowerPoint. This can benefit you in many ways. For example, you can show an employer that you have received certified training in Microsoft Office 2000, or you can advance further in education or in your organization. Earning this certification makes you more competitive with the knowledge and skills that you possess. It is also personally satisfying to know that you have reached a skill level that is validated by Microsoft Corporation.

You can also be certified as an **Expert** user of Microsoft Office. The difference between Expert and Core users is the level of competency. Core users can perform a wide range of basic tasks. Expert users can do all those same tasks, plus more advanced tasks, such as special formatting.

Where Does Testing Take Place?

To be certified, you will need to take an exam from a third-party testing company called an **Authorization Certification Testing Center**. Call **800-933-4493** to find the location of the testing center nearest you. Learn more about the criteria for testing and what is involved. Tests are conducted on different dates throughout the calendar year.

South-Western Educational Publishing has developed an entire line of training materials suitable for Microsoft Office certification. To learn more, call **800-824-5179**. Also, visit our Web site at **www.swep.com**.

TABLE OF CONTENTS

UNIT — INTRODUCTION

UNIT — INTRODUCTION TO MICROSOFT WORD

UNIT   INTRODUCTION TO MICROSOFT EXCEL

UNIT   INTRODUCTION TO MICROSOFT ACCESS

UNIT INTRODUCTION TO MICROSOFT POWERPOINT

UNIT

INTRODUCTION

lesson 1 — 1.5 hrs.

Office 2000 Basics
and the Internet

Estimated Time for Unit: 1.5 hours

OFFICE 2000 BASICS AND THE INTERNET

OBJECTIVES

Upon completion of this lesson, you should be able to:

■ Explain the concept of an integrated software package.

■ Start an Office application from Windows 98.

■ Open an existing document.

■ Save and close an Office document.

■ Know the shortcuts for opening recently used documents.

■ Use the Help system.

■ Use the Office Assistant.

■ Quit an Office application.

■ Access the Internet and use a Web browser.

⏱ Estimated Time: 1.5 hours

Introduction to Office 2000

Office 2000 is an integrated software package. An ***integrated software package*** is a program that combines several computer applications into one program. Office 2000 consists of a word processor application, a spreadsheet application, a database application, a presentation application, a schedule/organization application, a desktop publishing application and a Web page application.

The word processor application (Word) enables you to create documents such as letters and reports. The spreadsheet application (Excel) lets you work with numbers to prepare items such as budgets or to determine loan payments. The database application (Access) organizes information such as addresses or inventory items. The presentation application (PowerPoint) can be used to create slides, outlines,

🌐 Web Site

For more information on Microsoft Word and other Microsoft products, visit Microsoft's Web site at *http://www.microsoft.com.*

speaker's notes, and audience handouts. The schedule/organization application (Outlook) increases your efficiency by keeping track of e-mail, appointments, tasks, contacts, events, and to-do lists. The desktop publishing application helps you design professional-looking documents. The Web page application (FrontPage) enables you to create and maintain your own Web site.

Because Office 2000 is an integrated program, the applications can be used together. For example, numbers from a spreadsheet can be included in a letter created in the word processor or in a presentation.

Starting an Office 2000 Application

An Office 2000 application can be started from the Programs menu on the Start menu or directly from the Start menu.

OPENING AN OFFICE APPLICATION FROM THE PROGRAMS MENU

To open an Office application from the Programs menu, click the Start button, select Programs, and then click the name of the application you want to open.

OPENING AN OFFICE APPLICATION FROM THE START MENU

To open an Office application and create a new blank document within the application at the same time, click the Start button. Then, click New Office Document on the Start menu. On the General tab of the New Office Document dialog box that appears (see Figure 1-1), double-click the icon for the type of blank document you want to create. The application for that type of document opens and a new blank document is created. For example, if you double-click the Blank Presentation icon, PowerPoint will open and a blank presentation will be displayed on the screen.

Hot Tip

If the Microsoft Office Shortcut Bar is installed, you can use it to open an Office application and create a blank document at the same time.

Concept Builder

You can also open a new file from within an application by choosing **New** on the **File** menu. The New dialog box appears, which is very similar to the New Office Document dialog box.

FIGURE 1-1
General tab in the New Office Document dialog box

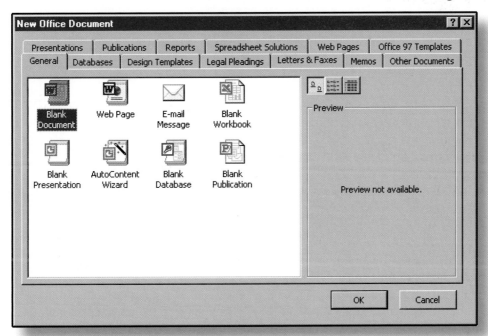

1. Click the **Start** button to open the **Start** menu.

2. Click **Programs**, and then **Microsoft Power-Point**. PowerPoint opens.

3. Click **Cancel** to close the PowerPoint dialog box.

4. Click the **Start** button; then, click **New Office Document**.

5. The New Office Document dialog box appears, as shown in Figure 1-1.

6. Click the **General** tab, if it is not already selected.

7. Double-click the **Blank Document** icon. Word starts and a blank document appears. Leave Word and PowerPoint open for use in the next Step-by-Step.

Opening, Saving, and Closing Office Documents

In Office applications, you *open*, *save*, and *close* files in the same way. Opening a file means loading a file from a disk onto your screen. Saving a file stores it on disk. Closing a file removes it from the screen.

OPENING AN EXISTING DOCUMENT

To open an existing document, you can choose Open on an application's File menu, which displays the Open dialog box (see Figure 1-2). Or, choose Open Office Document on the Start menu, which displays the Open Office Document dialog box.

FIGURE 1-2
Open dialog box

The Open (or Open Office Document) dialog box enables you to open a file from any available disk and folder. The Look in box, near the top of the dialog box, is where you locate the disk drive that contains the file you want to open. Below that is a list that shows you the folders or resources that are on the disk. Double-click a folder to see what files and folders are contained within. To see all the files or office documents in the folder instead of just those created with a particular application, choose All Files or Office Files from the *Files of type* drop-down list box located near the bottom of the dialog box. The bar on the left side of the dialog box provides a shortcut for accessing some of the common places to store documents.

When you have located and selected the file you want to open, click the Open button. If you click the down arrow next to the Open button, a menu is displayed. You can choose to open the document as a ***read-only file*** that can be viewed but not changed, open a copy of the document, or open the document in your browser if it is saved in Web page format.

STEP-BY-STEP ▷ 1.2

1. With Word on the screen, choose **Open** on the **File** menu. The Open dialog box appears, as shown in Figure 1-2.

2. Click the down arrow to the right of the *Look in* box to display the available disk drives.

3. Click the drive that contains your student data files and locate the **Employees** folder, as shown in Figure 1-3.

4. Double-click the **Employees** folder. The folders within the Employees folder appear (see Figure 1-4).

5. Double-click the **Rita** folder. The names of the Word files in the Rita folder are displayed.

6. Click the down arrow at the right of the *Files of type* box and select **All Files**. The names of all files in the Rita folder are displayed.

7. Click **Schedule Memo** to select it and then click **Open** to open the file.

8. Leave the file open for the next Step-by-Step.

FIGURE 1-3
Look in box

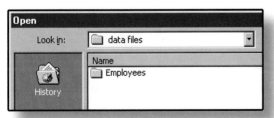

FIGURE 1-4
Employees folder

You can see how folders can help organize and identify documents. The Rita folder also contains a spreadsheet with the work schedule for the first two weeks in September. In the next Step-by-Step, you will start Excel, the spreadsheet application of Office 2000, and open the spreadsheet that goes with the memo.

S TEP-BY-STEP ▷ 1.3

1. Click the **Start** button.

2. Click **Open Office Document**.

3. Click the down arrow at the right of the *Look in* box and click the drive that contains the student data files.

4. Double-click the **Employees** folder; then, double-click the **Rita** folder.

5. Double-click **September Schedule** to open the file. The Office 2000 spreadsheet application, Excel, opens and *September Schedule* appears on the screen.

6. Leave the file open for the next Step-by-Step.

Saving a File

Saving is done two ways. The Save command saves a file on a disk using the current name. The Save As command saves a file on a disk using a new name. The Save As command can also be used to save a file to a new location.

FILENAMES

Unlike programs designed for the early versions of Windows and DOS, filenames are not limited to eight characters. With Windows 98, a filename may contain up to 255 characters and may include spaces. However, you will rarely need this many characters to name a file. Name a file with a descriptive name that will remind you of what the file contains. The authors of this book have chosen names that are descriptive and easy to use. The filename can include most characters found on the keyboard with the exception of those shown in Table 1-1.

TABLE 1-1
Characters that cannot be used in filenames

CHARACTER	NAME	CHARACTER	NAME
*	asterisk	<	less than sign
\	backslash	.	period
[]	brackets	;	semicolon
:	colon	/	slash
,	comma	"	quotation mark
=	equal sign	?	question mark
>	greater than sign	|	vertical bar

S TEP-BY-STEP ▷ 1.4

1. *September Schedule* should be on the screen from the last Step-by-Step.

2. Choose **Save As** on the **File** menu. The Save As dialog box appears, as shown in Figure 1-5.

IN-6

3. In the *File name* box, key **Sept Work Sched**, followed by your initials.

4. Click the down arrow to the right of the *Save in* box and choose where you want to save the file.

5. Choose **Save** to save the file with the new name.

6. Leave the document open for the next Step-by-Step.

FIGURE 1-5
Save As dialog box

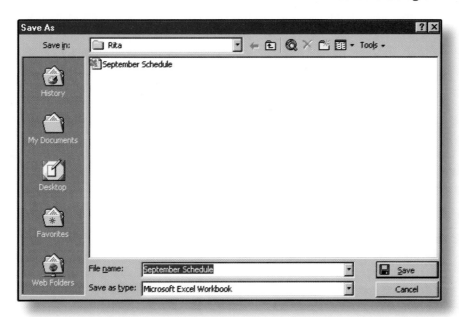

Closing an Office Document

You can close an Office document either by choosing Close on the File menu or by clicking the Close button on the right side of the menu bar. If you close a file, the application will still be open and ready for you to open or create another file.

S TEP-BY-STEP ▷ 1.5

1. Choose **Close** on the **File** menu. *Sept Work Sched* closes.

2. Click the **Microsoft Word** button on the taskbar to make it active. *Schedule Memo* should be displayed.

3. Click the **Close** button (X) in the right corner of the menu bar to close *Schedule Memo*.

4. Leave Word open for the next Step-by-Step.

Hot Tip

When you first use an Office 2000 application, the menus only display the basic commands. To see an expanded menu with all the commands, click the arrows at the bottom of the menu. As you work, the menus are adjusted to display the commands used most frequently, adding a command when you choose it and dropping a command when it hasn't been used recently.

Shortcuts for Loading Recently Used Files

Office offers you two shortcuts for opening recently used files. The first shortcut is to click Documents on the Start menu. A menu will open listing the 15 most recently used documents. To open one of the recently used files, double-click on the file you wish to open.

The second shortcut can be found on each Office application's File menu. The bottom part of the File menu shows the filenames of the four most recently opened documents. The filename with the number 1 beside it is the most recently opened document. When a new file is opened, each filename moves down to make room for the new number 1 file. To open one of the files, you simply choose it as if it were a menu selection. If the document you are looking for is not on the File menu, use Open to load it from the disk.

> **Hot Tip**
>
> If the file is on a floppy disk, you must be sure that the correct disk is in the drive.

Office 2000 Help

This lesson has covered only a few of the many features of Office 2000 applications. For additional information, use the Office 2000 Help system as a quick reference when you are unsure about a function. To get specific help about topics relating to the application you are using, access help from the Help menu on the menu bar. Then, from the Help dialog box, shown in Figure 1-6, you can choose to see a table of contents displaying general topics and subtopics, key a question in the Answer Wizard, or search the Help system using the Index.

Many topics in the Help program are linked. A *link* is represented by colored, underlined text. By clicking a link, the user "jumps" to a linked document that contains additional information.

FIGURE 1-6
Help feature

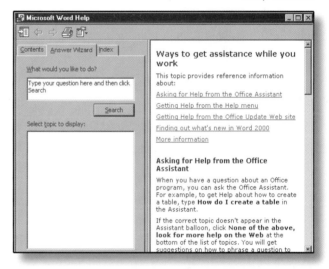

Using the buttons on the toolbar controls the display of information. The Hide button removes the left frame of the help window from view. The Show button will restore it. Back and Forward buttons allow you to move back and forth between previously displayed help entries. Use the Print button to print the help information displayed. The Options button offers navigational choices, as well as options to customize, refresh, and print help topics.

The Contents tab is useful if you want to browse through the topics by category. Click a book icon to see additional help topics. Click a question mark to display detailed help information in the right frame of the help window.

STEP-BY-STEP ▷ 1.6

1. Open the Word Help program by choosing **Microsoft Word Help** on the **Help** menu.

2. Click the **Hide** button on the toolbar to remove the left frame.

3. Click the **Show** button to display it again.

4. The Answer Wizard tab is displayed and the right frame displays *Ways to get assistance*

while you work. Your screen should appear similar to Figure 1-6.

5. Click the **Getting Help from the Help menu** link in the right frame.

6. Read the help window and leave it open for the next Step-by-Step.

Hot Tip

If the Office Assistant appears, turn it off by clicking **Options** in the balloon, clearing the *Use Office Assistant* check box, and clicking **OK**.

Using the Answer Wizard tab, you can key in a question about what you would like to do. Then click one of the topics that appears in the box below to display the information in the right frame.

When you want to search for help on a particular topic, use the Index tab and key in a word. Windows will search alphabetically through the list of help topics to try to find an appropriate match, as shown in Figure 1-7. Double-click a topic to see it explained in the right frame of the help window.

FIGURE 1-7
Index tab of the Help system

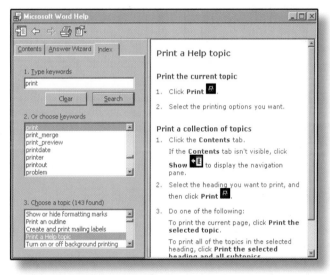

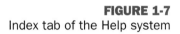

1. Click the **Index** tab.

2. Key **print** in the *Type keywords* box and click **Search**.

3. In the *Choose a topic* box, scroll down until you find **Print a Help topic** and click it to display information in the right frame as shown in Figure 1-7.

4. Read the help window; then, print the information by following the instructions you read.

5. Click the **Back** button to return to the previous help entry.

6. Click the **Forward** button to advance to the next help entry.

7. Close the Help program by clicking the **Close** button.

Office Assistant

The Office Assistant is a feature found in all the Office 2000 programs that offers a variety of ways to get help. The Assistant, shown in Figure 1-8, is an animated character that offers tips, solutions, instructions, and examples to help you work more efficiently. The default Office Assistant character is a paperclip. A *default* setting is the one used unless another option is chosen.

The Office Assistant monitors the work you are doing and anticipates when you might need help. It appears on the screen with tips on how to save time or use the program's features more effectively. For example, if you start writing a letter in Word, the Assistant pops up to ask if you want help, as shown in Figure 1-9.

If you have a specific question, you can use the Office Assistant to search for help. To display the Office Assistant if it is not on the screen, choose Show the Office Assistant from the Help menu. Key your question and click Search. The Assistant suggests a list of help topics in response.

FIGURE 1-8
Office Assistant

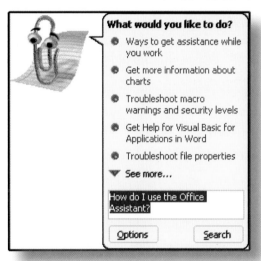

FIGURE 1-9
Office Assistant

STEP-BY-STEP ▷ 1.8

1. Choose **Show the Office Assistant** on the **Help** menu. The Office Assistant appears.

2. Key **How do I use the Office Assistant?** in the text box.

3. Click **Search**. A list of help topics is displayed, as shown in Figure 1-8.

4. Click **Ways to get assistance while you work**. The Microsoft Word Help box appears.

5. Click the **Asking for Help from the Office Assistant** link.

6. Read about the Office Assistant and print the information.

7. Click the **Close** box to remove the Help window from the screen.

8. Open a new Word document.

9. Key **Dear Zebedee,** and press **Enter**.

10. A message from the Office Assistant appears, asking if you want help writing your letter, as shown in Figure 1-9.

11. Click **Cancel**.

12. Close the Word document without saving.

13. Leave Word on the screen for the next Step-by-Step.

Quitting an Office Application

The Exit command on the File menu provides the option to quit Word or any other Office application. You can also click the Close button (X) on the right side of the title bar. Exiting an Office application takes you to another open application or back to the Windows 98 desktop.

STEP-BY-STEP ▷ 1.9

1. Open the **File** menu. Notice the files listed toward the bottom of the menu. These are the four most recently used files mentioned in the previous section.

2. Choose **Exit**. Word closes and Excel is displayed on the screen.

3. Click the **Close** button in the right corner of the title bar. Excel closes and the desktop appears on the screen. The taskbar shows an application is still open.

4. Click the **PowerPoint** button on the taskbar to display it on the screen. Exit PowerPoint. The desktop appears on the screen again.

Accessing the Internet

The **Internet** is a vast network of computers linked to one another. The Internet allows people around the world to share information and ideas through Web pages, newsgroups, mailing lists, chats, e-mail, and electronic files.

Connecting to the Internet requires special hardware and software and an Internet Service Provider. Before you can use the Internet, your computer needs to be connected and you should know how to access the Internet.

The **World Wide Web** is a system of computers that share information by means of hypertext links on "pages." The Internet is its carrier. To identify hypertext documents, the Web uses addresses called **Uniform Resource Locators (URLs)**. Here are some examples of URLs:

http://www.whitehouse.gov
http://www.microsoft.com
http://www.thomson.com/swpco

The Web toolbar, shown in Figure 1-10, is available in all Office 2000 programs. It contains buttons for opening and searching documents. You can use the Web toolbar to access documents on the Internet, on an **Intranet** (a company's private Web), or on your computer. To display the Web toolbar in an application, choose View, Toolbars, Web.

FIGURE 1-10
Web toolbar

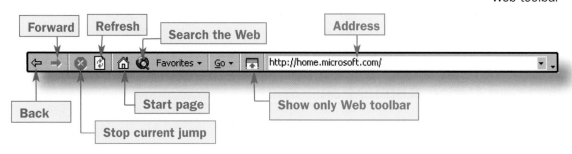

The Back button takes you to the previous page and the Forward button takes you to the next page. Click the Stop Current Jump button to stop loading the current page. The Refresh Current Page button reloads the current page. Click the Start Page button to load your **home page**, the first page that appears when you start your browser. The Search the Web button opens a page in which you can type keywords and search the Web. The Favorites button is a list to which you can add your favorite sites so that you can return to them easily. From the Go button's menu, you can choose to go to different sites or key in an address using the Open command. Click Show Only Web Toolbar when you want to hide all the toolbars except the Web toolbar. When you know the specific address you want to jump to, key it in the *Address* box.

To view hypertext documents on the Web, you need special software. A **Web browser** is software used to display Web pages on your computer monitor. Microsoft's **Internet Explorer** is a browser for navigating the Web that is packaged with the Office 2000 software. When you click the Start Page button, Search the Web button, or key an URL in the *Address* box of the Web toolbar, Office automatically launches your Web browser. Depending on your type of Internet connection, you may have to connect to your Internet Service Provider first. Figure 1-11 shows a Web page using Word as a browser.

Concept Builder

There are two basic types of Internet connections. *Dial-up access* uses a modem and a telephone line to communicate between your computer and the Internet. Most individual users and small businesses have dial-up access. *Direct access* uses a special high-speed connection between a computer network and the Internet. This access is faster but more expensive than dial-up access. Many businesses and institutions have direct access.

FIGURE 1-11
Web browser

Hot Tip

Since this page is updated every day, your page may not look exactly like the one shown.

STEP-BY-STEP ▷ 1.10

1. Connect to your Internet Service Provider if you're not connected already.

2. Open Word. Choose **Toolbars** on the **View** menu, and **Web** from the submenu if the Web toolbar isn't displayed already.

3. Click the **Start Page** button on the Web toolbar. The Start Page begins loading, as shown in Figure 1-11. Wait a few moments for the page to load. (Your start page may be different from the one shown, since this page can be changed easily by choosing Set Start Page on the *Go* button menu.)

4. Click the **Show Only Web Toolbar** button on the toolbar.

5. Click the **Search the Web** button. A new page loads where you can search for a topic on the Web.

6. Click the **Back** button to return to the Start Page.

7. Close all the Word windows that are open. (If a message appears asking you if you want to save changes, click **No**.)

8. Disconnect from your Internet Service Provider.

Hot Tip

Toolbars display buttons for basic commands only. To see additional buttons, click **More Buttons** on the toolbar and choose from the list that appears. When you use a button from the list, it is added to the toolbar. If you haven't used a button recently, it is added to the More Buttons list.

Hot Tip

You can display the Web toolbar in any Office application and use it to access the World Wide Web.

Concept Builder

To search for topics on the Web using Microsoft's Search page, key your topic in the *Search* box, choose a search engine, and click **Search**.

Summary

In this lesson, you learned:

■ Microsoft Office 2000 is an integrated software package. The professional version consists of a word processor application, a spreadsheet application, a database application, a presentation application, a schedule/organizer application, and a Web page application. The documents of an integrated software package can be used together.

■ Office applications can be started from the Programs menu and from the Start menu.

■ You can open an existing document from the File menu or from the Start menu. The Open dialog box will be displayed enabling you to open a file from any available disk or directory.

■ No matter which Office application you are using, files are opened, saved, and closed the same way. Filenames may contain up to 255 characters and may include spaces.

■ Recently used files can be opened quickly by choosing the filename from the bottom of the File menu. Or, click the Start button, and select Documents to list the 15 most recently used files. To exit an Office application, choose Exit from the File menu or click the Close button (X) on the title bar.

- The Office 2000 Help program provides additional information about the many features of Office 2000 applications. You can access the Help program from the menu bar and use the Contents, Answer Wizard, and Index tabs to get information.

- The Office Assistant is a help feature found in all Office applications. It offers tips, advice, and hints on how to work more effectively. You can also use it to search for help on any given topic.

LESSON 1 REVIEW QUESTIONS

WRITTEN QUESTIONS

Write a brief answer to the following questions.

1. List four of the applications that are included in Office 2000.

2. What is one way to start an Office application?

3. What is the difference between the Save and Save As commands?

4. If the Web toolbar is not on the screen, how do you display it?

5. What are two of the options you can choose in the Help dialog box?

TRUE/FALSE

Circle T if the statement is true or F if the statement is false.

T   F   1.   In all Office applications, you open, save, and close files in the same way.

T   F   2.   A read-only file is a printed copy of a document.

T   F   3.   The Office Assistant is available in all Office 2000 programs.

T   F   4.   The Web uses addresses called URLs to identify hypertext links.

T   F   5.   A default setting is one that cannot be changed.

LESSON 1 PROJECTS

PROJECT 1-1

You need to save a copy of September's work schedule in Gabriel, Mark, and Sandy's folders as well as in Rita's.

1. Use the **New Office Document** command to open a new Word document.

2. Use the **Open Office Document** command to open the **September Schedule** file in Excel.

3. Use the **Save As** command to save the file as **Sept Work Sched**, followed by your initials, in Gabriel's folder.

4. Repeat the process to save the file in Mark and Sandy's folders as well.

5. Close **Sept Work Sched** and exit Excel.

6. Close the Word document without saving and exit Word.

PROJECT 1-2

1. Open Word and access the Help system.

2. Click the **Index** tab.

3. Key **tip** in the *Type keywords* box to find out how to show the Tip of the Day when Word starts.

4. Print the information displayed in the right frame.

5. Click the **Answer Wizard** tab.

6. In the *What would you like to do?* box, key **What do I do if the Office Assistant is distracting?**

7. Click **Search**.

8. In the *Select topic to display* box, select **Troubleshoot the Office Assistant**.

9. In the right frame, click on the link **The Office Assistant is distracting**.

10. Print the information about what to do if the Office Assistant is distracting.

11. Close the Help system and exit Word.

PROJECT 1-3

1. Connect to your Internet Service Provider.

2. Open your Web browser.

3. Search for information on the Internet about Microsoft products.

4. Search for information about another topic in which you are interested.

5. Return to your home page.

6. Close your Web browser and disconnect from the Internet.

Extra Challenge

If you are using Microsoft Internet Explorer as your Web browser, choose **Web Tutorial** on the **Help** menu and use the tutorial to learn more about the Internet.

CRITICAL THINKING

ACTIVITY 1-1

Describe how you would use each of the Office 2000 applications in your personal life. Imagine that you are a business owner and describe how each of the Office 2000 applications would help you increase productivity.

ACTIVITY 1-2

Use the Office 2000 Help system to find out how to change the Office Assistant from a paper clip to another animated character. Then find out how you can download additional Assistants.

ACTIVITY 1-3

Open your Web browser. Compare the toolbar of your browser with the Web toolbar shown in Figure 1-10. Use the Help system if necessary and describe the function of any buttons that are different. Then describe the steps you would take to print a Web page.

UNIT

INTRODUCTION TO MICROSOFT® WORD

Estimated Time for Unit: 9 hours

WORD BASICS

OBJECTIVES

Upon completion of this lesson, you should be able to:

- Create a new document.
- Identify parts of the Normal view screen.
- Understand menus and toolbars.
- Enter text.
- Save a document.
- Navigate through a document.
- Locate and open an existing document.
- Preview a document.
- Print a document.
- Print in landscape orientation.

⏱ Estimated Time: 1 hour

Introduction to Word Processing

Word *processing* is using a computer and software program, such as Word, to produce documents such as letters and reports. These documents can be used in your school, career, personal, and business activities. Thanks to today's advanced computers and easy-to-use software, word processing can be done by almost anyone who can use a computer.

One of the most popular word processing programs is Word. You can use Word to create simple documents such as memos, complex documents such as newsletters with pictures, and even documents that can be published as Web pages.

The Word lessons in this unit contain step-by-step exercises for you to complete using a computer and Word. After completing all of the exercises, you will be able to create and revise your own word processing documents.

Creating a New Word Document

Start Word by clicking the Start button and choosing Microsoft Word from the Programs menu. A screen displaying copyright information will appear briefly, followed by a blank page where documents are created and edited.

STEP-BY-STEP ▷ 1.1

1. With Windows 98 running, click **Start** on the taskbar.

2. At the top of the Start menu, click **New Office Document**. The New Office Document dialog box appears.

3. Click the **General** tab, if necessary.

4. Click the **Blank Document** icon and click **OK**. Microsoft Word opens and a blank page appears in Normal view, as shown in Figure 1-1. The document is titled *Document1* until you save it with a new name.

Blank Document

5. Leave the document open for the next Step-by-Step.

Hot Tip

If the document does not appear in Normal view, choose Normal from the View menu.

FIGURE 1-1
Document in Normal view

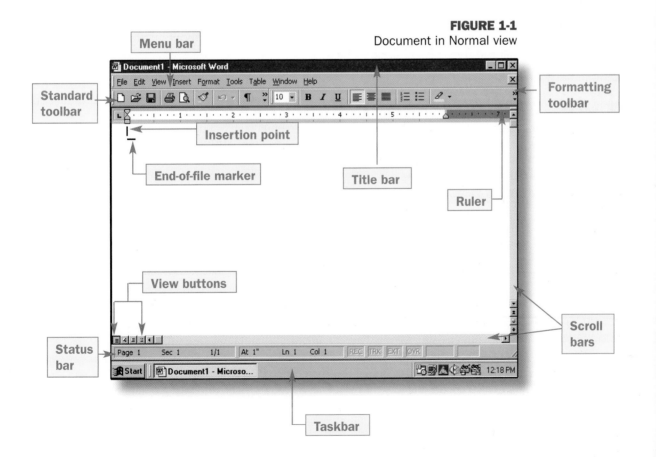

Understanding the Normal View Screen

Look carefully at the parts of the Normal view screen labeled in Figure 1-1 and find them on your screen. Many of these elements appear in other Office applications as well, and you will want to become familiar with them. The most important features of the Normal view screen are discussed below.

At the very top of the screen is the *title bar* where the names of the program and the current file are located. The *menu bar*, directly below the title bar, contains menu titles from which you can choose a variety of word processing commands. The *Standard toolbar*, located below the menu bar, contains buttons you can use to perform common tasks, such as printing and opening documents. The *Formatting toolbar* shares the same row as the Standard toolbar and contains buttons for changing character and paragraph formatting, such as alignment and type styles.

Using the *ruler*, located beneath the toolbar, you can quickly change indentions, tabs, and margins. The *end-of-file marker* is a horizontal line that shows the end of the document. Just above the end-of-file marker is the blinking *insertion point*, which shows where text will appear when you begin keying. The *view buttons* at the lower left corner of the document window allow you to quickly change views.

The *scroll bars*, located at the bottom and right sides of the window, allow you to move quickly to other areas of the document. Located at the bottom of the window is the *status bar* that tells you what portion of the document is shown on the screen and the location of the insertion point, as well as displays the status of certain Word features. The Windows 98 *taskbar* is located at the bottom of the screen. It shows the Start button, the Quick Launch toolbar, and all open programs.

The mouse pointer looks like an I-beam in the text area of the window, but when you move it out of the text area toward the toolbars, it becomes an arrow to allow you to easily point and click on toolbar buttons and menu names.

Viewing the Document Screen

There are four ways to view your document on the screen: Normal, Web Layout, Print Layout, and Outline. You have already learned about Normal view. Table 1-1 describes the features of each view and when you would want to use them.

To switch between views, choose the view you want from the View menu or click one of the view buttons at the bottom left of the document window.

TABLE 1-1
Document screen views

VIEW	DESCRIPTION
Normal	Shows a simplified layout of the page so you can quickly type, edit, and format text. Headers and footers, page boundaries, and backgrounds are not displayed.
Web Layout	Simulates the way a document will look when it is viewed as a Web page. Text and graphics appear the way they would in a Web browser, and backgrounds are visible.
Print Layout	Shows how a document will look when it is printed. You can work with headers and footers, margins, columns, and drawing objects that are all displayed.
Outline	Displays headings and text in outline form so you can see the structure of your document and reorganize easily. Headers and footers, page boundaries, graphics, and backgrounds do not appear.

Using Menus and Toolbars

A **menu** in Word is like a menu in a restaurant. You look at the Word menus to see what the program has to offer. Each title in the menu bar represents a separate **pull-down menu**. By choosing a command from a pull-down menu, you give Word instructions about what you want to do.

When you first use Word, each menu displays only basic commands. To see an expanded menu with all the commands, click the arrows at the bottom of the menu. As you work, Word adjusts the menus to display the commands used most frequently, adding a command when you choose it and dropping a command when it hasn't been used recently. Figure 1-2 compares the short and expanded versions of the Edit menu.

Toolbars provide another quick way to choose commands. The toolbars use **icons**, or small pictures, to remind you of each button's function. Toolbars can also contain pull-down menus. Unless you specify otherwise, only the Standard and Formatting toolbars are displayed, but many more are available. To see a list of the Word toolbars you can use, right-click on a toolbar.

As with the menus, toolbars initially display buttons only for basic commands. To see additional buttons, click More Buttons (the button with two right arrows >>) on the toolbar and choose from the list that appears, as shown in Figure 1-3. When you use a button from the list, it is added to the toolbar. If you haven't used a button recently, it is returned to the More Buttons list.

FIGURE 1-2
Short menu vs. expanded menu

FIGURE 1-3
More Buttons list

Text Entry and Word Wrap

To enter text in a new document, you begin keying at the insertion point. As you key, the insertion point moves to the right and data in the status bar changes to show your current position on the line. If the text you are keying extends beyond the right margin, it automatically moves to the next line. This feature is called *word wrap* because words are "wrapped around" to the next line when they will not fit on the current line.

Press Enter only to end a line at a specific place or to start a new paragraph. To insert a blank line, press Enter twice.

STEP-BY-STEP ▷ 1.2

1. Key the text from Figure 1-4 and watch how the words at the ends of lines wrap to the next line as they are keyed.

2. If you key a word incorrectly, just keep keying. You will learn how to correct errors later in this lesson.

3. Leave the document open for the next Step-by-Step.

FIGURE 1-4
Text for Step-by-Step 1.2

```
Each day, you should take time to plan and organize the day's work. You
can avoid wasted effort and meet your goals when a daily time plan is
made.

When making a daily time plan, list all tasks you need to complete that
day and rank the tasks in order of importance. Record tasks on a
calendar that must be completed that day and draw a line through each
task as it is completed.

Weekly and monthly time plans also can help you organize your schedule
and avoid wasting time. Weekly and monthly time plans can be made
following the same steps as those you used for completing a daily time
plan.
```

Navigating Through a Document

In order to correct errors, insert new text, or change existing text, you must know how to relocate the insertion point in a document. You can move the insertion point in a document using the mouse or using keyboard commands. For short documents, it might be faster to move the insertion point using the mouse. To relocate the insertion point, place the I-beam where you want the insertion point and then click the left mouse button. The blinking insertion point appears.

When working with a long document, you might find it tedious to use the mouse pointer to move the insertion point. Scrolling through a document of several pages using the mouse can take a long time. In this case, it is faster to use the keyboard to move the insertion point. Table 1-2 shows the keys you can press to move the insertion point both short and long distances.

TABLE 1-2
Keyboard shortcuts for moving the insertion point

PRESS	TO MOVE THE INSERTION POINT
Right arrow	Right one character
Left arrow	Left one character
Down arrow	To the next line
Up arrow	To the previous line
End	To the end of a line
Home	To the beginning of a line
Page Down	To the next screen
Page Up	To the previous screen
Ctrl+right arrow	To the next word
Ctrl+left arrow	To the previous word
Ctrl+End	To the end of the document
Ctrl+Home	To the beginning of the document

S TEP-BY-STEP ▷ 1.3

1. Move the mouse pointer to the end of the first line in the first paragraph. Click once. The insertion point moves to the end of the line.

2. Move the insertion point to the end of the document by pressing **Ctrl+End**.

3. Move the mouse pointer to the left of the first letter of the first word in the document.

4. Click once to place the insertion point before the first letter.

5. Move to the fourth word in the first line by pressing **Ctrl+right arrow** four times.

6. Click **End** to move to the end of the sentence.

7. Click **down arrow** to move to the next line.

8. Click **Ctrl+Home** to move to the beginning of the document.

9. Leave the document open for the next Step-by-Step.

Saving a File

The document you see on the screen is temporarily stored in the computer's ***random access memory (RAM).*** When the computer is turned off, the document is erased from RAM. Therefore, you must save the document to a disk if you want to retrieve it later. Saving is done two ways. You can use the Save command or the Save As command. When you save a file, Word stores the document on a hard or floppy disk, where it remains until you remove it. It is a good practice to save the document at intervals (every 10 to 15 minutes) to avoid accidentally losing your work and wasting time recreating a document.

When you save a file for the first time, choose Save As from the File menu or click the Save button on the toolbar. The Save As dialog box appears, as shown in Figure 1-5. Click the down arrow to the right of the *Save in* box and click the drive where you will save your file. Select the contents of the *File name* box, key a file name, and choose Save. After you have already saved a file, you can use Save As to save it again using a new name. Use Save As also to save a document to a different location or with a different format.

The next time you want to save changes to your document, click the Save button on the toolbar or choose Save from the File menu. These commands update the file and do not open the dialog box.

Folders can help you organize files on your disks. To create a new folder, click the Create New Folder button in the Save As dialog box. A New Folder dialog box appears, as shown in Figure 1-6. Give the folder a name. After you click OK, Word automatically opens the new folder so you can store your current document in it if you wish.

Concept Builder

The AutoRecover feature automatically saves a temporary copy of your document every 10 minutes. The temporary copy will open automatically when you start Word after a power failure or similar problem.

Concept Builder

To save a Word document as an HTML file that can be viewed using a Web browser, choose Save as Web Page from the File menu.

FIGURE 1-5
Save As dialog box

FIGURE 1-6

New Folder dialog box

STEP-BY-STEP ▷ 1.4

1. Click the **Save** button on the toolbar. The Save As dialog box appears, as shown in Figure 1-5.

2. Click on the down arrow at the right of the *Save in* box to display the available disk drives.

3. Choose the drive where you want to save the file.

4. Click the **Create New Folder** button. The New Folder dialog box appears, as shown in Figure 1-6.

5. In the *Name* box, key **Lesson 1**. Click **OK**.

6. In the *File name* box, select *Each day* and key **Time Plan** followed by your initials.

7. Click **Save**. Word saves the file in the folder you created.

8. Word returns you to the Normal view screen. Choose **Close** from the **File** menu to close the document.

Locating and Opening an Existing Document

With Word on the screen, you can open an existing document by choosing Open from the File menu or the Open button on the standard toolbar. This displays the Open dialog box where you can open a file from any available disk and folder.

STEP-BY-STEP ▷ 1.5

1. With Word on the screen, choose **Open** from the **File** menu. The Open dialog box appears.

2. Click the down arrow to the right of the *Look in* box to display the available disk drives.

3. Click the drive that corresponds to the file you

saved in the last Step-by-Step and locate **Time Plan**.

4. Click **Open** to open the file.

5. Leave the document open for the next Step-by-Step.

Previewing Your Document

The Print Preview command enables you to look at a document as it will appear when printed. You can access the Print Preview command from the File menu, or you can click the Print Preview button on the toolbar. When you issue this command, Word opens a preview window similar to the one shown in Figure 1-7. The pointer changes to a magnifying glass with a plus (+) sign in the middle. Simply position the magnifying glass where you want to view text up close and click. The text will be enlarged. The magnifying glass changes to a minus (-) sign. Click the document again and the document will return to the size that fits in the window.

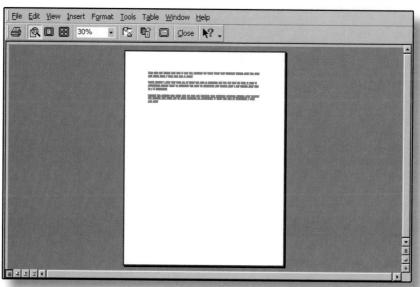

FIGURE 1-7
Print Preview

The Print Preview toolbar, shown in Figure 1-8, contains options for looking at your document. You can print your document, view one page or multiple pages of your document, control the percentage of zoom, display the ruler, shrink text to fit a page, show the full screen, close Print Preview, and use Help.

Use the Print button to print the document using default settings. The Magnifier button changes the pointer from the magnifying glass to the regular pointer so you can edit your document right in Print Preview. The One Page button shows one page in print preview. The Multiple Pages button displays from one to six pages in Print Preview.

Use the Zoom control to choose a percentage of magnification in which to view the document. You can view one page at as much as 500% and you can view as many as 12 pages or more (depending on your monitor size) at 10%. The Page Width option shows the document at its actual page width. The Text Width option shows the document at a width that displays all the text across the page. The Whole Page option displays one page. The Two Pages option displays two pages at a time.

The View Ruler button displays rulers along the left and top of the Print Preview screen. You can use these rulers to set margins, set tabs, and adjust indents. The Shrink to Fit button changes the font size of a document so that more text will fit on a page.

The Full Screen button maximizes the window so that you can view an entire page on the screen at a larger percentage of magnification than the regular Whole Page view can. The Close Preview button exits Print Preview and returns you to your document view. Click the Context Sensitive Help button when you need help using these buttons.

FIGURE 1-8
Print Preview toolbar

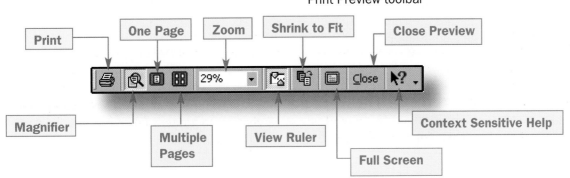

Print

One Page

Zoom

Shrink to Fit

Close Preview

Magnifier

Multiple Pages

View Ruler

Full Screen

Context Sensitive Help

STEP-BY-STEP ▷ 1.6

1. Click the **Print Preview** button on the toolbar.

2. Click the text part of the page with the plus sign magnifying glass. The page is enlarged.

3. Click with the minus sign magnifying glass. The page returns to full-page view.

4. Click the **View Ruler** button. The rulers appear (or disappear).

5. Click the **Full Screen** button. The window is maximized.

6. Click the **Close Full Screen** button. You are returned to full-page view.
 Close Full Screen

7. Click the down arrow beside the **Zoom** box. Click **50%**.
 31%

8. Click the down arrow again and click **150%**.

9. Click the down arrow again and click **Whole Page**. You are returned to full-page view.

10. Click the **Close** button on the toolbar to return to the Normal view screen.
 Close

Printing Your Document

You can print a full document, a single page, or multiple pages from a document on the screen at any time. The Print dialog box, as shown in Figure 1-9, appears when you choose Print from the File menu. The Print dialog box has various options for printing files. You can also print by clicking the Print button on the toolbar in the Normal view screen or in Print Preview, but the Print dialog box won't appear. Clicking the button causes Word to skip the Print dialog box and begin printing immediately using the default settings, which are to print all pages.

To print certain pages of a document, simply click the *Pages* option in the *Page range* box and then key the range of pages you want to print separated by a hyphen. For example, to print pages 3 through 5 of a document, key *3-5*. When you want to print individual pages, separate them with a comma. For example, to print only pages 3 and 5, key *3,5*. Choose the *Current page* option to print the page where the insertion point is located. Click the *Selection* option to print only the selected text.

FIGURE 1-9
Print dialog box

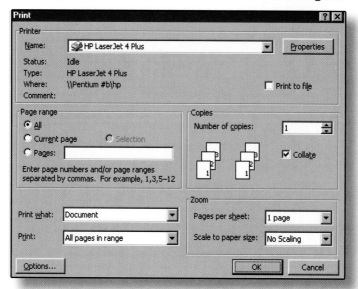

The *Copies* box allows you to specify the number of copies of the document or pages you are printing. Click the *Collate* check box to print the first copy of the pages in order (for example, from 1 to 5), then to start the second copy of pages (from 1 to 5). Turn off this option if you want to print all copies of page 1, then all copies of page 2, and so on.

The *Print* box in the lower portion of the dialog box allows you to choose to print *All pages in range*, only the *Odd pages*, or only the *Even pages*. Use the options in the *Zoom* box to control how many pages are printed on one sheet or scale your document to another size when printing.

S TEP-BY-STEP ▷ 1.7

1. Choose **Print** from the **File** menu. The Print dialog box appears.

2. Print the document using the default settings by choosing **OK**.

3. Choose **Close** from the **File** menu to close the document. (Choose **Yes** to save any changes if you are prompted.)

Printing in Landscape Orientation

Documents printed in ***portrait orientation***, as seen in Figure 1-10, are longer than they are wide. By default, Word is set to print pages in portrait orientation. In contrast, documents printed in ***landscape orientation***, as seen in Figure 1-11, are wider than they are long. Most documents are printed in portrait orientation. Some documents, however, such as documents with graphics or numerical information, look better when printed in landscape orientation.

To print a document in landscape orientation, access the Page Setup dialog box from the File menu box. Click the Paper Size tab and choose the *Landscape* option in the *Orientation* box.

FIGURE 1-10
Portrait orientation

FIGURE 1-11
Landscape orientation

Professional Dress Style Show

*Tuesday, April 2
at 6 p.m.
Monarch Hotel
Tickets are $10
Proceeds benefit the
Business Women's Club scholarship fund*

**Does your new management position leave you
feeling like you're in over your head?**

Come to our seminar, "Skills for New Managers"

February 3, 8-12 a.m., Hilton Hotel Blue Room
Seminars Unlimited

S TEP-BY-STEP ▷ 1.8

1. Open **IW Step1-8** from your student data files. Use Print Preview to view the document before you make any changes. Close Print Preview.

2. Save the document as **Seminar** followed by your initials.

3. Choose **Page Setup** from the **File** menu. The Page Setup dialog box appears.

4. Click the **Paper Size** tab.

5. In the *Orientation* box, choose the **Landscape** option.

6. Preview the document.

7. Save, print, and close the document.

Office Assistant

The Office Assistant is an animated Help character that offers tips, solutions, instructions, and examples to help you work more efficiently. The Assistant monitors the work you are doing and anticipates when you might need help. It appears on the screen with tips on how to save time or use the program's features more effectively. If you have a specific question, you can use the Office Assistant to search for help. To display the Office Assistant if it is not on the screen, choose Show the Office Assistant from the Help menu. Key your question and click Search. The Assistant suggests a list of help topics in response.

1. Choose **Show the Office Assistant** from the **Help** menu. The Office Assistant appears.

2. Key **What does the Office Assistant do?** in the text box.

3. Click **Search**. A list of help topics is displayed.

4. Click **Display tips and messages through the Office Assistant**. The Microsoft Word Help box appears.

5. Click **Hide, show, or turn off the Office Assistant** link.

6. Read the information about the Office Assistant and print it.

7. Click the Close box to remove the Help window from the screen.

8. Right-click on the Office Assistant and choose **Hide** on the shortcut menu.

Summary

In this lesson, you learned:

■ Word is a word processing program that can be used to create documents such as letters, memos, forms, and even Web pages. When you start Word, the Normal view screen appears.

■ When text is entered, the word wrap feature automatically wraps words around to the next line if they will not fit on the current line. When corrections or additions need to be made, the insertion point can be placed anywhere within a document using the keyboard or mouse.

■ The document that appears on the screen is stored in the computer's RAM. Therefore, it must be saved to a floppy or hard disk if it is to be retrieved later.

■ You can locate and open an existing document through the Open dialog box.

■ The Print Preview command enables you to look at a document as it will appear when printed. An entire document or part of a document can be printed at any time.

■ The Print dialog box appears when you choose Print from the File menu. You can also print by clicking the Print button on the toolbar, which skips the Print dialog box and causes your document to begin printing immediately.

■ Documents printed in landscape orientation are wider than they are long.

LESSON 1 REVIEW QUESTIONS

MULTIPLE CHOICE

Select the best response for the following statements.

1. The Normal view screen does not contain the following:
   A. Title bar
   B. View buttons
   C. Text box
   D. Insertion point

2. What dialog box do you use to save a file for the first time?
   A. Save
   B. Locate File
   C. Save As
   D. Save File

3. Clicking the Print button on the toolbar causes Word to
   A. Begin printing immediately using default settings
   B. Display the Print dialog box
   C. Switch to the Print Preview screen
   D. Show the document on the screen as it will appear when printed

4. To see a list of the Word toolbars you can
   A. Click the arrows at the bottom of a menu
   B. Choose Display from the Toolbar menu
   C. Click More Buttons (>>) on the toolbar
   D. Right-click on a toolbar

5. In Print Preview the insertion point changes to a
   A. Pointer
   B. Magnifying glass
   C. I-beam
   D. Hand

FILL IN THE BLANKS

Complete the following sentences by writing the correct word or words in the blanks provided.

1. The toolbars use _____ to remind you of each button's functions.   *Icons*

2. To insert a blank line in a document, press the _____ key twice.   *Enter*

3. Documents printed in _____ orientation are wider than they are long.   *Landscape*

4. The blinking _____ shows where text will appear when you begin keying.   *insertion po...*

5. _____ can help you organize files on your disks.   *Folder*

LESSON 1 PROJECTS

PROJECT 1-1

The department store where you work is having a clearance sale after the holidays. Before printing flyers you need to add some text and change the orientation.

1. Open **IW Project1-1** from the student data files.

2. Save the document as **Holiday** followed by your initials.

3. Place the insertion point between the two sentences at the end of the document and key this text:

   `Hurry down to Wilmore's to take advantage of our low prices on holiday merchandise.`

4. Place the insertion point at the end of the last sentence and key this text:

   `Don't miss your chance!`

5. Change the orientation of the document to landscape.

6. Preview the document.

7. Save, print, and close the document.

PROJECT 1-2

You work for the Career Placement Center and are preparing informational pamphlets as a resource for people seeking employment. Your supervisor gives you some paragraphs about interviewing and asks you to key them as a first step toward creating a pamphlet.

1. Create a new Word document.

2. Key the following text:

   `Preparing for a Job Interview`

   `A job interview gives you the chance to sell yourself to a possible employer. To make a good impression, you should prepare for the interview in advance. First, you should learn about the company you are interviewing with and prepare any questions you have about the company.`

   `Prepare a folder containing information you may need during the interview such as names and addresses of former employers, names and addresses of references, a copy of your resume, school records, and your Social Security card.`

3. Save the document as **Interview** followed by your initials.

4. Print the document and close it.

5. Exit Word.

CRITICAL THINKING

ACTIVITY 1-1

You notice that there is a Favorites folder in the Open and Save as dialog boxes and you want to find out more about it. Use the Help system to print information about the feature and answer the following questions:

- What is stored in the Favorites folder?

- What is an advantage to using the Favorites folder?

- How do you add something to the Favorites folder?

ACTIVITY 1-2

With Windows 98, a file name may contain up to 255 characters and include spaces. You should name a file with a descriptive name that will remind you of what the file contains and make it easy to retrieve.

Read each item below. From the information given, develop a file name for each document. Key the file name beside the appropriate number on a new Word document. Each file must have a different name. Strive to develop descriptive file names. Choose a file name for the document you created. Print and close.

1. A letter to the Spinnaker Publishing Company requesting a catalog.

2. A report entitled "Changing Attitudes Concerning Bird Sanctuaries" written by the wildlife preserve company, Future Dreams, which will be used to develop a grant proposal.

3. A letter that will be enclosed with an order form to Spinnaker Publishing Company to place an order.

4. A letter of complaint to the Spinnaker Publishing Company for sending the wrong merchandise.

5. An announcement for a reception to be given in honor of a retiring executive, Seth Alan Grey.

6. A memorandum to all employees explaining job openings and salary increases within the national company, Canyon Enterprises.

7. Minutes of the May board of directors meeting of Towering Insurance Company.

8. A press release written by Future Dreams to the media about a one-day event called *Live in Harmony with Nature*.

9. A mailing list for sending newsletters to all employees of Canyon Enterprises.

10. An agenda for the June board of directors meeting of Towering Insurance Company.

BASIC EDITING

OBJECTIVES

Upon completion of this lesson, you should be able to:

- Select text.

- Delete and type over text.

- Undo and redo recent actions.

- Cut, copy, and paste text.

- Use drag and drop to move or copy text.

🕐 **Estimated Time: 1 hour**

Selecting Text

Selecting is highlighting a block of text. Blocks can be as small as one character or as large as an entire document. After selecting a block of text, you can edit the entire block at once. This speeds operations such as large deletions and changes to line spacing. You can select text using the mouse, using the keyboard, using the keyboard in combination with the mouse, and using the Edit menu.

To select text with the mouse, position the I-beam to the left of the first character that begins the text you want to select. Hold down the left button on the mouse, drag the pointer to the end of the text you want to select, and release the button. To remove the highlight, click the left mouse button.

To quickly select a single word, click the left mouse button twice rapidly on the word. This is called *double-clicking*. To quickly select a paragraph, click three times rapidly in the paragraph. This is called *triple-clicking*.

You can select text one complete line at a time by using only the keyboard. Hold down the Shift key and press the down arrow to select one line. Press the down arrow again and again to add more lines to the selected block.

Other shortcuts use both the mouse and the keyboard. *Shift-clicking* is holding down the Shift key while clicking the mouse. You will use Shift-clicking in a later lesson to select two or more drawing objects. You can also use the Select All command from the Edit menu to select an entire document. Table 2-1 summarizes ways to select text.

TABLE 2-1
Selecting blocks of text

TO SELECT THIS	DO THIS
Word	Double-click the word.
Line	Click one time in the left margin beside the line.
Line (or lines)	Position the insertion point at the beginning of a line, press and hold Shift, and press the down arrow once to select one line or several times to select more lines.
Sentence	Press and hold down Ctrl and click in the sentence.
Paragraph	Triple-click anywhere in the paragraph. or Double-click in the left margin of the paragraph.
Multiple paragraphs	Double-click in the left margin beside the paragraph, then drag to select following paragraphs.
Entire document	Triple-click in the left margin. or Hold down Ctrl and click one time in the left margin. or Choose Select All from the Edit menu.
Objects (two or more)	Press Shift and click the objects.

STEP-BY-STEP ▷ 2.1

1. Open the **Time Plan** file you last used in Step-by-Step 1.7.

2. Save the document as **Time Plan2** followed by your initials.

3. Click one time in the margin to the left of the word *Each* to select the first line.

4. Click one time anywhere in the document to remove the highlight.

5. Double-click the word *Each* to select it.

6. Click anywhere to remove the highlight.

7. Triple-click anywhere in the first paragraph to select it.

8. Remove the highlight.

9. Position the insertion point before the *y* in the word *you* in the first sentence. Click and drag to select the words *you should take time*.

10. Remove the highlight.

11. Choose **Select All** from the **Edit** menu to select the entire document.

12. Remove the highlight.

13. Leave the document open for the next Step-by-Step.

Using the Backspace and Delete Keys

You might find, as you read over your text, that you need to delete characters or words. There are two ways to delete characters. You can quickly remove them using either the Backspace key or the Delete key. Pressing Backspace deletes the character to the left of the insertion point. Pressing Delete removes the character to the right of the insertion point. If you hold down either of these keys, it will continue to remove characters until you release the key. You can also easily remove a number of characters or words by selecting them and then pressing either Backspace or Delete.

S TEP-BY-STEP ▷ 2.2

1. Place the insertion point after the word *should* in the first sentence of the document.

2. Press **Backspace** until *you should* and the extra blank space following the comma disappear.

3. In the first sentence of the second paragraph, select the words *that day*.

4. Press **Delete**. The words disappear.

5. Use Backspace and Delete to correct any additional mistakes you have made.

6. Save and leave the document open for the next Step-by-Step.

Using Overtype

In **Overtype mode**, the text you key replaces existing text, or "types over" it. Overtype mode is especially useful for correcting misspelled words or for replacing one word with another one of the same length. For example, you can replace the *ie* in *thier* with *ei* to correct the spelling of *their* without having to insert or delete any letters or spaces.

Double-click OVR on the status bar as shown in Figure 2-1 to turn Overtype mode on or off. When Overtype is on, *OVR* will be shown in black. After replacing text, turn off Overtype mode by double-clicking OVR again so you do not key over any text you want to keep.

FIGURE 2-1
Overtype mode

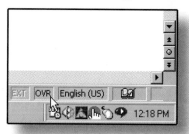

Using Undo, Redo, and Repeat

When working on a document, you will sometimes delete text accidentally or change your mind about editing or formatting changes you made. This is when the Undo command is useful. The Undo command will reverse a number of recent actions. To use the Undo command, click the Undo button on the toolbar or choose Undo from the Edit menu. The Undo command on the menu will include a description of your most recent action, such as Undo Clear or Undo Typing.

You can keep choosing the Undo command to continue reversing recent actions. Or you can click the down arrow next to the Undo button on the toolbar to see a drop-down list of your recent actions. The most recent action appears at the top of the list, as shown in Figure 2-2. You can choose from the list the action you want to undo.

Similar to the Undo command is the Redo button on the toolbar or the Redo command in the Edit menu. Use this command to reverse an Undo action. As with the Undo command, when you click the down arrow next to the Redo button, a list of recent actions appears. Choose from the list the action you want to Redo.

You can use the Repeat command to repeat your last action. Choose Repeat from the Edit menu. If your last action cannot be repeated, the command Can't Repeat is grayed out on the menu.

FIGURE 2-2
Undo list

Hot Tip

When you choose an item from the Undo or Redo drop-down list, Word will also undo or redo all the actions listed above it on the list.

STEP-BY-STEP ▷ 2.3

1. Position the insertion point after the period at the end of the second paragraph.

2. Insert a blank line and key the following text:

   As you mark off each performed task, you will feel a sense of accomplishment, which will motivate you to complete more tasks.

3. Double-click **OVR** on the status bar. *OVR* appears in black, as shown in Figure 2-1.

4. Move the insertion point back to the left of the *f* in the word *feel* in the sentence you just keyed. Key **gain**.

5. Move the insertion point to the left of the *p* in *performed* in the same sentence. Key **completed**.

6. Double-click **OVR** in the status bar to turn off the Overtype mode.

7. Click the arrow beside the **Undo** button on the toolbar. A drop-down list appears, as shown in Figure 2-2.

8. Scroll down the list—all choices will be high-lighted as you scroll—and choose **Typing c**. (The description should read *Undo 9 actions*.) The word *completed* changes back to *performed*.

9. Click the down arrow beside the **Redo** button on the toolbar. A drop-down list appears.

Hot Tip

If the Redo button is not visible, you can display it by clicking More Buttons (>>) on the toolbar and then choosing it from the list of buttons.

10. Scroll down the list and choose **Typing d**. (The description should read *Redo 9 actions*.) The word *performed* changes back to *completed*.

11. Select the word *accomplishment*.

12. Press **Delete**.

(continued on next page)

13. Choose **Undo Clear** from the **Edit** menu. The word *accomplishment* reappears.

14. Place the insertion point at the beginning of the document.

15. Key the words **Time Plan** and press **Enter**.

16. Choose **Repeat Typing** from the **Edit** menu. The words are repeated on the next line.

17. Undo the last two actions.

18. Save and leave the document open for the next Step-by-Step.

Copying and Moving Text

At some point when you are editing a document, you will probably want to move text around or copy it to a different location. The feature that makes these moving and copying operations so easy is the Clipboard. The ***Clipboard*** is a temporary storage place in memory. You send text to the Clipboard by using either the Cut or Copy command from the Edit menu or by clicking the Cut or Copy buttons on the toolbar. Then, you can retrieve that text by using the Paste command or the Paste button. When you cut or copy more than one item the Clipboard toolbar appears, as shown in Figure 2-3.

The Clipboard will store the text you send to it (up to 12 items) until you clear the Clipboard. To paste an item, click the icon. You can paste Clipboard text as many times as you want or paste all the items stored by using the Paste All button. The Clipboard does not provide long-term storage, as saving a file does. When you turn off the computer, the text in the Clipboard is lost. To clear the Clipboard manually, click the Clear Clipboard button.

Hot Tip

When you close the Clipboard toolbar three times in a row without using it, it will no longer automatically display. You can then display it manually or just use the Cut, Copy, and Paste buttons on the toolbar to copy and move text.

FIGURE 2-3
Clipboard toolbar

Moving Text

When you want to move text from one location to another, use the Cut and Paste commands. The Cut command removes the selected text from your document and places it on the Clipboard. When you paste the text, it is copied from the Clipboard to the location of the insertion point in the document. This operation is often referred to simply as cutting and pasting.

1. Display the Clipboard by choosing **Toolbars** from the **View** menu and **Clipboard** from the submenu.

2. Click the **Clear Clipboard** button to clear any items that are on the Clipboard.

3. Select the last sentence of the document.

4. Choose **Cut** from the **Edit** menu. The sentence you selected disappears from the screen. It has been placed on the Clipboard.

5. Select the first paragraph.

6. Click the **Cut** button on the toolbar. The paragraph is also removed and placed on the Clipboard. Your Clipboard should resemble the one shown in Figure 2-3.

7. Position the insertion point at the end of the last sentence of the last paragraph.

8. Insert a blank line.

9. Move the pointer to the first icon on the Clipboard. A pop-up box appears that contains the first sentence you cut.

10. Move your pointer to the second icon and part of the text for the paragraph you cut will appear. Click the icon. The paragraph appears at the insertion point.

11. Click the **Close** button to close the Clipboard.

12. Save and leave the document open for the next Step-by-Step.

Copying Text

The Copy command is similar to the Cut command. When you choose the Copy command, however, a copy of your selected text is placed on the Clipboard while the original text remains on the screen. As before, retrieve the copied text from the Clipboard.

STEP-BY-STEP ▷ 2.5

1. Select the first sentence of the last paragraph, which begins *Each day....*

2. Click the **Copy** button on the toolbar.

3. Position the insertion point at the beginning of the first paragraph.

4. Click the **Paste** button on the toolbar. The sentence is copied.

5. Save and leave the document open for the next Step-by-Step.

Hot Tip

You can also access the Cut, Copy, and Paste commands by right-clicking the mouse button on the selected text and choosing the commands from the shortcut menu.

Using Drag and Drop to Copy or Move Text

When copying or moving text a short distance within a document, you can use a quick method called ***drag and drop***. To use this method to move text, select the text you want to move. Then, place the mouse pointer on the selected text, click, and hold down the mouse button. A small box will appear below the pointer. Using the mouse, drag the text to the location where you want to move it. As you begin dragging, a dotted insertion point appears. Place the dotted insertion point where you want the text and release the mouse button.

To use the drag and drop method to copy text, perform the same steps as when moving text, but hold down Ctrl while dragging. A box appears below the pointer and a + (plus) sign displays beside the box. When you release the mouse button, the text is placed at the dotted insertion point location while the originally selected text remains unchanged.

STEP-BY-STEP ▷ 2.6

1. Select the last sentence of the document, which begins *You can avoid....*

2. Position the pointer over the selected text.

3. Click and hold. A dotted insertion point will appear at the pointer and a box will appear below the pointer.

4. Drag the pointer to the end of the second paragraph. Position the pointer after the period ending the paragraph and release the mouse button. The sentence is moved.

5. Select the first sentence of the second paragraph that begins *As you mark....*

6. Position the pointer over the selected text and click and hold.

7. Hold down **Ctrl** and drag to place the dotted insertion point after the word *work* at the end of the last paragraph. Release the mouse button and then **Ctrl**. The sentence is copied.

8. Delete the last paragraph.

9. Select the last sentence that begins *Weekly and monthly...* and click the **Cut** button on the toolbar.

10. Display the Clipboard, which now has three items. Clear the Clipboard.

11. Close the Clipboard. Adjust spacing as necessary between sentences and paragraphs.

12. Save, print, and close.

Summary

In this lesson, you learned:

- You can speed operations by selecting blocks of text.

- You can delete text using Backspace and Delete. Overtype mode allows you to replace existing text with the new text that is keyed. Overtype is especially useful for correcting misspelled words.

- When you click the down arrow next to the Undo button, a drop-down list of your recent actions appears. You can choose from the list the action you want to undo. You can redo an action using the Redo button. You can repeat an action using the Repeat command on the Edit menu.

- You send text to the Clipboard by using either the Cut or Copy command from the Edit menu or toolbar. Then, you can retrieve that text by using the Paste command.

- When copying and moving text a short distance, you can use a quick method called drag and drop.

LESSON 2 REVIEW QUESTIONS

TRUE/FALSE

Circle T if the statement is true or F if the statement is false.

T F 1. Selecting is highlighting a block of text.

T **F** 2. Pressing Backspace deletes the character to the right of the insertion point.

T **F** 3. Use Overtype mode to reverse a recent action.

T F 4. The Repeat command will repeat your last action.

T **F** 5. The Clipboard provides long-term storage just as saving a file does.

WRITTEN QUESTIONS

Write a brief answer to the following questions.

1. How do the Cut and Copy commands differ?

2. Describe the drag and drop method for copying text.

   select text & position insert pt in the text. Hold down control key + left mouse button & drag text to new loc. Release mouse + ctrl key

3. What is Shift-clicking?

   method of selecting holding [mouse button & shift key

4. When is the Undo command useful?

   reversing editing & formatting action

5. Describe the two ways to delete characters.

LESSON 2 PROJECTS

PROJECT 2-1

You are an administrative assistant at Granville University. The files of some students who have applied for the Summer Language Workshop are not complete and you are creating a checklist to send that identifies the items still needed.

1. Open **IW Project 2-1** from the student data files.

2. Save the document as **SLW Checklist** followed by your initials.

3. Key the following paragraph between the title and the first paragraph.

   We are pleased that you have applied to be part of the Summer Language Workshop at Granville University. The six-week program gives qualified high school juniors and seniors an opportunity to study a foreign language and earn college credits.

4. Move the items on the checklist to place them in alphabetic order.

5. Copy the entire document and place it at the bottom of the page, leaving four blank lines between documents.

6. Preview the document. Print from Preview.

7. Save and close.

PROJECT 2-2

Your business, Web Essentials, designs and creates Web pages. You have developed some tips for companies that have Web sites. However, the document needs to be corrected before being distributed.

1. Open **IW Project2-2** from the student data files.

2. Save the file as **Web Site** followed by your initials.

3. Make the corrections indicated by the proofreader's marks in Figure 2-4.

4. Save, print, and close.

FIGURE 2-4

How to Publicize Your Web Site

Now that your company has a Web Site, you need to publicize it so that people will visit your site. Here are ways you can publicize your site. *^eight*

1. Submit the URL to as many search engines as possible, such as Lycos (http://www.lycos.com) and WebCrawler (http://www.webcrawler.com).
2. Submit the URL to as many Internet directories as possible, such as Yahoo (http://www.yahoo.com) and Starting Point. *(http://www.stpt.com)*
3. Submit the URL to Web sites that list What's New and What's Cool pages. Look for sites that are related to your company. For example, if your company sells widgets for home phones, search for Web sites that list new products for the home. *In addition to the What's New on the Web sites*
4. Trade links with related Web Sites. For example, you could ask the owners of the Home Electronics Online site to add a link to your page, and you can add a link on your Web site to theirs.
5. Send out press releases to newspapers, television stations, radio stations, and *relevant* magazines announcing your site and any unique information or services it provides consumers.
6. Print the URL ~~of your site~~ on all your business correspondence including business cards, letterhead, and brochures. Also include the URL in any printed or broadcast advertising.
7. Advertise your site online by sponsoring a Web page or purchasing advertising space on a relevant Web Site.
8. Include the URL in your e-mail and newsgroup signature file.

PROJECT 2-3

You work at Shade's Auto Dealership. They are sponsoring a golf tournament to benefit the local food bank. Key an information sheet to post on the bulletin board.

1. Open **IW Project2-3** from the student data files.

2. Save the document as **Golf Tournament** followed by your initials.

3. Insert a blank line after the first paragraph and key the following text. Use what you've learned to correct errors as you key.

   ```
   Where: Forest Hills Country Club
   When: June 22-23
   Time: Tee times begin at 8 a.m. each day
   Cost: $50 entry fee per person

   Sign up at the Country Club office or at Shade's Auto Dealership.
   ```

4. Use Overtype to replace **When:** with **Date:**.

5. Delete **Where** and key **Location**.

6. Change the tee times to 9 a.m.

7. Undo the change.

8. Move the last sentence of the first paragraph to make it the last sentence of the last paragraph.

9. Save, print, and close the document.

CRITICAL THINKING

SCANS

ACTIVITY 2-1

You are opening a new T-shirt shop in the mall and will be hiring several employees. You need to adopt employee policies so new employees will know the rules of the company. Your policies will cover tardiness, absenteeism, dress code, employee evaluations, telephone answering procedures, and using the telephone for personal calls. Choose three of those issues (or choose your own) and write a paragraph about each one. Be sure to include penalties for not following the policies.

ACTIVITY 2-2

A co-worker asks you some questions about using the Clipboard to copy and paste items. Use Help to answer them.

■ What happens when the Clipboard is full and I try to copy an additional item?

■ How do I reset the count on the Clipboard so that it will display automatically again?

■ Which other Office programs can I paste items into using the Clipboard?

3

BASIC FORMATTING

OBJECTIVES

Upon completion of this lesson, you should be able to:

■ Change font, font style, size, color, underline style, and font effects.

■ Highlight text and change the case.

■ Align text and change the vertical alignment.

■ Copy format and style.

■ Use Click and Type to insert text.

⏱ Estimated Time: 1 hour

Using Fonts

Designs of type are called *fonts*, or typefaces. Just as clothing comes in different designs, fonts have different designs. Like clothing, fonts can be dressy or casual. When you are creating a document, you should consider what kind of impression you want the text to make. Do you want your document to look dressy and formal? Or do you want it to look casual and informal? The fonts shown in Figure 3-1 would result in four very different looking documents.

It is possible to use many different fonts in one document. However, using more than two or three fonts makes a document look cluttered and hard to read. The fonts available to you are those that are supported by your printer or installed on your computer. Because there are hundreds of different kinds of printers in use, the fonts mentioned in this book may not be available on your printer. If you do not have some of the fonts suggested for use in this book, use available fonts.

If you look closely at the first line in Figure 3-2, you can see small lines at the ends of the lines that make up the characters. These lines are called *serifs*. If a font has these serifs, it is called a serif font. If a font does not have serifs, it is called a *sans serif* font. Serif fonts are generally considered to be "dressier" than sans serif fonts and are often used for the body of a document. Sans serif fonts are often used for titles, headings, and page numbers.

FIGURE 3-1
Different fonts

This font is called Arial.

This font is called Impact.

This font is called Brush Script.

This font is called Times New Roman.

FIGURE 3-2
Serif vs. sans serif font

Serif Font: Aa Bb Cc Dd

Sans Serif Font: Aa Bb Cc Dd

 Did You Know?

Sans is French for "without."

Changing the Font

Word offers two ways to change the font: using the Font dialog box and using the Font box on the formatting toolbar. To display the Font dialog box, shown in Figure 3-3, choose Font from the Format menu. Click the Font tab to access the Font section of the dialog box. The box under *Font* shows the current font. Below that, other fonts are listed. Use the scroll bars to locate the font you want. Then, click on it. The text in the *Preview* box will change to the chosen font. To change the font using the Font box on the formatting toolbar, simply click the down arrow at the right of the box, scroll to the font of your choice, and click it.

You can change the font of text already keyed by selecting it first and then choosing a new font. Or, change the font of text not yet keyed by first choosing the font and then keying the text.

FIGURE 3-3
Font dialog box

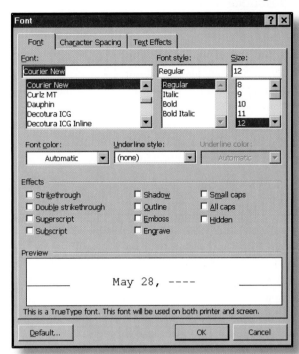

S TEP-BY-STEP ▷ 3.1

1. Open **IW Step3-1** from the student data files.

2. Save the document as **Diet** followed by your initials.

3. Choose **Select All** from the **Edit** menu to select all the text.

4. Choose **Font** from the **Format** menu. The Font dialog box appears, as shown in Figure 3-3.

5. Click the **Font** tab if necessary.

6. In the *Font* box, scroll down and click **Times New Roman**. Notice the *Preview* box shows text in the new font.

7. Click **OK**. The text in your document changes to Times New Roman.

8. Click anywhere in the document to remove the highlight.

9. Select the title of the document, *Reducing Fat in the American Diet*.

10. Click the down arrow at the right of the **Font** box in the formatting toolbar. A list of fonts appears.

11. Choose a sans serif font, such as Arial, from the list of fonts. The title appears in the selected font. Click the mouse button to remove the highlight.

12. Save and leave the document open for the next Step-by-Step.

Changing Font Style

Not only can you change the font, but you can also change the font style. *Font style* refers to certain standard changes in the appearance of a font. Common font styles are bold, italic, and underline. These styles can be applied to any font. You may also combine styles, creating bold italics, for example. Figure 3-4 illustrates some of the styles available in Word.

When you begin keying a document, you are using a regular style. This is the style you will likely use for the body of most documents. However, you might want to use other styles for particular features in your documents. For example, you can emphasize a title by applying a bold style to it.

Word allows you to change font styles using the Font dialog box, toolbar buttons, or shortcut keys. The easiest way to change the style is to select the text and click the bold, italic, or underline button on the toolbar. The style will be applied to, or removed from, the selected text. To combine styles, click two buttons in succession, such as bold and then italic to create bold italic.

To change the font style using the Font dialog box, select the text and choose Font from the Format menu. Click the Font tab if necessary. Under *Font style*, click one of the styles listed. The text in the *Preview* box changes to the chosen font style. While the toolbar buttons may be the fastest way to change font style, using the Font dialog box can save you time because you can change the font, font style, size, and other characteristics of text at the same time.

Another way to change font style is to use keyboard shortcuts. Table 3-1 shows keyboard shortcuts that can be used to change font styles.

FIGURE 3-4
Different font styles

This is Times New Roman regular.

This is Times New Roman bold.

This is Times New Roman italic.

This is Times New Roman bold italic.

This is Times New Roman <u>underlined.</u>

 Hot Tip

A faster way to reach the Font dialog box is to right-click in your document and choose Font from the shortcut menu.

TABLE 3-1
Keyboard shortcuts for choosing font style

TYPE STYLE	PRESS
Bold	Ctrl+B
Italic	Ctrl+I
<u>Underline</u>	Ctrl+U

S TEP-BY-STEP ▷ 3.2

1. Select the title.

2. Choose **Font** from the **Format** menu. In the *Font Style* box, click **Bold**.

3. Click **OK**. The title changes to bold style.

4. Select the word *fat* in the first paragraph, second sentence.

5. Click the **Italic** button on the formatting toolbar. The text changes to italic.

6. Save and leave the document open for the next Step-by-Step.

Changing Font Size

Font size is determined by measuring the height of characters in units called *points*. There are 72 points in an inch. A standard font size for text is 12 point. The higher the point size, the larger the characters. Figure 3-5 illustrates the Arial font in 10, 14, and 18 point. You can change font size by using the Font Size box on the toolbar or in the Font dialog box.

FIGURE 3-5
Different font sizes

This is Arial 10 point.

This is Arial 14 point.

This is Arial 18 point.

Changing the Color of Text

Word allows you to change text on your screen to colors. Colors are fun to use and can add interesting effects to your documents. If you have a color printer, you can even print your document as it appears on your screen. If you have a printer with black ink or toner only, the document will print in black and shades of gray.

To change the color of text on your screen, select the text and choose Font from the Format menu. You can choose the color you want in the *Font color* box of the Font dialog box. Or you can click the down arrow next to the Font Color button on the toolbar and choose a color from the palette that appears.

STEP-BY-STEP ▷ 3.3

1. Select the entire document.

2. Choose **Font** from the **Format** menu. In the *Size* box, scroll down and click **14**.

3. Click **OK**. Remove the highlight.

4. Select the title.

5. Click the arrow to the right of the **Font Size** box in the formatting toolbar. A list of font sizes appears.

6. Choose **18**. The title appears in 18 point size.

7. With the title still selected, choose **Font** from the **Format** menu. The Font dialog box appears.

8. Click the down arrow under *Font color*. A palette of colors appears. Click **Green**. Notice the text in the *Preview* box changes to green.

9. Click **OK**. Remove the highlight. The title appears in green.

10. Save and leave the document open for the next Step-by-Step.

Changing Underline Style and Color

In the Font dialog box, you can choose an underline style from the *Underline style* list by clicking the down arrow. Examples of underlining options include a single line, a double line, a dotted line, a thick line, and a wavy line. You can change the color of the underline by clicking the *Underline color* down arrow and selecting a color from the palette.

Changing Font Effects

Word offers font effects to help you enhance your text. These font effects are shown in Table 3-2. To select a font effect, choose one of the options in the *Effects* section of the Font dialog box.

TABLE 3-2
Font effects

SELECTED FONT EFFECTS	RESULT
Strikethrough	~~No turning back~~
Superscript	The mountain is ^{high}
Subscript	The pool is $_{deep}$
Shadow	By invitation only
Outline	Thursday
Emboss	DECEMBER 13
Small Caps	CALYPSO STREET
All Caps	GLENMERLE
Hidden	Nothing

STEP-BY-STEP ▷ 3.4

1. Select the title.

2. Choose **Font** from the **Format** menu.

3. Under *Effects*, choose **Shadow**.

4. Click **OK**. The words now have a shadow effect. Remove the highlight.

5. Select the *Introduction* heading.

6. Right-click on the heading and choose **Font** from the shortcut menu to display the Font dialog box.

7. Click the down arrow in the *Underline style* box. Choose the double-line style from the list.

8. Click the down arrow in the *Underline color* box. Choose blue from the palette.

9. Click **OK**. The heading is now double-under-lined in blue.

10. Save and leave the document open for the next Step-by-Step.

Extra Challenge

Create a new document. Key your name. Copy and paste your name on the same page four times. Select each one and change the font, size, style, and color to your choice so you end up with your name in four different appearances. Experiment with the available Effects in the Font dialog box.

Highlighting

To emphasize an important part of the document, you can *highlight* it in color. To highlight text or graphics, select the item and click the down arrow next to the Highlight button on the toolbar. Then choose the color you want from the palette that appears as shown in Figure 3-6. Or, if the Highlight button is already the color you want, click it and then select the text or graphics to be highlighted.

Changing Case

Case refers to whether letters are capitalized or not. Uppercase letters are capitalized. Lowercase letters are not capitalized. To convert the case of text, simply select the text and choose Change Case from the Format menu. The Change Case dialog box shown in Figure 3-7 appears, listing five choices for changing case. *Sentence case* changes selected text to look like a sentence, capitalizing the first letter of the first word and lowercasing the rest of the text. The *lowercase* option lets you change all selected text to lowercase. The *UPPERCASE* option lets you change all selected text to uppercase. The *Title Case* option changes selected text to initial caps—each word in the title is capitalized and other characters are lowercased. The *tOGGLE cASE* option reverses the case of the selected text. All capital letters are lowercased and all lowercase text is uppercased. To choose a case option, click the appropriate option button.

FIGURE 3-6
Highlight color palette

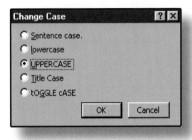

FIGURE 3-7
Change Case dialog box

S TEP-BY-STEP ▷ 3.5

1. In the last paragraph under *Dietary Guidelines for Americans*, select the second sentence that begins *Thus the guidelines....*

2. Click the down arrow next to the **Highlight** button on the toolbar. A palette of colors appears, as shown in Figure 3-6.

3. Choose the middle color on the top row, *Turquoise*. The selected text appears turquoise on the screen.

4. Select the title.

5. Choose **Change Case** from the **Format** menu. The Change Case dialog box appears, as shown in Figure 3-7.

6. Choose **Title Case**.

7. Choose **OK**. All words begin with a capital letter.

8. Select the words *In The* in the title.

9. Choose **Change Case** from the **Format** menu and choose **lowercase** in the Change Case dialog box.

10. Choose **OK**. The capitals change to lowercase letters.

11. Save and leave the document open for the next Step-by-Step.

Aligning Text

A**lignment** refers to how text is positioned between the margins. As Figure 3-8 shows, text can be aligned left, center, right, or justified. Left alignment is the default setting. The type of alignment you use can significantly alter a document's appearance.

Documents are normally aligned left or justified. Long documents are easier to read when aligned left. Centering is often used for invitations, titles, and headings. Right alignment may be used for page numbers and dates.

To align text, click in the paragraph you want to align, or select it. Choose Paragraph from the Format menu. In the Paragraph dialog box, shown in Figure 3-9, choose an alignment from the drop-down list in the *Alignment* box. However, the easiest way to change alignment is to click the alignment buttons on the formatting toolbar.

FIGURE 3-8
Text alignment

This text is left-aligned.

This text is centered.

This text is right-aligned.

This text is justified because text is aligned at both the left and right margins. This text is justified because text is aligned at both the left and right margins.

FIGURE 3-9
Paragraph dialog box

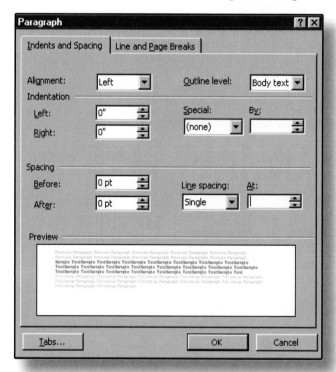

STEP-BY-STEP ▷ 3.6

1. Select the title.

2. Choose **Paragraph** from the **Format** menu. The Paragraph dialog box appears, as shown in Figure 3-9.

3. Beside *Alignment*, click the down arrow to the right of *Justified*. Click **Centered**.

4. Click **OK**. The title is centered.

5. Select the date above the title.

6. Click the **Align Right** button on the toolbar. (If the button is not dis-

played, choose it from the More Buttons menu.) The date is right-aligned.

7. Insert two blank lines between the date and the title.

8. Click in the paragraph that begins *Today....*

9. Click the **Align Left** button on the toolbar. The paragraph is aligned left.

10. Save and leave the document open for use in Step-by-Step 3.8.

Changing Vertical Alignment

You can also change the vertical alignment of text in a document. You can align text with the top of the page, center the text, or distribute the text equally between the top and bottom margins. Choose Page Setup on the File menu to display the Page Setup dialog box. The Page Setup dialog box is divided into four sections. Each section has a tab you can click to access the section. You can change settings in more than one section before clicking OK.

To change vertical alignment, click the Layout tab, as shown in Figure 3-10. In the *Vertical alignment* box, click the down arrow and choose Top, Center, Justified, or Bottom. Then click OK.

FIGURE 3-10
Page Setup dialog box

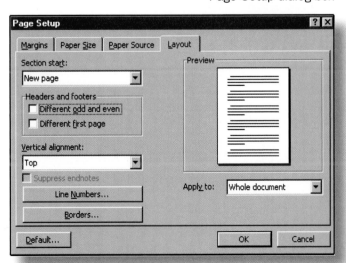

1. Create a new Word document.

2. Key the following text:

   Your name
   HD 1163
   Reducing Fat in the American Diet

3. Center the text.

4. Change the font to Arial and the font size to 18.

Hot Tip

Fonts you have used recently are grouped at the top of the Font drop-down list. This saves time when selecting fonts using the Font list on the toolbar.

5. Choose **Page Setup** from the **File** menu. The Page Setup dialog box appears, as shown in Figure 3-10.

6. Click the **Layout** tab if necessary.

7. Click the down arrow in the *Vertical alignment* box and choose **Center** from the list. Click **OK**.

8. Save the document as **Diet Title** followed by your initials.

9. Preview the document to see that the text is aligned vertically.

10. Print and close the document.

Using Click and Type

Click and Type is a useful feature that you can use to quickly insert text or other items into a blank area of a document. It saves you from having to manually insert blank lines or tabs in order to position the insertion point where you want it. Just double-click on the document where you want to insert text and begin keying.

To turn the feature on, choose Options from the Tools menu, click the Edit tab, and click the *Enable click and type* check box. Click and Type can be used only in Print Layout or Web Layout views. You can tell what formatting will be applied by watching the pointer as you move it to different areas of the document. For example, an I-beam on top of a *Center* icon, as shown in Figure 3-11, indicates the text will be centered.

FIGURE 3-11
Use Click and Type to start keying anywhere

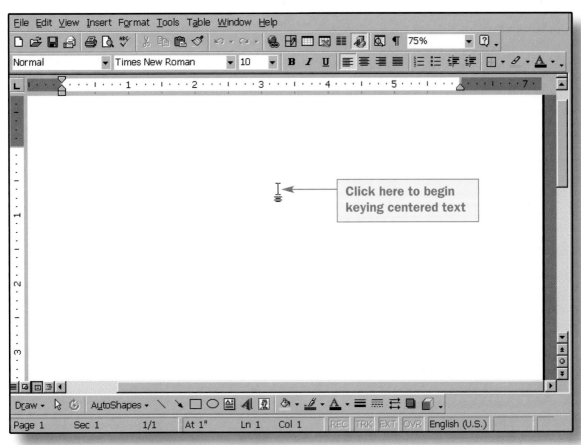

File Edit View Insert Format Tools Table Window Help

Normal ▼ Times New Roman ▼ 10 ▼ B I U

Click here to begin keying centered text

Draw ▼ AutoShapes ▼

Page 1   Sec 1   1/1   At 1"   Ln 1   Col 1   REC TRK EXT OVR English (U.S.)

STEP-BY-STEP ▷ 3.8

1. Create a new Word document.

2. Switch to Print Layout view.

3. Scroll down until 4.5 inches is visible on the left ruler.

4. Move the pointer to the middle of the document around the 4.5-inch mark and double-click.

5. Key the following text:

```
Your name
HD 1163
Reducing Fat in the American Diet
```

6. Change the font to Arial and the font size to 18.

7. Preview the document to see that the text is centered and aligned vertically just as it was in the last Step-by-Step when you did it manually.

8. Close the document without saving.

Copying Format and Style

Often you will spend time formatting a paragraph with indents or tabs or styles such as bold and italic and then find that you need the same format in another part of the document. The Format Painter button on the toolbar allows you to copy the format and style of a block of text, rather than the text itself. You can use the command to quickly apply a complicated format and style to text. To use the Format Painter command, select the formatted text you want to copy. Then, click the Format Painter button and select the text you want to format. The text changes to the copied format.

STEP-BY-STEP ⊳ 3.9

1. With the *Diet* document on the screen, select the heading, *Introduction*. Change the font size to 16.

2. With the title still selected, click the **Format Painter** button on the toolbar. The pointer changes to a paintbrush and I-beam.

3. Scroll down and select the heading, *Dietary Guidelines for Americans*. The font size, underline style, and underline color formatting that were copied are applied.

4. Copy the same formatting to the heading, *Fat in the American Diet*.

5. Save, print, and close the document.

Hot Tip

To apply a format multiple times, double-click the Format Painter button. When you're finished, click the Format Painter button one time to return the insertion point to an I-beam and deactivate the command.

Summary

In this lesson, you learned:

- Serif fonts are generally considered to be "dressier" than sans serif fonts and are often used for the text portion of a document. Sans serif fonts are often used for titles, headings, and page numbers. Common font styles are bold, italic, and underline. These styles can be applied to any font.

- Font size is measured in points. A point is about 1/72nd of an inch. The higher the point size, the larger the characters. You can change the color of text, style of underline, color of underline, and font effects from the Font dialog box. Changing case changes the selected text from uppercase to lowercase or vice versa.

- You can align text by choosing Paragraph from the Format menu or by clicking the buttons on the formatting toolbar. You can also change the vertical alignment in the Page Setup dialog box.

- Use Click and Type to start keying text anywhere on a page.

- Use the Format Painter button to copy the format and style of a block of text.

LESSON 3 REVIEW QUESTIONS

MATCHING

Match the correct term in Column 2 to its description in Column 1.

Column 1

D 1. Small lines at the ends of characters

H 2. Unit for measuring type size

E 3. Designs of type

F 4. Whether letters are capitalized or not

G 5. How text is positioned between margins

Column 2

A. Font style

B. Format

C. Font size

D. Serifs

E. Fonts

F. Case

G. Alignment

H. Points

WRITTEN QUESTIONS

Write a brief answer to the following questions.

1. Describe serif and sans serif fonts.

2. Name three common font styles.

reg bold italic broad

3. Name five ways to change the appearance of text in the Font dialog box.

font, font style, size, line, [for effects]

4. How do you align text?

5. What does the Format Painter button do?

copy the present style of a line of text rather than text [itself]

LESSON 3 PROJECTS

PROJECT 3-1

Your organization has raised money to commission a granite historical marker commemorating the founder of your city. Prepare a document that will indicate the design of the marker.

1. Open **IW Project3-1** from the student data files.

2. Save the document as **Marker** followed by your initials.

3. Change all text to title case.

4. Change all the text to Times New Roman, 20-point, engraved, 25% gray font.

5. Change the name *Lewis C. Staples* to Arial, 22-point, small caps, 40% gray font.

6. Copy the format from *Lewis C. Staples* to *Oxford, Virginia.*

7. Center all the text in the document and then align it vertically using center alignment.

8. Save, preview, print, and close.

PROJECT 3-2

Your company is preparing guidelines for proofreading outgoing correspondence. Make changes to the document so it is more appealing to read.

1. Open **IW Project3-2** from the student data files.

2. Save the document as **Guidelines** followed by your initials.

3. Change the text of the whole document to Footlight MT Light 12 point. (If that font is not available, choose another serif font.)

4. Center the title and change it to Tahoma, 16 point, bold, plum color, with a double-wavy underline. (If that font is not available, choose another sans serif font.)

5. Change the heading *Check Facts* to Tahoma (or the same font you used in step 4), 14 point, italic, and teal color.

6. Copy the format of the heading *Check Facts* to the other two headings.

7. Apply the Justify alignment to all text paragraphs. (Do not apply this alignment to the heading.)

8. Save, preview, print, and close.

CRITICAL THINKING

ACTIVITY 3-1

An effective way to capture a reader's attention is to animate text. Use the Help system to figure out how to animate text, how to remove animation from text, and how to display or hide animation.

ACTIVITY 3-2

SCANS

You work for a photo lab. In addition to film developing, they also do reprints, enlargements, slides, black and white, copy and restoration, posters, and passport photos. Your manager wants to include a list of services available with each customer's order and he asks you to create it. Briefly explain each service, how much it costs, and how much time it takes to complete. Make effective use of fonts, font size, style, color, effects, and alignment.

CONTROLLING TEXT

OBJECTIVES

Upon completion of this lesson, you should be able to:

- Adjust indents and line spacing.
- Set the margins of a document.
- Set and use tabs.
- Sort text.
- Create bulleted, numbered, and outline numbered lists.
- Change and customize lists.

⏱ Estimated Time: 1 hour

Changing Indents and Spacing

An *indent* is the space you insert between text and a document's margin. You can indent text from the left margin, from the right margin, or from both the left and right margins. You can indent text by using the indent markers on the ruler, shown in Figure 4-1.

The first-line indent marker is the upper triangle at the left edge of the ruler. The lower triangle is the hanging indent marker. The rectangle below the hanging indent is the left indent marker. The right indent marker is the lower triangle located at the right edge of the ruler. To indent text, select the text or position the insertion point in the text you want to indent, and then simply drag one of these markers to the desired point on the ruler.

FIGURE 4-1
Indent markers

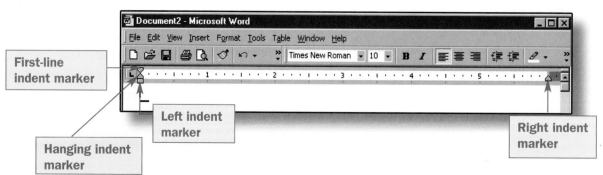

Because the first-line indent and the hanging indent are close together, they sometimes move at the same time. To move them at the same time, click the left indent marker, then drag. To move the hanging indent marker without moving the first-line indent marker, click in the point of the marker and drag.

Setting a First-Line Indent

Changing the first-line indent gives you many different ways to vary the look of your text. Using the first-line indent marker, you can indent paragraphs as you enter text as shown in Figure 4-2. After you set a first-line indent in one paragraph, all subsequent paragraphs you key will have the same first-line indent. First-line indents help you to locate the beginning of a new paragraph.

Hot Tip

You can also indent text using the Decrease Indent and Increase Indent buttons on the toolbar and the Left, Right, and Special boxes in the *Indentation* section of the Paragraph dialog box.

Hot Tip

You can place your mouse pointer over the indent markers on the ruler without clicking and the names of the indents will appear.

FIGURE 4-2
First-line indent

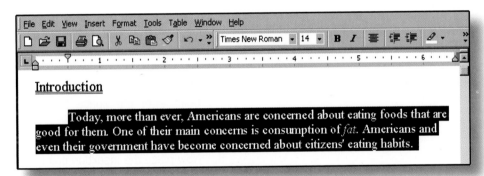

Setting a Hanging Indent

You can also create *hanging indents* in which the first full line of text is followed by indented lines, as shown in Figure 4-3. To set a hanging indent, drag the hanging indent marker to the right of the first-line indent marker. Hanging indents are useful for lists or documents such as glossaries.

FIGURE 4-3
Hanging indent

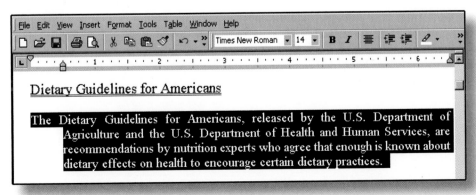

Indenting from Both Margins

Indenting from both margins, as shown in Figure 4-4, sets off paragraphs from the main body of text. You might use this type of indent for long quotations.

FIGURE 4-4
Indent from both margins

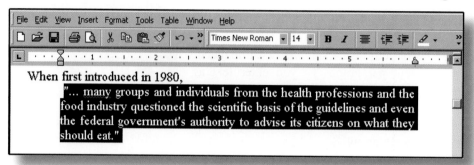

STEP-BY-STEP ▷ 4.1

1. Open the **Diet** document that you last used in Step-by-Step 3.8.

2. Save the document as **Diet2** followed by your initials.

3. Select the first paragraph or position the insertion point anywhere in the paragraph.

4. Click on the first-line indent marker and drag it to the .5-inch mark, as shown in Figure 4-2. You have created a first-line indent.

5. Select the paragraph after the *Dietary Guidelines for Americans* heading.

6. Click and drag the hanging indent marker to the .5-inch mark, as shown in Figure 4-3. You have created a hanging indent.

7. In the next paragraph, place the insertion point after the space following *1980,* and press **Enter**.

8. Now place the insertion point after the space following *eat."* and press **Enter**.

9. Click in the quotation.

10. Click the left indent marker and drag both the first-line indent and hanging indent markers to the .5-inch mark. You have created a left indent.

11. Drag the right indent marker to the 6-inch mark, as shown in Figure 4-4. You have created a right indent.

12. Save and leave the document open for the next Step-by-Step.

Adjusting Spacing

To help make a document more readable or appealing, you can adjust the spacing. There are several options—you can adjust the line spacing, the paragraph spacing, or the character spacing.

Line spacing refers to the amount of space between lines of text, as shown in Figure 4-5. By default, Word single-spaces text. Single-spacing has no extra space between each line. Single-spacing is often used for business letters or desktop publications.

FIGURE 4-5
Line spacing options

The line spacing of this paragraph is single. The line spacing of this paragraph is single.

The line spacing of this paragraph is 1.5 lines. The line spacing of this paragraph is 1.5 lines.

The line spacing of this paragraph is double. The line spacing of this paragraph is double.

To make text more readable, you can add space between lines of text. The 1.5 lines option adds half a line of space between lines. Double-spaced text has a full blank line between each line of text.

Change line spacing by choosing Paragraph from the Format menu to display the Paragraph dialog box (shown in Figure 4-6) and then make changes in the *Line spacing* box. You can also change to a common line space by using the keyboard shortcut keys shown in Table 4-1.

FIGURE 4-6
Paragraph dialog box

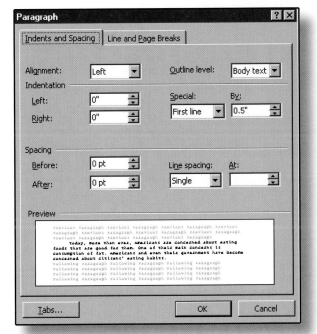

TABLE 4-1
Spacing keyboard shortcuts

LINE SPACE OPTION	SHORTCUT
Single	Ctrl+1
1.5 lines	Ctrl+5
Double	Ctrl+2

Another way to increase the readability of a page is to add spaces between the paragraphs. You can add space before or after paragraphs by accessing the Paragraph dialog box and changing the values in the *Before* or *After* box of the *Spacing* area.

You can adjust the spacing between characters by selecting the text and choosing Font from the Format menu. In the Font dialog box, click the Character Spacing tab, shown in Figure 4-7. When you choose Expanded or Condensed in the *Spacing* box, all the characters are altered by the same amount—the space chosen in the *By* box.

FIGURE 4-7
Character Spacing tab of Font dialog box

STEP-BY-STEP 4.2

1. Select the first paragraph of the document.

2. Choose **Paragraph** from the **Format** menu. The Paragraph dialog box appears, as shown in Figure 4-6.

3. In the *Spacing* section, click the down arrow in the *Line spacing* box.

4. Click **Double**. Notice the text under Preview changes to double-spaced.

5. Choose **OK**. The paragraph is double-spaced.

6. Select the paragraphs under the *Dietary Guidelines for Americans* heading up to (but not including) *The Seven Dietary Guidelines for Americans are:*.

7. Choose **Paragraph** from the **Format** menu. The Paragraph dialog box appears.

8. In the *Spacing* box beside *Before,* click the up arrow; **0 pt** should change to **6 pt**.

9. Choose **OK**. The extra space is inserted before each selected paragraph.

10. Select the title.

11. Choose **Font** from the **Format** menu. The Font dialog box appears.

12. Click the **Character Spacing** tab.

13. In the *Spacing* box, choose **Expanded**. In the *By* box, click the up arrow until **1 pt** is displayed. The dialog box should appear similar to Figure 4-7.

14. Click **OK**. The characters in the title have slightly more spacing between them.

15. Save the document and leave it open for the next Step-by-Step.

 Hot Tip

You can access the Paragraph dialog box quickly by right-clicking and choosing Paragraph from the shortcut menu.

Setting Margins

M*argins* are the blank areas around the top, bottom, and sides of a page. If you do not specify the amount of space to use as margins, Word will set the space to a standard setting, called the default margins. Sometimes, however, you will want different margins. For example, if you plan to bind a document along the left side of the page, you will need a larger left margin to make room for the binding.

The margins of a document are changed in the Margins section of the Page Setup dialog box, shown in Figure 4-8. To change the margin settings, select the current entry beside *Top* and key a new measurement. Press Tab to go to *Bottom*, the next setting. As you press Tab, notice that the Preview document's margins change to show the new margin settings. After you change the measurements for Top, Bottom, Left, and Right, click OK.

FIGURE 4-8
Page Setup dialog box

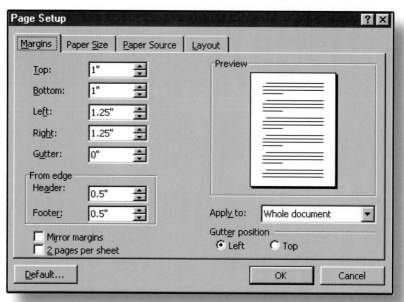

STEP-BY-STEP ▷ 4.3

1. Preview the document to see the existing margins. Close Print Preview.

2. Choose **Page Setup** from the **File** menu. The Page Setup dialog box appears. Click the **Margins** tab, as shown in Figure 4-7.

3. Change the Top margin to 1.25 inches by keying **1.25**.

4. Press **Tab** to go to the Bottom margin setting. Notice the sample document's margins change as you press Tab.

5. Key **.75** in the Bottom margin setting.

6. The Left and Right margin settings should be **1** inch.

7. Click **OK**.

8. Preview the document to see the new margins, as shown in Figure 4-9. Close Print Preview.

9. Save, print, and close the document.

Concept Builder

If you want to bind a document, you can insert space in the *Gutter* box to make room for the binding. You can change the amount of space between the edge of the page and header and footer text by keying a different measurement in the *From edge* box.

FIGURE 4-9
Print Preview reflecting changed margins

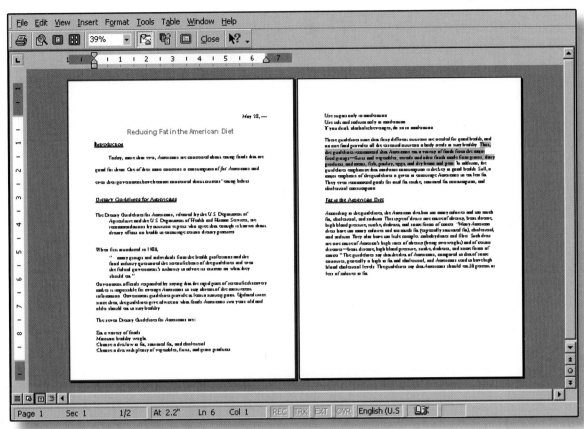

Setting Tabs

T*abs* mark the place where the insertion point will stop when you press the Tab key. Tabs are useful for creating tables or aligning numbered items. Text can be aligned with decimal, left, right, or center tabs, as shown in Figure 4-10. Notice that different tab symbols appear over the different types of tab settings. Left-aligned default tabs are set in Word every half inch.

FIGURE 4-10
Types of tabs

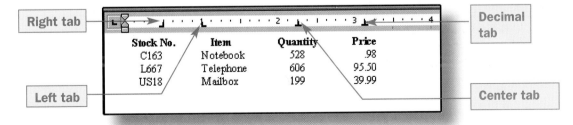

Tabs may be preceded by solid, dotted, or dashed lines called *leaders*, which fill the blank space before the tab setting. Sometimes these are used with tables of contents. Leaders can be used with any tab.

To set tabs, select the text or place your insertion point in the paragraph you want to be affected by the tab and choose Tabs from the Format menu. The Tabs dialog box appears, as shown in Figure 4-11. Key the tab stop position, choose a kind of tab alignment, and then choose what kind of leader you want, if any. Click Set to set the tab. After setting the tabs you want, click OK. If you are keying text, all additional paragraphs after the first one will have the same tab settings.

The Clear button allows you to clear a tab listed in the *Tab stop position* box. Use the Clear All button to clear all the tabs listed.

Another way to set tabs is by clicking the tab box at the far left of the ruler. Each time you click, it changes to another type of tab—left, right, center, or decimal. When it changes to the tab you want, click on the ruler at the measurement where you want to set the tab and the tab appears. To remove a tab, drag it off the ruler.

Concept Builder

The tab box on the ruler also has options for additional tabs—bar, first-line indent, and hanging indent.

FIGURE 4-11
Tabs dialog box

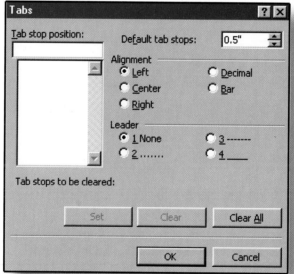

S TEP-BY-STEP ▷ 4.4

1. Open **IW Step4-4** from the student data files.

2. Save the document as **Supplies** followed by your initials.

3. Display the ruler, if it isn't showing already, by choosing **Ruler** from the **View** menu.

4. Select all data except the title.

5. Click the tab box on the ruler to display the left tab symbol if necessary. Click the 1.5-inch mark on the ruler to insert a left tab. The first column of text is left aligned at the 1.5-inch mark.

6. Choose **Tabs** from the **Format** menu. The Tabs dialog box appears as shown in Figure 4-10.

7. Click **Clear** to clear the -0.5 tab.

8. Key **4.75** in the *Tab stop position* box.

9. In the *Alignment* section, choose **Decimal** and in the *Leader* section, choose **2 ....** .

10. Click **Set**.

11. Click **OK**. The dialog box closes and text in the second column is lined up at the tab you set.

12. Save and leave the document open for the next Step-by-Step.

Extra Challenge

You can practice setting tabs by creating a list of your own. Include three columns of information: the item, the approximate price, and a phrase describing why you need the item. Use at least two different kinds of tabs.

Sorting Text in a Document

Sorting arranges a list of words in ascending order (*a* to *z*) or in descending order (*z* to *a*). It can also arrange a list of numbers in ascending (smallest to largest) or in descending (largest to smallest) order. Sorting is useful for putting lists of names or terms in alphabetic order.

To sort text in a document, choose Sort from the Table menu. The Sort Text dialog box appears, as shown in Figure 4-12. In this dialog box, you can choose the options for the sort.

FIGURE 4-12
Sort Text dialog box

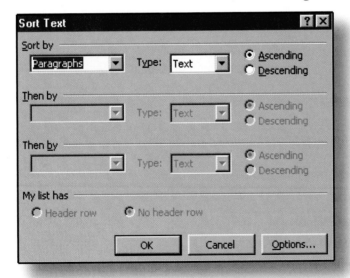

1. Select the list if necessary. Do not select the title.

2. Sort the list in ascending order by price following these steps:
   a. Choose **Sort** from the **Table** menu. The Sort Text dialog box appears, as shown in Figure 4-11.
   b. In the *Sort by* box, choose **Paragraphs** if necessary.
   c. In the *Type* box, choose **Number**.
   d. Choose **Ascending** if necessary.
   e. Click **OK**. The list is sorted in ascending order by price.

3. Sort the list in ascending alphabetic order following these steps:
   a. With the list still selected, choose **Sort** from the **Table** menu. The Sort Text dialog box appears.
   b. In the *Sort by* box, choose **Paragraphs** if necessary.
   c. In the *Type* box, choose **Text** if necessary.
   d. Choose **Ascending** if necessary.
   e. Click **OK**. The list is sorted in ascending alphabetic order.

4. Save, print, and close the document.

Using Bullets and Numbering

The Bullets and Numbering dialog box provides three options for creating a list—bulleted, numbered, and outline numbered. The process for creating a bulleted list or a numbered list is very similar. An outline numbered list is a little different.

Bulleted and Numbered Lists

Sometimes it is helpful to create a bulleted or numbered list in a document—for example, when it is difficult to distinguish between groups of items that are bunched together in a sentence. A numbered list is used when items appear sequentially, such as instructions. A bulleted list is often used when the order of items does not need to be emphasized. Bullets are any small character that appears before an item. Pictures, symbols, and icons can all be used as bullets.

To create a bulleted or numbered list, click the Bullets or Numbering button on the toolbar and begin keying. Each time you press Enter, a new bullet or number automatically appears. To finish a list, press Enter twice. Alternatively, to convert existing text into a bulleted or numbered list, select the text and click the Bullets or Numbering button on the toolbar.

Concept Builder

Word will automatically format your text as a bulleted list if you key a hyphen (-) or asterisk (*), space or tab, key text, and then press Enter. A numbered list is automatically formatted when you key 1, period, space or tab, key text, and then press Enter.

STEP-BY-STEP ▷ 4.6

1. Start a new Word document.

2. Key **To Do List** and press **Enter**.

3. Click the **Numbering** button on the toolbar. The number 1 appears and then a tabbed space so you can begin keying a numbered list.

4. Key **Go to the bank on Thursday.**

5. Press **Enter**. Notice how Word automatically formats the next number in the list.

6. Key the remaining items in the to do list shown below.

   2. Water the plants on Friday.
   3. Key the February report.

7. After you key the third item, press **Enter** twice to stop the numbered list formatting.

8. Key **Items for Meeting** and press **Enter**.

9. Click the **Bullets** button on the toolbar. A bullet appears with a tabbed space so you can begin keying a bulleted list. Notice the bullet is indented further than the numbered list. You will learn how to change this later.

10. Key **Murphy file**.

11. Press **Enter**. Notice how Word automatically continues formatting a bulleted list.

12. Key the remaining items under *Items for Meeting* shown below.

   • Research report
   • Notes from the meeting on January 13th

13. After keying the third item in the list, press **Enter** twice to stop the bulleted list formatting.

14. Save the document as **Lists** followed by your initials.

15. Print and close.

Outline Numbered Lists

A list is multileveled when it contains two or more levels of bullets and numbering. You can create multilevel lists, such as outlines, by choosing the Outline Numbered tab in the Bullets and Numbering dialog box. As shown in Figure 4-13, it contains predefined formats for multilevel lists. Click the format you want to use for your multilevel list and begin keying.

As you key a multilevel list, you will need to indent some items more than others. Click the Increase Indent and Decrease Indent buttons on the formatting toolbar to help you build the hierarchy of your multilevel list.

 Hot Tip

You can also press the Tab button to indent an item or press Shift+Tab to decrease the indent on an item.

FIGURE 4-13

Outline Numbered tab of the Bullets and Numbering dialog box

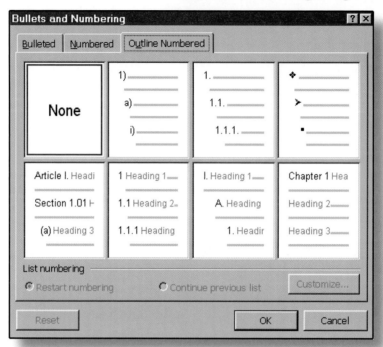

STEP-BY-STEP ▷ 4.7

1. Open **IW Step4-7** from the student data files.

2. Save the document as **Outlines** followed by your initials.

3. Select the four items under *Payroll Deductions*.

4. Click the **Bullets** button on the formatting toolbar. The items are formatted into a bulleted list.

5. Select the four items under *Income Sources*.

6. Click the **Numbering** button on the formatting toolbar. The items are formatted into a numbered list. Don't worry if the bulleted list and numbered list are not aligned—you will learn how to change that later.

7. Place the insertion point on the blank line below the heading *Employment Benefits.*

8. Choose **Bullets and Numbering** from the **Format** menu. The Bullets and Numbering dialog box appears.

9. Click the **Outline Numbered** tab, as shown in Figure 4-12.

10. Click the second format on the top row and choose **OK**. The number *1)* and an indent appear.

11. Key **Insurance** and press **Enter**.

12. Click the **Increase Indent** button. The indent is increased and the letter *a)* appears.

13. Key **Medical** and press **Enter**.

14. Key **Life** and press **Enter** and key **Dental** and press **Enter**.

15. Click the **Decrease Indent** button. The indent is decreased and the number *2)* appears.

16. Key the remaining items as shown below.

```
2) Vacation
   a)Holidays
   b)Personal Days
```

```
3) Leave
   a)Sick
   b)Emergency
```

17. Save and leave the document open for the next Step-by-Step.

Changing and Customizing Lists

Using the Bullets and Numbering dialog box, you can change the appearance of lists in the same way as you chose a predefined format for the multilevel list. Select the list you want to change and choose Bullets and Numbering from the Format menu to access the Bullets and Numbering dialog box. Click the Bulleted or Numbered tab and click the format you want.

To change the appearance of a bulleted list, choose Bullets and Numbering from the Format menu. Choose the bullet style you want in the Bulleted tab, shown in Figure 4-14.

FIGURE 4-14

Bulleted tab of the Bullets and Numbering dialog box

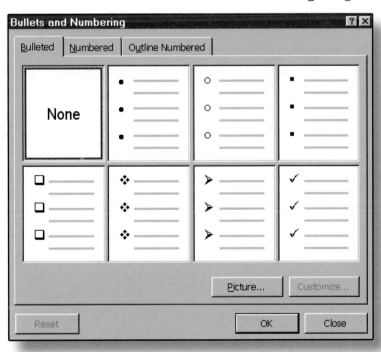

To customize a bulleted list, click the Customize button. As shown in Figure 4-15, you can change the bullet character, bullet position, or text position in the Customize Bulleted List dialog box. The *Preview* box shows how the list will look.

To change the appearance of a numbered list, choose the Numbered tab, shown in Figure 4-16. Click the numbered style you want and choose whether you want to restart the numbering or continue the previous list.

Concept Builder

You can insert a picture or other graphical bullet by clicking Picture in the Bulleted tab of the Bullets and Numbering dialog box. Picture bullets are often used when creating documents for the Web.

FIGURE 4-15
Customize Bulleted List dialog box

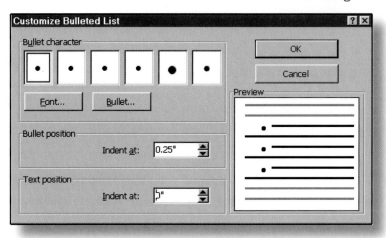

FIGURE 4-16
Numbered tab of the Bullets and Numbering dialog box

To customize a numbered list, click the Customize button. As shown in Figure 4-17, you can change the number format, number style, number position, and text position in the Customize Numbered List dialog box. The *Preview* box shows how the list will look.

FIGURE 4-17
Customize Numbered List dialog box

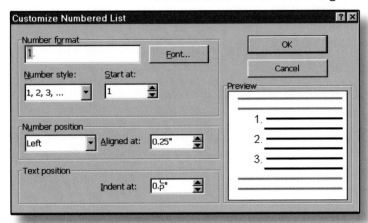

STEP-BY-STEP ▷ 4.8

1. Select the four bulleted items under *Payroll Deductions*. (The bullets will not be selected.)

2. Choose **Bullets and Numbering** from the **Format** menu. The Bullets and Numbering dialog box appears.

3. Click the **Bulleted** tab if necessary.

4. Click the second bullet option on the second row (❖), and choose **OK**. The bullets change character.

5. Select the four numbered items under *Income Sources*. (The numbers will not be selected.)

6. Choose **Bullets and Numbering** from the **Format** menu. The Bullets and Numbering dialog box appears.

7. Click the **Numbered** tab if necessary.

8. Click the first choice on the second row.

9. Click the **Customize** button. The Customize Numbered List dialog box appears.

10. In the *Number position* section, change *Aligned at:* to **.25 inches**.

11. In the *Text position* section, change *Indent at:* to **.5 inches**.

12. Click **OK**. The numbered list changes to an alphabetic list and is aligned with the bulleted list.

13. Save, print, and close the document.

 Extra Challenge

Open the *Lists* document you created in Step-by-Step 4.6. Change the bulleted list so that it is aligned with the numbered list and change the bullet character.

Summary

In this lesson, you learned:

- You can indent text from the left margin, right margin, or from both the left and right margins.

- Single-spacing has no extra space between each line. Double-spacing has one full line space between each line of text.

- If you do not specify the amount of space to use as margins, Word will set the space to a standard setting, called the default margins.

- Text can be aligned with decimal, left-aligned, right-aligned, or centered tabs. Leaders can be used with any kind of tab. Sorting arranges a list of words or numbers in ascending order or descending order.

- Use the Bullets or Numbering buttons on the toolbar to create bulleted or numbered lists. To change the appearance of your list, choose Bullets and Numbering from the Format menu to access the Bullets and Numbering dialog box.

LESSON 4 REVIEW QUESTIONS

TRUE/FALSE

Circle T if the statement is true or F if the statement is false.

T F 1. An indent is the space you place between text and a document's margins.

T F 2. Tabs are useful for adding space before or after a paragraph.

T F 3. A list of numbers in ascending order goes from largest to smallest.

T F 4. Pictures, symbols, and icons can all be used as bullets.

T F 5. If you do not specify margins, your document will not have any.

MULTIPLE CHOICE

Select the best response for the following statements.

1. What type of text has a full blank line between each line of text?
   A. Single-spaced
   B. Indented
   C. Double-spaced
   D. Paragraph

2. A line of periods or dashes preceding a tab is called a
   A. Tab symbol
   B. Leader
   C. Decimal line
   D. Default dot

3. The upper triangle at the left edge of the ruler indicates the
    A. First-line indent marker
    B. Decrease indent marker
    C. Hanging indent marker
    D. Left indent marker

4. To customize your bulleted list, you can change
    A. Bullet character
    B. Bullet position
    C. Text position
    D. All of the above

5. Which tab in the Bullets and Numbering dialog box contains predefined formats for multilevel lists?
    A. Numbered
    B. Bulleted
    C. Outline Numbered
    D. All of the above

LESSON 4 PROJECTS

PROJECT 4-1

1. Open **IW Project4-1** from the student data files.

2. Save the document as **Porch Lights** followed by your initials.

3. Sort the paragraphs in ascending alphabetic order.

4. Create a numbered list from all the text (not including the headings).

5. Customize the list so the numbers are aligned at 0 inches and the text is indented at .25 inches.

6. Change the line spacing of the text so there is 6 pt spacing before each paragraph.

7. Change the left and right margins to 1 inch.

8. Save, print, and close the document.

PROJECT 4-2

1. Open **IW Project4-2** from the student data files.

2. Save the document as **Shipping** followed by your initials.

3. Place the insertion point two lines below the paragraph.

4. Set left tabs at 1.75 inches, 3 inches, and 4.75 inches.

5. Key the headings **Company**, **Cost**, **Weight Limit**, and **Delivery Time** in bold using the tabs.

6. Press **Enter**. Clear all the current tabs.

7. Set a decimal tab with dot style leaders at 1.94 inches.

8. Set a center tab with dot style leaders at 3.5 inches.

9. Set a right tab with dot style leaders at 5.63 inches.

10. Using the tabs just set, key the following information in a table:

```
Lightning    $11.75    1 lb 4 oz    1:00 p.m.
Pronto       $9.99     10 oz.       12:30 p.m.
Zippy        $14.50    2 lbs        10:00 a.m.
Speed Air    $12.95    none         3:00 p.m.
```

11. Sort the list in ascending order.

12. Indent the first line of the first paragraph .5 inches.

13. Change the spacing of the table to 1.5 inches.

14. Save, print, and close the document.

PROJECT 4-3

1. Open the **Interview** file that you last used in Project 1-2.

2. Save the document as **Interview2** followed by your initials.

3. Change all the text to 12 point.

4. Bold and center the title in 14 point Arial.

5. Key a colon after the words *such as* in the first sentence of the second paragraph and then delete the rest of the sentence.

6. Key the following items as a bulleted list with the bullet character shown:

```
❖ Social Security card
❖ Names and addresses of former employers
❖ Names and addresses of references
❖ A copy of your resume
❖ School records
```

7. Double-space the first paragraph and the first line of the second paragraph. Indent the first line of the first and second paragraphs .25 inches.

8. Sort the bulleted list in ascending order and change the spacing to 1.5.

9. Save, print, and close the document.

CRITICAL THINKING

ACTIVITY 4-1

You have keyed a bulleted list of items for a project at work, but the bulleted characters keep showing up as clock faces. Use Help to figure out what the problem is and how to solve it.

ACTIVITY 4-2

You work as an administrative assistant at a local commercial college. The professor who teaches an introductory computer class asks you to key a list of basic Word features that he can use in class. Create an outline numbered list of the Word features you have learned so far. Use different levels and customize the format however you want.

LESSON 5

HELPFUL WORD FEATURES

OBJECTIVES

Upon completion of this lesson, you should be able to:

■ Use AutoFormat As You Type, AutoComplete, and AutoText.

■ Make corrections using AutoCorrect, automatic spell checking, and automatic grammar checking.

■ Check the spelling and grammar of a document.

■ Insert the date and time.

■ Insert hyphens.

■ Use the Thesaurus.

■ Find specific text and replace it with other text.

🕐 **Estimated Time: 1 hour**

Using Automatic Features

Word offers many types of automated features that can help you create documents. AutoCorrect corrects errors as you type, AutoFormat As You Type applies built-in formats as you type, AutoText inserts frequently used text, and AutoComplete guesses words as you are typing. Word also has automatic features that check your spelling and grammar.

AutoCorrect

AutoCorrect is a feature that automatically corrects errors as you type. It corrects common capitalization, typing, spelling, and grammatical errors. AutoCorrect is also useful for quickly inserting text. For example, you can specify that when you key the letters *bc*, they will always be replaced with Barkewiecz Corporation. Unless you specify otherwise, this feature is turned on. You can turn it off or make adjustments in the AutoCorrect dialog box (shown in Figure 5-1) by choosing AutoCorrect from the Tools menu and removing the checkmarks beside the features you want to disable.

 Concept Builder

You can click the Exceptions button in the AutoCorrect dialog box to specify any capitalization that you don't want Word to correct automatically.

FIGURE 5-1
AutoCorrect dialog box

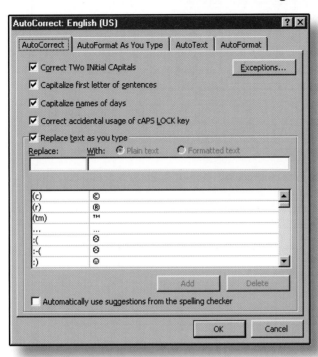

S TEP-BY-STEP ▷ 5.1

1. Open **IW Step5-1** from the student data files.

2. Save as **To Do Memo** followed by your initials.

3. Place the insertion point on the first blank line after the list of things to do on Day 1 and key the following (with the misspelled word *hte*): **type notes taken at hte marketing meeting.** Notice that AutoCorrect automatically capitalized *Type* as the first word in a sentence immediately after you keyed it. AutoCorrect also recognized that you meant to key *the* and automatically changed *hte* to the correct spelling.

4. Choose AutoCorrect from the Tools menu. The AutoCorrect dialog box appears, as shown in Figure 5-1.

5. In the *Replace* box, key your three initials in lowercase. Press **Tab** to move to the *With* box.

6. In the *With* box, key your full name. Click the **Add** button.

7. Click **OK** to close the AutoCorrect dialog box.

8. Select *Student's Name* beside *To:*.

9. Key your initials in lowercase and then a space. AutoCorrect replaces the initials with your full name.

10. Save the document and leave it open for the next Step-by-Step.

AutoFormat As You Type

When you use the AutoFormat As You Type feature, Word automatically applies built-in formats to text as you type. For example, if you type the number 1, a period, press Tab, and then key text, Word automatically formats the text for a numbered list. Similarly, if you type a bullet, press Tab, and key text, Word formats that text as a bulleted list. Word also changes fractions and numbers such as *3/4* to $^3/4$ and *31st* to 31st as you key.

To choose which automatic formatting options you want, choose AutoCorrect from the Tools menu and then click the AutoFormat As You Type tab, as shown in Figure 5-2.

FIGURE 5-2
AutoFormat As You Type tab of the AutoCorrect dialog box

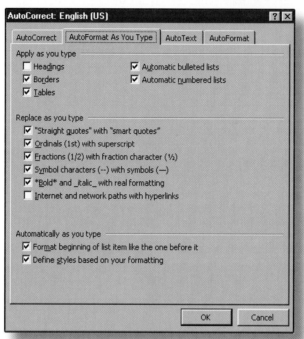

STEP-BY-STEP 5.2

1. On the second item under *Day 4*, delete the period and key **(8 1/2 x 11).** Notice that Auto-Format As You Type changes the fraction from *1/2* to $^1/2$ after you key it.

2. Place the insertion point on the blank line below *Day 5*. Key the following text and notice that AutoFormat As You Type automatically formats the text for a numbered list as you key:

   1. Key and distribute letters to partners about new parking arrangements.

3. Press **Enter**. Notice that AutoFormat As You

Type automatically formats the next number in the list. Key the following text beside number 2:

   2. Pick me up from the airport at 3:38 p.m. Let me know if there are any important items I need to take care of before 5 p.m.

4. On the first item under *Day 5*, change the period to a comma and key **which begin on the 3rd**. Notice that AutoFormat As You Type changes *3rd* to *3rd* after you key it.

5. Save and leave the document open for the next Step-by-Step.

AutoText

Using AutoText, you can store frequently used text, such as a name, address, or slogan, so you don't have to rekey it each time. You can use the built-in AutoText entries that are available or create your own. To insert an entry, choose AutoText from the Insert menu. A submenu appears listing categories of common AutoText entries such as Mailing Instructions and Salutation. Clicking one of these items opens another submenu with the choices that you can insert in your document.

Concept Builder

Choose View, Toolbars, AutoText to display the AutoText toolbar and quickly access available AutoText entries or create your own.

To create your own entry, choose AutoText from the Insert menu and then AutoText from the submenu. The AutoCorrect dialog box appears with the AutoText tab displayed, as shown in Figure 5-3. Key your entry and click Add. You can also add an entry to your document, delete an entry, or display the AutoText toolbar using this dialog box.

FIGURE 5-3
AutoText tab of the AutoCorrect dialog box

STEP-BY-STEP ▷ 5.3

1. Place the insertion point at the right tab underneath *Date:* at the top of the memo.

2. Choose **AutoText** from the **Insert** menu and **Subject Line** from the submenu. Click **Subject:** and the text is automatically inserted in the document at the insertion point.

3. Choose **AutoText** from the **Insert** menu and **AutoText** from the submenu. The AutoCorrect dialog box appears, as shown in Figure 5-3.

4. Key your name in the *Enter AutoText entries here* box.

5. Click **Add** to add your name to the AutoText entries. Click **OK** to close the dialog box.

6. Save and leave the document open for the next Step-by-Step.

AutoComplete

AutoComplete guesses certain words you are keying from the first few letters and then suggests the entire word. For example, if you key *Dece*, the word *December* appears in a ScreenTip above the insertion point, as shown in Figure 5-4. To accept the suggested word, press Enter, and the word *December* appears. To ignore the suggested word, just keep keying. Word can AutoComplete words such as days of the week, months, the current date, or AutoText entries—including ones you have created.

FIGURE 5-4
ScreenTip

To:	Student's Name
From:	Jan December
Date:	18 Dece
Subject:	Things To Do Next Week

STEP-BY-STEP ▷ 5.4

1. Delete your name beside *To:*.

2. Begin keying your name in the same place. When the AutoComplete suggestion appears with your name, press **Enter** to accept it.

3. Select *Date*. Key **18 Dece** and press **Enter** to accept the AutoComplete suggestion when it appears, as shown in Figure 5-4.

4. Select *Day 1*. Key **Mond** and press **Enter** to accept the AutoComplete suggestion when it appears.

5. Replace each of the other *Day* headings with the consecutive days of the week, accepting each AutoComplete suggestion when it appears.

6. Save and leave the document open for the next Step-by-Step.

Automatic Spell Checking

Automatic spell checking identifies misspellings and words that are not in Word's dictionary by underlining them with a wavy red line immediately after you key them. To correct a misspelled word that is underlined, position the pointer on the word and click with the right mouse button. A shortcut menu appears with a list of correctly spelled words. Click with the left mouse button on the suggestion that you want, and it replaces the misspelled word. The automatic spell checker can be turned on and off or adjusted by accessing the Spelling & Grammar tab of the Options dialog box (see Figure 5-5) through the Tools menu. To check spelling manually, click the Spelling button on the toolbar.

Did You Know?

The automatic spell checker sometimes identifies words as being misspelled that aren't, such as names. This is because the spell checker could not find the word in its dictionary.

FIGURE 5-5

Spelling & Grammar tab of the Options dialog box

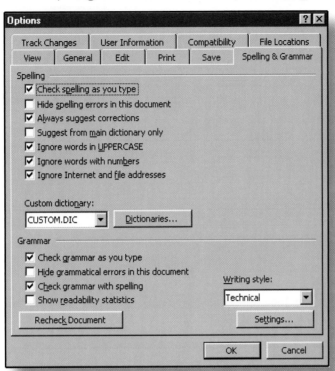

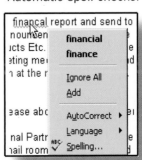

STEP-BY-STEP 5.5

1. Choose **Options** from the **Tools** menu. Click the **Spelling & Grammar** tab, as shown in Figure 5-5.

2. In the *Spelling* section, click to insert a checkmark in the *Check spelling as you type* box if the box is not already checked.

3. Click **OK**.

4. Place the insertion point between the words *formatting* and *report* on the first item under *Monday*.

5. Key the misspelled word *financal* followed by a space. The automatic spell checker detected the misspelled word and underlined it in red.

6. Position the I-beam on the underlined misspelled word and click the right mouse button. A shortcut menu appears, as shown in Figure 5-6.

7. With the left mouse button, click on **financial**, the correct spelling. The misspelled word is replaced with the correctly spelled word and the wavy red underline disappears.

8. Save and leave the document open for the next Step-by-Step.

FIGURE 5-6

Automatic spell checker

Automatic Grammar Checking

Similar to the automatic spell checker feature, automatic grammar checking checks your document for grammatical errors. When it finds a possible error, Word underlines the word, phrase, or sentence with a wavy green line. To see the suggested corrections, right-click the word or phrase. Choose a suggestion or Grammar from the shortcut menu. For more information about the particular grammar error that has been identified, you can choose About this Sentence.

The automatic grammar checker looks for capitalization errors, commonly confused words, misused words, passive sentences, punctuation problems, and other types of grammar problems.

Concept Builder

Although the grammar checker is a helpful tool, you still need to have a good working knowledge of English grammar. The grammar checker can identify a possible problem, but it's up to you to decide if the change should be made depending on the context of the sentence.

STEP-BY-STEP ▷ 5.6

1. Choose **Options** from the **Tools** menu. In the Options dialog box, click the **Spelling & Grammar** tab.

2. In the *Grammar* section, click to insert a checkmark beside *Check grammar as you type* if the box is not already checked. Click **OK**.

3. Create a third item under *Friday* and key the following passive sentence:

   ```
   Call Mack and see if the travel
   arrangements were made by him
   for next week.
   ```

4. Press **Enter** twice after you key the sentence. The grammar checker automatically identifies the sentence as a problem and underlines it in green.

5. Position the I-beam on the green underlined part of the sentence and click the right mouse button. A shortcut menu appears, as shown in Figure 5-7.

6. Choose the suggested change at the top of the shortcut menu, **he made travel arrangements**. The sentence is corrected.

7. Create a numbered list from the items under each day, as has been done for *Friday* already.

8. Save, print, and close the document.

Did You Know?

A *passive* sentence is one in which the subject of the sentence is acted upon, like the sentence in Step-by-Step 5.6, step 3. An *active* sentence is one in which the subject of the sentence acts, like the sentence in step 6. You should always strive to write active sentences.

FIGURE 5-7
Automatic grammar checker

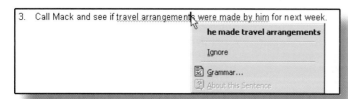

Using the Spelling and Grammar Checker

In addition to checking your spelling as you type and making some corrections automatically, Word also lets you check your document's spelling and grammar after you finish keying it. You can check an entire document or portions of a document by clicking the Spelling and Grammar button on the toolbar or by choosing the Spelling and Grammar command from the Tools menu.

The Spelling and Grammar dialog box shown in Figure 5-8 contains options that allow you to check the spelling and grammar of words, ignore words, make changes, or add words to your own custom dictionary. When Word finds an error, you can correct it through the Spelling and Grammar dialog box and continue the check. You can also click the Office Assistant button—the button with a question mark—in the dialog box to get information about the possible error. Table 5-1 explains each of the available options in the Spelling and Grammar dialog box.

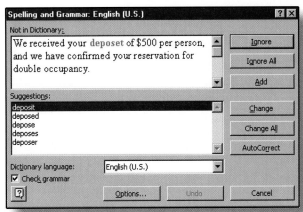

FIGURE 5-8
Spelling and Grammar dialog box

TABLE 5-1
Spelling and Grammar dialog box options

OPERATION	ACTION
Ignore	Ignores only the word displayed in red or green.
Ignore All	Ignores all instances of the same word or occurrences of the rule.
Change	Changes only the selected word.
Change All	Changes all instances of the same word.
Add	Adds the selected word to the custom dictionary.
Suggestions	Displays a list of proposed spellings or grammar changes.
AutoCorrect	Adds a word to your AutoCorrect list.
Options	Allows you to change default spelling and grammar check settings.
Undo	Reverses your last spelling change.
Cancel/Close	Before you make a spelling change, Cancel stops the spelling check. At the end of a spell check, Close stops the spelling check and saves all the changes you have made. After your first spelling change, the button name *Cancel* changes to *Close*.

1. Open **IW Step 5-7** from the student data files.

2. Save the document as **Tour Letter** followed by your initials.

3. Press **Ctrl+Home** to move the insertion point to the beginning of the document.

4. Click the **Spelling and Grammar** button on the toolbar. The Spelling and Grammar dialog box appears, as shown in Figure 5-8.

5. The word *deposet* is displayed in red type in the dialog box. Note that suggested words are listed in the Suggestions box.

6. Click the word **deposit**.

7. Click **Change**. Word replaces the misspelled word and continues checking.

8. The word *has* is displayed in green. The word *have* is in the Suggestions box. Click **Change**.

9. The word *valad* is displayed in red. The word *valid* is in the Suggestions box. Click **Change**.

10. The word *recomends* is displayed in red. The word *recommends* is in the Suggestions box. Click **Change**.

11. The word *a* is displayed in green. Click **Change** to change it to *an*.

12. The word *departur* is displayed in red. The word *departure* and another word is suggested. Click **Change All**. Word replaces the error each time it occurs in the document and continues checking.

13. The word *Cassaundra* is displayed in red. Click **Ignore**.

14. The message *The spelling and grammar check is complete* appears.

15. Click **OK**. The insertion point returns to the beginning of the document.

16. Save and leave the document open for the next Step-by-Step.

Inserting the Date and Time

You can easily insert the current date and time into a word processing document. Choose Date and Time from the Insert menu to display the Date and Time dialog box, shown in Figure 5-9. Select one of the many different formats available. You can choose a different language and also whether or not the date will be updated automatically each time you open a document. When creating a letter or memo you would want the date to remain fixed for record keeping purposes. However, if you were inserting the date in a template or a report issued on a regular basis you would probably want to have the current date displayed each time you open the document.

Hot Tip

To automatically insert the current date using AutoComplete, begin keying the name of the current month. When a box pops up, press Enter to insert the month. Key a space and a box pops up with the current date. Press Enter to insert the entire date in the document.

FIGURE 5-9
Date and Time dialog box

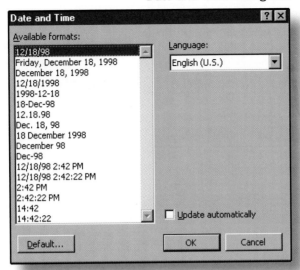

STEP-BY-STEP ▷ 5.8

1. Place the insertion point on the first blank line of the document.

2. Choose **Date and Time** from the **Insert** menu. The Date and Time dialog box appears, as shown in Figure 5-9.

3. Click on the format *25 September 1998*.

4. *English (US)* should be chosen in the *Language* box.

5. There should not be a check in the *Update automatically* box.

6. Click **OK**. The current date is inserted in the letter.

7. Save and leave the document open for the next Step-by-Step.

Inserting Hyphens

Hyphens give documents a professional look. You can hyphenate text automatically by using the Language command on the Tools menu and clicking Hyphenation. In the Hyphenation dialog box, shown in Figure 5-10, select the *Automatically hyphenate document* check box.

You can also insert hyphens manually. If you want to control where a word or phrase breaks if it falls at the end of a line, you can use an optional hyphen. To insert an optional hyphen, click where you want to insert the hyphen in the word or phrase and press Ctrl+Hyphen.

Concept Builder

Increasing the hyphenation zone in the Hyphenation dialog box will reduce the number of hyphens in a document. Decreasing the hyphenation zone will reduce the raggedness of the right margin by inserting more hyphens.

If you want to make sure that text separated by a hyphen doesn't divide over two lines, use a nonbreaking hyphen. For example, use a nonbreaking hyphen when numbers separated by a hyphen must remain on the same line. To insert a nonbreaking hyphen, press Ctrl+Shift+-.

FIGURE 5-10
Hyphenation dialog box

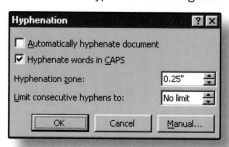

S TEP-BY-STEP ▷ 5.9

1. Choose **Language** from the **Tools** menu. Then choose **Hyphenation** from the submenu. The Hyphenation dialog box appears, as shown in Figure 5-10.

2. Click to place a check in the *Automatically hyphenate document* box.

3. Click **OK**. Text in the document is automatically hyphenated.

4. Save and leave the document open for the next Step-by-Step.

C Concept Builder

You can insert optional or nonbreaking hyphens and other special characters by choosing Symbol from the Insert menu and clicking the Special Characters tab. To insert symbols, such as ® or Σ, click the Symbol tab in the same dialog box.

Using the Thesaurus

C

The **Thesaurus** is a useful feature for finding a synonym (a word with a similar meaning) for a word in your document. For some words, the Thesaurus also lists antonyms, or words with opposite meanings. Use the Thesaurus to find the exact word to express your message or to avoid using the same word repeatedly in a document. To use the Thesaurus, select the word you want to look up and choose Language from the Tools menu and Thesaurus from the submenu. The Thesaurus dialog box appears, as shown in

Concept Builder

Even synonyms can have different shades of meaning. Be sure the synonym makes sense in context before replacing a word.

Figure 5-11. In the *Meanings* box, click the word that best describes what you want to say. Then choose from the words listed in the *Replace with Synonym* box and click Replace. Table 5-2 describes the options in the Thesaurus dialog box.

FIGURE 5-11
Thesaurus dialog box

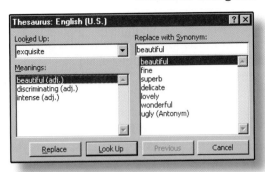

TABLE 5-2
Thesaurus dialog box options

OPERATION	ACTION
Replace	Click to replace the original word with the word in the *Replace with Synonym* box.
Look Up	Shows a listing of possible synonyms and meanings.
Previous	Click to show the last word you looked up in the current Thesaurus session. Does not show words from a previous dialog box.
Cancel	Click to close the dialog box.

STEP-BY-STEP ▷ 5.10

1. Select the word *exquisite* in the first paragraph.

2. Choose **Language** from the **Tools** menu and choose **Thesaurus** from the submenu. The Thesaurus dialog box appears, as in Figure 5-11. The *Meanings* box contains a list of the meanings of *exquisite*.

3. The meaning **beautiful (adj.)** should be selected. The box under *Replace with Synonym* contains a list of synonyms for *exquisite* using the *beautiful* meaning.

4. Click **wonderful**.

5. Click **Replace**. The word *exquisite* is replaced with the word *beautiful* in the document. Notice that the paragraph is automatically re-hyphenated when you make changes.

6. Select the word *establish* in the second sentence of the fourth paragraph.

7. Using the *ascertain (v.)* meaning, replace *establish* with the synonym *determine*.

8. Save and leave the document open for the next Step-by-Step.

Using Find and Replace

C Find and Replace are useful editing commands that let you find specific words in a document quickly and, if you wish, replace them instantly with new words. Both commands are chosen from the Edit menu. First you will learn about Find, then about Replace.

The Find Command

Using the Find command, you can quickly search a document for every occurrence of a specific word or phrase you key in the *Find what* box. The Find command moves the insertion point from its present position to the next occurrence of the word or phrase for which you are searching.

Find can locate whole or partial words. For example, it can find the word *all* or any word with *all* in it, such as *fall, horizontally,* or *alloy.* You can display options by clicking the More button in the Find and Replace dialog box, explained in Table 5-3, to narrow your search criteria.

TABLE 5-3
Find dialog box options

OPERATION	ACTION
Search	Lets you search from the location of the insertion point up, from the location of the insertion point down, or all (the entire document).
Match case	Searches for words with the same case as that keyed in the *Find what* box.
Find whole words only	Finds only the word *all*—not words with *all* in them.
Use wildcards	Makes it possible to search for words using a question mark or asterisk, called a wildcard, along with a word or characters in the Find dialog box. Each question mark represents a single character in the same position in a word. Each asterisk represents two or more characters. See Table 5-4.
Sounds like	Locates words that sound alike but are spelled differently. For example, if you key the word *so,* Word would also find the word *sew.*
Find all word forms	Lets you find different forms of words. For example, if you search for the word *run,* Word would also find *ran, runs,* and *running.*
Find Next	Goes to the next occurrence of the word.
Cancel	Stops the search and closes the dialog box.
More/Less	Displays the Find and Replace options/Hides the options.
Format	Lets you search for formatting, such as bold, instead of searching for a specific word. It also allows you to search for words with specific formatting, such as the word *computer* in bold.
Special	Lets you search for special characters that may be hidden, such as a paragraph mark, or special characters that are not hidden, such as an em dash (—).

TABLE 5-4
Using wildcards

TO FIND	KEY
Both *Caleb* and *Kaleb*	?aleb
Any five-letter word beginning with *a* and ending with *n*	a???n
June and *July*	Ju*
Kindness, tenderness, selfishness	*ness

S TEP-BY-STEP ▷ 5.11

1. Place the insertion point at the beginning of the document.

2. Choose **Find** from the **Edit** menu. The Find and Replace dialog box appears.

3. Click the **More** button. The Find and Replace dialog box looks like Figure 5-12.

4. In the *Find what* box, key **con***.

5. In the *Search Options* section, check the **Use wildcards** option.

6. Choose **Find Next**. Word selects and stops on the word *confirmed*. (If the Find and Replace dialog box is covering the word *confirmed*, click on the title bar and drag the box down until the word is displayed.)

7. Choose **Find Next**. Word stops on the word *consulting*.

8. Click **Cancel**.

9. Move the insertion point to the beginning of the document.

10. Choose **Find** from the **Edit** menu.

11. Key **tour** in the *Find what* box.

12. Click the **Use wildcards** option to remove the checkmark.

13. Click the **Find whole words only** option.

14. In the *Search* box, choose **All**, if necessary.

15. Click **Find Next**. The word *tour* is selected.

16. Click **Find Next** again. The second occurrence of the word *tour* is selected. (You may need to move the dialog box to view the selected word.)

17. Click **Find Next** again. The message *Word has finished searching the document* appears. Click **OK**.

18. Click **Cancel**. The Find and Replace dialog box disappears.

19. Save and leave the document open for the next Step-by-Step.

(continued on next page)

FIGURE 5-12
Find tab in the Find and Replace dialog box

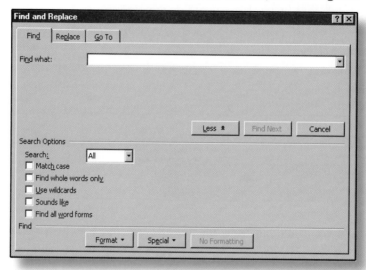

The Replace Command

The Replace command is an extended version of the Find command. Replace has all the features of Find. In addition, the Replace command, shown in Figure 5-13, allows you to replace a word or phrase in the *Find what* box with another word or phrase you key in the *Replace with* box. The replacements can be made individually using the Replace button, or all occurrences can be replaced at once using the Replace All button.

FIGURE 5-13
Replace tab in the Find and Replace dialog box

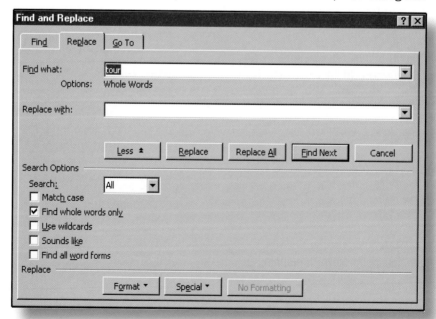

S TEP-BY-STEP ▷ 5.12

1. Press **Ctrl+Home** to move the insertion point to the beginning of the document.

2. Choose **Replace** from the **Edit** menu. The Find and Replace dialog box appears with the word *tour* in the *Find what* box, as shown in Figure 5-13.

3. Key **December** in the *Find what* box.

4. Key **June** in the *Replace with* box.

5. Click **Replace All**. The following message appears: *Word has completed its search of the document and has made 1 replacement.*

6. Click **OK**.

7. Click **Close** to close the Find and Replace dialog box.

8. Save, print and close the document.

Summary

In this lesson, you learned:

■ The AutoFormat As You Type feature automatically applies built-in formats to text as you type. AutoComplete guesses certain words you are keying from the first few letters and then suggests the entire word. You can use AutoText to store frequently used text so you don't have to rekey it each time.

■ Automatic grammar checking automatically checks your document for grammatical errors. When Word finds an error, it underlines the word, phrase, or sentence with a green wavy line.

■ Automatic spell checking identifies misspellings and words that are not in its dictionary by underlining them in red immediately after you key them. AutoCorrect automatically corrects capitalization and common spelling errors as you type.

■ The Spelling and Grammar dialog box contains options that allow you to check the spelling and grammar of words, ignore words, make changes, or add words to your own custom dictionary.

■ The Date and Time command is especially useful to include the date in a letter or memo.

■ You can hyphenate text automatically by using the Language command on the Tools menu and clicking Hyphenation. You can hyphenate text manually by inserting optional and nonbreaking hyphens.

■ The Thesaurus is a useful feature for finding a synonym (a word with a similar meaning) for a word in your document. For some words, the Thesaurus also lists antonyms.

■ The Find command moves the insertion point from its present position to the next occurrence of the word or phrase for which you are searching. Replace has all the features of Find. In addition, it allows you to replace a word or phrase in the *Find what* box with another word or phrase you key in the *Replace with* box.

FILL IN THE BLANKS

Complete the following sentences by writing the correct word or words in the blanks provided.

1. Checking the *Update automatically* box will display the _____ date each time you open the document. *current*

2. A wavy green underline in a document indicates a possible _____ error. *grammar*

3. To make sure that text separated by a hyphen doesn't divide over two lines, use a _____ hyphen. *non-breaking*

4. The Thesaurus is useful for finding a(n) _____ for a word in your document. *synonym*

5. The Replace command is an extended version of the _____ command. *FIND*

MATCHING

Match the correct term in Column 2 to its description in Column 1.

Column 1	Column 2
B 1. Guesses words as you are typing	**A.** Exclamation point
D 2. Changes fractions and numbers such as 3/4 to $^3/_4$ as you key	**B.** AutoComplete
H 3. Stores frequently used entries	**C.** Automatic grammar checking
F 4. Uses a wavy red underline	**D.** AutoFormat As You Type
G 5. A wildcard	**E.** AutoCorrect
	F. Automatic spell checking
	G. Asterisk
	H. AutoText

PROJECT 5-1

You need to make some additions to the guidelines for proofreading outgoing correspondence that your company is preparing.

1. Open the **Guidelines** file that you last used in Project 3-2.

2. Save the document as **Guidelines2** followed by your initials.

3. Insert a blank line at the end of the document and key the heading **Check Spelling** in the same format as the others.

4. Key the following text underneath the heading:

```
Always check the spelling of a document. The following words are
commonly misspelled:
business
address
environment
manual
column
February
calendar
grammar
noticeable
receive
```

5. Notice that AutoCorrect automatically capitalized each word. Use automatic spell checking to correct any words you misspelled while keying.

6. Use the Thesaurus to replace the word *helpful* in the second paragraph with a word that makes sense in context.

7. Hyphenate the document. Apply justified alignment to the new paragraph (*Always check the spelling . . .*).

8. Replace all occurrences of the word *entire* with the word *whole*.

9. Save, print, and close the document.

PROJECT 5-2

You are the secretary for Marina Bay Business and Professionals Association and need to make some changes to the minutes before submitting them at the upcoming meeting.

1. Open **IW Project5-2** from your student data files.

2. Save the document as **Marina Minutes** followed by your initials.

3. Check the document's spelling and grammar and correct any errors.

4. Insert the current date on the blank line beneath *Minutes of the Business Meeting*.

5. Using AutoComplete, insert your name at the beginning of the list of members who attended the meeting.

6. Replace all occurrences of *club* (not clubhouse) with *association*.

7. In the *Old Business* paragraph, find a synonym for the word *aim* that makes sense in context.

8. In the first *New Business* paragraph, find a synonym for the word *help* in the third sentence that makes sense in context.

9. In the *Announcements* paragraph, complete the first sentence by keying **the 7th of next month.**

10. Save, print, and close.

CRITICAL THINKING

ACTIVITY 5-1

You just started working for a publishing company where each manuscript is checked for readability statistics. Use the Help system to find out how to determine the reading level of a document and which readability scores are used.

ACTIVITY 5-2

SCANS

You work for Candlelight Time, a regional chain of candle stores. A new store will be opening soon and your supervisor asks you to key a letter to potential customers announcing the grand opening and offering a free candle to the first 100 customers. Make the letter at least three paragraphs long. Use any helpful automatic features. Insert the current date, check the spelling and grammar, and hyphenate the document.

DESKTOP PUBLISHING WITH WORD

What Is Desktop Publishing?

D*esktop publishing* is the process of combining text and graphics, using a computer, to create attractive documents. With inexpensive personal computers and software, desktop publishing has become one of the fastest growing software applications.

Desktop publishing skills can give you an advantage in school and in your career. With desktop publishing, you can design a newsletter for a school organization, an advertisement for a business, or a program for a fund-raising event. Employers consider desktop publishing experience a valuable asset because it shows that you can use a computer to communicate information.

Creating Columns

Sometimes a document can be more effective if the text is in multiple columns. A newsletter is an example of a document that often has two or more columns. Columns are easy to create in Word. Choose Columns from the Format menu. The Columns dialog box appears, as shown in Figure 6-1. In this dialog box, specify the number of columns you want and how much space you want between the columns. Unless you specify otherwise, all columns will be equal width. You can also specify whether you want a line separating the columns. You can convert existing text into columns or create the columns before keying text. Text that you key will fill up one column before flowing into the next.

To format a document into columns quickly without accessing the Columns dialog box, click the Columns button on the toolbar. A drop-down menu, as shown in Figure 6-2, lets you choose the number of columns you want, up to four.

If you are in Normal view when you choose the Columns command, Word automatically switches to Print Layout view so the columns appear side by side.

FIGURE 6-1
Columns dialog box

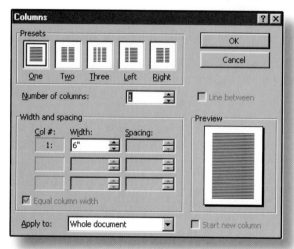

FIGURE 6-2
Columns button and drop-down menu on the toolbar

STEP-BY-STEP ▷ 6.1

1. Open **IW Step6-1** from your student data files.

2. Save the document as **Hampton Hills** followed by your initials.

3. Use Print Preview to view the document. Close Print Preview.

4. Click the **Columns** button on the toolbar and choose the 3 Columns option, as shown in Figure 6-2. Notice the view changes to Print Layout so the columns appear side by side.

5. Use Print Preview to view the document and see that the text fills only two and a half columns. Close Print Preview.

6. Choose **Columns** from the **Format** menu. The Columns dialog box appears as shown in Figure 6-1.

7. In the *Presets* box, choose **Two**.

8. In the *Width and spacing* box under *Spacing*, click the up arrow until it reads **0.6"**.

9. Click in the box beside *Line between* to insert a checkmark. Click **OK**.

10. Use Print Preview to view the columns. Close Print Preview.

11. Save and leave the document open for the next Step-by-Step.

Drawing Graphics

Word allows you to enhance documents by adding graphics. **Graphics** are pictures that help illustrate the meaning of the text, make the page more attractive, or make the page more functional. Word includes drawing tools that enable you to create your own graphics and add them to your documents.

Figure 6-3 shows a document created with Word. The letter takes on a more professional appearance with the addition of a letterhead that includes a graphic created with Word's drawing tools.

FIGURE 6-3
Letterhead created in Word

Drawing Toolbar

To draw graphics, you must be in Print Layout view. When you are ready to create your graphic, click the Drawing button on the toolbar to display the Drawing toolbar at the bottom of the document window.

The Drawing toolbar, shown in Figure 6-4, contains buttons for drawing and manipulating objects, such as lines, arcs, rectangles, circles, and freeform shapes.

FIGURE 6-4
Drawing toolbar

STEP-BY-STEP 6.2

1. Select the second block of text under the heading *Independence Day Parade . . .* that begins with *Keep children and animals . . .* and ends with *. . .will be towed.*

2. Click the **Bullets** button on the Formatting toolbar.

3. Position the insertion point on the first blank line after the paragraph under the *Bicycle Safety Class Announced* heading.

4. Click the **Drawing** button on the toolbar. The Drawing toolbar appears.

5. Save and leave the document open for the next Step-by-Step.

The Drawing toolbar contains many tools. Some of them are used for drawing, and some buttons are used for manipulating or modifying what you've drawn. Table 6-1 summarizes the basic drawing tools that appear in the Drawing toolbar.

TABLE 6-1
Drawing tools

BUTTON	NAME	FUNCTION
	Rectangle tool	Draws rectangles and squares. To use, click and hold the mouse button, then drag to draw. To create a perfect square, hold down the Shift key as you drag.
	Line tool	Draws straight lines. To use, position the pointer where you want the line to begin, then click and hold the mouse button and drag to where you want the line to end.
	Oval tool	Draws ovals and circles. To use, click and hold the mouse button, then drag to draw the oval or circle. To create a perfect circle, hold down the Shift key as you drag.
	Select Objects	Lets you select and manipulate objects. To use, click on the arrow. The insertion point assumes the pointer shape.

STEP-BY-STEP ▷ 6.3

1. Click the **Rectangle** tool button. Your mouse pointer changes to a crosshair.

2. Position the pointer on the upper right side portion of the paragraph about bicycle safety.

3. Press and hold the mouse button and drag to draw an upright rectangle about $1^1/2$ inches tall and $3/4$ inch wide. Some of the lines of text will disappear under the box. Release the mouse button when your rectangle is approximately the same size and in the same position as the one in Figure 6-5.

4. Click the **Rectangle** tool button. Click and drag to draw a rectangle (the be-

ginning of a traffic light) inside the one on your screen as in Figure 6-6.

5. Click the **Oval** tool button. The pointer changes to a crosshair.

6. Hold down the **Shift** key. In the margin to the right of the rectangles, draw a perfect circle with a diameter of about $3/4$ inch. Do not be concerned at this point that the circle is not positioned correctly.

7. Save and leave the document on the screen for the next Step-by-Step.

FIGURE 6-5
Drawing a graphic

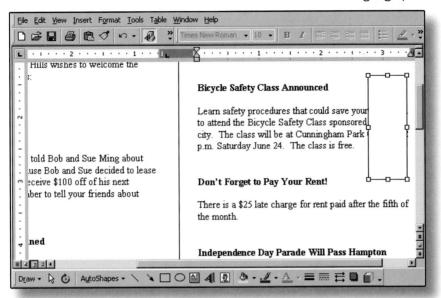

FIGURE 6-6
You can draw many different objects using the drawing tools

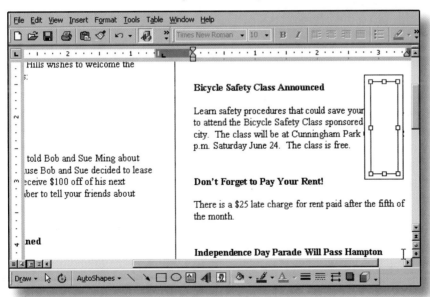

Manipulating Objects

Once you have drawn an object, it does not have to be the final product. There are many ways to manipulate an object. You can resize, copy, move, layer, group, flip, rotate, and change the appearance of an object to make it what you want it to be.

Selecting an Object

When you first drew the objects in Step-by-Step 6.3, you probably noticed the little squares that appeared at the edges of the graphic when you released the mouse button. (See Figure 6-5.) These small squares are called *handles*. They indicate that the object is selected, and they allow you to manipulate the selected object. When you choose another tool, the selection handles around an object disappear.

Before you can copy, move, delete, or manipulate an object, you have to select it. To select an object, position the insertion point over the object and click. The selection handles appear around the object, and you can then manipulate the object. A four-sided arrow appears with the arrow pointer.

To deselect an object, click another object or anywhere in the window. To delete an object, select it and press Delete or Backspace.

Resizing an Object

Handles do more than indicate that an object is selected. They are also used to resize an object. Often during the process of creating a drawing, you will realize that the line, rectangle, or circle you just drew isn't quite the right size. Resizing is easy. Simply select the object to make the handles appear and then drag one of the handles inward or outward to make the object smaller or larger.

Hot Tip

Hold down the Shift key and drag a corner handle to maintain an object's proportions.

Cutting, Copying, and Pasting Objects

You can cut, copy, and paste objects the same way you do text. The Cut and Copy commands place a copy of the selected image on the Clipboard. Pasting an object from the Clipboard places the object in your drawing. You can then move it into position.

S TEP-BY-STEP ▷ 6.4

1. Click on the circle you drew to select it. Handles appear.

2. Place the pointer in the middle of the circle and press and hold down the left mouse button. Drag the circle into the upper part of the rectangle. Resize the circle by dragging the handles until the circle fits snugly inside the top of the rectangle, as shown in Figure 6-7.

3. With the circle still selected, click the **Copy** button on the toolbar.

4. Click the **Paste** button on the toolbar. A copy of the circle appears.

5. Click the **Paste** button again. Another copy of the circle appears.

6. The last circle you pasted is still selected. Drag the circle into the rectangle and place it at the bottom of the rectangle. When you release the mouse button, the selection handles will reappear.

7. In the same manner, drag the remaining circle into place below the first circle. Your screen should look like Figure 6-8. If necessary, adjust the size of your rectangles so that all three circles fit in it snugly.

8. Save and leave the document open for the next Step-by-Step.

FIGURE 6-7
Object handles

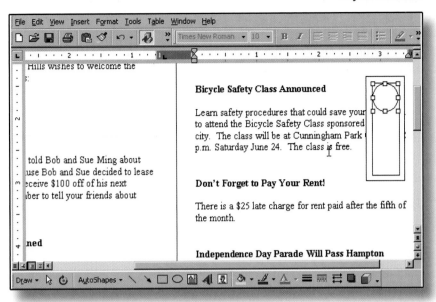

FIGURE 6-8
You can move an object by selecting it and dragging it to the new location

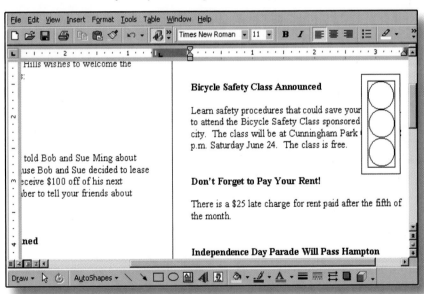

Changing the Appearance of Objects

Color adds life to your drawings. Word allows you to easily fill objects with color or change the color of lines. To change the color, select the object you want to fill or the line you want to change, and click the Fill Color button or the Line Color button on the Drawing toolbar. When you click the down arrow on one of these buttons, a color box appears, as shown in Figures 6-9 and 6-10.

To choose a color from the color box, simply click the color you want. Your selected object appears in this color. To find out the name of the colors in the color box, position the mouse pointer over a color square. The color name appears below the pointer.

Another way to change the appearance of drawings is to change the line style. You can change the style of a line or the lines that make up an object such as a rectangle. Word gives you many choices for line styles including thick and thin lines, dotted lines, and arrows. To change the line style, select the line you want to change and click the Line Style button on the Drawing toolbar. When you click the Line Style button, a menu of line styles appears, as shown in Figure 6-11. Click a line style and your selected line or object's line will change to your choice.

You can change lines to dash styles and different arrow styles using the Dash Style and Arrow Style buttons.

FIGURE 6-9
Fill Color button
with color box

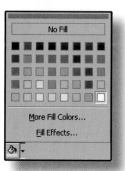

FIGURE 6-10
Line Color button
with color box

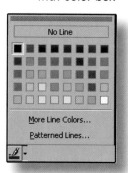

FIGURE 6-11
Line style menu

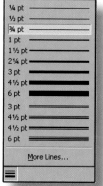

S TEP-BY-STEP ▷ 6.5

1. Select the top circle on your drawing of a traffic light.

2. Click the down arrow on the **Fill Color** button on the Drawing toolbar. The color box appears.

3. Position the mouse pointer on the **Red** color square. The word *Red* appears below the pointer.

4. Click the **Red** color square. The circle is filled with the color red.

5. Select the second circle on your drawing.

6. Click the down arrow on the **Fill Color** button and click the color **Yellow**. The second circle becomes yellow.

7. Select the third circle on your drawing and fill it with the color **Green**.

8. Select the second rectangle you drew—the one containing the three colored circles.

9. Click the down arrow on the **Line Color** button on the Drawing toolbar. The color box appears.

10. Click the color **Light Orange**.

11. Click the **Line Style** button. A box of line styles appears.

12. Click the **6 pt** thick line. The line on your drawing thickens.

13. With the rectangle still selected, use the Fill Color button to fill the rectangle with the color

Black. Your drawing of the traffic light is complete, as shown in Figure 6-12.

14. Save the document and leave it open for the next Step-by-Step.

FIGURE 6-12
Completed drawing

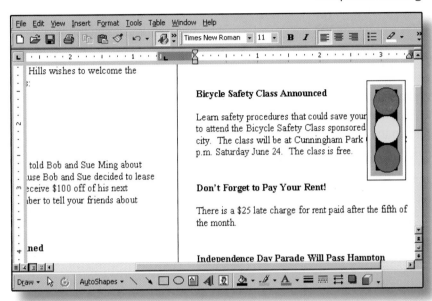

Layering Objects

Each object you create can be changed, moved, or deleted at any time. This is an advantage of drawing on a computer rather than on paper. With a computer, you can lift your mistakes right off the screen and try again.

The objects you create are laid on top of each other. When you create an object, it is placed on top of other objects that already have been drawn. Sometimes you will need to rearrange the order in which objects are layered. Word provides four commands for doing this: Send to Back, Bring to Front, Send Backward, and Bring Forward.

FIGURE 6-13
Draw button menu

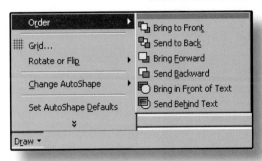

These commands are in the Draw menu on the Drawing toolbar, as shown in Figure 6-13. The Send to Back command moves the selected object or objects to the bottom layer. The Bring to Front command moves the selected object or objects to the top layer. The Send Backward command moves the selected object toward the back one step (or layer) at a time. The Bring Forward command brings an object toward the front one step at a time.

Word also allows you to change the stacking order of text and objects. Just as its name suggests, the Bring to Front of Text command places the selected object in front of text. The Send Behind Text command sends the selected object behind the text. These commands are also located in the Draw menu.

STEP-BY-STEP ▷ 6.6

1. Select the red circle.

2. Click the **Draw** button on the Drawing toolbar. Choose **Order** from the menu and then **Send to Back** on the submenu. The red circle is sent behind the black rectangle.

   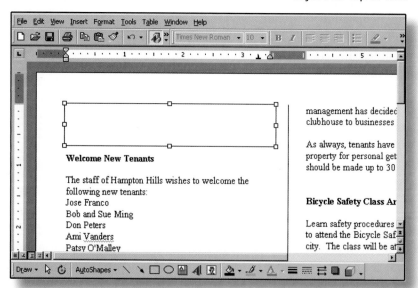

3. With the red circle still selected, click the **Draw** button. Choose **Order** on the menu and then **Bring to Front** on the submenu. The red circle is brought to the front of the black rectangle.

4. Position the insertion point at the beginning of the document.

5. Select the title, *Hampton Hills*, and change the font size to 14 point. Remove the highlight.

6. Click the **Rectangle** button and draw a rectangle approximately 3$\frac{1}{2}$ inches wide and $\frac{3}{4}$

inches tall to frame the text as shown in Figure 6-14. The text disappears behind the rectangle. Leave the rectangle selected.

7. Click the arrow beside the **Fill Color** button and choose **No Fill**. Now you can see the text again.

8. Change the Fill Color to **Gray-25%** and change the Line Color to **Gray-25%**.

9. With the rectangle still selected, click the **Draw** button. Choose **Order** on the menu and then click **Send Behind Text** on the submenu. The text appears in front of the gray rectangle.

10. Click outside the rectangle to deselect it.

11. Save and leave the document open for the next Step-by-Step.

FIGURE 6-14
Object on top of text

Selecting More Than One Object

Sometimes you will want to select more than one object. Word gives you two ways to select more than one object. The first is called *Shift-clicking*. The second method is to draw a selection box around a group of objects.

SHIFT-CLICKING

To Shift-click, hold down the Shift key and click each of the objects you want to select. Use Shift-clicking when you need to select objects that are not close to each other or when the objects you need to select are near other objects you do not want to select. If you select an object by accident, click it again to deselect it.

DRAWING A SELECTION BOX

Using the Select Objects tool, you can drag a selection box around a group of objects. Objects included in the selection box will be selected. Use a selection box when all of the objects you want selected are near each other and can be surrounded with a box. Be sure your selection box is large enough to enclose all the selection handles of the various objects. If you miss a handle, that item will not be selected.

COMBINING METHODS

You can also combine these two methods. First, use the selection box, and then Shift-click to include objects that the selection box might have missed.

Grouping Objects

As your drawing becomes more complex, you will find it necessary to "glue" objects together into groups. *Grouping* allows you to work with several objects as though they were one object. To group objects, select the objects you want to group and choose Group from the Draw menu on the Drawing toolbar. Objects can be ungrouped using the Ungroup command.

STEP-BY-STEP ▷ 6.7

1. Click the **Select Objects** button if necessary.

2. Click and drag a selection box around the traffic light drawing. All the objects in the drawing are selected.

3. Click outside the drawing to remove the selection handles.

4. Select the orange and black rectangle by clicking somewhere on the orange or black.

5. Hold down the **Shift** key and click the white rectangle behind it.

6. Still holding down the **Shift** key, click in the center of each circle.

7. Release the **Shift** key.

8. Click the **Draw** button on the toolbar and choose **Group** from the menu. Your drawing is now grouped into one object instead of five separate objects.

9. Save your document and leave it open for the next Step-by-Step.

Flipping and Rotating Objects

You can modify an object by flipping or rotating it. Flipping reverses orientation or direction of the selected object. Word has two flipping options available through the Drawing toolbar: Flip Horizontal changes the orientation of an object from right to left, and Flip Vertical reverses the orientation from top to bottom. The three rotating commands include the Rotate Right command, the Rotate Left command, and the Free Rotate command. The Rotate Right command moves a graphic in 90 degree increments to the right. The Rotate Left command rotates the graphic in 90 degree increments to the left. The Free Rotate command lets you rotate a graphic to any angle.

To flip or rotate an object, select it, click Draw on the Drawing toolbar, and choose Rotate or Flip from the menu. Choose the command you want from the submenu, as shown in Figure 6-15.

Concept Builder

When you choose the Free Rotate command, the object becomes surrounded with green handles that you click and drag to rotate the object.

FIGURE 6-15
Flip and rotate commands

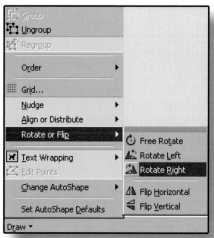

STEP-BY-STEP ▷ 6.8

1. Select the traffic light object if necessary.

2. Click the **Draw** button and then choose **Rotate or Flip** on the menu. Click **Rotate Right** on the submenu. The traffic light rotates 90 degrees to the right and is now on its side.

3. Click the **Draw** button and choose **Rotate or Flip** on the menu. Click **Flip Horizontal** on the submenu. The object doesn't appear to move, but it has reversed its position and the red light is now on the far left instead of on the right.

4. Click the **Draw** button, **Rotate or Flip**, and **Flip Horizontal** again. The red light is now on the right.

5. Click the **Draw** button, **Rotate or Flip**, and **Rotate Right**. The object rotates to the right and the traffic light is now upside down with the red light on the bottom.

6. Click the **Draw** button, **Rotate or Flip**, and **Flip Vertical**. The object doesn't appear to move, but it has reversed position and the red light is now on the top again.

7. Save and leave the document open for the next Step-by-Step.

Wrapping Text Around Graphics

The graphic you drew is covering up some text beneath it. To make text wrap around a graphic, select the graphic and choose Object from the Format menu. In the Format Object dialog box, click the Layout tab to see the wrapping options, as shown in Figure 6-16. The *Wrapping style* samples show how text will flow around your graphic object.

You can also wrap text around an object by choosing Text Wrapping from the Draw menu on the Drawing toolbar. A submenu of choices appears, as shown in Figure 6-17.

FIGURE 6-16
Format Object dialog box

FIGURE 6-17
Text wrapping options

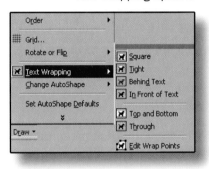

S TEP-BY-STEP ▷ 6.9

1. Select the traffic light drawing.

2. Choose **Object** from the **Format** menu. The Format Object dialog box appears.

3. Click the **Layout** tab, as shown in Figure 6-16.

4. In the *Wrapping style* section, click the **Square** button and click **OK**. The text is wrapped around the object.

5. Save, print, and close the document.

Summary

In this lesson, you learned:

■ You can create documents with multiple columns. You can specify the number of columns and whether you want a line separating them.

■ Graphics can enhance documents by illustrating text or making the page more attractive or functional. Word allows you to draw graphics to add to word processing documents using the Drawing toolbar.

- Graphics created in Word are made up of one or more objects. Word provides a Drawing toolbar with tools that let you draw lines, rectangles, ovals, and more. There also are many options for working with graphic objects.

- Drawing objects can be manipulated by resizing, copying, moving, layering, grouping, flipping, rotating, and changing their appearance. To manipulate an object, click to select it and handles will appear.

- To wrap text around an object, select it and choose Object from the Format menu.

LESSON 6 REVIEW QUESTIONS

FILL IN THE BLANKS

Complete the following sentences by writing the correct word or words in the blanks provided.

1. The process of combining text and graphics, using a computer, to create attractive documents is called _____. *desktop publishing*

2. The _____ toolbar contains tools you can use to draw and manipulate objects. *Drawing*

3. To resize an object, select it and drag one of the _____. *handles*

4. Using the _____ command, you can rotate a graphic to any angle. *free rotate*

5. In the Format Object dialog box, click the _____ tab to see the text wrapping options. *layout*

MATCHING

Match the correct term in Column 2 to its description in Column 1.

Column 1		Column 2
D	1. Reverses the orientation of an object.	A. Layering
F	2. Working with several objects as one.	B. Drawing
G	3. Selecting more than one object.	C. Rotating
A	4. Objects on top of others.	D. Flipping
E	5. Positioning text around an object.	E. Wrapping
		F. Grouping
		G. Shift-clicking

LESSON 6 PROJECTS

PROJECT 6-1

A friend is selling his house and asks you to create a poster to accompany an information sheet that lists all the features of his house. He will have these available for interested buyers.

1. Create the poster in Figure 6-18 using what you've learned in this lesson. Follow the instructions shown on the poster.

2. Save the document as **Sale Poster** followed by your initials.

3. Print and close the document.

FIGURE 6-18

PROJECT 6-2

You are hosting an Independence Day party at your house. Since you have recently moved and many people have not been to your new home, you decide to include a map in the invitation.

1. Use what you have learned in this lesson to create the map shown in Figure 6-19.

2. Save the document as **House Map** followed by your initials.

3. Print and close the document.

FIGURE 6-19

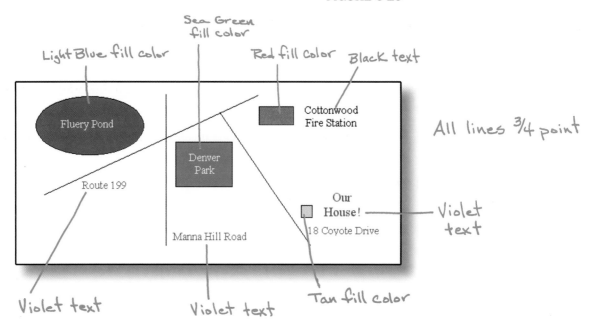

PROJECT 6-3

A computer crashed at work and some of the files were corrupted. Unfortunately, you can no longer access the file that contained the company letterhead and must re-create it using a hard copy.

1. Re-create the letterhead shown in Figure 6-20 using what you learned in this lesson.

2. Save the document as **Color Brick** followed by your initials.

3. Print and close.

FIGURE 6-20

CRITICAL THINKING

ACTIVITY 6-1

The computers in the office where you work are not currently networked. Next week a computer consultant is coming to install a network. Your supervisor wants to send him a layout of the computers in the office so he can get an idea of what is involved in the project. Use the drawing tools to create a layout of the office. Be sure to indicate where each computer is and where the printers are located. Use fill color and line color to make the document more effective.

ACTIVITY 6-2

Your supervisor suggests that you add a "drop cap" to enhance a desktop publishing document. Use the Help system to find out what a drop cap is, how to create one in a document, and how to remove one.

MORE DESKTOP PUBLISHING WITH WORD

OBJECTIVES

Upon completion of this lesson, you should be able to:

- Insert WordArt.
- Use 3-D effects.
- Insert text boxes.
- Insert and scale clip art.
- Add borders and shading.

Estimated Time: 1 hour

Inserting WordArt

C   WordArt is an Office 2000 feature that lets you transform text into a graphic object. The WordArt Gallery, shown in Figure 7-1, contains predefined styles such as curved and stretched text. After you choose a style, the WordArt object is inserted into your document and becomes an object you can change using the other tools on the Drawing toolbar.

FIGURE 7-1
WordArt Gallery

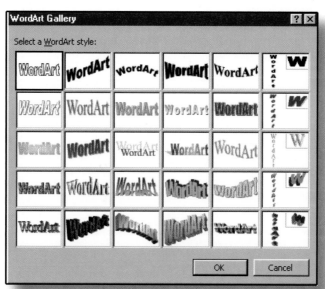

To insert WordArt, click the Insert Word-Art button on the Drawing toolbar. Choose the WordArt style of your choice in the WordArt Gallery and click OK. The Edit WordArt Text dialog box appears, as shown in Figure 7-2, where you key the text you want to use in your WordArt. You can also change the text's font, size, and style. When you are done, click OK and your WordArt object appears.

Along with your WordArt object, a WordArt toolbar appears that you can use to edit the WordArt. Using the toolbar, shown in Figure 7-3, you can edit the text, choose a different style from the WordArt Gallery, format the Word-Art, or change its shape. You can also use buttons to rotate the WordArt, wrap text around it, or change the letter heights, alignment, or character spacing.

Did You Know?

White space is the blank parts of a page. White space frames the headings, columns, and graphics of a document. It acts as a cushion for the eye against too much text and enhances readability.

FIGURE 7-2
Edit WordArt Text dialog box

FIGURE 7-3
WordArt toolbar

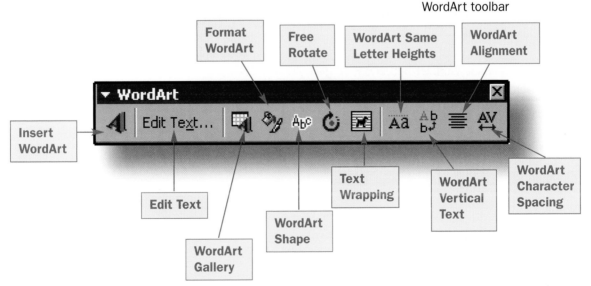

1. Open the **Hampton Hills** file you last used in Step-by-Step 6.9.

2. Save the file as **Hampton Hills2** followed by your initials.

3. Delete the gray rectangle around *HAMPTON HILLS Newsletter.*

4. Delete the words *HAMPTON HILLS Newsletter* and the two blank lines below it.

5. Click the **Insert WordArt** button on the toolbar. The WordArt Gallery appears, as shown in Figure 7-1.

6. Click the fourth style on the second row and choose **OK**. The Edit WordArt Text dialog box appears, as shown in Figure 7-2.

7. Key **Hampton Hills Newsletter**.

8. Change the font, size, and style to Arial, 40 point, bold and click **OK**. The WordArt object and the WordArt toolbar appear, as shown in Figure 7-3.

9. Choose **Zoom** from the **View** menu, choose **75%** and click **OK**.

10. Click the **Format WordArt** button on the WordArt toolbar.

11. In the Format WordArt dialog box, click the **Layout** tab.

12. Click the **Advanced** button. The Advanced Layout dialog box appears.

13. Click the **Text Wrapping** tab.

14. In the *Wrapping style* section, click the **Top and bottom** button.

15. In the *Distance from text* section, click the up arrow beside Bottom until **0.5"** appears in the box.

16. Click **OK** twice to return to your document.

17. Drag the WordArt object to the top of the page.

18. Click outside the object to deselect it and choose **Columns** from the **Format** menu.

19. Click the **Line between** box to remove the checkmark and choose **OK**.

20. Preview the document. Your screen should look similar to Figure 7-4. Exit Preview.

21. Adjust the placement of the WordArt object, if necessary. If the Clubhouse Reservations heading is at the bottom of the first column, insert a blank line to move it to the top of the second column with its corresponding text.

22. Save and leave the document open for the next Step-by-Step.

FIGURE 7-4
Newsletter with WordArt title

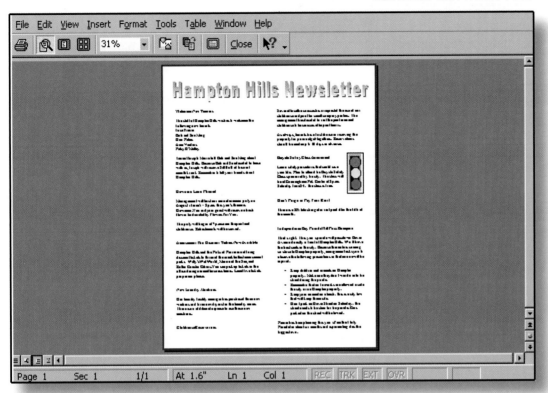

Using 3-D Effects

Another way to enhance an object is to use 3-D effects. You can add a 3-D effect to a drawing object by selecting it and clicking the 3-D button on the Drawing toolbar. A pop-up menu appears, as shown in Figure 7-5.

To modify a 3-D object, click the 3-D Settings button on the 3-D menu and a 3-D Settings toolbar appears, as shown in Figure 7-6. Use the buttons on the toolbar to tilt the object and change the depth, direction, lighting, surface, or color.

FIGURE 7-5
3-D menu

FIGURE 7-6
3-D Settings toolbar

1. Click the WordArt object to select it.

2. Click the **3-D** button on the Drawing toolbar. A pop-up menu appears, as shown in Figure 7-5.

3. Click the third style on the first row, *3-D Style 3*.

4. Click the **3-D button** and click **3-D Settings**. The 3-D Settings toolbar appears, as shown in Figure 7-6.

5. Click the **Tilt Up** button.

6. Click the down arrow next to the 3-D Color button. A palette of colors appears.

7. Choose the **Pale Blue** color (the sixth box on the last row).

8. Click the **Lighting** button and choose the top center light.

9. Close the 3-D Settings toolbar.

10. Deselect the WordArt object.

11. Preview the document.

12. Save and leave the document open for the next Step-by-Step.

Inserting Text Boxes

Text boxes are useful for adding labels or call outs to a document. Once a text box is inserted in a document, it can be treated similarly to a graphic. You can format, resize, or change the position of a text box using the same commands as you would with a drawing object. To format a text box, choose Text Box from the Format menu. To resize a text box, click the handles and drag. To move a text box, click and drag it to the location you want.

To add a text box, choose Text Box from the Insert menu or click the Text Box button on the Drawing toolbar and a crosshair pointer appears. Click and drag to create a text box that appears along with the Text Box toolbar, as shown in Figure 7-7. An insertion point appears inside the text box so you can key the text that you want. Text within a text box can be formatted just as regular text can be.

FIGURE 7-7
Text box and Text Box toolbar

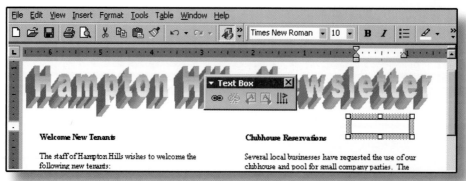

STEP-BY-STEP ▷ 7.3

1. Click the **Text Box** button on the Drawing toolbar.

2. Place the crosshair pointer below and to the right of the newsletter title.

3. Click and drag to create a text box approximately $1\frac{1}{2}$ inches by $\frac{1}{2}$ inch, as shown in Figure 7-7.

4. Key **June 2000** in the text box.

5. Change the text to Arial, 10 point, bold. If the text does not fit, drag the handles to resize the box.

6. With the text box selected, click the **down arrow** next to the Fill Color button on the Drawing toolbar and choose **Pale Blue**.

7. Click the down arrow next to the Line Color button and choose **No Line**.

8. Select the text, click the down arrow next to the Font Color button and choose **Dark Blue**.

9. Choose **Text Box** from the **Format** menu. The Format Text Box dialog box appears.

10. Click the **Layout** tab. In the *Wrapping style* section, click **Tight**.

11. Click **OK**. Click outside the text box to deselect it.

12. Choose **Zoom** from the **View** menu, click **100%**, and click **OK**.

13. Drag to position the text box so it looks like Figure 7-8.

14. Save and leave the document open for the next Step-by-Step.

FIGURE 7-8
Completed text box

Is Newsletter

June 2000

Clubhouse Reservations

Several local businesses have requested the use of our clubhouse and pool for small company parties. The management has decided to rent the pool area and clubhouse to businesses after pool hours.

Working with Clip Art

Y ou may sometimes want to use art from another source rather than draw it yourself. Graphics that are already drawn and available for use in documents are called **clip art**. Clip art libraries offer artwork of common objects that can speed up and possibly improve the quality of your work. Figure 7-9 illustrates how clip art adds flair to a meeting poster.

FIGURE 7-9
Poster with clip art

Inserting Clip Art

To insert clip art, choose Picture from the Insert menu and ClipArt from the submenu. The Insert ClipArt dialog box appears, as shown in Figure 7-10. There are three media tabs from which to choose—Pictures, Sounds, and Motion Clips. The Pictures tab includes not only clip art, but other images such as photographs and bitmaps. You can also import clips from other sources into the Clip Gallery or even connect to the Web to access more clips.

To find a clip art image, type one or more words in the *Search for clips* box. Or, with the Pictures tab displayed, click on a category and the available clip art will be shown. When you click on the clip you want, a toolbar menu appears, as shown in Figure 7-11.

Click the *Insert clip* button to insert the image in your document at the location of your insertion point. Click the *Preview clip* button to view the image without adding it to your document. To add a clip to your favorites or to another category, click the *Add clip to Favorites or other category* button. To see similar clips, click the *Find similar clips* button.

Concept Builder

If a category of images is displayed in the Picture tab, you can click on the other media tabs to see what sounds or motion clips are available in the same category.

FIGURE 7-10
Insert ClipArt dialog box

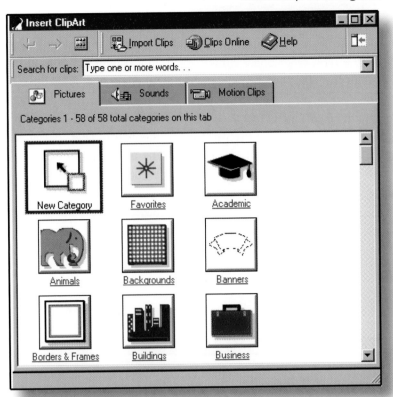

FIGURE 7-11
Clip art toolbar menu

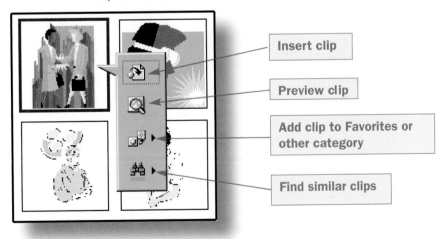

Insert clip

Preview clip

Add clip to Favorites or other category

Find similar clips

1. In the first column, place the insertion point at the beginning of the first line under the *Welcome New Tenants* heading.

2. Choose **Picture** from the **Insert** menu and then click **ClipArt** on the submenu. The Insert ClipArt dialog box appears, as shown in Figure 7-10.

3. In the list of categories, scroll down and click **People at Work**.

4. Click the picture of two people shaking hands, shown in Figure 7-12 outlined in blue. (Your

screen may not look exactly like the figure.) If that picture is not available, click another appropriate one. A toolbar menu appears.

5. Click the **Insert clip** button. Close the Insert ClipArt dialog box to see the picture that has been inserted in your document.

6. Save and leave the document open for the next Step-by-Step.

FIGURE 7-12
People at Work category

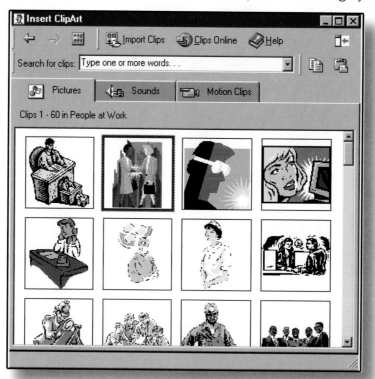

Editing Clip Art

Although clip art is already created, you can alter the way it appears on the page. When the clip art is selected, the Picture toolbar appears, as shown in Figure 7-13. Using the buttons, you can change the image to black and white or grayscale, increase or decrease the contrast or brightness, crop the image, or reset its original properties. You can also format it by clicking the Format Picture button on the Picture toolbar. The Format Picture dialog box appears, as shown in Figure 7-14.

When you resize a graphic using the handles, the length and width may not maintain the same proportions. To change the size, or *scale*, of a graphic so that its proportions are correct, choose the Size tab where you can key an exact size or percentages of length and width scale.

FIGURE 7-13
Picture toolbar

FIGURE 7-14
Format Picture dialog box

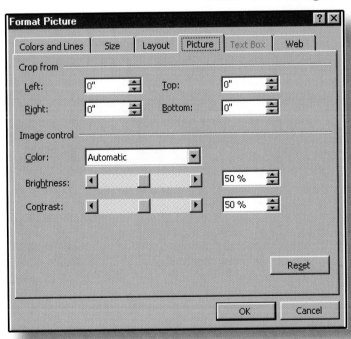

1. Click the picture to select it. The Picture toolbar appears, as shown in Figure 7-13.

2. Click the **Format Picture** button. The Format Picture dialog box appears, as shown in Figure 7-14.

3. Click the **Size** tab. In the *Scale* section beside *Height*, click the down arrow until **35%** appears in the box. Notice that the *Width* percentages and *Size* measurements change also.

4. In the *Size* box, the *Height* should be 1.32" and the *Width* should be 0.99". If your dialog box has different measurements in the *Size* box, delete the current data and key these measurements to resize the graphic.

5. Click **OK**. The clip art is smaller.

6. Click the **Text Wrapping** button on the Picture toolbar.

7. Click **Square** on the submenu.

8. Your document should appear similar to Figure 7-15.

9. Save and leave the document open for the next Step-by-Step.

FIGURE 7-15
Scaled clip art

Using Borders and Shading

Borders and shading add interest and emphasis to text. However, be sure to use them sparingly and wisely. Too many borders or shades on a page can make it look cluttered and hard to read.

Adding Borders to Paragraphs

Borders are single, double, thick, or dotted lines that appear around one or more words or paragraphs and are used to emphasize the text. You can specify whether the border appears on all four sides like a box, on two sides, or on only one side of the paragraph. Other options include shadow, 3-D, and custom borders. Select the text you want to border and choose Borders and Shading from the Format menu. In the Borders tab of the Borders and Shading dialog box, shown in Figure 7-16, specify the border setting, style and width of line, and color for your border. After selecting your options, you can see a sample in the *Preview* box.

FIGURE 7-16
Borders tab of the Borders and Shading dialog box

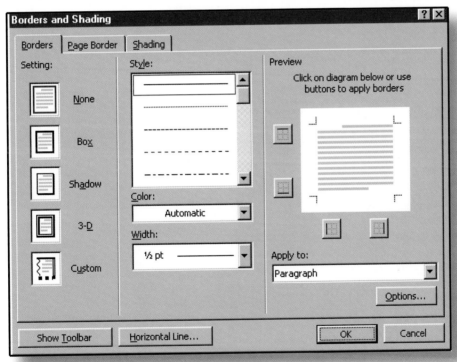

Adding Shading to Paragraphs

You can also add shading—grays or colors—or patterns, such as diagonal stripes, to paragraphs or lines of text. However, to maintain readability of a paragraph that contains several sentences, it is best to add only light shades (25% or less) to text. You can create interesting effects by adding patterns to short titles or names. Simply select the text you want to shade and access the Shading section of the Borders and Shading dialog box, shown in Figure 7-17. Here, you can choose the shade, pattern, and color you want. The *Preview* box shows you a sample of what your shading choices will look like.

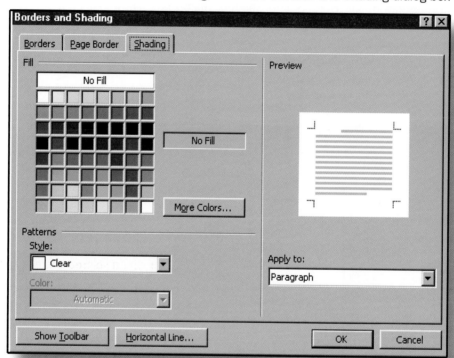

FIGURE 7-17
Shading tab of the Borders and Shading dialog box

Adding Borders to Pages

Just as you can add borders to paragraphs, you can add borders to entire pages. In the Borders and Shading dialog box, choose the Page Borders tab where you can choose the setting, line style and width, and color of border that you want. In the Art box, you can choose predefined art borders. Click the Options button and you can specify the amount of space between the border and the text or the edge of the page.

STEP-BY-STEP ▷ 7.6

1. Select the heading *Don't Forget to Pay Your Rent!*, the blank line, and the sentence below it.

2. Choose **Borders and Shading** from the **Format** menu. The Borders and Shading dialog box appears, as shown in Figure 7-16.

3. Click the **Borders** tab if necessary.

4. In the *Setting* section, click the **Box** button.

5. In the *Width* box, click the arrow and choose the **1½ pt** width from the menu.

6. In the *Color* box, choose **Blue**. A blue single-lined border appears around the heading and text, as shown in the Preview box.

7. Click the **Shading** tab, as shown in Figure 7-17. In the *Fill* section, choose **Light Yellow**. Choose **20%** in the *Style* box.

8. Click **OK**. In addition to the border, the text now contains a light yellow 20% shade, as shown in Figure 7-18.

9. Save, print, and close the document.

Extra Challenge

Create a new document and use WordArt to create a logo for your school or organization.

FIGURE 7-18
Border with a colored pattern shade

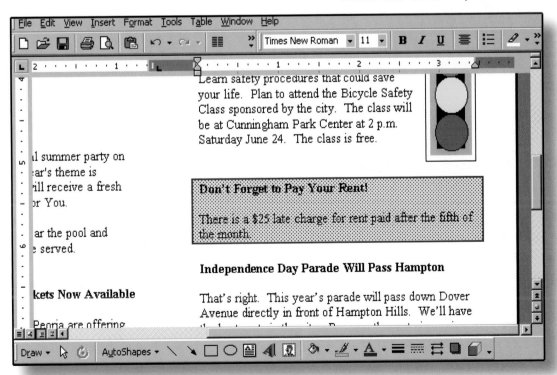

Summary

In this lesson, you learned:

- From the WordArt Gallery you can choose a style and insert a WordArt object into your document. Use the WordArt toolbar to edit the WordArt.

- Using 3-D effects can enhance an object. Buttons on the 3-D Settings toolbar can be used to tilt the object, change the depth, direction, lighting, surface, or color.

- Text boxes can be created to contain special text. They can be formatted, resized, or moved just as drawing objects can.

- You can insert clip art using the Microsoft Clip Gallery and scale it to fit your document.

- Borders and shading add interest and emphasis to text.

LESSON 7 REVIEW QUESTIONS

WRITTEN QUESTIONS

Write a brief answer to the following questions.

1. What is clip art?

    collection of graphics already drawn

2. Why should you use only light shades on entire paragraphs?

    As darker shadows hard to read

3. How do you modify a 3-D object?

   [handwritten] Click 3D Setting button on 3-D menu to display 3-D Settings toolbar — use the buttons on the toolbar to modify

4. Name three things you can do using the WordArt toolbar.

   [handwritten] edit text, choose diff style fp WordArt gallery, format WordArt, change shape - rotate w/ caps - lights, align

5. What are text boxes useful for?

   [handwritten] adding labels or callouts to doc.

TRUE/FALSE

Circle T if the statement is true or F if the statement is false.

T **F** 1. To scale a graphic means to change its size and maintain the correct proportions.

T **F** 2. Text within a text box can be formatted just as regular text can be.

T **F** 3. With WordArt you can transform text into a graphic object.

T **F** 4. Applying 3-D effects is a good way to enhance a text paragraph.

T **F** 5. Borders are lines that emphasize clip art.

PROJECT 7-1

You work as an assistant to the marketing director at Canyon Bank. He has keyed some preliminary text for an informational brochure and asks you to format it attractively.

1. Open **IW Project7-1** from your student data files.

2. Save the document as **Canyon Bank** followed by your initials.

3. Select all text and change the font size to 10 point.

4. Change the top margin to 1 inch and the left, right, and bottom margins to .5 inches.

5. Format the document into three columns with no lines between columns.

6. Change the spacing between columns to .4 inches. If you are prompted to switch to Page Layout view, click **Yes**.

7. Select the first paragraph. Change the font to 10 point Arial italic.

8. Delete the title and the three blank lines below it.

9. Insert a WordArt object for the title, **Maintaining a Checking Account**. Use the third style on the third row and change the font and size to Impact 32 point.

10. Drag the title into position centered at the top of the page. Preview to make sure there is about half an inch margin space around the top and sides of the title.

11. Wrap text around the WordArt object using the *Top and bottom* style. Leave .4 inches distance from the text on the bottom.

12. Position the insertion point in the blank line before the heading, *Using Your Checking Account.*

13. Search for and insert an appropriate clip art picture that relates to money. Scale the graphic if necessary and center it within the column.

14. Select the Canyon Bank mailing address in the second column before the heading, *Managing Your Account.* Create a dark green shadow border using the 2 ¼ pt single line and fill it with a 20% green shade.

15. Center the text within the box.

16. Save, print, and close.

PROJECT 7-2

You work as a freelance desktop publisher. One of your accounts is Pet Essentials, a pet store with a newsletter of the same name that is distributed to customers in the store. Each month the manager gives you a file with the newsletter text and asks you to format it into a one-page newsletter.

1. Open **IW Project7-2** from your student data files.

2. Save the document as **Pet Essentials** followed by your initials.

3. Format the document with 3 columns with a line and .4 inches between each column. If the *Helpful Hints* heading is not at the top of column 2, add line spaces as needed at the bottom of column 1 to move the heading to column 2. If the *Cats in History: Ancient Egypt* heading is not at the top of column 3, add line spaces as needed at the bottom of column 2 to move the heading to column 3.

4. Create a WordArt title for the newsletter called **Pet Essentials**:
   A. Use the first design in the last row and change the text to Broadway in 48 point.
   B. Choose **3-D Style 3** for the WordArt title.

5. Insert clip art of a cat before the *Cats in History* heading. Scale it to fit the column size.

6. Choose Top and Bottom text wrapping style and center the clip art within the column.

7. Create a text box with the current month and year in it to the right of the title.

8. Change the text in the text box to green, bold, 11 point Arial.

9. Change the fill color and line color of the text box to light green.

10. Place a green, 1½ point border around the information about vaccine costs and fill it with light green shading.

11. Save, print, and close the document.

SCANS

ACTIVITY 7-1

You have recently started working at Story's End, a retail bookstore. The manager is interested in producing a monthly newsletter to distribute to customers and asks you to design it. She suggests including such things as new arrivals, bestseller lists, and upcoming events happening at the store. She tells you to use as many columns as needed and to include any clip art, logos, borders, and shading that will enhance the appearance. Create a newsletter for next month and print a sample for her to see.

ACTIVITY 7-2

You notice buttons on the Drawing toolbar that are not familiar and are interested in discovering what other features are available. Use Help to find out about AutoShapes and Shadow so that you can experiment when creating your own drawings.

WORKING WITH DOCUMENTS

OBJECTIVES

Upon completion of this lesson, you should be able to:

- Switch between documents.
- Copy and paste text between documents.
- Insert page breaks.
- Work with multipage documents.
- Insert headers and footers.
- Create footnotes and endnotes.
- Create a section with formatting that differs from other sections.
- Apply styles.
- Create and modify an outline.

🕐 **Estimated Time: 1 hour**

Switching Between Documents

One of the most useful features of Word is its ability to open more than one document at a time. While you are working on one document, you can create or open another document and work on it for a while. You can switch back and forth as often as you like. Suppose, for example, you are creating a résumé in one document. While the résumé document is on the screen, you can create a new document in which to key the cover letter you will send with the résumé. If you want to send a list of references, you can even create a third document in which to key the references.

Concept Builder

All the programs in Office 2000 allow you to open new documents while you are working on other documents.

When you open or create a new document, Word displays it on top of the document that is already open. The new document window becomes the active window and a button corresponding to the document is displayed on the taskbar. It is easy to move back and forth between documents: Just click the taskbar button for the document you want to work on, and it will become the active window. You can also choose a document you want from the Window menu.

1. Open the **Diet2** document that you last used in Step-by-Step 4.3.

2. Save the document as **Diet Final** followed by your initials.

3. Open the **Diet Title** document that you created in Step-by-Step 3.7. It becomes the active window.

4. Save the document as **Diet Title2** followed by your initials.

5. Notice that buttons for both documents are displayed on the taskbar. Click the **Diet Final** button on the taskbar to make it the active window.

6. Click the **Window** menu. On the menu, you will see your two documents listed, with a check mark beside *Diet Final*. Click **2 Diet Title2**. The menu will close and *Diet Title2* will once again be the active window.

7. Leave the *Diet Title2* window on the screen for the next Step-by-Step.

Copying and Pasting Text Between Documents

Just as you can copy or move text within a document, you can copy or move data from one document to another. For example, you might copy a paragraph from one document to another, or you might move a whole section from one report to another.

1. Click the **Diet Final** button on the taskbar to make that document active.

2. Select the date.

3. Click the **Copy** button on the toolbar. A copy of the text is placed on the Clipboard.

4. Click **Diet Title2** on the taskbar to display the document.

5. Move the insertion point to a new line after the existing text.

6. Click the **Paste** button on the toolbar. The text you copied from *Diet Final* is placed in *Diet Title2*.

7. Use the Format Painter to copy the format of the previous title page information to the date that you just inserted.

8. Save the document and print it. Close the document. Leave the **Diet Final** document open for the next Step-by-Step.

Inserting Page Breaks

When a document has more text than will fit on one page, Word must select a place in the document to end one page and begin the next. The place where one page ends and another begins is called a ***page break***. Word automatically inserts page breaks where they are necessary. You also can insert a page break manually. For example, you might want to insert a page break manually to prevent an automatic page break from separating a heading from the text that follows it.

To insert a page break manually, choose Break from the Insert menu. Choose *Page break* in the Break dialog box that appears, as shown in Figure 8-1.

In Normal view, an automatic page break is a dotted line across the page. A manual page break is also shown by a dotted line across the page, but it has the words *Page Break* in the middle, as shown in Figure 8-2. To delete manual page breaks, select the page break line and press Backspace or Delete.

FIGURE 8-1
Break dialog box

FIGURE 8-2
Page break

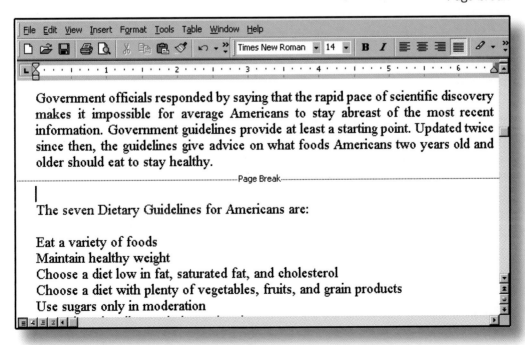

S TEP-BY-STEP ▷ 8.3

1. Display the **Diet Final** document.

2. Switch to Normal view if necessary.

3. Place the insertion point in the blank line above the paragraph that begins *The seven Dietary Guidelines....*

4. Choose **Break** from the **Insert** menu. The Break dialog box appears, as shown in Figure 8-1.

5. In the *Break types* area, *Page break* should be selected. Choose **OK**. The dotted line with the words *Page Break* in the middle indicates that a manual page break has been inserted, as shown in Figure 8-2. The heading and list now appear on page 2 of the document.

6. Save and leave the document open for the next Step-by-Step.

Working with Multipage Documents

When a document is only one page long, it isn't hard to edit or format the text. These tasks become more challenging in multipage documents because you cannot see the whole document on your screen at once. Word provides several tools that are useful for formatting and editing long documents.

Splitting Windows

Word lets you view two parts of your document at once by using the Split command from the Window menu. Suppose you want to see text at the beginning of a document while you are editing at the end of the document. By splitting your document, you can see both parts of the document. Each area of the document, called a *pane,* contains separate scroll bars to allow you to move through that part of the document.

S TEP-BY-STEP ▷ 8.4

1. Press **Ctrl+Home** to go to the beginning of the document.

2. Choose **Split** from the **Window** menu. A horizontal bar appears with the mouse pointer as a positioning marker.

3. Position the bar so that the document window is divided into two equal parts.

4. Click the left mouse button. The document window splits into two separate panes, each with independent scroll bars and rulers, as shown in Figure 8-3.

5. Press the down scroll arrow in the bottom pane of the split window. Notice that the document scrolls downward while the text in the upper pane remains still.

6. Choose **Remove Split** from the **Window** menu. The window returns to one pane.

7. Leave the document open for the next Step-by-Step.

FIGURE 8-3
Document divided with the Split command

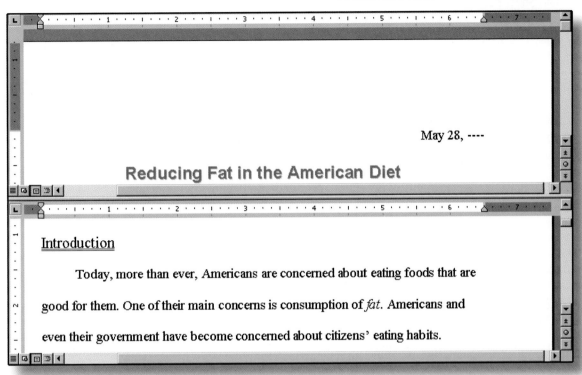

Using the Go To Command

One of the quickest ways to move through a document is to use the Go To command. Go To allows you to skip to a specific part of a document. To skip to a specific page, choose Go To from the Edit menu. The Go To tab of the Find and Replace dialog box appears, as shown in Figure 8-4. Page is the default setting in the *Go to what* box, so key the page number where you want to move in the *Enter page number* box. After you click Go To, Word will move the insertion point to the beginning of the page you specified.

Hot Tip

As you drag the vertical scroll box, a ScreenTip pops up and shows you the page number in relation to the position of the scroll box in the scroll bar. Try it!

FIGURE 8-4
Go To command

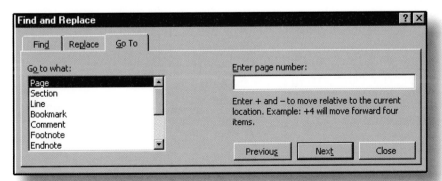

Viewing Hidden Characters

The Show/Hide ¶ command allows you to view hidden formatting characters as shown in Figure 8-5. These are characters such as paragraph returns or end-of-line marks. Being able to see these hidden characters can help you edit your text.

FIGURE 8-5
Visible formatting characters

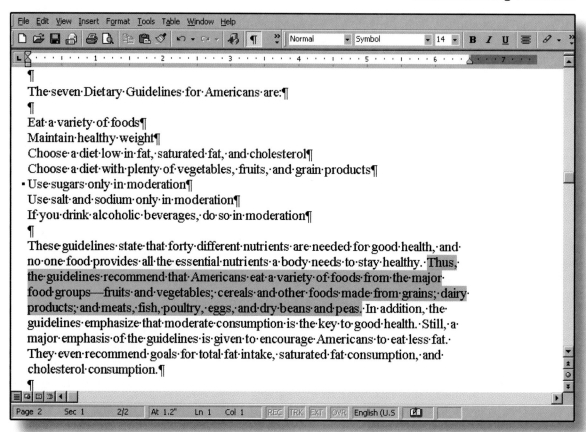

Using the Word Count Command

FIGURE 8-6
The Word Count dialog box

While you work on a document, you may want to know how many words it contains. The Word Count command counts the pages, words, characters, paragraphs, and lines in your document quickly. The insertion point can be located anywhere in the document when you use Word Count. You can count the words in a specific section of text by first selecting the text and then using Word Count. To use Word Count, choose Word Count from the Tools menu. A dialog box appears listing Word Count's findings, as shown in Figure 8-6.

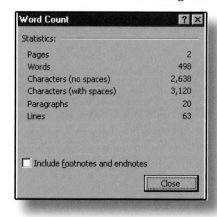

INTRODUCTION TO MICROSOFT WORD

STEP-BY-STEP ▷ 8.5

1. Choose **Go To** from the **Edit** menu. The Find and Replace dialog box appears, as shown in Figure 8-4.

2. In the *Enter page number* box, key **2** and click **Go To**. The insertion point moves to the beginning of page 2.

3. Click **Close**. The Find and Replace dialog box disappears.

4. Click the **Show/Hide ¶** button on the toolbar. Word makes the paragraph returns and spacebar characters visible.

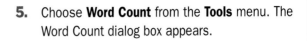

5. Choose **Word Count** from the **Tools** menu. The Word Count dialog box appears.

6. Click **Close**.

7. Click the **Show/Hide ¶** button. The characters are hidden.

8. Save and leave the document open for the next Step-by-Step.

Inserting Headers and Footers

Headers and footers allow you to include the same information, such as your name and the page number, on each page of a document. A *header* is text that is printed at the top of each page. A *footer* is text that is printed at the bottom of the page. Figure 8-7 shows both a header and a footer. Word has many header and footer options. You can even create separate headers and footers for even and odd pages.

Insert headers and footers by choosing Header and Footer from the View menu. Headers and footers have their own formatting toolbar that appears when you choose the Header and Footer command. The toolbar, shown in Figure 8-8, contains formatting buttons you can use to insert the date, time, and page numbers. Other buttons make it easy to access the Page Setup dialog box and to switch between the header and footer.

FIGURE 8-7
Header and footer

Calypso Project Status Report   September 25, 2000

Page 1

FIGURE 8-8
Header and Footer toolbar

By default, Word assumes you want the same header and footer on all pages in a document. However, you can choose to have one header/footer on the first page with a different header/footer on all other pages. Also, you can choose one header/footer on odd-numbered pages with another header/footer on even-numbered pages. To create alternate headers and footers, choose Header and Footer from the View menu. Click Page Setup from the Header and Footer toolbar. In the *Headers and footers* box of the Layout tab, choose *Different odd and even* or *Different first page*. Click OK and enter your alternate headers and footers in the panes provided.

STEP-BY-STEP ▷ 8.6

1. Move the insertion point to the beginning of the document.

2. Choose **Header and Footer** from the **View** menu. Your document is changed to Print Layout view and your insertion point is in the header pane. A Header and Footer toolbar appears.

3. Click the **Page Setup** button on the header and footer toolbar. The Page Setup dialog box appears.

4. Click the **Margins** tab. Change the left and bottom margins to 1.25 inches. Click **OK**.

5. Key **your name** in the header pane. Notice that the text is automatically formatted to 10 point Courier New.

6. Press **Tab**. Click the **Insert Date** button on the header and footer toolbar. The date appears.

7. Press **Tab**. Click the **Insert Page Number** button on the header and footer toolbar. The number *1* is inserted.

8. Switch to the Footer pane by clicking the **Switch Between Header and**

Footer button. The insertion point appears in the footer pane.

9. Press **Tab** to move the insertion point to the centered tab.

10. Key **Reducing Fat in the American Diet**. Notice that the text is automatically formatted to 10 point Courier New.

11. Select the footer data you just keyed. Change the font to Times New Roman 9 point.

12. Click the **Switch Between Header and Footer** button to go back to the header. Change the font of the header data to Times New Roman 9 point.

13. Click the **Close** button on the header and footer toolbar.

14. Choose **Print Layout** from the **View** menu.

15. Scroll to the top and bottom of the page. The header and footer text you keyed is shown in light gray text.

16. Save and leave the document open for the next Step-by-Step.

You can also insert page numbers quickly into a header or footer by choosing Page Numbers from the Insert menu. The Page Number dialog box opens, as shown in Figure 8-9. Choose whether to display the page number in a header or footer, the alignment you want, and whether or not to show a page number on the first page. Your choices are reflected in the *Preview* box. To format the page number, click the Format button to open the Page Number Format dialog box, shown in Figure 8-10.

FIGURE 8-9
Page Numbers dialog box

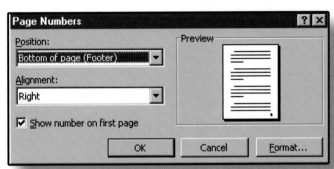

FIGURE 8-10
Page Number Format dialog box

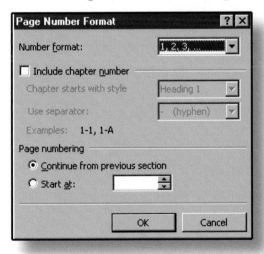

Extra Challenge

Open a previously created document and insert the page number right-aligned at the bottom of the page (in a footer). Experiment with the different number formats available.

Creating Footnotes and Endnotes

A *footnote* or *endnote* is used to document quotations, figures, or summaries, or to provide other text that you do not want to include in the body of your document. Footnotes are printed at the bottom of each page, and endnotes are printed at the end of the document.

To insert a footnote or endnote, position the insertion point at the place in the document where you need a reference and choose Footnote from the Insert menu. The Footnote and Endnote dialog box appears, as shown in Figure 8-11. Specify in the *Insert* section whether you want an endnote or footnote. In the *Numbering* section, choose to reference your endnote or footnote with AutoNumber or a Custom mark. Click the Symbol button to choose a symbol. Click the Options button to choose different types of Auto-Numbers, such as 1, 2, 3 or i, ii, iii. When you click OK, the footnote or endnote pane opens as shown in Figure 8-12. You can then key the footnote or endnote in the pane.

After you create a footnote, a number or the custom mark you chose will appear in the document. The corresponding footnote will print at the end of the page or the endnote will print at the end of the document.

You can view footnotes you've created by choosing Footnotes from the View menu.

FIGURE 8-11
Footnote and Endnote dialog box

FIGURE 8-12
Footnote pane

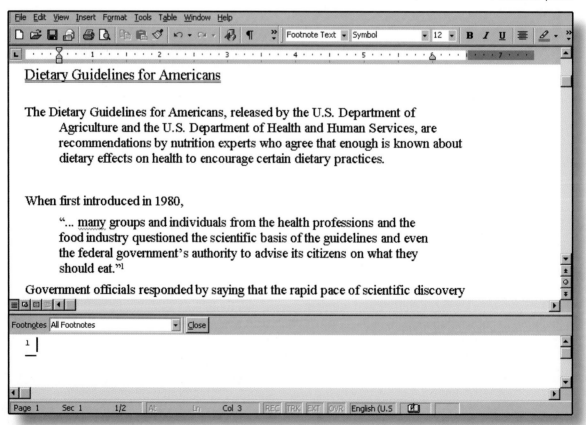

S TEP-BY-STEP 8.7

1. Switch to Normal view. Place the insertion point after the quotation mark in the second paragraph under the heading *Dietary Guidelines for Americans*.

2. Choose **Footnote** from the **Insert** menu. The Footnote and Endnote dialog box appears, as shown in Figure 8-9. AutoNumber is chosen by default in the *Numbering* section. This indicates that your footnotes will be numbered.

Hot Tip

You can delete a footnote or endnote by selecting the footnote number or symbol in the text and pressing Delete. The remaining footnotes/endnotes, if any, will be renumbered automatically.

3. Click **OK**. The Footnote pane appears at the bottom of the document window with the insertion point blinking after the number *1*.

4. Key **"Dietary Guidelines for Americans: No-nonsense Advice for Healthy Eating,"** ***FDA Consumer*****, November 1985, p. 14.** (Key the period.) The footnote may be shown in a different font; you'll change it later.

5. Click **Close** in the Footnote pane.

6. Place the insertion point after the quotation mark in the last paragraph of the document.

7. Choose **Footnote** from the **Insert** menu. Click **OK**.

8. Key **U.S. Department of Agriculture and U.S. Department of Health and Human Services, "Nutrition and Your Health: Dietary Guidelines for Americans," Home and Garden Bulletin No. 232, 3d edition, 1990, p. 3.** (Key the period.)

9. Select all text in the footnote pane. Change the font to Times New Roman 10 point.

10. Click **Close**.

11. Switch to Print Layout view and scroll to see the footnote at the bottom of each page.

12. Save, print, and close the document.

Concept Builder

In Print Layout view, you can key a footnote directly at the bottom of a page without using the footnote pane.

Creating a Section with Formatting That Differs from Other Sections

In Word, the default is the same page layout for an entire document. You can divide a document into two or more *sections* to create different layouts within one document. You will want to create sections within a document when the page layout must be different for only part of the document. For example, you might want to format only part of a page with columns. From section to section, you can have different headers and footers, page numbers, margins, print orientation, and other formatting features.

To create a new section, choose Break from the Insert menu. The Break dialog box appears, as shown in Figure 8-13. To start the new section on the next page, choose *Next page*. To start the new section on the same page, choose *Continuous*. To start the new section break on the next odd-numbered or even-numbered page, choose *Odd page* or *Even page*.

In Normal view, a section break is shown by a double dotted line across the page with the words *Section Break* in the middle, as shown in Figure 8-14. To delete section breaks, place the insertion point on the section break line and press Delete.

FIGURE 8-13
Break dialog box

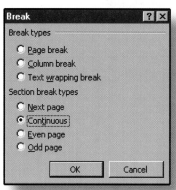

FIGURE 8-14
Continuous section break

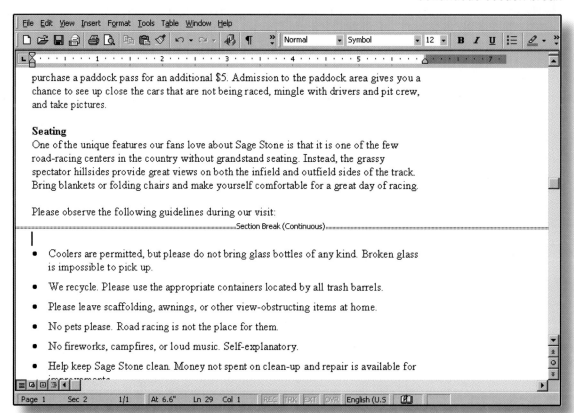

S TEP-BY-STEP ▷ 8.8

1. Open the **IW Step8-8** data file.

2. Save the document as **Sage Stone** followed by your initials.

3. Switch to Normal view if necessary and place the insertion point on the blank line before the bulleted list.

4. Choose **Break** from the **Insert** menu. The Break dialog box appears.

5. Click **Continuous** in the *Section break types* box as shown in Figure 8-13.

6. Click **OK**. A double dotted line with the words *Section Break (Continuous)* in the middle indicates that a continuous section break is inserted, as shown in Figure 8-14.

7. Select the bulleted list.

8. Choose **Columns** from the **Format** menu. The Columns dialog box appears.

9. Format the list into two columns with .3" of space between them.

10. Click **OK**. Word switches to Print Layout view.

11. Save and leave the document open for the next Step-by-Step.

Applying Styles

In Word, a *style* is a predefined set of formatting options that have been named and saved. Using styles in a document can save time and add consistency to a document. For example, one particular style could specify 10-point Arial font, bold font style, and single line spacing. By applying that style you can format text in one step instead of several and be certain that all text with that style looks the same. To apply a style, select text and choose an existing style from the Style box list on the toolbar. Or, choose Style from the Format menu. The Style dialog box appears, as shown in Figure 8-15, where you can see a preview and a description of each style.

FIGURE 8-15
Style dialog box

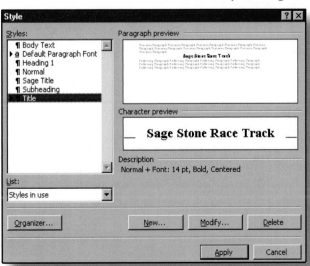

1. Select the title.

2. Choose **Style** from the **Format** menu. The Style dialog box appears, as shown in Figure 8-15.

3. In the *Styles* box, click **Sage Title**. Read the description and look at the preview.

4. Click **Apply**. The Sage Title style is applied to the title.

5. Select the subheading *Schedule*.

6. Choose **Subheading** from the *Style* list box on the toolbar. The subheading *Schedule* is changed to the Subheading style.

7. Copy the format of *Schedule* to the other two subheadings.

8. Save, print, and close the document.

Organize a Document in Outline View

Outlines are useful for creating a document with a hierarchical structure. To create an outline in Word, first switch to Outline view by clicking the Outline View button at the bottom left of the document window. When you do, the Outlining toolbar is displayed and an outline symbol appears so that you can key a heading, as shown in Figure 8-16. A plus symbol before a heading (⊞) indicates that there are subheadings or body text below it. A minus symbol (⊟) indicates that there are not any subheadings or body text below the heading.

FIGURE 8-16
Outlining toolbar

Creating an Outline

When you key the first heading and press Enter, Word formats it with the built-in heading style Heading 1. Word has nine built-in styles that are assigned for each different level of heading. As you are keying your outline, you can assign a heading to a different level. Click the Demote button on the Outlining toolbar to move a heading to the next lower level. Click the Promote button to move a heading to the next higher level. Click the Demote to Body Text button to style a heading as body text.

Hot Tip

Pressing Tab will demote a heading to the next lower level and pressing Shift+Tab will promote a heading to the next higher level.

Modifying an Outline

Once you have keyed an outline, you can easily modify it. Use the Up and Down buttons on the toolbar to move a heading to a different location. Or click the heading's outline symbol (⊞ or ⊟) and drag it to a new location. When you move a heading that way, all the subordinate text underneath it moves with it. Click the Expand or Collapse buttons to view only the headings you want and make it easier to reorganize the outline. When you switch to a different view, outline indentations disappear but the style formatting for the headings is still visible.

Concept Builder

The outline symbols (⊞ and ⊟) on the screen in Outline view are there to show you the document's structure. They will not appear when you print.

STEP-BY-STEP ▷ 8.10

1. Create a new Word document and switch to Outline view. The Outlining toolbar and an outline symbol appear, as shown in Figure 8-16.

2. Key **Recycling** next to the minus symbol (⊟). The text is formatted as Heading 1.

3. Press **Enter**. Click the **Demote** button to move down a level and key **Why recycle?**

4. Press **Enter**. Press **Tab** to move down a level and key **Save landfill space**.

5. Continue keying text from Figure 8-17 using the Demote and Promote buttons to move up and down levels.

6. Save the document as **Recycle** followed by your initials.

7. Place the insertion point on the *Why recycle?* heading and click the **Collapse** button to show only the headings.

8. Click on the plus symbol (⊞) next to the *Conserve natural resources* heading to select it.

9. Begin dragging the plus symbol up. As you do a horizontal line appears. Drag until the line is between the headings *Why recycle?* and *Save landfill space*, as shown in Figure 8-18. When you release the mouse button, the *Conserve natural resources* heading is moved to the new location.

10. Place the insertion point on the *Why recycle?* heading and click the **Expand** button. Notice that all the text underneath the *Conserve natural resources* heading moved along with it.

11. Place the insertion point on the text *Oil kills freshwater organisms that fish eat.*

12. Click the **Move Up** button. The text moves up.

13. Save, print, and close the document.

(continued on next page)

FIGURE 8-17
Text to key for Step-by-Step 8.10

⊹ **Recycling**
  ⊹ *Why recycle?*
    ⊹ **Save landfill space**
      ▫ Landfill space is becoming scarce.
      ▫ Recycled items do not take up space in the landfills.
    ⊹ **Conserve natural resources**
      ▫ Recycling paper products saves trees.
      ▫ Recycling aluminum saves energy that would be used to make new aluminum.
    ⊹ **Avoid pollution**
      ▫ Oil dumped down sewers, in alleys, and in landfills contains toxic substances that contaminate water underground and on the surface.
      ▫ Oil kills freshwater organisms that fish eat.
      ▫ Litter is ugly and can be hazardous.

FIGURE 8-18
Moving a heading in Outline View

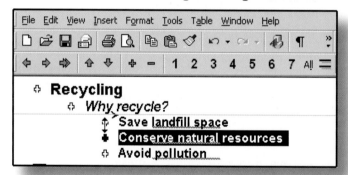

Assigning Outline Levels to Paragraphs

When you work in Outline view, the built-in heading styles change the appearance of your text. However, sometimes you may want to impose a hierarchical structure on your document without any visible formatting. You can do this by assigning outline levels to the paragraphs of your text. You can then still work in Outline view to see the indentations, but the text will appear without any character formatting. To assign an outline level to a paragraph, switch to Print Layout view and select the paragraph. Choose Paragraph from the Format menu and then the Indents and Spacing tab. Click the level you want in the Outline level box.

S TEP-BY-STEP ▷ 8.11

1. Open **IW Step8-11** from the data files.

2. Save as **Harris Clarke** followed by your initials.

3. Switch to Print Layout view if necessary.

4. Select the title *Harris Clarke Securities Online Service*.

5. Choose **Paragraph** from the **Format** menu and choose the **Indents and Spacing** tab if necessary.

6. In the *Outline level* box, choose **Level 1**.

7. Click **OK**.

8. Follow the same procedure to make *Getting Online* and *Online Information* into **Level 2** headings.

9. Make *Activate*, *Login*, *Accounts*, and *Markets* into **Level 3** headings.

10. Switch to Outline view. Your document should look similar to Figure 8-19.

11. Save, print and close the document.

FIGURE 8-19
The document in Step-by-Step 8.11 in Outline View

⊕ Harris Clarke Securities Online Service
　▫ Using our Internet service, you have a financial management tool at your fingertips. You can access your account activity, get market information, and enhance the relationship you have with your financial consultant.
　⊕ Getting Online
　　⊕ Activate
　　　▫ To activate your service, contact one of our representatives in the Online Help department at 1-800-555-HELP. Our help line is available 24 hours a day.
　　⊕ Login
　　　▫ You will be assigned a ten-character password. You can save this password on the login screen so that you do not have to key it each time you sign on.
　⊕ Online Information
　　⊕ Accounts
　　　▫ You can customize how you view your account activity. It is possible to view single or multiple transactions, switch between accounts, sort information, and specify a time range.
　　⊕ Markets
　　　▫ Market data is available at any time. You can chart securities, get expanded quote information, and access special reports.

Summary

In this lesson, you learned:

- It is easy to move back and forth between documents by clicking a document's icon in the taskbar.

- You can copy and paste text between documents just as you can within a document.

- By splitting your document, you can see two separate parts of the document. Each area of the document is called a pane. Go To allows you to jump to a specific page in a document.

- Hidden formatting characters include spaces, paragraph returns, and end-of-line marks. The Word Count command counts the pages, words, characters, paragraphs, and lines in your document quickly.

- Word automatically inserts page breaks where they are necessary. You also can insert a page break manually by choosing Break from the Insert menu and choosing Page Break.

- Headers and footers have their own formatting toolbar that appears when you choose the Header and Footer command. The Header and Footer toolbar contains formatting buttons you can use to insert the date, time, and page numbers.

- A footnote or endnote is used to document quotations, figures, summaries, or other text that you do not want to include in the body of your document. Footnotes are printed at the bottom of each page, and endnotes are printed at the end of the document.

- To create different page layouts within one document, divide the document into sections. Styles are predefined sets of formatting options that add consistency to a document. You can define a new style, apply a style, and modify a style.

- Outlines are useful for creating a document with a hierarchical structure. You can work in Outline view and see the visible formatting or assign outline levels to paragraphs, which does not change the document's appearance.

LESSON 8 REVIEW QUESTIONS

MULTIPLE CHOICE

Select the best response for the following statements.

1. What command do you use to skip to a specific part of a document?
   A. Find
   B. Move To
   C. Go To
   D. Skip To

2. Using the Show/Hide ¶ command, you can view hidden
   A. Orphans
   B. Formatting characters
   C. Window panes
   D. Bullets

3. A footnote can be used to document
   A. Quotations
   B. Figures
   C. Summaries
   D. All of the above

4. Text printed at the top of the page is called a(n)
   A. Header
   B. Footer
   C. Footnote
   D. Endnote

5. To have more than one page layout in a document, divide the document into
   A. Styles
   B. Sections
   C. Summaries
   D. Splits

FILL IN THE BLANKS

Complete the following sentences by writing the correct word or words in the blanks provided.

1. When you open a new document, a button corresponding to the document is displayed on the _____. *taskbar*

2. You can view two parts of your document at once by using the _____ command. *Split*

3. To count words in a document, choose the Word Count command from the _____ *Tools* menu.

4. A(n) _____ *style* is a predefined set of formatting options that have been named and saved.

5. A(n) _____ before a heading in Outline view indicates that there are subheadings or body text below it. *plus symbol*

PROJECT 8-1

1. Open the **Guidelines2** file that you last used in Project 5-1.

2. Save the document as **Guidelines Final** followed by your initials.

3. Insert a manual page break before the *Check Spelling* heading.

4. Create a continuous section break and format the list of words into two columns.

5. Open **IW Project8-1** from the student data files.

6. Select all the text and copy it.

7. Switch to the **Guidelines Final** document and paste the text below the first paragraph under the *Be Consistent* heading.

8. Insert the page number right-aligned in a footer. In the Page Numbers dialog box, click the Format button. Specify that page numbers start with **1**.

9. Save, print, and close the document. Close the **IW Project8-1** document.

PROJECT 8-2

1. Open the **Porch Lights** file that you last used in Project 4-1.

2. Save the document as **Porch Lights2** followed by your initials.

3. Create a header with the current date right-aligned.

4. Place the insertion point after the first sentence in #5. Create a numbered footnote that says: **Call for more information on our Web hosting offer.**

5. Place the insertion point after the word *FREE* at the end of #6. Create a footnote that says: **You can lower the price once without any extra charge.**

6. Apply the **Heading 2** style to the phrase *Constantly available information.*

7. Apply the **Heading 2** style to the phrase that follows each number in the rest of the document.

8. Save, print, and close the document.

CRITICAL THINKING

ACTIVITY 8-1

You want to delete a footnote from a document. Then you decide to convert all your footnotes in a document to endnotes. Use the Help system to find out how to do so.

ACTIVITY 8-2

You work for Alan's Tree & Garden Center, a retail nursery and tree farm that specializes in drought tolerant plants. Since many customers are not sure what they should purchase when landscaping their yards, you mention to the manager that it would be helpful to have a brochure available with some basic information. He suggests that you create an outline of what should be included. Use Word to create an outline for a brochure that includes information about the business and the products and services offered as well as information about trees, plants, shrubs, and soil.

LESSON 9

INCREASING EFFICIENCY USING WORD

OBJECTIVES

Upon completion of this lesson, you should be able to:

- Create and use templates and wizards.
- Insert, format, and revise tables.
- Create and print envelopes and labels.
- Use mail merge.
- Save a document as a Web page and apply a theme.
- Understand integration basics.
- Insert a hyperlink in a document.

⏱ Estimated Time: 1 hour

Using Templates and Wizards

Suppose you are a sales representative and you must file a report each week that summarizes your sales and the new contacts you have made. Parts of this report will be the same each week, such as the document's format and the headings within the report. It would be tedious to re-create the document each week. Word solves this problem by allowing you to create a template or use an existing Word template for documents that you use frequently. A **template** is a file that contains page and paragraph formatting and text that you can customize to create a new document similar to but slightly different from the original. A report template would save all formatting, font choices, and text that do not change, allowing you to fill in only the new information each week.

Opening an Existing Template

Word contains many templates you can use to create documents. To open an existing Word template, choose New from the File menu. The New dialog box contains a number of tabs for document types (Figure 9-1). Each tab contains several templates for that document type. You can use a template as is or modify it and save it as a new template.

To open a template you want to use as is, click its name and click OK. Word opens a new blank document with the settings and text specified by the template already in place. Replace the data in the template with your own data and save.

To open a template and modify it, click the template name, click the Template option button, and click OK. After you have finished modifying the template, save it again with the same or a new name.

FIGURE 9-1
New dialog box

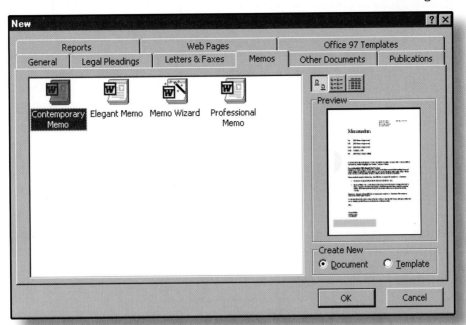

STEP-BY-STEP ▷ 9.1

1. Choose **New** from the **File** menu. The New dialog box appears.

2. Click the **Memos** tab. Click the *Contemporary Memo*, as shown in Figure 9-1.

3. In the *Create New* box, choose **Document**, if necessary.

4. Choose **OK**. The Contemporary Memo template appears on your screen.

5. Switch to Normal view.

6. Click *[Click **here** and type name]* beside *To:* and key **Wyatt Brown**.

7. Click *[Click **here** and type name]* beside *CC:* and key **Angela Hegstrom**.

8. Click *[Click **here** and type name]* beside *From:* and key your name.

9. Click *[Click **here** and type subject]* beside Re: and key **How to Use Memo Templates**.

10. Save the file as **Memo Document** followed by your initials.

11. Print and close the document.

Extra Challenge

Create a document using any other available template.

Creating a Template

As stated above, you can create a template by modifying an existing one, or you can create a template from your own document. To create a template using a new, blank document, choose New from the File menu. On the General tab, click Blank Document. Click the Template option in the *Create New* box and click OK. To create a template from an existing document, open the document and choose Save As from the File menu. In the Save As dialog box key a file name and choose Document Template in the *Save as type* box. When you save your document, it will be saved as a template in the Templates folder of the Office folder on the hard drive. If you save a template somewhere other than this default location, it will not appear in the New dialog box when you want to use it.

STEP-BY-STEP ▷ 9.2

1. Choose **New** from the **File** menu. The New dialog box appears.

2. Click the **General** tab and click the **Blank Document** icon.

3. Click the **Template** option in the *Create New* box.

4. Click **OK**. A blank document titled *Template1* appears on your screen.

5. Choose **Picture** from the **Insert** menu. Click **ClipArt** on the submenu. The Insert ClipArt dialog box appears.

6. In the *Search for clips* box, key **keys** and press **Enter**.

7. Click one of the images of keys that is available and choose **Insert clip** from the toolbar.

8. Close the Insert ClipArt dialog box. The image is in the document and the Picture toolbar appears.

9. Select the image and click the **Format Picture** button on the Picture toolbar. The Format Picture dialog box appears.

10. Scale the image down so that it will be the appropriate size for use in a letterhead.

11. Center the image.

12. Using whatever fonts are available to you, create a letterhead like the one illustrated in Figure 9-2.

13. Change the top margin to .5 inches, the left and right margins to 1.75 inches, and the bottom margin to 1 inch. Adjust and realign the graphic, if necessary.

14. When you finish creating the letterhead, move the insertion point to below the letterhead.

15. Choose **Save As** from the **File** menu.

16. In the *File name* box, key **Keys Template** followed by your initials and then click **Save**.

17. Close the file.

Hot Tip

Word saves regular word processing documents with the *.doc* extension and saves template files with the *.dot* extension.

Hot Tip

If the Picture toolbar does not appear when you select an image, choose **Toolbars** from the **View** menu and **Picture** from the submenu.

FIGURE 9-2
Letterhead template

Creating a Document Using a Template

You can use the template you created as many times as needed. To use a template, choose New from the File menu. In the New dialog box, click the General tab and then click the template's icon and click OK to bring up a copy of your template titled *Document1*. (Yours might be *Document2* or *Document3* depending on how many new documents you have created since starting Word.) After you make changes to this document, choose Save As to save it to your data disk as a regular Word document with the .doc extension.

S TEP-BY-STEP ▷ 9.3

1. Choose **New** from the **File** menu. The New dialog box appears.

2. Click the **General** tab.

3. Click **Keys Template** and choose **OK**. A copy of the template opens, named *Document1*.

4. Save the document as **Keys Letter** followed by your initials.

5. Insert five blank lines and key the letter shown in Figure 9-3 in Arial 10 pt.

6. Preview the document to make sure it is centered properly on the page.

7. Print and close the document.

(continued on next page)

FIGURE 9-3
Text to Key for Step-by-Step 9.3

March 6, —

Ms. Claire Denver
9007 Landridge Boulevard
White Plains, NY 10602-9007

Ms. Denver:

Thank you for your request for more information on Keys Catering
Services. I understand that you are planning a reception for your son's
engagement.

Keys Catering Services has been providing quality catering since 1990,
and we have catered at more than 300 events—including engagement and
wedding receptions. We have an excellent reputation for quality,
reliability, and service. We are able to provide varied services and
menu items ranging from an elegant French dinner to a casual Mexican
fiesta.

I've enclosed a brochure that describes our catering services. Please
contact me for more information. I would like to be of further service
to you.

Again, thank you for your interest in Keys Catering Services.

Sincerely,

Chris Keys
Owner

Enclosures

Using Wizards

A *wizard* is similar to a template, but it asks you questions and creates a document based on your answers. The word processing wizards available to you include memos, letters, faxes, reports, and Web pages. To start a wizard, choose New from the File menu. In the New dialog box, click one of the tabs, click a document wizard, and choose OK. The *Preview* box shows a sample of what your document will look like. The wizard will begin by asking you a question or asking you to key information. Sometimes you will choose between two or more alternatives. You can click on each choice and an example of the choice is shown in the dialog box. Click Next to go to the next step. Click Back to go to the previous step. Click Finish at the end, and the wizard will create the document for you. Once you have created the document, you can add specific text and modify existing text in your document.

S TEP-BY-STEP ▷ 9.4

1. Choose **New** from the **File** menu. The New dialog box appears.

2. Click the **Letters & Faxes** tab and click the **Fax Wizard** icon. Choose **OK**. The Fax Wizard dialog box appears. Click **Next>**.

3. Click the *Just a cover sheet with a note* option. Click **Next>**.

4. Click *I want to print my document so I can send it from a separate fax machine*. Click **Next>**.

5. In the *Name* box, key **Mr. Griffin Moss**.

6. In the *Fax Number* box, key **606-555-9163**. Click **Next>**.

7. Choose the **Professional** style. Click **Next>**.

8. In the *Name* box, key **Calliope Rose**.

9. In the *Company* box, key **Rose Investments**.

10. In the *Mailing Address* box, key

    2016 Future Street
    Dallas, TX 75298-2016

11. In the *Phone* box, key **214-555-3447**.

12. In the *Fax* box, key **214-555-8822**. Click **Next>**.

13. Click **Finish**. The Wizard creates the document.

14. On the *Phone* line, click *[Click **here** and type phone number]* and key **606-555-2382**.

15. On the *Pages* line, click *[Click **here** and type number of pages]* and key **2**.

16. On the *Re:* line, click and key **Investments**.

17. Double-click the box beside **For Review**.

18. Click beside *Comments* and key **Please consider the following investments. I will call you next week to discuss them.**

19. Save the file as **Fax Cover Sheet** followed by your initials.

20. Print and close the document.

21. Delete your template from the hard drive of your computer:
    a. Choose **New** from the **File** menu.
    b. Locate the **Keys Template** file, probably in the General tab.
    c. Right-click the **Keys Template** file.
    d. Click **Delete** on the shortcut menu.
    e. Click **Yes**. The template file is deleted. Close the New dialog box.

 Extra Challenge

Use the Fax Wizard to create a personal fax cover sheet for yourself or for your school.

Inserting and Formatting Tables

A **table** is an arrangement of text or numbers in rows and columns, similar to a spreadsheet. Tables are sometimes easier to use than aligning text with tabs.

To create a table, choose Insert from the Table menu and then Table from the submenu. Specify the number of columns and rows you want in the Insert Table dialog box, shown in Figure 9-4. To enter text in a table, position the insertion point in the cell where you want to begin. A **cell** is where a row and column intersect. Key the text and then use the Tab or an arrow key to move to the next cell where you want to insert data. Use the Enter key only if you want to insert a second line in a cell.

FIGURE 9-4
Insert Table dialog box

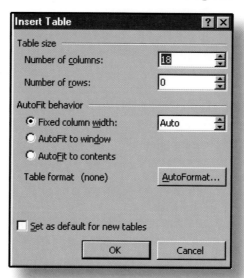

STEP-BY-STEP ▷ 9.5

1. Open **IW Step9-5** from the student data files.

2. Save the document as **Voting Memo** followed by your initials.

3. Position the insertion point on the second blank line below the second paragraph.

4. Choose **Insert** from the **Table** menu. Then, choose **Table** from the submenu. The Insert Table dialog box appears, as shown in Figure 9-4.

5. In the *Number of columns* box, key **3**.

6. In the *Number of rows* box, key **10**.

7. Click **OK**. The table is inserted.

8. Key the data into the table as shown in Figure 9-5.

9. Save and leave the document open for the next Step-by-Step.

FIGURE 9-5
Data in a table

Precinct	Place	Address
1	Westerner Elementary School	4590 Sunrise Street
2	Jefferson Junior High School	3501 City Avenue
3	Plainsman High School	1200 Ranch Road
4	Buffalo High School	1780 Buffalo Road
5	Garrett Middle School	5881 Rodeo Road
6	Winters Elementary School	3559 Prairie Way
7	Coronado Elementary School	7900 5th Street
8	Mission Middle School	2398 Verde Street
9	West Texas High School	6503 26th Street

Revising a Table

After you have created a table, you can revise it by inserting and deleting rows and columns and changing formats within cells. Change formats by clicking in a specific table cell or by selecting entire rows or columns and then changing the format. To select an entire row, click to the left of the row (outside the table). To select an entire column, position your pointer just above the column and click when your pointer changes to a downward-pointing arrow.

To insert a row, select a row and choose Insert from the Table menu and then choose Rows Above or Rows Below depending on where you want them to appear in relation to the selected row. To insert a column, select a column and choose Insert from the Table menu and then choose Columns to the Left or Columns to the Right. A new column will be inserted to the left or to the right of the one you selected. Similarly, you can delete a column or row by selecting it and choosing Delete from the Table menu and then choosing Columns or Rows.

You can change column width or row height manually by clicking on the border of the column or row and dragging the border to expand or decrease width or height.

STEP-BY-STEP ▷ 9.6

1. Click to the left of *Precinct*—outside the table—to select the first row.

2. Click the **Center** button on the toolbar. All three of the headings are centered.

3. With the first row still selected, change the font size to 14 point.

4. Position your pointer at the top of the *Precinct* column. When your pointer changes to a downward-pointing arrow, click to select the entire column.

5. Choose the **Center** button on the toolbar. The data in the entire column is centered.

(continued on next page)

6. With the first column still selected, choose **Insert** from the **Table** menu and **Columns to the Right** from the submenu. A new column is inserted to the right of the first column.

7. You decide you do not need this column after all. Click anywhere in the new column. Choose **Delete** from the **Table** menu and **Columns** from the submenu. The new column is deleted. Notice that the table structure also changes.

8. Drag the right border of the *Precinct* column to the left to reduce the column width. The column should be only slight wider than the column heading. Each table entry should now fit on one line with no runovers.

9. Click to the left of the Precinct 9 row to select it.

10. Choose **Insert** from the **Table** menu and **Rows Below** from the submenu. A new row is inserted below the one you selected.

11. In the new row, key the following data:

```
10   Lincoln Elementary School
900  Holly Avenue
```

12. Save and leave the document open for the next Step-by-Step.

Formatting a Table

You can easily change the alignment, font, style, and size of data in a column or row much the same way you've changed the appearance of text in previous lessons. You select the row or column and choose the command you want from the toolbar or menus.

You can also change the borders and shading of table cells using the Borders and Shading command in the Format menu just as you did earlier in this lesson. Add a border or shading to one cell by clicking in it and then selecting a border or shading option. Add a border or shading to an entire row or column by selecting the row or column and then selecting the border or shading option.

Word has many different pre-designed formats that you can apply to your table. Place the insertion point in any cell in the table and choose Table AutoFormat. Click the AutoFormat button and select one of the formats from the Table AutoFormat dialog box, shown in Figure 9-6.

Many of the commands on the Table menu are available on the Tables and Borders toolbar. To display it, open the View menu, choose Toolbars, and then click Tables and Borders. You can add or change borders and shading using the Border or Shading button, and you can also apply a number of alignment and other formatting options.

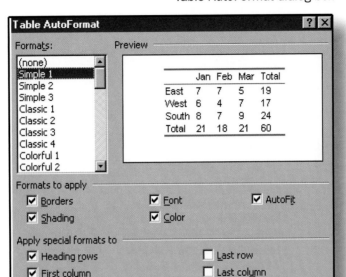

FIGURE 9-6
Table AutoFormat dialog box

Modifying Table Structure

You can make other modifications to the structure of a table using tools on the Tables and Borders toolbar. You can *split* cells to transform one column or row into two or more. You can *merge* cells to create one large cell out of several small cells. To split or merge cells, select the cells and click the Split Cells or Merge Cells button on the Tables and Borders toolbar.

The Table Properties dialog box, shown in Figure 9-7, gives you a number of other options for modifying the table. To open this dialog box, choose Table Properties on the Table menu. You can choose to wrap text around the table, change the cell and table alignment, and specify the height and width of columns and rows in this dialog box.

To add interest to your table, you can rotate the text within a cell so that it reads vertically rather than horizontally. You can rotate text quickly by clicking the Change Text Direction button on the Tables and Borders toolbar. Or, you can choose Text Direction from the Format menu. In the Text Direction - Table Cell dialog box, shown in Figure 9-8, choose the Orientation you want and click OK.

FIGURE 9-7
Table Properties dialog box

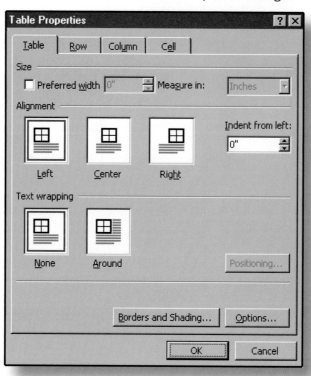

FIGURE 9-8
Text Direction - Table Cell dialog box

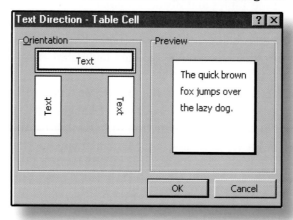

STEP-BY-STEP ▷ 9.7

1. Choose **Toolbars** from the **View** menu and then click **Tables and Borders** on the submenu.

2. Select the first row and insert a row above it.

3. In the new first row, key **Cast Your Vote!**

4. Select the new first row and click the **Merge Cells** button on the Tables and Borders toolbar. The new text is now centered across the entire table.

5. Select all the cells with numbers in them.

6. Choose **Text Direction** from the **Format** menu. The Text Direction - Table Cell dialog box appears, as shown in Figure 9-8.

7. In the *Orientation* box, choose the vertical text option on the left and click **OK**. The text changes to a vertical direction. The row heights also increase. Boldface the numbers.

8. Choose **Table Properties** from the **Table** menu. The Table Properties dialog box appears.

9. Click the **Row** tab.

10. In the *Size* section, key **0.35** in the *Specify height* box.

11. Click the **Table** tab. Your screen appears similar to Figure 9-7.

12. In the *Alignment* section, click **Center**. Click **OK**.

13. Select all the data in the table (excluding headings).

14. Access the **Cell** tab of the Table Properties dialog box.

15. In the *Vertical alignment* section, choose **Center**. Click **OK**.

16. Click the arrow next to the **Border Color** button and choose **Dark Green** from the palette of colors.

17. Select the entire table and click the arrow next to the **Outside Border** button on the Tables and Borders toolbar. Choose the **All Borders** button on the palette of border choices. All table borders are now dark green.

18. With the table still selected, click the arrow next to the **Shading Color** button and choose **Light Green** from the palette of colors.

19. Close the Tables and Borders toolbar.

20. Save, print, and close the file.

Extra Challenge

Use the Borders and Shading command to change the colors of the table to red, white, and blue. You might also want to change some text colors to red, white, or blue. Save this file with a new name so you don't overwrite the *Voting Memo* file.

Creating and Printing Envelopes

C It is easy to address envelopes using Word. Choose Envelopes and Labels from the Tools menu to display the Envelopes and Labels dialog box. In the Envelopes tab, shown in Figure 9-9, key the delivery address and return address. To change the envelope size or fonts, choose Options to display the Envelope Options dialog box, shown in Figure 9-10.

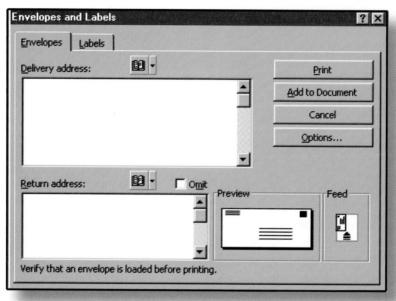

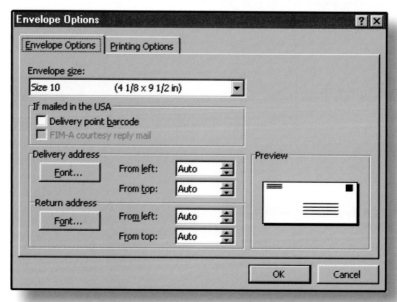

STEP-BY-STEP ▷ 9.8

1. Create a new Word document.

2. Choose **Envelopes and Labels** from the **Tools** menu. The Envelopes and Labels dialog box appears.

3. Click the **Envelopes** tab, shown in Figure 9-9.

4. In the *Delivery address* box, key

   Stephan Stordahl
   33 Wafarer Way
   Bozeman, MT 59715

5. In the *Return address* box, key your name and address.

6. Click the **Options** button. The Envelope Options dialog box is displayed, as shown in Figure 9-10.

7. In the *Delivery address* box, click **Font** to display the Envelope Address dialog box.

8. Change the font to **Comic Sans MS** and click **OK**. Click **OK** again to return to the Envelopes and Labels dialog box.

9. In the Envelopes and Labels dialog box, click **Print**. (Print the envelope on plain paper if desired.)

10. When a message appears asking if you want to save the new return address as the default return address, click **No**.

11. Leave the blank Word document open for the next Step-by-Step.

Creating and Printing Labels

Creating labels is very similar to creating envelopes. Access the Labels tab of the Envelopes and Labels dialog box, as shown in Figure 9-11. Type the address you want to appear on the labels. You can choose to print a full page of the same label or just one label. To choose a label type other than the one shown in the *Label* section, click the Options button to display the Label Options dialog box, shown in Figure 9-12.

FIGURE 9-11

Labels tab of the Envelopes and Labels dialog box

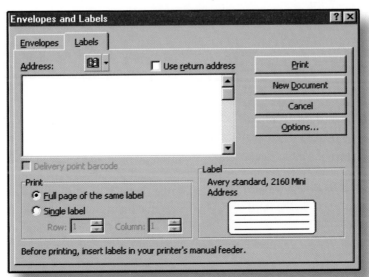

FIGURE 9-12
Label Options dialog box

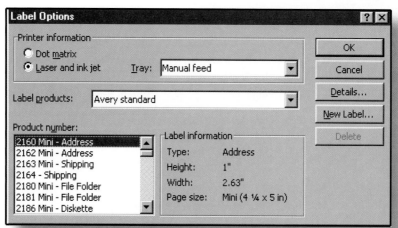

STEP-BY-STEP ▷ 9.9

1. Choose **Envelopes and Labels** from the **Tools** menu. The Envelopes and Labels dialog box appears.

2. Click the **Labels** tab, as shown in Figure 9-11.

3. In the *Address* box, key

```
Earle Langeland
4040 Surfer Lane
Santa Cruz, CA 90670
```

4. Click the **Options** button to display the Label Options dialog box, shown in Figure 9-12.

5. In the *Product number* box, scroll down to choose **5160 - Address**. Click **OK**.

6. In the Envelopes and Labels dialog box, click **Print**. (Print the labels on plain paper.)

7. Close the Word document without saving.

Using Mail Merge

Mail **merge** is combining a document with information that personalizes it. For example, you might send a letter to each member of a professional organization. In each letter the information is the same, but the names of the recipients will be different. One letter may begin "Dear Mr. Bodleian" or "Dear Ms. Dreary." The document with the information that doesn't change is called the ***main document***. The ***data source*** contains the information that will vary in each document.

The Mail Merge Helper will guide you through the mail merge process. Choose Mail Merge from the Tools menu to display the Mail Merge Helper dialog box, shown in Figure 9-13. In the first step, you choose what kind of document you want to create—a form letter, mailing labels, envelopes, or a catalog. In the second step, you choose whether you want to create a new data source, open an existing one, or use addresses from an electronic address book. In the third step, you merge the main document with the data source.

FIGURE 9-13
Mail Merge Helper dialog box

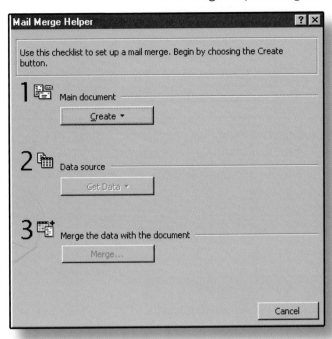

If you choose to create a data source, the Create Data Source dialog box opens, as shown in Figure 9-14, where you can choose which field names you want to use. You will later insert the field names, or *merge fields*, in the main document where you want to print the information from the data source. After you have chosen the field names and chosen where you want to save the data source, the Data Form dialog box appears as shown in Figure 9-15 so that you can enter data.

FIGURE 9-14
Create Data Source dialog box

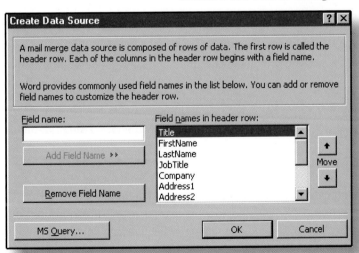

FIGURE 9-15
Data Form dialog box

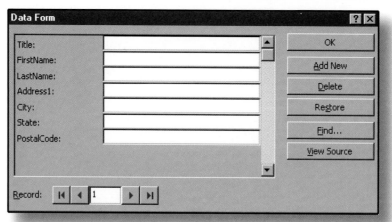

1. Create a new Word document.

2. Choose **Mail Merge** from the **Tools** menu. The Mail Merge Helper dialog box appears, as shown in Figure 9-13.

3. In the *Main document* section, click **Create**; then choose **Envelopes**.

4. Click **Active Window** in the message box that appears.

5. In the *Data source* section, click **Get Data**; then choose **Create Data Source**. The Create Data Source dialog box appears, as shown in Figure 9-14.

6. In the *Field names in header row* box, click **Job Title**.

7. Click the **Remove Field Name** button.

8. Using the same process remove the field names Address2, Country, HomePhone, and WorkPhone. Click **OK**. The Save As dialog box appears.

9. Save the data source as **Mail Merge** followed by your initials.

10. Click **Edit Data Source** in the message box that appears. The Data Form dialog box appears, as shown in Figure 9-15.

11. Key all the data records shown in Figure 9-16. Click **Add New** to start a new data record and click **OK** to return to the main document when you are finished.

12. Choose **Mail Merge** from the **Tools** menu to display the Mail Merge Helper dialog box.

13. In the *Main document* section, click the **Setup** button. The Envelope Options dialog box appears. Click **OK**.

14. The Envelope address dialog box appears. Click the **Insert Merge Field** button and choose **Title** from the drop-down list.

15. Use the same process to insert the rest of the merge fields as shown in Figure 9-17. (Be sure to add spaces where necessary and insert a comma between the City and State merge fields.)

16. Click **OK**. The merge fields are inserted in the main document and the Mail Merge Helper dialog box is displayed.

17. In the Merge the data with the document section, click **Merge**. The Merge dialog box appears, as shown in Figure 9-18.

18. Click **Merge**. The information from the data source is inserted into the merge fields to create an envelope for each data record.

19. Scroll down to see each envelope. Save the document as **Envelopes** followed by your initials.

20. Print and close.

21. Save the document with the merge fields as **Mail Merge Main Doc** and close it. When you get a message asking if you want to save the Mail Merge data source, click **Yes**.

FIGURE 9-16
Data records to key for Step-by-Step 9.10

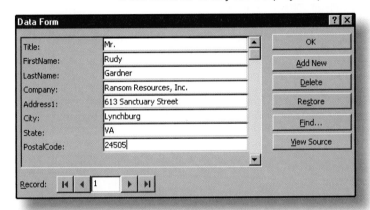

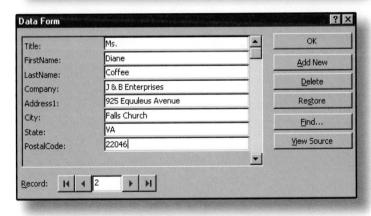

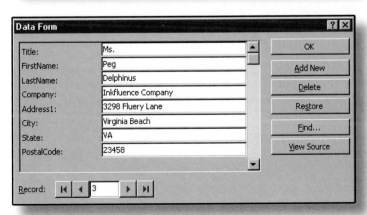

(continued on next page)

FIGURE 9-17
Envelope address dialog box

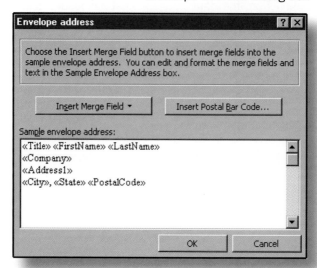

FIGURE 9-18
Merge dialog box

Creating a Web Page

Web pages are documents that can be viewed by Web browsers, such as Internet Explorer. Using Office 2000, you can convert Word documents to Web pages by choosing Save as Web Page from the File menu. When you use this command, Word converts your document to HTML format and supplies HTML tags for most common document features such as tables and fonts.

A good way to enhance a Web page is to add a theme. A ***theme*** is a preformatted design that you can apply to a document to change its appearance without changing the content. A theme changes the color scheme, font, and formatting of your document to provide a new look. Choose Theme from the Format menu to open the Theme dialog box, shown in Figure 9-19.

When you convert a document to a Web page, Word switches to Web Layout view so you can see what the document will look like when opened in a browser. To actually preview a document in your browser choose Web Page Preview from the File menu. The browser opens and displays your document.

FIGURE 9-19
Theme dialog box

FIGURE 9-19
Theme dialog box

STEP-BY-STEP ▷ 9.11

1. Open the **Porch Lights2** file that you last used in Project 8-2.

2. Choose **Save as Web Page** from the **File** menu. The Save as Web Page dialog box appears.

3. In the *File name* box, key **Porch Lights Web** followed by your initials. Click **Save**. Word switches to Web Layout view.

4. Remove the date in the header.

5. Change the numbered list to a bulleted list.

6. Choose **Theme** from the **Format** menu. The Theme dialog box appears, as shown in Figure 9-19.

7. In the *Choose a Theme* box, scroll down and choose **Rice Paper**. The preview box shows the design elements for that theme. Click **OK**.

8. The *Rice Paper* theme has been applied to your document.

9. Choose **Web Page Preview** from the **File** menu. Your browser opens and the document is displayed. Your screen should appear similar to Figure 9-20.

10. Save, print, and close the document.

(continued on next page)

FIGURE 9-20
Web page displayed in a Web browser

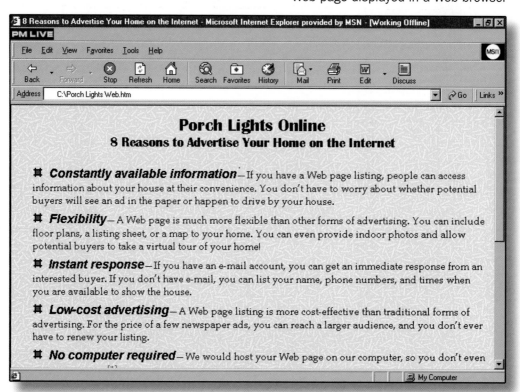

Send a Word Document via E-mail

There are several ways you can use e-mail in conjunction with Word. You can e-mail a message using Word as your e-mail editor, e-mail a copy of a document directly from Word, or e-mail a Word document as an attachment.

To e-mail a message using Word as your e-mail editor, choose New from the File menu and then click E-mail Message on the General tab. After you click OK, a document window appears with an e-mail header on top as shown in Figure 9-21. Fill in the recipient information, key your message, and click Send. The message is e-mailed and the document window closes. The message will be sent in HTML format and can be viewed by any browser or e-mail program that can read HTML.

The process for e-mailing a document directly from Word is similar to e-mailing a message. After you have created or opened a document, click the E-mail button on the Standard toolbar. An e-mail header appears where you fill in the recipient information. Then click the Send a Copy button. A copy of the document is e-mailed, but the original stays open so you can continue working on it. The e-mail information is saved with the document and appears in the e-mail header next time you send a copy of the document.

To e-mail a document as an attachment, open or create a document and then choose Send To on the File menu. Choose Mail Recipient (as Attachment) on the submenu, enter the recipient information, and click Send.

Hot Tip

If Mail Recipient (as Attachment) is not available on the submenu, choose **Options** from the **Tools** menu. Click the **General** tab and select the *Mail as attachment* check box.

FIGURE 9-21
E-mail message in Word

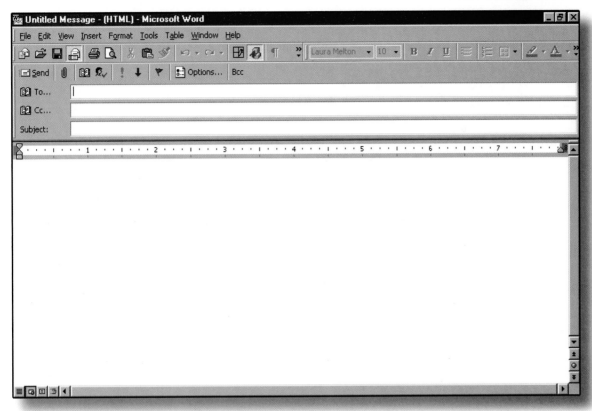

Integration Basics

As you have learned, Office 2000 is an integrated program. **Integration** means combining parts into a whole. You can integrate data within an application. For example, in Word you can insert a hyperlink that connects two documents together or embed an object in a document.

To insert a hyperlink in a document, select the text you want to make a hyperlink and choose Hyperlink from the Insert menu. The Insert Hyperlink dialog box appears, as shown in Figure 9-22. Choose whether you want to link to another document or a Web page. Click OK and a hyperlink is inserted in the document. The text you selected is displayed in blue with a blue underline. Click it to go to the linked location.

Another way to integrate within Word is to use the Paste Special command. For example, you can copy a table from one document and choose Paste Special from the Edit menu to insert it in another document. In the Paste Special dialog box, shown in Figure 9-23, choose Microsoft Word Document Object. When you choose the Paste link option, any changes you make to the original table file will be updated in the document where you pasted it.

Another way to integrate data is to use more than one Office application to complete a project. For example, you can add a chart from an Excel worksheet to a PowerPoint presentation. Or you can use information from an Access database to create form letters in Word. Tables from Word documents can become Excel data. Sharing data among applications can be done easily by simply cutting, copying, and pasting. Other ways to integrate data are by embedding, linking, creating form letters, and creating mailing labels.

When you are moving data, the file you are moving data *from* is called the **source file** and the file you are moving data *to* is called the **destination file**. The process of sharing data varies, depending on what applications are involved. Word, Excel, and Access documents have unique formats. For example, data from an Excel worksheet is arranged in cells, information in an Access database is collected in fields, and text in a Word document does not follow any particular format. When you move data between applications by cutting or copying and pasting, Office changes the format of the information you are moving so that it may be used in the destination file. For example, information copied from fields in an Access database will be pasted in an Excel worksheet in columns and rows.

FIGURE 9-22
Insert Hyperlink dialog box

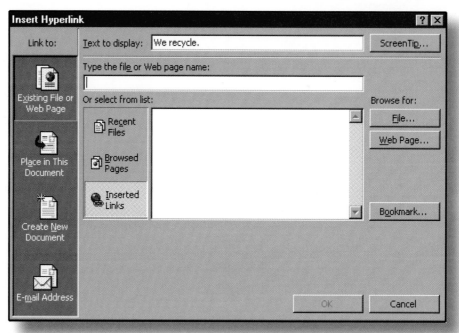

FIGURE 9-23
Paste Special dialog box

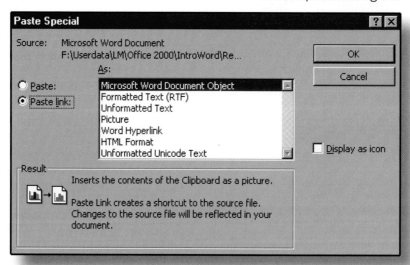

STEP-BY-STEP ▷ 9.12

1. Open the **Sage Stone** file that you last used in Step-by-Step 8.9.

2. Save the document as **Sage Stone Link** followed by your initials.

3. In the second bulleted item, select the sentence **We recycle.**

4. Click **Hyperlink** on the **Insert** menu. The Insert Hyperlink dialog box appears, as shown in Figure 9-21.

5. Under *Browse for:* click the **File** button.

6. In the Link to File dialog box, locate the **Recycle** file that you last used in Step-by-Step 8.10.

7. Click **OK** to return to the Insert Hyperlink dialog box.

8. Click **OK**. The hyperlink is inserted in document. The text you selected is blue with a blue underline.

9. Click the hyperlink. The **Recycle** document opens.

10. Close the **Recycle** document.

11. Notice in the **Sage Stone Link** document that the hyperlink has changed color to indicate that it has been used. Save and close.

12. Open **IWStep9-12** from the student data files.

13. Save the file as **SSTable** followed by your initials.

14. Select the entire table and copy it.

15. Switch to the **Sage Stone Link** document.

16. Insert another blank line at the end of the docu-ment and choose **Paste Special** from the **Edit** menu. The Paste Special dialog box appears.

17. Choose **Microsoft Word Document Object** and click **Paste Link** as shown in Figure 9-23 Click **OK**. The table is pasted in the document.

18. Save and close **Sage Stone Link**.

19. In the **SSTable** document, switch the Rip Tarber Stock Championship so it is on Labor Day and the Stock Classic Starter so it is on Memorial Day.

20. Save and close **SSTable**. Open **Sage Stone Link**. The changes you made in the table are reflected in the document.

21. Save, print, and close the document.

Summary

In this lesson, you learned:

- Templates allow you to save the format, font choices, and text of commonly produced documents. Wizards are similar to templates, but they ask you questions and create the document based on your answers.

- Tables are used to show data in columns and rows. They are usually easier to use than aligning text with tabs. You can easily change the format of tables to best display your data.

- You can quickly create envelopes or labels by choosing the Envelopes and Labels command from the Tools menu.

- Mail merge lets you insert changing information into a standard document. Use mail merge to create form letters, envelopes, and labels.

- Choose Save as Web Page from the File menu to save a Word document as a Web page. Apply a theme to change the color scheme, font, and formatting.

- Integration is sharing data within an application or between applications to complete a project. You can insert a hyperlink in a Word document that links it to another file or Web page.

- Data is moved from a source file to a destination file. When data is moved between applications, Office changes the format so the information fits the destination file.

LESSON 9 REVIEW QUESTIONS

WRITTEN QUESTIONS

Write a brief answer to the following questions.

1. What is a wizard?

2. What are the steps for inserting a table?

3. How do you change the address font on an envelope?

   in env tab of env & lbl - click optns - Font - change font

4. What is mail merge?

   comb standard doc w/ info personalizing it

5. How do you insert a hyperlink into a document?

   select text you want to make hyperlink & choose hyperlink from insert menu - in dialog box choose the file to link to the click ok -

TRUE/FALSE

Circle T if the statement is true or F if the statement is false.

T **(F)** 1. A template file can only be used once.

(T) F 2. A cell is where a row and column intersect.

T **(F)** 3. The data source contains the information that stays the same in a mail merge.

T **(F)** 4. A theme links one document to another.

(T) F 5. The file you are moving data from is called the source file.

PROJECT 9-1

1. Open the **Color Brick** file that you last used in Project 6-3.

2. Save the letterhead as a template with the name **Color Brick Template** followed by your initials and close.

3. Open **Color Brick Template** by selecting **New** from the **File** menu and locating the file in the New dialog box.

4. Save the document as **Auken Letter** followed by your initials.

5. Insert five blank lines below the letterhead and key the letter below in Times New Roman 12 pt.

```
May 4, —

Mr. Van Auken
125 Mercy Street
Greenville, SC  29695-6500

Mr. Auken:

The possibilities are endless! The revolutionary new brick colors you've
heard about will be shown at the Home Expo this year. And you're invited
to join me for a peek at these amazing products!

I can't wait to show you the beautiful new brick colors and the unique
ways you can use them. And, of course, the quality and durability are
super. I want to show you examples of these bricks in use. Our
purchasing options make it possible to use these bricks for wonderful
accents and designs on commercial and residential buildings!

The show will be May 20-23. If you have a free moment, call me before
the show, and I'll schedule a time when we can meet. But even if you
can't schedule the time in advance, please visit Booth 504A. You'll see
what all the excitement in building is about!

Sincerely,


Davy Willows
Salesperson
```

6. Save, print, and close the document.

7. Create an envelope to mail the letter to Mr. Auken.

8. Delete the **Color BrickTemplate** from the Templates directory on the hard drive of your computer.

PROJECT 9-2

1.   Open the **Canyon Bank** file that you last used in Project 7-1.

2.   Save the document as **Canyon Bank2** followed by your initials.

3.   Place the insertion point at the end of the third column. Insert a blank line and key the following heading in bold.

     `Types of Checking Accounts`

4.   Insert a blank line, and then insert a table with 9 rows and 3 columns. Use the **Contemporary** AutoFormat.

5.   Key and format the data in the table as shown in Figure 9-24. Adjust column widths if needed to make sure the table data fits on the page. Use Times New Roman 9 point.

6.   Select the words *other services available* in the last paragraph of the third column.

7.   Create a hyperlink to the **Harris Clarke** document you created in Step-by-Step 8.11.

8.   Save, print, and close the document.

FIGURE 9-24

	Bonus	Regular
Check Writing Fee	No	No
ATM Fee	No	No
Monthly Fee	No	$0-$8
Min. Balance	$1,500	$750
Interest	Yes	No
Direct Deposit Discount	No	Yes
Free Debit Card	No	No
Overdraft Protection	Yes	No

CRITICAL THINKING

ACTIVITY 9-1

Your supervisor asks you to insert a graphic on an envelope and to attach the envelope to a document you are editing so she can print it later. Use the Help system to find out how to do as she has requested.

ACTIVITY 9-2

You work for a real estate agency that is interested in creating a Web page with information about the company. Create a Web page and add a theme. Link it to at least one other page or Web site.

Introduction to Microsoft Word

COMMAND SUMMARY

FEATURE	MENU CHOICE	TOOLBAR BUTTON	LESSON
Align Text	Format, Paragraph		3
AutoCorrect	Tools, AutoCorrect		5
AutoFormat	Tools, AutoCorrect, AutoFormat		5
AutoText	Insert, AutoText		5
Borders	Format, Borders and Shading		7
Bold	Format, Font		3
Bulleted list	Format, Bullets and Numbering		4
Case	Format, Change Case		3
Clip art	Insert, Picture, Clip Art		7
Close	File, Close		1
Columns	Format, Columns		6
Copy	Edit, Copy		2
Copy format and style	*insert csc9.tif*		3
Create a new document	File, New		1, 9
Cut	Edit, Cut		2
Date & time, insert	Insert, Date & Time		5
Drawing graphics	View, Toolbars, Drawing		6
Envelopes	Tools, Envelopes and Labels		9
Find	Edit, Find		5
Font	Format, Font	Times New Roman	3
Font color	Format, Font		3
Font effects	Format, Font		3
Font size	Format, Font	10	3
Footnotes and endnotes	Insert, Footnote		8
Grammar check	Tools, Spelling and Grammar		5
Go to	Edit, Go To		8
Italic	Format, Font		3

FEATURE	MENU CHOICE	TOOLBAR BUTTON	LESSON
Header and footer	View, Header and Footer		8
Highlight		[icon]	3
Hyperlink, insert	Insert, Hyperlink	[icon]	9
Hyphenation	Tools, Language, Hyphenation		5
Labels	Tools, Envelopes and Labels		9
Line spacing	Format, Paragraph		4
Mail merge	Tools, Mail Merge		9
Margins	File, Page Setup		4
Numbered list	Format, Bullets and Numbering	[icon]	4
Open existing document	File, Open	[icon]	1
Outline, create	View, Outline		8
Outline numbering	Format, Bullets and Numbering		4
Page break	Insert, Break		8
Page Numbers	Insert, Page Numbers or View, Header and Footer		8
Paste	Edit, Paste	[icon]	2
Preview document	File, Print Preview	[icon]	1
Print document	File, Print	[icon]	1
Remove Split Window	Window, Remove Split		8
Replace	Edit, Replace		5
Reverse action	Edit, Undo	[icon]	2
Reverse Undo	Edit, Redo	[icon]	2
Ruler	View, Ruler		1
Save	File, Save	[icon]	1
Section breaks	Insert, Break		8
Select entire document	Edit, Select All		2
Shading	Format, Borders and Shading		7
Show/Hide ¶		[icon ¶]	8
Spell check	Tools, Spelling and Grammar	[icon ABC]	5
Split a window	Window, Split		8
Sort	Table, Sort	[icon]	4
Start Word	Start, New Office Document		1
Styles	Format, Style	Heading 1	8

FEATURE	MENU CHOICE	TOOLBAR BUTTON	LESSON
Table, Autoformat	Table, Autoformat		9
Table, insert	Table, Insert, Tables		9
Table, modify	Table, Properties		
Tabs	Format, Tabs		4
Text box	Insert, Text Box		7
Theme for Web page	Format, Theme		9
Thesaurus	Tools, Language, Thesaurus		5
Type over text		OVR	2
Underline	Format, Font	U	3
Vertical alignment	File, Page Setup		3
Web page	File, Save as Web Page		9
Word count	Tools, Word Count		8

REVIEW QUESTIONS

MATCHING

Match the correct term in Column 2 to its description in Column 1.

Column 1	Column 2
_____ 1. List of options from which to choose	**A.** fonts
_____ 2. Designs of type	**B.** default
_____ 3. Text printed at the top of each page	**C.** taskbar
_____ 4. Setting used unless another option is chosen	**D.** menu
_____ 5. Where a row and column intersect in a table	**E.** scale
	F. header
	G. cell

WRITTEN QUESTIONS

Write a brief answer to the following questions.

1. What is the difference between the Save and the Save As command?

2. What are leaders?

3. How do you resize an object?

4. What does the Split command do?

5. How does Word identify possible grammar errors?

APPLICATIONS

APPLICATION 1

1. Open **IW App1** from the student data files.

2. Save the document as **Island West** followed by your initials.

3. Check the document for spelling and grammar errors. Make changes as needed.

4. Find the word **Property** and replace it with **Properties** each time it occurs in the document.

5. Move the heading *How do I get more information?* and the paragraph that follows to the end of the document.

6. Replace the word *excellent* in the third paragraph with a synonym that makes sense in context.

7. Change the line spacing of the document to 1.5.

8. Change the orientation to landscape.

9. Create a WordArt title named **Island West Properties**. Choose the fifth style on the second row.

10. Center align the document vertically on the page.

11. Change each of the headings to the **Heading 1** style.

12. Indent the last heading and paragraph 1 inch on each side and center the heading.

13. Create a **3 pt Dark Red** border around the last heading and paragraph filled with **Light Yellow**.

14. Save, print, and close.

APPLICATION 2

1. Use the Professional Memo template and key the following:

   ```
   To: All Employees
   From: Jack Hightower
   Date: [current date]
   Re: Job Shadows
   ```

2. Delete the *CC:* line.

3. In the text part key the following:

   Job Shadow Day

   Next Friday our company is participating in the Job Shadow program. Students from local high schools are given the opportunity to spend a day "shadowing" an employee at a business in which they are interested. If you are willing to be involved, please contact me by Monday. Thanks.

4. Replace *Company Name Here* with **Hazel Grey & Associates**. Adjust the cell containing the name so that it appears on one line.

5. Save the memo as **Job Shadow** followed by your initials.

6. Print and close.

APPLICATION 3

1. Open **IW App3** from the student data files.

2. Save the document as **Bagel Mania** followed by your initials.

3. Change all the text to 12 point Times New Roman.

4. Change the left and right margins to 1 inch.

5. Center the title and change it to uppercase, Arial, 16 point, bold, with shadow effect.

6. Center the subtitle and change it to Arial, 14 point, italics, with outline effect.

7. Apply a .5-inch first-line indent to the first paragraph.

8. Sort the list of bagels in ascending order.

9. Insert a continuous section break before and after the list of bagels.

10. Format the list of bagels into 3 columns with .4 inches between them.

11. Change the *Breakfast Bagels* heading to 14 point, bold, small caps, dark teal, with a teal dotted underline. (Choose the second dotted underline.)

12. Copy the format of the *Breakfast Bagels* heading to the *Lunch Bagels* heading.

13. Number the items in the breakfast and lunch bagel lists. Start over with number 1 for the second list.

14. Change the line spacing of the first paragraph to 1.5, the types of bagels to double spacing, and the breakfast and lunch lists with 6 pt After spacing.

15. Align the prices in the breakfast and lunch lists at a 6.25-inch decimal tab.

16. Center and italicize *Come again!* and change the text to 14 point.

17. Save, print and close the file.

APPLICATION 4

1. Open **IW App4** from the student data files.

2. Save the file as **Zephyr Theatre** followed by your initials.

3. Make the numbered list into a bulleted list.

4. Select the heading *Performance Schedule* and all the text that follows.

5. Cut the selected text and paste it in a new document.

6. Save the new document as **Performance Schedule** followed by your initials.

7. Change the theme to *Sumi Painting*.

8. Save it as **Schedule Web** followed by your initials and close it.

9. Switch to the **Zephyr Theatre** document.

10. Change the theme to *Sumi Painting* and use the Save as Web Page command to save the document as **Theatre Web**.

11. Insert a piece of theatre related clip art at the top of the page, scale it, and use square text wrapping.

12. Create a hyperlink to the **Schedule Web** file using the last line of text, *Schedule of Performances*.

13. Save and close the document.

14. Open **Theatre Web** in your Web browser. Print the page.

15. Click the hyperlink to switch to the schedule page.

16. Print the page and close the browser.

ON-THE-JOB SIMULATION

You work at the Java Internet Café, which has been open a short time. The café serves coffee, other beverages, and pastries and offers Internet access. Seven computers are set up on tables along the north side of the store. Customers can come in and have a cup of coffee and a Danish and explore the World Wide Web.

Because of your Microsoft Office experience, your manager asks you to create and revise many of the business's documents.

SCANS

JOB 1

Many customers ask questions about the terms they come across while using the Internet. Your manager asks you to create a sign with definitions of the most common terms. The sign will be posted near each computer.

1. Open a new Word document.

2. Create the poster shown in Figure UR-1.

3. Save the document as **Terms** followed by your initials.

4. Print and close.

Internet Terminology

*Arial Bold
26 pt.
Dark Blue*

*Terms:
Dark Blue*

Browser: A program used on a computer connected to the Internet that provides access to the World Wide Web (WWW). There are two kinds of Web browsers: text-only and graphical. Graphical browsers are best because they allow you to see images and document layouts.

*Text:
Arial
14 pt.*

Download: To transfer a file from a remote computer to your computer through a modem and a telephone line.

E-mail (electronic mail): The use of a computer network to send and receive messages. With an Internet connection, you can compose messages and send them in seconds to a friend with an Internet connection in your city or in another country.

FAQ (Frequently Asked Questions): In USENET, a document posted to a newsgroup. It contains a list of the most common questions and answers for assisting new users.

Internet: A worldwide system of linked computer networks that eases data communication such as file transfer, e-mail, and newsgroups.

Newsgroup: An online discussion group that's devoted to a single topic. Members post e-mail messages to the group, and those reading the group messages send reply e-mail messages to the author or to the group.

USENET: A collection of more than 1,500 newsgroups.

World Wide Web (WWW): A global system that uses the Internet as its carrier. You navigate from "page" to page by clicking underlined links, which display other pages that contain their own links.

*3/4 point dotted
line box dark blue
6 pt. from text*

JOB 2

Many customers become curious when they see computers through the windows of the coffee shop. The café servers are often too busy to explain the concept as soon as the customer enters the store. Your manager asks you to revise the menu to include a short description of the café. These menus will be printed and placed near the entrance.

1. Open **IW Job2** from the student data files.

2. Key the text below.

   The Java Internet Café is a coffee shop with a twist. As you can see, there are seven computers on tables at the north side of the café. These computers provide high-speed Internet access to our customers. Whether you're a regular on the Net or a novice, our system is designed to allow you easy exploration of the World Wide Web. You've heard about it; now give it a try. Ask your server to help you get started.

3. Save the document as **Java Menu** followed by your initials.

4. Change the left and right margins to 1 inch.

5. Change the font of the paragraph you just keyed to Arial 11 point, if necessary.

6. Insert one blank line after the paragraph and key the title **Menu** centered.

7. Change the font of *Menu* to Arial 18 point bold. You'll paste the menu information from Excel later.

8. Insert and center the following footer.

   Sit back, sip your coffee, and surf the net.

9. Change the font to Arial 14 point bold.

10. Save, print, and close the document. Close Word.

UNIT

INTRODUCTION TO MICROSOFT® EXCEL

Estimated Time for Unit: 16 hours

EXCEL BASICS

OBJECTIVES

Upon completion of this lesson, you should be able to:

- Define the terms *spreadsheet* and *worksheet*.

- Identify the parts of the worksheet.

- Move the highlight in the worksheet.

- Select cells and enter data in the worksheet.

- Edit cells.

- Save a worksheet.

- Print a worksheet.

⏱ Estimated Time: 1.5 hours

What Is Excel?

Excel is the spreadsheet application of the Office 2000 programs. A ***spreadsheet*** is a grid of rows and columns containing numbers, text, and formulas. The purpose of a spreadsheet is to solve problems that involve numbers. Without a computer, you might try to solve this type of problem by creating rows and columns on ruled paper and using a calculator to determine results (see Figure 1-1). Computer

FIGURE 1-1
Spreadsheet prepared on paper

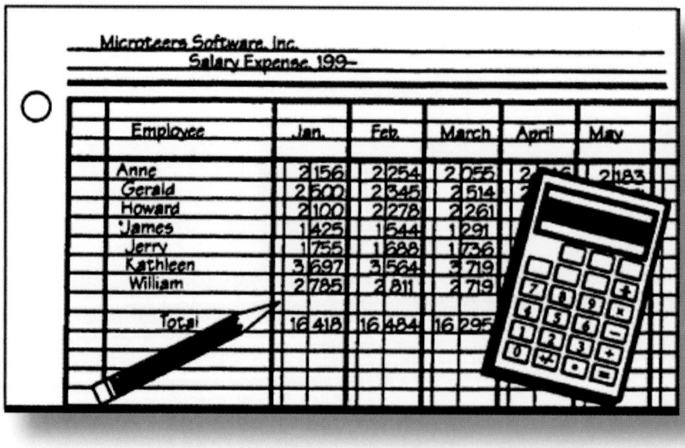

spreadsheets also contain rows and columns, but they perform calculations much faster and more accurately than spreadsheets created with pencil, paper, and calculator.

Spreadsheets are used in many ways. For example, a spreadsheet can be used to calculate a grade in a class, to prepare a budget for the next few months, or to determine payments to be made on a loan. The primary advantage of spreadsheets is the ability to complete complex and repetitious calculations accurately, quickly, and easily. For example, you might use a spreadsheet to calculate your monthly income and expenses.

Besides calculating rapidly and accurately, spreadsheets are flexible. Making changes to an existing spreadsheet is usually as easy as pointing and clicking with the mouse. Suppose, for example, you have prepared a budget on a spreadsheet and have overestimated the amount of money you will need to spend on gas and electric and other utilities. You may change a single entry in your spreadsheet and watch the entire spreadsheet recalculate the new budgeted amount. You can imagine the work this change would require if you were calculating the budget with pencil and paper.

Excel uses the term *worksheet* to refer to computerized spreadsheets. Sometimes you may want to use several worksheets that relate to each other. A collection of related worksheets is referred to as a *workbook*.

Starting Excel

Excel is started from the desktop screen in Windows. One way to start Excel is to click the Start button, select Programs, and then choose Microsoft Excel. When Excel starts, a blank worksheet titled *Book1* appears on the screen. You will see some of the basic parts of the screen that you learned about in the Introduction: the title bar, the menu bar, and the toolbar. However, as shown in Figure 1-2, Excel has its own unique buttons and screen parts.

FIGURE 1-2
Excel opening screen

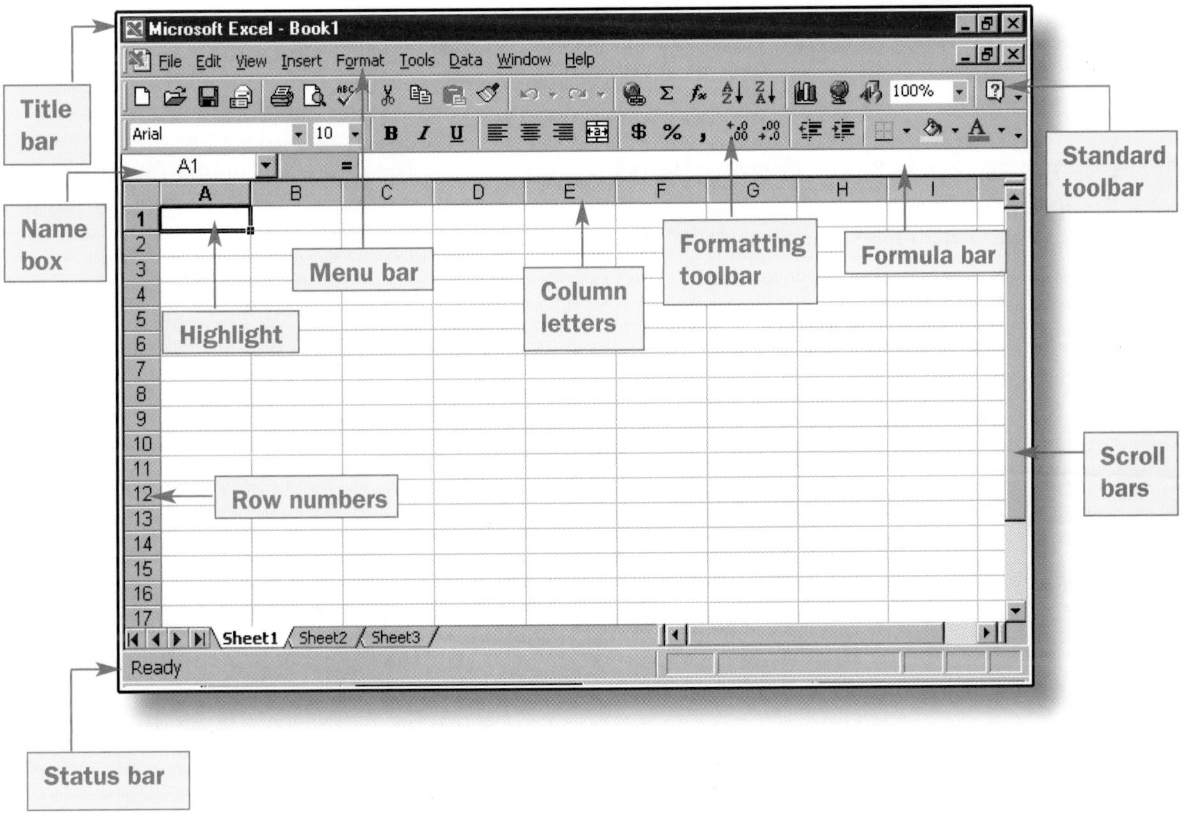

S TEP-BY-STEP ▷ 1.1

1. With Windows running, click the **Start** button, click **Programs**, and then choose **Microsoft Excel**.

2. Microsoft Excel starts and a blank worksheet titled *Book1* appears, as shown in Figure 1-2. Maximize the window, if necessary.

3. Leave the blank worksheet on the screen for use in the next Step-by-Step.

PARTS OF THE WORKSHEET

Columns of the worksheet appear vertically and are identified by letters at the top of the worksheet window. *Rows* appear horizontally and are identified by numbers on the left side of the worksheet window. A *cell* is the intersection of a row and column and is identified by a *cell reference*, the column letter and row number (for example, C4, A1, B2).

The mouse pointer is indicated by a thick plus sign when it's in the worksheet. If you move the pointer up to the toolbars and menus, the pointer turns into an arrow. In Word, the insertion point indicates the point at which a character is keyed. In the worksheet the entry point is indicated by a *highlight*, which appears on screen as a dark border around a cell.

The cell that contains the highlight is the *active cell*, which is distinguished by a dark border. Your screen currently shows a border around cell A1, the active cell. You may change the active cell by moving the highlight from one cell to another. The *formula bar* appears directly below the toolbar in the worksheet and displays a formula when the cell of a worksheet contains a calculated value. On the far left side of the formula bar is the *name box* or cell reference area that identifies the active cell.

> **Hot Tip**
>
> The column letter and row number of the active cell are bolded for easy reference.

Opening an Existing Worksheet

To open an existing worksheet, choose Open on the File menu, or click the Open button on the toolbar. In the Open dialog box, specify the file you want to open.

When you start Excel, the program displays a new worksheet temporarily titled *Book1*. This worksheet is eliminated if you open another file.

> **Did You Know?**
>
> Excel has several template files that you may use to solve common spreadsheet problems (such as invoices, expense statements, and purchase orders). To open these files, choose **New** on the **File** menu. On the templates tab, open the file that applies to the problem you would like to solve.

S TEP-BY-STEP ▷ 1.2

Suppose that you have volunteered to help a local environmental awareness group by conducting a census of species of birds. For the remainder of this lesson, you will complete a worksheet that accounts for each species of bird.

1. Choose **Open** on the **File** menu. The Open dialog box appears.

2. In the *Look in* box, select the drive and/or folder containing the student data files for this course. The files appear in the display window.

3. Double-click the filename **IE Step1-2**. The worksheet appears on the screen similar to Figure 1-3.

4. Leave the worksheet on the screen for the next Step-by-Step.

I E - 4

FIGURE 1-3
Opening a worksheet

	A	B	C	D	E	F	G
1	BIRD CENSUS						
2							
3	Species	Week 1	Week 2	Week 3	Week 4	Monthly Total	
4							
5	Boat-Tailed Grackles	9	12	6		27	
6	Goldfinches	6	10	7		23	
7	Black-Capped Chickadees	12	8	17		37	
8	Red-Headed Woodpeckers	2	5	8		15	
9	Eastern Bluebirds	1	3	2		6	
10	English Sparrows	21	15	1		37	
11						0	
12							
13	Total Birds Sighted	51	53	41	0	145	

Moving the Highlight in a Worksheet

The easiest way to move the highlight to a cell on the screen is to move the mouse pointer to the cell and click. When working with a large worksheet, you may not be able to view the entire worksheet on the screen. You can scroll throughout the worksheet using the mouse by dragging the scroll box in the scroll bar to the desired position. You can also move the highlight to different parts of the worksheet using the keyboard or the Go To command in the Edit menu.

USING KEYS TO MOVE THE HIGHLIGHT

You can move the highlight by pressing certain keys or key combinations as shown in Table 1-1. Many of these key combinations may be familiar to you if you use Microsoft Word. As in Word, when you hold down an arrow key, the highlight will move repeatedly and quickly.

USING THE GO TO COMMAND TO MOVE IN THE WORKSHEET

You may want to move the highlight to a cell that does not appear on the screen. The fastest way to move to the cell is by choosing Go To on the Edit menu or by pressing the shortcut key, F5. The Go To dialog box appears, as shown in Figure 1-4. Key the cell reference in the *Reference* box and click OK. The highlight will move to the cell.

TABLE 1-1
Key combinations for moving around the worksheet

TO MOVE	PRESS
Left one column	Left arrow
Right one column	Right arrow
Up one row	Up arrow
Down one row	Down arrow
To the first cell of a row	Home
To cell A1	Ctrl+Home
To the last cell containing data	Ctrl+End
Up one window	Page Up
Down one window	Page Down

Did You Know?

You may also go to specific text or numbers in the worksheet by choosing the **Find** command on the **Edit** menu. The Find dialog box opens. In the *Find what* text box, key the data you would like to locate in the worksheet and then click **Find Next**. The highlight will move to the next cell that contains the data.

1. The highlight should be in cell A1. Notice that the column letter A and the row number 1 are bold.

2. Move to the last cell in the worksheet that contains data by pressing **Ctrl+End**. The highlight moves to cell F13 in the lower right side of the worksheet.

3. Move to the first cell of row 13 by pressing **Home**. The highlight appears in cell A13, which contains the words *Total Birds Sighted*.

4. Move up three rows by pressing the up arrow key three times. The highlight appears in cell A10, which contains the words *English Sparrows*.

5. Choose **Go To** on the **Edit** menu. The Go To dialog box appears as shown in Figure 1-4.

6. Key **B3** in the Reference box.

7. Click **OK**. The highlight moves to B3.

8. Leave the worksheet on the screen for the next Step-by-Step.

Teamwork

Have a classmate call out cell references so you can practice moving the highlight to the correct cell using the methods you have learned.

FIGURE 1-4
Go To dialog box

Selecting a Group of Cells

Often, you will perform operations on more than one cell at a time. A selected group of cells is called a *range*. In a range, all cells touch each other and form a rectangle. The range is identified by the cell in the upper left corner and the cell in the lower right corner, separated by a colon (for example, A3:C5). To select a range of cells, place the highlight in the cell that is one corner of the range and drag the highlight to the cell in the opposite corner. As you drag the highlight, the range of selected cells will become shaded (except for the cell you originally selected). The column letters and row numbers of the range you select are bold. If you select a range of cells that is too large to be entirely displayed on the screen, a label appears diagonally to the last highlighted cell that tells how many rows and columns are included in the range, as shown in Figure 1-5.

FIGURE 1-5
Selecting a range of 19 rows and 7 columns

	A	B	C	D	E	F	G	H
4								
5	Boat-Tailed Grackles	9	12	6		27		
6	Goldfinches	6	10	7		23		
7	Black-Capped Chickadees	12	8	17		37		
8	Red-Headed Woodpeckers	2	5	8		15		
9	Eastern Bluebirds	1	3	2		6		
10	English Sparrows	21	15	1		37		
11						0		
12								
13	Total Birds Sighted	51	53	41	0	145		

Cell contents: = BIRD CENSUS

Sum=580

S TEP-BY-STEP ▷ 1.4

1. With the highlight in **B3**, hold down the left mouse button and drag to the right until **F3** is highlighted.

2. Release the mouse button. The range B3:F3 is selected. Notice that the column letters B through F and the row number 3 are bolded.

3. Move the highlight to **B5**.

4. Hold down the mouse button and drag down and to the right until **F13** is highlighted.

5. Release the mouse button. The range B5:F13 is selected.

6. Leave the worksheet open for the next Step-by-Step.

Entering Data in a Cell

Worksheet cells may contain text, numbers, formulas, or functions. Text consists of alphabetical characters such as headings, labels, or explanatory notes. Numbers can be values, dates, or times. Formulas are equations that calculate a value. Functions are special formulas that place either values or characters in cells. (Formulas and functions are discussed in later lessons.)

 Hot Tip

The Enter and Cancel buttons will not appear unless you key data into a cell. You can click the Edit Formula button to edit a formula.

IE-7

You enter data by keying the text or numbers in a cell, and then either clicking the Enter button on the formula bar or pressing the Enter key on the keyboard. If you choose not to enter the data you have keyed, you can simply click the Cancel button in the formula bar or press Esc and the keyed data will be deleted.

If you make a mistake, choose Undo on the Edit menu or click the Undo button on the toolbar to reverse your most recent change. To undo multiple actions, click the down arrow to the right of the Undo button on the toolbar. A list of your previous actions is displayed and you can choose the number of actions you want to undo.

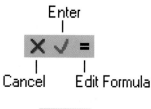

STEP-BY-STEP ▷ 1.5

1. Move the highlight to **E5** and key **15**. As you key, the numbers appear in the cell and in the formula bar.

2. Press **Enter**. The highlight moves to E6.

3. Key **4**.

4. Click **Enter**. Notice that the totals in F6 and E13 change as you enter the data.

5. Undo the action by clicking the down arrow button to the right of the **Undo** button on the toolbar. A menu appears listing the actions you have just performed.

6. Choose **Typing "4" in E6** on the menu, as shown in Figure 1-6. The data will be removed from E6 and the data in F6 and E13 change back to the previous totals.

7. Now enter the following data into the remaining cells in column E:

Cell	Data
E6	5
E7	20
E8	4
E9	10
E10	16

8. In addition to the species above, you sighted a blue heron. Key **Heron** in cell **A11**.

9. Enter **1** in **E11**. Leave the worksheet on the screen for the next Step-by-Step.

FIGURE 1-6
Undo multiple actions by clicking the arrow to the right of the Undo button

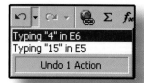

Hot Tip

If you need help while working with any of Excel's features, use the Office Assistant. The Assistant is an animated character that offers tips, solutions, instructions, and examples to help you work more efficiently. It appears on the screen with tips on how to manage spreadsheet data and workbook files. If you have a specific question, you can use the Office Assistant to search for help. To display the Office Assistant if it is not on the screen, choose **Show the Office Assistant** on the **Help** menu. Key your question and click **Search**. The Assistant displays a list of help topics in response. (See page IN-10 for more information on the Office Assistant, and step-by-step instructions on using it.)

Changing Data in a Cell

As you enter data in the worksheet, you may change your mind about data or make a mistake. If so, you may edit, replace, or clear existing data in cells of the worksheet.

EDITING DATA

Editing is performed when only minor changes to cell data are necessary. Data in a cell may be edited in the formula bar by using the Edit key on your keyboard, F2. To edit data in a cell, select the cell by placing the highlight in the cell and pressing F2. An insertion point similar to the one in Word will appear in the cell and you can make changes to the data. Press Enter to reenter the data.

You may prefer to use the mouse pointer to edit a cell. First, click the cell you want to edit; then click in the formula bar at the place you want to change the data. After you have made the changes you need, click the Enter button.

REPLACING DATA

Cell contents are usually replaced when you must make significant changes to cell data. To replace cell contents, select the cell, key the new data, and enter the data by clicking the Enter button or by pressing the Enter key.

CLEARING DATA

Clearing a cell will empty the cell of all its contents. To clear an active cell, you may either press the Delete key or Backspace key, or choose Clear on the Edit menu. Choosing Clear gives you a submenu where you can delete the format of the cell, the contents of the cell, or a note with the cell.

 Did You Know?

A worksheet is usually part of a collection of worksheets called a workbook. A tab near the bottom of the screen identifies a particular worksheet. You may move, copy, or delete a worksheet by *right*-clicking the worksheet tab and then selecting the operation you desire from the shortcut menu.

Hot Tip

If you plan to replace similar data appearing in more than one cell, you may want to try using the **Replace** command on the **Edit** menu. The Replace dialog box opens. In the *Find what* text box, key the data you would like to change in the worksheet. In the *Replace with* text box, key the data you would like to appear in place of the existing data. When you click **Find Next**, the highlight will move to the place where the data appears. Then, click **Replace** to substitute the new data for the existing data. If you click **Replace All**, Excel will automatically substitute the new data in all areas of the worksheet.

STEP-BY-STEP ▷ 1.6

1. Move the highlight to **D10**.

2. Press **F2**. An insertion point appears in the cell.

3. Make sure the insertion point is positioned after the *1* and key **8**.

4. Press **Enter**. The number *18* appears in the cell.

5. Move the highlight to **A11**.

6. Key **Blue Heron** and click the **Enter** button on the formula bar. The words *Blue Heron* replace the word *Heron* in the cell.

7. Move the highlight to **A3**.

8. Press the **Delete** key. The contents are cleared from the cell. Your screen should appear similar to Figure 1-7. Leave the worksheet on the screen for the next Step-by-Step.

(continued on next page)

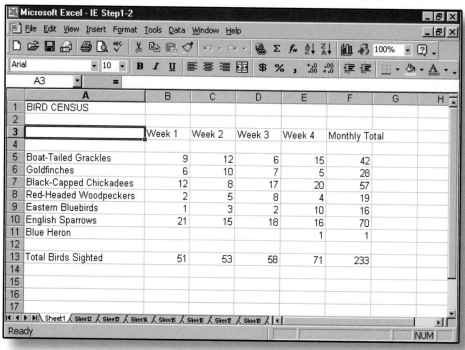

FIGURE 1-7
Changing data in a cell

Zoom View

You can magnify or reduce the view of your worksheet by using the Zoom button on the Standard toolbar (or by using the Zoom command on the View menu). The default magnification is 100%. If you would like to get a closer view of your worksheet, select a larger percentage from the drop-down list. Reduce the view by selecting a smaller percentage from the drop-down list. If you would like a different magnification than those available on the drop-down list, you may key your desired percentage directly in the Zoom box.

 Did You Know?

You may save a file in a new folder by clicking the **New Folder** button in the Save As dialog box. When the New Folder dialog box appears, key a name for the new folder and click **OK**.

Saving a Worksheet

You save worksheets using the process you learned in the Introduction. The first time you save a worksheet, the Save As dialog box appears in which you name the worksheet. Once a worksheet has been saved, the Save command will update the latest version.

STEP-BY-STEP 1.7

1. Click the down arrow on the **Zoom** button on the Standard toolbar.

2. Click **200%**. The view of the worksheet will double in size.

3. Click the **Zoom** button's down arrow again, and then click **50%**. The view of the worksheet will shrink to half of its default size.

4. Click the **Zoom** button's down arrow once more, and then click **100%**. The worksheet will return to its default size.

5. Choose **Save As** on the **File** menu. The Save As dialog box appears.

6. Key **Bird Survey**, followed by your initials, in the *File name* text box.

7. Click **Save**. Leave the worksheet open for the next Step-by-Step.

Printing a Worksheet

Printing a worksheet is similar to printing any document. There are options available to print part of a worksheet or to change the way your worksheet looks. You will learn more about these options in Lesson 3. For now, you will print the entire worksheet using the default settings.

STEP-BY-STEP 1.8

1. Choose **Print** on the **File** menu. The Print dialog box appears.

2. Click **OK**. The worksheet begins printing.

3. Choose **Close** on the **File** menu. If you are asked to save changes, click **Yes**. The worksheet closes.

Summary

In this lesson, you learned:

- The purpose of a spreadsheet is to solve problems involving numbers. The advantage of using a spreadsheet is that you can complete complex and repetitious calculations quickly and easily.

- A worksheet consists of columns and rows intersecting to form cells. Each cell is identified by a cell reference, which is the letter of the column and number of the row.

- You can move to different cells of the worksheet by clicking on the cell with the mouse pointer, using a series of keystrokes, or by scrolling with the mouse.

- Both text and numerical data may be entered into the worksheet. You can alter data by editing, replacing, or deleting.

TRUE/FALSE

Circle T if the statement is true or F if the statement is false.

T (F)   1.   The primary advantage of the worksheet is to summarize text documents.

(T) F   2.   A cell is the intersection of a row and column.

T (F)   3.   The Go To command saves a file and exits Excel.

T (F)   4.   Saving a worksheet file differs significantly from saving a Word file.

(T) F   5.   The best way to make minor changes to existing data in a cell is to key new data and press the Enter key.

WRITTEN QUESTIONS

Write a brief answer to the following questions.

1.   What term describes a cell that is ready for data entry?

The cell that is ready for data entry is the active cell

2.   How are columns identified in a worksheet?

Col idenf by letters

3.   What indicates that a cell is ready to accept data?

The cell that is ready for data is highlighted

4. What keys should be pressed to move the highlight to the last cell of the worksheet that contains data?

cntr + end

5. What key is pressed to clear data from an active cell?

delete key

LESSON 1 PROJECTS

PROJECT 1-1

Write the letter of the keystroke from Column 2 that matches the highlight movement in Column 1.

Column 1	Column 2
f 1. Left one column	A. Ctrl+Home
c 2. Right one column	B. Page Up
h 3. Up one row	C. Right arrow
j 4. Down one row	D. Home
d 5. To the first cell of a row	E. Ctrl+Page Up
a 6. To cell A1	F. Left arrow
g 7. To the last cell containing data	G. Ctrl+End
b 8. Up one window	H. Up arrow

_____ 9. Down one window   I. Ctrl+Page Down

_____ 10. To the previous worksheet in a workbook   J. Down arrow

_____ 11. To the next worksheet in a workbook   K. Page Down

PROJECT 1-2

The file *IE Project1-2* contains information concerning the percent of home ownership in the 50 states. Make the following corrections and additions to the worksheet.

1. Open **IE Project1-2** from the student data files.

2. Save the file as **Home Owner**, followed by your initials.

3. Enter **GA** in **A15**.

4. Enter **64.90%** in **B15**.

5. Enter **65.00%** into **C15**.

6. Edit the data in **A16** to be **HA**.

7. Edit the data in **B16** to be **53.90%**.

8. Delete the data in **A3**.

9. Save, print, and close the file.

PROJECT 1-3

Residential Developers, Inc., has developed a worksheet to help prospective home buyers estimate the cost of homes in four different neighborhoods. The cost of homes within neighborhoods tends to fluctuate based on the square footage of the home. Each of the four neighborhoods tends to have a different cost per square foot.

1. Open **IE Project1-3** from the student data files.

2. Save the file as **Developments**, followed by your initials.

3. Enter the square footages in the following cells to estimate the home costs. The estimated home cost in each neighborhood will change as you enter the data.

Cell	Enter
C7	1250
C8	1500
C9	2200
C10	2500

4. After selling several houses in the Lake View neighborhood, Residential Developers, Inc., has figured that the cost per square foot is $67.00, rather than $65.00. Edit B7 to show **$67.00**.

5. Save, print, and close the file.

CRITICAL THINKING

ACTIVITY 1-1

The purpose of a spreadsheet is to solve problems that involve numbers. Identify two or three numerical problems in each of the following categories that might be solved by using a spreadsheet.

1. Business

2. Career

3. Personal

4. School

ACTIVITY 1-2

You have already selected a range of cells that is so large it extends several screens. You realize that you incorrectly included one column of cells you do not want within the selected range.

To reselect the range of cells, you must page up to the active cell (the first cell of the range) and drag through several screens to the last cell in the range. You are wondering if there is a better way to reduce the selected range without having to page up to the original screen.

Use the Help function of Office to find how to select fewer cells without canceling your original selection. In your word processor, write a brief explanation of the steps you would take to change the selected range.

CHANGING THE APPEARANCE OF A WORKSHEET

OBJECTIVES

Upon completion of this lesson, you should be able to:

■ Change column width.

■ Position text within a cell by wrapping, rotating, indenting, and aligning.

■ Change the appearance of cells using fonts, styles, colors, and borders.

■ Designate the format of a cell to accommodate different kinds of text and numerical data.

⏱ **Estimated Time: 1.5 hours**

Worksheet Appearance

Worksheets are useful only when they are understandable to the user. It is important that data in a worksheet is accurate, but it is also important that it is presented in a way that is visually appealing.

Changing Column Width

Sometimes the data you key will not fit in the column. When data is wider than the column, Excel responds by doing one of the following:

■ Displaying a series of number signs (######) in the cell.

■ Cutting off the data (the right portion of the data will not be displayed).

■ Letting the data run outside of the column.

■ Converting the data to a different numerical form (for example, changing long numbers to exponential form).

Hot Tip

You can change the width of several columns at a time by selecting the columns, then dragging the right edge of one of the column headings.

You can widen the column by placing the mouse pointer on the right edge of the column heading (the column letter). The pointer then changes into a double-headed arrow. To widen the column, drag to the right until the column is the desired size. When you drag to change the width of a column or height of a row, a label appears near the pointer displaying the new measurements.

Another way to change column width is to use the Column Width dialog box, shown in Figure 2-1. Place the highlight in the column you would like to change. Then, choose Column on the Format menu and click Width on the submenu. In the Column Width dialog box, key the desired width and click OK.

Concept Builder

You can also change the height of a row by dragging the bottom edge of the row heading.

FIGURE 2-1
Column Width dialog box

STEP-BY-STEP ▷ 2.1

1. Open **IE Step2-1** from the student data files. Notice that the data in D3 extends partially into column E.

2. Save the worksheet as **3Q Budget**, followed by your initials.

3. Place the mouse pointer on the right edge of the column D heading. The pointer turns into a double-headed arrow.

4. Drag the double-headed arrow to the right until the label reads *Width: 10.00*, as shown in Figure 2-2, and release the mouse button. The entire word *September* now fits within column D.

5. Select columns **B** through **D**.

6. Choose **Column** on the **Format** menu, then

choose **Width** on the submenu. The Column Width dialog box appears (see Figure 2-1).

7. Key **10** in the *Column width* text box.

8. Click **OK**. The widths of the selected columns have been changed to 10. Leave the worksheet on the screen for the next Step-by-Step.

9. Scroll down one screen and place the mouse pointer on the bottom edge of the row 18 heading. The pointer turns into a double-headed arrow.

10. Drag the double-headed arrow down until the label reads *Height 18.00 (24 pixels)*.

11. Save the file and leave the worksheet on the screen for the next Step-by-Step.

FIGURE 2-2
Column width measurement label

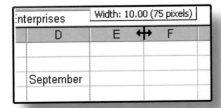

LETTING EXCEL FIND THE BEST FIT

Suppose you have a column full of data of varying widths. You want the column to be wide enough to display the longest entry, but no wider than necessary. To let Excel determine the best width of a column, place the highlight in the cell and choose Column on the Format menu, then choose AutoFit Selection on the submenu.

Hot Tip

Another way to find the best fit is to place the mouse pointer on the right edge of the column heading and double-click when the double-headed arrow appears.

STEP-BY-STEP ▷ 2.2

1. Place the highlight in cell **A20**. Notice that the words *Cumulative Surplus* are cut off.

2. Choose **Column** on the **Format** menu, then choose **AutoFit Selection** on the submenu.

Column A widens to show all the data in A20. Save and leave the worksheet on the screen for the next Step-by-Step.

Positioning Text within a Cell

Unless you specify otherwise, Excel enters text as left-justified without wrapping. However, you may change the position of text within a cell in several ways. (See Table 2-1.)

TABLE 2-1
Positioning text within a cell

TEXT POSITION	FUNCTION	EXAMPLE OF USE
Wrapped	Begins a new line within the cell	Moves text to a new line when it is longer than the width of the cell
Rotated	Displays text at an angle	Turns the text so that it might be displayed in a narrower column
Indented	Moves the text several spaces to the right	Creates subheadings below primary headings
Left-Justified	Begins the text on the left side of the cell	The default justification for textual data
Centered	Places the text in the middle of the cell	Creates column headings
Right-Justified	Begins the text on the right side of the cell	The default justification for numerical data
Merge and Center	Merges multiple cells into one cell and places the text in the middle of the merged cell	Creates a title across the top of a worksheet

TEXT WRAP

Text that is too long for a cell will spill over into the next cell if the next cell is empty. If the next cell is not empty, the text that does not fit into the cell will not display. You can choose to have text wrap within a cell in the same way text wraps within a word-processing document using the text wrap option. The row height will automatically adjust to show all of the lines of text. This is referred to as *wrapped text*.

To turn on the text wrap option, select the cells in which you intend to wrap text. Then choose Cells on the Format menu. In the Format Cells dialog box, click the Alignment tab, as shown in Figure 2-3. In the Text control section click the *Wrap text* box to turn on the text wrap option.

Hot Tip

You can also access the Format Cells dialog box by right-clicking an active cell or range and choosing Format Cells on the shortcut menu.

FIGURE 2-3
The *Wrap text* option on the Alignment tab in the Format Cells dialog box

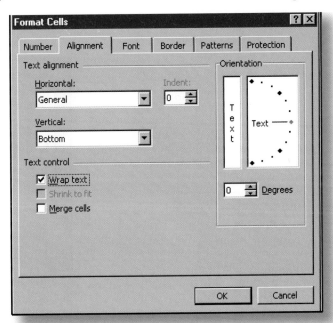

STEP-BY-STEP ▷ 2.3

1. Move the highlight to cell **A22**.

2. Choose **Cells** on the **Format** menu. The Format Cells dialog box appears.

3. Click the **Alignment** tab.

4. Click the **Wrap text** box in the Text control section to insert a check mark (✔).

5. Click **OK**. The text wraps in the cell and the cell height adjusts automatically.

6. Save and leave the worksheet on the screen for the next Step-by-Step.

ROTATE TEXT

Sometimes column headings are longer than the data in the columns. Excel allows you to save space by rotating the text to any angle. Using *rotated text* can also help give your worksheet a more professional look.

 Concept Builder

Rotated text can also be used when labeling charts.

To rotate text, select the cells containing the text you want to rotate and choose Cells on the Format menu. When the Format Cells dialog box appears, choose the Alignment tab, as shown in Figure 2-3. In the *Orientation* box, click a degree point, drag the angle indicator, or type the angle you want in the *Degrees* text box.

STEP-BY-STEP ▷ 2.4

1. Highlight **B3:D3**.

2. Choose **Cells** on the **Format** menu. The Format Cells dialog box appears.

3. Click the **Alignment** tab, if it is not already selected.

4. In the *Orientation* section, key **45** in the *Degrees* text box. The Text indicator moves to a 45-degree angle, as shown in Figure 2-4.

5. Click **OK**. The text in B3 through D3 is now displayed at a 45-degree angle.

6. Change the width of columns **B** through **D** to **8**.

7. Save and leave the worksheet on the screen for the next Step-by-Step.

FIGURE 2-4
Orientation section of Alignment tab

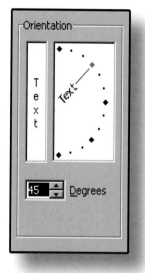

INDENTING TEXT

Indented text within cells can help distinguish categories or set apart text. Instead of trying to indent text by keying spaces, Excel allows you to click the Increase Indent on the toolbar to accomplish this task easily. To move the indent in the other direction, click the Decrease Indent button.

ALIGNING TEXT

You can align the contents of a cell several ways: left, centered, right, justified, and centered across several columns. Excel automatically left aligns all text entries. All numbers are right-aligned unless a different alignment is specified.

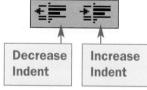 **Concept Builder**

You can indent text in a cell up to 16 levels.

To change the alignment of a cell, place the highlight in the cell and click one of the four alignment buttons on the toolbar.

For other alignment options, choose Cells on the Format menu and then click the Alignment tab. In the Format Cells dialog box, click the alignment you want from the *Horizontal* or *Vertical* list boxes, and click OK.

Hot Tip

When you highlight cells in a row and choose the Merge and Center button, the cells are merged and contents are centered.

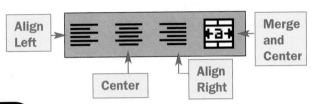

Align Left

Center

Align Right

Merge and Center

STEP-BY-STEP ▷ 2.5

1. Move the highlight to **A5**.

2. Click the **Increase Indent** button on the toolbar.

3. Indent the text in **A6**.

4. Highlight **A10:A16** and indent the text.

5. Select **B3:D3**.

6. Click the **Center** button on the tool-bar. The headings are centered.

7. Highlight **A7**.

8. Click the **Align Right** button. *Total Income* is aligned at the right of the cell.

9. Right align cells **A17**, **A19**, and **A20**.

10. Select **A1:D1**.

11. Click the **Merge and Center** button. *Asparagus Enterprises* is centered across cells A1 through D1.

12. Merge and center the *Third Quarter Budget* across **A2:D2**.

13. Save and leave the worksheet on the screen for the next Step-by-Step.

Changing Cell Appearance

The appearance of a cell's contents may be changed to make it easier to read. You can alter the appearance of cell contents by changing the font, size, style, color, alignment, format, and borders.

FONTS AND FONT SIZES

The font and font size you choose may significantly affect the readability of the worksheet. The number, types, and sizes of fonts available depend largely on what fonts are installed on your computer. You can choose different fonts for different parts of a worksheet.

Font

Font size

Changing fonts and sizes in a worksheet is similar to changing the fonts and sizes in a word-processing document. Highlight the cells you want to change and choose the font and size you want from the toolbar. You can also choose Cells on the Format menu. In the Format Cells dialog box, click the Font tab. As shown in Figure 2-5, the Format Cells dialog box has options for changing the font, font style, font size, and color.

FIGURE 2-5
Font tab in the Format Cells dialog box

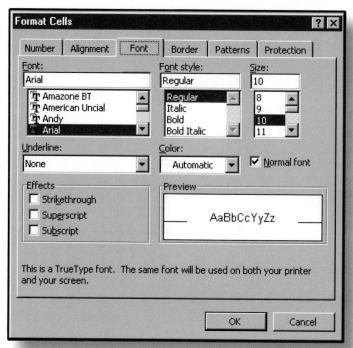

STYLE

Bolding, italicizing, or underlining can add emphasis to the contents of a cell. Highlight the cell or cells you want to change and click the appropriate style button on the toolbar. To return the contents of the cell to a regular style, simply click the button again.

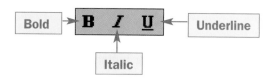

STEP-BY-STEP ▷ **2.6**

1. Select **B3:D3**.

2. Click the down arrow beside the Font box `Times New Roman ▾` on the toolbar. Scroll down and choose **Times New Roman** (or a similar font).

3. Click the **down arrow** beside the `8 ▾` Font Size box and choose **8**.

4. Move the highlight to **A1**.

5. Choose **Cells** on the **Format** menu. The Format Cells dialog box appears.

6. Click the **Font** tab.

7. In the *Font* list box, scroll down and click **Times New Roman**.

8. In the *Font style* list box, click **Bold**.

9. In the *Size* list box, scroll down and click **14**.

10. Click **OK**.

11. Highlight **A2**.

12. Click the **Bold** button on the toolbar.

13. Bold the following cells using the same procedure: **A4**, **A7**, **A9**, **A17**, **A19**, and **A20**.

14. Widen column A to **18**.

15. Select the range **B6:D6**.

16. Click the **Underline** button on the toolbar.

17. Underline **B16:D16**.

18. Select **A5:A6**.

19. Click the **Italic** button.

20. Italicize **A10:A16**.

21. Save and leave the worksheet on the screen for the next Step-by-Step.

Extra Challenge

Experiment by changing the font, size, and style of text in the worksheet. Use the Undo button to undo changes you make.

COLOR

Changing the color of cells or cell text is another way to add emphasis. To change the color of a cell using the toolbar, move the highlight to the cell and click the down arrow beside the Fill Color button on the toolbar. A menu of colors appears, as shown in Figure 2-6. Click the color you want, and the cell is filled with that color.

To change the color of text using the toolbar, move the highlight to the cell you want to change and click the down arrow beside the Font Color button. A menu of colors appears as shown in Figure 2-7. Click the color you want and the text is changed to your color choice.

You can also change the color of cells and text using the Format Cells dialog box. Choose Cells on the Format menu, and then click the Patterns tab. Click on a color in the *Cell shading* section. You can also click the down arrow beside the *Pattern* box and choose a pattern from the menu.

FIGURE 2-6
Fill Color button color palette

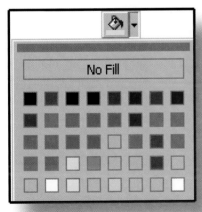

FIGURE 2-7
Font Color button color palette

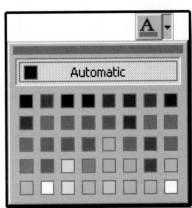

1. Select **A1:D1** (which is now merged into one cell).

2. Click the down arrow beside the **Font Color** button. A menu of colors appears.

3. Click the **Green** square in the second row of the color menu. (As you point to each square, a label will tell you the color.) The title changes to green text.

4. With A1:D1 still selected, click the down arrow beside the **Fill Color** button. A menu of colors appears.

5. Click the **Gray-25%** square in the fourth row. The cell becomes light gray.

6. Save and leave the worksheet on the screen for the next Step-by-Step.

Extra Challenge

Change the text and cell color of all the headings.

BORDERS

You can add emphasis to a cell by placing a border around its edges. You can place the border around the entire cell or only on certain sides of the cell. You can add borders two ways. First, you can insert a border by highlighting the cell and choosing the Cells command on the Format menu. In the Format Cells dialog box, click the Border tab. Choose the border placement, style, and color (see Figure 2-8), and

Concept Builder

Selecting cells and clicking the Borders button (instead of the down arrow) applies the last border that was chosen using the toolbar.

then click OK. In addition, you can insert a border quickly by clicking the down arrow of the Borders button on the formatting toolbar. A box of border choices appears, as shown in Figure 2-9. Click one of the options to add the border you want.

FIGURE 2-8
Border tab in the Format Cells dialog box

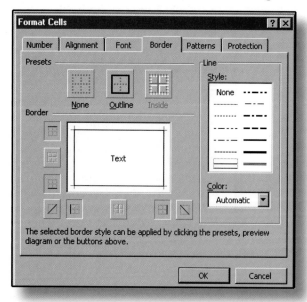

FIGURE 2-9
Borders button

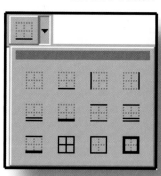

S TEP-BY-STEP ▷ 2.8

1. Highlight **A4**.

2. Choose **Cells** from the **Format** menu. The Format Cells dialog box appears.

3. Click the **Border** tab.

4. In the *Style* box, click the thin, solid line (last choice in the first column).

5. In the *Presets* section, click the **Outline** button.

6. Click **OK**. When the highlight is moved, a border outlines the cell.

7. Highlight **A9**.

8. Click the down arrow beside the **Borders** button. From the menu that appears, choose **Outside Borders** (third choice on the last row).

9. Save and leave the worksheet on the screen for the next Step-by-Step.

Cell Formats

Format affects the way data is shown in a cell. The default format is called *General,* which accommodates both text and numerical data. However, you can use several other formats (see Table 2-2). You can format a cell by highlighting the cell or range and choosing Cells on the Format menu. In the Format Cells dialog box, click the Number tab and select a format (see Figure 2-10) from the *Category* list. Then, click OK. You can format data for currency, percentage, or commas, and to increase and decrease decimals, by clicking corresponding buttons on the toolbar.

CLEARING CELL FORMATS

You have learned how to change the appearance of a worksheet by bolding, italicizing, and underlining. You have also learned to add color and borders. You can remove the formats you apply to a cell or range of cells, by selecting the cell or range, choosing Clear on the Edit menu, and then clicking Formats on the submenu. This removes the formatting *only.*

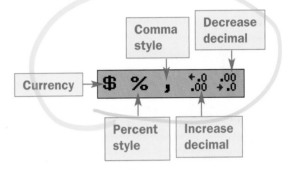

Hot Tip

Sometimes you will use a certain type of number format, alignment, font, border, or pattern on a consistent basis. If you know you will be using these styles again, you may want to define that style so you can apply it later. To define a style, select the cell that has the combination of formats you want. Choose **Style** on the **Format** menu, and name your style in the Style name box. Then, click **Add** and **Close**.

To apply a style you have created, select the cells to be formatted. Then, choose **Style** on the **Format** menu, and select the style you want from the *Style name* box. Click **OK**.

TABLE 2-2
Cell formats

FORMAT NAME	EXAMPLE	DISPLAY DESCRIPTION
General	1000	The default format; displays either text and numerical data as keyed
Number	1000.00	Displays numerical data with a fixed number of places to the right of the decimal point
Currency	$1,000.00	Displays numerical data preceded by a dollar sign
Accounting	$1,000.00 $ 9.00	Displays numerical data in a currency format that lines up the dollar sign and decimal point vertically within a column
Date	6/8/99	Displays text and numerical data as dates
Time	7:34 PM	Displays text and numerical data as times
Percentage	35.2%	Displays numerical data followed by a percent sign
Fraction	35 7/8	Displays numerical data as fractional values
Scientific	1.00E+03	Displays numerical data in exponential notation
Text	45-875-33	Displays numerical data that will not be used for calculation, such as serial numbers containing hyphens
Special	79410	Displays numerical data that requires a specific format, such as ZIP codes or phone numbers
Custom	000.00.0	Displays formats designed by the user, including formats with commas or leading zeros

FIGURE 2-10
Number tab in the Format Cells dialog box

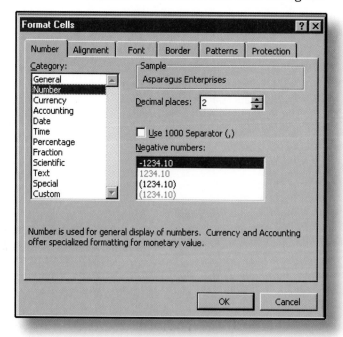

STEP-BY-STEP ▷ 2.9

1. Select **B5:D5**.

2. Choose **Cells** on the **Format** menu. The Format Cells dialog box appears.

3. Click the **Number** tab.

4. Click **Currency** in the *Category* list box.

5. Click **OK**.

6. Change the width of columns **B** through **D** using AutoFit Selection.

7. Change the format of **B20:D20** to **Currency**.

8. Select the range **B6:D19**.

9. Open the Format Cells dialog box and click the **Number** tab.

10. Click **Number** in the *Category* list box.

11. Click the **Use 1000 Separator (,)** box so that it is checked.

12. Click **OK**. Your screen should look similar to Figure 2-11.

13. Select **A1:D8**.

14. Choose **Clear** on the **Edit** menu, and then click **Formats** on the submenu. Notice that formats you have applied have now been removed.

15. Click the **Undo** button. The formats will be restored.

16. Print the worksheet. Then, save and close the file.

Applying an AutoFormat

AutoFormats are formats that have already been created within Excel. For example, certain AutoFormats will automatically bold headings and place dollar signs in front of numbers. Others will add colors to the worksheet.

To apply an AutoFormat, you should first select the range to be formatted. After you choose AutoFormat on the Format menu, a gallery of formats will appear in the dialog box. Choose the format that you would like to use and then click OK.

FIGURE 2-11
By changing the appearance of a worksheet, you can make it easier to use

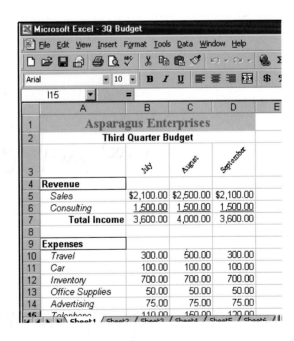

Summary

In this lesson, you learned:

■ Worksheet columns may be widened to accommodate data that is too large to fit in the cell.

■ You can wrap, rotate, indent, or align to change the position of text within the cell of a worksheet.

- The appearance of cell data may be changed to make the worksheet easier to read. Font, font size, and style (bolding, italicizing, and underlining) may be changed. Color and borders may also be added.

- The appearance of the cell may be changed to accommodate data in a variety of numerical formats.

LESSON 2 REVIEW QUESTIONS

TRUE/FALSE

Circle T if the statement is true or F if the statement is false.

T F 1. A series of number signs (######) appearing in a cell indicates that the data is wider than the column.

T F 2. Wrapped text will begin a new line within the cell of a worksheet when the data exceeds the width of a column.

T F 3. The Merge and Center button will combine several cells into one cell and place the text in the middle of the merged cell.

T F 4. You can place a border around the entire cell or only on certain sides of the cell.

T **F** 5. The default format for data in a cell is *Text*.

WRITTEN QUESTIONS

Write a brief answer to the following questions.

1. What cell format displays numerical data preceded by a dollar sign?

    currency cell display

2. What is one way to let Excel determine the best width of a column?

    Chose col fr format menu the choose AutoFit Selection or place mouse on headings + double click Rightedg for heading + double click porotn a

3. What is one reason for rotating text?

   saving space
   adding professional look
   labeling charts

4. What is the difference between the Fill Color and Font Color buttons?

   Fill color changs color of cells
   font color changs color of text

5. What are the four cell alignment buttons available on the toolbar?

   Algn L   Merge
   "   R   Center

LESSON 2 PROJECTS

PROJECT 2-1

Write the letter of the cell format option in Column 2 that matches the worksheet format described in Column 1.

Column 1	Column 2
1. Displays both text and numerical data as keyed	A. Accounting
2. Displays numerical data with a fixed amount of places to the right of the decimal point	B. Time
3. Displays numerical data preceded by a dollar sign; however, dollar signs and decimal points do not necessarily line up vertically within the column	C. Scientific
	D. Fraction

_K_ 4. Displays numerical data with a dollar sign and decimal point that line up vertically within a column

_G_ 5. Displays text and numerical data as dates

_B_ 6. Displays text and numerical data as times

_I_ 7. Displays numerical data followed by a percent sign

_D_ 8. Displays the value of .5 as 1/2

_C_ 9. Displays numerical data in exponential notation

_E_ 10. Displays numerical data that will not be used for calculation, such as serial numbers containing hyphens

_J_ 11. Displays formats designed by the user

_L_ 12. Displays text in numerical format such as ZIP codes

E. Text

F. General

G. Date

H. Number

I. Percentage

J. Custom

K. Currency

L. Special

PROJECT 2-2

In this project, you will improve the appearance of the worksheet so that you may present your results.

1. Open **IE Project2-2** from the student data files.

2. Save the file as **Bird Census**, followed by your initials.

3. Bold **A1**.

4. Bold the range **B3:F3**.

5. Rotate the text in **B3:E3** by 45 degrees.

6. Change the width of columns **B** through **E** to **6**.

7. Wrap the text in **F3**.

8. Bold the range **A13:F13**.

9. Italicize the range **A5:A11**.

10. Right align **A13**.

11. Center align the data in cells **B3** through **F3**.

12. Change the font size in **A1** to **14**.

13. Merge and center cells **A1:F1**.

14. Place a single, thin line border around the heading *Bird Census*.

15. Save, print, and close the file.

PROJECT 2-3

The file *IE Project2-3* is a worksheet containing the inventory of The Pager Shop. The headings and numerical data have already been keyed in the worksheet. You are to make the spreadsheet easier to read and more attractive.

1. Open **IE Project2-3** from the student data files.

2. Save the file as **Pager Shop**, followed by your initials.

3. Center the text in cells **B4:D5**.

4. Indent the text in **A7:A10**.

5. Change the width of columns **B**, **C**, and **D** to **10**.

6. Bold **B12** and **D12**.

7. Change the size of text in **A1** to **12** point. Merge and center **A1:D1**.

8. Change the size of text in **A2** to **11** point. Merge and center **A2:D2**.

9. Change the color of cells **A1:D1** to green (use the *Green* in the second row).

10. Change the color of text in **A2:D2** to yellow (use the *Light Yellow* in the last row).

11. Format **C7:D10** and **D12** for **Currency** with two decimal places.

12. Change the color of text in **B12** and **D12** to the same green used in the title cells.

13. Save, print, and close the worksheet.

PROJECT 2-4

A college student would like to estimate her long-distance phone bill for calls she made home. Each time she makes a phone call, she notes the time of day and the number of minutes she spoke. She has prepared a worksheet to calculate the cost of the phone calls she has made. She must now format and print the worksheet.

1. Open **IE Project2-4** from the student data files.

2. Save the file as **Long Distance**, followed by your initials.

3. Key **Estimate of Long Distance Bill** in **A1**.

4. Bold **A1**.

5. Change the size of the text in **A1** to **12** point.

6. Merge and center **A1:D1**.

7. Change the color of the range **A1:D1** to blue.

8. Change the color of the text in **A1** to white.

9. Underline the contents of **B3:C3**.

10. Center the contents of **B3:C3**.

11. Format **C4:D6** for **Currency** with two decimal places.

12. Format **D7** for **Currency** with two decimal places.

13. Underline the contents of **D6**.

14. Save, print, and close the file.

PROJECT 2-5

A balance sheet is a corporate financial statement that lists the assets (resources available), liabilities (amounts owed), and equity (ownership in the company). *IE Project2-5* contains the balance sheet of Microsoft Corporation to be formatted.

1. Open **IE Project2-5** from the student data files.

2. Save the file as **Microsoft**, followed by your initials.

3. Change the column width of column **C** to **5**.

4. Change the size of the text in **A1** to **12** point.

5. Change the size of the text in **A2:A3** to **10** point.

6. Bold **A1:C1**.

7. Merge and center **A1:E1**, **A2:E2**, **A3:E3**, and **A4:E4**.

8. Bold **A6**, **A7**, **A20**, **D6**, **D7**, **D15**, and **D20**.

9. Underline **B10**, **B15**, **E12**, **E18**, and **E19**.

10. Format **B8**, **E8**, **B20**, and **E20** for **Accounting** with no decimal places and no dollar ($) symbol.

11. Format **B9:B11**, **B13:B15**, **E9:E13**, and **E16:E19** for **Accounting** with no decimal places and no symbol.

12. Save, print, and close the file.

PROJECT 2-6

The file *IE Project2-6* is a mileage chart between major cities in the United States. In this project you will make the data easier to read.

1. Open **IE Project2-6** from the student data files.

2. Save the file as **Mileage**, followed by your initials.

3. Format **B2:O15** for **Number** with no decimal places and a comma separator.

4. Bold **B1:O1** and **A2:A15**.

5. Change the width of column **A** to **10**.

6. Rotate **B1:O1** to **-75 degrees**.

7. Change the width of columns **B** through **O** to **5**.

8. Save, print, and close the file.

CRITICAL THINKING

ACTIVITY 2-1

To be useful, worksheets must be easy to view, both on screen and on the printed page. Identify ways to accomplish the following:

1. Emphasize certain portions of the worksheet.

2. Make text in the worksheet easier to read.

3. Distinguish one part of the worksheet from another.

4. Keep printed worksheet data from "spilling" onto another page.

ACTIVITY 2-2

You have been spending a lot of time formatting worksheets that you have created. Your friend tells you that you could save some time by using the AutoFormat operation contained in Excel. She did not have time to explain how AutoFormat works and so you are left curious.

Use the Help function of Excel to find information on applying an AutoFormat to a range of cells. When you have finished, open **IE Activity2-2** and apply an AutoFormat of your choice to the data in the worksheet. When you have finished, save the file as **Autoformat**, followed by your initials.

ORGANIZING THE WORKSHEET

Basics of Worksheet Organization

Data in a worksheet should be arranged in a way that is easily accessed and observed. Data is rarely useful in its orginal format. You may reorganize data by moving it to another part of the worksheet. You may also reduce data entry time by copying data to another part of the worksheet. If you decide that certain data is not needed you may delete entire rows or columns. If you would like to include additional information in a worksheet, you may insert another row or column.

Copying Data

When creating or enlarging a worksheet, you may want to use the same text or numbers in another part of the worksheet. Rather than key the same data over again, you can copy the data.

There are several ways to copy data in a worksheet. In this lesson, you will learn to copy and paste, use the drag-and-drop method, and fill cells. These operations can significantly decrease the amount of time needed to prepare a worksheet.

🎯 **Hot Tip**

Data copied into a cell will replace data already in that cell. Check your destination cells for existing data before copying.

COPY AND PASTE

Choosing the Copy command on the Edit menu or clicking the Copy button on the toolbar copies the contents of a cell or cells to the Clipboard. A revolving border appears around the selection, as shown in Figure 3-1. The Copy command will not affect the data in the original cell(s).

Copy

✂ 📋 📋

Cut   Paste

FIGURE 3-1
Copy data to another part of the worksheet

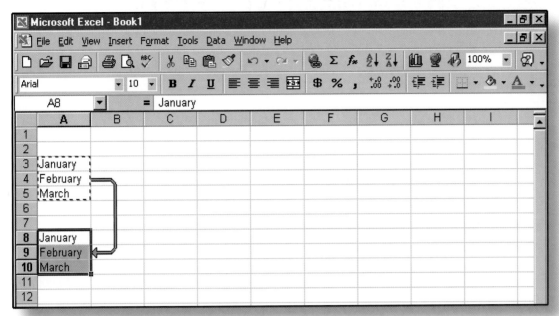

Next, place the highlight in the cell where you want the data to be copied. Then, choose Paste on the Edit menu or click the Paste button on the toolbar. The copied data will be pasted from the Clipboard to the cell or cells.

The data stored on the Clipboard will remain until it is replaced with new data. If you would like to make multiple copies, choose the Paste command again.

Hot Tip

If you are pasting a range of cells, it is not necessary to select the entire range; you need only highlight the upper left corner of the range into which data will be pasted.

STEP-BY-STEP ▷ 3.1

1. Open **IE Step3-1** from your student data files.

2. Save the file as **Utility**, followed by your initials.

3. Select the range **A3:D6**.

4. Choose **Copy** on the **Edit** menu. A revolving border surrounds the range.

5. Highlight **A8**.

6. Choose **Paste** on the **Edit** menu. The range of cells is copied from A3:D6 to A8:D11. (The border around A3:D6 will continue to revolve until you start the next step.)

7. Key **Natural Gas** in **A7**.

8. Key **100 cf** in **B7** to indicate the amount of cubic feet in hundreds.

9. Key **Cost / 100 cf** in **C7** to indicate the cost per hundred cubic feet.

10. Copy **D2** and paste it to **D7**.

11. Save the worksheet and leave it on the screen for the next Step-by-Step.

USING THE DRAG-AND-DROP METHOD

Excel allows you to quickly copy data using the drag-and-drop method. First highlight the cells you want to copy. Then, move the pointer to the top border of the highlighted cells. The cross turns into an arrow pointer. While holding down the Ctrl key, drag the cells to a new location and release the mouse button. As you press the Ctrl key, a small plus sign (+) appears above the mouse pointer. As you drag the mouse pointer, a pop-up label appears showing where the new location of the highlighted cells will be when you release the mouse button.

STEP-BY-STEP ▷ 3.2

1. Select the range **A8:D11**.

2. Move the pointer to the top edge of cell A8 until it turns into an arrow pointer.

3. Press and hold down the **Ctrl** key. The plus sign appears.

4. Click and drag down until the pointer is in cell **A13** and the pop-up label reads *A13:D16*.

5. Release the mouse button, and then the Ctrl key. The data is copied from A8:D11 to A13:D16.

6. Key **Water** in **A12**.

7. Key **1000 gallons** in **B12**.

8. Key **Cost / 1000 gal** in **C12** to indicate the cost per 1000 gallons of water.

9. Use the drag-and-drop method to copy **D7** to **D12**.

10. Bold the contents of cells **A7:C7** and **A12:C12**. Your screen should look similar to Figure 3-2.

11. Save and leave the worksheet on the screen for the next Step-by-Step.

FIGURE 3-2
Copying and pasting speed data entry

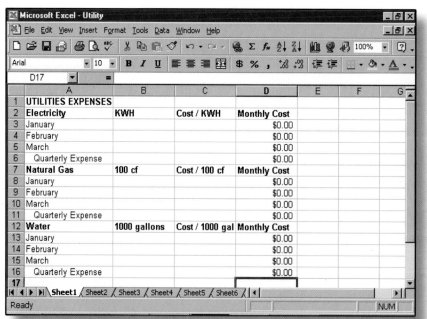

THE FILL COMMAND

Filling copies data into adjacent cell(s). The Fill command on the Edit menu has several options on the submenu, including Down, Right, Up, and Left. Choose Down to copy data into the cell(s) directly below the original cell, as shown in Figure 3-3. Fill Up copies data into the cell(s) directly above the original cell.

Fill Right and Fill Left copies data into the cell(s) to the right or left of the original cell. All options make multiple copies if more than one destination cell is selected. For example, the Down option can copy data into the next several cells below the original cell. Filling data is somewhat faster than copying and pasting because filling requires choosing only one command. However, filling can be used only when the destination cells are adjacent to the original cell.

Hot Tip

Sometimes you may want to fill in a series of numbers or dates. For example, you might want a column to contain months such as January 2001, February 2001, March 2001, and so on. To fill cells with a series of data, begin by entering at least two cells with data. Then select the starting cells and drag the fill handle over the range of cells you want to fill.

FIGURE 3-3

Fill Down copies data to adjacent cells below the original cell

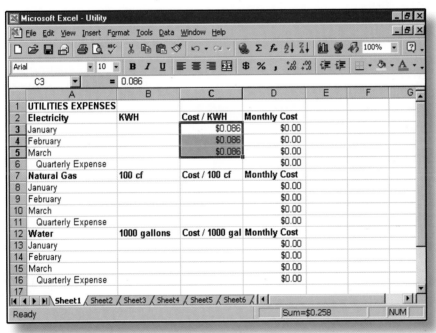

STEP-BY-STEP ▷ 3.3

1. The cost of electricity for all three months is $0.086 per kilowatt hour. Enter **.086** in **C3**.

2. Drag from **C3** to **C5** to select the range to be filled.

3. Choose **Fill** on the **Edit** menu, then choose **Down** on the submenu. The contents of C3

are copied to cells C4 and C5.

4. Enter **.512** in **C8** to record the cost per 100 cubic feet of natural gas.

5. Use the **Fill Down** command to copy the data from **C8** to **C9** and **C10**.

(continued on next page)

6. Enter **.69** in **C13** to record the cost per 1000 gallons of water.

7. Use the **Fill Down** command to copy the data from **C13** to **C14** and **C15**.

8. Enter the following utility usage data into the worksheet:

Electricity	KWH
January	548
February	522
March	508

Natural Gas	100 cf
January	94
February	56
March	50

Water	1000 gallons
January	9
February	10
March	12

9. After completing the worksheet, notice that the monthly costs have been calculated based on the data you entered. Your screen should look similar to Figure 3-4.

10. Save and leave the worksheet on your screen for the next Step-by-Step.

FIGURE 3-4
Using the Fill Down command

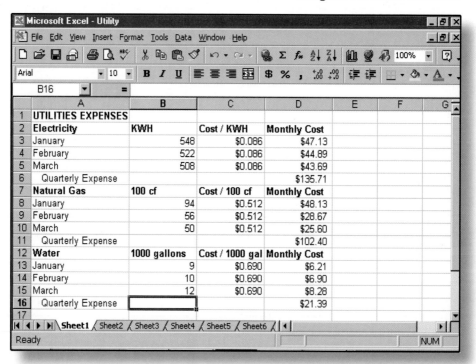

Moving Data

There may be a time when you want to move data to a new location in a worksheet. You can move data two ways. The first method, cutting and pasting, is most appropriate when you want to move data to an area of the worksheet that is not currently in view on the screen. You've learned that the Copy command places a copy of the data on the Clipboard that can then be pasted into another area of the worksheet. The Cut command also places selected data on the Clipboard; however, the Cut command removes the data from its original position in the worksheet. After cutting data, place the highlight in the cell where you want the data to appear and choose Paste on the Edit menu or click the Paste button on the toolbar.

Concept Builder

The drag-and-drop method is the easiest way to move data in a worksheet because you can do it without touching a key or using a menu.

The drag-and-drop method can also be used to move data in the worksheet. The procedure is the same as you learned earlier in this lesson, except you do not hold down the Ctrl key as you would when you are copying data.

STEP-BY-STEP ▷ 3.4

1. Select the range **A12:D16**.

2. Click the **Cut** button on the toolbar. A revolving border surrounds the data in the range.

3. Highlight **A14**.

4. Click the **Paste** button on the toolbar. The data moves to the range A14:D18.

5. Select the range **A7:D11**.

6. Move the pointer to the top edge of A7 until it turns into an arrow.

7. Click the mouse and drag down to **A8** until the pop-up label reads *A8:D12*.

8. Release the mouse button. The data moves to the range A8:D12. Your screen should look similar to Figure 3-5.

9. Save and leave the worksheet on the screen for the next Step-by-Step.

FIGURE 3-5

The Cut command moves data to another part of the worksheet

	A	B	C	D
1	UTILITIES EXPENSES			
2	Electricity	KWH	Cost / KWH	Monthly Cost
3	January	548	$0.086	$47.13
4	February	522	$0.086	$44.89
5	March	508	$0.086	$43.69
6	Quarterly Expense			$135.71
7				
8	Natural Gas	100 cf	Cost / 100 cf	Monthly Cost
9	January	94	$0.512	$48.13
10	February	56	$0.512	$28.67
11	March	50	$0.512	$25.60
12	Quarterly Expense			$102.40
13				
14	Water	1000 gallons	Cost / 1000 gal	Monthly Cost
15	January	9	$0.690	$6.21
16	February	10	$0.690	$6.90
17	March	12	$0.690	$8.28

Inserting and Deleting Cells, Rows, and Columns

You can also change the appearance of a worksheet by adding and removing rows and/or columns. In the previous Step-by-Step, you could have inserted rows between the types of utilities rather than move existing data.

To insert a row, choose Rows on the Insert menu. A row will be added above the highlight. To insert a column, choose Columns on the Insert menu. A column will be added to the left of the highlight.

When entering a long column of data, you may discover that you omitted a number at or near the top of the worksheet column. Rather than move the data to make room for the omitted data, it may be easier to insert a cell. Choose Cells on the Insert menu and the Insert dialog box opens. Designate whether you want existing cells to be shifted to the right or down.

When you want to delete a row or column, place the highlight in the row or column you want to delete. Then, choose Delete on the Edit menu. The Delete dialog box appears, as shown in Figure 3-6. Choose *Entire row* to delete the row, or choose *Entire column* to delete the column.

The easiest way to delete a row is to click on the row number to highlight the entire row. Then, choose Delete on the Edit menu. This process skips the Delete dialog box. You can easily delete a column the same way. Simply click the column letter to highlight the entire column, and then choose the Delete command. The Delete command erases all the data contained in the row or column. If you accidentally delete the wrong column or row, you can choose Undo to restore the data. Use Redo to cancel the Undo action.

FIGURE 3-6
Delete dialog box

You may also delete an individual cell by using the Delete command on the Edit menu. Suppose that you accidentally entered a number twice while entering a long column of numbers. To eliminate the duplicate data, highlight the cell and choose Delete on the Edit menu. In the Delete dialog box (see Figure 3-6), click *Shift cells up* and then click OK. The cell is removed and the data in the cell below it is moved up one cell.

STEP-BY-STEP ▷ 3.5

1. Highlight any cell in row **2**.

2. Choose **Rows** on the **Insert** menu. Excel inserts a new, blank row 2. The original row 2 becomes row 3.

3. Highlight any cell in column **B**.

4. Choose **Columns** on the **Insert** menu. A blank

column appears as column B. The original column B becomes column C.

5. Enter **Date Paid** in **B3**.

6. Highlight any cell in column **B**.

7. Choose **Delete** on the **Edit** menu. The Delete dialog box appears as shown in Figure 3-6.

8. Click **Entire column** and click **OK**.

9. Click the row **3** number (left of *Electricity*). The entire row is selected.

10. Choose **Delete** on the **Edit** menu. Row 3 is deleted.

11. Click the **Undo** button on the toolbar. The row is restored.

12. Highlight **B17**.

13. Chose **Cells** on the **Insert** menu.

14. Click **Shift cells down** and click **OK**. The data in B17:B18 will be shifted to B18:B19.

15. Highlight **B17** if it is not currrently selected, and choose **Delete** on the **Edit** menu.

16. Click **Shift cells up** and click **OK**. The data in B18:B19 will be shifted back to B17:B18.

17. Save and leave the worksheet on the screen for the next Step-by-Step.

Freezing Titles

Often a worksheet can become so large that it is difficult to view the entire worksheet on the screen. As you scroll to other parts of the worksheet, titles at the top or side of the worksheet may disappear from the screen, making it difficult to identify the contents of particular columns. For example, the worksheet title *Utilities Expenses* in previous Step-by-Steps may have scrolled off the screen when you were working in the lower part of the worksheet.

Freezing will keep row or column titles on the screen no matter where you scroll in the worksheet. As shown in Figure 3-7, rows 1 and 2 are frozen so that when you scroll down, rows 3 through 13 are hidden. To freeze titles, place the highlight below the row you want to freeze or to the right of the column you want to freeze. Then, select Freeze Panes on the Window menu. All rows above the highlight and columns to the left of the highlight will be frozen. Frozen titles are indicated by a darkened gridline that separates the frozen portion of the worksheet from the unfrozen portion. To unfreeze a row or column title, choose the Unfreeze Panes command on the Window menu; the darkened gridline disappears and the titles will be unfrozen.

FIGURE 3-7
Freezing titles

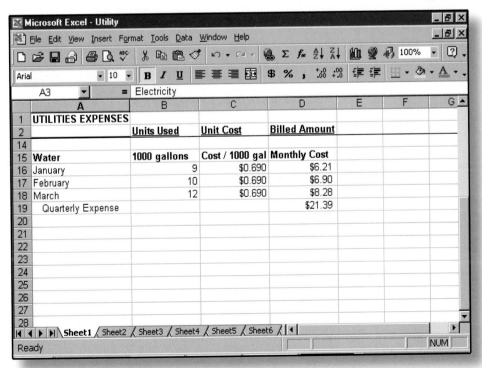

S TEP-BY-STEP ▷ 3.6

1. Enter the following column titles into the designated cells:

Cell	Column Title
B2	Units Used
C2	Unit Cost
D2	Billed Amount

2. Underline and bold the contents of **B2**, **C2**, and **D2**.

3. Highlight **A3**.

4. Choose **Freeze Panes** on the **Window** menu. The title and column headings in rows 1 and 2 are now frozen. A darkened gridline appears between rows 2 and 3.

5. Scroll to the lower part of the worksheet to highlight cell **D19**. You will notice that the column headings remain at the top of the screen no matter where you move.

6. Choose **Unfreeze Panes** on the **Window** menu. The title and column headings are no longer frozen.

7. Save the file and leave it on the screen for the next Step-by-Step.

Protecting a Worksheet

Protecting a worksheet prevents anyone from making changes to it by accident. Data cannot be added, removed, or edited until the protection is removed.

To protect a worksheet, choose Protection on the Tools menu. Then, choose Protect Sheet on the submenu. When the Protect Sheet dialog box appears, as shown in Figure 3-8, make sure the *Contents* box is checked. You can provide extra protection by keying a password. No one will be able to unprotect or change the worksheet without entering your password. If you do not enter a password, the contents can be unprotected and changed by anyone.

If you attempt to change the data in the worksheet after it has been protected, Excel displays a message telling you the cells cannot be changed. If you want to change the worksheet, you must first unprotect it by choosing Unprotect Sheet on the Protection command's submenu.

FIGURE 3-8
Protect Sheet dialog box

1. Choose **Protection** on the **Tools** menu, then choose **Protect Sheet** on the submenu. The Protect Sheet dialog box appears, as shown in Figure 3-8.

2. Click the **Contents** box if it is not checked already.

3. Click **OK**. The worksheet is now protected.

4. To check protection, move the highlight to **B4**, a cell within the protected range.

5. Enter **550**. A message appears telling you the cell is protected and that you may read, but not edit, the data.

6. Click **OK** to close the message.

7. Choose **Protection** on the **Tools** menu. Then, choose **Unprotect Sheet** on the submenu to turn the protection off. Leave the worksheet on the screen for the next Step-by-Step.

Printing Options

In Lessons 1 and 2, you printed a worksheet using the default settings. There are, however, other options for printing parts of a worksheet or changing the way a worksheet prints.

PRINTING OPTIONS IN THE PRINT DIALOG BOX

You can print part of a worksheet using the Print command. To define the part of the worksheet you want to print, select the range to be printed and choose Print on the File menu. When the Print dialog box appears (see Figure 3-9), click *Selection* in the *Print what* section.

FIGURE 3-9
Print dialog box

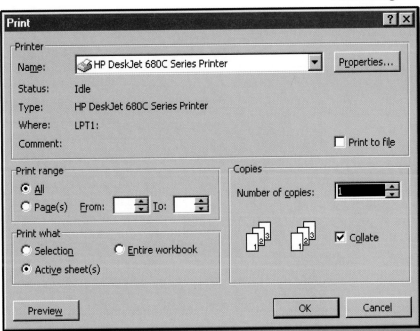

In the *Print what* section, you can also choose to print the active sheet(s), or the entire workbook. In addition, the Print dialog box lets you choose the number of copies to print. The *Page range* options let you specify whether you want to print all pages of the worksheet or certain pages.

SETTING PAGE BREAKS

If you are having difficulty placing data on a printed page in a way that is easily viewed, you may want to manually place page breaks in your worksheet. To force a page break above a selected cell, choose Page Break on the Insert menu. To remove a page break, select a cell below the page break and then choose Remove Page Break on the Insert menu.

DESIGNING THE PRINTED PAGE

The Page Setup command on the File menu allows you to set page margins, and page lengths and widths, designate page numbers, and determine whether column letters, row numbers, and gridlines should be printed. The Page Setup dialog box is divided into four tabbed sections, shown in Figure 3-10. These sections are discussed below.

FIGURE 3-10
Page Setup dialog box

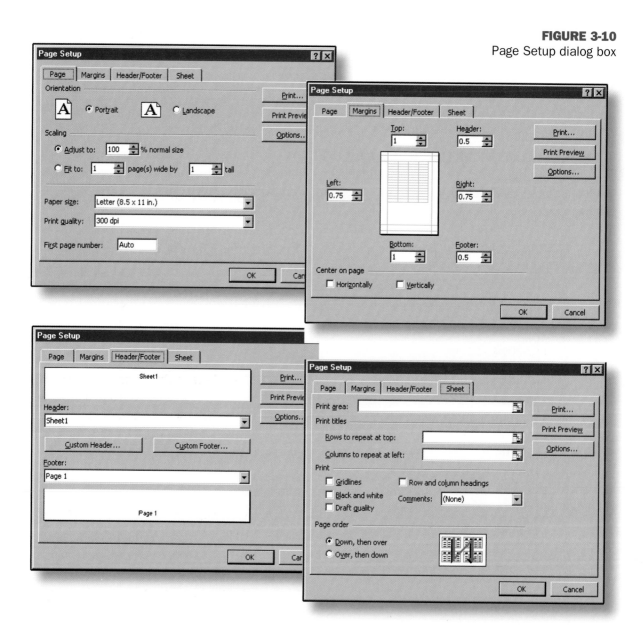

- **Page**. Page orientation (portrait or landscape), scaling, paper size, and print quality are designated under the Page tab. In addition, you can designate the page number of the first page of the worksheet.

- **Margins**. The Margins tab of the dialog box allows you to change the margins of the printed page by keying the margin size in the appropriate box. You can also choose to center the worksheet horizontally and/or vertically on the page.

- **Header/Footer**. Under the Header/Footer tab, you can key text to be printed at the top and bottom of each page.

- **Sheet**. Under the Sheet tab, you can set the print area and title the worksheet. You can also choose whether gridlines, row headings, and column headings are printed.

 Did You Know?

Sometimes you may want to print the same worksheet for different people with different information needs. A custom view will save print settings so that you may convert the spreadsheet to the view desired. To create a custom view, specify the page setup and print settings. Then, select **Custom Views** on the **View** menu. Click **Add** in the Custom Views dialog box, and then key the name you would like to use for the custom view. Click **OK** to save the view format and settings. You may apply the customized view at any time by opening the Custom Views dialog box, selecting the view you want, and then clicking **Show**.

S TEP-BY-STEP ▷ 3.8

1. Choose **Page Setup** on the **File** menu. The Page Setup dialog box appears.

2. Click the **Page** tab if it's not chosen already.

3. In the *Orientation* section, click the **Landscape** button. In the *Scaling* section, click the up arrow until **130** appears in the *Adjust to* box.

4. Click the **Margins** tab.

5. Click the down arrow on the *Bottom* box until **0.5** appears.

6. In the *Center on page* section, check **Horizontally** and **Vertically**.

7. Click the **Header/Footer** tab.

8. Click the down arrow in the *Header* text box.

9. Click **Utility, Page 1**.

10. Click the **Sheet** tab.

11. In the *Print* section, check **Gridlines** and **Row and column headings**.

12. Click the **Collapse Dialog** button at the right side of the **Print area** text box. The dialog box will disappear.

13. Drag from **A1** to **D19**.

14. Click the **Expand Dialog** button at the right side of the Page Setup—Print area dialog box. The Page Setup dialog box will appear and *A1:D19* appears in the Print area text box.

15. Click **OK**.

16. Save and leave the worksheet on the screen for the next Step-by-Step.

PREVIEWING A WORKSHEET BEFORE PRINTING

The Print Preview command shows how your printed pages will appear before you actually print them. To access the Print Preview screen (see Figure 3-11), choose Print Preview on the File menu or click the Print Preview button on the toolbar.

The buttons across the top of the screen provide options for viewing your worksheet. Choose Next and Previous to see other pages of your worksheet. Use the Zoom button or click the magnifying glass mouse pointer on the page to get a magnified view. Click the Margins button to change the margins of the worksheet, or click the Setup button to go to the Page Setup dialog box discussed earlier. Click Page Break Preview to adjust the page breaks and control what appears on each page when the worksheet is printed. When you have finished previewing the printed pages, you can return to the worksheet by choosing Close, or print the worksheet by choosing the Print button.

FIGURE 3-11
Print Preview screen

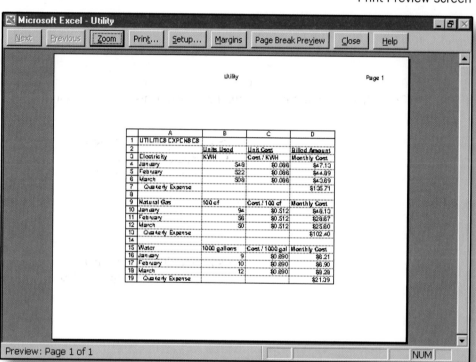

STEP-BY-STEP ⟩ 3.9

1. Select **A1:D19**.

2. Choose **Print** on the **File** menu. The *Print dialog* box appears.

3. Click **Selection** in the *Print what* box.

4. Click **OK**. The selection will print.

5. Click the **Print Preview** button on the toolbar. The Print Preview screen appears, as shown in Figure 3-11.

6. Click the **Zoom** button. A portion of the previewed page becomes larger so that it can be examined in more detail.

7. Click **Setup**.

8. Click the **Sheet** tab, if it's not open already.

9. In the *Print* box, click the **Gridlines** box and the **Row and column headings** box to remove the check marks.

10. Click **OK**.

I E - 4 6

11. Click the **Print** button. The Print dialog box appears.

12. Print the active sheet by clicking **OK**.

13. Save and close the file.

 Extra Challenge

Use the formatting commands you learned in Lesson 2 to make the spreadsheet more attractive.

Summary

In this lesson, you learned:

■ The data in a worksheet can be moved or copied to another location by using the Cut, Copy, Paste, and Fill commands on the Edit menu. These commands save time by eliminating the need to rekey large quantities of data. The drag-and-drop method can also be used to copy and move data in worksheets.

■ Inserting or deleting rows and columns can change the appearance of the worksheet. When a worksheet becomes large, the column or row titles will disappear from the screen as you scroll to other parts of the worksheet. You can keep the titles on the screen at all times by freezing them.

■ A worksheet can be protected from accidental change by choosing Protect Sheet on the Protection submenu on the Tools menu. You can unprotect a worksheet if changes are necessary.

■ You can designate a portion of the worksheet to print using the Selection option in the Print dialog box. The Page Setup command controls the page size and the margins that will be printed. To view the worksheet as it will appear before actually printing it, use the Print Preview command.

LESSON 3 REVIEW QUESTIONS

TRUE/FALSE

Circle T if the statement is true or F if the statement is false.

T F 1. If you copy data into cells already containing data, the existing data will be replaced by the copied data.

T F 2. The Fill commands are available only if you plan to copy to cells adjacent to the original cell.

T F 3. Deleting a row or column will erase the data contained in the row or column.

T **F** 4. The Freeze Panes command will freeze rows above and columns to the right of the highlight.

T F 5. You can preview a worksheet before printing by clicking the Print Preview button on the toolbar, or by choosing the Print Preview command in the File menu.

WRITTEN QUESTIONS

Write a brief answer to the following questions.

1. What key do you press to copy data using the drag-and-drop method?

   press ctrl key to copy

2. How do you make multiple copies of data that has been copied to the Clipboard already?

   place the insertion point where you want data & choose PASTE again

3. What should you do if you accidentally delete a column or row?

   Choose undo from Edit menu or undo on the tool bar

4. What command keeps the titles of a worksheet on the screen no matter where the highlight is moved?

   Freeze Panes

5. Which menu contains the Protection command?

   is on the tools menu

LESSON 3 PROJECTS

PROJECT 3-1

Write the letter of the worksheet command in Column 2 that will solve the worksheet problem in Column 1.

Column 1

B 1. You are tired of keying repetitive data.

E 2. A portion of the worksheet would be more useful in another area of the worksheet.

C 3. You forgot to key a row of data in the middle of the worksheet.

G 4. You no longer need a certain column in the worksheet.

H 5. Column headings cannot be viewed on the screen when you are working in the lower part of the worksheet.

D 6. You would like to prevent others from entering data in a worksheet.

A 7. Your boss would rather not view your worksheet on the screen and has requested a copy on paper.

F 8. You would like to print only the selected area of a worksheet.

Column 2

A. Print command or Print button on the toolbar

B. Fill command or Copy command

C. Rows or Columns command

D. Protection command

E. Cut command, Paste command

F. Selection option in the Print dialog box

G. Delete command

H. Freeze Panes command

PROJECT 3-2

IE Project3-2 contains a list of assets of Pelican Retail Stores. Perform the following operations to make the worksheet more useful to the reader.

1. Open **IE Project3-2** from the student data files.

2. Save the file as **Pelican Stores**, followed by your initials.

3. Insert a column to the left of column **B**.

4. Widen column **A** to **45** spaces.

5. Move the contents of **D4:D17** to **B4:B17**.

6. Change columns **B** and **C** to **10** spaces.

7. Insert a row above row **4**.

8. Indent the contents of **A11**, **A15**, and **A18**.

9. Underline the contents of **B5:C5**.

10. Save, print, and close the file.

PROJECT 3-3

IE Project3-3 is a mileage chart that you worked with in a previous project. Because the distances between cities do not change, you would like to protect the contents of the worksheet so that the data will not be altered. In addition, you would like the page in landscape orientation so that you are able to print the chart on one page.

1. Open **IE Project3-3** from the student data files.

2. Save the file as **Mileage2**, followed by your initials.

3. Freeze the column headings in row **1** and the row headings in column **A**. (*Hint:* Place the highlight in **B2** before choosing the Freeze Panes command.)

4. Protect the contents of the worksheet. Do not specify a password.

5. Change the printed page orientation from portrait to landscape.

6. Save, print, and close the file.

PROJECT 3-4

The file *IE Project3-4* accounts for the inventory purchases of a small office supply store. The worksheet is not currently organized by suppliers of the inventory.

1. Open **IE Project3-4** from the student data files.

2. Save the file as **Supply Inventory**, followed by your initials.

3. Organize the worksheet so that it looks like the table below. The new worksheet should have inventory items organized by supplier, with proper headings inserted. Some of the data is out of order and needs to be moved. Remember to bold appropriate data.

Item	Ordering Code	Quantity
Mega Computer Manufacturers		
Mega X-39 Computers	X-39-25879	20
Mega X-40 Computers	X-40-25880	24
Mega X-41 Computers	X-41-25881	28
Xenon Paper Source		
Xenon Letter Size White Paper	LT-W-45822	70
Xenon Letter Size Color Paper	LT-C-45823	10
Xenon Legal Size White Paper	LG-W-45824	40
Xenon Legal Size Color Paper	LG-C-45825	5
MarkMaker Pen Co.		
MarkMaker Blue Ball Point Pens	MM-Bl-43677	120
MarkMaker Black Ball Point Pens	MM-Bk-43678	100
MarkMaker Red Ball Point Pens	MM-R-43679	30

4. The following inventory item has been accidentally excluded from the worksheet. Add the item by using the Fill Down command and then editing the copied data.

Item	Ordering Code	Quantity
MarkMaker Green Ball Point Pens	MM-G-43680	30

5. Delete the following items.

Item	Ordering Code	Quantity
Mega X-39 Computers	X-39-25879	20
MarkMaker Blue Ball Point Pens	MM-Bl-43677	120

6. Undo the last Delete command.

7. Change the page orientation to landscape.

8. Save, print, and close the file.

PROJECT 3-5

1. Open **IE Project3-5** from the student data files.

2. Save the file as **Time Record**, followed by your initials.

3. Delete rows **4** and **5**.

4. Insert the following information on the time record. (Note: The AutoComplete function may automatically enter some of the work descriptions for you as you begin to enter the data. To accept the data as it appears, press Enter.)

Date	From	To	Admin.	Meetings	Phone	Work Description
9-Dec	8:15 AM	12:00 PM		1.00	2.75	Staff meeting and call clients
10-Dec	7:45 AM	11:30 AM	2.00		1.75	Paperwork and call clients
11-Dec	7:45 AM	11:30 AM			3.75	Call clients
13-Dec	8:00 AM	12:00 PM	2.00	2.00		Mail flyers and meet w/KF

5. Freeze headings above row **8**.

6. Insert a blank row above row **16**. Insert the following information:

Date	From	To	Admin.	Meetings	Phone	Work Description
12-Dec	7:45 AM	11:30 AM	2.00		1.75	Paperwork and call clients

7. Copy **D15** to **D16**.

8. Preview the worksheet and zoom in to see the total hours worked.

9. Change the orientation of the worksheet to landscape. Center horizontally and vertically on the page.

10. Save, print, and close the worksheet.

PROJECT 3-6

The file *IE Project3-6* contains the grades of several students taking Biology 101 during the spring semester. The instructor has asked that you, the student assistant, help maintain the grade records of the class.

1. Open **IE Project3-6** from the student data files.

2. Save the file as **Class Grades**, followed by your initials.

3. Merge and center **A1:I1**. Merge and center **A2:I2**.

4. Column A contains the last names of students in the class.
   A. Add a column between the current columns **A** and **B** to hold the first names of the students.
   B. Enter **First Name** in **B3** of the new column.
   C. Enter the following names in the new column you created:

Row	Entry
4	Ashley
5	Kevin
6	Cindy
7	Raul
8	Haley
9	Cameron

5. Protect the worksheet to prevent accidental changes.

6. Preview the worksheet.

7. Change the worksheet to landscape orientation and centered horizontally on the page.

8. Change the header to read *Sheet 1, Page 1*.

9. Remove the footer, if any exists.

10. Save, print, and close.

PROJECT 3-7

You are a member of the Booster Club, an organization that raises money to purchase sports equipment for the local high school. You have been allocated $1,210 to purchase sports equipment for the school. You prepare a worksheet to help calculate the cost of various purchases. (*Note*: The AutoComplete function may enter some of the data for you as you begin to enter the data. To accept the data as it appears, press Enter.)

1. Open the file **IE Project3-7** from the student data files.

2. Save the file as **Booster Club**, followed by your initials.

3. Bold and center the column headings in row **2**.

4. Insert a row above row **3**.

5. Freeze the column headings in row **2**.

6. Insert a row above row **8** and key **Bats** in **A8** (the new row).

7. Use the Fill Down command to copy the formula in **E4** to **E5:E11**. Do not copy the formula into E12.

8. Format the **Cost (D4:D11)** and **Total (E4:E12)** columns for currency with two decimal places.

9. Key the data for Sport and Cost, as given in the following table. Use the Fill Down command as needed to copy repetitive data. Widen the columns if necessary.

Item	Sport	Cost
Basketballs	Basketball	28
Hoops	Basketball	40
Backboards	Basketball	115
Softballs	Softball	5
Bats	Softball	30
Masks	Softball	35
Volleyballs	Volleyball	25
Nets	Volleyball	125

10. You have $1,210 to spend on equipment. The organization has requested you to purchase the items listed below. Any remaining cash should be used to purchase as many basketballs as possible.

Basketballs	5
Hoops	2
Backboards	2
Softballs	20
Bats	5
Masks	1
Volleyballs	7
Nets	1

11. Increase the number of basketballs and watch the dollar amount in the total. You should use $1,203.00 and have $7.00 left over.

12. Unfreeze column headings.

13. Save, print, and close the file.

PROJECT 3-8

IE Project3-8 contains attendance data for a neighborhood swimming pool. Format the worksheet in a way that you find appealing. You may move data in the worksheet. You may also change the column width, color, alignment, borders, format, and font of the data. When you have finished, name and save the file as **Swimming Pool**, followed by your initials. Then print and close the file.

CRITICAL THINKING

ACTIVITY 3-1

As a zoo employee, you have been asked to observe the behavior of a predatory cat during a three-day period. You are to record the number of minutes the animal displays certain behaviors during the time that the zoo is open to visitors. Set up a worksheet that can be used to record the number of minutes that the cat participates in these behaviors during each of the three days.

■ Sleeping

■ Eating

■ Walking

■ Sitting

■ Play

Make your worksheet easy to read by using bolded fonts, italicized fonts, varied alignment, and color.

LESSON 4

WORKSHEET FORMULAS

OBJECTIVES

Upon completion of this lesson, you should be able to:

- Enter and edit formulas.
- Distinguish between relative, absolute, and mixed cell references.
- Use the AutoSum button and the point-and-click method of entering formulas.
- Display formulas in the worksheet.
- Perform immediate and delayed calculations.

Estimated Time: 2.5 hours

What Are Formulas?

Worksheets can use numbers entered in certain cells to calculate values in other cells. The equations used to calculate values in a cell are known as ***formulas***. Excel recognizes the contents of a cell as a formula when an equal sign (=) is the first character in the cell. For example, if the formula =8+6 were entered in cell B3, the value of 14 would be displayed in B3 of the worksheet. The formula bar displays the formula =8+6, as shown in Figure 4-1.

FIGURE 4-1
Formula result displays in the cell

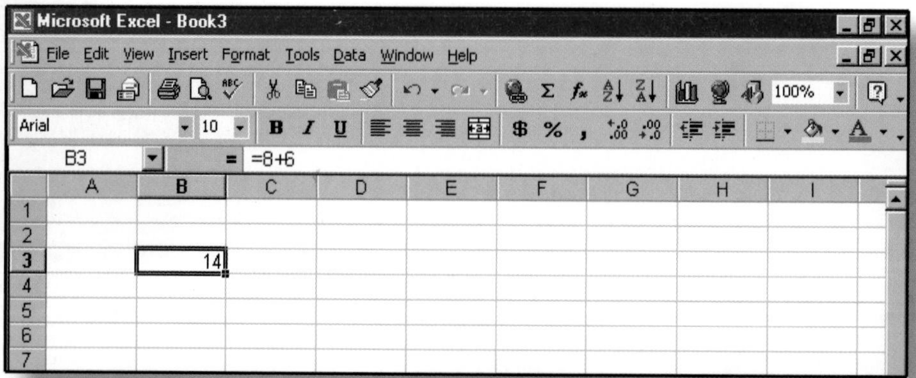

Structure of a Formula

A worksheet formula consists of two components: operands and operators. An *operand* is a number or cell reference used in formulas. You can key cell references in uppercase (A1) or lowercase (a1). An *operator* tells Excel what to do with the operands. For example, in the formula =B3+5, B3 and 5 are operands. The plus sign (+) is an operator that tells Excel to add the value contained in cell B3 to the number 5. The operators used in formulas are shown in Table 4-1. After you have keyed the formula, enter it by pressing the Enter key or by clicking the check mark (✔) on the formula bar.

TABLE 4-1
Formula operators

OPERATOR	OPERATION	EXAMPLE	MEANING
+	Addition	B5+C5	Adds the values in B5 and C5
-	Subtraction	C8-232	Subtracts 232 from the value in C8
*	Multiplication	D4*D5	Multiplies the value in D4 by the value in D5
/	Division	E6/4	Divides the value in E6 by 4
^	Exponentiation	B3^3	Raises the value in B3 to the third power

S TEP-BY-STEP ▷ 4.1

1. Open **IE Step4-1** from the student data files.

2. Save the worksheet as **Calculate**, followed by your initials.

3. Highlight **C3**.

4. Key **=A3+B3** and press **Enter**. The formula result *380* appears in the cell.

5. In **C4**, key **=A4-B4** and press **Enter**.

6. In **C5**, key **=A5*B5** and press **Enter**.

7. In **C6**, key **=A6/B6** and press **Enter**.

8. Check your results by comparing them to Figure 4-2. Leave the file open for use in the next Step-by-Step.

FIGURE 4-2
Entering formulas

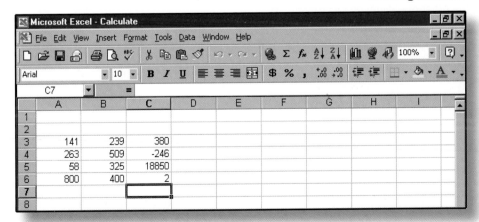

ORDER OF EVALUATION

Formulas containing more than one operator are called complex formulas. For example, the formula =C3*C4+5 will perform both multiplication and addition to calculate the value in the cell. The sequence used to calculate the value of a formula is called the *order of evaluation*.

Formulas are evaluated in the following order:

1. Contents within parentheses are evaluated first. You may use as many pairs of parentheses as you want. Excel will evaluate the innermost set of parentheses first.

2. Mathematical operators are evaluated in order of priority, as shown in Table 4-2.

3. Equations are evaluated from left to right if two or more operators have the same order of evaluation. For example, in the formula =20-15-2, the number 15 would be subtracted from 20; then 2 would be subtracted from the difference (5).

TABLE 4-2
Order of evaluation priority

ORDER OF EVALUATION	OPERATOR	SYMBOL
First	Exponentiation	^
Second	Positive or negative	+ or -
Third	Multiplication or division	* or /
Fourth	Addition or subtraction	+ or −

STEP-BY-STEP ▷ 4.2

1. In **D3**, key **=(A3+B3)*20**. The values in A3 and B3 will be added, and then the result will be multiplied by 20.

2. Press **Enter**. The resulting value is 7600.

3. You can see the importance of the parentheses in the order of evaluation by creating an identical formula without the parentheses. In E3, key **=A3+B3*20**, the same formula as in D3 but without the parentheses.

4. Press **Enter**. The resulting value is 4921. This value differs from the value in D3 because Excel multiplied the value in B3 by 20 before adding the value in A3. In D3, the values in A3 and B3 were added together and the sum multiplied by 20.

5. Save the worksheet and leave it open for the next Step-by-Step.

Editing Formulas

Excel will not let you enter a formula with an incorrect structure. A dialog box explaining the error appears. For example, if a formula with an open parenthesis, but no closed parenthesis is entered, a message describing the error and how to correct the error will appear. You can then correct the formula by editing in the formula bar. You can also edit formulas already entered in the worksheet. To edit a formula, highlight the cell, then press the Edit key (F2); or, click in the formula bar and key or delete data as necessary.

STEP-BY-STEP ▷ 4.3

1. Move the highlight to **E3**. The formula is shown in the formula bar.

2. Place the insertion point after the = in the formula bar and click.

3. Key **(**.

4. Press **Enter**. An error message appears asking whether you would like to accept a suggested change or correct the error yourself.

5. Choose **No** so that you may correct the error yourself. A dialog box describing the error appears.

6. Click **OK**.

7. Now move the insertion point in the formula bar between the *3* and the *.

8. Key **)**.

9. Press **Enter**. The value changes to 7600.

10. Save the file and leave it on the screen for the next Step-by-Step.

Relative, Absolute, and Mixed Cell References

Three types of cell references are used to create formulas: relative, absolute, and mixed. A *relative cell reference* adjusts to its new location when copied or moved. For example, in Figure 4-3, the formula =A3+A4 is copied to B5 and the formula changes to =B3+B4. In other words, this formula is instructing Excel to add the two cells directly above. When the formula is copied or moved, the cell references change, but the operators remain the same.

Absolute cell references do not change when moved or copied to a new cell. To create an absolute reference, you insert a dollar sign ($) before the column letter and/or the row number of the cell reference you want to stay the same. For example, in Figure 4-4, the formula =$A$3+$A$4 is copied to B7 and the formula remains the same in the new location.

FIGURE 4-3
Copying a formula with relative cell references

FIGURE 4-4
Copying a formula with absolute cell references

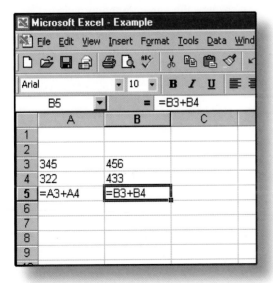

Cell references containing both relative and absolute references are called *mixed cell references*. When formulas with mixed cell references are copied or moved, the row or column references preceded by a dollar sign will not change; the row or column references not preceded by a dollar sign will adjust relative to the cell to which they are moved. As shown in Figure 4-5, when the formula =A$3+A$4 is copied to B7, the formula changes to =B$3+B$4.

FIGURE 4-5
Copying a formula with mixed cell references

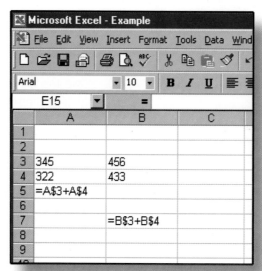

STEP-BY-STEP ▷ 4.4

1. Place the highlight in **D3**. The formula =(A3+B3)*20 (shown in the formula bar) contains only relative cell references.

2. Use Fill Down to copy the formula in **D3** to **D4**.

3. Place the highlight in **D4**. The value in D4 is 15440 and the formula in the formula bar is =(A4+B4)*20. The operators in the formula remain the same, but the relative cell references changed to reflect a change in the location of the formula.

4. Enter =**$A$3*($B$3-200)** in **D5**. The value in D5 is 5499. The formula contains absolute cell references, which are indicated by the dollar signs that precede row and column references.

5. Copy the formula in **D5** to **D6**. The value in D6 is 5499, the same as in D5.

6. Move the highlight to **D5**. Now move the highlight to **D6**. Because the formula in D5 contains absolute cell references, the formula is exactly the same as the formula in D6.

7. Enter =**$A$4+B4** in **E4**. This formula contains mixed cell references (relative and absolute). The value in E4 is 772.

8. Copy the formula in **E4** to **E5**. Notice the relative reference B4 changed to B5, but the absolute reference to A4 stayed the same. The value in E5 is 588.

9. Copy the formula in **E5** to **F5**. Again, notice the relative reference changed from B5 to C5. The absolute reference to A4 stayed the same. The value in F5 is 19113.

10. Save, print, and close the file.

Creating Formulas Quickly

You have already learned how to create formulas by keying the formula or editing existing formulas. In this section, formulas are created quickly by using the point-and-click method and by clicking the AutoSum button.

POINT-AND-CLICK METHOD

Earlier, you constructed formulas by keying the entire formula in the cell of the worksheet. You can include cell references in a formula more quickly by clicking on the cell rather than keying the reference. This is known as the *point-and-click method*. The point-and-click method is particularly helpful when you have to enter long formulas that contain several cell references.

To use the point-and-click method to create a formula, simply substitute keying a cell reference with clicking the cell. For example, to enter the formula =A3+B3 in a cell, you would first highlight the cell that will contain the formula. Then, press =, click A3, press +, click B3, and press Enter.

STEP-BY-STEP 4.5

The manager of the Fruit and Fizz Shop would like to determine the total sales of juice and soda during the month, plus what percentage each type of juice and soda is of the total items sold. Prices of individual servings are as follows:

	Large	Small
Juice	$1.50	$ .90
Soda	$ .80	$ .50

1. Open **IE Step4-5** from the student data files.

2. Save the file as **Drinks**, followed by your initials.

3. Key =(1.5* in **D6**. ($1.50 is the price for a large juice.)

4. Click **B6**. (You will see a moving border around the cell.)

5. Key)+(.9*. ($.90 is the price for a small juice.)

6. Click **C6**.

7. Key).

8. Press **Enter**. The amount $567.00 will appear in the cell.

9. Use Fill Down to copy the formula in **D6** to **D7** and **D8**. The value in D7 is $393.90. The value in D8 is $142.50.

10. Key =(.8* in D9. ($.80 is the price for a large soda.)

11. Click **B9**.

12. Key)+(.5*. ($.50 is the price for a small soda.)

13. Click **C9**.

14. Key) and press **Enter**. The value in D9 is $282.20.

15. Use Fill Down to copy the formula in **D9** to **D10** and **D11**. Your screen should look similar to Figure 4-6.

16. Save and leave the file on your screen for the next Step-by-Step.

(continued on next page)

FIGURE 4-6
Inserting formulas using the point-and-click method

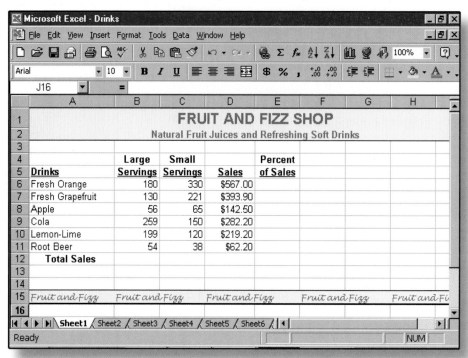

THE AUTOSUM BUTTON

Worksheet users frequently need to sum long columns of numbers. The AutoSum button on the toolbar makes this operation simple. The AutoSum button is identified by the Greek letter *sigma* (Σ). To use AutoSum, place the highlight in the cell where you want the total to appear. Click the AutoSum button, and Excel scans the worksheet to determine the most logical column or row of adjacent cells containing numbers to sum. Excel then displays an outline around the range it has selected. This range is identified in the highlighted cell. If you prefer a range other than the one Excel selects, drag to select those cells. Click Enter to display the sum in the cell.

The sum of a range is indicated by a special formula in the formula bar called a function formula. For example, if the sum of the range D5:D17 is entered in a cell, the function formula will be =SUM(D5:D17). The SUM function is the most frequently used type of function formula. Function formulas will be discussed in greater detail in the next lesson.

S TEP-BY-STEP ⟹ 4.6

1. Highlight **D12**.

2. Click the **AutoSum** button. The range D6:D11 is outlined. Excel has correctly selected the

range of cells you would like to sum. The formula =SUM(D6:D11) appears in the formula bar.

INTRODUCTION TO MICROSOFT EXCEL

3. Press **Enter**. D12 displays *$1,667.00*, the sum of the numbers in column D.

4. Highlight **E6**.

5. Press **=**.

6. Click **D6**.

7. Press **/**.

8. Key **$D$12** and press **Enter**.

9. Copy the formula in **E6** to **E7:E12**. Your screen should look similar to Figure 4-7.

10. Save and leave the worksheet on your screen for the next Step-by-Step.

FIGURE 4-7
Using the AutoSum button

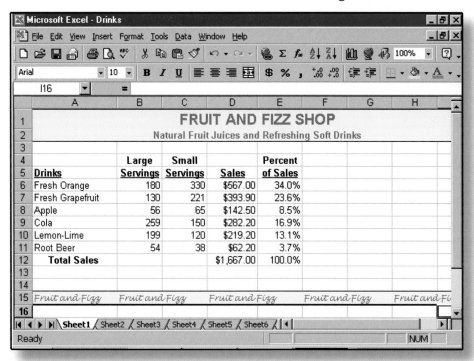

Previewing a Calculation

You may want to determine a calculated amount from worksheet data before entering a formula. By using a feature called Auto Calculation, you may determine, for example, the number of entries within a range or the average of amounts in a range. To use Auto Calculation to determine the sum of data contained in a range, select the range and then right-click on the status bar at the bottom of the screen. A menu will appear. By clicking Sum, the summation of data in the range will appear in the status bar.

Hot Tip

Auto Calculation may also be used to determine the minimum or maximum value that lies within a range.

1. Select the range **B6:C6**.

2. *Right*-click anywhere in the status bar. A menu will appear.

```
  None
  ‾‾‾‾‾‾‾‾‾
  Average
  Count
  Count Nums
  Max
  Min
✓ Sum
```

3. If it is not already checked, click **Sum** until a check mark appears. The number of large and small orange juices served, 510, will appear in the status bar.

4. Select the range **B6:C11**. The total number of large and small drinks, 1,802, appears in the status bar. Click outside the range to deselect it and remain in this screen for the next Step-by-Step.

Extra Challenge

Auto Calculation may be used to check the formula results. D12 contains a function formula that determines the sum of D6:D11. To check the results of the formula, right-click the status bar and click sum. Then select D6:D11. The sum in the status bar should equal the value in D12.

Formula Helpers

The Options dialog box, displayed by choosing Options on the Tools menu, contains several tabbed sections that define features in the worksheet. For example, the *Formulas* box in the *Window options* section on the View tab (see Figure 4-8) will replace the values in the cells of the worksheet with the formulas that created them. If a cell does not contain a formula, Excel displays the data entered in the cell. To display values determined by the formulas again, click to remove the check mark from the *Formulas* box. The *Manual* button on the Calculation tab will prevent worksheet formulas from calculating until you press the F9 key.

FIGURE 4-8
View tab in the Options dialog box

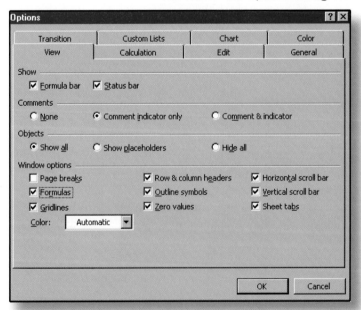

SHOWING FORMULAS ON THE WORKSHEET

In previous Step-by-Steps, you were able to view formulas only in the formula bar. Cells of the worksheet contained the values determined by formulas rather than the formulas themselves. When creating a worksheet containing many formulas, you may find it easier to organize formulas and detect formula errors when you can view all formulas at once.

DELAYED CALCULATIONS

Values in the worksheet are usually calculated as a new formula is entered, but you can also calculate the formula at a specific moment. Delayed calculation (also called manual calculation) can be useful when you are working with a large worksheet that will take longer than usual to calculate; or you may want to view the difference in a particular cell after you have made changes throughout the worksheet.

To delay calculation, click the *Manual* button on the Calculation tab of the Options dialog box (see Figure 4-9). Then, press F9 to start calculation. To return to automatic calculation, click the *Automatic* button in the *Calculation* section of the tab.

FIGURE 4-9
Calculation tab in the Options dialog box

Options
Transition	Custom Lists	Chart	Color
View	Calculation	Edit	General

Calculation
- ○ Automatic
- ○ Automatic except tables
- ● Manual
- ☑ Recalculate before save
- [Calc Now (F9)]
- [Calc Sheet]

- ☐ Iteration
  - Maximum iterations: 100
  - Maximum change: 0.001

Workbook options
- ☑ Update remote references
- ☐ Precision as displayed
- ☐ 1904 date system
- ☑ Save external link values
- ☑ Accept labels in formulas

[OK] [Cancel]

STEP-BY-STEP ▷ 4.8

1. Choose **Options** on the **Tools** menu. The Options dialog box appears, as shown in Figure 4-8.

2. Click the **View** tab.

3. In the *Window options* box, click the **Formulas** box until a check mark appears.

4. Click **OK**.

(continued on next page)

5. Scroll to the right so that columns D and E appear on the screen. All formulas are now visible.

6. Press **Ctrl+`**. Cells with formulas now show values again.

7. Choose **Options** on the **Tools** menu.

8. Click the **Calculation** tab in the Options dialog box (see Figure 4-9).

9. Click the **Manual** button in the **Calculation** section.

10. Click **OK**. Calculation is now delayed.

11. Change the following values in the worksheet.
   a. Key **182** in **B6**.
   b. Key **220** in **C7**.
   c. Key **125** in **C10**.

12. Press **F9** while watching the screen. Calculations occur as you press the key. The total sales in cell D12 should be $1,671.60.

13. Access the Options dialog box and the Calculation tab.

14. Click the **Automatic** button in the **Calculation** section and click **OK**.

15. Change the page orientation to landscape.

16. Save, print, and close the file.

Extra Challenge

Open the file you previously saved as *Drinks*. The current number of orange juices sold is 182. Determine how many large orange juices must be sold in order to achieve over $1,700 in sales by entering larger amounts in cell B5. When you have determined the amount, close the file.

Summary

In this lesson, you learned:

- Worksheet formulas perform calculations on values referenced in other cells of the worksheet.

- Relative cell references adjust to a different location when copied or moved. Absolute cell references describe the same cell location in the worksheet regardless of where it is copied or moved. Mixed cell references contain both relative and absolute cell references.

- Formulas may be created quickly by using the point-and-click method. This method inserts a cell reference by clicking rather than keying its column letter and row number.

- A group of cells may be summed quickly by using the AutoSum button on the toolbar. Excel will insert the SUM formula function and determine the most likely range to be summed.

LESSON 4 REVIEW QUESTIONS

TRUE/FALSE

Circle T if the statement is true or F if the statement is false.

T **(F)** 1. An operator is a number or cell reference used in formulas.

T **(F)** 2. In a complex formula, subtraction will be performed before multiplication.

(T) F 3. Operations within parentheses will be performed before operations outside parentheses in a formula.

T **(F)** 4. An absolute cell reference will change if the formula is copied or moved.

T **(F)** 5. Manual calculation is performed by pressing the F2 key.

WRITTEN QUESTIONS

Write a brief answer to the following questions.

1. Which operator has the highest priority in the order of evaluation in a worksheet formula?

   Exponentiation

2. What type of cell reference adjusts to its new location when it is copied or moved?

   Relative cell references adjust to their new location

3. Write an example of a formula with a mixed cell reference.

   = $B3 + D$4
   Mixed references an absolote ref + a relative ref.

4. Explain how to enter the formula =C4+B5+D2 using the point-and-click method.

    Key =, click cell CF Key +, click
    BS Key +, click D2 Key & press Ent

5. Which keystrokes will display formulas in the worksheet?

    Contr +

LESSON 4 PROJECTS

PROJECT 4-1

Match the letter of the worksheet formula in Column 2 to the description of the worksheet operation performed by the formula in Column 1.

Column 1	Column 2
D 1. Adds the values in A3 and A4	**A.** =A3/(27+A4)
H 2. Subtracts the value in A4 from the value in A3	**B.** =A3^27
J 3. Multiplies the value in A3 times 27	**C.** =A3^27/A4
E 4. Divides the value in A3 by 27	**D.** =A3+A4
B 5. Raises the value in A3 to the 27th power	**E.** =A3/27
F 6. Divides the value in A3 by 27, then adds the value in A4	**F.** =A3/27+A4
	G. =(A3*27)/A4
A 7. Divides the value in A3 by the result of 27 plus the value in A4	**H.** =A3-A4

8. Multiplies the value in A3 times 27, then divides the product by the value in A4 _G_

9. Divides 27 by the value in A4, then multiplies the result by the value in A3 _I_

10. Raises the value in A3 to the 27th power, then divides the result by the value in A4 _C_

I. =A3*(27/A4)

J. =A3*27

PROJECT 4-2

1. Open **IE Project4-2** from the student data files.

2. Save the file as **Formulas**, followed by your initials.

3. Enter formulas in the specified cells that will perform the requested operations below. After you enter each formula, write the resulting value in the space provided.

Resulting Value		Cell	Operation
_____	1.	C3	Add the values in A3 and B3
_____	2.	C4	Subtract the value in B4 from the value in A4
_____	3.	C5	Multiply the value in A5 by the value in B5
_____	4.	C6	Divide the value in A6 by the value in B6
_____	5.	B7	Sum the values in the range B3:B6
_____	6.	D3	Add the values in A3 and A4, then multiply the sum by 3
_____	7.	D4	Add the values in A3 and A4, then multiply the sum by B3
_____	8.	D5	Copy the formula in D4 to D5
_____	9.	D6	Subtract the value in B6 from the value in A6, then divide by 2
_____	10.	D7	Divide the value in A6 by 2, then subtract the value in B6

4. Save, print, and close the file.

I E - 6 9

PROJECT 4-3

You are a fundraiser for Zoo America. Because winter is typically a slow time for the zoo, you decided to have a special fundraiser during the holiday. Zoo employees will set up booths at holiday events to sell T-shirts, sweatshirts, and coffee mugs. You have been asked to create a worksheet that calculates the bills of individuals who purchase these items. You are required to charge a sales tax of 7% on each sale. The file *IE Project4-3* is a worksheet lacking formulas required to calculate the bills. Complete the worksheet following these steps:

1. Open **IE Project4-3** from the student data files.

2. Save the file as **Zoo**, followed by your initials.

3. Enter formulas in **D6**, **D7**, **D8**, and **D9** to calculate the total of each item when quantities are entered in column C.

4. Enter a formula in **D10** to sum the totals in **D6:D9**.

5. Enter a formula in **D11** to calculate a sales tax of 7% of the subtotal in **D10**.

6. Enter a formula in **D12** to add the subtotal and sales tax.

7. Change the worksheet for manual calculation.

8. Format **D6:D12** for currency with two places to the right of the decimal point.

9. Underline the contents of **D9** and **D11**. The worksheet is now ready to accept data unique to the individual customer.

10. A customer purchases two tiger T-shirts, three dolphin T-shirts, one sweatshirt, and four coffee mugs. Enter the quantities in column **C** and press **F9** to calculate.

11. Make sure that you have entered the formulas correctly. If any of the formulas are incorrect, edit them and recalculate the worksheet.

12. When you are confident that the worksheet is calculating as you intended, save the file.

13. Print the customer's bill and close the file.

PROJECT 4-4

Part 1

Alice Grant has been saving and investing part of her salary for several years. She decides to keep track of her investments on a worksheet. The file *IE Project4-4* contains the investments of Alice Grant. She owns several types of investments:

■ **Money Market Account** — a bank savings account that does not require notification before money is withdrawn.

■ **Stocks** — shares of ownership in a corporation.

■ **Mutual Fund** — a collection of several stocks and/or bonds (borrowings) of corporations that are combined to form a single investment.

Alice's stock and mutual fund shares are sold on a major exchange and the value of the shares may be looked up in the newspaper after any business day.

1. Open **IE Project4-4** from the student data files.

2. Save the file as **Investments**, followed by your initials.

3. Calculate the values of the stocks in column **D** by entering formulas in **D6** through **D8**. The formulas should multiply the number of shares in column B times the price of the shares in column C.

4. Calculate the values of the mutual funds in column **D** by entering formulas in **D10** and **D11**. Similar to the stocks, the formulas should multiply the number of shares in column B times the price of the shares in column C.

5. Enter a formula in **D12** that sums the values in **D4** through **D11**.

6. Alice wants to determine the percentage of each investment with respect to her total investments. Enter the following formula **=D4/$D$12** in **E4**.

7. You may have noticed that the formula you entered in E4 contains an absolute cell reference. If this formula is copied into other cells, the absolute reference to D12 will remain the same. Copy the formula in **E4** to cells **E6** through **E8**, and cells **E10** through **E12**.

8. Save the file.

Part 2

After glancing at the newspaper, Alice realizes that the values of her investments have changed significantly. She decides to update the worksheet containing her investment records.

9. Change the worksheet to manual calculation.

10. Enter the following updated share price amounts:

Investment	Price
MicroCrunch, Corp.	$16.00
Ocean Electronics, Inc.	$20.25
Photex, Inc.	$14.50
Prosperity Growth Fund	$ 5.50
Lucrative Mutual Fund	$13.00

11. Perform manual calculation by pressing **F9**.

12. Save and print the worksheet. Close the file.

I E - 7 1

ACTIVITY 4-1

You have been offered three jobs, each paying a different salary. You have been told the gross pay (the amount before taxes), but have not been told your net pay (the amount after tax has been taken out).

Assume that you will have to pay 10% income tax and 7% Social Security tax. Develop a spreadsheet with formulas that will determine the amount of net pay. The format should be similar to the following:

	A	B	C	D	E
1	DETERMINATION OF MONTHLY NET PAY				
2	Job Offer	Gross Pay	Income Tax	Social Security Tax	Net Pay
3	Job 1	$14,500			
4	Job 2	$15,600			
5	Job 3	$16,100			

Your worksheet should include:

■ Formulas in C3:C5 that multiply the gross pay in column **B** times **.10**.

■ Formulas in D3:D5 that multiply the gross pay in column **B** times **.07**.

■ Formulas in E3:E5 that subtract the amounts in columns **C** and **D** from the amount in column **B**.

When you finish, save the file as **Job Offer**, followed by your initials, print, and close the file.

ACTIVITY 4-2

One of the most difficult aspects of working with formulas in a worksheet is getting them to produce the proper value after they are copied or moved. This requires an understanding of the differences between absolute and relative cell references.

If you experience difficulty after moving or copying formulas, you may not always have a text available to help you correct the problem. Use the Help system to locate an explanation of the differences between absolute and relative cell references. Print the explanation.

FUNCTION FORMULAS

Upon completion of this lesson, you should be able to:

- Identify the parts of a function formula.

- Use function formulas to solve mathematical problems.

- Use function formulas to solve statistical problems.

- Use function formulas to solve financial problems.

- Use function formulas to insert times and dates in a worksheet.

⏱ **Estimated Time: 2 hours**

Function Formulas

*F**unction formulas*** are special formulas that do not use operators to calculate a result. They perform complex calculations in specialized areas of mathematics, statistics, logic, trigonometry, accounting, and finance. Function formulas are also used to convert worksheet values to dates and

Did You Know?

There are more than 300 function formulas in Excel.

times. In this section, you will learn the more frequently used function formulas. A more comprehensive explanation of many Excel functions appears in the *Excel Function Reference* at the the end of this unit.

Parts of Function Formulas

A function formula contains three components: the equal sign, a function name, and an argument. The equal sign tells Excel a function formula will be entered into the cell. The function name identifies the operation to be performed. The *argument* is a value, cell reference, range, or text that acts as an operand in a function formula. The argument is enclosed in parentheses after the function name. If a function formula contains more than one argument, commas separate the arguments. The range of cells that make up the argument is separated by a colon.

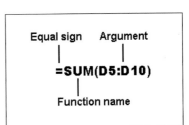

Equal sign   Argument

=SUM(D5:D10)

Function name

In the previous lesson, you created a function formula by using the AutoSum button. When pressed, the AutoSum button inserted an equal sign followed by the word *SUM*. The range of cells to be summed was designated within parentheses, for example, =SUM(D5:D10). In this function formula, the word *SUM* is the function name that identifies the operation. The argument is the range of cells that will be added together.

Function formulas may be entered in the worksheet in two ways. First, the function formula may be entered directly into the cell by keying an equal sign, the function name, and the argument.

Function formulas may also be entered through dialog boxes by choosing Function on the Insert menu or by clicking the Paste Function button on the toolbar. The Paste Function dialog box and Formula Palette guide you through inserting a function in a cell (see Figure 5-1).

FIGURE 5-1
Paste Function dialog box and Formula Palette

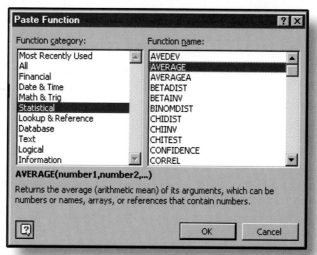

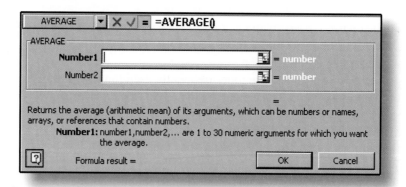

The Paste Function dialog box makes it easy to browse through all of the available functions to select the one you want. The dialog box also provides a brief explanation of any function you choose. Choose a function classification by clicking it in the *Function category* box. Then, choose an individual function formula within the category from the *Function name* box. A description of the function formula appears near the bottom of the dialog box. Click OK to go to the Formula Palette.

In the *Formula Palette*, you may select a cell or range to appear in the argument. You can enter arguments in two ways. First, you can key the argument on the Formula Palette. Alternatively, you can click the Collapse Dialog button at the end of the *Number* text boxes, and then select the cell or range directly from the spreadsheet. When you have finished specifying the argument, click the Expand Dialog button to restore the Formula Palette, then click OK, and your choices will be inserted as a function in the highlighted cell.

Collapse Dialog

Expand Dialog

ENTERING A RANGE IN A FORMULA BY DRAGGING

Ranges are often included in function formulas. You may enter a range into a formula quickly by dragging on the worksheet. For example, suppose you wanted to enter the function formula =SUM(E5:E17). You would first enter =SUM(. Then, drag from E5 to E17. The formula is completed by keying the closing parenthesis, and pressing Enter.

MATHEMATICAL AND TRIGONOMETRIC FUNCTIONS

Mathematical and trigonometric functions manipulate quantitative data in the worksheet. Some mathematical operations, such as addition, subtraction, multiplication, and division, do not require function formulas. However, mathematical and trigonometric functions are particularly useful when you need to determine values such as logarithms, factorials, sines, cosines, tangents, and absolute values.

You have already learned to use one of the mathematical and trigonometric functions when you used the AutoSum button to create SUM functions. Two other mathematical functions, the square root and rounding functions, are described in Table 5-1. Notice that two arguments are required to perform the rounding operation.

TABLE 5-1
Mathematical functions

FUNCTION	OPERATION
SQRT(number)	Displays the square root of the number identified in the argument. For example, =SQRT(C4) will display the square root of the value in C4.
ROUND(number,num_digits)	Displays the rounded value of a number to the number of places designated by the second argument. For example, =ROUND(14.23433,2) will display 14.23. If the second argument is a negative number, the first argument will be rounded to the left of the decimal point. For example =ROUND(142.3433,-2) will display 100.
LN(number)	Displays the natural logarithm of a number. For example, =LN(50) will display 1.69897.

S TEP-BY-STEP ▷ 5.1

1. Open **IE Step5-1** from the student data files.

2. Save the file as **Functions**, followed by your initials.

3. Highlight **B8**.

4. Enter **=SUM(B3:B7)**. (The same operation could have been performed using the AutoSum button on the toolbar.)

5. Highlight **B9** and choose **Function** on the

(continued on next page)

Insert menu. The Paste Function dialog box appears, similar to Figure 5-1.

6. Click **Math & Trig** in the *Function category* box.

7. Scroll down and click **SQRT** in the *Function name* box.

8. Click **OK**. The Formula Palette appears.

9. Enter **B8** in the *Number* text box. You will notice the value in B8, 2466, appears to the right of the *Number* box. The value that will appear in B9, 49.65883607, appears at the bottom of the dialog box.

10. Click **OK**. The function formula in B9 is =SQRT(B8).

11. Highlight **B10**.

12. Click the **Paste Function** button on the toolbar. The Paste Function dialog box opens.

13. Click **Math & Trig** in the *Function category* box if it is not selected already.

14. Click **ROUND** in the *Function name* box.

15. Click **OK**. The Formula Palette appears.

16. Enter **B9** in the *Number* box.

17. Enter **2** in the *Num_digits* box.

18. Click **OK**. The function formula in B10 is =ROUND(B9,2). Your screen should appear similar to Figure 5-2.

19. Save and leave the worksheet open for the next Step-by-Step.

FIGURE 5-2
Entering mathematical functions

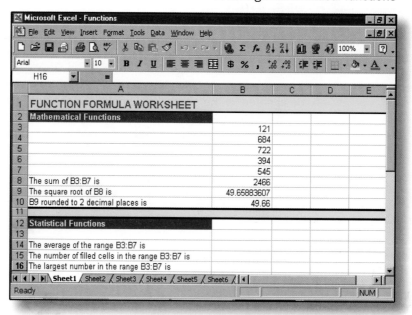

STATISTICAL FUNCTIONS

Statistical functions are used to describe large quantities of data. For example, function formulas can be used to determine the average, standard deviation, or variance of a range of data. Statistical functions can also be used to determine the number of values in a range, the largest value in a range, and the smallest value in a range. Table 5-2 shows some of the statistical functions available in Excel. Notice that all the statistical functions contain a range for the argument. The range is the body of numbers the statistics will describe.

TABLE 5-2
Statistical functions

Lesson ⑤ Function Formulas

FUNCTION	OPERATION
AVERAGE(number1,number2...)	Displays the average of the range identified in the argument. For example, =AVERAGE(E4:E9) displays the average of the numbers contained in the range E4:E9.
COUNT(value1,value2...)	Displays the number of cells with numerical values in the argument range. For example, =COUNT(D6:D21) displays 16 if all the cells in the range are filled.
MAX(number1,number2...)	Displays the largest number contained in the range identified in the argument.
MIN(number1,number2...)	Displays the smallest number contained in the range identified in the argument.
STDEV(number1,number2...)	Displays the standard deviation of the numbers contained in the range of the argument.
VAR(number1,number2...)	Displays the variance for the numbers contained in the range of the argument.

STEP-BY-STEP ▷ 5.2

1. To find the average of values in B3:B7, place the highlight in **B14**.

2. Click the **Paste Function** button on the toolbar. The Paste Function dialog box appears.

3. Click **Statistical** in the *Function category* box.

4. Click **AVERAGE** in the *Function name* box.

5. Click **OK**. The Formula Palette appears.

6. Click the **Collapse Dialog** button at the right side of the *Number1* text box.

7. Select **B3:B7** by dragging directly on the worksheet.

8. Click the **Expand Dialog** button on the right side of the formula bar.

9. Click **OK**.

10. To find the number of filled cells in B3:B7, highlight **B15**.

11. Access the Paste Function dialog box.

12. Click **Statistical** in the *Function category* box if it is not already selected, and click **COUNT** in the *Function name* box.

13. Click **OK**.

14. Enter **B3:B7** in the *Value1* box.

(continued on next page)

15. Click **OK**.

16. To find the largest number in B3:B7, highlight **B16**.

17. Enter **=MAX(B3:B7)**.

18. To find the smallest number in B3:B7, highlight **B17**.

19. Enter **=MIN(B3:B7)**.

20. To find the standard deviation of B3:B7, highlight **B18** and enter **=STDEV(B3:B7)**.

21. To find the variance of B3:B7, highlight **B19** and enter **=VAR(B3:B7)**. Your screen should look similar to Figure 5-3.

22. Save the worksheet and leave it open for the next Step-by-Step.

FIGURE 5-3
Entering statistical functions

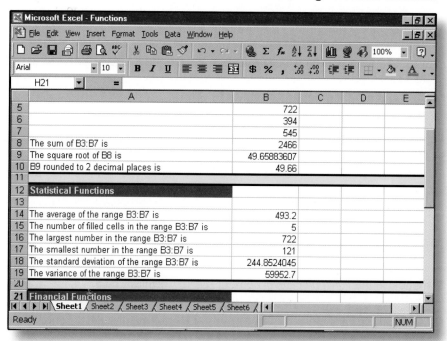

FINANCIAL FUNCTIONS

Financial functions are used to analyze loans and investments. The primary financial functions are future value, present value, and payment, which are described in Table 5-3.

TABLE 5-3

Financial functions

Lesson ⑤ Function Formulas

FUNCTION	OPERATION
FV(rate,nper,pmt,pv,type)	Displays the future value of a series of equal payments (third argument), at a fixed rate (first argument), for a specified number of periods (second argument). (The fourth and fifth arguments are optional.) For example, =FV(.08,5,100) determines the future value of five $100 payments at the end of five years if you can earn a rate of 8%.
PV(rate,nper,pmt,fv,type)	Displays the present value of a series of equal payments (third argument), at a fixed rate (first argument), for a specified number of payments (second argument). (The fourth and fifth arguments are optional.) For example, =PV(.1,5,500) displays the current value of five payments of $500 at a 10% rate.
PMT(rate,nper,pv,fv,type)	Displays the payment per period needed to repay a loan (third argument), at a specified interest rate (first argument), for a specified number of periods (second argument). (The fourth and fifth arguments are optional.) For example, =PMT(.01,36,10000) displays the monthly payment needed to repay a $10,000 loan at a 1% monthly rate (a 12% year rate divided by 12 months), for 36 months (three years divided by 12).*

* The rate and term functions should be compatible. In other words, if payments are monthly rather than annual, the annual rate should be divided by 12 to determine the monthly rate.

STEP-BY-STEP ▷ 5.3

Scenario 1: You plan to make six yearly payments of $150 into a savings account that earns 3.5% annually. Use the FV function to determine the value of the account at the end of six years.

1. Enter **.035** in **B24**. The value 3.5% appears in the cell.

2. Enter **6** in **B25**.

3. Enter **-150** in **B26**. The value $(150.00) appears in the cell. (A negative number is entered when you pay cash; positive numbers indicate that you receive cash. In this case, you are paying cash to the bank.)

4. Move the highlight to **B27** and access the Paste Function dialog box.

5. Click **Financial** in the *Function category* box and click **FV** in the *Function name* box.

6. Click **OK**.

7. Key **B24** in the *Rate* box.

8. Key **B25** in the *Nper* box.

9. Key **B26** in the *Pmt* box.

10. Click **OK**. The savings account will have grown to the amount shown in B27 after six years.

11. Save the file.

(continued on next page)

Scenario 2: You have a choice of receiving $1,200 now or eight annual payments of $210 that will be invested at your bank at 3% interest for the entire eight years. Use the PV function to determine which is the most profitable alternative.

1. Enter **.03** in **B29**.

2. Enter **8** in **B30**.

3. Enter -**210** in **B31**. (A negative number is entered when you pay cash. In this case, you are paying cash to the bank.)

4. Enter **=PV(B29,B30,B31)** in **B32**. The best decision is to take the delayed payments because the present value, $1,474.14, is greater than $1,200.

5. Save the file.

Scenario 3: You need to borrow $5,000. Your banker has offered you an annual rate of 12% interest for a five-year loan. Use the PMT function to determine what your monthly payments on the loan would be.

1. Enter **.01** in **B34**. (A 1% monthly rate [12% divided by 12 months] is used because the problem requests monthly, rather than annual, payments.)

2. Enter **60** in **B35**. (A period of 60 months [5 years times 12 months] is used because the problem requests monthly, rather than annual, payments.)

3. Enter **5000** in **B36**.

4. Enter **=PMT(B34,B35,B36)** in **B37**. The value (*$111.22*) will be red in the cell. The number is negative because you must make a payment. Under the conditions of this loan, you will pay a total of $1,673.20 ([$111.22 * 60 months]-$5,000 principal) in interest over the life of the loan.

5. Your screen should look similar to Figure 5-4.

6. Save, print, and close the file.

FIGURE 5-4
Entering financial functions

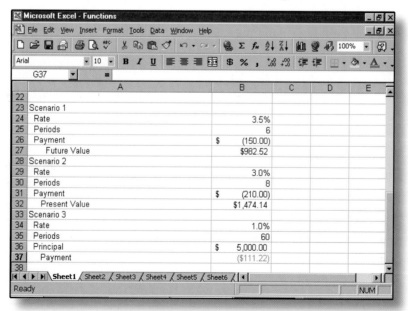

DATE, TIME, AND TEXT FUNCTIONS

Functions may also be used to insert dates and certain kinds of text into a worksheet. For example, date and time functions may be used to convert serial numbers to a month, a day, or a year. A date function may also be used to insert the current date or current time.

A text function can be used to convert text in a cell to all uppercase or lowercase letters. Text functions can also be used to repeat data contained in another cell. These functions are described in Table 5-4.

Did You Know?

Lookup (LOOKUP, VLOOKUP, HLOOKUP) and reference (AD-DRESS, COLUMN, ROW) functions may be used to find cell contents or cell locations and use them as data in another part of the worksheet. For example, you might use the LOOKUP function to display the name of a person that you have located in a worksheet by entering a Social Security number.

TABLE 5-4
Date, time, and text functions

FUNCTION	OPERATION
DATE(year,month,day)	Displays the date in a variety of formats such as *12/17/99* or *December 17, 1999*.
NOW()	Displays the current date or time based on the computer's clock. For example, =NOW() in a cell will display the current date and time, such as 5/23/01 *10:05*.
REPT(text,number_times)	Displays the text (first argument) a specified number of times (second argument). For example, REPT(B6,3) will repeat the text in cell B6 three times.

STEP-BY-STEP ▷ 5.4

1. Open **IE Step5-4** from the student data files.

2. Replace the words *NEXT YEAR* in **A1** with next year's date (such as 2001).

3. Insert today's date in **B13**. Move the highlight to **B13** and click the **Paste Function** button.

4. Click **Date & Time** in the *Function category* box.

5. Click **NOW** in the *Function name* box.

6. Click **OK**.

7. Click **OK**. The function formula *=NOW()* appears in the formula bar. The current date and time appear in B13.

8. To format the date, choose **Cells** on the **Format** menu.

9. Click the **Number** tab if it is not selected already.

10. Click **Date** in the *Category* box if it is not selected already.

11. Choose the format that displays the day in numerical form, the month in abbreviated form, followed by the last two digits of the year, such as 14-Mar-98. Click **OK**.

12. Copy the contents of **B13** to **C13**.

13. With the highlight in **C13**, choose **Cells** on the **Format** menu to insert the current time.

(continued on next page)

14. Click the **Number** tab if it is not selected already.

15. Click **Time** in the *Category* box.

16. Choose the format which displays the time in numerical form followed by either AM or PM, such as 1:30 PM, and click **OK**. The time appears in C13.

17. To repeat the text in A1 in B14, place the highlight in **B14**.

18. Access the Paste Function dialog box.

19. Click **Text** in the *Function category* box and click **REPT** in the *Function name* box.

20. Click **OK**.

21. Enter **A1** in the *Text* box, and enter **1** in the *Number_times* box.

22. Click **OK**. The title will be repeated in B14. If the title of the worksheet is changed, the text in B14 will instruct the user to rename the file.

23. Save the file under the name appearing in B14. Your screen should look similar to Figure 5-5.

24. Print and close the file.

FIGURE 5-5
Using function formulas to insert dates

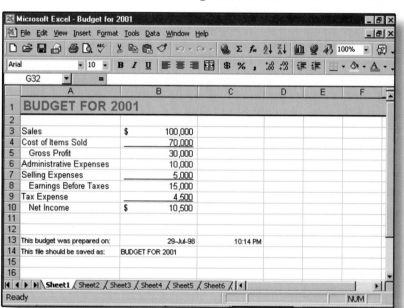

LOGICAL FUNCTIONS

Logical functions, such as the IF function, may be used to display text or values if certain conditions exist. In the IF function, the first argument sets a condition for comparison called a logical test. The second argument determines the value that will be displayed if the logical test is true. The third argument determines the value that will be displayed if the logical test if false.

For example, a teacher might use the IF function to determine whether a student has passed or failed a course. The function formula IF(C4>60,"PASS","FAIL") will display "PASS" if the value in C4 is greater then 60. The formula will display "FAIL" if the value in C4 is not greater than 60.

STEP-BY-STEP ▷ 5.5

1. Open **IE Step5-5** from the student data files, and save the file as **Optics**, followed by your initials.

2. Occidental Optics has noticed that its shipping costs have increased because retailers are asking for smaller amounts of optical solutions on a more frequent basis. To offset these costs, Occidental has decided to charge a $25 shipping fee for orders of quantities less than 5 cartons. The company decides to use an IF function to determine whether or not the fee is applied to an order. In cell **D6**, enter **=IF(B6<5,25,0)**.

3. Copy the function formula in D6 to **D7:D15**. Your screen should appear similar to Figure 5-6.

4. Save, print, and close the file.

FIGURE 5-6
Using and IF function

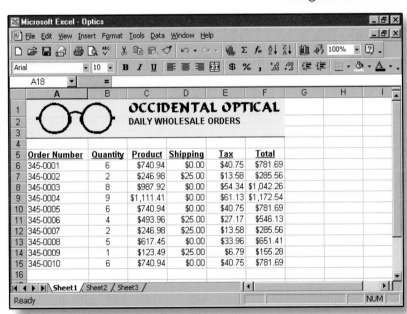

Summary

In this lesson, you learned:

■ Function formulas are special formulas that do not require operators.

■ Excel has more than 300 function formulas.

■ Function formulas may be used to perform mathematical, statistical, and financial operations.

■ Function formulas may also be used to format text and insert dates and times.

TRUE/FALSE

Circle T if the statement is true or F if the statement is false.

T **F** 1. Function formulas do not have operators.

T **F** 2. The AutoSum button creates the function formula =SUM in the highlighted cell.

T **F** 3. The SMALL function formula displays the smallest number contained in the range identified in the argument.

T **F** 4. It is necessary to use the Formula Palette to insert a function formula in a worksheet.

T **F** 5. The NOW() function will insert either the current date or current time into a spreadsheet cell.

FILL IN THE BLANKS

Complete the following sentences by writing the correct word or words in the blanks provided.

1. The _argument_ is enclosed in parentheses in a function formula.

2. The _SUM_ function formula is inserted in a cell when you click the AutoSum button.

3. The _Formula Palette_ is a dialog box in which you specify elements to be included in the function formula.

4. _Financial_ functions perform various operations, such as finding present and future values.

5. _Statistical_ functions describe large quantities of data such as the average, standard deviation, or variance of a range of data.

LESSON 5 PROJECTS

PROJECT 5-1

Write the appropriate function formula to perform each of the described operations. You may refer to Tables 5-1 through 5-3 to help you prepare the function formulas.

=MIN(1. Determine the smallest value in A4:A90.

_____ 2. Determine the standard deviation of the values in K6:K35.

_____ 3. Determine the average of the values in B9:B45.

_____ 4. Determine the yearly payments on a $5,000 loan at 8% for 10 years.

_____ 5. Determine the value of a savings account at the end of 5 years after making $400 yearly payments; the account earns 8%.

_____ 6. Round the value in C3 to the tenths place

_____ 7. Determine the present value of a pension plan that will pay you 20 yearly payments of $4,000; the current rate of return is 7.5%.

_____ 8. Determine the square root of 225.

_____ 9. Determine the variance of the values in F9:F35.

_____ 10. Add all the values in D4:D19.

_____ 11. Determine how many cells in H7:H21 are filled with data.

_____ 12. Determine the largest value in E45:E92.

PROJECT 5-2

The file *IE Project5-2* contains a worksheet of student grades for one examination.

1. Open **IE Project5-2** from the student data files.

2. Save the file as **Course Grades**, followed by your initials.

3. Determine the number of students taking the examination by entering a function formula in **B26**.

4. Determine the average exam grade by entering a function formula in **B27**.

5. Determine the highest exam grade by entering a function formula in **B28**.

6. Determine the lowest exam grade by entering a function formula in **B29**.

7. Determine the standard deviation of the exam grades by entering a function formula in **B30**.

8. Format cells **B27** and **B30** for numbers with one digit to the right of the decimal.

9. Print and close the file.

PROJECT 5-3

SCANS

   Generic National Bank makes a profit by taking money deposited by customers and lending it to others at a higher rate. In order to encourage depositing and borrowing, you have developed a worksheet that informs depositors about the future value of their investments. Another portion of the worksheet determines the yearly payments that must be made on their loans. The incomplete worksheet is in *IE Project5-3*. Complete the worksheet by following these steps:

1. Open **IE Project5-3** from the student data files.

2. Save the file as **Bank**, followed by your initials.

3. Enter a PMT function formula in **B11** that will inform borrowers of the yearly payment. Assume that the loan principal (or present value) will be entered in B5, the lending rate will be entered in B7, and the term of the loan will be entered in B9. (*#DIV/0!*, indicating an error due to division by zero, will appear in the cell because no data is in the argument cell references yet.)

4. A potential borrower inquires about the payments on a $5,500 loan for four years. The current lending rate is 11%. Determine the yearly payment on the loan. (The amount in B11 will appear as a negative because it is an amount that must be paid.)

5. Print the portion of the worksheet that pertains to the loan (A1:C14) so that it may be given to the potential borrower.

6. Enter an FV function formula in **B24** informing depositors of the future value of periodic payments. Assume the yearly payments will be entered in B18, the term of the payments will be entered in B20, and the interest rate will be entered in B22. ($0.00 will appear because no data is in the argument cell references yet.)

7. A potential depositor is starting a college fund for her son. She inquires about the value of yearly deposits of $450 at the end of 15 years. The current interest rate is 7.5%. Determine the future value of the deposits. (Remember to enter the deposit as a negative because it is an amount that must be paid.)

8. Print the portion of the worksheet that applies to the deposits (A14:C26) so that it may be given to the potential depositor.

9. Save and close the file.

PROJECT 5-4

The Tucson Coyotes have just completed seven preseason professional basketball games. Coach Patterson will soon be entering a press conference in which he is expected to talk about the team's performance for the upcoming season.

Part 1

Coach Patterson would like to be well-informed concerning player performance before entering the press conference. The file *IE Project5-4* contains scoring and rebound data for games against seven opponents. Complete the following spreadsheet so that Coach Patterson can form opinions on player performance.

1. Open **IE Project5-4** from the student data files.

2. Save the file as **Game Stats**, followed by your initials.

3. Enter a formula in **J5** that sums the values in **B5:I5**.

4. Copy the formula in **J5** to **J6:J11**.

5. Enter a formula in **J18** that sums the values in **B18:I18**.

6. Copy the formula in **J18** to **J19:J24**.

7. Enter a function formula in **B12** that averages the game points in **B5:B11**.

8. Enter a function formula in **B13** that determines the standard deviation of the game points in **B5:B11**.

9. Enter a function formula in **B14** that counts the number of entries in **B5:B11**.

10. Copy the formulas in **B12:B14** to **C12:I14**.

11. Enter a function formula in **B25** that averages the rebounds in **B18:B24**.

12. Enter a function formula in **B26** that determines the standard deviation of the rebounds in **B18:B24**.

13. Enter a function formula in **B27** that counts the number of entries made in **B18:B24**.

14. Copy the formulas in **B25:B27** to **C25:I27**.

15. Save and print the file.

Part 2

Based on the worksheet you prepared, indicate in the blanks that follow the names of the players that are likely to be mentioned in the following interview:

Reporter: You have had a very successful preseason. Three players seem to be providing the leadership needed for a winning record.

Patterson: Basketball teams win by scoring points. It's no secret that we rely on (1), (2), and (3) to get those points. All three average at least 10 points per game.

Reporter: One of those players seems to have a problem with consistency.

Patterson: (4) has his good games and his bad games. He is a young player and we have been working with him. As the season progresses, I think you will find him to be a more reliable offensive talent.

(*Hint:* One indication of consistent scoring is the standard deviation. A high standard deviation may indicate high fluctuation of points from game to game. A low standard deviation may indicate that the scoring level is relatively consistent.)

Reporter: What explains the fact that (5) is both an effective scorer and your leading rebounder?

Patterson: He is a perceptive player. When playing defense, he is constantly planning on how to get the ball back to the other side of the court.

Reporter: Preseason injuries can be heartbreaking. How has this affected the team?

Patterson: (6) has not played since being injured in the game against Kansas City. He is an asset to the team. We are still waiting to hear from the doctors on whether he will be back soon.

Reporter: It is the end of the preseason. That is usually a time when teams make cuts. Of your healthy players, (7) is the lowest scorer. Will you let him go before the beginning of the regular season?

Patterson: I don't like to speculate on cuts or trades before they are made. We'll just have to wait and see.

1. _____

2. _____

3. _____

4. _____

5. _____

6. _____

7. _____

When you have finished filling in the blanks, close the file.

CRITICAL THINKING

ACTIVITY 5-1

You are considering the purchase of a car and would like to compare prices offered by several dealerships. Some dealerships have a car that includes the accessories you desire, others will need to add the accessories for an additional price. Prepare a worksheet similar to the following format:

	A	B	C	D
1	A COMPARISON OF PRICES BY DEALERSHIP			
2				
3	Dealership	Base Price	Accessories	Total
4	Bernalillo New and Used Cars	$16,300	$500	
5	Los Alamos Auto	$15,800	$400	
6	Mountain Auto Sales	$16,000	$400	
7	Sandia Car Sales	$17,100	$120	
8	Truchas Truck and Auto	$16,500	$550	
9				
10	Highest Price			
11	Lowest Price			
12	Average Price			

Perform the following operations to provide information that will be useful to making the car purchase decision.

- Enter formulas in **D4:D8** that will add the values in column **B** to the values in column **C**.

- Enter a function formula in **D10** that will determine the highest price in **D4:D8**.

- Enter a function formula in **D11** that will determine the lowest price in **D4:D8**.

- Enter a function formula in **D12** that will determine the average price in **D4:D8**.

When you have finished, save the file as **Car Purchase**, followed by your initials, and print your results.

MAKING THE WORKSHEET USEFUL

OBJECTIVES

Upon completion of this lesson, you should be able to:

■ Insert a comment in the worksheet.

■ Apply conditional formatting.

■ Paint formats from one part of the worksheet to another.

■ Sort data in a worksheet.

■ Name a range of data.

■ Use the outline mode to view a portion of the worksheet.

■ Insert a picture in a worksheet.

Estimated Time: 2 hours

Introduction

Excel comes with a number of tools that make worksheets easier to use. You can add a comment to a cell to provide further explanation of the data contained in the cell. A range of data can be made easier to identify by giving it a name. You can summarize a large quantity of data by using the outline mode. You can also make data more illustrative by sorting it or by applying "conditional" formatting to it if it meets a specified criterion.

Inserting a Cell Comment

A *cell comment* is a message that explains or identifies information contained in the cell. For example, when abbreviations have been entered in cells, a cell comment can be used to spell out the words. In addition, comments can be used to explain the calculations in cells that contain formulas.

Cell comments are inserted by choosing Comment on the Insert menu. A comment box appears with the user name's followed by a colon. Key the comment (see Figure 6-1), and then click outside the comment box to close it. A red triangle appears in the corner of the cell to indicate that it contains a comment. To read a cell comment, point to the cell that contains it and the comment is displayed.

To edit a comment, select the cell that contains the comment and choose Edit Comment on the Insert menu. To delete a comment, choose Clear on the Edit menu and then choose Comments on the submenu.

Concept Builder

You can view all the comments at once by choosing Comments on the View menu.

FIGURE 6-1
Inserting a cell comment

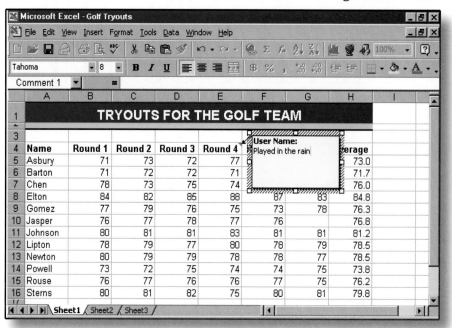

Name	Round 1	Round 2	Round 3	Round 4			erage
Asbury	71	73	72	77			73.0
Barton	71	72	72	71			71.7
Chen	78	73	75	74			76.0
Elton	84	82	85	88	87	83	84.8
Gomez	77	79	76	75	73	78	76.3
Jasper	76	77	78	77	76		76.8
Johnson	80	81	81	83	81	81	81.2
Lipton	78	79	77	80	78	79	78.5
Newton	80	79	79	78	78	77	78.5
Powell	73	72	75	74	74	75	73.8
Rouse	76	77	76	76	77	75	76.2
Sterns	80	81	82	75	80	81	79.8

STEP-BY-STEP ▷ 6.1

1. Open **IE Step6-1** from the student data files.

2. Save the worksheet as **Golf Tryouts**, followed by your initials.

3. Highlight **E4**.

4. Choose **Comment** on the **Insert** menu. The cell comment box appears.

5. Key **Played in the rain** in the cell comment box, as shown in Figure 6-1.

6. Click outside the cell comment box. A small red triangle appears in the upper right corner of the cell, indicating that the cell contains a comment.

7. Point to cell **E4** with your mouse pointer. The cell comment appears on the screen.

8. Enter the following comments in the designated cells:

Cell	Comment
F7	Includes four penalty strokes
G10	Absent due to illness
H10	Based on five rounds

9. Save and leave the worksheet on the screen for the next Step-by-Step.

Conditional Formatting

Conditional formatting applies a font, border, or pattern to a cell when certain conditions exist in that cell. For example, a businessperson may want attention brought to a number that exceeds an amount requiring approval, or to a date that indicates a passed deadline.

Conditional formats are applied by choosing Conditional Formatting on the Format menu, and then specifying the cell conditions and the format used if the conditions become true. For example, the dialog box in Figure 6-2 indicates that when the value is less than or equal to 76, the cell contents will be shaded green and bolded.

FIGURE 6-2
Conditional Formatting dialog box

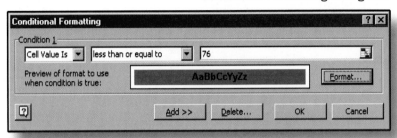

STEP-BY-STEP ▷ 6.2

The golf coach has decided that a player must average a score of less than or equal to 76 to qualify for the team. In this Step-by-Step, you indicate those who made the team by highlighting their names in green.

1. Highlight **H5**.

2. Choose **Conditional Formatting** on the Format menu. The Conditional Formatting dialog box appears.

3. In the second text box, select **less than or equal to**.

4. In the third text box key **76**.

5. Click **Format**. The Format Cells dialog box appears.

6. Click the **Font** tab if it is not already selected, and click **Bold** in the *Font style* box.

7. Click the **Patterns** tab and click a green color in the *Color* box.

8. Click **OK** to close the Format Cells box. The formats you selected will appear in the Conditional Formatting preview box. Click **OK** again to close the Conditional Formatting dialog box. The contents of H5 should appear green and bolded.

9. Save the file and leave the worksheet on the screen for the next Step-by-Step.

Painting Formats

Format painting allows you to copy the format of a worksheet cell without copying the contents of the cell. For example, after formatting one cell for a percentage, you may format other cells for a percentage by painting the format.

To paint a format, begin by highlighting a cell that has the format you prefer. Click the Format Painter button on the toolbar, and then highlight the range of cells that you would like to format.

S TEP-BY-STEP ▷ 6.3

1. Highlight **H5**.

2. Click the **Format Painter** button on the toolbar.

3. Drag from **H6** to **H16**. Your screen should look similar to Figure 6-3.

4. Save the file and leave the worksheet on the screen for the next Step-by-Step.

FIGURE 6-3
Applying conditional formats

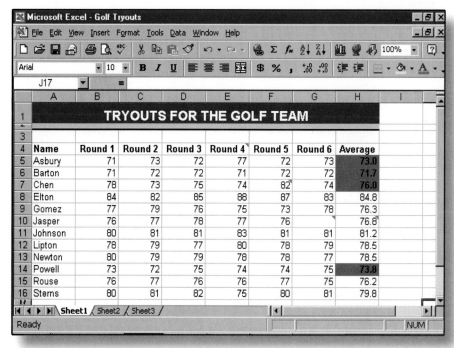

FIGURE 6-4
Sort dialog box

Sorting Data

Sorting will reorganize data to place it in an order that is more meaningful. In an ascending sort, data with letters will be in alphabetic order (A to Z) and data with numbers from lowest to highest. You may also sort in descending order in which data with letters will be sorted from Z to A and data with numbers will be sorted from highest to lowest.

If you have a column heading for data, you most likely will not want it to be sorted along with the data contained in the column. To prevent Excel from including the heading in the sort, select the *Header row* button in the Sort dialog box (see Figure 6-4).

I E - 9 2

INTRODUCTION TO MICROSOFT EXCEL

STEP-BY-STEP ▷ 6.4

1. Click **H4** to indicate that you want to sort by the data contained in column H.

2. Choose **Sort** on the **Data** menu. The Sort dialog box appears similar to Figure 6-4. *Average* should appear in the *Sort by* box.

3. Click **Ascending** if it is not already selected.

4. Click **OK**. The data will be sorted from lower to higher scores. Your screen should appear similar to Figure 6-5.

5. Click **A4** to make the Name data the new sort criterion.

6. Click the **Sort Ascending** button on the Standard toolbar. The data will be sorted alphabetically by player name.

7. Save, print, and close the file.

FIGURE 6-5
Sorting data in a worksheet

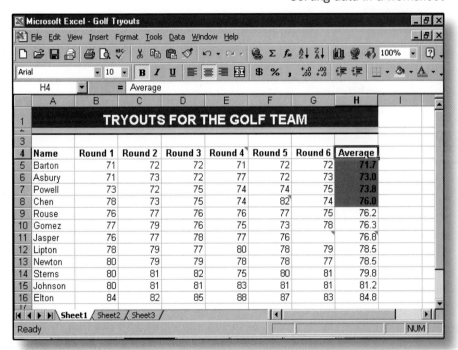

Naming a Range of Data

Ranges may be referred to by a word instead of cell addresses. If you work frequently with a range of data, it may be easier to remember a range name rather than cell references separated by a colon. For example, a range of expenses contained in B4:B28 might be named "expenses." To determine the sum of items in this range, the function formula =SUM(expenses) would display the same amount as the function formula =SUM(B4:B28).

A range is named by first selecting the range. Then enter a name in the *Name* box located to the left of the Formula bar. Whenever the range is selected, the range name appears in the *Name* box.

STEP-BY-STEP ▷ 6.5

1. Open **IE Step6-5** from the student data files.

2. Save the file as **Combustion**, followed by your initials.

3. Select **B6:B14**.

4. Enter **Jan** in the *Name* box. Your screen should appear similar to Figure 6-6.

5. Press **Enter**.

6. Enter **=SUM(Jan)** in **B15**. The sum of B6:B14 will appear.

7. Save and leave the worksheet on the screen for the next Step-by-Step.

FIGURE 6-6
Identifying a range in the *Name* box

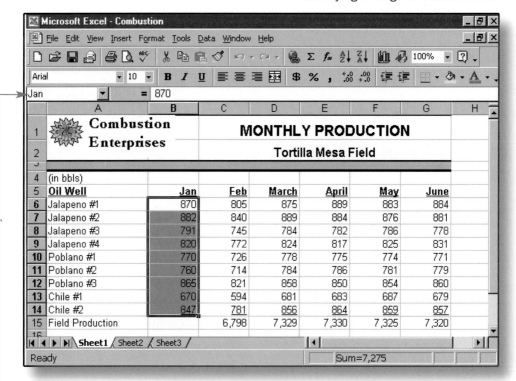

Name box

INTRODUCTION TO MICROSOFT EXCEL

Applying Outlines to a Worksheet

Outlines are useful in summarizing large worksheets. The Auto Outline command will search the worksheet for cells with formula results. It will then hide the data that determines the formula results. Only cells with titles, headings, and formula results will be displayed.

Outlines are applied by selecting the Group and Outline command on the Data menu and then selecting the Auto Outline command on the submenu. While in outline mode, the worksheet displays *detail symbols* (plus and minus signs) in the margins of the worksheet area (see Figure 6-7). To decrease the level of detail, click the minus detail symbol. The rows or columns used in formula calculations will be hidden (as shown in Figure 6-8).

To increase the level of detail, click the plus detail symbol. To exit the outline mode, select Clear Outline from the Group and Outline command on the Data menu.

 Hot Tip

You may also temporarily remove a row or column from the screen by hiding it. To hide a selected row or column, select either **Row** or **Column** on the **Format** menu, and then click **Hide** on the submenu. To redisplay a hidden row, select cells in the row above or below the hidden row, open the **Format** menu, select **Row**, and click **Unhide** on the submenu. To display a hidden column, select cells in the column to the left or to the right of the hidden column, open the **Format** menu, select **Column**, and click **Unhide** on the submenu.

FIGURE 6-7

Detail symbols displayed in outline mode

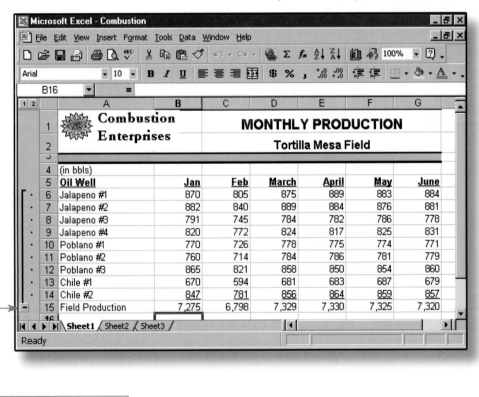

Click to decrease detail level

FIGURE 6-8
Decreasing the level of detail displayed

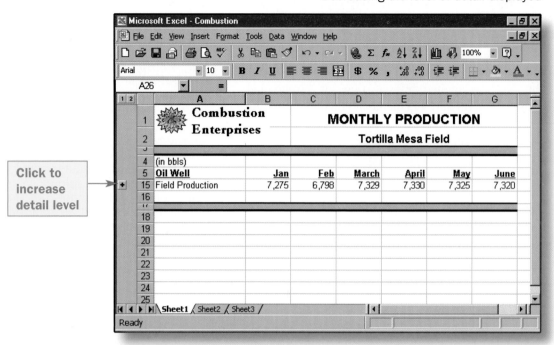

Click to
increase
detail level

STEP-BY-STEP ▷ 6.6

1. Choose the **Group and Outline** command on the **Data** menu, and then select **Auto Outline** on the submenu. Your screen should appear similar to Figure 6-7.

2. Click the minus sign in the margin on the left side of the screen. Excel will hide rows 6 through 14 because they are used to determine the amounts in row 15. Your screen should appear similar to Figure 6-8.

3. Click the plus sign in the margin on the left side of the screen. Rows 6 through 14 will reappear.

4. Choose **Group and Outline** on the **Data** menu, and then select **Clear Outline** on the submenu.

5. Save, print, and close the file.

Creating Links between Worksheets in a Workbook

You may remember that the worksheet you are working with is just one of a collection of worksheets contained in workbook. The worksheets in a workbook are indicated by tabs at the bottom of a screen (with default titles of Sheet1, Sheet2, etc.).

In some cases you may need several worksheets to solve one numerical problem. For example, in a business that has several divisions, you may want to keep the financial results of each division on a separate worksheet. Then, on a separate worksheet, you might want to combine the results of each division to show the combined results of all divisions.

To use data from one worksheet in another worksheet of a workbook, select the destination cell and then enter an = (or click the = button on the formula bar). Then, click the sheet tab that contains the source data you would like to link, select the cell, or range of cells, and press Enter. The data will then be linked to the destination sheet. Any changes to the source data will also change the value in the destination cell.

Insert and Delete Worksheets

Worksheets may be added to or deleted from a workbook. To insert a worksheet, click the tab of the worksheet that will *follow* the new sheet. Then click Worksheet on the Insert menu. A new worksheet will be inserted before the sheet you selected.

To delete a worksheet, click any cell in the worksheet and then click Delete Sheet on the Edit menu. Click OK to confirm the deletion. You can also *right*-click on any tab and select Insert or Delete on the shortcut menu.

S TEP-BY-STEP ▷ 6.7

1. Open **IE Step6-7** from the student data files. Notice that the sheet tabs indicate separate worksheets entitled *Western* and *Eastern*. Save the workbook as **Corporate Sales**, followed by your initials.

2. Click the sheet tab **Sheet3**. This worksheet will summarize the sales that appear on the Western and Eastern worksheets.

3. *Right*-click the **Sheet3** tab and then click **Rename** on the shortcut menu.

4. Key **Corporate**, and then press **Enter**. The word "Corporate" will appear on the third tab.

5. Select cell **B3** and enter **=**.

6. Click the **Western** tab.

7. Select cell **B6**. The cell address preceded by the sheet name, *=Western!B6* appears in the formula bar.

8. Press **Enter**. You are returned to the Corporate sheet, and $543,367 will appear in B3.

9. Select cell **B4**, and enter **=**.

10. Click the **Eastern** tab.

11. Select cell **B6**. The cell address *=Eastern!B6* appears in the formula bar.

12. Press **Enter**. Your screen should appear similar to Figure 6-9.

13. The company anticipates adding a Northern Division. Click the **Eastern** tab.

14. Click **Worksheet** on the **Insert** menu. A tab named *Sheet1* will appear.

15. *Right*-click the **Sheet1** tab and then click **Rename** on the shortcut menu.

16. Key **Northern**, and then press **Enter**.

17. Save the file. Print the **Corporate** sheet, and then close the file.

FIGURE 6-9
Linking data on a summary worksheet

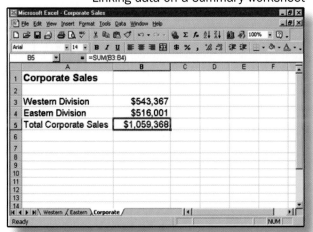

Inserting a Picture in a Worksheet

You may want to change the appearance of a worksheet by adding a picture. For example, some corporations like to include their corporate logo on the worksheet. In addition, pictures are sometimes added to illustrate data contained in a worksheet. For instance, you might want to insert a smile in a worksheet that indicates good financial results (see Figure 6-10).

FIGURE 6-10
Pictures improve worksheet appearance

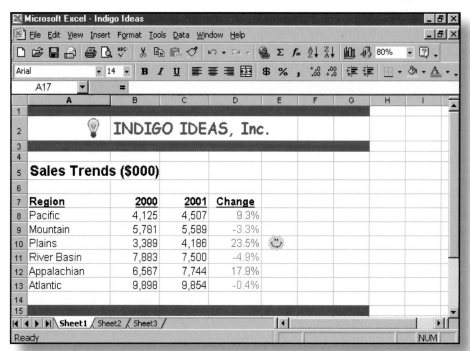

FIGURE 6-11
Insert ClipArt dialog box

You may insert a picture from the Clip Art Gallery in the Office software or from a file that contains a picture. To insert a picture from the Clip Art Gallery, select Picture on the Insert menu, and then select Clip Art on the submenu. The Insert ClipArt dialog box opens, similar to Figure 6-11. Make a clip art selection from one of the categories.

You insert a picture from a file by selecting Picture on the Insert menu, and then selecting From File.

STEP-BY-STEP ▷ 6.8

1. Open **IE Step6-8** from the student data files, and save it as **Botany**, followed by your initials.

2. Choose **Picture** on the **Insert** menu, and then select **From File** on the submenu. The Insert Picture dialog box appears.

3. Choose **Rose** from the student data files.

4. Click the **Insert** button. Your screen should appear similar to Figure 6-12.

5. Scroll down so that the lower sizing handles on the picture are visible.

6. Drag the middle lower sizing handle upward until the dark line at the bottom of row 6 is visible.

7. Drag the middle right sizing handle to the left until the edge of the picture is at the right side of column A. Your screen should appear similar to Figure 6-13.

8. Save the file and leave it open for the next Step-by-Step.

FIGURE 6-12
Inserting a picture

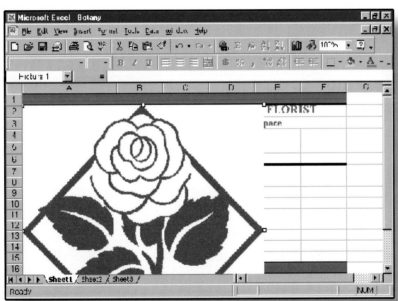

(continued on next page)

FIGURE 6-13
Picture size is changed by dragging the sizing handles

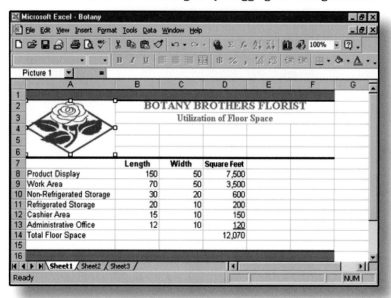

Editing a Picture

Once a picture has been inserted in a worksheet, you may move it or edit it to fit your needs. Many of the edit functions are contained on the Picture toolbar (see Figure 6-14), which can be displayed by right-clicking on the toolbar and selecting Picture. Table 6-1 explains methods for editing pictures.

FIGURE 6-14
Picture toolbar

TABLE 6-1
Editing pictures

ACTION	SELECT THE PICTURE AND THEN:
Move the picture	Drag it to the desired position.
Restore the picture to its original format	Click the Restore button on the Picture toolbar.
Resize the picture	Drag the sizing handles on the sides of the picture.
Crop the picture (trim the edges)	Click the Crop button on the toolbar and then drag the sizing handles.
Change the brightness of the picture	Click the More Brightness or Less Brightness button on the Picture toolbar.
Change the contrast of the picture	Click the Increase Contrast or Decrease Contrast button on the Picture toolbar.
Make a color in the picture transparent	Click the Set Transparent Color button on the Picture toolbar, and then click a color in the picture.

STEP-BY-STEP ▷ 6.9

1. If the Picture toolbar is not already displayed, *right*-click on the toolbar and then click **Picture**.

2. Click the **Set Transparent Color** button on the Picture toolbar. The cursor will change to the set transparent color icon.

3. Click on a white part of the picture. You will now be able to see the gridlines of the work-sheet behind the picture.

4. Click the **More Brightness** button on the Picture toolbar five times. The picture will change from a maroon to a pink color.

5. Close the Picture toolbar.

6. Save, print, and close the file.

Inserting Hyperlinks to Files and Web Pages

You can insert hyperlinks in a worksheet that "jump" to other files or Web pages on the Internet. For example, you may want to create a link to another Excel file that contains the source data for information used in your current worksheet. You may also want to create a link to a Web page that contains information that relates to items contained in the worksheet.

To create a hyperlink, first select text or a graphic. Then, right-click the item and select Hyperlink on the shortcut menu. When the Insert Hyperlink dialog box appears, key the filename or Web page address into the *Type the file or Web page name* text box. After you click OK, you will be returned to the spreadsheet and the pointer will appear as a pointed finger when it is passed over the linked item.

If you create a hyperlink to a file, that file will be opened when the text or graphic is clicked in the worksheet. If you create a hyperlink to a Web page, that page will be opened in your browser when you click the text or graphic that has been linked.

Summary

In this lesson, you learned:

- Cell comments provide messages that explain the contents of a cell. They are designated by a red triangle in the upper right corner of the cell.

- Conditional formatting will cause a cell or range to change font, borders, or patterns when specific mathematical or logical conditions exist in that cell.

- Format painting will copy the format of a cell to other cells without copying the contents of the cell.

- Data in a worksheet may be sorted in alphabetic or numeric order.

- Ranges of data may be referred to by a name rather than cell references.

- Large worksheets may be outlined to summarize the data.

LESSON 6 REVIEW QUESTIONS

TRUE/FALSE

Circle T if the statement is true or F if the statement is false.

T **F** 1. Cell comments can be seen in the worksheet at all times.

T **F** 2. The Comment command is located on the Tools menu.

T F 3. Cells with comments are identified with a small red triangle in the upper right corner of the cell.

T **F** 4. The Format Painter button on the toolbar is represented by a clipboard.

T **F** 5. When sorting, the worksheet is always ordered with the smallest values listed first.

FILL IN THE BLANKS

Complete the following sentences by writing the correct word or words in the blanks provided.

1. _Conditional formatting_ will bold the contents of a cell if the value exceeds a certain amount.

2. A message that explains or identifies data contained in a cell, but does not appear in the cell, is a _Cell comment_ .

3. Cell comments appear when the _highlight_ is placed on the worksheet cell.

4. Cell formats can be copied without copying cell content by a process called _format painting_ .

5. When a large worksheet contains formula results, the data may be summarized by using the _Group Outline_ command on the Data menu.

LESSON 6 PROJECTS

PROJECT 6-1

The file *IE Project6-1* contains the salaries and annual ratings of Level 10 employees for Impact Corporation. Level 10 employees are currently paid between $30,000 and $35,000 per year. However, the management is concerned that salaries within that range do not relate to the level of performance of the individuals.

Part 1

In this part, you will sort the data by the employee's annual rating. Then you will indicate the following three salary categories using conditional formatting:

Salary Range	Conditional Format
$30,000 to $31,666	Yellow
$31,667 to $33,333	Red
$33,334 to $35,000	Blue

1. Open **IE Project6-1** from the student data files.

2. Save the file as **Impact**, followed by your initials.

3. Sort the data in **A6:E20** by the **Annual Rating** in descending numerical order.

4. Highlight **D6**.

5. Choose **Conditional Formatting** on the **Format** menu.

6. In the second text box of *Condition 1*, select **between** if it is not already selected.

7. Key **30,000** in the third text box, and **31,666** in the fourth text box.

8. Format *Condition 1* with a yellow color.

9. Begin *Condition 2* by clicking **Add >>**.

10. In the second text box of *Condition 2*, select **between** if it is not already selected.

11. Key **31,667** in the third text box, and **33,333** in the fourth text box.

12. Format *Condition 2* with a red color.

13. Begin *Condition 3* by clicking **Add >>**.

14. In the second text box of *Condition 3*, select **between** if it is not already selected.

15. Key **33,334** in the third text box, and **35,000** in the fourth text box.

16. Format *Condition 3* with a blue color.

17. Exit the Conditional Formatting dialog box.

18. Paint the format in **D6** to **D7:D20**.

19. Save the file.

Part 2

If salaries are allocated based on annual ratings, those with higher ratings should appear near the top of the worksheet and have salaries formatted in blue. Those with lower ratings should appear near the bottom of the worksheet and have salaries formatted in yellow. When a salary does not reflect their annual rating, the color format of the employee may appear to be out of place.

Based on the worksheet you have prepared, determine which employees you believe are currently underpaid. Then insert your recommended salary in a comment for the cell that contains the current salary. Save, print, and close the file when you have completed the project.

PROJECT 6-2

The file *IE Project6-2* contains the top 100 grossing American films. The films are currently in alphabetical order by film name.

Part 1

Column D of *IE Project6-2* contains the number of dollars that the film grossed. Column E shows the amounts in column D in today's dollars (adjusted for inflation). Determine the most successful film in history by sorting the data.

1. Open **IE Project6-2** from the student data files.

2. Save the file as **Movies**, followed by your initials.

3. Sort the data in descending order by the **Gross Adjusted for Inflation** data.

4. Save and print the file.

Part 2

Suppose you would like to rent videotapes of successful movies that have been released in the last few years. Re-sort the data to show the most recently released movies at the top of the worksheet.

1. Sort the data by **Release Date** in descending order.

2. Save, print, and close the file.

PROJECT 6-3

You have worked for Xanthan Gum, Corp. for several years and been informed that you are now eligible for promotion. Promotions at Xanthan are determined by supervisor ratings and a written examination. To be promoted, you must score an average of 80 or above in four categories:

- Supervisor rating of leadership potential
- Supervisor rating of understanding of duties
- Supervisor rating of willingness to work hard
- Written test score

After receiving your supervisor ratings, you decide to prepare a spreadsheet to determine the minimum written test score needed for promotion.

1. Open **IE Project6-3** from the student data files.

2. Save the file as **Xanthan**, followed by your initials.

3. In cell **B6**, enter **70** as the supervisor rating; in **B7**, enter **85**; and in **B8**, enter **80**.

4. Enter a formula in **B11** that determines the average of the values in **B6:B9**.

5. Format **B11** for a number with zero places to the right of the decimal.

6. Format **B11** for the following conditions:

Condition	Format
B11 is less than 80	The pattern of B11 is red
B11 is greater than or equal to 80	The pattern of B11 is green

7. Enter the following possible test scores in **B9**: **75**, **80**, **85**, **90**, **95**. Which ones will result in a promotion?

8. Save, print, and close the file, showing the minimum test score you'll need to get in order to be promoted.

PROJECT 6-4

An employee of Paper Container Products would like to view the spreadsheet of the company's quarterly sales without the detail of each geographic region and each quarter.

1. Open **IE Project6-4** from the student data files.

2. Save the file as **Paper**, followed by your initials.

3. Use the Auto Outline command to convert the worksheet to outline mode.

4. Hide the quarterly information by clicking the minus sign above the column letters at the top of the worksheet.

5. Restore the quarterly data by clicking the plus sign at the top of the worksheet.

6. Hide the regional data by clicking the minus sign at the left of the worksheet.

7. Print the summarized worksheet.

8. Restore the regional data by clicking the plus sign at the left of the worksheet.

9. Use the **Clear Outline** command to exit the outline mode.

10. Save and close the file.

CRITICAL THINKING

SCANS

ACTIVITY 6-1

A manufacturing company prepares a budget each month. At the end of the month a report that compares the actual amount spent to the budgeted amount is prepared.

	A	B	C	D
1	**Manufacturing Expense Report**			
2		Budgeted Amount	Actual Amount	Budget Variance
3	Labor Expense	$54,000	$55,500	-$1,500
4	Raw Material A Expense	$45,000	$44,000	$1,000
5	Raw Material B Expense	$31,000	$32,000	-$1,000
6	Overhead Expense	$100,000	$95,000	$5,000
7				

How could conditional formatting be used to give emphasis to conditions in which the budget has been exceeded?

WORKING WITH OTHER SOFTWARE TOOLS

OBJECTIVES

Upon completion of this lesson, you should be able to:

- Move and copy data between applications.
- Link data from other applications.
- Use the Drawing tools to enhance a worksheet.
- Save a worksheet as a Web page.

⏱ **Estimated Time: 2 hours**

Integrating Data Between Applications

You have already learned how easy it is to move and copy data among documents created in any one of the Office applications using the Cut, Copy, and Paste commands. The process of copying and pasting data between applications is similar to copying and pasting data within an application. Office makes the process easy by adjusting the format of the data being copied to fit the application where it is being pasted.

Word to Excel

Suppose you want to place data from a Word table in an Excel worksheet in order to perform calculations on the data. Office lets you integrate information from a word processing file with an Excel worksheet in one of two ways:

1. If the text from Word is set up as a table or with data separated by tabs, Excel will place the text in separate cells in the worksheet.

2. If the text is in a single block, all of the text will be pasted into the currently highlighted cell of the worksheet.

STEP-BY-STEP ▷ 7.1

1. Open a new blank worksheet.

2. Start Word; then, open the **IE Step7-1** document from the student data files.

3. Click anywhere in the table of the Word document.

(continued on next page)

4. Choose **Select** on the **Table** menu, and then select **Table** on the submenu. Your screen should appear similar to Figure 7-1.

5. Click the **Copy** button.

6. Click the **Microsoft Excel** button on the taskbar to switch to Excel.

7. Click the **Paste** button.

8. Adjust the column widths and row heights so that the worksheet looks similar to Figure 7-2.

9. Save the worksheet as **Large Corps**, followed by your initials.

10. Print the worksheet, and then close the file.

11. Close **IE Step7-1** in Word.

FIGURE 7-1
Copying a table from a Word document to an Excel worksheet

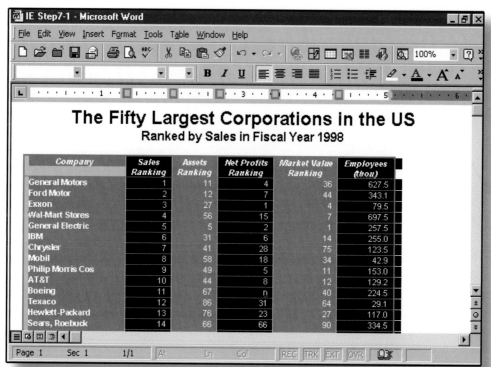

FIGURE 7-2
Excel accommodates both content and formats from other software tools

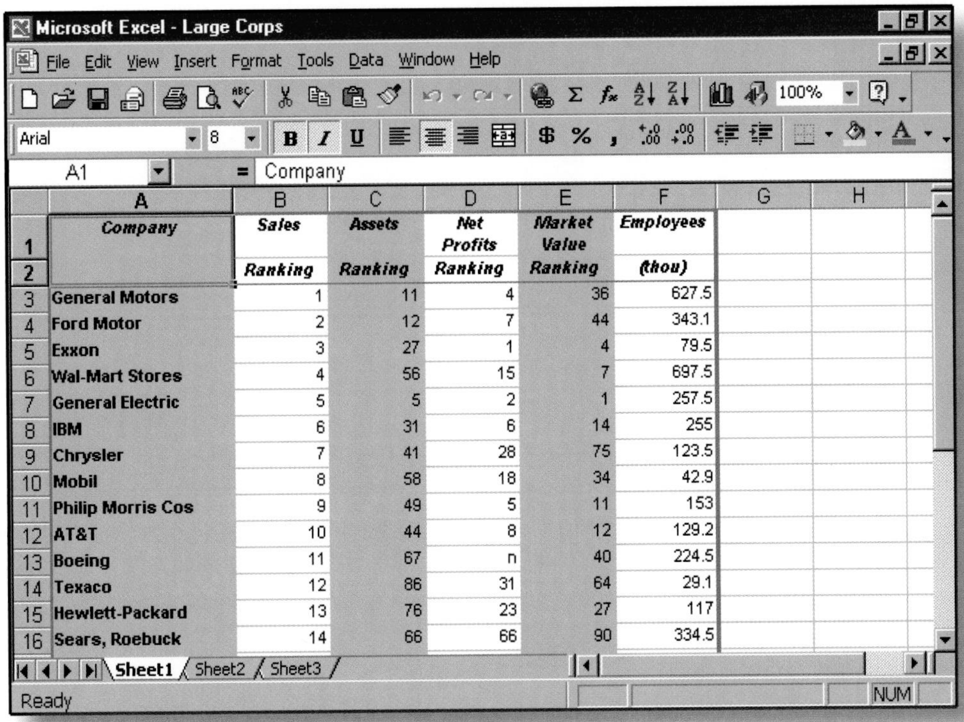

Company	Sales Ranking	Assets Ranking	Net Profits Ranking	Market Value Ranking	Employees (thou)
General Motors	1	11	4	36	627.5
Ford Motor	2	12	7	44	343.1
Exxon	3	27	1	4	79.5
Wal-Mart Stores	4	56	15	7	697.5
General Electric	5	5	2	1	257.5
IBM	6	31	6	14	255
Chrysler	7	41	28	75	123.5
Mobil	8	58	18	34	42.9
Philip Morris Cos	9	49	5	11	153
AT&T	10	44	8	12	129.2
Boeing	11	67	n	40	224.5
Texaco	12	86	31	64	29.1
Hewlett-Packard	13	76	23	27	117
Sears, Roebuck	14	66	66	90	334.5

Did You Know?

You can open files created in other applications, such as LOTUS 1-2-3, dBASE, and Quattro Pro, in Excel. After editing the file, you may either save the file in its original format or as an Excel file. To save in a specific format, select **Save As** on the **File** menu. Then, select the file format type from the *Save as type* drop-down list box.

Excel to Word

Another common integration operation is to paste numbers from a worksheet into a word processing document. When Excel data is copied to Word, Word automatically places it in a table.

1. Open Word; then, open the **IE Step7-2** Word document from the student data files.

2. In Excel, open the **IE Step7-2** workbook from the student data files. If necessary, increase the window size so the entire document is visible.

3. Highlight the range **A1:D7**. Your screen should appear similar to Figure 7-3.

4. Click the **Copy** button on the toolbar.

5. Click the **Microsoft Word** button on the taskbar to switch to Word.

6. Place the insertion point between the first and second paragraphs.

7. Click the **Paste** button on the toolbar. The data from the worksheet appears in the letter.

8. Save the letter as **Insurance Letter**, followed by your initials. Your screen should appear similar to Figure 7-4.

9. Print the **Insurance Letter** document, and then close it.

10. Switch to Excel and save the file as **Insurance Rates**, followed by your initials. (If a Summary Info dialog box appears, click **OK** to continue the save process.) Leave the worksheet on the screen for the next Step-by-Step.

FIGURE 7-3
Copying worksheet data to a Word document

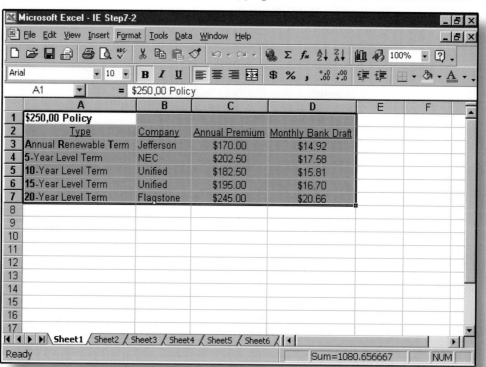

FIGURE 7-4

Word places Excel data in a table

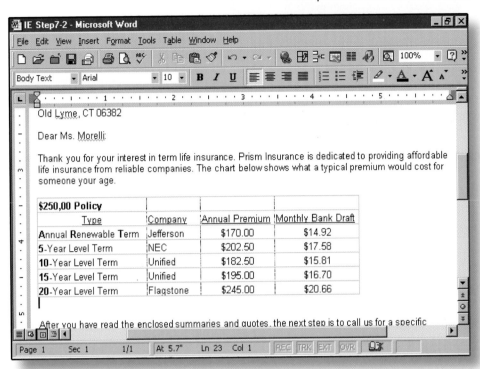

$250,00 Policy			
Type	Company	Annual Premium	Monthly Bank Draft
Annual Renewable Term	Jefferson	$170.00	$14.92
5-Year Level Term	NEC	$202.50	$17.58
10-Year Level Term	Unified	$182.50	$15.81
15-Year Level Term	Unified	$195.00	$16.70
20-Year Level Term	Flagstone	$245.00	$20.66

Linking Data

Some spreadsheets are updated periodically. For example, suppose you are the treasurer of an organization that files a monthly financial report. Your report is basically the same each month except for the month's cash flow (money received and spent) numbers. Each month you update the cash flow data in an Excel worksheet to reflect the monthly activities. Then you report the data by pasting it into a Word document.

You can avoid copying and pasting the data each month by a process called *linking*. In this process, data changed on the original file, known as a *source* file, is automatically updated in the file to which it is copied, known as the *destination* file. Linking is performed by using the Paste Special command. When you link data, the information you insert in the destination document is connected to information in the source file. The linked data is not actually part of the destination file, but contains a description of where the application in which the destination file was created should go to find the data. Then, each time changes are made and saved to the source document, the changes are reflected in the destination document when it is opened.

Figure 7-5 shows the Paste Special dialog box that appears when data from an Excel worksheet is pasted into a Word document using the Paste Special command. The *Paste Link* option places the worksheet data into the document and creates the link to the actual worksheet.

FIGURE 7-5

Paste Special dialog box

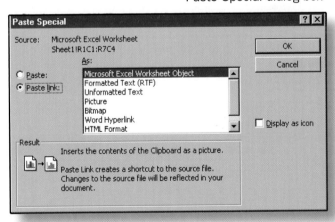

1. In Word, open **IE Step7-3** from the student data files.

2. Save the document as **Insurance Letter 2**, followed by your initials.

3. Switch to **Insurance Rates** in Excel.

4. Select **A1:D7**, if it is not already selected.

5. Click the **Copy** button.

6. Switch to Word. Place the insertion point between the first and second paragraphs.

7. Choose **Paste Special** on the **Edit** menu. The Paste Special dialog box appears.

8. Click **Paste link**.

9. Click **Microsoft Excel Worksheet Object** in the **As** box. The Paste Special dialog box should look similar to Figure 7-5.

10. Click **OK**. The worksheet data appears in the Word document. The data is linked to *Insurance Rates*. Any changes made to *Insurance Rates* will be reflected in *Insurance Letter 2*.

11. Save and print **Insurance Letter 2**.

12. Switch to Excel and leave **Insurance Rates** on the screen for the next Step-by-Step.

UPDATING A LINK

Excel data in a linked Word document will be automatically updated every time a destination file is opened.

If you do not want links to be changed automatically, you may change the destination to be updated manually. On the Edit menu, select Links. In the Links dialog box, click *Manual* from the *Update* options (see Figure 7-6). When you are ready to update, select Links on the Edit menu and then click Update Now.

FIGURE 7-6
Links dialog box

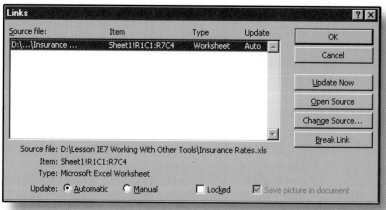

S TEP-BY-STEP ▷ 7.4

1. The *Insurance Rates* Excel file should be open on the screen. Change the cost of the annual premium in **C3** to **$175** for the Annual Renewable Term, and **$188.50** in **C5** for the 10-Year Level Term. The monthly bank draft amounts for those two types of policies will change automatically.

2. Save **Insurance Rates**.

3. Switch to **Insurance Letter 2** in Word.

4. Select **Links** on the **Edit** menu, and click the **Update Now** button. Click **OK** to close the Links dialog box. Notice that the annual premium and monthly bank draft costs (money deducted from a bank account automatically) in *Insurance Letter 2* are now updated.

5. Save, print, and close **Insurance Letter 2**.

6. Switch to Excel and close **Insurance Rates**.

Using Draw in the Worksheet

The Drawing tools in Excel can be used to insert lines and objects that help make a worksheet more informative. For example, you might use a text box to explain a value in the worksheet. Or, you might use an object such as a rectangle or circle to create a corporate logo.

The Drawing toolbar is accessed by clicking the Drawing button on the Standard toolbar. The Drawing toolbar normally appears near the bottom of the screen.

S TEP-BY-STEP ▷ 7.5

1. Open **IE Step7-5** from the student data files.

2. Save the file as **Oil Production**, followed by your initials.

3. Click the **Drawing** button on the Standard toolbar. The Drawing toolbar appears near the bottom of the screen.

4. Click the **Text Box** button on the Drawing toolbar. The highlight turns into a ⊥.

5. Drag from **E18** to **G20**. A text box appears.

6. Key **Bad weather caused February production to be low.** in the text box.

7. Click the **3-D** button on the Drawing toolbar. A pop-up menu appears.

8. Click the upper left three-dimensional box that appears in the pop-up menu.

9. Click the **Arrow** button on the Drawing toolbar. The highlight turns into a +.

10. Drag from the left side of the text box to the contents of **C15**. Your screen should appear similar to Figure 7-7.

11. Save the file and leave it on the screen for the next Step-by-Step.

 Did You Know?

You can modify or delete lines and 3-D objects you have created in an Excel worksheet. To delete a line or object, click on it, and then press Delete. To change or modify a line or object, click on it, and then modify your line or select a new 3-D object by clicking the line, arrow, or 3-D button on the Drawing toolbar.

(continued on next page)

FIGURE 7-7
Using the Drawing tools

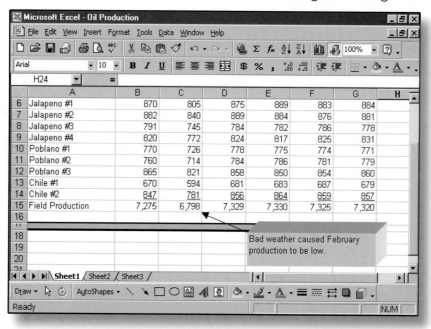

Editing Objects with Draw

Once objects have been created using the Drawing tools, they may be changed. In most cases, changes can be made by clicking on the object and then using a button on the Formatting or Drawing toolbars.

STEP-BY-STEP ⟹ 7.6

1. Click the arrow that points to C15. Handles appear at the ends of the arrow.

2. Click the **Line Style** button on the Drawing toolbar. A submenu with different line thicknesses appears. Your screen should appear similar to Figure 7-8.

3. Click the **1¹/₂** point line. The line thickness of the arrow will become thicker.

4. Click inside the 3-D box you created earlier. Handles will appear at each corner and side.

5. Click the **Shadow** button on the Drawing toolbar. A menu similar to the one in Figure 7-9 appears.

6. Click **Shadow Style 6** on the menu. The box

will change from a 3-D box to a rectangle with a shadow along the lower right sides.

7. Select the text within the shadowed box.

8. Click the **Bold** button on the Formatting toolbar.

9. Click the down arrow to the right of the **Font Color** button on the Drawing toolbar, then click the orange-colored box. When you have finished, your screen should appear similar to Figure 7-10.

10. Click the **Drawing** button on the Standard toolbar to hide the Drawing toolbar.

11. Save and then print the file. Leave it on the screen for the next Step-by-Step.

FIGURE 7-8
Line Style button options

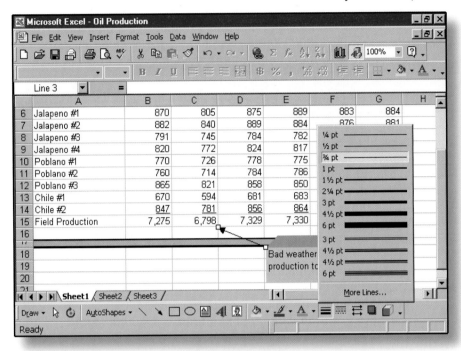

FIGURE 7-9
Shadow options on the Drawing toolbar

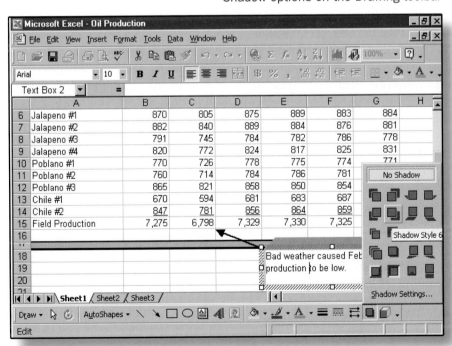

(continued on next page)

FIGURE 7-10
Editing objects

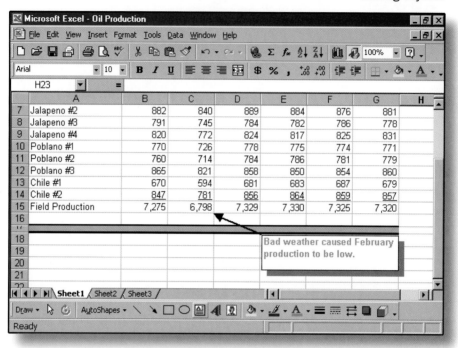

Using Worksheets on the Web

In some cases, you may want to share worksheet information with others. You can share Excel worksheet data on the Internet if you save the worksheet in HyperText Markup Language (HTML) format. HTML is easily viewed in popular Internet browsers, such as Internet Explorer and Netscape Navigator.

By previewing, you can see how your worksheet will appear as a Web page. Choose Web Page Preview on the File menu. When you have finished previewing the Web page, close your browser window and edit your worksheet as needed.

STEP-BY-STEP ▷ 7.7

1. Choose **Web Page Preview** on the **File** menu. After a few moments, Internet Explorer will open and the worksheet will appear as a Web page.

2. Close Explorer and return to the worksheet.

3. Choose **Save as Web Page** on the **File** menu. The Save As dialog box similar to Figure 7-11 appears. Notice that *Web Page* appears in the *Save as type* box.

4. In the *File name* box, enter **OP Web Page**, followed by your initials.

5. Click **Save**. You will be returned to the Excel spreadsheet.

6. Launch your Explorer by clicking the **Launch Internet Explorer Browser** in the Quick Launch toolbar.

7. In Explorer, choose **Open** on the **File** menu. The Open dialog box of Explorer appears, similar to Figure 7-12.

8. In the text box, enter the path for **OP Web Page**.

9. Click **OK**. Your screen should appear similar to Figure 7-13.

10. Print **OP Web Page** from your Internet browser, and then exit your browser.

11. Save and close the worksheet file.

 Did You Know?

If you can't remember the exact path of a file, you can use the Browse button in the Open dialog box of Internet Explorer. When you click the Browse button and select a folder, all files in that folder are displayed. Simply select the specific file you wish to open.

FIGURE 7-11
Saving a worksheet in HTML format

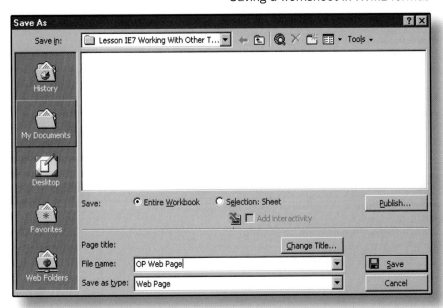

FIGURE 7-12
Open dialog box of Explorer

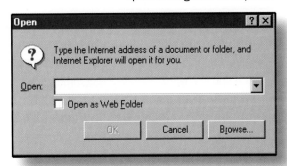

(continued on next page)

FIGURE 7-13
Placing an Excel worksheet on a Web page

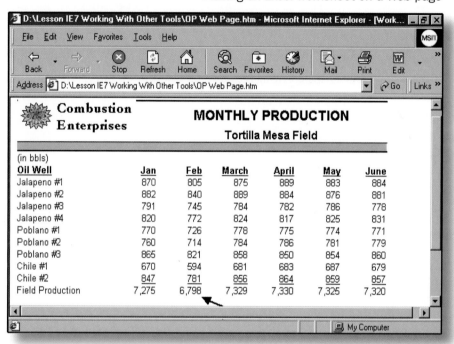

Checking Spelling on a Worksheet

Excel has a dictionary tool that will check the spelling of words on a worksheet. Excel uses the same dictionary that is available in Microsoft Word. To spell-check a worksheet, select the Spelling command on the Tools menu, or click the Spelling button on the Formatting toolbar.

STEP-BY-STEP ⟹ 7.8

1. Open **IE Step7-8** from the student data files, and save it as **Euro**, followed by your initials.

2. Click the **Spelling** button on the Formatting toolbar. The Spelling dialog box appears. The Spelling tool has correctly identified *Austia* as a misspelled word and has offered several suggestions for change.

3. Click **Austria** in the Suggestions box. Then, click **Change**. The Spelling tool will correct the change and move to the next word that is misspelled.

4. Click **Finland**, and then click **Change**.

5. Next, the Spelling tool has identified *Markka* as a misspelled word. However, *Markka* is the correct spelling of the Finnish currency. (The term was incorrectly identified because it is not a commonly used English word.)

6. Click **Ignore**. A dialog box indicating that the spelling check is complete appears. Click **OK**.

7. Save and print the file. Leave the file on screen for the next Step-by-Step.

Sending a Workbook as Email

If you have electronic mail capability, you can send an Excel workbook in an email message. Excel workbooks may be sent in one of two ways: The workbook can be sent in the body of an email message, or it can be sent as an attachment file to an email message.

STEP-BY-STEP ▷ 7.9

1. Click the **E-mail** button on the Standard toolbar.

2. If you are asked, click **Send single sheet as a message body**. An email form will appear with Euro.xls in the subject box, similar to Figure 7-14.

3. Enter an email address in the *To:* box.

4. Click **Send this Sheet**.

5. Close the file without saving.

Extra Challenge

The Euro file contains the permanent conversion rates for the 11 countries participating in the common European currency, the Euro. Open the file you saved as Euro and try entering amounts in the local currency (column C) to find out how many Euros may be obtained when converting currency. When you have finished, close the file without saving it.

FIGURE 7-14
Emailing a worksheet

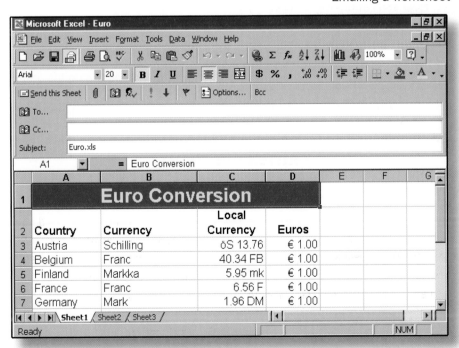

Summary

In this lesson, you learned:

■ Office pastes Word information that is separated by tabs into individual Excel worksheet cells. Text in a single block is pasted into the currently highlighted cell of the worksheet. Excel data that is copied to a Word document is automatically placed in a table.

■ Excel data can be linked to a Word document using the Paste Special command. The document is automatically updated with changes made to the spreadsheet.

■ You can use the Drawing tools to create lines and objects in a worksheet.

■ A worksheet may be saved as a Web page for use on the Internet.

LESSON 7 REVIEW QUESTIONS

TRUE/FALSE

Circle T if the statement is true or F if the statement is false.

T F 1. A common integration operation is to paste numbers from a worksheet into a Word document.

T F 2. When copying text from Word that is set up as a table, Excel will place the text in separate cells in the worksheet.

T F 3. Linking is performed by using the Copy Special command.

T F 4. The Drawing toolbar is accessed by clicking the Drawing button on the Standard toolbar.

T F 5. Excel worksheets must be saved as a Web page before they can be viewed on the Internet.

WRITTEN QUESTIONS

Write a brief answer to the following questions.

1. What is the advantage of linking data?

When the source file is changed, linked data in the destination file will change also. Linked data does not need to be updated in the destination file

2. What selections should you make in the Paste Special dialog box to link Excel data in a Word document?

Click the Paste Link button + designate Microsoft Excel Worksheet Object in the AS Box

3. The file that accepts linked data from a source file is referred to as what kind of file?

destination file

4. What types of objects may be created in an Excel file by using the Drawing toolbar?

Lines, arrows, metaghs, ovals or free-form items

5. When saving an Excel file as a Web page, the worksheet data will be converted to what file format?

to Hyper-Text Markup Language (HTML)

LESSON 7 PROJECTS

PROJECT 7-1

Chemical Solutions, Inc. orders catalyst liquids from American Catalyst Supplies once a month. To reduce paperwork, the company would like to link data that is periodically updated on an Excel worksheet to a letter created in Word in which they outline the order for catalyst liquids.

1. If necessary, start Word, and open the **IE Project7-1** Word document from the student data files.

2. Save the file as **Reorder Letter**, followed by your initials.

3. If necessary, start Excel, and open the **IE Project7-1** workbook from the student data files.

4. Save the file as **Raw Material**, followed by your initials.

5. Select **A3:D6** and click the **Copy** button on the Standard toolbar.

6. Switch to Word and place the insertion point between the first and second paragraphs.

7. Paste an updatable link in the Word document.

8. Switch to Excel and change the quantity in **B4** to **16**, **B5** to **13**, and **B6** to **20**.

9. Save **Raw Material**.

10. Switch to Word. The quantities and total cost should be updated.

11. Save and print the **Reorder Letter**. Then, close both files.

PROJECT 7-2

Skyline Skate Rink has established a Web site to advertise its services. Its pricing structure is stored on an Excel worksheet. The rink's manager would like to save the information as a Web page so that it may be placed on the Internet.

1. Open **IE Project7-2** from the student data files.

2. Save the file as **Skate Rink**, followed by your initials.

3. Save the file as a Web page entitled **Price Web Page**.

4. Open Internet Explorer and view *Price Web Page*.

5. Print the Web page from your Internet browser.

6. Close your Internet browser, and close **Skate Rink**.

CRITICAL THINKING

ACTIVITY 7-1

SCANS

You have created an Excel worksheet that will be used by several other people. Certain parts of the spreadsheet are complicated and may not be understood by all worksheet users.

You know that all worksheet users have access to the Internet, and you would like to create a convenient way for them to contact you if they have any questions about the worksheet. Specifically, you would like to insert a link to your e-mail address.

Use the Help system to find information on how to create a hyperlink to an e-mail address in a worksheet. In Microsoft Word, write a brief explanation outlining the steps required to create such a hyperlink.

WORKSHEET CHARTS

OBJECTIVES

Upon completion of this lesson, you should be able to:

- Identify the purpose of charting worksheet data.

- Identify the types of worksheet charts.

- Create a chart sheet and save a chart.

- Switch between charts and worksheets, zoom, and rename a chart.

- Preview and print a chart.

- Create an embedded chart.

- Edit a chart and change the type of chart.

⏱ **Estimated Time: 2.5 hours**

What Is a Worksheet Chart?

A *chart* is a graphical representation of data contained in a worksheet. Charts make the data of a worksheet easier to understand. For example, the worksheet in Figure 8-1 shows the populations of four major American cities for three years. You may be able to detect the changes in the populations by carefully examining the worksheet. However, the increases and decreases in the populations of each city are easier to see when the contents of the worksheet are illustrated in a chart, such as the one shown in Figure 8-2.

Types of Worksheet Charts

In this lesson, you will create four of the most commonly used worksheet charts: column chart, line chart, pie chart, and scatter chart. These charts, and several other types of charts, are illustrated in Figure 8-3.

COLUMN CHART

A *column chart* uses bars of varying heights to illustrate values in a worksheet and is useful for showing relationships among categories of data. For example, the column chart in Figure 8-2 has one vertical column to show the population of a city for each of three years and shows how the population of one city compares to populations of other cities.

FIGURE 8-1

Worksheet data that's well-suited for illustration in a chart

	A	B	C	D
1	**CITY POPULATIONS**			
2				
3	(in thousands)			
4		**1970**	**1980**	**1990**
5	Boston	641	563	574
6	Dallas	844	905	1007
7	Phoenix	584	790	983
8	St. Louis	622	453	397

FIGURE 8-2

Using a chart to illustrate the relationships among data

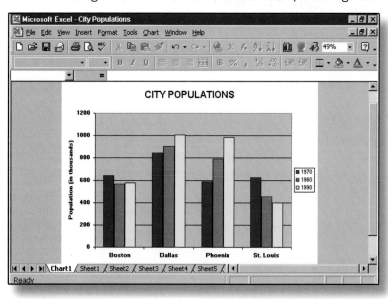

FIGURE 8-3

Charts available in Excel

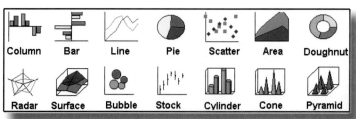

LINE CHART

A *line chart* is similar to the column chart except columns are replaced by points connected by a line. The line chart is ideal for illustrating trends over time. For example, Figure 8-4 is a line chart that shows the growth of the U.S. federal debt from 1984 to 1998. The vertical axis represents the level of the debt and the horizontal axis shows the years. The line chart makes it easy to see how the federal debt has grown over time.

PIE CHART

Pie charts show the relationship of a part to a whole. Each part is shown as a "slice" of the pie. For example, a teacher could create a pie chart of the distribution of grades in a class, as shown in Figure 8-5. Each slice represents the portion of grades given for each letter grade.

SCATTER CHART

Scatter charts, sometimes called XY charts, show the relationship between two categories of data. One category is represented on the vertical (Y) axis, and the other category is represented on the horizontal (X) axis. It is not practical to connect the data points with a line because points on a scatter chart usually do not relate to each other, as they do in a line chart. For example, the scatter chart in Figure 8-6 shows a data point for each of 12 individuals based on their height and weight. In most cases, a tall person tends to be heavier than a short person. However, because some people are tall and skinny, and others are short and stocky, the relationship between height and weight cannot be represented by a line.

Did You Know?

Businesses often use column, bar, and line charts to illustrate growth over several periods. For example, the changes in yearly production or income over a 10-year period can be shown easily in a column chart.

Did You Know?

Businesses often use pie charts to indicate the magnitude of expenses in comparison to other expenses. Pie charts are also used to illustrate the company's market share in comparison to its competitors.

FIGURE 8-4
Line chart is ideal for illustrating trends of data over time

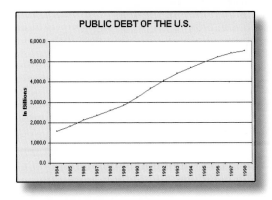

FIGURE 8-5
Each "slice" of a pie chart represents part of a larger group

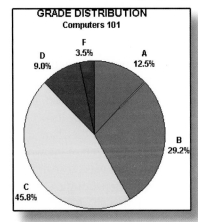

Creating a Chart from a Worksheet

You can create and display charts in two ways: by placing the chart on a chart sheet or by embedding the chart in the worksheet. A *chart sheet* is a separate sheet in the workbook on which you can create and store a chart. You can name the chart sheet to identify its contents and access it by clicking its tab. Use a chart sheet when it is inconvenient to have the chart and data on the same screen or when you plan to create more than one chart from the same data.

An *embedded chart* is created within the worksheet. The primary advantage of an embedded chart is that it may be viewed at the same time as the data from which it is created. When you print the worksheet, the chart will be printed on the same page.

CREATING A CHART ON A CHART SHEET

Create a new chart sheet by first highlighting the data from the worksheet that is to be included in the chart. Then, choose Chart on the Insert menu. The *Chart Wizard*, an on-screen guide that helps you prepare a chart, appears. The Chart Wizard presents four steps for preparing a chart:

FIGURE 8-6

Scatter charts show the relationship between two categories of data

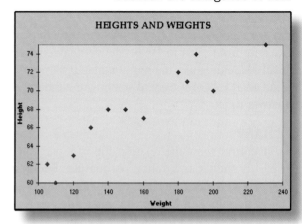

- **Step 1, Select the Chart Type**—Select a type of chart, such as column, line, or pie.

- **Step 2, Chart Source Data**—Confirm the range of data to be included in the chart. The range should also include the textual data that you plan to use as labels in the chart. You may also designate whether there is more than one series of data to be charted. A *data series* is a group of related information in a column or row of a worksheet that will be plotted on a chart.

- **Step 3, Chart Options**—Designate the characteristics of the chart. The parts of a worksheet chart are identified in Figure 8-7. Table 8-1 describes the chart options that are specified under a separate tab in the Step 3 dialog box of the Chart Wizard.

- **Step 4, Chart Location**—Specify whether the chart will be embedded within the worksheet or appear on a separate sheet. When you create a chart on a separate sheet, it is identified by a name on a tab that appears near the bottom of the screen. The tab of the chart appears directly to the left of the tab of the worksheet from which the chart was created. If you do not name the chart in Step 4 of the Chart Wizard, Excel names the first chart sheet *Chart1*. If additional charts are created from the worksheet, they become *Chart2*, *Chart3*, and so on.

Hot Tip

To determine the part of a chart, place the mouse pointer on that area. The name of the chart part will appear near the pointer.

Hot Tip

You can change options you selected in previous steps of the Chart Wizard by clicking the Back button at the bottom of the dialog box.

After you have completed these steps, a chart appears on screen.

FIGURE 8-7
Parts of a worksheet chart

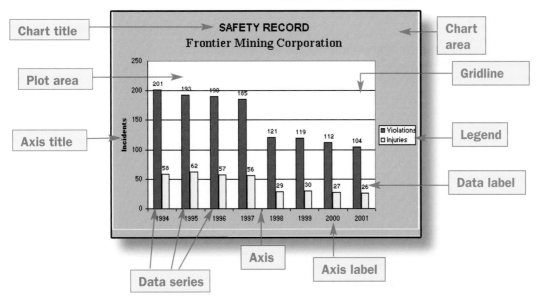

TABLE 8-1
Characteristics related to chart options

CHART OPTION TAB	OPTION FUNCTION
Titles	Headings that identify the contents of the chart or the axes in the chart; most charts have a chart title and titles for each axis
Axes	Lines that establish a relationship between data in a chart; most charts have a horizontal or X axis and a vertical or Y axis
Gridlines	Lines through a chart that relate the data in a chart to the axes
Legend	List that identifies patterns or symbols used in a chart
Data Labels	Text or numbers that identify the values depicted by the chart objects directly on the chart
Data Table	Data series values displayed in a grid below the chart

S TEP-BY-STEP ▷ 8.1

1. Open **IE Step8-1** from the student data files. Column A contains educational levels and Column B contains the median incomes of those with that level of education.

2. Select the range **A3:B8**. The highlighted items are the data to be included in the chart that you will create.

(continued on next page)

3. Choose **Chart** on the **Insert** menu. The Step 1 of 4 Chart Wizard dialog box opens, as shown in Figure 8-8.

4. Click **Column** in the *Chart type* list, if it is not already selected.

5. From the *Chart sub-type* options, click the first chart sub-type box if it is not already selected. The description will identify the selected chart as a "Clustered Column. Compares values across categories."

6. Preview the chart you are about to create by clicking and holding the **Click and Hold to View Sample** button.

7. Click **Next**. The Step 2 of 4 Chart Wizard dialog box appears. In this dialog box, Excel has created a sample chart.

8. Click **Next**. The Step 3 of 4 dialog box appears. The tabs at the top of the dialog box indicate options that may be changed in the chart.

9. Click the **Titles** tab if it is not selected already.

10. Key **YOUR EDUCATION PAYS** in the *Chart title* text box.

11. Key **Education Level** in the *Category (X) axis* text box.

12. Key **Median Income** in the *Value (Y) axis* text box. As you enter the titles, they will appear in the sample chart area on the right side of the dialog box. When you finish, the dialog box should appear similar to Figure 8-9.

13. Click the **Legend** tab.

14. Click the **Show legend** text box until no check mark appears in the box. This chart uses only one series of data and does not need a legend to distinguish among data.

15. Click **Next**. The Step 4 of 4 Chart Wizard dialog box appears.

16. Click **As new sheet**.

17. Enter **Column** in the text box. The dialog box should look similar to Figure 8-10.

18. Click **Finish**. Your screen displays a chart sheet with the chart you created. Near the bottom of the page, a sheet tab titled *Column* appears. The chart should appear similar to Figure 8-11. Leave the file open for the next Step-by-Step.

FIGURE 8-8
Step 1 of the Chart Wizard

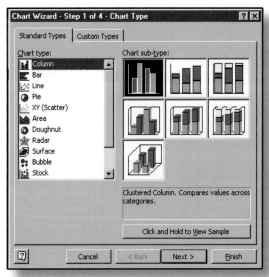

FIGURE 8-9
Enter chart titles on the Titles tab

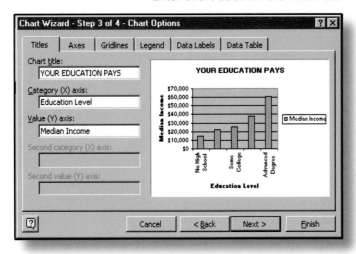

FIGURE 8-10
Step 4 of the Chart Wizard

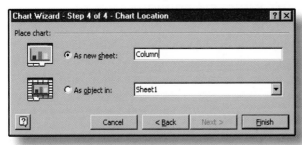

FIGURE 8-11
Finished chart sheet

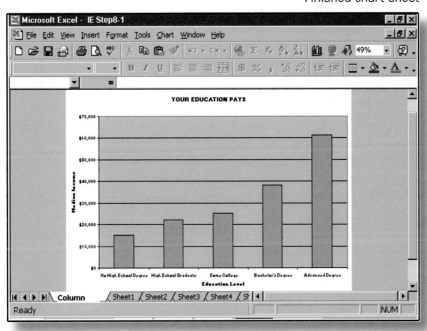

The chart illustrates the value of education in attaining higher income. Notice that the columns get higher on the right side of the chart, indicating that those who stay in school will be rewarded with higher incomes.

Excel may also display the Chart toolbar which contains buttons that are useful in editing a chart. As you work more with charts you may want to use these buttons. If you do not want the Chart toolbar displayed, you can close it.

SAVING A CHART

A chart is considered part of a workbook. When you save the workbook, you will also save the charts you have created. Save the worksheet and its chart(s) by choosing Save on the File menu. It does not matter if you are on the worksheet containing the data or the chart sheet.

STEP-BY-STEP ▷ 8.2

1. Choose **Save As** on the **File** menu.

2. Save the file as **Education Pays**, followed by

your initials. Leave the file open for the next Step-by-Step.

SWITCHING BETWEEN CHART SHEETS AND WORKSHEETS

A chart sheet is closely related to the worksheet from which it is created. If you change the data in a worksheet, these changes will automatically be made in the chart created from the worksheet.

To return to the worksheet from which a chart was created, click the tab of the worksheet. The chart may be accessed once again by clicking the sheet tab with the chart name on it.

ZOOM COMMAND

You can use the Zoom command on the View menu to enlarge a chart sheet or worksheet to see it in greater detail, or reduce it to see more on your screen. You can use the preset zoom settings or key in your own between 10% and 400% of the actual size. When you choose the Fit Selection option, the sheet will automatically be sized to fit the screen. You can choose the Zoom command from the View menu or click the Zoom box on the toolbar.

STEP-BY-STEP ▷ 8.3

1. Click the **Sheet1** tab near the bottom of the screen. The worksheet appears.

2. Edit the contents of **A5** to be **High School Degree**.

3. Click the **Column** sheet tab. The chart sheet appears. The label for the second column has changed.

4. To see the labels more closely, click the down arrow

on the Zoom button. Click **75%**. Scroll to view all areas of the chart.

5. To reduce the sheet to fit the screen, choose **Zoom** on the **View** menu. The Zoom dialog box appears.

6. Click **Fit selection** from the *Magnification* options. Click **OK**.

7. Save and leave the file on the screen for the next Step-by-Step.

RENAMING A CHART SHEET

Renaming a chart sheet is particularly useful after you have prepared several charts from one worksheet. These charts may become difficult to distinguish by their chart sheet number and are easier to recognize with more descriptive names. Change the name of the chart sheet by choosing the Sheet command on the Format menu and choosing Rename on the submenu. You may also change the name of the sheet by right-clicking the sheet tab and then clicking Rename on the shortcut menu.

Hot Tip

You may delete chart sheets that are no longer needed by right-clicking the chart sheet tab, and clicking Delete on the shortcut menu.

STEP-BY-STEP ▷ 8.4

1. Right-click the **Column** sheet tab.

2. Click **Rename** on the shortcut menu.

3. Key **Income Chart** on the sheet tab.

4. Click outside the sheet tab.

5. Save and leave the file on the screen for the next Step-by-Step.

Previewing and Printing a Chart

You preview and print a chart the same way you do a worksheet. You can click the Print Preview button to preview the sheet. You click the Print button to send the sheet directly to the printer.

STEP-BY-STEP ▷ 8.5

1. Click the **Print Preview** button. The chart appears in the preview window.

2. Click the **Print** button in the Print Preview window.

3. Click **OK**.

4. Save and close the file.

Creating an Embedded Chart

An embedded chart appears within a worksheet rather than on a separate sheet. An embedded chart is created in the same way as a chart on a sheet with one exception. In the last step of the Chart Wizard (step 4), you will click the *As object in* button rather than the *As new sheet* button, as shown in Figure 8-10.

In the next Step-by-Step, you will embed a pie chart in a worksheet. Pie charts compare items within one group to other items within the same group. For example, in a group of pet owners, you can show what percent own dogs, cats, or fish. Pie

Concept Builder

Embedded charts are useful when you want to print a chart next to the data the chart illustrates. When a chart will be displayed or printed without the data used to create the chart, a separate chart sheet is usually more appropriate.

charts differ from column or line charts because they use only one series of numeric data. In the column chart you created, you selected two columns of data to compare the level of education to median incomes. To create a pie chart, select a column of data, and then choose the Chart command on the Insert menu.

Because embedded charts are displayed directly on the worksheet, there is the possibility that they can interfere with other worksheet data by covering it or by appearing in an area that is inconvenient for printing. You can move an embedded chart by dragging it to a different part of the worksheet. You can also change the size of an embedded chart by dragging the *image handles*, which are small black squares that appear at the corners and sides of an embedded chart.

STEP-BY-STEP ▷ 8.6

Great Plains Grains is a company that sells a variety of agricultural products. The managers would like to determine which products comprise the largest portion of their sales by illustrating the segment sales in a pie chart.

1. Open **IE Step8-6** from the student data files.

2. Save the file as **Segment Sales**, followed by your initials.

3. Select the range **A7:B10**.

4. Choose **Chart** on the **Insert** menu.

5. Click the **Pie** chart type.

6. Click the chart sub-type in the upper left portion of the *chart sub-type* section, if it is not already selected. The description will identify the selected chart as a "Pie.

Displays the contribution of each value to a total."

7. Click **Next**. The Step 2 Chart Wizard dialog box appears.

8. Click **Next**. The Step 3 Chart Wizard dialog box appears.

9. Click the **Titles** tab if it is not selected already.

10. Key **Annual Sales by Segment** in the *Chart title* text box.

11. Click the **Legend** tab.

12. Make sure the **Show Legend** box is *not* checked.

13. Click the **Data Labels** tab.

14. Click the **Show label and percent** button.

FIGURE 8-12
Creating an embedded pie chart

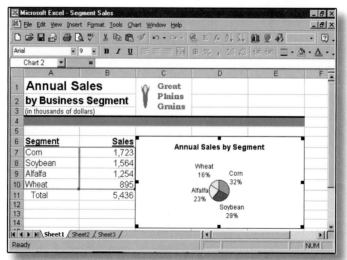

15. Click **Next**. The Step 4 Chart Wizard dialog box appears.

16. Click **As object in** if it is not already selected.

17. Click **Finish**.

Creating Other Types of Charts

In previous Step-by-Steps you created a column chart and pie chart. Now you will learn to create a three-dimensional chart and a scatter chart.

THREE-DIMENSIONAL CHARTS

Excel allows you to make charts look as though they are three-dimensional. Area, bar, column, cone, cylinder, line, surface, pie, and pyramid charts are available in three-dimensional formats.

18. Use the image handles to fit the chart within **C5:E14**. Your screen should look similar to Figure 8-12.

19. Print the file and leave the worksheet on your screen for the next Step-by-Step.

 Hot Tip

You may print the chart with or without the worksheet data you used to create the chart. To print the chart only, select the chart by clicking on it, and then choose Print on the File menu. To print the chart and the worksheet data, deselect the chart by clicking outside of it, and then choose Print on the File menu.

STEP-BY-STEP ▷ 8.7

1. Save the file as **Segment Sales 3D**, followed by your initials.

2. Right-click the white space in the pie chart embedded in the worksheet. A shortcut menu appears.

3. Choose **Chart Type** on the menu. The Chart Type dialog box appears.

4. Click the middle chart in the top row of the

chart sub-type area. The chart description "Pie with a 3-D visual effect" appears at the bottom of the dialog box.

5. Click **OK**. You are returned to the worksheet. Your screen should look similar to Figure 8-13.

6. Click outside the chart to deselect the chart.

7. Save, print, and then close the worksheet.

FIGURE 8-13
3-D pie chart

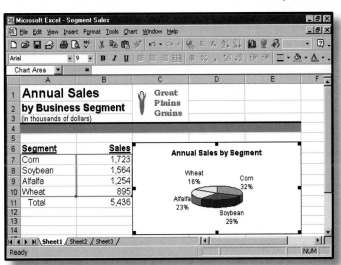

SCATTER CHARTS

Scatter charts are sometimes referred to as *XY charts* because they place data points between an X and Y axis. Scatter charts might be harder to prepare because you must designate which data should be used as a scale on each axis.

STEP-BY-STEP ▷ 8.8

Coronado Foundries produces manufactured goods. During the manufacturing process, a certain amount of scrap will be produced. Management expects that as more goods are produced, more scrap will also be produced. They would like to produce a chart to illustrate the expected relationship.

1. Open **IE Step8-8** from the student data files.

2. Save the file as **Scrap Report**, followed by your initials.

3. Select the range **B6:C16**.

4. Choose **Chart** on the **Insert** menu. The Step 1 Chart Wizard dialog box appears.

5. Click the chart type **XY (Scatter)**.

6. Click the first chart sub-type if it is not already selected. The description will identify the selected chart as a "Scatter. Compares pairs of values."

7. Click **Next**. The Step 2 Chart Wizard dialog box appears.

8. Click **Next**. The Step 3 Chart Wizard dialog box appears.

9. Click the **Titles** tab if it is not selected already.

10. Key **Production and Scrap Report** in the *Chart title* box.

11. Key **Units of Production** in the *Value (X) axis* box.

12. Key **Units of Scrap** in the *Value (Y) axis* box.

13. Click the **Legend** tab.

14. Make sure the **Show Legend** box is not checked.

15. Click **Next**. The Step 4 Chart Wizard dialog box appears.

16. Click **As new sheet** if it is not already selected.

17. Key **Scatter Chart** in the *As new sheet* text box.

18. Click **Finish**. A scatter chart appears on a chart sheet. You may be able to tell that factories with larger production also tend to generate more scrap. Notice that the data points are concentrated in the right portion of the chart. To spread the data out, you may adjust the scale of the chart.

19. To adjust the X axis to the left, double-click the X (horizontal) axis. The Format Axis dialog box appears.

20. Click the **Scale** tab.

21. Key **4000** in the *Minimum* box.

22. Click **OK**. The portion of the chart to the left of 4000 on the X axis, which did not have any data points, has been removed.

23. To adjust the Y axis downward, double-click the Y (vertical) axis. The Format Axis dialog box appears.

24. Click the **Scale** tab if it is not already chosen.

25. Enter **250** in the *Maximum* box.

26. Click **OK**. The portion of the chart above 250 has been removed. The chart sheet on your screen should look similar to Figure 8-14.

27. Save, print, and close the file.

FIGURE 8-14
Scatter charts can show labeled points between two axes

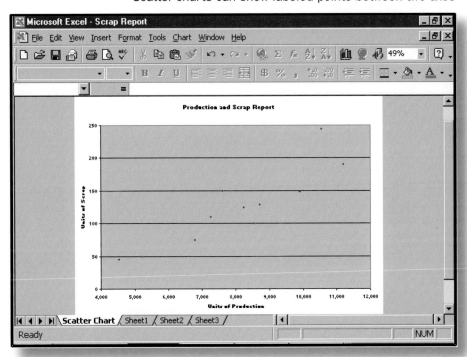

Editing a Chart

The Chart Wizard creates charts in a way that may be useful to many Excel users. However, you may want to edit the chart to suit your specific needs. For example, you may want to change a title font or the color of a column. Figure 8-15 shows six areas of the chart and some of the characteristics that may be changed. Clicking with the left mouse button selects the chart part. Double-clicking with the left mouse button produces one of the dialog boxes identified in Table 8-2. Within the dialog box, you can access tabbed areas to edit specific chart characteristics. Clicking the right mouse button produces a shortcut menu with options such as clearing data, inserting data, or changing chart types.

FIGURE 8-15
Six parts of the chart

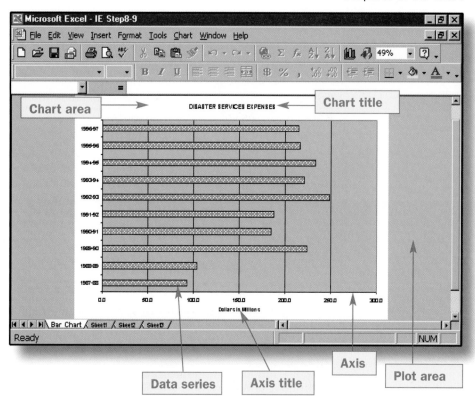

TABLE 8-2
Charts may be edited using one of six Format dialog boxes

FORMAT DIALOG BOX	TABBED AREAS OF THE DIALOG BOX
Format Chart Title	Patterns – designates the border and color of the chart title
	Font – designates the font, font size, and color of characters in the chart title
	Alignment – designates the justification and orientation of the chart title
Format Axis Title	Patterns – designates the border and color of the axis title
	Font – designates the font and font size of characters in the axis title
	Alignment – designates the justification and orientation of the axis title
Format Axis	Patterns – designates the border and color of the axis
	Scale – designates characteristics of the axis scale
	Font – designates the font and font size of characters in the axis
	Number – designates the format of numbers in the labels in the axis (for example, currency, text, date)
	Alignment – designates the orientation of the labels in the axis

TABLE 8-2
(continued)

FORMAT DIALOG BOX	TABBED AREAS OF THE DIALOG BOX
Format Data Series	Patterns – designates the border and color of the data series
	Axis – designates whether the data is plotted on a primary or secondary axis
	Y Error Bars – designates the treatment of points that extend beyond the scale of the chart
	Data Labels – designates the words or values that may appear on the points of a graph
	Series Order – designates which data series will appear first in clustered charts
	Options – designates the other characteristics unique to the chart type
Format Plot Area	Patterns – designates the border and color of the plot area
Format Chart Area	Patterns – designates the border and color of the chart background
	Font – designates the font and font size of characters in the chart area

STEP-BY-STEP ▷ 8.9

1. Open **IE Step8-9** from the student data files. This is a worksheet containing the disaster services expenses of the American Red Cross.

2. Save the file as **Red Cross**, followed by your initials.

3. Click the **Bar Chart** sheet tab. The sheet contains a chart that indicates the level of disaster services expense for each period.

4. To add a subtitle, click the chart title **DISASTER SERVICES EXPENSES**. A shaded border with handles surrounds the title.

5. Click to the right of the last S in the title. An insertion point appears.

6. Press **Enter**. The insertion point becomes centered under the first line of the title.

7. Key **American Red Cross**. The subtitle appears in the chart.

8. To change the font size of the horizontal axis labels, double-click the horizontal axis. The Format Axis dialog box appears.

9. Click the **Font** tab. The axis labels are currently 10 point.

10. Choose **12** in the *Size* box.

11. Click **OK**. You are returned to the chart sheet. The horizontal axis labels are now larger.

12. To change the color of the bars, double-click one of the bars. The Format Data Series dialog box appears.

13. Click the **Patterns** tab if it is not already selected.

(continued on next page)

14. Click any bright red in the *Area* box. A bright red color appears in the *Sample* box.

15. Click **OK**. You are returned to the chart sheet. The chart appears with bright red bars. Your

screen should appear similar to Figure 8-16. Leave the chart sheet on the screen for the next Step-by-Step.

FIGURE 8-16
Modifying parts of the chart

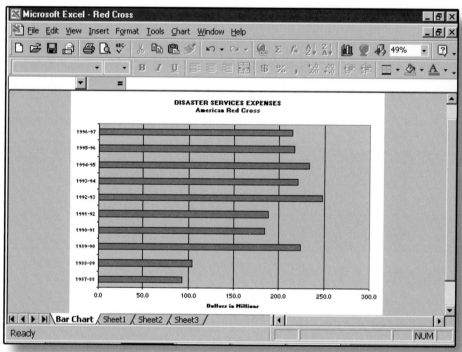

Changing the Type of Chart

After creating a chart, you can change it to a different type by choosing the Chart Type command on the Chart menu (or by clicking the chart area or plot area with the *right* mouse button and then choosing the Chart Type command). The Chart Type dialog box is the same dialog box that appears in the Step 1 Chart Wizard dialog box (see Figure 8-8).

Concept Builder

Not all charts are interchangeable. For example, data that is suitable for a pie chart is often not logical in a scatter chart. However, most line charts are easily converted into column or bar charts.

1. Choose **Chart Type** on the **Chart** menu.

2. Click **Line** in the *Chart type* box.

3. Click the middle box in the first column of the *Chart sub-type* box if it is not already selected. The description will identify the selected chart as a "Line with markers displayed at each data value."

4. Click **OK**. The new line chart appears similar to Figure 8-17.

5. Rename the chart sheet as **Line Chart**.

6. Save, print, and close the file.

Extra Challenge

Convert the line chart you just created into a column chart. Save the file as *Red Cross Column*.

FIGURE 8-17
Changing a column chart into a line chart

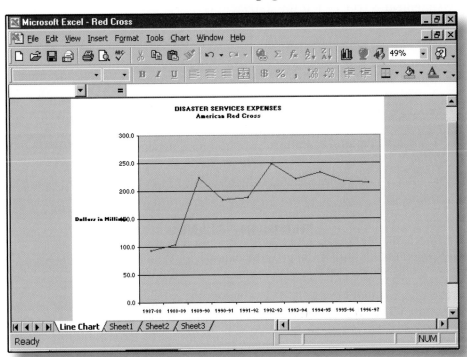

Summary

In this lesson, you learned:

■ A chart is a graphical representation of worksheet data. You can create several types of worksheet charts, including column charts, line charts, pie charts, and scatter charts. Several types of charts can also be created three-dimensionally.

- Charts may be embedded within a worksheet or created on a chart sheet. A chart sheet is an area separate from the Excel worksheet in which a chart is created and stored. An embedded chart is created within a worksheet.

- The Chart Wizard is a four-step, on-screen guide that helps you prepare a chart from an Excel worksheet. The Chart Wizard is used to prepare a chart whether the chart is to appear in the worksheet or in a chart sheet.

- A chart created from a worksheet is considered part of that worksheet. When you save the worksheet, you will also save the charts you have created from the worksheet.

- You can edit your chart by clicking one of six areas of the chart that accesses a Format dialog box. You can change the type of chart in the Chart Type dialog box.

LESSON 8 REVIEW QUESTIONS

TRUE/FALSE

Circle T if the statement is true or F if the statement is false.

T F 1. Charts are a graphical representation of worksheet data.

T F 2. Column charts are the best way to represent data groups that are part of a whole.

T F 3. Line charts are good for representing trends over a period of time.

T F 4. A scatter chart produces a "cloud" of data points not connected by lines.

T F 5. When the worksheet data changes, charts created from the worksheet also change.

FILL IN THE BLANKS

Complete the following sentences by writing the correct word or words in the blanks provided.

1. A(n) _pie_ chart is represented by a circle divided into portions.

2. In a worksheet chart, the _legend_ shows patterns or symbols that identify the different types of data.

3. The _Format_ menu contains the command for renaming a chart sheet.

4. A(n) _embedded_ is a chart that is created on the same sheet as the data being charted.

5. _Data labels_ represent the values depicted by chart objects like data points or columns.

LESSON 8 PROJECTS

PROJECT 8-1

The file *IE Project8-1* contains the populations of the world's largest cities. Create a column chart to illustrate the data.

1. Open **IE Project8-1** from the student data files.

2. Save the file as **Population**, followed by your initials.

3. Create a column chart from the data in **A5:B12** in a chart sheet.

4. Title the chart **World's Largest Cities**.

5. Title the Y axis **Population in Millions**. No X axis title is needed.

6. Include major horizontal gridlines.

7. Do not include a legend in the chart.

8. Name the chart sheet **Column Chart**.

9. Preview the chart.

10. Save, print, and close the file.

PROJECT 8-2

You have been running each morning to stay in shape. Over the past 10 weeks you have recorded your running times in file *IE Project8-2*.

1. Open **IE Project8-2** from the student data files.

2. Save the file as **Training**, followed by your initials.

3. Create an embedded line chart with markers at each data value from the data in **A5:B14**.

4. Do not include a chart title.

5. Title the Y axis **Time in Minutes**. No X axis title is needed.

6. Include major horizontal gridlines in the chart.

7. Do not include a legend in the chart.

8. Use the chart handles to position the chart in the range **C3:I15** on the worksheet.

9. Save the file. Print the worksheet with the embedded chart, and close the file.

PROJECT 8-3

The file *IE Project8-3* contains the number of McDonald's hamburger restaurants in different regions of the world.

1. Open **IE Project8-3** from the student data files.

2. Save the file as **McDonalds**, followed by your initials.

3. Create a pie chart in a chart sheet from the data in **A6:B10**.

4. Title the chart **Systemwide Locations**.

5. Place a legend on the right side of the chart that identifies each geographical region.

6. Include percentages as data labels next to each slice.

7. Name the chart sheet **Pie Chart**.

8. Edit font sizes so the chart title is **24** points, the slice percentages are **18** points, and the legend is **18** points.

9. Switch to the worksheet. Edit the content of **A9** to be **Others** rather than Europe.

10. Switch back to the chart sheet to see that the legend has been updated with the edited data.

11. Save the file. Print the chart and close the file.

PROJECT 8-4

The file *IE Project8-4* contains the monthly cash flow of a young family. To better explain their expenses to family members, a member of the household decides to create a pie chart in which each slice represents an expense category that contributes to total expenses.

1. Open **IE Project8-4** from the student data files.

2. Save the file as **Family Expenses**, followed by your initials.

3. Create a three-dimensional pie chart on a chart sheet from the data in **A6:B13**.

4. Title the pie chart **Where Our Money Goes**.

5. Do not include a legend in the chart.

6. The pie chart should include the data labels and percentages for each slice.

7. Name the chart sheet **3D Pie Chart**.

8. Change the font size of the chart title to **18** points.

9. Change the font size of the data labels to **14** points.

10. Preview the chart. As you view the chart determine in what areas you believe most spending occurs.

11. Save the file. Print the chart, and close the file.

PROJECT 8-5

The file *IE Project8-5* contains the study time and examination scores for several students. The instructor is attempting to determine if there is a relationship between study time and examination scores.

1. Open **IE Project8-5** from the student data files.

2. Save the file as **Study Time**, followed by your initials.

3. Create a scatter chart without connecting lines in a chart sheet from the data in **B4:C21**.

4. Title the chart **Comparison of Exam Grades to Study Time**.

5. Title the X axis **Hours of Study**.

6. Title the Y axis **Examination Grades**.

7. Do not include gridlines, a legend, or data labels in the chart.

8. Name the chart sheet **Scatter Chart**.

9. Change the font size of the chart title to **20** points.

10. Change the font size of the axis titles to **14** points.

11. Change the font size of the axis labels to **12** points.

12. Change the minimum value of the vertical scale (Y axis) to **50**.

13. Preview the chart. As you view the chart, determine whether you believe a relationship exists between study time and examination results.

14. Save the file. Print the chart, and close the file.

PROJECT 8-6

You operate the concession stand at the home baseball games of Mountain College, and have noticed a decrease in popularity of certain items as the season has progressed. The sales for each game have been kept on a worksheet. Now you would like to use the worksheet to create a chart that illustrates the change in sales levels for each product during the season.

1. Open **IE Project8-6** from the student data files.

2. Save the file as **Concession Sales**, followed by your initials.

3. Create a column chart on a chart sheet from the data in **A4:E9**.

4. Title the chart **Concession Sales**.

5. No X axis title is needed. Title the Y axis **Sales in Dollars**.

6. Include a legend at the right of the chart to identify the game number.

7. Name the chart sheet **Column Chart**.

8. Access the Format Plot Area dialog box and change the color in the *Area* box to white.

9. Change the font of the chart title to **18** points.

10. Change the font size of the X (horizontal) axis labels to **14** points and apply boldface to the labels.

11. Change the font size of the Y (vertical) axis labels to **12** points.

12. Change the font size of the Y axis title to **14** points.

13. Change the font size of the legend labels to **12** points.

14. Preview the chart. While you view the chart, determine which product has decreased in sales over the last four games.

15. Save the file. Print the chart, and close the file.

PROJECT 8-7

The file *IE Project8-7* contains the income statement of Radiation Software Corporation for several years. You would like to illustrate the corporation's growth by charting the sales and income levels.

1. Open **IE Project8-7** from the student data files.

2. Save the file as **Radiation**, followed by your initials.

3. Create a line chart with markers in a chart sheet from the data in **A5:F7**.

4. Title the chart **Revenue and Income of Radiation Software Corporation**.

5. Title the Y axis **(in Thousands)**. No X axis title is needed.

6. Place a legend that distinguishes revenue from income at the bottom of the chart.

7. Name the chart sheet **Revenue Chart**.

8. Change the font size of the chart title to **18** points.

9. Change the font size of the X (horizontal) axis and Y (vertical) axis labels to **14** points.

10. Change the font size of the Y axis title to **12** points.

11. Change the font size of the legend labels to **14** points.

12. Save the file. Print the chart. As you view the printed chart, determine whether the company's sales have decreased, increased, or remained stable.

13. Change the type of chart to a clustered column chart.

14. Save, print the chart, and close the file.

CRITICAL THINKING

ACTIVITY 8-1

For each scenario, determine what type of worksheet chart you believe would be the most appropriate to represent the data. Justify your answer by describing why you believe the chart is most appropriate.

Scenario 1. A scientist has given varying amounts of water to 200 potted plants. After 35 days, the height of the plant and the amount of water given to the plant was recorded in a worksheet.

Scenario 2. A corporation developed a new product last year. A manager in the corporation recorded the number of units sold each month. He noticed that sales in summer months are much higher than sales in the winter and would like to prepare a chart to illustrate this to other sales managers.

Scenario 3. A high school principal has students that come from five middle schools. She has recorded the name of the middle school and the number of students drawn from each of the middle schools. She would like to illustrate how some of the middle schools supply significantly more students than other middle schools.

COMMAND SUMMARY

FEATURE	MENU COMMAND	TOOLBAR BUTTON	LESSON
Align Text	Format, Cells, Alignment		2
Bold Text	Format, Cells, Font	**B**	2
Borders Around Cells	Format, Cells, Border		2
Cell Comment	Insert, Comment		6
Center Text Across Range of Cells	Format, Cells, Alignment, Center Across Selection		2
Chart Creation	Insert, Chart		8
Column Width Automatic	Format, Column, AutoFit Selection		2
Column Width Specific	Format, Column, Width		2
Conditional Formatting	Format, Conditional Formatting		6
Copy by Filling	Edit, Fill		3
Copy data	Edit, Copy		3
Decrease Decimal	Format, Cells, Number		2
Decrease Indent			2
Delay Calculations	Tools, Options, Calculation		4
Design a Printed Page	File, Page Setup		3
Drawing Toolbar, Display	View, Toolbars, Drawing		6
Fill Cell with Color	Format, Cells, Pattern		2
Font Change	Format, Cells, Font	Arial	2
Font Color	Format, Cells, Font	**A**	2
Font Size	Format, Cells, Font	10	2
Format Painting			6

FEATURE	MENU COMMAND	TOOLBAR BUTTON	LESSON
Freeze Titles	Window, Freeze Panes		3
Function Formula or Paste Function	Insert, Function	f_x	5
Increase Decimal	Format, Cells, Number		2
Increase Indent			2
Insert Column	Insert, Columns		3
Insert Row	Insert, Rows		3
Italicize Text	Format, Cell, Font	I	2
Move Data	Edit, Cut, then Edit, Paste		3
Open a Worksheet File	File, Open		3
Paste data	Edit, Paste		3
Preview a Chart	File, Print Preview		8
Preview a Worksheet	File, Print Preview		3
Protect a Worksheet	Tools, Protection, Protect Sheet		3
Rotating Text	Format, Cells, Alignment		2
Save a Named Worksheet	File, Save		3
Save an Unnamed Worksheet	File, Save As		3
Show Formulas in Worksheet	Tools, Options, View		4
Sort Data in Ascending Order	Data, Sort		6
Sort Data in Descending Order	Data, Sort		6
Sum a Range	Insert, Function	Σ	4
Underline Text	Format, Cell, Font	U	2
Unfreeze Titles	Window, Unfreeze Panes		3
Wrapping Text	Format, Cells, Alignment, Wrap text		2

TRUE/FALSE

Circle the T if the statement is true or F if the statement is false.

T F 1. The active cell reference will appear in the toolbar.

T F 2. To select a group of cells, click each cell individually until all cells in the range have been selected.

T F 3. The Save As dialog box appears every time you save a worksheet.

T F 4. The formula =B$4+C$9 contains mixed cell references.

T F 5. A chart may be printed from the chart sheet.

FILL IN THE BLANKS

Complete the following sentences by writing the correct word or words in the blanks provided.

1. A(n) _____ cell reference will remain the same when copied or moved.

2. The Manual button under the Calculation tab in the Options dialog box delays calculation until the _____ key is pressed.

3. The _____ toolbar button will add a range of numbers in a worksheet.

4. A(n) _____ chart uses bars to represent values in a worksheet.

5. The _____ tab in the Options dialog box is used to display formulas rather than values in the worksheet.

APPLICATIONS

APPLICATION 1

The worksheet in *IE App1* is a daily sales report that is submitted by a gas station manager to the owner. Change the appearance of the worksheet to make it easier to read.

1. Open **IE App1** from the student data files.

2. Save the file as **Gas Sales**, followed by your initials.

3. Change the size of the text in **A1** to **16** points.

4. Bold **A1**.

5. Change the width of column **A** to **20**.

6. Change the width of columns **B** through **D** to **15**.

7. Merge and center **A1:D1**.

8. Format **B2** for a Date in which the month is alphabetic and the day and year are numeric (Month XX, XXXX).

9. Enter **May 28, 2000** in **B2**.

10. Merge and center **B2:D2**.

11. Format **B3** for Time in which the hours and minutes are numeric and followed by AM or PM (XX:XX XM).

12. Enter **8:05 PM** in **B3**.

13. Merge and center **B3:D3**.

14. Change the size of the text in **A2:D8** to **14** points.

15. Wrap the text in **C5**.

16. Underline and center **B5:D5**.

17. Format **B6:B8** as a Number with a comma separator and no decimal places.

18. Format **C6:D8** for Currency with 2 decimal places.

19. Save, print, and close the file.

APPLICATION 2

An income statement describes how profitable a company has been during a certain period of time. *IE App2* is the income statement of Dole Food Company, Inc. Format the income statement in a way that makes it more readable to the financial statement user. The financial statement should have the following qualities:

- The heading should be in a bold font that is larger than the font of the items in the body of the financial statement.

- The heading should be separated from the body of the financial statement by at least one row.

- Columns of the worksheet should be wide enough to view all of the contents.

- The first (revenues) and last (net income) numbers in the financial statement should be preceded by dollar signs.

- All numbers should use a comma as the 1000 separator.

- Color should be added to make the file visually appealing.

When you have finished, save the file as **Dole**, followed by your initials. Then, print and close the file.

APPLICATION 3

The file *IE App3* is a worksheet that contains a list of members of the Computer Science Club and service points the members earned during the year. In preparation for their end-of-year banquet, the club secretary would like to prepare a worksheet that identifies the exceptional members (those with service points exceeding 1000) and outstanding members (those with service points between 800 and 1000). Format the worksheet with the following qualities.

- Sort the data by column B, the number of service points, with those with the most points at the top of the worksheet.

- The title **Exceptional and Outstanding Members** should be inserted at the top of the worksheet.

- A bold subtitle **Exceptional Members** should be inserted above William Griffin's name.

- A bold subtitle **Outstanding Members** should be inserted above Matthew Carcello's name.

- A bold subtitle **Other Active Members** should be inserted above Mohamed Abdul's name.

- The service points should be formatted as a Number with a comma separator and no decimal places.

- The school colors are blue and red. Add these colors and bolding to make the worksheet visually appealing.

When you have finished, save the file as **CSClub**, followed by your initials. Then, print and close the file.

APPLICATION 4

The revenue and expenses of Escape Computer Network Corporation are recorded in *IE App4*. You would like to illustrate the distribution of the corporation's costs for the year.

1. Open **IE App4** from the student data files.

2. Save the file as **Escape**, followed by your initials.

3. Create an exploded pie chart with three-dimensional effects, in a chart sheet using the data in **A13:B19**.

4. Title the chart **Expenses for the Year**.

5. Place a legend at the bottom of the chart to identify the slices.

6. Include percentages next to each slice.

7. Name the chart sheet **Pie Chart**.

8. Edit font sizes so the chart title is **22** points, the slice percentages are **18** points, and the legend is **14** points.

9. Preview the chart. As you view the chart, determine the largest categories of expense.

10. Save the file, print the chart, and close the file.

ON-THE-JOB SIMULATION

You work at the Java Internet Café, which has been open a short time. The café serves coffee, other beverages, and pastries and offers Internet access. Computers are set up on tables in the store, so customers can come in and have a cup of coffee and a Danish, and explore the World Wide Web. You need to create a menu of coffee prices and computer prices. You will do this by integrating Microsoft Excel and Microsoft Word.

JOB 1

1. Open a new Excel worksheet.

2. Key the data shown in Figure 1 into the worksheet, and format as shown.

FIGURE UR-1

	A	B	C	D
1	Coffee Prices			
2				
3	House coffee	$1.00	Café breve	$2.25
4				
5	Café au lait	$1.50	Café latte	$2.25
6				
7	Cappuccino	$1.75	Con panna	$2.50
8				
9	Espresso	$2.00	Espresso doppio	$2.75

3. Change the width of columns **A** and **C** to **29** and columns **B** and **D** to **9**.

4. Left align data in columns **B** and **D**.

5. Change the font to **Arial**, **14** points.

6. Format the data in columns **B** and **D** for currency with 2 places to the right of the decimal.

7. Save the file as **Coffee Prices**, followed by your initials.

8. Highlight and copy **A1** through **D9**.

9. Open Word and the **IE Simulation** document from the student data files.

10. Insert one blank line below the **Menu** heading and paste link the worksheet.

11. Save the document as **Java Café Menu**, followed by your initials.

12. Switch to Excel.

13. Open **Computer** from the student data files.

14. Rename and save it as **Computer Prices**, followed by your initials.

15. Highlight and copy **A1** through **B11**.

16. Switch to Word and *Java Café Menu*.

17. Insert a blank line after the *Coffee Prices* menu listings.

18. Paste link the *Computer Prices* worksheet.

19. Preview the document. Adjust the placement of the data if necessary, so that all data fits on one page.

20. Save, print, and close **Java Café Menu**.

21. Switch to Excel and close **Computer Prices** and **Coffee Prices** without saving changes.

JOB 2

The menu you created has been very successful. However, your manager asks you to make a few changes.

1. Open the **Coffee Prices** and **Computer Prices** files you saved in Job 1.

2. Make the changes to the *Coffee Prices* and *Computer Prices* worksheets as shown in Figure 2.

Java Internet Café

2001 Zephyr Street
Boulder, CO 80302-2001
303.555.JAVA JavaCafe@Cybershop.com

The Java Internet Café is a coffee shop with a twist. As you can see, there are seven computers on tables at the north side of the café. These computers provide high-speed Internet access to our customers. Whether you're a regular on the Net or a novice, our system is designed to allow you easy exploration of the World Wide Web. You've heard about it; now give it a try. Ask your server to help you get started.

Menu

Coffee Prices

House coffee	$1.00 ~.75~	Café breve	$2.25
Café au lait	$1.50	Café latte	$2.25
Cappuccino	$1.75 ~2.00~	Con panna	$2.50
Espresso	$2.00	Espresso doppio	$2.75

Computer Prices

Membership fee -- includes own account with personal ID, password, and e-mail address	$10 per month
28,800 bps Internet access (members) -- includes ⟨World⟩ Wide Web, FTP, Telnet, and IRC plus e-mail	$4 per hour
28,800 bps Internet access (non-members) -- includes World Wide Web, FTP, Telnet, and IRC	$6 per hour
Color scanner -- includes Internet access, use of software and the CD-ROM library	$5 per 1/2 hour
Laser printer -- inquire about duplexing capabilities	$.25 per page

Sit back, sip your coffee, and surf the net.

3. Save and close *Coffee Prices* and *Computer Prices*. Exit Excel.

4. Switch to Word and open **Java Café Menu**.

5. Notice the file has been updated since you made changes to the two worksheet files. Make the correction in the footer.

6. Save as **Java Café Menu 2**, followed by your initials.

7. Print and close. Exit Word.

Excel Function Reference

There are hundreds of functions available in Excel. This reference illustrates some of the more commonly used functions. The functions are grouped by the categories you see in the Paste Function dialog box. For each function there is an example of how it is used and how it should appear when entered in an Excel worksheet.

FINANCIAL FUNCTIONS—DEPRECIATION FUNCTIONS

FUNCTION	USE	TASK	EXAMPLE	
			THE FUNCTION FORMULA:	WILL DISPLAY:
DATE(year,month,day)	Displays the serial number of a date	Display the serial number for December 15, 2001	=DATE (2001,12,15)	37240 (in text format)
DATEVALUE(date_text)	Converts a text date to a serial number	Display the serial number for September 9, 2001	=DATEVALUE ("9/9/2001")	37143
DAY(serial_number)	Converts a serial number to a day of the month	Identify the day in October 9, 2001.	=DAY("10/9/2001")	9
HOUR(serial_number)	Converts portion of the serial number at the right of the decimal to an hour of the day at 7 p.m.	Display the hour of the day contained in a serial number for 12/15/2001	=HOUR(37240.8)	19
MONTH(serial_number)	Converts a serial number to a month	Display the month number contained in a serial number for 9/9/2001	=MONTH(37143)	9
NOW()	Displays the serial number of the current date and time	Display the serial number (assuming you are using the computer on December 15, 2001 at noon).	=NOW()	37240.5
TIME(hour,minute,second)	Displays the serial number of a time	Display the serial number of the 14th hour, 45th minute, 15th second.	=TIME(14,45,15) 0.601475	2:45 PM (in time format); (in text format)
TODAY()	Displays the serial number of today's date	Display the serial number of the day (assuming you are using the computer on December 15, 2001)	=TODAY()	37240 (in text format); 12/15/01 (in date format)
YEAR(serial_number)	Converts a serial number to a year	Display the year contained in a serial number for 9/9/2001	=YEAR(37143)	2001

Arguments
Date_text: date in text form (within quotations)
Day: day of the month stated as a number between 1 and 31
Month: month stated as a number between 1 and 12

Serial_number: Microsoft Excel 2000 uses a default date system in which dates are represented as the number of days after December 31, 1899. For example, January 3, 1900, is represented as 3, and February 7, 1999, is represented as 36198 when the cell is formatted for text. Numbers to the right of a decimal represent time. For example, 36198.5 indicates February 7, 1999, at 12:00 p.m.

Year: year stated as a number between 1900 and 9999

FINANCIAL FUNCTIONS

FUNCTION	USE	TASK	EXAMPLE	
			THE FUNCTION FORMULA:	**WILL DISPLAY:**
FV(rate,nper,pmt,pv,type)	Displays the future value of an investment	Find the value of 10, $1000 end-of-year payments invested at a 7% rate.	=FV(7%,10,1000,0,0)	$13,816.45
NPV(rate,value1,value2,...)	Displays the net present value of an investment	Find the net present value of an investment that requires a $10,000 outlay but pays $4,000 the first year, $3,000 the second, and $2,000 the third when an 8% rate is desired.	=NPV(8%,-10000, 5000,4000,2500)	$40.34
PMT(rate,nper,pv,fv,type)	Displays the periodic payment of an annuity	Find the end of year payment for a $100,000 loan at 8% for 10 years.	=PMT(8%, 10,10000,0,0)	($1,490.29)
PV(rate,nper,pmt,fv,type)	Displays the present value of an investment	Find the value of an investment that pays $5,000 at the end of every year for 30 years. Your expected rate of return is 8%.	=PV(8%,30,5000,0,0)	($56,288.92)

Arguments

Nominal_rate: the nominal (stated) rate of interest

Nper: the total number of payment periods in an annuity

Npery: the number of compounding periods per year

Pmt: the payment made each period

Pv: the present value

Fv: the future value

Type: 0 indicates payments at the end of the period, 1 indicates payments at the beginning of the period

DATE AND TIME FUNCTIONS

FUNCTION	USE	TASK	EXAMPLE	
			THE FUNCTION FORMULA:	**WILL DISPLAY:**
DB(cost,salvage,life, period,month)	Displays depreciation for a specified period using the declining balance method	Find the second year depreciation for a 6-year-old machine costing $10,000 with $1,000 salvage.	=DB(10000,1000, 6,2,12)	$2,172.39

DATE AND TIME FUNCTIONS

FUNCTION	USE	TASK	EXAMPLE	
			THE FUNCTION FORMULA:	WILL DISPLAY:
SLN(cost,salvage,life)	Displays the straight-line depreciation for the period	Find the yearly depreciation for a 6-year-old machine costing $10,000 with $1,000 salvage.	=SLN(10000,1000,6)	$1,500.00
SYD(cost,salvage,life, period)	Displays the sum-of-years' digits depreciation for a period	Find the second year depreciation for a 6 year machine costing $10,000 with $1,000 salvage.	=SYD(10000, 1000,6,2)	$2,142.86

Arguments
Cost: initial cost of the asset
Month: the number of months in the first year of depreciation
Life: the number of periods an asset is depreciated
Period: the period in which depreciation is to be calculated
Salvage: the value of the asset at the end of its useful life

LOGICAL FUNCTIONS

FUNCTION	USE	TASK	EXAMPLE	
			THE FUNCTION FORMULA:	WILL DISPLAY:
AND(logical1,logical2,...)	Displays TRUE if all arguments are TRUE	Determine whether the value in B7 is both below 100, and above 50.	=AND(B7<100, B7>50)	TRUE (if the value in B7 is 78); FALSE (if the value in B7 is 120)
IF(logical_test,value_if _true,value_if_false)	Designates a logical test	Determine whether a student passes an examination by exceeding a score of 60. The grade is recorded in B7.	=IF(B7>60,"PASS", "FAIL")	PASS (if the value in B7 is 90); FAIL (if the value in B7 is 55)
NOT(logical)	Reverses the logic of an argument	Determine whether the value in B7 does not equal 0.	=NOT(B7=0)	TRUE (if the value in B7≠0); FALSE (if the value in B7=0)
OR(logical1,logical2,...)	Displays TRUE if any argument is TRUE	Determine whether the value in B7 is either below 100, or above 50.	=OR(B7<100,B7>50)	TRUE (if the value in B7 is 120 or 25); FALSE (if the value in B7 is 75)

Arguments

Logical: statement that may be evaluated as true or false

Logical_test: statement that may be evaluated as true or false

Value_if_false: the value displayed in the cell if the statement is false

Value_if_true: the value displayed in the cell if the statement is true

LOOKUP AND REFERENCE FUNCTIONS

In the statistical examples, assume the following range of cells in a worksheet:

	A	B	C
1	INCOME STATEMENT		
2		This Year	Last Year
3	Sales	$100,000	$90,000
4	Cost of Goods Sold	$45,000	$43,000
5	Administrative Expenses	$20,000	$15,000
6	Net Income	$35,000	$32,000

FUNCTION	USE	TASK	EXAMPLE	
			THE FUNCTION FORMULA:	**WILL DISPLAY:**
COLUMN(reference)	Displays the column number of a reference	Use the column number of cell B3 in a calculation.	=COLUMN(B4)	2 (because column B is the second column)
COLUMNS(array)	Displays the number of columns in a reference	Use the number of columns in a range in a calculation.	=COLUMNS(A2:C6)	3 (because the range contains three columns)
HLOOKUP(lookup_value,table_array,row_index_num,...)	Displays the value of an indicated cell in the top row of an array	Display the contents of the third row in a column	=HLOOKUP("This Year",A2:C6,3)	45000 (because this amount is in the third row of the range under "This Year")
ROW(reference)	Displays the row number of a reference	Use the row number of cell B4 in a calculation.	=ROW(B4)	4 (because row 4 is the fourth row)
ROWS(array)	Displays the number of rows in a reference	Use the number of rows in a range in a calculation.	=ROWS(A2:C6)	5 (because the range contains 5 rows)

Arguments

Array: an array (rectangular representation of a group of values) or range of cells

Col_index_num: the column number in the table_array

Lookup_value: value to be found in the first row or column

Table_array: the range or range name to be searched

Reference: cell address

Row_index_num: the row number in the table_array

MATHEMATICAL FUNCTIONS (SEE MATH & TRIG CATEGORY)

FUNCTION	USE	TASK	EXAMPLE	
			THE FUNCTION FORMULA:	WILL DISPLAY:
ABS(number)	Displays the absolute value of a number	Determine the absolute value of the value in B7	=ABS(B7)	7 (if the value in B7 is either 7 or -7)
CEILING(number, significance)	Rounds a number to the higher multiple of significance	Round the price in B7 to the next highest dime.	=CEILING(B7,0.1)	$1.60 (if the value in B7 is either $1.59 or $1.51)
COS(number)	Displays the cosine of a number	Determine the cosine of the value in B7	=COS(B7)	.070737 (if the value in B7 is 1.5).
EXP(number)	Displays *e* raised to the power of a given exponent	Determine the base (*e*) when raised to the power of B7.	=EXP(B7)	4.481689 (if the value in B7 is 1.5)
FLOOR(number, significance)	Rounds a number to the lower multiple of significance	Round the price in B7 down to the next lower dime.	=FLOOR(B7,0.1)	$1.50 (if the value in B7 is either $1.59 or $1.51)
LN(number)	Displays the natural logarithm of a number	Determine the natural logarithm of the value in B7.	=LN(B7)	2.70805 (if the value in B7 is 15)
PI()	Displays the value of Pi	Determine the area of a circle with a radius length in B7.	=PI()*(B7^2)	73.5398 (if the radius value in B7 is 5)
POWER(number,power)	Displays the number raised to a power	Determine the cube of the value in B7.	=POWER(B7,3)	125 (if the value in B7 is 5)
PRODUCT(number1, number2,...)	Displays the product of the arguments	Determine the product of 7 times the value in B7.	=PRODUCT(B7,7)	35 (if the value in B7 is 5)
ROUND(number, num_digits)	Rounds a number to the specified digit	Round the price in B7 to the nearest dime.	=ROUND(B7,1)	$1.60 (if the value in B7 is $1.55); $1.50 (if the value in B7 is $1.54)
SIN(number)	Displays the sine of an angle	Determine the sine of the value in B7	=SIN(B7)	.99749 (if the value in B7 is 1.5)
SQRT(number)	Displays a positive square root	Determine the square root of the value in B7.	=SQRT(B7)	8 (if the value in B7 is 64)
SUM(number1,number2,...)	Adds the arguments	Determine the sum of the values in B7 and B8, plus 9.	=SUM(B7,B8,9)	20 (if the value in B7 is 5 and the value in B8 is 6)

FUNCTION	USE	TASK	EXAMPLE	
			THE FUNCTION FORMULA:	WILL DISPLAY:
TAN(number)	Displays the tangent	Determine the tangent of the value in B7.	=TAN(B7)	.969668 (if the value in B7 is .77)
TRUNC(number, num_digits)	Truncates a number to an integer	Truncate the value in B7 to the tenths digit.	=TRUNC(B7,1)	1.8 (if the value in B7 is 1.811 or 1.899)

Arguments
Number: any real number
Num_digits: the number of digits to be rounded (for example, 1 = tenths, 2 = hundredths)
Power: the exponent to which a base number is raised

STATISTICAL FUNCTIONS
In the statistical examples, assume the following range of cells in a worksheet:

	B
3	5
4	6
5	7
6	6
7	6
8	9

FUNCTION	USE	TASK	EXAMPLE	
			THE FUNCTION FORMULA:	WILL DISPLAY:
AVERAGE(number1, number2,...)	Displays the average of arguments	Determine the average of the range B3:B8.	=AVERAGE(B3:B8)	6.5
COUNT(value1, value2,...)	Displays the number of filled cells in a range	Determine the number of cells containing values in the range B3:B8.	=COUNT(B3:B8)	6
MAX(number1, number2,...)	Displays the maximum value in a data set	Determine the maximum value in the range B3:B8.	=MAX(B3:B8)	9
MEDIAN(number1, number2,...)	Displays the median of a range	Determine the median of the range B3:B8.	=MEDIAN(B3:B8)	6
MIN(number1, number2,...)	Displays the minimum value in a data set	Determine the minimum value in the range B3:B8.	=MIN(B3:B8)	5
MODE(number1, number2,...)	Displays the most common value in a data set	Determine the mode of the range B3:B8.	=MODE(B3:B8)	6
PERCENTILE(array,K)	Displays the percentile of values in a range	Determine the break for the 90th percentile of the range B3:B8.	=PERCENTILE (B3:B8,0.9)	8

FUNCTION	USE	TASK	EXAMPLE	
			THE FUNCTION FORMULA:	WILL DISPLAY:
STDEV(number1, number2,…)	Estimates the standard deviation	Determine the standard deviation of the range B3:B8.	=STDEV(B3:B8)	1.3784
VAR(number1, number2,…)	Estimates the variance	Determine the variance of the range B3:B8.	=VAR(B3:B8)	1.9

Arguments
number1,number2,…: group of numbers, an array, or a range
array: range of data
K: percent value between 0 through 1

TEXT FUNCTIONS

FUNCTION	USE	TASK	EXAMPLE	
			THE FUNCTION FORMULA:	WILL DISPLAY:
DOLLAR(number, decimals)	Converts a number to text in currency format	Convert the value in B7 to a dollar format rounded to cents.	=DOLLAR(B7,2)	$1,721.07 (if the value in B7 is 1721.0735)
EXACT(text1,text2)	Checks whether two text entries are identical	Compare the similarity of the word in B7 to the word in B8.	=EXACT(B7,B8)	FALSE (if the text in B7 is "there" and B8 is "their"); TRUE (if the text in B7 is "there" and B8 is "there")
LOWER(text)	Converts text to lower case	Convert the text in B7 to lower case.	=LOWER(B7)	Fall (if the text in B7 is "Fall" or "FALL")
PROPER(text)	Capitalizes the first letter in each word	Convert the text in B7 to proper case.	=PROPER(B7)	February (if the text in B7 is "february" or "FEBRUARY")
REPT(text,number_times)	Repeats text a designated number of times	Create a customized border.	=REPT("#-",5)	#-#-#-#-#-
UPPER(text)	Converts text to upper case	Convert the text in B7 to upper case	=UPPER(B7)	SELL! (if the text in B7 is "sell!" or "Sell!")

Arguments
Decimals: the number of digits to the right of the decimal point
Number: any real number
Number_times: the number of times an action will take place

UNIT

INTRODUCTION TO MICROSOFT® ACCESS

Estimated Time for Unit: 9 hours

ACCESS BASICS

OBJECTIVES

Upon completion of this lesson, you should be able to:

■ Understand databases.

■ Start Access and open a database.

■ Identify parts of the Access screen.

■ Identify the database objects.

■ Understand database terminology.

■ Create a new database and a new table.

■ Design, modify, name, and save a table.

■ Navigate a database and enter records.

■ Print a table and exit Access.   ⏱ **Estimated Time: 1.5 hours**

Database Basics

Access is a program known as a ***database management system***. A computerized database management system allows you to store, retrieve, analyze, and print information. You do not, however, need a computer to have a database management system. A set of file folders can be a database management system. Any system for managing data is a database management system. There are distinct advantages, however, to using a computerized database management system.

A computerized database management system (often abbreviated DBMS) is much faster, more flexible, and more accurate than using file folders. A computerized DBMS is also more efficient and cost-effective. A program such as Access can store thousands of pieces of data in a computer or on a disk. The data can be quickly searched and sorted to save time normally spent digging through file folders. For example, a computerized DBMS could find all the people with a certain ZIP code faster and more accurately than you could by searching through a large list or through folders.

Starting Access

To start Access, click the Start button on the taskbar. Select Programs, and then click the Microsoft Access icon to load Access. After a few moments, the Access startup dialog box appears, as shown in Figure 1-1. The dialog box gives you the option of creating a new database or opening an existing one. You can also choose to use a Database Wizard to guide you through the process of creating a database.

FIGURE 1-1
Access startup dialog box

STEP-BY-STEP ⇨ 1.1

1. With Windows 98 running, click **Start** on the taskbar.

2. Point to **Programs** on the **Start** menu, and click **Microsoft Access**.

3. Access opens and the Access startup dialog box appears as shown in Figure 1-1. Leave the dialog box on the screen for the next Step-by-Step.

Opening a Database

You can open an existing database from the startup dialog box or from the File menu. To open a database from the startup dialog box, click the *Open an existing file* option and choose a database from the file list. To create a new database, click the *Blank Access database* or *Access database wizards, pages, and projects* option. If you choose *Blank Access database*, you must manually create the database. If you choose *Access database wizards, pages, and projects*, you will be guided through the creation of the database. You will learn more about creating databases later in this lesson.

When you open an existing database, the Database window appears, like that shown in Figure 1-2. The Objects bar on the left side of the window lists the types of database objects. The database objects window lists the various functions for creating the selected object and any objects that already exist. In Figure 1-2, for example, three functions for creating a table and one table named *service club members* are listed. You will learn about database objects later in this lesson.

FIGURE 1-2
Database window

STEP-BY-STEP ▷ 1.2

1. Click the **Open an existing file** option, if it is not already selected.

2. Make sure the **More Files** option is highlighted in the list box, and click **OK**.

3. Open the file **IA Step1-2** from the student data files. The Database window appears, as shown in Figure 1-2. Leave the database open for the next Step-by-Step.

The Access Screen

Like other Office 2000 applications, the Access screen has a title bar, menu bar, and toolbar. At the bottom of the screen is the status bar. Click the down arrow in the Objects bar to view the other objects. Figure 1-3 shows the Access screen with the *IA Step1-2* database open.

As you use Access, various windows and dialog boxes will appear on the screen. Unlike Word and Excel, Access does not have a standard document view. Instead, the screen changes based on how you are interacting with the database.

 Did You Know?

As in other Office programs, you can access the Office Assistant for help. To display the Office Assistant, choose **Show the Office Assistant** on the **Help** menu. Key in a question and click **Search**.

Database Objects

When a database is saved, the file that is saved contains a collection of objects. These objects work together to store data, retrieve data, display data, print reports, and automate operations. The Objects bar

FIGURE 1-3
Access screen

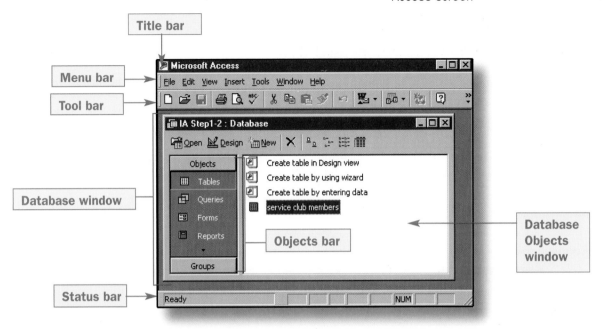

FIGURE 1-3
Access screen

in the Database window displays a button for each type of object. Click the down arrow on the bar to view the additional objects.

Table 1-1 briefly explains the purpose of each type of object.

TABLE 1-1
Database objects

OBJECT	DESCRIPTION
Table	Tables store data in a format similar to that of a worksheet. All database information is stored in tables.
Query	Queries search for and retrieve data from tables based on given criteria. A query is a question you ask the database.
Form	Forms allow you to display data in a custom format. You might, for example, create a form that matches a paper form.
Report	Reports also display data in a custom format. Reports, however, are especially suited for printing and summarizing data. You can even perform calculations in a report.
Page	Data access pages are a new object in Access 2000. They let you design other database objects so that they can be published to the Web.
Macro	Macros automate database operations by allowing you to issue a single command that performs a series of operations.
Module	Modules are like macros but allow much more complex programming of database operations. Creating a module requires the use of a programming language.

C

1. Make sure **Tables** is selected on the Objects bar. Highlight the **service club members** table in the database objects window, and click the **Open** button. The table appears, as shown in Figure 1-4.

2. Choose **Close** on the **File** menu to close the table. The database objects window is visible again.

3. Click **Queries** on the Objects bar. There is one query object named *Lubbock*. This query locates members who live in Lubbock.

4. Click **Forms** on the Objects bar. There is one form object named *service members form*.

5. Choose **Close** on the **File** menu to close the database. Leave Access open for the next Step-by-Step.

FIGURE 1-4
Database table

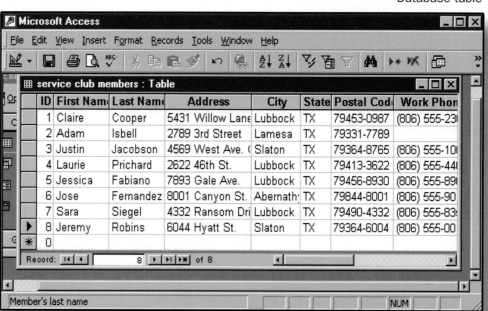

Database Terminology

Four terms are essential to know when working with databases. These terms relate to the way data is organized in a table. A ***record*** is a complete set of data. In the service club members table, each member is stored as a record. In a table, a record appears as a row, as shown in Figure 1-5.

Each record is made up of ***fields***. For example, the first name of each member is placed in a special field that is created to accept first names. In a table, fields appear as columns. In order to identify the fields, each field has a ***field name***. The data entered into a field is called an ***entry***. In the service club members database, for example, the first record has the name *Claire* as an entry in the First Name field.

FIGURE 1-5
Records and fields

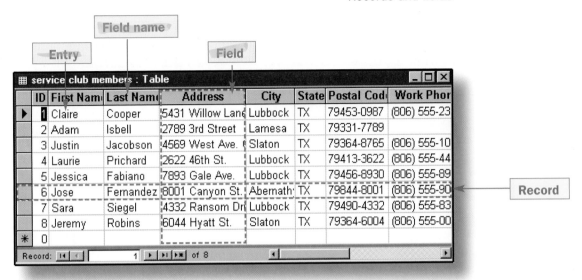

Creating a Database

The first step in creating a database is to create the file that will hold the database objects. To do this, you choose New on the File menu. The New dialog box appears, as shown in Figure 1-6. With the General tab already selected, choose Database and the File New Database dialog box appears. This is where you will name the file and store it with your other data files. Choose Create and the Database window appears, as shown in Figure 1-7. It will not contain any objects yet, because none have been created.

FIGURE 1-6
New dialog box

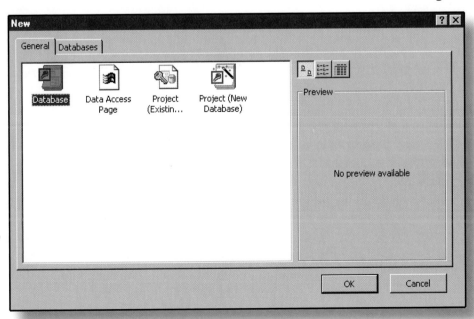

FIGURE 1-7
Database window

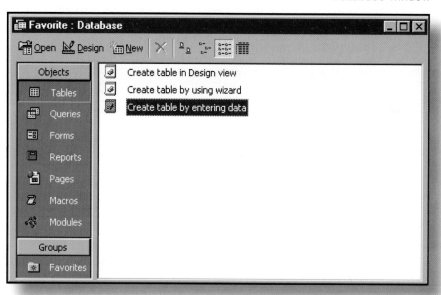

STEP-BY-STEP ▷ 1.4

1. Choose **New** on the **File** menu. The New dialog box appears, as shown in Figure 1-6.

2. With the **General** tab selected, choose **Database**, and then click **OK**. The File New Database dialog box appears.

3. Save the database as **Favorite**, followed by your initials, and then click **Create**. Your Database window should look like that shown in Figure 1-7.

4. Double-click **Create table by entering data**. A new table appears in Datasheet view, as shown in Figure 1-8.

5. Choose **Close** on the **File** menu to go back to the Database window. Leave the window open for the next Step-by-Step.

Extra Challenge

Create a new database. In the New dialog box, choose the **Databases** tab. Select one of the database formats already designed for you and add your own information.

FIGURE 1-8
New table in Datasheet view

Table1 : Table					
Field1	Field2	Field3	Field4	Field5	Fi
▶					

Record: ◄◄ ◄   3   ► ►► ►* of 30

Creating Tables

Because all other database objects rely on the existence of a database table, creating a table is the next step after creating a database. In many database management systems, data is stored using more than one table. To create a table, click Tables on the Objects bar. Click the New button and the New Table dialog box appears, as shown in Figure 1-9.

The New Table dialog box lists several ways to create a table. The most common way is to create the table in **_Design view_**. This is the view where you will design new tables and modify the design of existing tables. You can also create a table in Design view by double-clicking _Create table in Design view_ in the Database window.

> **C ▶ Hot Tip**
>
> You can create a table manually in Design view. Or, you can select the _Table Wizard_ option in the New Table dialog box. A series of wizards guides you step-by-step through the process of creating a table.

FIGURE 1-9
New Table dialog box

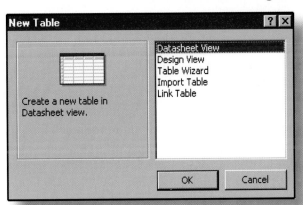

New Table

Create a new table in Datasheet view.

Datasheet View
Design View
Table Wizard
Import Table
Link Table

OK   Cancel

S TEP-BY-STEP ▷ 1.5

1. Click **Tables** on the Objects bar, if necessary, and then click **New**. The New Table dialog box appears, as shown in Figure 1-9.

2. Choose the **Design View** option and click **OK**. The Design view window opens. Leave the window on the screen for the next Step-by-Step.

Designing a Table

Now you are ready to design your table. You create the table's fields in the Design view window. As you can see in the window on your screen, each field in a table is divided into three sections: Field Name, Data Type, and Description. You will insert data in each of these three sections to create a table.

FIELD NAMES

First you have to decide what data you need to store. You should divide the data into categories to create fields. For example, suppose you want to create a database of your family members' birthdays. Some fields to include would be the person's name, address, and birth date. An example of a record would be: Halie Jones (name), 3410 Vicksburg Ave., Dallas, TX 75224(address), and 10/28/89 (birth date).

You key the names of these fields in the Field Name column of the Table design window. It is helpful if you create meaningful field names that identify the types of data stored.

DATA TYPE

After keying the field name, press the Tab key to move to the Data Type column. Then, determine the type of data to be stored in each field and choose an appropriate data type. The *data type* tells Access what kind of information can be stored in the field. Table 1-2 briefly describes the basic data types.

Choosing the correct data type is important. For example, you might think a telephone number or ZIP code should be stored in a field with a Number data type. However, you should only use Number data types when you intend to do calculations with the data. You won't be adding or subtracting ZIP codes. Numbers that will not be used in calculations are best stored as Text.

For a table of favorite restaurants, the name of the restaurant and address would be stored in fields of Text type, which is the default data type. The typical meal cost is ideal for the Currency type. The date you last ate at the restaurant would be Date type, and a Yes/No data type could specify whether reservations are required.

To choose a data type, click the arrow that appears in the Data Type column when the insertion point is in that column or when you key the first letter of the word. This button is called a drop-down arrow. A menu appears allowing you to choose a data type.

 Did You Know?

You can set a default value for a field that usually contains the same value. For example, if most of the people in a database of names and addresses live in Texas, you can enter TX as the default value of the State field. The State field will automatically contain TX, unless you change it.

DESCRIPTION

The last step in designing a table is to key a description for each field. The description explains the data in the field. For example, a field for the *Restaurants* database named Last Visit could have a description such as Date I Last Ate at the Restaurant. The description clarifies the field name. It does not appear in a table, but does display in the status bar when you select the field.

TABLE 1-2
Data types

DATA TYPE	DESCRIPTION
Text	The Text data type allows letters and numbers (alphanumeric data). A text field can hold up to 255 characters. Data such as names and addresses is stored in fields of this type.
Memo	The Memo data type also allows alphanumeric data. A memo field, however, can hold thousands of characters. Memo fields are used for data that does not follow a particular format. For example, you might use a Memo field to store notes about a record.
Number	The Number data type holds numeric data. There are variations of the Number type, each capable of storing a different range of values.
Date/Time	The Date/Time data type holds dates and times.
Currency	The Currency data type is specially formatted for dealing with currency.
AutoNumber	The AutoNumber data type is automatically incremented by Access for each new record added. Counters are used to give each record in a database a unique identification.
Yes/No	The Yes/No data type holds logical values. A Yes/No field can hold the values Yes/No, True/False, or On/Off.
OLE Object	The OLE Object data type is used for some of the more advanced features. It allows you to store graphics, sound, and even objects such as spreadsheets in a field.
Hyperlink	The Hyperlink data type is used to store a hyperlink as a UNC path or URL.
Lookup Wizard	The Lookup Wizard creates a field that allows you to choose a value from another table or from a list of values.

STEP-BY-STEP ▷ 1.6

1. Key **Name** in the first row of the Field Name column.

2. Press **Tab** (or **Enter**). The data type will default to Text, which is appropriate for the name of the restaurant.

3. Press **Tab** to move to the Description column.

4. Key **Name of restaurant** and press **Enter** to move to the next row.

5. Key the other fields and descriptions shown in Figure 1-10. All of the fields are the Text data type.

(continued on next page)

FIGURE 1-10
Defining fields in a table

FIGURE 1-10
Defining fields in a table

Field Name	Data Type	Description
Name	Text	Name of restaurant
Address	Text	Address of restaurant
Phone	Text	Phone number of restaurant
▶ Specialty	Text	Restaurant's specialty foods

6. Key **Last Visit** in the Field Name column and press **Tab**.

7. Click the arrow in the Data Type field and choose **Date/Time** from the drop-down menu that appears, as shown in Figure 1-11.

8. Press **Tab**.

9. Key **Date I last ate at the restaurant** in the Description column. Press **Tab**.

10. Key **Reservations** in the Field Name column, choose **Yes/No** as the data type, and key **Are reservations required?** in the Description column.

11. Leave the Design view window on the screen for the next Step-by-Step.

FIGURE 1-11
Data types

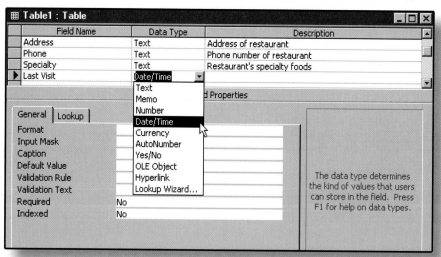

Naming and Saving a Table

After designing a table, you must give it a name and save the design. To save a table, choose Save on the File menu. The Save As dialog box appears, as shown in Figure 1-12. Key a name for the table and click OK. A message appears asking you if you want to create a *primary key*, which is a special field that assigns a unique identifier to each record. You can have Access create the primary key for you, in which case each record is automatically assigned a unique number. Or you can designate an existing field to be a primary key. For example, in a table containing the names and addresses of customers, you might create a field that contains a customer identification number. You could set this as the primary key, since it will be a unique number for each customer.

FIGURE 1-12
Save As dialog box

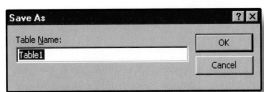

S TEP-BY-STEP ▷ **1.7**

1. Choose **Save** on the **File** menu. The Save As dialog box appears, as shown in Figure 1-12.

2. Key **Restaurants** in the *Table Name* box and click **OK**.

3. You will be asked if you want to create a primary key. Click **No**.

4. Choose **Close** on the **File** menu to close the Design view window and return to the Database window. Note that your *Restaurants* table now appears as an object, as shown in Figure 1-13.

5. Leave the Database window open for the next Step-by-Step.

FIGURE 1-13
Database window showing *Restaurants* table as an object

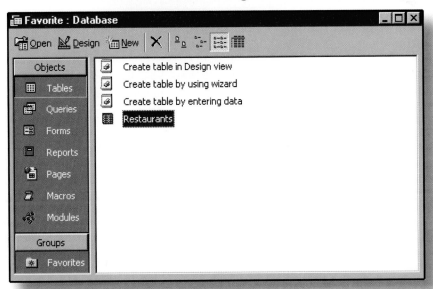

Modifying Tables

To modify the design of a table, you must be in Design view. Go to Design view by highlighting the name of the table in the Database window and clicking the Design button. In Design view, you can make changes to the names of fields, data formats, and descriptions.

You can add fields to the end of the list, or you can insert a new row for a field between existing fields. To insert a new row, place the insertion point in the row *below* where you want the new row to appear. Then, choose Rows on the Insert menu. You can delete a field by placing the insertion point in the row you want to delete and choosing Delete Rows on the Edit menu. You can also insert and delete rows by clicking the Insert Rows or Delete Rows button on the standard toolbar.

It is important to make sure you don't delete the wrong data in Design view; but if you do, you can click the Undo Delete button on the toolbar. The Undo Delete button reverses your last command.

You can delete an entire table by highlighting the table in the Database window and choosing Delete on the Edit menu.

When you finish changing fields, choose Save on the File menu or click the Save button on the toolbar.

 Did You Know?

A primary key field is a unique identifier for a record. To set a field as a primary key, open the table in Design view and click the row selector for the desired field. Click the Primary Key button on the toolbar.

STEP-BY-STEP 1.8

1. Highlight the **Restaurants** table in the Database window if it's not selected already.

2. Click the **Design** button. The table appears in Design view.

3. Click in the first blank row's Field Name column to place the insertion point there. You may need to scroll down.

4. Key **Meal Cost** in the Field Name column. Press **Tab**.

5. Choose **Currency** as the data type. Press **Tab**.

6. Key **Typical meal cost** as the description.

7. Place the insertion point in the **Last Visit** field name.

8. Click the **Insert Rows** button on the toolbar. A blank row is inserted above the *Last Visit* field.

9. In the blank row, key **Favorite Dish** as the field name, choose **Text** as the data type, and key **My favorite meal** as the description.

10. Place the insertion point in the **Reservations** field name.

11. Click the **Delete Rows** button on the toolbar. The Reservations field is deleted.

12. Click the **Undo Delete** button on the toolbar. The Reservations field re-appears.

13. Click the **Save** button on the toolbar to save the design changes. Remain in this screen for the next Step-by-Step.

Navigating and Entering Records in Datasheet View

Once a table is created and designed, you can enter records directly into the table using ***Datasheet view***. In Datasheet view, the table appears in a form similar to a spreadsheet, as you saw earlier in the lesson. As with a spreadsheet, the intersection of a row and a column is called a cell. To get to Datasheet view, select the table in the Database window and click the Open button, or click the View button on the toolbar while in Design view. You can switch back to Design view by clicking the View button again.

View, Datasheet

View, Design

The techniques used to enter records in the table are familiar to you. Press Enter or Tab to move to the next field as you enter the data. Access will consider the data types as you enter data. For example, you must enter a valid date in a Date/Time field and you must enter a number in a Number field. If you don't, an error message appears.

After entering records in a table in Datasheet view, you do not need to save the changes. Access saves them for you automatically. Remember to always save changes to the table design in Design view.

You can use the mouse to move the insertion point to a particular cell in the table. You can also use the keys in Table 1-3 to navigate through a table.

Did You Know?

You can switch to the Datasheet or Design view using options on the View menu.

Always save changes to the table design in the Design View

TABLE 1-3
Navigating in Datasheet View

KEY	DESCRIPTION
Enter, Tab, or right arrow	Moves to the following field
Left arrow or Shift+Tab	Moves to the previous field
End	Moves to the last field in the current record
Home	Moves to the first field in the current record
Up arrow	Moves up one record and stays in the same field
Down arrow	Moves down one record and stays in the same field
Page Up	Moves up one screen
Page Down	Moves down one screen

C

1. Click the **View** button in the Design view window to switch to Datasheet view. The *Restaurant* table looks like that shown in Figure 1-14. Notice how the View button now displays a different icon to indicate that clicking it will switch you back to Design view.

2. Key **Rosa's** in the Name field. Press **Tab**.

3. Key **8722 University Ave.** in the Address field. Press **Tab**.

4. Key **555-6798** in the Phone field. Press **Tab**.

5. Key **Mexican** in the Specialty field. Press **Tab**.

6. Key **Chicken Fajitas** in the Favorite Dish field. Press **Tab**.

7. Key today's date in the Last Visit field. Press **Tab**. (If you do not key the year, it will be added automatically.)

8. The Reservations field has a check box in it. Click the check box or press the spacebar to place a check in the box. Press **Tab**.

9. Key **5.95** as the typical meal cost. Press **Tab**. Leave the database table open for the next Step-by-Step.

Extra Challenge

Create a database of your own favorite local restaurants. Use the fields from this *Restaurants* exercise, and any others that may apply.

FIGURE 1-14
Datasheet view

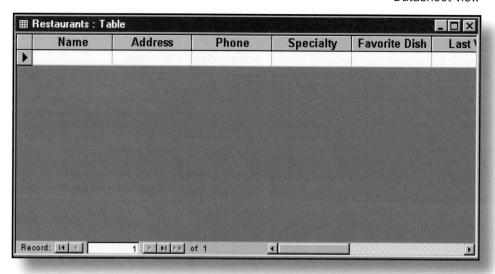

Printing a Table

You can print a database table in Datasheet view. Choose the Print command on the File menu to display the Print dialog box. As shown in Figure 1-15, you can choose to print all the records, only those selected, or for long tables you can specify the pages to print. Click the Setup button and the Page Setup dialog box appears, as shown in Figure 1-16. Here you can change the margins. To change the orientation, click the Properties button in the Print dialog box.

You can also click the Print button on the toolbar to print the database table. However, the Print dialog box will not appear for updates to the page setup.

FIGURE 1-15
Print dialog box

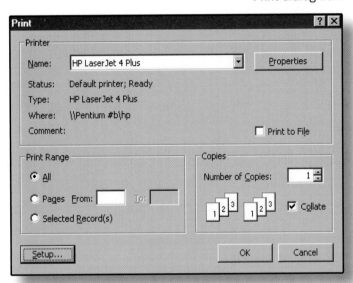

FIGURE 1-16
Page Setup dialog box

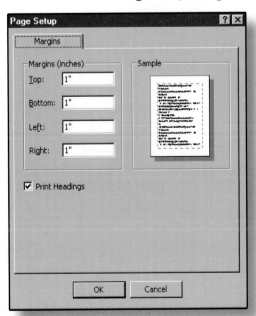

S TEP-BY-STEP ▷ 1.10

1. Choose **Print** on the **File** menu. The Print dialog box appears, as shown in Figure 1-15.

2. Click **Setup**. The Page Setup dialog box appears, as shown in Figure 1-16.

3. For the margins, key **.5** in the Left box and **.5** in the Right box.

4. Click **OK**.

5. In the Print dialog box, click **Properties**. The Properties dialog box appears.

6. From the *Orientation* options, click **Landscape**.

7. Click **OK**.

8. In the Print dialog box, click **All** from the *Print Range* options, if it isn't already selected. Click **OK**.

9. Close the table. The record has been saved in the table automatically.

Exiting Access

As in other Office 2000 programs, you exit Access by choosing the Exit command on the File menu. Exiting Access takes you back to the Windows 98 desktop. Remember to remove any floppy disks, and properly shut down Windows 98 before turning off the computer.

S TEP-BY-STEP ▷ 1.11

1. Choose **Close** on the **File** menu. The database closes.

2. Choose **Exit** on the **File** menu. The Windows 98 desktop appears.

Summary

In this lesson, you learned:

■ Access is a program known as a database management system. A computerized database management system allows you to store, retrieve, analyze, and print information. Start Access from the Programs menu.

■ You can open an existing database from the File menu or by clicking the toolbar button. The Access screen has a title bar, menu bar, and toolbar. Access, however, does not have a standard document view.

■ A database is a collection of objects. The objects work together to store data, retrieve data, display data, print reports, and automate operations. The object types are tables, queries, forms, reports, macros, and modules.

■ A record is a complete set of data. Each record is made up of fields. Each field is identified by a field name. The actual data entered into a field is called an entry.

■ Creating a database creates a file that will hold database objects. To store data, a table must first be created. In Design view, you can create fields and assign data types and descriptions to the fields. Once a table has been created and designed, you can enter records in Datasheet view.

■ As in other Office 2000 applications, you exit Access by choosing the Exit command from the File menu.

LESSON 1 REVIEW QUESTIONS

TRUE/FALSE

Circle T if the statement is true or F if the statement is false.

T F 1. A computerized DBMS is more efficient than paper filing.

T F 2. Opening a database automatically displays the data in the table.

T F 3. Access has a standard document view that remains on the screen as long as a database is open.

T F 4. A database file is a collection of database objects.

T F 5. Fields are identified by field names.

WRITTEN QUESTIONS

Write a brief answer to the following questions.

1. Which window appears after you open a database?

2. List three types of database objects.

3. Which database object allows you to search for and retrieve data?

4. What is the term for the data entered in a field?

5. Which view is used to design tables?

LESSON 1 PROJECTS

PROJECT 1-1

1. Start Access.

2. Open the **Favorite** database.

3. Open the **Restaurants** table in Datasheet view.

4. Insert the records shown in Figure 1-17.

5. Print the table in landscape orientation.

6. Close the table.

FIGURE 1-17

Access Basics

Lesson 1

Name	Address	Phone	Specialty	Favorite Dish	Last Visit	Reservations	Meal Cost
Health Hut	3440 Slide Rd.	555-6096	Healthy foods	Fruit Delight	6/30/98	☐	$5.50
Stella's	7822 Broadway	555-8922	Italian	Lasagna	7/6/98	☑	$9.95
Tony's BBQ	2310 82nd St.	555-3143	BBQ	Baby Back Ribs	5/1/98	☑	$10.95
Morning Glory	5660 Salem	555-6621	Breakfast	Daybreak Muffins	7/12/98	☐	$2.95
Salads and Stuff	8910 Main St.	555-3440	Salads	Chicken Caesar Salad	4/29/98	☐	$5.95
Saltlick Steakhouse	2100 Highway 281	555-6700	Steaks	Rib Eye	3/10/98	☑	$13.50
Alamo Diner	451 San Jacinto	555-9833	American	Cheeseburger	8/4/98	☐	$5.50

PROJECT 1-2

SCANS

1. With the *Favorite* database open, create a new table named **Stores** using the field names, data types, and descriptions shown in Figure 1-18.

FIGURE 1-18

Field Name	Data Type	Description
Name	Text	Store name
Address	Text	Store address
Phone	Text	Store's telephone number
Specialty	Text	What the store sells
Credit Cards	Yes/No	Does the store accept credit cards?
▶ Hours	Date/Time	Hours of operation

Field Properties

General | Lookup

Format
Input Mask
Caption
Default Value
Validation Rule
Validation Text
Required   No
Indexed   No

The field description is optional. It helps you describe the field and is also displayed in the status bar when you select this field on a form. Press F1 for help on descriptions.

2. Save the table as **Stores** and close it. No primary key is necessary.

3. Open the table in Datasheet view and enter the record shown in Figure 1-19.

FIGURE 1-19

Name	Address	Phone	Specialty	Credit Cards	Hours
Electronics Plus	6443 Elgin St.	555-2330	Electronics	☑	10am to 6pm
				☐	

4. After keying the Hours field entry, a message appears telling you the value you entered isn't appropriate for the field. Click **OK** and delete the data in the Hours field.

5. Close Datasheet view and open the table in Design view.

6. Change the data type for the Hours field to **Text**.

7. Insert a new row above the Hours field and key a new field named **Checks** with the **Yes/No** data type, and **Does the store accept personal checks?** as the description.

8. Save the changes and close Design view.

9. Open the table in Datasheet view and click the check box (for *yes*) in the Checks field.

10. Key **10am to 6pm** in the Hours field.

11. Enter the records shown in Figure 1-20.

FIGURE 1-20

Name	Address	Phone	Specialty	Credit Cards	Checks	Hours
Music Master	2700 Canton	555-9820	Music-CDs	☑	☐	11am to 9pm
Rag Doll	2136 Quaker	555-4560	Ladies clothes	☑	☑	10am to 5:30pm
Vision Computers	6720 Data Drive	555-2300	Computers	☑	☑	10am to 7pm
Athletics X-Press	8904 Richmond	555-7811	Shoes	☑	☑	12pm to 7pm
College Clothiers	3340 University	555-3570	Clothes	☐	☑	12pm to 6pm

12. Change the left and right margins to **.5** inches and print the table.

13. Close the table.

PROJECT 1-3

1. Open the **Stores** table in Design view.

2. Delete the **Checks** field.

3. Change the data type for the Credit Cards field to **Text**.

4. Save the changes and close Design view.

5. Open the table in Datasheet view.

6. Change the left and right margins to **.75"** and print the table.

7. Close the table and database.

PROJECT 1-4

1. Create a new database named **Music**.

2. With the *Music* database open, create a new table named **Pop** using the field names, data types, and descriptions shown in Figure 1-21.

FIGURE 1-21

Pop : Table			
Field Name	**Data Type**	**Description**	
Name	Text	Musical artist's name	
Title	Text	Title of CD or tape	
Year	Number	Year title was released	
▶ Type	Text	CD or tape?	

3. Save the table as **Pop**. No primary key is necessary.

4. Switch to Datasheet view and enter the records shown in Figure 1-22.

5. Print and close the table.

Web Site

To find information on your favorite music, artists, concerts, software, instruments, or music education, access Music Search at *http://www.musicsearch.com*. Web sites and addresses change regularly, so if you can't find the information at this site, try another.

FIGURE 1-22

Name	Title	Year	Type
Dire Straits	Money for Nothing	1988	CD
Mariah Carey	Music Box	1993	CD
Van Morrison	Moondance	1970	Tape
Kenny G.	Silhouette	1988	CD
Natalie Merchant	Blind Man's Zoo	1989	CD
Billy Joel	Glass Houses	1980	Tape
▶		0	

PROJECT 1-5

1. With the *Music* database open, open the **Pop** table in Design view.

2. Delete the **Type** field.

3. Save the change.

4. Switch to Datasheet view and add the records as shown in Figure 1-23.

5. Print the table.

6. Close the table and database.

FIGURE 1-23

Name	Title	Year
Pretenders	The Isle Of View	1995
Jackson Browne	Looking East	1996
Genesis	Three Sides Live	1994
▶		0

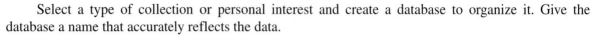

SCANS

ACTIVITY 1-1

Select a type of collection or personal interest and create a database to organize it. Give the database a name that accurately reflects the data.

Create and design a table for your data using the Table Wizard. Carefully consider what fields your database will need.

To start the Table Wizard, double-click *Create table by using wizard* in the Database window and follow the screens to create your table. In the first screen, choose the Personal category and one of the Sample tables. In the Sample Fields column, select the fields for your new table. When finished with the first screen, click the Next button. In the second screen, enter the name of your table and click Next. On the third screen, choose *Enter data directly into the table* and click the Finish button. The table will appear in Datasheet view. Enter at least two records in the table. Change the margins if necessary and print the table. Close the table and exit Access.

ACTIVITY 1-2

When creating a database with many of the same types of fields, it is helpful to know how to copy the definition of a field. Use the Help feature and search for the steps to copy a field's definition within a table. Write down these basic steps.

MANIPULATING DATA

Upon completion of this lesson, you should be able to:

■ Edit a record and undo a change.

■ Select records and fields.

■ Delete a record.

■ Cut, copy, and paste data.

■ Change the layout of a datasheet.

🕑 **Estimated Time: 1.5 hours**

Editing Records

 T o make editing records easier, Access provides navigation buttons on your screen. The navigation buttons are used to move around the datasheet. These buttons may not be necessary when working with databases as small as those you used in the previous lesson. As databases get larger, however, the navigation buttons become very useful. Figure 2-1 shows the locations of the navigation buttons.

FIGURE 2-1
Navigation buttons

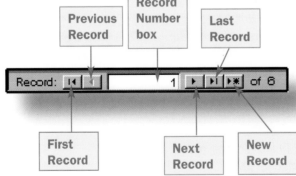

The First Record button is used to move quickly to the top of the table and the Last Record button is used to move to the bottom of the table. There are also buttons used to move to the next or previous record. To move to a specific record number, click the Record Number box and key the number of the record in the field. Press Tab to move to the record. To add a new record, click the New Record button.

The current record is indicated by an arrow to the left of the record. The computer keeps track of the current record using a ***record pointer***. When you move among records in Datasheet view, you are actually moving the record pointer.

If you use the Tab key to move to a cell, Access highlights the contents of the cell. As in a spreadsheet, you can replace the contents of the cell by keying data while the existing data is highlighted. If you click a cell with the mouse, the insertion point appears in the cell, allowing you to edit the contents.

Undoing Changes to a Cell

There are three ways to undo changes to a cell. If you make a mistake keying data in a cell, you can choose Undo Typing on the Edit menu or click the Undo button on the toolbar. Your last action is reversed. If you have already entered the data in a cell and moved to the next cell (or any cell), choose Undo Current Field/Record on the Edit menu or press the Esc button to restore the contents of the entire record. If you make changes to a record and then move to the next record, you can restore the previous record by choosing Undo Saved Record on the Edit menu.

S TEP-BY-STEP ▷ 2.1

1. Open **IA Step2-1** from the student data files.

2. Open the **Calls** table in Datasheet view. The purpose of this table is to keep a log of telephone calls.

3. Click the **Last Record** button at the bottom of the table to move the record pointer to the last record.

4. Click the **First Record** button to move the record pointer to the first record.

5. Click the **Next Record** button to move the record pointer to the next record.

6. In the second record, the time is shown as 11:00 AM when it should be 10:30 AM. Press **Tab** until the **Call Time** field is highlighted.

7. Key **10:30** in the Call Time field and press **Tab**. (The field is formatted for AM.)

8. Move the mouse pointer to the **Subject** field in the third record. Click to place the pointer at the beginning of the field. The entire field will be highlighted.

9. Key **Computers** and press **Tab**.

10. Press **Esc**. The word *Computers* changes back to *Hardware*.

11. The entry in the Notes field of the third record is highlighted. Press **Delete.** The entry is deleted.

12. Click the **Undo** button on the toolbar. The Notes field entry reappears.

13. Leave the table on the screen for the next Step-by-Step.

Selecting Records and Fields

You can quickly select records and fields by clicking the record or field selectors. *Field selectors* are at the top of a table and contain the field name. Figure 2-2 shows the Name field selected. *Record selectors* are located to the left of a record's first field. Clicking in the upper left corner of the datasheet selects all records in the database.

You can select more than one field by clicking the field selector in one field, holding down the Shift key, and clicking the field selector in another field. The two fields, and all the fields in between, will be selected. You can use the same method to select multiple records. You can also select multiple fields or records by clicking and dragging across the field or record selectors.

FIGURE 2-2
Record and field selectors

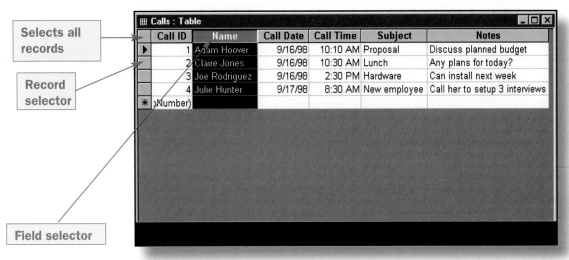

Selects all records

Record selector

Field selector

STEP-BY-STEP ▷ 2.2

1. Click the **Name** field selector to select the entire column.

2. Click the **Subject** field selector to select the column.

3. Select the **Name** field again.

4. Hold down the **Shift** key and click the **Call Time** field selector. The Name, Call Date, and Call

Time fields are selected, as shown in Figure 2-3.

5. Click the record selector of the **Claire Jones** record. The entire record is selected.

6. Select the **Julie Hunter** record. Leave the table on the screen for the next Step-by-Step.

(continued on next page)

FIGURE 2-3
Selecting multiple columns

Calls : Table					
Call ID	Name	Call Date	Call Time	Subject	Notes
1	Adam Hoover	9/16/98	10:10 AM	Proposal	Discuss planned budget
2	Claire Jones	9/16/98	10:30 AM	Lunch	Any plans for today?
3	Joe Rodriguez	9/16/98	2:30 PM	Hardware	Can install next week
4	Julie Hunter	9/17/98	8:30 AM	New employee	Call her to setup 3 interviews
*	(Number)				

Record: 14 ◄ 1 ► ►I ►* of 4

Deleting Records

To delete an entire record, select the record and choose
Delete Record on the Edit menu or press the Delete key. You
can also click the Delete Record button on the toolbar. A
message box appears, as shown in Figure 2-4, warning you
that you are about to delete a record. Click Yes to permanently delete the record or No to cancel the deletion. Once
you've deleted a record using the Delete Record command,
you cannot use the Undo command or Esc key to restore it.

You cannot delete fields in Datasheet view the same
way you delete records. As you learned in Lesson 1, you can
delete fields in Design view.

Hot Tip

You can delete more than one
record by holding down the Shift
key, clicking the field selector in
each field, and then selecting
Delete Record.

FIGURE 2-4
Message warning you that you are about to delete a record

> **Microsoft Access**
>
> ⚠ **You are about to delete 1 record(s).**
>
> If you click Yes, you won't be able to undo this Delete operation.
> Are you sure you want to delete these records?
>
> [Yes]   [No]

S TEP-BY-STEP ▷ 2.3

1. Click the **Previous Record** button to move to the *Joe Rodriguez* record.

2. Click the **Delete Record** button on the toolbar. A message appears, as shown in Figure 2-4, warning you that you are about to delete the record.

3. Click **Yes**. The record is deleted. Notice that the numbers in the Call ID field do not renumber when a record is deleted. The reason is that the number in the Call ID field is automatically assigned when the record is created and does not change. Leave the table on the screen for the next Step-by-Step.

Cutting, Copying, and Pasting Data

The Cut, Copy, and Paste commands in Access work the same way as in other Office applications. You can use the commands to copy and move data within a table or between tables. To cut or copy an entire record, select the record and choose Cut or Copy on the Edit menu or click the Cut or Copy buttons on the toolbar.

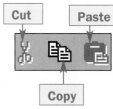

Using Cut, Copy, and Paste can sometimes be tricky. You must be aware that data pasted in a table will overwrite the existing data. If you want to copy an entire record and paste it into a table as a new record, use the Paste Append command on the Edit menu. You can also highlight the blank record at the bottom of a table and choose Paste on the Edit menu or the Paste button on the toolbar. When you select a record and choose the Cut command, you will get the same message as when you use the Delete command. The difference is that with the Cut command, you can restore the record to the end of the table by using the Paste or Paste Append command.

Did You Know?

You can move and copy an entire object. In the Database window, select the object (table, query, form, or report) and choose **Cut** or **Copy** on the **Edit** menu. Open the database in which you want to paste the object, and choose **Paste** on the **Edit** menu.

Did You Know?

If you delete data or objects from a database, the database can become fragmented and use disk space inefficiently. Compacting rearranges how the database is stored on disk and optimizes the performance of the database. Access combines compacting and repairing into one process. Specify the database you want to compact and repair, choose **Database Utilities** on the **Tools** menu, and select **Compact and Repair Database**.

S TEP-BY-STEP ▷ 2.4

1. Select the **Adam Hoover** record.

2. Click the **Copy** button on the toolbar.

3. Click the **New Record** button, and then click the **Paste** button on the toolbar. The new record appears at the bottom of the database.

(continued on next page)

4. Change the date and time of record **5** to **September 17** at **5:00 PM**.

5. In the **Notes** field, delete the existing text and key **Proposal ready on Monday morning.**

6. Select the **Claire Jones** record.

7. Click the **Cut** button on the toolbar. The message saying that you are about to delete a record appears.

8. Click **Yes**.

9. Select the empty record at the end of the table.

10. Click the **Paste** button on the toolbar. The *Claire Jones* record appears as shown in Figure 2-5.

11. Leave the table on the screen for the next Step-by-Step.

FIGURE 2-5
Using the Cut and Paste buttons to add a record

Call ID	Name	Call Date	Call Time	Subject	Notes
1	Adam Hoover	9/16/98	10:10 AM	Proposal	Discuss planned budget
4	Julie Hunter	9/17/98	8:30 AM	New employee	Call her to setup 3 interviews
5	Adam Hoover	9/17/98	5:00 PM	Proposal	Proposal ready on Monday mornii
5	Claire Jones	9/16/98	10:30 AM	Lunch	Any plans for today?

⊞ Calls : Table

⁎ ɔNumber)

Record: ◄◄ ◄ 4 ► ►► ►⁎ of 4

Changing Datasheet Layout

You can make many changes to the datasheet layout, including changing row height and column width, rearranging columns, and freezing columns.

Changing Row Height

You can adjust the row height in a datasheet, but the adjustment affects all the rows. To change the height, position the pointer on the lower border of a row selector, and it will turn into a double arrow, as shown in Figure 2-6. Using the double arrow, click and drag the row border up or down to adjust the row height.

FIGURE 2-6
Adjusting the row height

Call ID
1
4
5
6
ɔNumber)

You can also specify an exact row height. Choose Row Height on the Format menu and the Row Height dialog box appears, as shown in Figure 2-7. Key a height in points (like font sizes) for the row.

FIGURE 2-7
Row Height dialog box

FIGURE 2-7
Row Height dialog box

STEP-BY-STEP ▷ 2.5

1. Position the mouse pointer on the lower border of the record selector for **Claire Jones**. You will know you have the pointer correctly positioned when it changes to a double arrow.

2. Drag the row border down slightly to increase the height of the row. When you release the mouse button, all rows are affected by the change.

3. Select the **Julie Hunter** record.

4. Choose **Row Height** on the **Format** menu. The Row Height dialog box shown in Figure 2-7 appears.

5. Key **30** in the Row Height box and click **OK**. The row height increases to a height that allows the data in the Subject and Notes field to be read more easily. Leave the table on the screen for the next Step-by-Step.

Changing Column Width

Often, the column widths provided by default are too wide or too narrow for the data in the table. Adjusting column width is similar to adjusting row height. To adjust the column width, place the mouse pointer in the field selector on the border of the column. The pointer changes to a double arrow. Click and drag to the width you want. Unlike rows, which must all have the same height, each field can have a different width.

When you choose Column Width on the Format menu, the Column Width dialog box appears, as shown in Figure 2-8. You can key a specific width or click the Best Fit button. The Best Fit button automatically selects the best width for the data in the column. Another way to choose the "best fit" is to place the mouse pointer on the field border and double-click when it turns into a double arrow.

Hot Tip

Instead of choosing Column Width on the Format menu, you can right-click the column and select Column Width on the shortcut menu that appears.

FIGURE 2-8
Column Width dialog box

STEP-BY-STEP ▷ 2.6

1. Position the pointer on the right border of the **Notes** field selector.

2. Drag to make the column wide enough to allow all the information to fit in the field.

3. Select the **Call ID** field.

4. Choose **Column Width** on the **Format** menu. The Column Width dialog box appears, as shown in Figure 2-8.

5. Click **Best Fit**. The column narrows.

6. Use the Best Fit option to adjust the width of the **Call Date** field.

7. Select the **Call Time** field.

8. Choose **Column Width** on the **Format** menu. The Column Width dialog box appears.

9. Key **16** in the Column Width box and click **OK**.

10. Change the width of the **Subject** field to **25**.

11. Print the table in landscape orientation. Leave the table on the screen for the next Step-by-Step.

Rearranging Columns

In Datasheet view, Access allows you to rearrange fields by dragging them to a new location. First, select the field you want to move. Then, click and hold down the mouse button on the field selector and drag the field to the new location. A vertical bar follows your mouse pointer to show you where the field will be inserted. Release the mouse button to insert the field in its new location.

STEP-BY-STEP ▷ 2.7

1. Select the **Call Date** field.

2. Click and drag the **Call Date** field to the left until the vertical bar appears between the Call ID and Name fields. Release the mouse button.

The Call Date column appears between the Call ID and Name columns, as shown in Figure 2-9.

3. Leave the table on your screen for the next Step-by-Step.

FIGURE 2-9
Rearranging fields

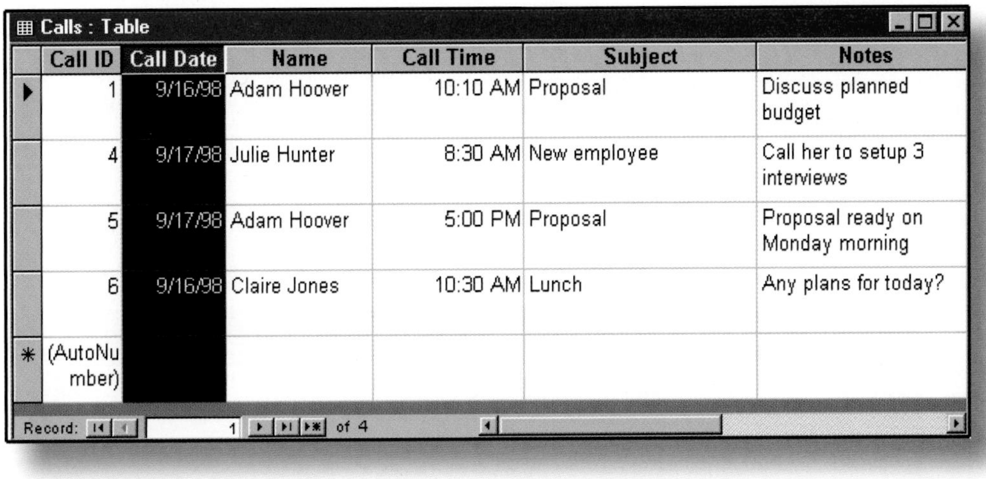

Lesson ② Manipulating Data

Call ID	Call Date	Name	Call Time	Subject	Notes
1	9/16/98	Adam Hoover	10:10 AM	Proposal	Discuss planned budget
4	9/17/98	Julie Hunter	8:30 AM	New employee	Call her to setup 3 interviews
5	9/17/98	Adam Hoover	5:00 PM	Proposal	Proposal ready on Monday morning
6	9/16/98	Claire Jones	10:30 AM	Lunch	Any plans for today?
*	(AutoNumber)				

Freezing Columns

If a table has many columns, it may be helpful to freeze one or more columns, allowing them to remain on the screen while you scroll to columns that are not currently visible.

To freeze columns, select the column or columns you want to freeze, and choose Freeze Columns on the Format menu. To unfreeze columns, choose Unfreeze All Columns on the Format menu.

STEP-BY-STEP ▷ 2.8

1. Select the **Call ID** field.

2. While holding down the **Shift** key, click the **Name** field. The Call ID, Call Date, and Name fields are all highlighted.

3. Choose **Freeze Columns** on the **Format** menu.

4. Click the horizontal scroll arrow at the bottom right of the table window to scroll to the Notes field. Notice that the frozen fields remain on the screen.

5. Choose **Unfreeze All Columns** on the **Format** menu.

6. Change the left and right margins to **.5"** and print the table in portrait orientation.

7. Choose **Close** on the **File** menu. You will be asked if you want to save changes to the layout of the table.

8. Click **Yes**. The Database window is visible on the screen. Leave the database open for the next Step-by-Step.

Changing Field Properties

When you defined fields for a table in Lesson 1, you specified only the field name, data type, and description. Now that you have created and used fields in a variety of situations, it is time to learn about field properties. ***Field properties*** allow you to further customize a field beyond merely choosing a data type.

You can view and change field properties in a table or form's Design view. Figure 2-10 shows the field properties available; you will learn about the most common ones. The field properties available will vary depending on the field's selected data type.

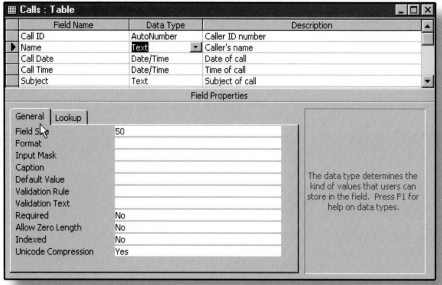

FIGURE 2-10
Field properties in Design view

FIELD SIZE

One of the most common field properties is Field Size. In fields of Text type, the Field Size is merely the number of characters allowed in the field. You can specify that the field allow up to 255 characters. The default size is 50.

In fields of Number type, the Field Size allows you to specify what internal data type Access will use to store the number. The available options are Byte, Integer, Long Integer, Single, Double, Replication ID, and Decimal. If you have computer programming experience, the available field sizes may be familiar to you. If the options

Did You Know?

If you decrease the size of a field, you may cut off any data over the set number of characters allowed in the field.

mean nothing to you, don't worry. There is an easy way to select the appropriate field size. If your field is to store whole numbers only, use the Long Integer field size. If your field will store fractional numbers with decimal places, choose the Double field size.

FORMAT

Use the Format field property to specify how you want Access to display numbers, dates, times, and text. For example, the default format for dates is *12/29/99*. Using the Format property, you can change the format to *29-Dec-99* or *Sunday, December 29, 1999*. You can also include the time with the date such as *12/29/99 9:15:30 AM*.

INPUT MASK

An input mask allows you to control the data pattern or format allowed in the field. You can also specify characters that will be put into the field automatically. For example, you can specify that a phone number be formatted with area code in parentheses, and the rest of the number split by a hyphen. When you key records, you won't have to key the parentheses or the hyphen; Access will put them in for you automatically. You can use the Input Mask Wizard to set the field's pattern or format for you.

CAPTION

The text you provide in the caption field property will be used *instead* of field names in forms, tables in Datasheet view, reports, and queries. For example, if the field name is *EmailName*, you could enter *E-mail address* in the caption field property. When you create a form that includes the field, the more descriptive name will appear as the field name.

DEFAULT VALUE

Another useful field property is Default Value. Use this field property when you have a field that usually contains the same value. For example, if most of the people in a database of names and addresses live in California, you can enter CA as the Default Value of the State field. The State field will automatically contain CA, unless you change it to another state.

Hot Tip

When you enter an even dollar amount in a formatted field, you only have to key the dollars. For example, you only have to key *3* and press Enter. The 3 you keyed will be formatted automatically to $3.00.

REQUIRED

The Required field property specifies whether you must enter a value in the field. For example, in an employee database, you might specify that each field requires a telephone number. If you try to enter a record without including a telephone number, Access will alert you that you must enter one.

DECIMAL PLACES

Number and Currency fields have a field property called Decimal Places. This property usually adjusts automatically depending on the data in the field. You can specify a number of decimal places here to override the automatic setting.

STEP-BY-STEP ▷ 2.9

1. Open the **Calls** table in Design view.

2. Select the **Name** field.

3. Under the Field Properties section beside *Field Size*, double-click **50** to highlight it. Key **40**.

4. In the *Caption* box, key **Caller's Name**.

5. Click in the *Required* field property box. A down arrow will appear at the right end of the box.

(continued on next page)

6. Click the down arrow and choose **Yes** from the menu.

7. Select the **Call Time** field.

8. Click in the *Format* field property box. A down arrow appears.

9. Click the down arrow. A menu of date and time formats appear.

10. Choose **Long Time**.

11. Choose **Yes** in the *Required* field property.

12. Select the **Notes** field.

13. Change the *Field Size* to **100**.

14. Save the table design. A message may appear stating that some data may be lost because you changed the setting for a field size to a shorter size. Click **Yes** to continue. Another message may appear asking if you want to test the changes. Click **Yes**.

15. Switch to Datasheet view to see the changes to the Call Time field. The Name field now contains the caption you entered. The other changes aren't visible.

16. Adjust the row height, if necessary, so you can see all the record data in each field. Print the table in landscape orientation.

17. Close the table and then close the database by clicking the **Close** button in the Database window.

Summary

In this lesson, you learned:

- The navigation buttons are used to move around the datasheet. They allow you to move to the first record, the last record, the previous record, or the next record. You can also use a navigation button to add a new record.

- There are three ways to undo changes to cells. If you make mistakes while keying data in a cell, you can click the Undo button. If you have already entered data and moved to the next cell, press Esc. To reverse all the changes to the previous record, choose Undo Saved Record on the Edit menu.

- To delete a record, use the Delete Record command. Entire records and fields can be selected by clicking the record and field selectors. Cut, Copy, and Paste are available in Datasheet view to move and copy data. The Paste Append command pastes a record at the end of the database.

- You can make many changes to a datasheet. You can change the row height and column width. You can also rearrange and freeze columns.

■ Field properties allow you to further customize a field beyond merely choosing a data type. Some of the more common field properties are Field Size, Input Mask, Caption, Default Value, Format, Required, and Decimal Places.

The easiest way to create a form is to use a Form Wizard. Using the Form Wizard, you select the fields and a style for the form. The Form Wizard then creates the form for you.

LESSON 2 REVIEW QUESTIONS

TRUE/FALSE

Circle the T if the statement is true or F if the statement is false.

T   F   1.   If you click a cell with the mouse, the insertion point appears in the cell.

T   F   2.   Holding down the Alt key allows you to select more than one field.

T   F   3.   In Access, you can use the Cut, Copy, and Paste commands.

T   F   4.   Changing the height of one row changes the height of all datasheet rows.

T   F   5.   You can delete records and fields in Datasheet view.

WRITTEN QUESTIONS

Write a brief answer to the following questions.

1.   What is the record pointer?

2.   How do you delete a record in Datasheet view?

3. What does the Paste Append command do?

4. Why would you want to freeze columns in Datasheet view?

5. In what view do you change field properties?

PROJECT 2-1

1. Open the **IA Project2-1** database from the student data files.

2. Open the **Employee Information** table in Datasheet view.

3. Go to record 7 and change the address to **4582 104th St**.

4. Go to record 11 and change the birth date to **12/14/61**.

5. Go to record 14 and change the first name to **Alex**.

6. Go to record 1 and change the last name to **Abraham**.

7. Undo your last change.

8. Delete record **5**.

9. Change the width of the **Address** field to **20** and the Zip Code field to **13**.

10. Change all other field widths using **Best Fit**.

11. Change the row height to **15**.

12. Change the left and right margins to **.5"** and print the table in landscape orientation.

13. Close the table. Click **Yes** if prompted to save changes to the layout of the table. Leave the database open for the next project.

PROJECT 2-2

1. Open the **Employee Information** table in Datasheet view.

2. Copy record **4** and paste it at the bottom of the table.

3. In the pasted record, change the First Name to **Mike,** the Title to **Account Executive**, the Birthdate to **9/28/61**, and the Salary to **2950.**

4. Move the **Birthdate** field to between the Zip Code and Department fields.

5. Freeze the **Employee Number**, **Last Name**, and **First Name** fields.

6. Scroll to the right until the **Birthdate** field is beside the **First Name** field.

7. Change the birth date of Hillary Davis to **10/28/68**.

8. Unfreeze the columns.

9. Change the left and right margins to **.5"** and print the table in landscape orientation.

10. Close the table. Click **Yes** if prompted to save changes to the layout of the table. Leave the database open for the next project.

PROJECT 2-3

1. Open the **Employee Information** table in Design view.

2. Format the **Salary** field for currency.

3. Select **Medium Date** from the Format field properties for the **Birthdate** field .

4. Key **Employee Number** as the Caption field property for the **Emp Number** field.

5. Make the **Zip Code** field **Required**.

6. Change the field size of the **Zip Code** field to **10.**

7. Save the table design. A message may appear asking if you want to continue. Click **Yes**. Another message may appear asking if you want to test the changes. Click **Yes**.

8. Switch to Datasheet view and insert the following records at the end of the table.

    ```
    16   Wells   Wendy   2610 21st St.   79832-2610   15-Feb-72   Sales   Secretary   $2,150.00
    17   Abbott  Donna   1824 Saratoga   79833-1900   12-Jan-59   Personnel   Manager   $2,880.00
    ```

9. Widen the **Salary** column and any other fields to show all data and column titles.

10. Change the left and right margins to **.5"** and print the table in landscape orientation.

11. Close the table. Click **Yes** if prompted to save changes to the layout of the table. Close the database.

Web Site

For information on careers, access the Occupational Outlook Handbook at *http://www.bls.gov/dolbls.htm.* Web sites and addresses change constantly. If you can't find the information at this site, try another.

CRITICAL THINKING

SCANS

ACTIVITY 2-1

Open the database you created for the Critical Thinking Activity in Lesson 1. Add two new records using the New Record buton. Select a field and make a change to the data. Delete an entire record. Copy one record and paste it into the table as a new record. If necessary, increase the column width and row height to see all the data. Rearrange the columns. Print and close the table.

ACTIVITY 2-2

You can use the Office Clipboard to collect and paste multiple items from the various Office programs. The Office Clipboard automatically copies multiple items when you do any of the following:

1. Copy or cut two different items in succession in the same program.

2. Copy one item, paste the item, and then copy another item in the same program.

3. Copy one item twice in succession.

Using the Help system, find the steps to collect and paste multiple items. Briefly write down the steps in numbered order.

CREATING AND MODIFYING FORMS

Creating Forms

Datasheet view is useful for many of the ways you work with a database table. Often, however, you may want a more convenient way to enter and view records. For example, the form shown in Figure 3-1 places all of the important fields from the Calls table into a convenient and attractive layout.

FIGURE 3-1
Forms can make entering and editing data easier

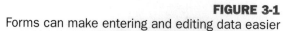
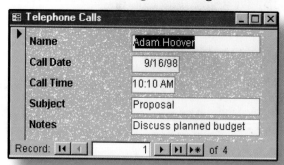

Forms can be created manually by placing fields on a blank form, arranging and sizing fields, and adding graphics. The Form Wizard makes the process easier. Creating a form manually gives you more flexibility, but in most cases the Form Wizard can create the form you need quickly and efficiently.

To create a form, click the Forms button on the Objects bar. Click the New button and the New Form dialog box appears, as shown in Figure 3-2. The New Form dialog box gives you several options for creating a form. In this lesson, you will use the Form Wizard option. The New Form dialog box also asks you to specify the table or query to use as a basis for the form. In more complex databases, you may have to choose among several tables or queries.

You can also create a form using the Form Wizard by double-clicking *Create form by using wizard* in the Database window.

FIGURE 3-2
New Form dialog box

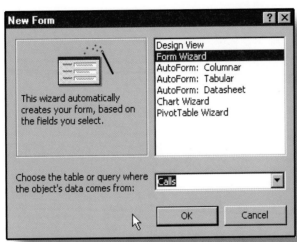

S TEP-BY-STEP ▷ 3.1

1. Open the **IA Step 3-1** database from the student data files. Click the **Forms** button on the Objects bar.

2. Click **New**. The New Form dialog box appears, as shown in Figure 3-2.

3. Choose the **Form Wizard** option and the **Calls** table from the drop-down list.

4. Click **OK**. The Form Wizard dialog box appears, as shown in Figure 3-3. Leave the Form Wizard dialog box on screen for the next Step-by-Step.

(continued on next page)

FIGURE 3-3
Form Wizard dialog box

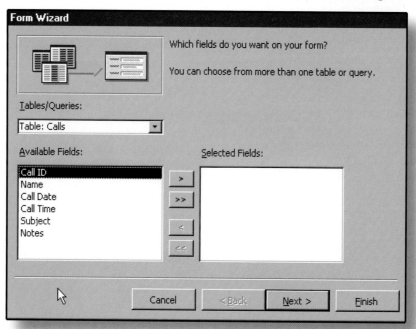

The next step is to choose the fields you want to appear on the form. To add a field to the form, click the field name in the *Available Fields* list and click the > button. To add all of the fields at once, click the >> button. If you plan to include almost all of the fields, click >> to include them all, then use the < button to remove the ones you do not want.

S TEP-BY-STEP ➩ 3.2

1. Click **>>**. All of the field names appear in the *Selected Fields* list.

2. Select the **Call ID** field in the *Selected Fields* list.

3. Click **<**. The **Call ID** field is moved back to the *Available Fields* list.

4. Click the **Next** button. The Form Wizard dialog box changes to ask you to select a layout for the form, as shown in Figure 3-4.

5. Leave the dialog box open for the next Step-by-Step.

FIGURE 3-4
Selecting a layout for a form

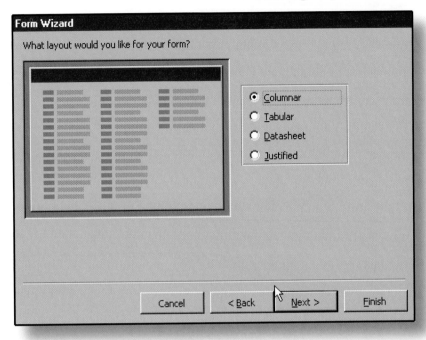

You have a choice of four different layouts for the form: *Columnar*, *Tabular*, *Datasheet*, and *Justified*. The *Columnar* layout is the most common type. The form in Figure 3-1 is an example of a *Columnar* layout. As data is entered, the insertion point moves down the fields.

The *Tabular* layout creates forms similar to Datasheet view. Both layouts display data in a tabular form. The *Tabular* layout gives you the ability to make a more attractive Datasheet view. Figure 3-5 shows an example of a form created using a tabular layout.

FIGURE 3-5
Tabular form layout

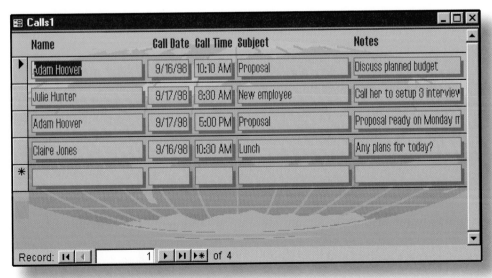

1. If not already selected, click the **Columnar** option.

2. Click **Next**. This dialog box asks you to choose a style, as shown in Figure 3-6.

3. Leave the dialog box open for the next Step-by-Step.

FIGURE 3-6
Choosing a style for a form

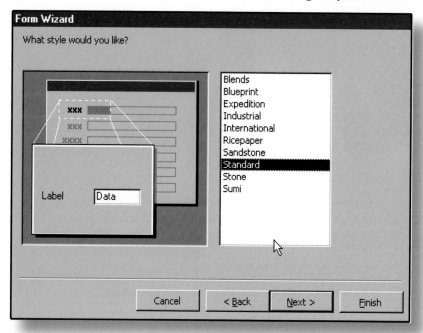

The style you select has no effect on the function of the form. Choosing a style allows you to personalize your form or give it flair. There are several styles from which to choose.

After you choose a style, you will be asked to name the form. The name you provide will appear in the Form section of the Database window. You are also given the option to begin using the form once it is created or to modify the form after the Form Wizard is done.

STEP-BY-STEP ▷ 3.4

1. Choose the **Standard** style from the list. The preview box shows you what this form style looks like. It should look similar to Figure 3-6.

2. Click the other styles to see what they look like.

3. Choose the **Sandstone** style and click **Next**. The final Form Wizard dialog box appears, as shown in Figure 3-7.

4. Key **Telephone Calls** in the title box.

FIGURE 3-7
Naming the form

FIGURE 3-8
A custom form

5. Click the **Open the form to view or enter information** button if it's not chosen already.

6. Click **Finish**. Access creates the form, which should look like that shown in Figure 3-8. Leave the form displayed for the next Step-by-Step.

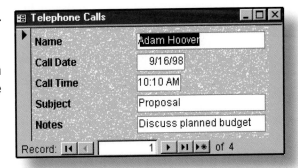

Using Forms

Using a form is basically the same as using Datasheet view. The same keys move the insertion point among the fields. You see the same set of navigation buttons at the bottom of the form, as shown in Figure 3-9. As with Datasheet view, you can move to a specific record by clicking in the Record Number box and entering the number of the record you want to see.

Table 3-1 summarizes the ways to move around when a form is displayed, including keyboard shortcuts.

To add a new record, click the Next Record button until the blank record at the end of the database appears, or click the New Record button. Key the new record. To edit an existing record, display the record and make changes in the fields of the form.

FIGURE 3-9
Navigation controls at the bottom of the form

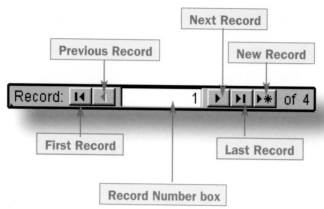

TABLE 3-1
Navigating a form

TO MOVE TO THE...	BUTTON	KEYBOARD SHORTCUT
First record	First Record button	Ctrl+Home
Last record	Last Record button	Ctrl+End
Next record	Next Record button	Page Down
Previous record	Previous Record button	Page Up

After entering or editing records in a form, you do not need to save the changes. Access saves them for you automatically. Remember to always save changes to the form design in Design view.

You can print forms much the same way you print tables. To print all the records in the form, choose Print on the File menu and the Print dialog box appears. In the Print dialog box, choose *All* from the *Print Range* options if you want to print all the records. Access will fit as many forms on each page as possible. To print only one record, display the record on the screen and choose Print on the File menu. Click the *Selected Record(s)* option from the *Print Range* options.

STEP-BY-STEP ▷ 3.5

1. Click the **New Record** button. A blank record appears in the form.

2. Enter the following information into the form:

   Name: **Excel Travel Agency**
   Call Date: **9/18/98**
   Call Time: **10:21 AM**
   Subject: **Seattle trip**
   Notes: **Flight 412 Departs 7:40 AM/Arrives 1:30 PM**

3. Click in the record number box. Delete the 5, key **4**, and press **Tab**.

4. Highlight the word **today** in the Notes field.

5. Key **Friday**.

6. Display record **5**, and choose **Print** on the **File** menu. The Print dialog box appears.

IA-48

7. Click the **Selected Record(s)** option from the *Print Range* options, and click **OK**. (The printed form may cut off the data in some of the fields.)

8. Choose **Close** on the **File** menu to close the form. Leave the database open for the next Step-by-Step.

Modifying Forms

Any form, whether created manually or with a Form Wizard, can be modified. You make changes to a form in Design view, which shows the structure of the form. To access Design view, select the form in the Database window, and then click the Design button. The form appears in Design view, as shown in Figure 3-10.

FIGURE 3-10
Design view

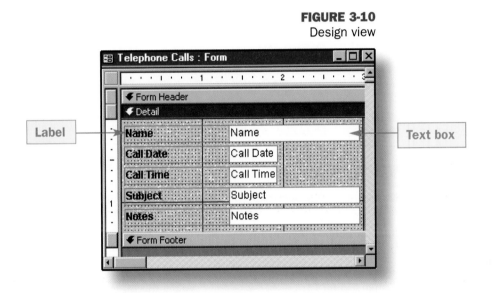

The form is divided into three sections: form header, detail, and form footer. The ***form header*** section displays information that remains the same for every record, such as the title for a form. A form header appears at the top of the screen in Form view and at the top of the first page of the forms when printed. The ***detail*** section displays records. You can display one record on the screen or as many as possible. A ***form footer*** section displays information that remains the same for every record, such as instructions for using the form. A form footer appears at the bottom of the screen in Form view or after the last detail section on the last page of the forms when printed.

The Toolbox, shown in Figure 3-11, has controls that you can use to modify and enhance the sections and objects on a form. The Label and Text Box tools are labeled because they are used frequently. There are three types of controls: bound, unbound, and calculated. A ***bound control*** is connected to a field in a table and is used to display, enter, and update data. An ***unbound control*** is not connected to a field and is used to display information, lines, rectangles, and pictures. The Label control, which is an unbound control, allows you to add text as a title or instructions to a form. Look again at Figure 3-10. Notice that the field name is contained in a Label control, and the field entry is contained in the Text Box control. A Text Box control is tied to, or *bound* to a field in the underlying table, whereas the Label control is not.

FIGURE 3-11
Toolbox

Label → Text box

In Design view, you can change the font, size, style, and other attributes of labels and text box data. Simply select the control, and use the buttons on the Formatting toolbar. Or, you can double-click a control to open its Properties dialog box and modify the attributes and other properties listed on the various tabs.

STEP-BY-STEP ⊳ 3.6

1. If not already selected, click **Forms** on the Objects bar. Choose the **Telephone Calls** form, and click the **Design** button. The form appears in Design view, as shown in Figure 3-10.

2. If necessary, display the Toolbox by clicking the **Toolbox** button. Click the **Line** button in the Toolbox.

3. Position the pointer in the **Detail** section between the Name label and the data field and click to place a line as shown in Figure 3-12.

4. Position the pointer at the right end of the line until a double arrow appears. Click and drag the right end of the line to the bottom of the form until it is vertical between the field labels and data fields as shown in Figure 3-13.

5. In the Detail section, click twice on the **Call Date** label. The Label properties window opens, as shown in Figure 3-14. If necessary, select the **All** tab.

FIGURE 3-12
Inserting a line

FIGURE 3-13
Repositioning the line object

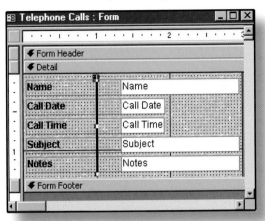

FIGURE 3-14
The Label screen

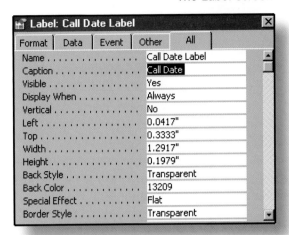

6. Change the caption to **Date** and close the Properties window.

7. Click twice on the **Call Time** label and change the caption to **Time**.

8. Position the pointer on the line between the **Form Header** section and **Detail** section until a double arrow appears as shown in Figure 3-15.

9. Click and drag the line down about a half inch to increase the height of the Form Header section.

10. Click the **Label** button in the Toolbox.

11. Position the pointer in the **Form Header** section and click and drag to draw a text box as shown in Figure 3-16.

12. Key **TELEPHONE CALLS** at the insertion point that appears in the text box.

13. Click outside the text box to view the title. Double-click on the text box to display the Label properties dialog box.

FIGURE 3-15
Resizing the Form Header

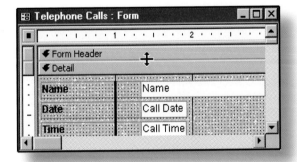

FIGURE 3-16
Inserting a text box

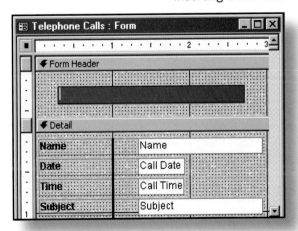

(continued on next page)

14. Scroll through the list of properties until you locate the *Font Name* and *Font Size* properties. Click in the **Font Name** text box, click the down arrow, and select **Arial Black**. Click in the **Font Size** box, click the down arrow, and change the size to **12**. Close the dialog box.

15. Position the pointer on the line at the bottom of the **Form Footer** section until a double arrow appears as shown in Figure 3-17.

16. Click and drag the line down about a half inch to increase the height of the Form Footer section.

17. Click the **Check Box** button in the Toolbox.

18. Position the pointer in the **Form Footer** and click to place a check box as shown in Figure 3-18. Your text box to the right of the check mark will contain a different number from the one showing in the figure.

FIGURE 3-17
Resizing the Form Footer

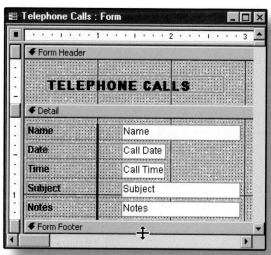

FIGURE 3-18
Form Footer with check box

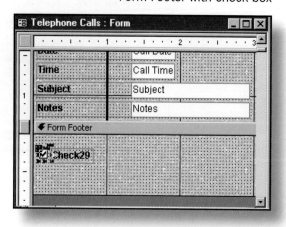

19. Double-click the text box to the right of the check mark. The Label properties dialog box appears.

20. Change the caption to **Return Call** and close the dialog box.

21. Click on the right border of the text box and drag to see all of the caption.

22. Choose **Close** on the **File** menu. A message appears asking if you want to save changes. Click **Yes**. You are returned to the Database window.

23. With the name of the form highlighted, click **Open**. The modified form appears on the screen.

24. If necessary, scroll to see all of the records. Go back to **record 1**, select **Print** on the **File** menu, make sure the **Selected Record(s)** option is selected, and click **OK**. Close the form and the database.

Hot Tip

To delete a line or other object on a form, make sure you are in Design view, click on the line or object to select it, and press the **Delete** key or choose **Delete** on the **Edit** menu.

Working with Calculated Controls

A *calculated control* on a form uses an expression to generate the data value for a field. For example, on an Orders form you might use the expression, Unit Cost multiplied by Units Ordered or =*Unit Cost*Units Ordered*, to determine the value in the Total Cost field.

To create a calculated control on a form, open the Properties dialog box for the text box that will contain the calculation. The Properties dialog box will look like that shown in Figure 3-19. In the Control Source text box, key the expression for calculating the field value. You can also key a name for the calculated field in the Name text box, and determine the numerical format in the Format text box. Open the form and the value for the calculated field is calculated for each record.

FIGURE 3-19

Text Box properties dialog box

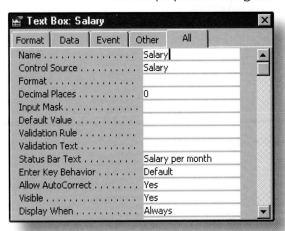

1. Open the **IA Step3-7** database from the student data files.

2. Click **Forms** on the Objects bar. Choose the **Employee Bonus** form and click the **Design** button. The form appears in Design view, as shown in Figure 3-20.

3. Position the pointer on the **Salary** text box as shown in Figure 3-20. Click twice to display the Text Box: Salary properties dialog box, as shown in Figure 3-19. If not already selected, choose the **All** tab.

4. Key **Bonus** in the **Name** box.

FIGURE 3-20
Design view

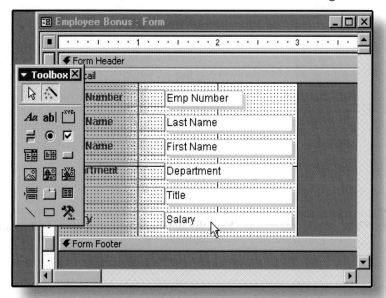

5. Key **=[Salary]*.10** in the **Control Source** box. The bonus field will be 10% of the employee's salary.

6. Click in the **Format** text box, click the down arrow, and choose **Currency**.

7. Close the properties dialog box. Click twice on the **Salary** label box which is to the left of the text box. The Label properties dialog box displays, as shown in Figure 3-21.

FIGURE 3-21
Label properties dialog box screen

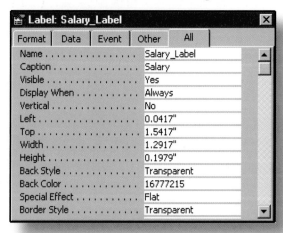

8. Change the **Caption** field to **Bonus** and close the dialog box. Switch to **Form** view by clicking the **View** button.

9. If necessary, scroll to see all the records. Print the form for record **2**. Close the form and leave the database open for the next Step-by-Step.

Working with Hyperlinks

As you learned in Lesson 1, you can define a field in a database table as a hyperlink data type. This type of field actually stores the path to another database object or a specified file, or the address to a Web site.

You can also insert a hyperlink in a form (or the report or page objects in a database) that links you to another object in the database, another file, or a Web site. For example, you might have a form in a company database that you use to enter information regarding employees, like their addresses, start dates, department, responsibilities, etc. You also maintain an Excel spreadsheet that tracks employees' salaries, bonuses, benefits, etc. You could insert a hyperlink in the database form that when clicked, immediately links you to the spreadsheet. The hyperlink provides you with an easy way to gain quick access to more information.

To insert a hyperlink, you must be in the form's Design view. Make sure the pointer is in the section of the form in which you want the hyperlink to appear, and then click the Insert Hyperlink button. In the Insert Hyperlink dialog box, select the file or Web page you want to link to, and then click OK.

Compacting and Repairing a Database

If you delete data or objects from a database, the database can become fragmented and use disk space inefficiently. Compacting rearranges how the database is stored on disk and optimizes the performance of the database. Access combines compacting and repairing into one process.

S TEP-BY-STEP ▷ 3.8

1. Click **Tables** on the Objects bar, and open the **Employee Information** table in Datasheet view or Design view. Be sure no one else has the database open before continuing.

2. Choose **Database Utilities** on the **Tools** menu.

3. Click **Compact and Repair Database**.

4. When finished, close the table and database.

 Hot Tip

Follow the steps above to compact and repair a database that is not open. Dialog boxes will display asking you to specify the database to compact and the new file name for the compacted database. If you use the same name, the original file will be replaced with the new compacted file.

Summary

In this lesson, you learned:

■ The easiest way to create a form is to use a Form Wizard. Using the Form Wizard, you select the fields and a style for the form. The Form Wizard then creates the form for you.

■ Any form, whether created manually or with a Form Wizard, can be modified. You make changes to a form using Design view, which shows the structure of the form.

■ The form in Design view is divided into three sections: form header, detail, and form footer. The form header section displays information that remains the same for every record, such as the title for a form. A form header appears at the top of the screen in Form view and at the top of the first page of records when printed. The detail section displays records. You can display one record on the screen or as many as possible. A form footer section displays information that remains the same for every record, such as instructions for using the form. A form footer appears at the bottom of the screen in Form view or after the last detail section on the last page of records when printed.

■ The Toolbox has controls that you can use to modify and enhance the sections within a form. There are three types of controls: bound, unbound, and calculated. A bound control is connected to a field in a table and is used to display, enter, and update data. An unbound control is not connected to a field.

■ A calculated control on a form uses an expression to calculate the data value for a field.

■ If you delete data or objects from a database, the database can become fragmented and use disk space inefficiently. Compacting the database rearranges how the database is stored on disk and optimizes the performance of the database.

LESSON 3 REVIEW QUESTIONS

TRUE/FALSE

Circle T if the statement is true or F if the statement is false.

T F 1. The style you select for a form has an effect on the function of the form.

T F 2. The Toolbox has tools that you can use to modify forms.

T F 3. You make modifications to a form in Datasheet view.

T F 4. If you delete data or objects from a database, the database can become fragmented and use disk space inefficiently.

T F 5. You can change a control's attributes by double-clicking it in Design view, and making changes in the control's Properties dialog box.

WRITTEN QUESTIONS

Write a brief answer to the following questions.

1. What are the four different layouts for a form?

2. How do you move to a specific record using a form?

3. What will happen if you use the same name for a newly compacted database?

4. What view is similar to a Tabular layout for a database?

5. In what view do you change the properties for a control?

PROJECT 3-1

1. Open the **IA Project3-1** database from the student data files. Create a new form with the Form Wizard using the **Employee Information** table.

2. Add the **First Name**, **Last Name**, **Department**, **Title**, and **Birthdate** fields.

3. Use the **Columnar** layout and the **Standard** style.

4. Title the form **Employee Birthdays**.

5. Go to record **3**, Trent Broach, and change the title to **Director of Sales**.

6. Go to record **15**, Donna Abbott, and change the *Birthdate* to **10-Jan-59**.

7. Print record **15**.

8. Close the form and leave the database open for the next project.

PROJECT 3-2

1. Open the **Employee Bonus** form in Design view.

2. Increase the size of the **Form Header** section.

3. Using the Label control, add a label box titled **EMPLOYEE BONUS**.

4. Change the *Font Name* to **Arial Black** and the *Font Size* to **12**.

5. Increase the size of the **Form Footer** section.

6. Using the Check Box control, add a check box titled **Eligible for Stock Plan**. If necessary, increase the size of the text box to see all the title.

7. When finished, save the changes and switch to **Form** view.

8. Open the modified form to view the changes. Display and print record **6**.

9. Close the form and database.

CRITICAL THINKING

ACTIVITY 3-1

Open the database you created for the Critical Thinking Activity in Lesson 1. Use the Form Wizard to create a Tabular form that includes the fields of your database table. Choose an attractive style for the form. Add a record to the table using the new form. Print the record and close the form. Close the database.

ACTIVITY 3-2

Using the Help feature, look up the definition of a subform and how it works. Write down a short definition and provide an example of a form and subform relationship used in a business setting. Be sure to mention the name of the field used to link the form and subform.

LESSON 4

FINDING AND ORDERING DATA

OBJECTIVES

Upon completion of this lesson, you should be able to:

- Find data in a database.
- Query a database.
- Use filters.
- Sort a database.
- Index a database.
- Establish relationships in a database.
- Create a query from related tables.

⏱ **Estimated Time: 1.5 hours**

Using Find

The Find command is the easiest way to quickly locate data in a database. The Find command allows you to search the database for specified information. There are several options that allow you flexibility in performing the search. These options appear in the Find and Replace dialog box, shown in Figure 4-1.

FIGURE 4-1
Find and Replace dialog box

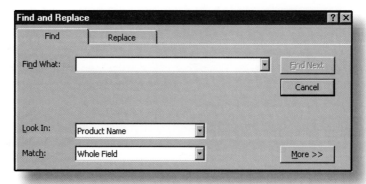

INTRODUCTION TO MICROSOFT ACCESS

You can access the Find and Replace dialog box by choosing Find on the Edit menu or by clicking the Find button on the toolbar. The Find command is available only when a datasheet or form is displayed.

To search for the data in a particular field, place your insertion point in the field you want to search and click the Find button. The Find and Replace dialog box opens with the *Look In* box containing the field name to search. Key the data for which you are searching in the *Find What* box.

The *Match* text box has a drop-down list that lets you choose what part of the field to search. If you want to match exactly the entire contents of a field, choose *Whole Field*. More commonly, however, you will not want to enter the field's entire contents. For example, if you are searching a database of books for titles relating to history, you might want to search for titles with the word *history* anywhere in the title. In that case, you would choose *Any Part of Field* from the list. You can also specify that the search look only at the first part of the field by choosing the *Start of Field* option. For example, if you need to search a table of names for people whose last name begins with *Mc,* the *Start of Field* option would be convenient.

Click the More button and note that the *Match Case* check box gives you the option of a case-sensitive search. Click the drop-down arrow for the *Search* text box to display a list in which you can specify whether you want to search up from the current record position, down from the current record position, or the entire table.

Click Find Next to display the next record that matches the criteria you've specified. When the entire database has been searched, a message appears stating that the search item was not found.

Hot Tip

Use the Find command when searching for one record at a time. Use the Filter tool when searching for multiple records. You will learn about filters later in this lesson.

STEP-BY-STEP ▷ 4.1

1. Open **IA Step4-1** from the student data files. This database includes a table of products. The products represent the inventory of a small office supply store.

2. Open the **Products** table in Datasheet view.

3. Place the insertion point in the **Product Name** field of the first record.

4. Click the **Find** button. The Find and Replace dialog box appears.

5. Key **Fax Machine** in the **Find What** box.

6. Be sure the **Product Name** field appears in the **Look In** box.

7. Click the down arrow to the right of the **Match** box and choose **Any Part of Field** from the list.

8. Click the **More** button to display more options.

   More >>

9. Be sure **All** appears in the **Search** box. The *Match Case* and *Search Fields As Formatted* options should not be selected.

10. Click the **Find Next** button. Product 32 is selected, as shown in Figure 4-2.

    Find Next

11. Click **Find Next** again. A message appears telling you that the search item was not found. There is only one fax machine in the product line. Click **OK**.

12. Click **Cancel** to close the Find and Replace box.

13. Close the table and leave the database open for the next Step-by-Step.

(continued on next page)

FIGURE 4-2
Finding data

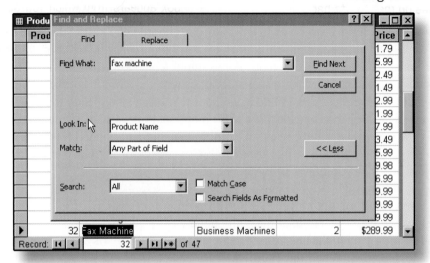

Using Queries

The Find command is an easy way of finding data. Often, however, you will need to locate data based on more complex criteria. For example, you may need to search for products with a value greater than $10. You cannot do that with the Find command. A special operation, called a *query*, will let you combine criteria to perform complex searches. For example, a query could locate products with a value greater than $10 of which fewer than three are in stock.

Queries allow you to "ask" the database almost anything about your data. In addition, you can create queries to display only the fields relevant to the search. For example, if you were querying a database of customers to locate those with a total purchased amount of $10,000 or more, you might want to display only the customers' names and total purchased amounts, rather than all the data in the table.

The first step in creating a query is to open the appropriate database and click Queries on the Objects bar. Then click the New button to create a new query. The New Query dialog box appears, as shown in Figure 4-3. The New Query dialog box gives you the option to create a query manually or to use one of several Query Wizards. In this lesson, you will learn to create a query manually. You use the Design View option in the New Query dialog box to do this.

FIGURE 4-3
New Query dialog box

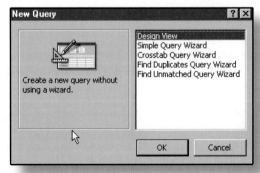

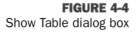

S TEP-BY-STEP ▷ 4.2

1. Click **Queries** on the Objects bar.

2. Click the **New** button. The New Query dialog box appears, as shown in Figure 4-3.

3. Choose **Design View**, if it is not already selected, and click **OK**. The Show Table dialog box appears from which you select a table to query, as shown in Figure 4-4. Leave the Show Table dialog box on the screen for the next Step-by-Step.

FIGURE 4-4
Show Table dialog box

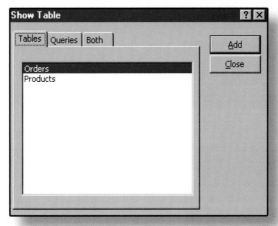

Because databases often include more than one table, you can choose the table you want to use in the Show Table dialog box. The Add button adds the fields from the highlighted table to your new query. After choosing a table and adding fields, click Close to close the Show Table dialog box. The fields you added now appear in a dialog box in the top pane of the query's design window, as shown in Figure 4-5.

FIGURE 4-5
Query window

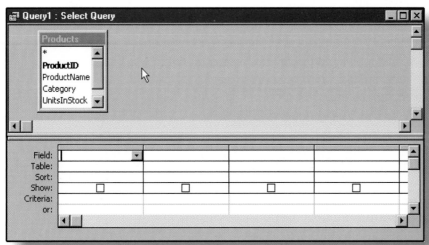

The query window is divided into two parts. The top part of the window shows the available tables and fields (the Products table and its fields are shown in Figure 4-5).

The bottom part of the window contains a grid that allows you to specify the information needed to create a query. To create a query, you must supply three pieces of information: the fields you want to search, what you are searching for (called the *search criteria*), and what fields you want to display with the results. The *Field* row is where you select a field to be part of the query. Click the down arrow to display the available fields. To include more than one field in a query, click in the next column of the *Field* row and choose another field.

The *Sort* row allows you to sort the results of the query. The *Show* checkbox determines whether the field is to be displayed in the query results. Normally, this will be checked. Occasionally, however, you may want to search by a field that does not need to appear in the query results.

For the fields you want to search, enter search conditions in the *Criteria* row. For example, if you want to find only records that contain the words *Office Supplies* in the Category field, you would key "Office Supplies" in the *Criteria* row of the Category field. When keying text in the *Criteria* row, always enclose it with quotation marks.

You can refine a search by using operators. For example, you might want to find all employees in a database table who make more than $30,000 a year, or you might want to search an inventory table for products of which there are less than five in stock. You can use the relational operators listed in Table 4-1 to conduct these types of searches.

TABLE 4-1
Relational operators

OPERATOR	DESCRIPTION
>	Greater than
<	Less than
=	Equal to
>=	Greater than or equal to
<=	Less than or equal to
<>	Not equal

You can also use the *And* or the *Or* operators. If you want to find records that meet more than one criteria, such as employees who make more than $30,000 a year *and* who have been with the company for less than two years, you would use the ***And operator***. Simply enter the criteria in the same Criteria row for the fields you want to search.

If you want to find records that meet one criteria or another, you would use the ***Or operator***. Enter the criteria in different rows for the fields you want to search.

After choosing the fields and entering search criteria, you should save the query by choosing Save on the File menu and keying a name for the query. To run a query, click the Run button in the query's Design view. Or, you can run a query directly from the Database window. Select the query, and then click the Open button.

Hot Tip

To modify a query, open it in Design view. You can change the fields to be searched, the search criteria, and the fields to be displayed in the query results.

S TEP-BY-STEP ▷ 4.3

1. With the **Products** table selected, click **Add**. The fields of the *Products* table appear in the query window. Click **Close** to close the Show Table dialog box.

2. In the query grid, click the down arrow in the **Field** row of the first column and choose **ProductName**, as shown in Figure 4-6.

3. Click the down arrow in the **Field** row of the second column and choose **UnitsInStock** from the menu.

4. In the **Criteria** row of the **Units in Stock** column, key **<3**. This tells Access to display any records with fewer than 3 items in stock.

5. In the third column, choose the **Retail Price** field.

6. In the **Field** row of the fourth column, key **[Retail Price]*.90**.

7. Click in the **Table** row and choose **Products**.

8. Click in the **Field** row again and highlight **Expr1**. Replace *Expr1* by keying **Discount Price**. (Microsoft Access enters the default field name Expr1. Unless replaced by a more appropriate name this is the column heading you will see in Datasheet view.)

9. With the cursor in the **Field** box, *right*-click and choose **Properties** on the shortcut menu. The Field Properties dialog box will display.

10. Click in the **Format** box on the General tab and scroll down to click **Currency**. Close the dialog box.

11. Choose **Save** on the **File** menu. You are prompted for a name for the query.

12. Key **Reorder Query** and click **OK**.

13. Choose **Close** on the **File** menu.

14. To run the query, highlight **Reorder Query** in the Database window and click **Open**. The results of the query appear, as shown in Figure 4-7.

15. Choose **Print** on the **File** menu to print the table with the query applied. Click **OK**.

16. Choose **Close** on the **File** menu to close the results of the query. Leave the database open for the next Step-by-Step.

C ▷ Did You Know?

You can save a table, form, or query as a Web page. Choose **Save As HTML** on the **File** menu. This command will start the *Publish to the Web Wizard*. Follow the steps through the wizard to create your Web page.

FIGURE 4-6
Selecting fields to query

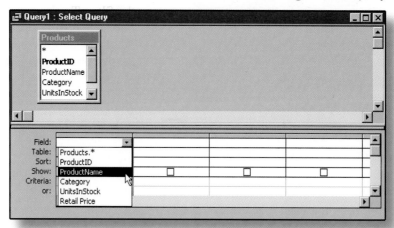

FIGURE 4-7
Running a query

Product Name	Units In Stock	Retail Price	Discount Price
Heavy Duty Stapler	2	$16.99	$15.29
Letter Sorter	2	$7.99	$7.19
Speaker Phone	2	$99.99	$89.99
Fax Machine	2	$289.99	$260.99
Cash Register	0	$269.99	$242.99
Photocopier	1	$699.00	$629.10
Typewriter	2	$129.99	$116.99
Computer Desk	2	$299.00	$269.10
Oak Office Desk	1	$399.00	$359.10
Bookshelf	2	$99.99	$89.99
Guest Chair	2	$159.00	$143.10

Filters

Queries are very powerful and flexible tools. In many cases, however, less power is adequate. *Filters* provide a way to display selected records in a database more easily than using queries. Think of a filter as a simpler form of a query. A filter "filters out" the records that do not match the specified criteria. When you use a filter, all of the fields are displayed, and the filter cannot be saved for use again later.

There are four types of filters: Filter By Form, Filter By Selection, Filter Excluding Selection, and Advanced Filter/Sort. The Filter By Form allows you to select records by keying the criteria into a form. To use Filter By Selection (the fastest and easiest option), you highlight a value or part of a value in a field as the criteria for the selection. The Filter Excluding Selection excludes the value you highlight as the criteria for the selection. To duplicate a query or create a more complicated selection use the Advanced Filter/Sort option.

To create a filter, a table must be open. Select Filter on the Records menu and then select one of the filter types from the submenu. If you select the Advanced Filter/Sort option, a Filter window like the one in Figure 4-8 appears. Notice that the Filter window is very similar to the query window. (Since there is only one table in this database, it's automatically added to the top part of the window.) Also notice that there is no *Show* row in the grid—all fields are displayed when you use a filter. In the grid, you select only those fields for which you want to enter criteria. When you have included all of the field specifications, choose Apply Filter/Sort on the Filter menu or click the Apply Filter button on the toolbar.

If you select Filter by Form, only the field names in the datasheet are displayed. When you click in a field, the filter arrow appears, as shown in Figure 4-9. Click the arrow and choose a data value from the list of all data values entered in the field. When finished, apply the filter. To create a filter by Selection you must first highlight the criteria in the table. Click Filter by Selection on the submenu and the filtered records display.

FIGURE 4-8
Design view for an advanced filter

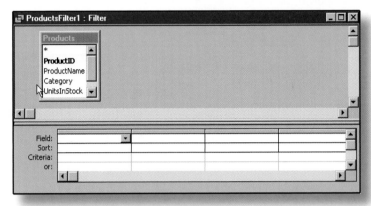

FIGURE 4-9
Filter by form

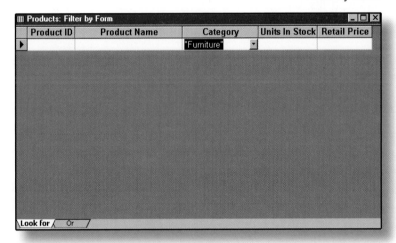

STEP-BY-STEP ▷ 4.4

1. In the Database window, click **Tables** on the Objects bar.

2. Open the **Products** table in Datasheet view.

3. Choose **Filter** on the **Records** menu, then select **Advanced Filter/Sort** on the sub-

menu. The Filter window appears, as shown in Figure 4-8.

4. Click the down arrow in the **Field** row of the first column and choose **Category** from the menu.

(continued on next page)

5. Key **"Furniture"** in the **Criteria** field of the first column. Include the quotation marks.

6. Click the **Apply Filter** button on the toolbar. The filter is applied, and only the products in the Furniture category are displayed, as shown in Figure 4-10.

7. Print the table with the filter applied.

8. Click the **Remove Filter** button to remove the filter and display all records.

9. Choose **Filter** on the **Records** menu, then select **Filter by Form** on the submenu. A form appears, as shown in Figure 4-9.

10. Click the down arrow in the **Category** field. (Furniture was the criteria in the previous filter.)

11. Choose **Desk Accessories** from the list of options.

12. Click the **Apply Filter** button on the toolbar. The filter is applied, and only the products in the Desk Accessories category are displayed, as shown in Figure 4-11.

13. Print the table with the filter applied.

14. Click the **Remove Filter** button.

15. To create a Filter by Selection, highlight **Calculator** in the **Product Name** field for record 27.

16. Choose **Filter** on the **Records** menu, then select **Filter by Selection** on the submenu. The filter is applied, and only the calculator products are displayed, as shown in Figure 4-12.

17. Print the table with the filter applied.

18. Click the **Remove Filter** button. Leave the table on the screen for the next Step-by-Step.

FIGURE 4-10
A filter displaying the Furniture category

Product ID	Product Name	Category	Units In Stock	Retail Price
39	Computer Desk	Furniture	2	$299.00
40	Oak Office Desk	Furniture	1	$399.00
41	Bookshelf	Furniture	2	$99.99
42	Executive Chair	Furniture	3	$259.99
43	Guest Chair	Furniture	2	$159.00
44	Desk Chair	Furniture	3	$129.99
45	4-Drawer Filing Cabinet	Furniture	4	$139.99
46	2-Drawer Filing Cabinet	Furniture	3	$79.99
47	Folding Table (8')	Furniture	4	$46.00
* (AutoNumber)				

Record: ◄ ◄ 1 ► ►I ►* of 9 (Filtered)

FIGURE 4-11
A filter displaying the Desk Accessories category

Product ID	Product Name	Category	Units In Stock	Retail Price
22	Letter Tray	Desk Accessories	4	$2.99
23	Desk Accessory Set	Desk Accessories	3	$21.99
24	Letter Sorter	Desk Accessories	2	$7.99
25	Drawer Tray	Desk Accessories	5	$3.49
26	Rotary Card File	Desk Accessories	3	$25.99
*	(utoNumber)			

FIGURE 4-12

A filter displaying the Calculator products

Product ID	Product Name	Category	Units In Stock	Retail Price
27	Scientific Calculator	Business Machines	3	$19.98
28	Basic Calculator	Business Machines	7	$6.99
29	Printing Calculator	Business Machines	3	$29.99
*	(utoNumber)			

Sorting

Sorting is an important part of working with a database. Often you will need records to appear in a specific order. For example, you may normally want a mailing list sorted by last name. But when preparing to mail literature to the entire mailing list, you may need the records to appear in ZIP code order. Access provides buttons on the toolbar to quickly sort the records of a table.

To sort a table, open the table and place the insertion point in the field by which you want to sort. Then click either the Sort Ascending or Sort Descending button. An *ascending sort* arranges records from A to Z or smallest to largest. A *descending sort* arranges records from Z to A or largest to smallest.

STEP-BY-STEP ▷ 4.5

1. The **Products** table should be open in Datasheet view. Suppose you want to sort the records from least in stock to most in stock. Place the insertion point in the first record of the **Units In Stock** field.

2. Click the **Sort Ascending** button. The records appear in order by Units In Stock.

3. Suppose you want to sort the records from most expensive to least expensive. Place the

insertion point in the first record of the **Retail Price** field.

4. Click the **Sort Descending** button. The products are sorted from most to least expensive.

5. Print the table and leave it open for the next Step-by-Step.

Sorting using the Sort Ascending and Sort Descending buttons is quick and easy. However, you will sometimes need to sort by more than one field. For example, suppose you want to sort the Products table by Category, but within each category you want the items to appear from most to least expensive. To perform this kind of sort, you must create a filter.

To use a filter to sort, create a filter as you normally do, but select an ascending or descending sort for the desired field or fields by clicking the down arrow in the *Sort* row. If the filter window has information left over from a previous sort or filter, you may need to click the cells with existing data and press the Backspace key to clear them.

S TEP-BY-STEP ▷ 4.6

1. Choose **Filter** on the **Records** menu, and then choose **Advanced Filter/Sort** on the submenu.

2. Choose the **Category** and **Retail Price** fields as shown in Figure 4-13. Click the down arrow in the **Sort** row and choose **Ascending** for the Category field, and **Descending** for the Retail Price field. You may need to clear some existing data from the filter window.

3. Click the **Apply Filter** button.

4. Scroll through the datasheet to see that the records have been sorted according to the specifications in the filter.

5. Print the table with the filter applied.

6. Leave the table and filter window open for the next Step-by-Step.

FIGURE 4-13
Sorting by more than one field

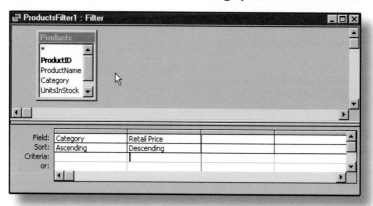

To filter and sort at the same time, you add the information for both to the same filter window. Choose Filter on the Records menu and select Advanced/Filter Sort. In the filter window select the field to which you want to apply a filter and the field to be sorted. Click the Apply Filter button on the toolbar.

1. Choose **Filter** on the **Records** menu, and then choose **Advanced Filter/Sort** on the submenu.

2. Suppose you want to display only the products with a retail price greater than $150. Key **>150** in the **Criteria** row of the **Retail Price** column. Leave the Category column as is.

3. Click the **Apply Filter** button. Only seven of the records meet the filter criteria and they are sorted by retail price within the categories, as shown in Figure 4-14.

4. Print the table with the filter applied.

5. Click the **Remove Filter** button to remove the filter. All of the records appear again.

6. Close the table. If prompted to save the design of the table, click **No**. Leave the database open for the next Step-by-Step.

FIGURE 4-14
Filtering and sorting records

Product ID	Product Name	Category	Units In Stock	Retail Price
34	Photocopier	Business Machines	1	$699.00
32	Fax Machine	Business Machines	2	$289.99
33	Cash Register	Business Machines	0	$269.99
40	Oak Office Desk	Furniture	1	$399.00
39	Computer Desk	Furniture	2	$299.00
42	Executive Chair	Furniture	3	$259.99
43	Guest Chair	Furniture	2	$159.00
*	(AutoNumber)			

Record: ◄◄ ◄ 1 ► ►I ►* of 7 (Filtered)

Indexing

Indexing is an important part of database management systems. In small databases, indexes do not provide much benefit. Large databases, however, rely on indexing to quickly locate data. In an Access database, you can specify that certain fields be indexed. Access can find data in an indexed field faster than it can find data in a field that is not indexed.

To index a field, go to Design view. For each field in Design view, you can specify whether you want the field to be indexed.

If indexing improves speed, why not index all of the fields? The reason is that each indexed field causes more work and uses more disk space. Before indexing a database, you should be sure that the benefit of indexing a field outweighs the negatives caused by indexing. As a general rule, index fields only in large databases, and index only those fields that are regularly used to locate records.

Setting a Primary Key

When you save a newly created table in a database, a message appears asking if you want to create a *primary key*, which is a special field that assigns a unique identifier to each record. You can have Access create the primary key for you, in which case, each record is automatically assigned a unique number. Or, you can set the primary key to an existing field within the table. The existing field should contain a unique value such as an ID number or part number. Primary keys must be set before creating table relationships, which are covered in the next section.

To designate a field as the primary key, open the table in Design view. Choose the field you want to set as the primary key by clicking the row selector. Click the Primary Key button on the toolbar. A primary key icon will now appear next to the primary key field.

S TEP-BY-STEP ▷ 4.8

1. In the **IA Step4-1** database, open the **Products** table in **Design** view.

2. Click the **row selector** for the **Product ID** field.

3. Click the **Primary Key** button on the toolbar. A key icon appears next to the **ProductID** field, as shown in Figure 4-15.

4. Close the table and a message appears asking you to save changes to the table. Click **Yes**. Leave the database open for the next Step-by-Step.

FIGURE 4-15
Setting the primary key

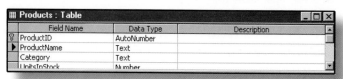

Relationships

By defining *relationships* between the different tables within a database, you can create queries, forms, and reports to display information from several tables at once. You can create a relationship between tables that contain a common field. For example, you might have a table that contains the name, telephone number, and other data on real estate agents. A second table might contain information, including the name of the listing agent, on properties for sale. You could set up a relationship between the two tables by joining the fields containing the agents' names. Then, you could create forms, queries, and reports that include fields from both tables.

The common fields must be of the same data type, although they can have different field names. In most relationships, the common field is also the primary key in at least one of the tables. It is referred to as the foreign key in the other table(s).

To ensure valid relationships between tables and prevent invalid data from being entered, Access utilizes *referential integrity* rules. These also help ensure that related data is not accidentally deleted or changed. To enforce referential integrity between tables, choose the Enforce Referential Integrity option when creating the relationship. If you break one of the rules with the related tables, Access displays a message and doesn't allow the change.

A *one-to-many relationship*, as illustrated in Figure 4-16, is the most common type of relationship. In a one-to-many relationship, a record in Table A can have matching records in Table B, but a record in Table B has only one matching record in Table A. In Figure 4-16, the Realtor field is the primary key in the Realtors table and the foreign key in the Houses table.

You define a relationship by clicking Relationships on the Tools menu or clicking the Relationships button on the toolbar. Add the tables you want to relate to the Relationships window. Next, you drag the key field from one table to the key field in the other table.

FIGURE 4-16
One-to-many relationship

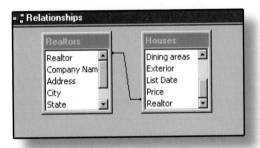

STEP-BY-STEP ▷ 4.9

1. The **IA Step4-1** Database window should still be open. Click **Relationships** on the **Tools** menu or click the **Relationships** button on the toolbar. If the Show Table dialog box does not appear, as shown in Figure 4-17, click **Show Table** on the **Relationships** menu.

2. Choose the **Products** table and click **Add**. Repeat this step for the **Orders** table.

3. When finished, click **Close**. The Relationships window should appear as shown in Figure 4-18.

4. Click the **ProductID** field in the **Products** table. Drag and drop it on the **Product ID** field in the **Orders** table. (*Remember:* The common fields don't have to have the same field name; they

just need to be of the same data type.) The Edit Relationships dialog box will appear as shown in Figure 4-19.

5. Check to be sure the Product ID field appears for both the Products and Orders tables. Click the **Enforce Referential Integrity** check box.

6. Click **Create**. The Relationships window appears as shown in Figure 4-20.

7. Close the Relationships window and a message appears asking if you want to save changes to the layout of Relationships. Click **Yes** to save the changes. Leave the database open for the next Step-by-Step.

(continued on next page)

FIGURE 4-17
Show Table dialog box

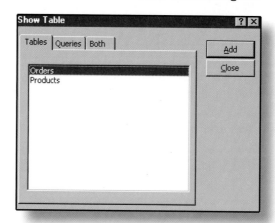

FIGURE 4-18
Relationships window

FIGURE 4-19
Edit Relationships dialog box

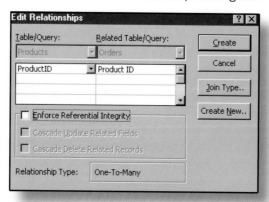

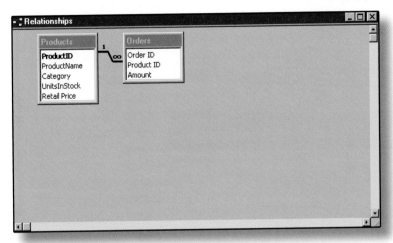

FIGURE 4-20
Table relationships

To print a database relationship, click Relationships on the Tools menu to display the Relationships window. Click Print Relationships on the File menu and a report listing the table relationships will display. Choose Print on the File menu or save the report for future reference.

STEP-BY-STEP ▷ 4.10

1. With the **IA Step4-1** Database window open, click **Relationships** on the **Tools** menu. The Relationships window appears (see Figure 4-20).

2. Click **Print Relationships** on the **File** menu. A report listing the table relationships will display as shown in Figure 4-21.

3. Click **Print** on the **File** menu and the Print dialog box appears. Click **OK** to print the report.

4. Close the Report window. A message displays asking if you want to save changes to the design of the report. Click **No**.

5. Close the Relationships window. Leave the database open for the next Step-by-Step.

FIGURE 4-21
Table relationships report

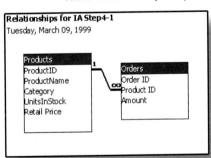

Viewing Related Records

To view the related records between two tables you can add a ***subdatasheet***. To insert a subdatasheet, open the table with the primary key in Datasheet view, and choose Subdatasheet on the Insert menu. In the Insert Subdatasheet window, choose the related table and click OK. The table with the primary key will reappear. Click the expand indicator icon (+) to the left of each row to display a subdatasheet of related records.

STEP-BY-STEP ▷ 4.11

1. Open the **Products** table in Datasheet view.

2. Click **Subdatasheet** on the **Insert** menu. The Insert Subdatasheet dialog box will appear as shown in Figure 4-22.

3. Choose the **Orders** table and click **OK**. The Products table will reappear.

4. Click the expand indicator button (**+**) to the left of Product ID number **3** to display a subdat-

sheet of related records as shown in Figure 4-23.

5. Click the indicator button again to close the subdatasheet. Close the **Products** table. A message displays asking if you want to save the changes to the Products table. Click **Yes** to save. Leave the database open for the next Step-by-Step.

FIGURE 4-22
Insert Subdatasheet dialog box

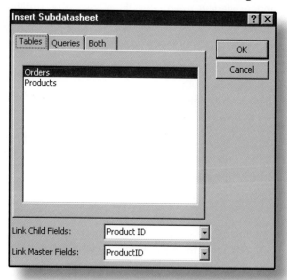

FIGURE 4-23
Subdatasheet of related records

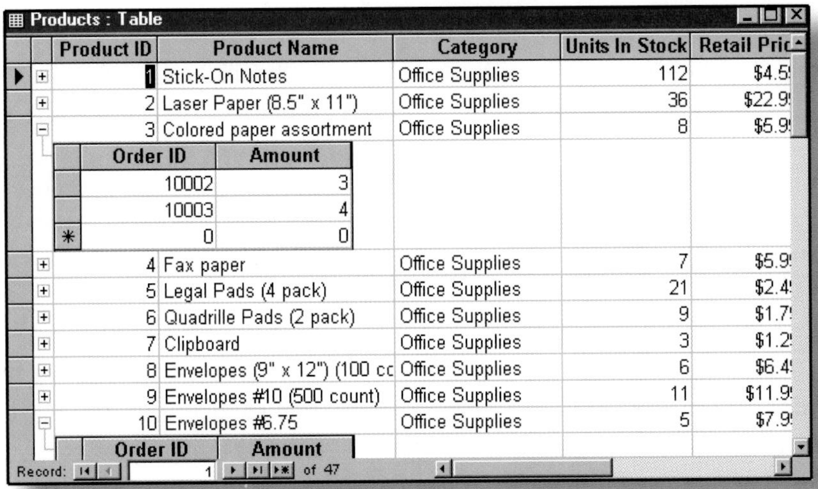

Creating a Multitable Query

After defining relationships in a database, you can create a **multitable query** to display the information from the related tables at once. For example, you might want to view customer information with the orders placed by the customers. To do this you would need data from both the Customers and Orders tables.

Except for a few additional steps, you will create a multitable query using the same procedure you've used to create queries. After opening the appropriate database, choose Queries on the Objects bar, and then click the New button to create a new query. The New Query dialog box appears. Choose the Design View option to create a query manually. In the Show Table dialog box, choose to add the related tables to the query. The fields in the related tables will appear in small boxes in the top part of the query window, as shown in Figure 4-24.

In the lower pane of the query window, specify the information needed from both tables to create the query. After choosing the fields and entering the search criteria, save the query.

FIGURE 4-24
Query window

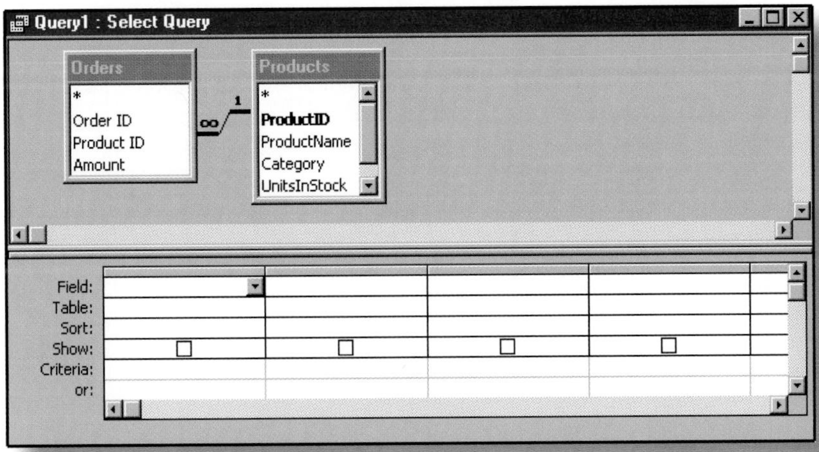

1. Click **Queries** on the Objects bar. Click the **New** button. The New Query dialog box appears.

2. Choose **Design View**, if it is not already selected, and click **OK**. The Show Table dialog box appears to allow you to choose the related tables for the query.

3. Select the **Orders** table, if necessary, and then click **Add**. The fields of the Orders table appear in the query window.

4. Select **Products** in the Show Table dialog box and click **Add**. The fields of the Products table appear in the query window.

5. Close the Show Table dialog box. The query window should look like Figure 4-24.

6. Click the down arrow in the **Field** row of the first column and choose **Orders.Order ID**, as shown in Figure 4-25.

7. Click the down arrow in the **Field** row of the second column and choose **Orders.Product ID**.

8. In the third column, choose **Products.Product Name**.

9. In the fourth column, choose **Orders.Amount**.

10. In the fifth column, choose **Products.Retail Price**.

11. Choose **Save** on the **File** menu, and enter **Invoice Query** as the name for the query. Click **OK**.

12. Click the **Run** button. The results of the query appear, as shown in Figure 4-26.

13. Choose **Print** on the **File** menu to print the table with the query applied. Click **OK**.

14. Choose **Close** on the **File** menu to close the query. Close the database.

FIGURE 4-25
Select fields to display in the query results

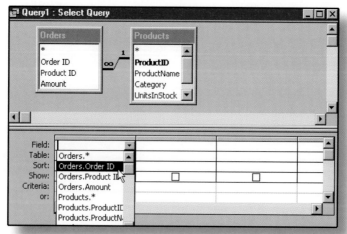

FIGURE 4-26
Results of a multitable query

Order ID	Product ID	Product Name	Amount	Retail Price
10000	10	Envelopes #6.75	2	$7.99
10001	31	Answering Machine	1	$49.99
10001	24	Letter Sorter	1	$7.99
10002	46	2-Drawer Filing Cabinet	1	$79.99
10002	11	3-ring binders (1")	10	$1.49
10002	3	Colored paper assortment	3	$5.99
10003	25	Drawer Tray	2	$3.49
10003	17	3-hole punch	1	$9.99
10003	3	Colored paper assortment	4	$5.99
10004	32	Fax Machine	1	$289.99
10004	20	Date Stamp	2	$2.49
10005	26	Rotary Card File	1	$25.99
10005	4	Fax paper	3	$5.99

Record: 1 of 13

Summary

In this lesson, you learned:

- The Find command is the easiest way to locate data in the database. The Find command searches the database for specified information.

- Queries allow more complex searches. A query allows you to search records using multiple and complex criteria and allows you to display selected fields. You can save a query and apply it again later.

- A filter is similar to a query; however, it displays all fields and cannot be saved. A filter can be used to sort records, or records can be sorted directly in a table without the use of a filter. Using a filter to sort records allows you to sort by more than one record.

- Indexing is an important part of database management systems. Indexing allows records to be located more quickly, especially in large databases.

- By defining relationships between the different tables within a database, you can create queries, forms, and reports to display information from several tables at once. A relationship is set up by matching data in key fields.

TRUE/FALSE

Circle the T if the statement is true or F if the statement is false.

T F   1.   The Find command can search for data in all fields.

T F   2.   The Find Next button in the Find dialog box finds the next record that matches the criteria you've specified.

T F   3.   A query automatically displays all fields in the table.

T F   4.   Filters cannot be saved for later use.

T F   5.   An ascending sort arranges records from Z to A.

WRITTEN QUESTIONS

Write a brief answer to the following questions.

1.   What is the easiest way to quickly locate data in a database?

2.   What are the three pieces of information you must supply when creating a query?

3.   What menu is used to access the command that creates a filter?

4. What button is used to sort records from largest to smallest?

5. What view allows you to index a field?

LESSON 4 PROJECTS

PROJECT 4-1

1. Open the **IA Project4-1** database file from the student data files.

2. Open the **Houses** table in Datasheet view.

3. Use the **Find** command to locate the first house with wood exterior.

4. Use the **Find** command to locate any remaining houses with wood exterior.

5. Close the table.

6. Create a query that displays houses with two bedrooms. Have the query display only the Address, Bedrooms, and Price fields. Save the query as **2 Bedrooms**.

7. Run the query and print the results. Close the query. Leave the database open for the next project.

PROJECT 4-2

1. Open the **Houses** table in the **IA Project4-1** database in Datasheet view.

2. Sort the table so that the houses are displayed from most expensive to least expensive.

3. Change the column width to **Best Fit** for all the columns.

4. Print the results of the sort in landscape orientation.

5. Create a filter to display only the houses listed with **Brad Gray** as the agent. You do not have to sort the records.

6. Print the results of the filter in landscape orientation.

7. Remove the filter to show all the records in the table. Leave the database open for the next project.

PROJECT 4-3

1. With the **Houses** table in the **IA Project4-1** database open, create a filter that displays three-bedroom houses only, sorted from least to most expensive.

2. Print the results of the filter in landscape orientation.

3. Remove the filter to show all records in the table.

4. Create a filter that displays only houses with two-car garages and brick exterior.

5. Print the results of the filter in landscape orientation.

6. Remove the filter to show all records in the table. Leave the database open for the next project.

PROJECT 4-4

1. With the **Houses** table in the **IA Project4-1** database open, use the **Find** command to locate the houses that were listed during December.

2. Create a query that displays the houses listed with **Nina Bertinelli** or **John Schultz** as the agent. Have the query display only the **Address**, **List Date**, **Price**, and **Agent** fields and sort the **Price** field from most to least expensive. Save the query as **Bertinelli/Schultz**.

3. Run the query and print the results. Close the query.

4. Open the **Houses** table and create a filter that sorts the houses from most to least bathrooms and the price from least to most expensive.

5. Print the results of the filter in landscape orientation.

6. Remove the filter to show all records in the table.

7. Close the table and the database.

CRITICAL THINKING

ACTIVITY 4-1

SCANS

You are a Realtor with three new clients who are ready to buy homes. List on paper each client's requirements in a home. For example, buyer #1 might want a three-bedroom house with a brick exterior and the maximum price is $90,000.

Using the **IA Project4-1** database and the **Houses** table, create a filter or query to locate the information for each client and print the results.

ACTIVITY 4-2

SCANS

Referential integrity is a set of rules that Access uses to check for valid relationships between tables. It also ensures that related data is not accidentally deleted or changed. Using the Help system, determine what conditions must be met before you can enforce referential integrity. Write a brief essay that explains the importance of referential integrity in a relational database, and why users of the database objects would benefit from it.

REPORTS AND MACROS

OBJECTIVES

Upon completion of this lesson, you should be able to:

■ Create a report using a Report Wizard.

■ Modify a report.

■ Create and run a macro.

🕐 **Estimated Time: 1.5 hours**

Reports

Databases can become large as records are added. Printing the database from Datasheet view may not always be the most desirable way to put the data on paper. Creating a **database report** allows you to organize, summarize, and print all or a portion of the data in a database. You can even use reports to print form letters and mailing labels. Figure 5-1 shows two examples of database reports. Database reports are compiled by creating a report object.

FIGURE 5-1
Database reports

Products by Units in Stock — Tiffany Matthews

UnitsInStock	Product Name	Product ID	Category	Retail
0	Cash Register	33	Business Machines	$22
1	Oak Office Desk	40	Furniture	$39
	Photocopier	34	Business Machines	$59
2	Bookshelf	41	Furniture	$8
	Computer Desk	39	Furniture	$29
	Fax Machine	32	Business Machines	$24
	Guest Chair	43	Furniture	$19
	Heavy Duty Stapler	15	Office Supplies	$1
	Letter Sorter	24	Desk Accessories	$
	Speaker Phone	30	Business Machines	$9
	Typewriter	35	Business Machines	$14
3	2-Drawer Filing Cabinet	46	Furniture	$8
	Clipboard	7	Office Supplies	$
	Desk Accessory Set	23	Desk Accessories	$1
	Desk Chair	44	Furniture	$18
	Executive Chair	42	Furniture	$25
	Printing Calculator	29	Business Machines	$2
	Rotary Card File	26	Desk Accessories	$2
	Scientific Calculator	27	Business Machines	$1
	Surge Protector	37	Computer Supplies	$1
4	4-Drawer Filing Cabinet	45	Furniture	$14
	Answering Machine	31	Business Machines	$4
	Disk Storage Box	38	Computer Supplies	$
	Folding Table (8')	47	Furniture	$4
	Letter Tray	22	Desk Accessories	$
	Scissors	16	Office Supplies	$
	Tape Dispenser	19	Office Supplies	$
5	Drawer Tray	25	Desk Accessories	$
	Envelopes #6.75	10	Office Supplies	$
6	Envelopes (9" x 12") (10	8	Office Supplies	$
	Standard Stapler	14	Office Supplies	$
7	3-hole punch	17	Office Supplies	$
	Basic Calculator	28	Business Machines	$
	Date Stamp	20	Office Supplies	$
	Fax paper	4	Office Supplies	$
8	Colored paper assortme	3	Office Supplies	$
9	3-ring binders (2")	12	Office Supplies	$
	3.5" HD Diskettes (Box o	36	Computer Supplies	$

Page

Employees by Department

Department	Last Name	First Name	Salary
Advertising			
	Abernathy	Mark	$2,375.00
	Barton	Brad	$2,590.00
	Denton	Scott	$2,600.00
	Doss	Derek	$2,200.00
Marketing			
	Martinez	Christine	$1,780.00
	Powell	Lynne	$2,970.00
	Powers	Sarah	$1,500.00
Personnel			
	Davis	Lee	$2,680.00
Public Relations			
	Smith	Shawna	$2,950.00
Sales			
	Best	Trent	$2,800.00
	Broach	Margie	$2,450.00
	Collins	Greg	$2,750.00
	Collins	Dave	$2,620.00
	Davis	Hillary	$2,620.00
	Sims	Jennifer	$1,550.00
	West	Debbie	$3,100.00

Page 1 of 1

Printing a database from Datasheet view is a form of a report. Printing from Datasheet view, however, offers you much less flexibility than creating a report and printing it. In this lesson, you will learn how to create report objects.

Creating a Report

The report database object lets you create reports that include selected fields, groups of records, and even calculations. As with other Access objects, you can create a report object manually or use the Report Wizard. In this lesson, you will create a report using the Report Wizard.

To create a report, click Reports on the Objects bar, and click the New button. The New Report dialog box appears, as shown in Figure 5-2.

In the New Report dialog box, you choose the method to create the report. To use a Report Wizard, choose *Report Wizard* from the list. Click the down arrow to select the table or query Access will use to create a report. Choose a table if you want to include the entire table in the report. Choose a query to include only certain data in the report. In many cases, you will want to create a query before creating a report.

FIGURE 5-2
New Report dialog box

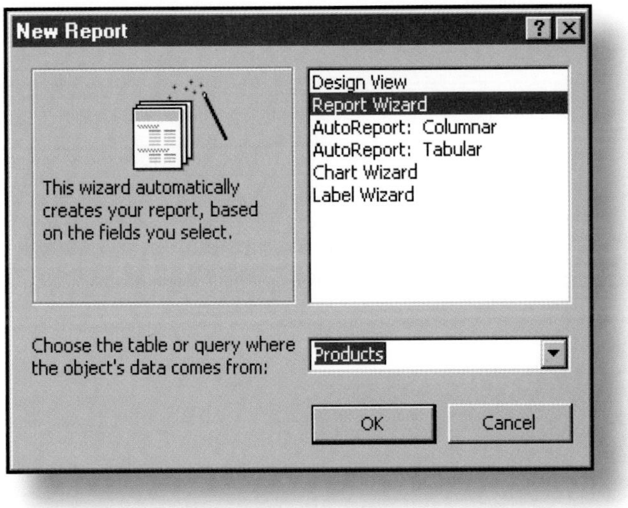

S TEP-BY-STEP ▷ 5.1

1. Open **IA Step5-1** from the student data files.

2. Click the **Reports** button on the Objects bar.

3. Click **New**. The New Report dialog box appears, as shown in Figure 5-2.

4. Choose **Report Wizard** from the list.

5. Click the down arrow and choose the table **Products** from the drop-down list. Click **OK**. The Report Wizard dialog box appears, as shown in Figure 5-3.

6. Leave the dialog box on the screen for the next Step-by-Step.

(continued on next page)

FIGURE 5-3
Starting the Report Wizard

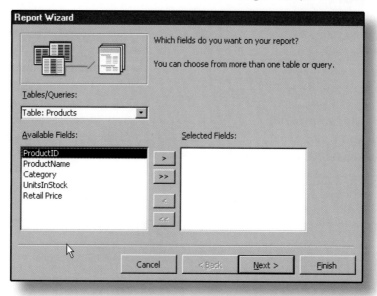

CHOOSING FIELDS FOR THE REPORT

You select fields for the report in the Report Wizard dialog box shown in Figure 5-3. You select fields the same way you did when creating a form using the Form Wizard.

STEP-BY-STEP ⟹ 5.2

1. Highlight **ProductName** in the *Available Fields* list. Click **>**. The ProductName field is now listed in the *Selected Fields* box.

2. The Category field is now highlighted in the *Available Fields* list. Click **>** three times to move the **Category**, **UnitsInStock**, and **Retail Price** fields to the *Selected Fields* box. Your screen should appear similar to Figure 5-4.

3. Click **Next**. The Report Wizard now gives you the option to group the report. Leave the dialog box on the screen for the next Step-by-Step.

> The >> button moves all fields in the *Available Fields* list to the *Selected Fields* box.

FIGURE 5-4
Choosing fields

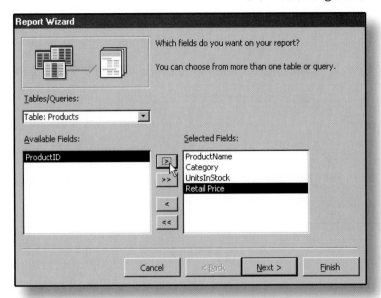

GROUPING AND SORTING THE REPORT

Grouping a report allows you to break it into parts based on the contents of a field. For example, you could organize a customers report into parts that group the customers by city. In the report you are creating now, you will group the report by product category. To group a report, choose the field(s) by which you want to group from the Report Wizard dialog box shown in Figure 5-5.

FIGURE 5-5
Grouping a report by fields

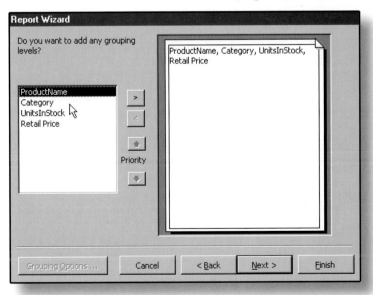

You can group by more than one field. When you group by more than one field, however, you must give the fields priority. For example, you could group customers by state first, then by city within each state.

Sorting the report goes hand-in-hand with grouping. The dialog box shown in Figure 5-6 allows you to specify fields by which the report will be sorted. As you can see, you can sort by multiple fields. Sorting orders the records in a group based on the chosen field or fields. For example, you could group a customers report by city and then sort it by company name. The records for each city would be listed in alphabetic order by company name.

FIGURE 5-6
Sorting a report

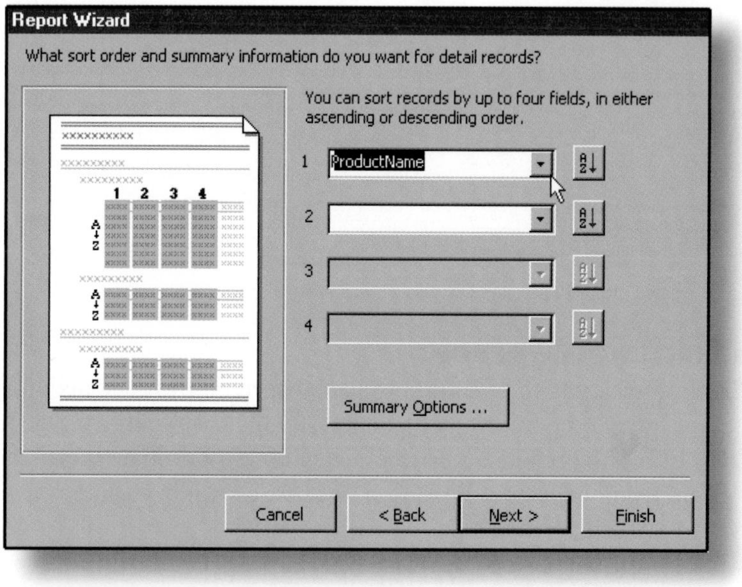

STEP-BY-STEP ▷ 5.3

1. Highlight **Category** and click **>**. Your screen should appear similar to Figure 5-7.

2. Click **Next**. The Report Wizard asks you which fields you want to sort by, as shown in Figure 5-6.

3. Choose **ProductName** as the first sort field by clicking the down arrow next to the number 1 box. For this report, you will sort by one field only. Leave the sort screen displayed for the next Step-by-Step.

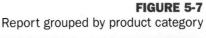

FIGURE 5-7

Report grouped by product category

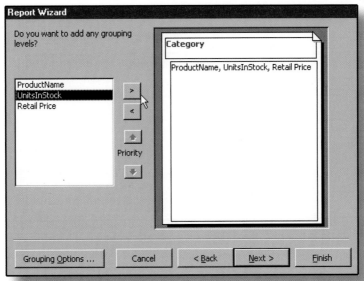

SUMMARY OPTIONS

One of the most useful features of reports is the ability to create summaries within it. Each group of records in a report can be followed by totals, averages, or other summary information. The Summary Options dialog box allows you to specify summaries for fields in the report.

STEP-BY-STEP ▷ 5.4

1. Click the **Summary Options** button. The Summary Options dialog box appears.

2. For the **UnitsInStock** field, click the **Sum** option. The report will total the UnitsInStock field.

3. For the **Retail Price** field, click the **Min** and **Max** options.

4. Choose the **Calculate percent of total for sums** option. (Access takes the total UnitsIn-

Stock for each category and calculates a percentage of the Grand Total.) Your screen should appear similar to Figure 5-8.

5. Click **OK** to close the Summary Options dialog box.

6. Click **Next**. The Report Wizard asks you to choose a layout and page orientation. Leave the Report Wizard on the screen for the next Step-by-Step.

(continued on next page)

I A - 8 9

FIGURE 5-8
Summary Options dialog box

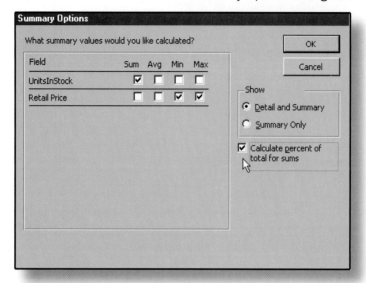

LAYOUT AND ORIENTATION

Next, you'll choose the layout and orientation for your report, as shown in Figure 5-9. The layout options let you choose how you want data arranged on the page. When you choose a layout, a sample is shown in the preview box. Choose from *Landscape* or *Portrait* orientation and click Next.

The next dialog box, shown in Figure 5-10, allows you to choose a style for the report. The style options are designed to give you some control over the report's appearance. The style you choose tells the reader of the report something about the data being presented. Some reports may call for a formal style, while others may benefit from a more casual style. When you choose a style, a sample is shown in the preview box.

FIGURE 5-9
Layout options

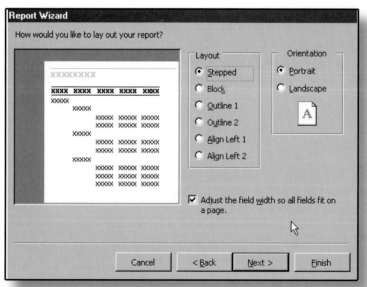

FIGURE 5-10
Style options

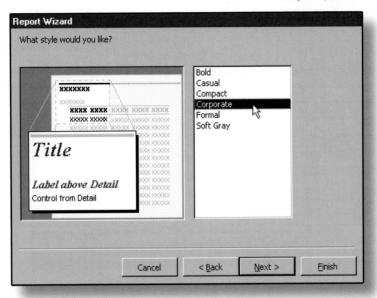

STEP-BY-STEP ▷ 5.5

1. Choose the **Outline 2** layout. The sample layout is shown in the preview box. Click the other options to look at the other layouts. When you have seen all of the available options, choose **Stepped** as the layout.

2. Choose **Portrait** as the page orientation, if it is not already selected.

3. Click **Next**.

4. Choose the **Casual** style. The sample style is shown in the preview box. Click on the other options to look at the other styles. When you have seen all of the available options, choose **Corporate** as the style.

5. Click **Next**. The final Report Wizard dialog box appears. Leave the Report Wizard on the screen for the next Step-by-Step.

Did You Know?

You can create a chart in either a form's or report's Design view. Click **Chart** on the **Insert** menu. On the form or report, click where you want the chart to appear. Follow the steps in the Chart Wizard to create the chart based on the tables and the fields you select.

NAMING THE REPORT

The final step is naming the report, as shown in Figure 5-11. Use a name that gives an indication of the report's output. A report name can be up to 64 characters including letters, numbers, spaces, and some special characters. For example, if a report from a database of customers prints only the customers with companies in your city, you might name the report *Local Customers*.

In addition to naming the report, this dialog box presents you with options for what you want to be displayed when the Report Wizard completes its work. Most of the time you will want to preview the report you just created, so that is the default option. After Access creates the report, it is shown on your screen in Preview mode. You may instead choose to make modifications to the report. You will get a brief look at how modifications are made later in this lesson.

After creating a report, you do not need to save it. Access saves it for you automatically with the title you entered in the Report Wizard. You will, however, need to save any modifications made later to the design of the report.

FIGURE 5-11
Naming the report

S TEP-BY-STEP ▷ 5.6

1. Key **Category Report** as the title of the report.

2. Make sure the option to preview the report is selected and click **Finish**. The report appears in a window, as shown in Figure 5-12.

3. Scroll through the report to see the various categories.

4. Click the **Print** button to print the report.

5. Choose **Close** on the **File** menu. The report will be saved automatically. Leave the Database window open for the next Step-by-Step.

 Did You Know?

To add a graphic to a report, open it in Design view, and click the **Image** button in the Toolbox. Click where you want to place the graphic in the report and the Insert Picture dialog box displays. Select the file where the picture is located. When finished, click **OK**. Access creates an image control that will display the graphic.

FIGURE 5-12
Previewing a report

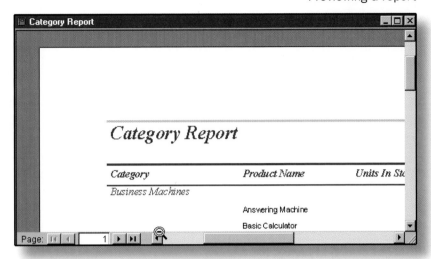

Modifying a Report

Any report, whether created manually or with the Report Wizard, can be modified. You make changes to a report using Design view, which shows the structure of a report. To open a report in Design view, select the report in the Database window, and then click the Design button. Figure 5-13 shows a report in Design view.

FIGURE 5-13
A report in Design view

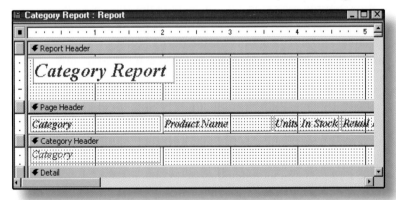

Like a form, the report is divided into sections, each identified by a band. Each section controls a part of the report and can be modified. Table 5-1 summarizes the purpose of each of the sections in the report.

TABLE 5-1
Report sections

SECTION	DESCRIPTION
Report Header	Contents appear at the top of the first page of the report.
Page Header	Contents appear at the top of each page of the report.
Category Header	Contents appear at the top of each group. Because your report is grouped by Category, the band is called Category Header.
Detail	Specifies the fields that will appear in the detail of the report.
Category Footer	Contents appear at the end of each group. The summary options appear in this band.
Page Footer	Contents appear at the end of each page of the report.
Report Footer	Contents appear at the end of the report.

Like a form, the sections in a report contain controls that represent each object on the report. These objects include field names, field entries, a title for the report, or even a graphical object, such as a piece of clip art. You can modify the format, size, and location of the controls in Design view to enhance the appearance of the data on the report.

In Design view, you can change the font, size, style, and other attributes of labels and text box data. Simply select the control, and use the buttons on the Formatting toolbar. Or you can double-click a control to open its Properties dialog box, and then change attributes and other properties.

The Toolbox, shown in Figure 5-14, has tools that you can use to modify reports. The Label tool, for example, allows you to add text.

FIGURE 5-14
Toolbox

STEP-BY-STEP ▷ 5.7

1. If not already selected, click **Reports** on the Objects bar. Choose the **Category Report** and click the **Design** button. The report appears in Design view, as shown in Figure 5-13.

2. Click the **Label** button in the Toolbox. (If the Toolbox is not displayed, *right*-click on the

report and choose **Toolbox** on the shortcut menu.)

3. In the **Report Header**, position the pointer to the right of the *Category Report* text, and click and drag to draw a text box as shown in Figure 5-15.

4. Key your name at the insertion point that appears in the text box. Click outside the text box to view the text.

5. Double-click the text box to display its properties dialog box, as shown in Figure 5-16. If not already selected, click the **All** tab.

6. Scroll through the list of properties until you locate the *Font Name* and *Font Size* properties. Click in the **Font Name** text box, click the down arrow, and select **Mistral** (or a comparable font). Then, click in the **Font Size** text box, click the down arrow, and choose **14**. Close the properties dialog box.

7. Scroll down to the **Report Footer** section. Position the pointer on the **Grand Total** label box as shown in Figure 5-17, and double-click to open its properties dialog box. If not already selected, click the **All** tab.

8. Change the *Caption* to **Total Units in Stock**. Change the *Font Size* to **12**. Close the dialog box.

9. In the **Detail** section, double-click the **Retail Price** box to open its properties dialog box, as shown in Figure 5-18. If not already selected, choose the **All** tab.

10. Click in the **Name** text box and key **Discount Price**. Click in the **Control Source** text box and key **=[Retail Price]*.90**. Change the *Format* property to **Currency**. Then, close the dialog box.

11. In the **Page Header** section, double-click the **Retail Price** label box to open its properties dialog box.

12. Change the *Caption* to **Discount Price** and close the dialog box.

13. With the **Discount Price** label still highlighted, increase the label size by dragging the handle on the right border to the right until you see the entire caption.

14. Click the **View** button to switch to **Print Preview**. If a message appears asking if you want to save changes, click **Yes**.

15. If necessary, scroll to the right to see your name on the report.

16. Choose **Print** on the **File** menu. In the Print dialog box, click **Pages** from the *Print Range* options. Specify that you want to print only page 1 by keying **1** in the *From* box and **1** in the *To* box. Click **OK**.

17. Close the report and leave the database open for the next Step-by-Step.

C **Hot Tip**

To delete a text box, click on the text box and press the **Delete** key or choose **Delete** on the **Edit** menu. To move a text box, click inside the box and drag. To resize a text box, click on the edge of the text box and drag.

(continued on next page)

[Handwritten note:] Create a link of a report + its've source by using graphical/obj. called controls. Controls can be text boxes that display name ft, labels that display titles + descriptions

I A - 9 5

FIGURE 5-15
Inserting text

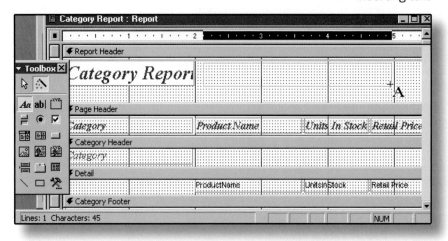

FIGURE 5-16
Label properties dialog box

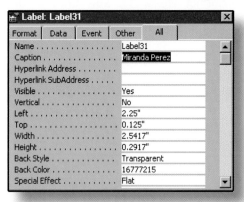

FIGURE 5-17
Modifying the Grand Total label

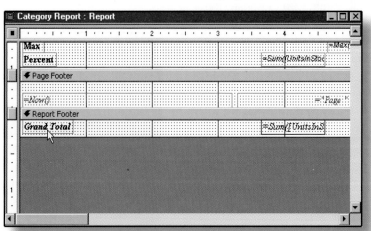

FIGURE 5-18
Text Box properties dialog box

Macros

One of the nice features of database management systems such as Access is the ability to automate tasks that are performed often. This is done by creating an object called a macro. A *macro* is a collection of one or more actions that Access can perform on a database. You can think of a macro as a computer program you create to automate some task you perform with the database.

Creating macros can be challenging, and there are many details to learn before you can become an expert. In this book you will get a taste of how macros work by creating a macro and running it.

Creating a Macro

To create a macro, click Macros on the Objects bar, and click the New button. The Macro window appears, allowing you to specify the actions to be performed by the macro. Figure 5-19 shows a macro in Design view with an example of actions that a macro can perform. The macro will perform the actions specified in the Action list.

FIGURE 5-19
Macro in Design view

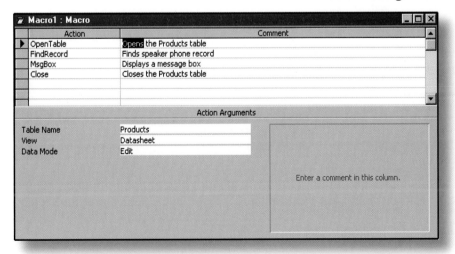

STEP-BY-STEP ▷ 5.8

1. Click **Macros** on the Objects bar.

2. Click **New**. A blank macro window appears.

Leave the window open for the next Step-by-Step.

Adding Actions to a Macro

You can choose an action by clicking the down arrow in the *Action* column cells. There are many available actions, some of which perform advanced operations. You can key an explanation of the action in the *Comment* column. The lower portion of the Macro window shows the action arguments for the chosen action. Action arguments contain detailed information that Access needs in order to perform the specified action. For example, if you choose the *OpenTable* action in the *Action* column, you would specify which table to open, such as the Products table, in the *Action Arguments* section.

Different actions require different detailed information in the *Action Arguments* section, as you will see in the next Step-by-Step. You will create a macro that will open the Products table, find the first speaker phone in the table, present a message box and beep, and close the table.

STEP-BY-STEP ▷ 5.9

1. Click the arrow in the **Action** column of the first blank row to display the list of available actions.

2. Scroll down and choose **OpenTable** from the menu.

3. In the **Comment** section, key **Opens the Products table**.

4. In the **Action Arguments** section, place the insertion point in the **Table Name** box. An arrow appears. Notice the box to the right of the *Action Arguments* contains an explanation of the data to be specified.

5. Click the arrow and choose **Products** from the list.

6. Leave the remaining *Action Arguments* at the default settings.

7. Place the insertion point in the second row of the **Action** column. Click the drop-down list arrow.

8. Scroll down and choose **FindRecord** from the list.

9. In the **Comment** section, key **Finds speaker phone record**.

10. In the **Action Arguments** section, key **Speaker Phone** in the **Find What** box.

11. In the **Match** box, choose **Any Part of Field** from the drop-down list.

12. Leave the next two action arguments at the default settings.

13. In the **Search As Formatted** box, choose **Yes** from the drop-down list.

14. In the **Only Current Field** box, choose **No** to search all the fields in each record.

15. In the **Find First** box, choose **Yes**, if it's not chosen already. Your screen should look similar to Figure 5-20.

16. Place the insertion point in the third row of the **Action** column, scroll down, and choose **MsgBox** from the list.

17. Key **Displays a message box** in the **Comment** section.

18. In the Action Arguments section, key **Record Found** in the **Message** box.

19. Choose **Yes** in the **Beep** box, if it is not already chosen.

20. Choose **Information** in the **Type** box.

21. Key **Results:** in the **Title** box.

22. Place the insertion point in the fourth row of the **Action** column and choose **Close** from the list.

23. Key **Closes the Products table** in the **Comment** section.

24. In the **Action Arguments** section, choose **Table** in the **Object Type** box.

25. Choose **Products** in the **Object Name** box.

26. Leave the window open for the next Step-by-Step.

FIGURE 5-20
Specifying *Action Arguments*

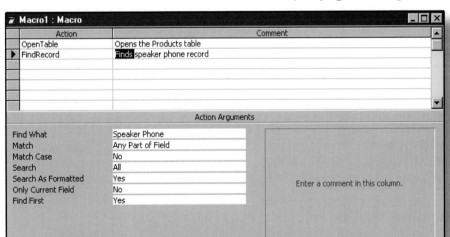

Saving and Running a Macro

After creating a macro, you will need to name and save it. This process is similar to the way you named and saved other database objects. Choose Save on the File menu and key a name. To close the macro, choose Close on the File menu. When you want to run a macro, highlight it in the Database window and click Run.

Extra Challenge

Modify the Speaker Phone macro to find the scientific calculator record. Save and run the macro.

STEP-BY-STEP 5.10

1. Choose **Save As** on the **File** Menu. The Save As dialog box appears.

2. Key **Speaker Phone** as the macro name and click **OK**.

3. Choose **Close** on the **File** menu to close the macro window. You are returned to the Database window.

4. Select **Macro** on the Objects bar. Highlight the **Speaker Phone** macro, if it is not already highlighted. Click the **Run** button. The *Products* table opens, the computer beeps, and the message box generated by the macro appears, as shown in Figure 5-21.

5. Click **OK** to close the message box. The table closes because of the Close action in the macro.

6. Open the **Speaker Phone** macro in Design view.

7. Highlight the row with the **MsgBox** action and choose **Delete** on the **Edit** menu.

8. Choose **Rows** on the **Insert** menu.

9. Click the down arrow in the **Action** column. Scroll down to choose the **PrintOut** action.

10. Key **Prints speaker phone record** in the **Comment** section.

11. In the **Action Arguments** section, choose **Selection** from the **Print Range** drop-down list.

12. Choose **Save** on the **File** menu to save the design changes.

13. Close the macro window.

14. Highlight the **Speaker Phone** macro, if it is not already highlighted. Click the **Run** button.

15. The *Products* table opens, the Speaker Phone record prints, and the table closes.

16. Close the database.

Hot Tip

If your computer does not beep when the message box appears, click the volume icon in the lower right-hand corner of your screen. In the Volume box, click the **Mute** box to remove the check mark. Rerun the macro to hear the beep.

FIGURE 5-21
Macro message box

Summary

In this lesson, you learned:

- Database reports allow you to organize, summarize, and print all or a portion of the data in a database. Database reports are compiled by creating a report object.

- The easiest way to create a report object is to use the Report Wizard. When using the Report Wizard, you first choose the table you want to base the report on and what fields of that table you want to include in the report. You can also choose to group the records and sort them.

- The Report Wizard also allows you to choose a style for your report. The style can give a report a casual or formal look.

- Reports are modified using Design view. Each report is divided into sections. Each section controls a different part of the report and can be modified.

- Macros automate tasks you perform often. The Macro window allows you to create a macro object.

LESSON 5 REVIEW QUESTIONS

TRUE/FALSE

Circle T if the statement is true or F if the statement is false.

T F   1.   Database reports are prepared by creating a report object.

T F   2.   The Report Wizard always includes all fields in a report.

T F   3.   Like file names, report names can contain only eight characters.

T F   4.   Action arguments contain detailed information about an action.

T F   5.   To run a macro, highlight it in the Database window and click Run.

WRITTEN QUESTIONS

Write a brief answer to the following questions.

1.   What are the two ways to create a report?

2. How does sorting affect a group?

3. What are sections in a report?

4. How do you use the Label tool to add text to a report?

5. When creating a macro, what action displays a message box?

LESSON 5 PROJECTS

PROJECT 5-1

1. Open **IA Step5-1** from the student data files. This is the database you used in this lesson.

2. Use the Report Wizard to create a report using all the fields in the **Products** table. Group the report by **UnitsInStock** and sort it by **ProductName**.

3. Choose the **Block** layout, **Portrait** orientation, and **Compact** style.

4. Title the report **Products by Units in Stock**. Select the option to preview the report.

5. Close the report after previewing.

6. Modify the report in Design view. Use the label tool to insert your name in the Report header. Save the changes.

7. Print the report.

8. Close the report and the database.

PROJECT 5-2

1. Open **IA Project5-2** from the student data files.

2. Use the Report Wizard to create a report. Use the **Employee Information** table and choose the **Last Name**, **First Name**, **Department**, and **Salary** fields.

3. Group the records by **Department** and sort by **Last Name**.

4. Choose the **Stepped** layout, **Portrait** orientation, and **Corporate** style.

5. Title the report **Employees by Department**. Select the option to preview the report.

6. Save the report.

7. Print and close the report. Leave the database open for the next project.

PROJECT 5-3

1. With the **IA Project5-2** database open, create a new macro that will open the **Employee Birthdays** form in Form view and find the **Shapiro** record. For the **FindRecord Action Arguments**, select **Any Part of Field** in the **Match** box, **No** in the **Match Case** box, **All** in the **Search** box, **Yes** in the **Search As Formatted** box, **No** in the **Only Current Field** box, and **Yes** in the **Find First** box. Then, have the macro print the Shapiro record only (*Print Range = Selection*), and close the Employee Birthdays form.

2. Save the macro as **Print Form Record** and close it.

3. Run the macro. Leave the database open for the next project.

PROJECT 5-4

1. Create a new macro in the **IA Project5-2** database that will open the **Managers** query in Datasheet view and find the **Marketing** record. (For the **FindRecord Action Arguments**, select **Any Part of Field** in the **Match** box, **No** in the **Match Case** box, **All** in the **Search** box, **Yes** in the **Search As Formatted** box, **No** in the **Only Current Field** box, and **Yes** in the **Find First** box. Then, have the macro print the Marketing record (Selection) only, and close the **Managers** query.

2. Save the macro as **Print Marketing Manager** and close it.

3. Run the macro. Close the database.

CRITICAL THINKING

ACTIVITY 5-1

Using the **IA Activity5-1** database file in the student data files and the **Houses** table, create a report listing all the information in the table. Also, create a macro that will open the **2 Bedrooms** query, find all of the two bedroom houses, print the results (*Print Range = All*), and close the query. Save the macro as **2 Bedroom Houses for Sale**. Run the macro and close the database.

ACTIVITY 5-2

Using the Help feature, look up the definition of a *subreport*. In your own words, write a brief essay that defines a subreport and provide an example of when you might use a subreport. For your example, assume you have a database containing tables on customers and product sales.

ACTIVITY 5-3

A *switchboard* is a form in a database that contains buttons representing macros you've created to open, close, and manage the objects in the database. Use the Help system to find out more about switchboards and how to create them. Write a brief essay explaining how you would use a switchboard in a database that you maintain.

INTRODUCTION TO MICROSOFT ACCESS

INTEGRATING ACCESS

Upon completion of this lesson, you should be able to:

■ Integrate Access with other Office applications.

■ Create a form letter.

■ Use query options to print only selected form letters.

■ Create and print mailing labels.

⏱ Estimated Time: 1.5 hours

Sharing Data

Because Office is an integrated suite of programs, you can easily move and copy data between applications. You can export an Access table to an Excel worksheet, or you can merge records in a table with a Word document. In this lesson, you'll learn how to share data between Access and other applications.

Word to Access

Suppose you have been given a list of names and addresses in a Word file. The names need to be entered into a database. You can easily paste the information into an Access table, where you can then edit and sort it, and create forms, queries, reports, and pages from it. If the text from Word is set up as a table or is separated by tabs, Access will automatically create the fields and enter the data as records. If the text is in a single block, all of the text will be pasted into the currently highlighted field.

Access to Word

You can also paste table records from an Access database into a Word document. The data is formatted with tabs when it enters the Word document. This feature could be used to create a table in Word, based on data from Access. Merging database records with a Word document is another method for integrating Access and Word, and is discussed later in this lesson.

Access to Excel

There are times when you might want to paste Access data into an Excel worksheet. Excel provides powerful calculation and data analysis features that can easily be applied to database records that are exported to an Excel workbook file. Each record in the table appears as a row in the worksheet, and each field is converted to a column.

Excel to Access

You can also paste data from an Excel worksheet into an Access database table. A worksheet is set up as columns and rows, much like a database table. The cells cut or copied from the worksheet will appear in the database beginning with the highlighted entry.

You could also use the Import Spreadsheet Wizard to insert Excel data in an Access table. Open the database file, select the Get External Data command on the File menu, and then select Import on the submenu. An Import dialog box opens, where you select the file you want to import. The Wizard then guides you through the process of placing the spreadsheet data in a table.

STEP-BY-STEP ▷ 6.1

1. Open the **IA Step6-1** database from the student data files.

2. Choose **Get External Data** on the **File** menu, and select **Import** on the submenu. The Import dialog box appears, similar to that shown in Figure 6-1.

3. Click the down arrow in the *Files of type* box and choose **Microsoft Excel** from the list.

4. Select the **New Products** Excel workbook from the student data files.

5. Click **Import**. The Import Spreadsheet Wizard dialog box opens, as shown in Figure 6-2. Notice the data from the New Products worksheet appears in the grid.

6. Click **Next** and a second wizard dialog box opens, asking if the first row of the spreadsheet contains the column headings.

7. Click **Next** since the first row does contain the column headings and the option is already selected. A third wizard dialog box appears asking where you would like to store your data.

8. The **In a New Table** option should already be selected. Click **Next** and a fourth wizard dialog box appears as shown in Figure 6-3.

9. Scroll to the right in the grid to view all the field columns in the table. Then, click **Next**. This wizard dialog box asks you to let Access add a primary key to the table.

10. Choose **No primary key** and click **Next**.

11. Key **New Products** in the *Import to Table* box. Click **Finish**.

12. A message appears stating that the wizard is finished importing the file. Click **OK**.

13. The New Products table should be listed in the Database window. Open the table in Datasheet view. Print the table.

14. Close the table and the database.

 Hot Tip

Backing up files on your computer should be a regular practice. To back up a database, you must close it first, and make sure that no other users have it opened. Using Windows Explorer, My Computer, Microsoft Backup, or other backup software, copy the database file to a backup medium, such as a floppy disk, a zip disk, tape, etc. To restore the database, simply copy the backup database file to the appropriate folder or disk.

FIGURE 6-1
Import dialog box

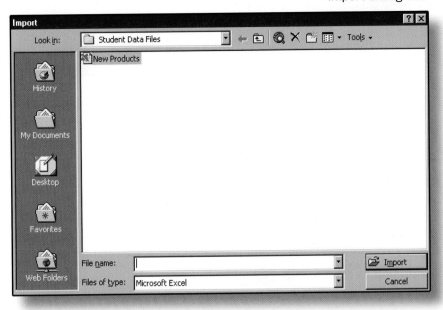

FIGURE 6-2
Import Spreadsheet Wizard dialog box

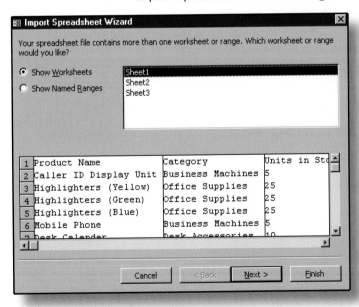

(continued on next page)

I A - 1 0 7

FIGURE 6-3
Import Spreadsheet Wizard lets you tailor Excel data

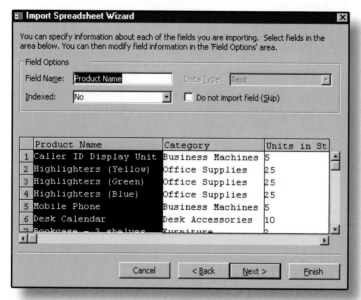

Form Letters

Another way to integrate Access and Word is through form letters. A ***form letter*** is a word processor document that uses information from a database in specified areas to personalize a document.

For example, you might send a letter to all the members of a professional organization using a form letter. In each letter, the information is the same but the names of the recipients will be different. One letter may begin "Dear Mr. Hartsfield" and another "Dear Ms. Perez."

Creating a Form Letter

To create form letters, you integrate information from a data source, such as an Access database, with a document from Word, called the main document. The ***main document*** contains the information that will stay the same in each form letter. The ***data source*** contains the information that will vary in each form letter. You insert the field names, or ***merge fields***, in the main document where you want to print the information from the data source. The merge fields you place in the Word document are enclosed in angle brackets (<< Field Name >>). When the main document and the data source are merged, the merge fields in the main document are replaced with the appropriate information from the data source to create personalized form letters.

Word provides a Mail Merge Helper that makes it easy to create a form letter. To access the Mail Merge Helper dialog box, shown in Figure 6-4, choose the Mail Merge command on Word's Tools menu. You will complete three steps in the Mail Merge Helper dialog box. To specify the main document, click Create in step 1, click Form Letters, and then click Active Window. The active document (the one displayed on the screen) is now the main document. To specify a data source, click Get Data in step 2, and click Open Data Source. When the Open Data Source dialog box appears, choose the file you want to use as the data source. If you want to query the database before merging, click the Query Options button in step 3. When you are ready to merge, click Merge.

FIGURE 6-4
Mail Merge Helper

The Mail Merge toolbar, shown in Figure 6-5, contains buttons to make the merging process easier. This toolbar is located above the ruler and below the formatting toolbar, but does not appear until you use the Mail Merge Helper. To insert merge fields, position the insertion point in the place in the main document where you want to insert information from the data source. Then click Insert Merge Field on the Mail Merge toolbar and click the appropriate field name from the data source. Insert all the merge fields you want until your main document is complete. Click the Merge to New Document button and the data from the database is inserted into the merge fields to create the form letters.

FIGURE 6-5
Mail Merge toolbar

STEP-BY-STEP ▷ 6.2

1. Open **Access** and the **Lakewood parents** database from the student data files. Open the **Fourth Grade** table.

2. Enlarge the table's window, if necessary, so all the fields and records are visible.

3. Open **Word** and the **Lakewood letter** document from the student data files.

4. Choose **Mail Merge** on the **Tools** menu. The Mail Merge Helper dialog box appears, as shown in Figure 6-4.

(continued on next page)

5. Click **Create**, and then choose **Form Letters**.

6. Click **Active Window**.

7. Click **Get Data**, and then choose **Open Data Source**. The Open Data Source dialog box appears.

8. Click the down arrow to the right of the **Files of type** list box. Click **MS Access Databases**.

9. Open the **Lakewood parents** database from the student data files. The Microsoft Access dialog box appears, as shown in Figure 6-6.

10. With the **Tables** tab displayed, highlight **Fourth Grade** and click **OK**.

11. When the Microsoft Word dialog box appears, as shown in Figure 6-7, click **Edit Main Document.** The *Lakewood letter* document appears on the screen.

12. Place the insertion point on the second line after the date.

13. Click the **Insert Merge Field** button on the Mail Merge toolbar.

14. Choose **Title** from the drop-down list.

15. Insert the rest of the merge fields shown in Figure 6-8 using the same method. (Be sure to add spaces where necessary and include a comma between the City and State merge fields.)

16. When finished, click the **Merge to New Document** button on the Mail Merge toolbar. The data from the database is inserted into the merge fields to create the form letters in a new file.

17. Scroll down the file to see the form letters.

18. Save the file as **Lake forms** and close it. Leave the **Lakewood letter** document open for the next Step-by-Step.

FIGURE 6-6
Microsoft Access dialog box

FIGURE 6-7

Microsoft Word dialog box

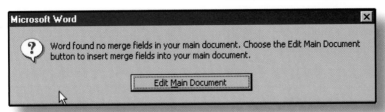

FIGURE 6-8

Inserted merge fields

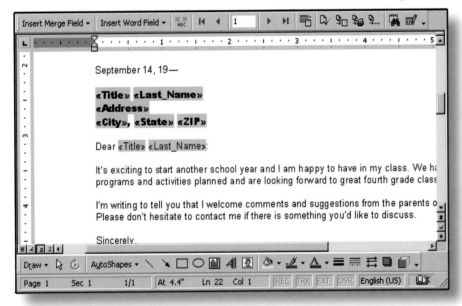

Using Query Options and Printing Form Letters

After the form letters have been created, they are ready to print. If you don't want to print every letter, you can click the Query Options button in the Mail Merge Helper. The Query Options dialog box will appear and you can then filter out only the records you want to merge and print.

STEP-BY-STEP ▷ 6.3

1. The **Lakewood letter** document should be open on your screen. Save it as **Lakewood letter 2**.

2. Click the **Mail Merge Helper** button on Word's Mail Merge toolbar. The Mail Merge Helper dialog box appears.

3. Click the **Query Options** button in Step 3. The Query Options dialog box appears.

4. You want to print only the letters to the parents of Ashlynn McNeal and Rafael Wade. In the **Field** box, click the down arrow and choose **Last Name**.

(continued on next page)

5. The *Comparison* box should read *Equal to*. In the **Compare to** box, key **McNeal**.

6. In the **And** box, click the down arrow and choose **Or**.

7. In the second **Field** box, click the down arrow and choose **Last Name**.

8. The *Comparison* box should read *Equal to*. In the **Compare to** box, key **Wade**. The Query Options dialog box should appear similar to Figure 6-9.

9. Click **OK**. The Mail Merge Helper dialog box reappears.

10. Click **Merge**. The Merge dialog box appears, as shown in Figure 6-10.

11. Click **Merge**. The two form letters you wanted to print are created in a new file.

12. Save the file as **Print form**.

13. Print the form letters by choosing **Print** on the **File** menu.

14. Click **OK**.

15. Close **Print form**. Save **Lakewood letter 2** and close it. Leave the **Fourth Grade** table and **Lakewood parents** database open.

FIGURE 6-9
Query Options dialog box

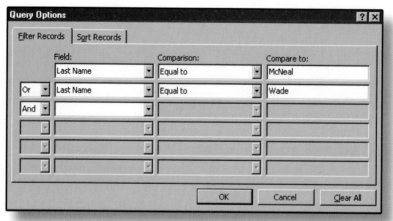

FIGURE 6-10
Merge dialog box

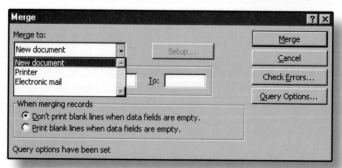

INTRODUCTION TO MICROSOFT ACCESS

Mailing Labels

Office makes it easy to create mailing labels from any data source that has name and address information. In this activity, creating mailing labels involves integrating the Word and Access applications. Creating mailing labels is very similar to creating form letters. The main difference is that mailing labels place information from more than one record on the same page. This is because mailing labels usually come in sheets that have as many as 30 labels per page.

To create mailing labels, you will be using the Mail Merge Helper again. This time, choose Mailing Labels on the Create menu in the Mail Merge Helper dialog box. After specifying a main document and a data source, you can choose the label options you want, insert merge fields that contain the address information, and print your mailing labels.

STEP-BY-STEP ▷ 6.4

1. Open a new Word document.

2. Choose **Mail Merge** on the **Tools** menu. The Mail Merge Helper dialog box appears.

3. Click **Create** and then click **Mailing Labels**.

4. Click **Active Window**.

5. Click **Get Data** and then click **Open Data Source**. The Open Data Source dialog box appears.

6. Click the down arrow to the right of the **Files of type** box. Click **MS Access Databases**.

7. Select **Lakewood parents** from the student data files, and click **Open**. The Microsoft Access dialog box appears.

8. With the Tables tab displayed, highlight **Fourth Grade** and click **OK**.

9. When the Microsoft Word dialog box appears, click **Set Up Main Document**. The Label Options dialog box appears, as shown in Figure 6-11.

10. From the **Printer Information** options, be sure **Laser and ink jet** is chosen, and then select

the **Tray** option that you wish to use with your printer.

11. The **Label products** box should have **Avery standard** chosen. In the **Product number** box, scroll down to highlight **5160 - Address**.

12. Click **OK**. The Create Labels dialog box appears.

13. Click the **Insert Merge Field** button and insert merge fields into the **Sample label** box, as shown in Figure 6-12. (Be sure to add spaces where necessary and include a comma between the City and State merge fields.)

14. Click **OK**. The Mail Merge Helper reappears.

15. Click **Merge**. The Merge dialog box appears.

16. Click **Merge**. The labels are displayed in a new file.

17. Save the file as **Mailing Labels**.

18. Print the labels.

19. Close **Mailing Labels**. Close the unsaved document without saving changes. Exit Word and Access.

(continued on next page)

FIGURE 6-11
Label Options dialog box

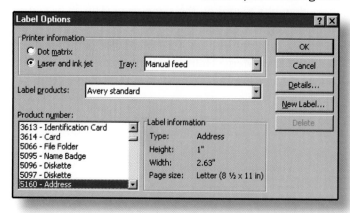

FIGURE 6-12
Create Labels dialog box

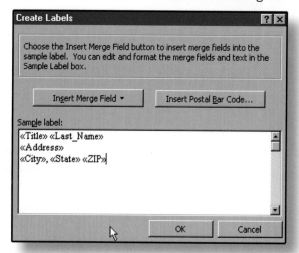

Summary

In this lesson, you learned:

■ Because Office is an integrated suite of programs, you can easily move and copy data between applications. No matter which applications you are using, the data is automatically formatted so that it can be used in the destination file.

■ A form letter is a word processor document that uses information from a database in specified areas to personalize a document. To create form letters, you insert merge fields in the main document that are replaced with information from the data source.

■ Creating mailing labels is very similar to creating form letters. The Mail Merge Helper and Mail Merge toolbar make it easy to create form letters or mailing labels.

LESSON 6 REVIEW QUESTIONS

TRUE/FALSE

Circle T if the statement is true or F if the statement is false.

T   F   1.   A merge field is a field name in the main document where you want to print the information from the data source.

T   F   2.   When moving and copying data with the Office suite of programs, the data is automatically formatted so it can be used in the destination file.

T   F   3.   The data source contains the information that stays the same in each form letter.

T   F   4.   The Mail Merge toolbar contains buttons to make the merging process easier.

T   F   5.   Click the Merge to New Document button to insert the data into the merge fields and create the form letters.

WRITTEN QUESTIONS

Write a brief answer to the following questions.

1.   Which button do you click to filter out only the records to merge and print in a form letter?

2.   Creating mailing labels involves integrating which two Office applications?

3.   What is the Main Document in a form letter?

4. After opening a new Word document, what option do you choose on the Tools menu to create mailing labels?

5. What is a form letter?

LESSON 6 PROJECTS

PROJECT 6-1

1. Open **IA Project6-1** from the student data files, and then open the **Employee Information** table.

2. Open **Word** and the **Dinner letter** document from the student data files.

3. Use the Mail Merge Helper to create a form letter by merging the **Dinner letter** document with data from the **Employee Information** table. Insert the merge fields as shown in Figure 6-13. When finished merging, scroll down to see the form letters.

4. Save the new document as **Dinner form** and close it.

5. Leave the **Dinner letter** open for the next project.

FIGURE 6-13

Lesson ⑥ Integrating Access

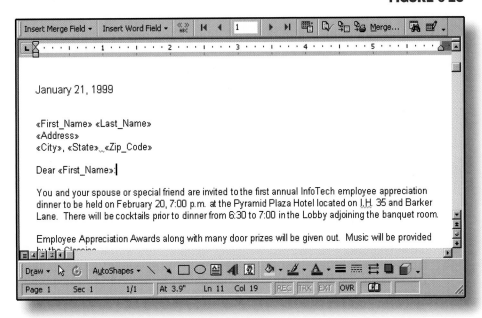

PROJECT 6-2

1. The Dinner letter should be open on your screen. Save it as **Dinner letter 2**.

2. Use the Mail Merge Helper to create a query to merge only the employees in the Public Relations department.

3. Save the new document as **PRForm**.

4. Print the form letters.

5. Close **PRForm**. Save **Dinner letter 2** and close. Leave the **Employee Information** table open.

PROJECT 6-3

1. Open a new Word document.

2. Use the Mail Merge Helper to create mailing labels. Merge the **Employee Information** table from the **IA Project6-1** database. Choose **Avery standard** in the **Label products** box. In the **Product number** box, scroll down to highlight **5160 – Address**.

3. Insert the merge fields as shown in Figure 6-14.

4. When finished, save the file as **Employee Labels**.

5. Print the labels.

6. Close **Employee Labels**. Close the unsaved document without saving changes. Exit Word and Access.

FIGURE 6-14

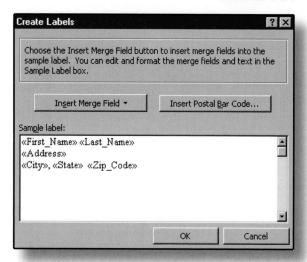

CRITICAL THINKING

ACTIVITY 6-1

Teachers need to send consent forms to each student's parents at the beginning of the year. This allows the students to participate in field trips or special activities away from the school. Create a consent form by merging the **Consent letter** with data from the **Third grade** table in the **Washington parents** database. The letter and database are stored in the student data files. Save the new document as **Consent form**. Merge and print letters for only the students with last names of **Davis**, **Hope**, **Shihab**, and **Ellis**. Save the new document as **Late form**.

ACTIVITY 6-2

Using the Help feature, look up the steps for adding a hyperlink to a form or report in a database. Write down the basic steps. Give an example of why you might add a hyperlink to either an Inventory, Customer, or Vendor database.

COMMAND SUMMARY

FEATURE	MENU COMMAND	TOOLBAR BUTTON	LESSON
Close	File, Close	✖	1
Close a Table	File, Close	✖	1
Column Width	Format, Column Width		2
Compact and Repair a Database	Tools, Database Utilities, Compact and Repair Database		2
Copy Record	Edit, Copy	📋	2
Cut Record	Edit, Cut	✂	2
Database (create)	File, New		1
Datasheet View	Open	▦	1
Delete Record	Edit, Delete Record	✖	2
Delete Row	Edit, Delete Row	⇥	1
Design View	Highlight name of Object, Design	◩ Design	1
Exit Access	File, Exit		1
Field Properties	Tables, Design	◩ Design	2
File, create	File, New, General tab, Database	▯	1
Filter, apply	Filter, Apply Filter/Sort	▽	3
Filter, create	Records, Filter		3
Filter, remove	Filter, Remove Filter/Sort	▽	3
Find Data	Edit, Find	🔍	3
First Record		◁	2
Form, create	Forms, New		2

FEATURE	MENU COMMAND	TOOLBAR BUTTON	LESSON
Form, modify	Forms, Design		2
Freeze Column	Format, Freeze Columns		2
Index Field	General tab, Indexed		3
Insert Merge Field			5
Insert Row			1
Last Record			2
Macro, create	Macro, New		4
Mailing Labels, create	Tools, Mail Merge, Create, Mailing Labels		5
Mail Merge Helper	Tools, Mail Merge		5
Merge to New Document			5
New Record			2
Next Record			2
Open Existing Database	File, Open		1
Paste Record	Edit, Paste		2
Previous Record			2
Print	File, Print		1
Query, create	Queries, New, Design View		3
Relationships, define	Tools, Relationships		3
Relationships, print	File, Print Relationships		3
Report, create	Reports, New		4
Report, modify	Reports, Design		4
Row Height	Format, Row Height		2
Save	File, Save		1

FEATURE	MENU COMMAND	TOOLBAR BUTTON	LESSON
Sort Ascending	Records, Sort, Sort Ascending	[A/Z↓]	3
Sort Descending`	Records, Sort, Sort Descending	[Z/A↓]	3
Start Access	Start, Programs, Microsoft Access		1
Subdatasheet	Insert, Subdatasheet		3
Table, create	Table, New		1
Table, modify	Highlight name of Table, Design	[Design]	1
Undo Changes in Cell	Edit, Undo Typing	[↶]	2
Undo Changes in Previous Cell	Edit, Undo Current Field/ Record or Esc key		2
Unfreeze All Columns	Format, Unfreeze All Columns		2

REVIEW QUESTIONS ▽

TRUE/FALSE

Circle T if the statement is true or F if the statement is false.

T F 1. A record appears as a column in Datasheet view.

T F 2. The navigation buttons are used to move around the datasheet.

T F 3. Queries allow the most complex searches.

T F 4. Sections are shown in Modify Report view.

T F 5. In the Label Options dialog box, you choose the data source you will be using for the mailing labels.

WRITTEN QUESTIONS

Write a brief answer to the following questions.

1. What data type is used to store dollar amounts?

2. What option makes Access choose the width of a column?

3. What button is used to cause the result of a filter to be displayed?

4. What is a macro?

5. In what document are merge fields inserted?

APPLICATION 1

1. Open the **IA App1** database from the student data files.

2. Open the **Stores** table in Datasheet view.

3. Move the **Hours** column between the **Specialty** and **Credit Cards** fields.

4. Move record **4** to the bottom of the table.

5. Close the table. Click **Yes** if prompted to save changes to the table.

6. Open the **Stores** table in Design view.

7. Insert a field between the **Specialty** and **Credit Card** fields. Name the field **Last Visit** with the **Date/Time** data type, and **Date of last visit** in the description field.

8. Choose **Medium Date** for the format of the **Last Visit** field.

9. Change the field size of the **Specialty** field to **25**.

10. Make the **Name** field **Required**.

11. Save the table design. A message may appear asking if you want to continue. Click **Yes**. Another message may appear asking if you want to test the changes. Click **Yes**.

12. Switch to Datasheet view and print the table in landscape orientation.

13. Close the table.

APPLICATION 2

1. The **IA App1** database should still be open. Create a new form with the Form Wizard using the **Stores** table.

2. Add the **Name**, **Specialty**, **Credit Cards**, and **Hours** fields.

3. Use the **Tabular** layout and the **Standard** style.

4. Title the form **Store Form**.

5. Insert the following record:

Name	Specialty	Credit Cards	Hours
Sports Authority	**Sporting Goods**	**Yes**	**9am to 9pm**

6. Print all the records in the form.

7. Close the form and the database.

APPLICATION 3

1. Open **IA App3** from the student data files.

2. Open the **Employee Information** table in Datasheet view.

3. Sort the table so that the employees's salaries are listed from lowest to highest.

4. Change the left and right margins to **.5"** and print the results of the sort in landscape orientation.

5. Create a query that displays the employees with a title of manager. Have the query display only the **Last Name**, **First Name**, **Department**, **Title**, and **Salary** fields. Save the query as **Managers**.

6. Run the query and print the results. Close the query.

APPLICATION 4

1. The **IA App3** database should still be open. Open the **Employee Information** table, and use the Find command to locate the employees with a title of Account Executive.

2. Create a filter to display only the employees in the Sales department.

3. Change the left and right margins to **.5"** and print the table in landscape orientation.

4. Show all the records in the table.

5. Close the table and the database.

1. Open the database you created in the Lesson 1 Critical Thinking Activity.

2. Create a report that prints the information from your database. If possible, group the report by some field in your database.

3. Give the report an appropriate name and print it.

4. Close the database.

APPLICATION 6

1. Open the **IA App6** database from the student data files.

2. Create a macro to open the **Products** table in Datasheet view, print all the pages, and close the table.

3. Save the macro as **Print Products Table**.

4. Run the macro.

5. Close the database.

You work at the Java Internet Café, which has been open a short time. The café serves coffee, other beverages, and pastries, and offers Internet access. Seven computers are set up on tables along the north side of the store. Customers can come in and have a cup of coffee and a Danish, and explore the World Wide Web.

All membership fees for March were due on March 1. A few members have not paid their monthly dues. Your manager asks you to write a letter to the members as a reminder.

JOB 1

1. Open **Word** and the **Payment Late Letter** from the student data files.

2. Save the document as **Payment Late Merge Letter**.

3. Open Excel and the **Computer Prices** workbook from the student data files.

4. In the spreadsheet, copy the range **A1** through **B11**, and paste it between the first and second paragraphs of the **Payment Late Merge Letter**. Make sure there is one blank line before and after the spreadsheet data.

5. Close **Computer Prices** without saving, and exit Excel.

6. Open **Access**, open the **Java members** database from the student data files, and then open the **Membership** table.

7. Scott Payton just paid his membership fee. Key **$10.00** in the March Paid field of his record.

8. Add the following new member to the end of the database:

   `Ms. Halie Shook, 1290 Wood Crest Apt. 224, Boulder, CO 80302, March Paid = $10`

9. Save the table and switch to Word.

10. Use the **Mail Merge Helper** to create form letters using the open database and Word document. Insert the merge fields as shown in Figure UR-1.

11. Use **Query Options** to create a query to merge the form letters for records with **0** in the **March Paid** field. (There should be three form letters.)

12. Merge the data into a new document.

13. Save the new document as **Payment form letter**.

14. Print the three form letters.

15. Close **Payment form letter**.

16. Save and close **Payment Late Merge Letter** and exit **Word**.

17. Close **Java members** and exit Access.

Java Internet Café

2001 Zephyr Street
Boulder, CO 80302-2001
303.555.JAVA JavaCafe@Cybershop.com

March 15, ----

«Name»
«Address»
«City_State_Zip»

Our records show that you have not paid your $10 membership fee, which was due March 1. We hope you plan to continue your membership with us. Membership lowers your hourly access fees and includes an e-mail account as explained below.

JOB 2

You need to create mailing labels for the form letters you printed yesterday.

1. Open a new Word document.

2. Use the **Mail Merge Helper** to create mailing labels for the three letters you printed yesterday.

3. Use the **Active Window** as the Main Document and the **Java members** database as the Data Source.

4. Choose the **5162 - Address** labels.

5. Insert the merge fields **Name**, **Address**, and **City_State_Zip** on the sample label.

6. Use **Query Options** to create a query to merge only the records with **0** in the **March Paid** field. Merge the data into a new document.

7. Highlight the labels and change the font size to **14** pt.

8. Save the labels document as **Late labels**.

9. Print the labels and close.

10. Close the unsaved document without saving changes and exit Word.

11. Close **Java Members** and exit Access.

UNIT

INTRODUCTION TO MICROSOFT® POWERPOINT

LESSON 1

POWERPOINT BASICS

OBJECTIVES

Upon completion of this lesson, you should be able to:

- Start PowerPoint.
- Open an existing presentation.
- Save a presentation.
- Navigate through a presentation.
- Use the menus and toolbars.
- Apply a design template.
- Change a slide layout.
- Insert clip art.
- Add a slide to a presentation.
- Change views.
- Print a presentation.
- Exit PowerPoint.

⏱ **Estimated Time: 1.5 hours**

Introduction to PowerPoint

PowerPoint is an Office 2000 application that can help you create a professional presentation. You can use PowerPoint to create slides, outlines, speaker's notes, and audience handouts. A presentation can include text, clip art, graphs, tables, charts, and even sound or video clips. Creating a presentation may seem like an intimidating task, but PowerPoint provides features such as design templates and wizards to help make the process easier.

As in all the Office 2000 programs, the Office Assistant is available with tips, solutions, instructions, and examples to help you work more efficiently. It anticipates when you might need help and appears on the screen with tips to guide you. If you have a specific question, you can use the Office Assistant to search for help. To display the Office Assistant, choose Show the Office Assistant from the Help menu. Key your question and click Search. The Assistant suggests a list of help topics in response.

> **Hot Tip**
>
> You can change the way the Office Assistant provides help by clicking Options, choosing the Options tab, and making selections. To choose a different animated character, click the Gallery tab.

Starting PowerPoint

PowerPoint, like other Office 2000 applications, is started from the desktop screen in Windows 98. To start PowerPoint, click the Start button, select Programs, then choose Microsoft PowerPoint. The PowerPoint dialog box appears as shown in Figure 1-1, and you can choose to create a new presentation or open an existing one.

Hot Tip

To skip this dialog box in the future, click *Don't show this dialog box again.*

FIGURE 1-1
PowerPoint dialog box

STEP-BY-STEP ▷ 1.1

1. Click the **Start** button to open the Start menu.

2. Click **Programs**, then choose **Microsoft Power-Point**.

3. PowerPoint starts and the PowerPoint dialog box appears, as shown in Figure 1-1.

4. Leave the dialog box on the screen for the next Step-by-Step.

Opening an Existing Presentation

When you want to open an existing presentation, choose the *Open an existing presentation* option in the PowerPoint dialog box. The box below it shows recently opened presentations. Choose the one you want and click OK. If the presentation you want is not shown, choose More Files and click OK. The Open dialog box appears where you locate and open the presentation (see Figure 1-2). When you locate the presentation you want to open, a preview of the first slide displays. Choose Open and the presentation will appear on the screen.

FIGURE 1-2
Open dialog box

Saving a Presentation

When you save a new presentation, choose Save As from the File menu or click the Save button on the toolbar to display the Save As dialog box. Click the down arrow to the right of the Save in box and click the drive where you will save your presentation. Select the contents of the *File name* box, key a file name, and choose Save.

The next time you want to save changes to your presentation, click the Save button on the toolbar or choose Save from the File menu. These commands update the file and do not open the dialog box.

Concept Builder

To save a presentation as an HTML file that can be viewed using a Web browser, choose Save as Web Page from the File menu.

STEP-BY-STEP ▷ 1.2

1. With the PowerPoint dialog box on the screen, choose **Open an existing presentation**, if it is not already selected.

2. Click **More files...**, if it is not already selected. Click **OK**. The Open dialog box appears.

3. Open **IP Step1-2** from the student data files.

4. A preview of the first slide appears in the box to the right. (See Figure 1-2.)

5. Click **Open.** The presentation opens with the first slide displayed on the screen in Normal view. (If it appears in another view, choose **Normal** from the **View** menu.)

6. Choose **Save As** from the **File** menu. The Save As dialog box appears.

7. Click the down arrow to the right of the *Save in* box and choose the drive where you want to save your presentation.

8. In the *File name* box, key **Penumbra** followed by your initials.

9. Click **Save**.

10. Leave the presentation open for the next Step-by-Step.

Navigating Through a Presentation

The presentation appears in Normal view, which you will learn more about later. To view the slides in a presentation, scroll up and down using the scroll bar. You can go directly to a slide by moving the scroll box up or down until the label to the left of the scroll bar shows the title and number of the slide you want to view (see Figure 1-3). When you release the mouse button, the slide appears on the screen.

Hot Tip

You can also press the Page Down key to view the next slide or press Page Up to view the previous slide.

FIGURE 1-3
Slide label on scroll bar

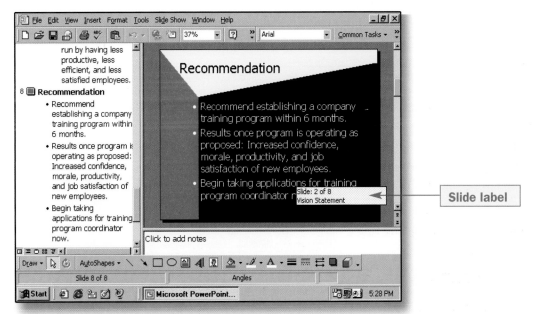

S TEP-BY-STEP ▷ 1.3

1. Click the down arrow at the bottom of the scroll bar on the right to scroll down and view each slide until slide 8, titled *Recommendation,* is displayed on the screen.

2. Go directly to the second slide by clicking the scroll box and moving it up until the label to the

left reads *Slide: 2 of 8 Vision Statement,* as shown in Figure 1-3. When you release the mouse button, slide 2 appears on the screen.

3. Leave the presentation open for the next Step-by-Step.

Using Menus and Toolbars

When you first use PowerPoint, the short menu only displays the basic commands. To see an expanded menu with all the commands, click the arrows at the bottom of the menu. As you work, PowerPoint adjusts the menus to display the commands used most frequently, adding a command when you choose it and dropping a command when it hasn't been used recently.

In Normal view, the three toolbars displayed on the screen by default include the Standard, Formatting, and Drawing toolbars, as shown in Figure 1-4. The Standard and Formatting toolbars share the same row. The Formatting toolbar has a button called Common Tasks that displays a menu of frequently performed functions when clicked, as shown in Figure 1-5. Toolbars display buttons only for basic commands. To see additional buttons, click More Buttons on the toolbar and choose from the list that appears. When you use a button from the list, it is added to the toolbar. If you haven't used a button recently, it is added to the More Buttons list.

Hot Tip

To hide or display a toolbar, right-click any toolbar on the screen and then choose a toolbar from the shortcut menu.

The status bar, shown in Figure 1-6, appears at the bottom of your screen. The button on the left side of the status bar shows which slide is displayed. The second button indicates the design currently in use. You can double-click it to bring up the Apply Design Template dialog box. The third button sometimes displays a spell-check icon that you can use to check the spelling of text in your presentation.

FIGURE 1-4
Standard, Formatting, and Drawing toolbars

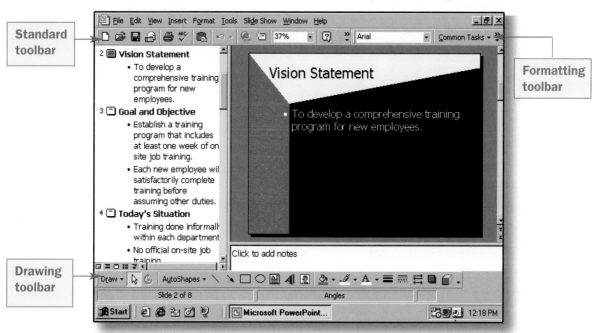

FIGURE 1-5
Common Tasks menu

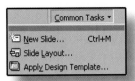

FIGURE 1-6
Status bar

Applying a Design Template

You can use a design template to change the appearance of your slides without changing the content. **Design templates** are predesigned graphic styles that can be applied to your slides. Using a design template, you can change the color scheme, font, formatting, and layout of your slides to create a different look.

To use a design template, access the Apply Design Template dialog box by choosing Apply Design Template from the Format menu. You can also click the Common Tasks button on the toolbar and choose Apply Design Template from the menu or double-click the second button on the status bar as explained earlier. This dialog box contains the names of the different design templates that come with the program. When you click the design template name, the sample slide on the right changes to show the new design, as shown in Figure 1-7. Choose Apply to change all your slides to the new design.

FIGURE 1-7
Apply Design Template dialog box

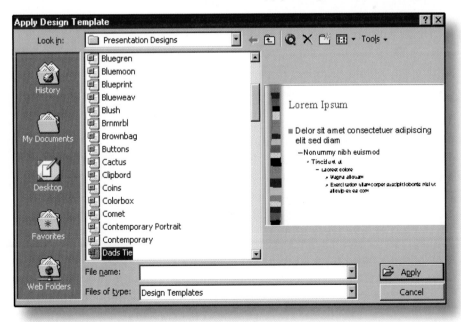

1. Click the **Common Tasks** button on the toolbar and choose **Apply Design Template** from the menu. The Apply Design Template dialog box appears.

2. In the box on the left, scroll down and click **Dads Tie**. The sample slide changes to the *Dads Tie* design, as shown in Figure 1-7.

3. Choose **Apply**. The current presentation is displayed on your screen with a new design. (If the Office Assistant appears with a message about resizing text, click **OK**.)

Concept Builder

PowerPoint automatically fits text within the existing text placeholder. If you want to turn this feature off, choose Options from the Tools menu, click the Edit tab and clear the *Auto-fit text to text placeholder* check box.

4. Scroll up and down to see that all the slides have been changed.

5. Display **slide 1**.

6. Click the title and reposition it attractively on the slide.

 Hot Tip

To move a text box, click to select it and drag. To resize, click the handles and drag.

7. Save and leave the presentation open for the next Step-by-Step.

Changing Slide Layout

W̲hen you want to easily change the layout of text or graphics on slides, you can use the program's preset layouts. PowerPoint includes 24 AutoLayouts you can choose from to create a new slide or change the layout of an existing slide. The different layouts include placeholders for text, columns, bulleted lists, clip art, tables, organization charts, objects, graphs, and media clips. A *placeholder* reserves a space in the presentation for the type of information you want. Just click on a placeholder and replace it with your own information. You can choose the layout that best fits the need of a particular slide.

Concept Builder

If you want to add text on a slide that does not have a placeholder for it, click the Text Box button on the Drawing toolbar.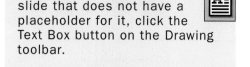

To change the layout for an existing slide, scroll to display the slide you want to change. Then, choose Slide Layout from the Format menu or click the Common Tasks button on the toolbar and choose Slide Layout from the menu. The Slide Layout dialog box contains small diagrams of the AutoLayouts, as shown in Figure 1-8. To change the layout, click a new layout and choose Apply.

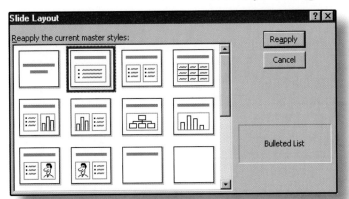

FIGURE 1-8
Slide Layout dialog box

S TEP-BY-STEP ▷ 1.5

1. Display slide 2.

2. Click the **Common Tasks** button on the toolbar
   and choose **Slide Layout** from the menu. The
   Slide Layout dialog box appears, as shown in
   Figure 1-8.

3. Click on the first layout in the third row. The
   box to the right of the layout choices should
   say *Text & Clip Art.*

4. Choose **Apply.** The Vision Statement slide is
   displayed with the existing text and a placeholder for clip art, as shown in Figure 1-9.

5. Save and leave the presentation open for the
   next Step-by-Step.

FIGURE 1-9
Clip art placeholder

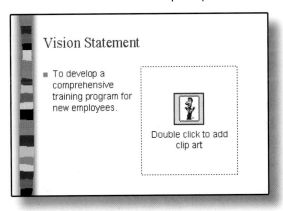

Inserting Clip Art

To insert clip art if there is already a clip art placeholder on the slide, double-click it. The Microsoft Clip Gallery appears, as shown in Figure 1-10, with numerous categories from which to choose.
You can also import clips from other sources into the Clip Gallery or even connect to the Web to access
more clips.

If there is not a placeholder, choose Picture from the Insert menu and Clip Art from the submenu.
The Insert ClipArt dialog box appears, which is very similar to the Microsoft Clip Gallery dialog box,
except it has three media tabs to choose from—Pictures, Sounds, and Motion Clips.

FIGURE 1-10
Microsoft Clip Gallery dialog box

To find a clip art image, type one or more words in the *Search for clips* box. Or, click on a category and the available clip art will be shown. When you click on the clip you want, a toolbar menu appears, as shown in Figure 1-11.

Click the *Insert clip* button to insert the image in your document at the location of your insertion point. Click the *Preview clip* button to view the image without adding it to your document. To add a clip to your favorites or to another category, click the *Add clip to Favorites or other category* button. To see similar clips, click the *Find similar clips* button.

Hot Tip

When you point to a picture a label pops up with information about it.

FIGURE 1-11
Clip art toolbar menu

STEP-BY-STEP ▷ 1.6

1. Double-click the clip art placeholder. The Microsoft Clip Gallery dialog box appears, as shown in Figure 1-10.

2. Scroll down the list of categories and click **People**.

3. Click the picture with the description **meetings**, as shown in Figure 1-11 with a box around it. (Your clip art choices may not match the figure exactly.) If that picture is not available, click another appropriate one. A clip art toolbar menu appears.

4. Click the **Insert clip** button.

5. The clip art you chose is displayed on the Vision Statement slide. (If a Picture toolbar appears, click X to close it.) Click the clip art and resize or move it to place it attractively on the slide if necessary.

Hot Tip

To move clip art, click the object and drag. To resize, click the handles and drag.

6. Save and leave the presentation open for the next Step-by-Step.

Adding a Slide

You can add a slide to a presentation by clicking the New Slide button on the toolbar, choosing New Slide from the Insert menu, or clicking the Common Tasks button on the formatting toolbar. This brings up the New Slide dialog box, which allows you to choose a layout for the new slide. The New Slide dialog box looks very similar to the Slide Layout dialog box and has the same 24 AutoLayouts from which to choose. When you choose a layout and click OK, the new slide is inserted into the presentation after the slide that is currently on the screen.

Another way to add a slide is to copy it from another presentation. Choose Slides from Files from the Insert menu. Locate the presentation you want to copy a slide from and click Display. Select the slide you want to copy and click Insert. The slide is inserted after the one displayed on the screen.

STEP-BY-STEP ▷ 1.7

1. Display the sixth slide titled *Available Options*. The button on the left of the status bar should read *Slide 6 of 8*.

2. Click the **New Slide** button on the toolbar. The New Slide dialog box appears.

3. Click the second layout in the first row, if it is not already chosen. The box to the right of the layout choices should say *Bulleted List*.

4. Click **OK**. A new slide with placeholders is displayed on the screen and the status bar now reads *Slide 7 of 9*.

5. Click where it reads *Click to add title.*

6. Key **Available Options**.

7. Click where it reads *Click to add text.*

8. Key **Equip each department to handle its own training.**

(continued on next page)

9. Press **Enter**, then **Tab**.

10. Key the remaining text shown in Figure 1-12.

11. Save and leave the presentation open for the next Step-by-Step.

FIGURE 1-12
Key text to make your new slide
appear like this figure

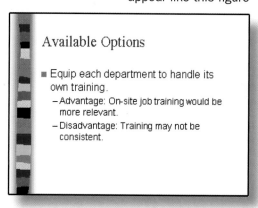

Available Options

■ Equip each department to handle its
own training.
– Advantage: On-site job training would be
more relevant.
– Disadvantage: Training may not be
consistent.

Changing Views

You can view a presentation five different ways. Each button on the bottom left of the screen, shown in Figure 1-13, corresponds with one of the five views. To change views, click the button for the view you want. You can also change views by choosing the desired view from the View menu.

You have been working in Normal view. This view has three panes—the largest, called the slide pane, displays one slide at a time and is useful for adding text or modifying the slide's appearance. The outline pane on the left shows the slide titles and main text in outline form. The notes pane on the bottom is where you can create notes that are helpful when presenting. To add speaker notes, click in the notes pane and begin keying.

 **Hot Tip**

To adjust the size of the different panes, click and drag the pane borders.

FIGURE 1-13
View buttons

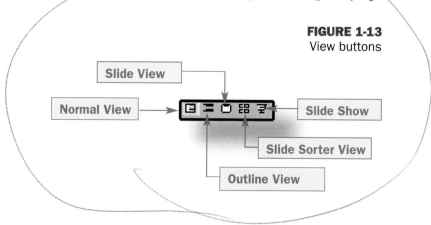

Slide View

Normal View

Slide Show

Slide Sorter View

Outline View

In Outline view the outline pane is enlarged so you can more easily develop and organize the content of your presentation. The slide and notes panes are still displayed on the right of the screen. In Slide view, one slide is shown on the screen. The pane on the left shows how many slides are in the presentation and indicates which slide is currently displayed. To move to another slide, just click the one you want.

Slide Sorter view, as shown in Figure 1-14, displays miniature versions of the slides on screen so that you can move and arrange slides easily by dragging. A Slide Sorter toolbar appears when you switch to this view to help you with timings, transitions, and animation. In Slide Show view, each slide fills the screen and you can run your presentation on the computer as if it were a slide projector to preview how it will look.

FIGURE 1-14
Slide Sorter view

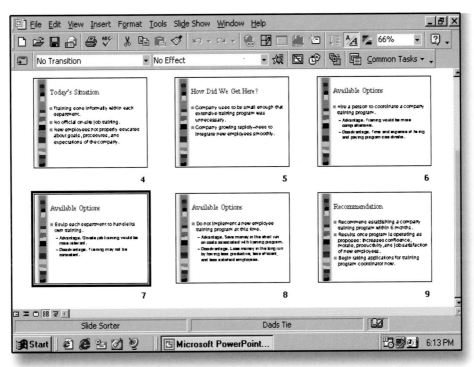

STEP-BY-STEP ▷ 1.8

1. Click the **Slide Sorter View** button. The screen appears as shown in Figure 1-14.

2. Click **slide 8** so that it is outlined in bold.

3. Click **slide 8** again and hold the mouse button down. Begin dragging to the right until a little box is visible at the bottom of the pointer and a line appears between slide 8 and slide 9.

(continued on next page)

4. Still holding the mouse button down, drag the pointer up to **slide 5** so the line is now between slide 5 and slide 6.

5. Release the mouse button. Slide 8 moves to become slide 6 and all other slides move down and are renumbered.

6. Click the **Outline View** button. The presentation appears in the form of an outline with the slide and notes panes on the right of the screen.

7. Click the **Slide View** button. One slide in the presentation appears on the screen.

8. Display slide 1 on the screen.

9. Click the **Slide Show** button.

10. The first slide appears on your screen as if you were giving a presentation. Click the left mouse button to advance through all the slides.

11. When all the slides have been displayed, a black screen is displayed. Click to exit the presentation and return to the PowerPoint screen.

12. Save and leave the presentation open for the next Step-by-Step.

Printing a Presentation

Choose Print from the File menu and the Print dialog box appears, as shown in Figure 1-15. The Print dialog box gives you the option of printing your presentation as slides using the Slide option, with notes using the Notes Pages option, or as an outline using the Outline View option. Using the Handouts option, you can print handouts with two, three, four, six, or nine slides per page and choose whether they are ordered horizontally or vertically.

FIGURE 1-15
Print dialog box

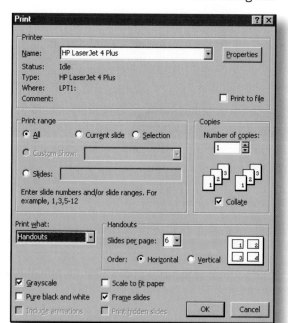

You can choose to print all the slides, only the current slide, or any combination of slides in your presentation. If you aren't printing your presentation in color, you can choose either the *Grayscale* or *Pure black and white* option. To make sure the slides will print on the page correctly, there is a *Scale to fit paper* option. With the *Frame slides* option, you can choose whether the border of the slides appears when printed.

Concept Builder

You can preivew what your presentation will look like when printed in black and white by choosing Black and White from the View menu.

S TEP-BY-STEP ▷ 1.9

1. Choose **Print** from the **File** menu. The Print dialog box appears, as shown in Figure 1-15.

2. In the *Print what* box, click the down arrow to the right and choose **Outline View**.

3. Click the check box to select the *Scale to fit paper* option.

4. Click **OK**. The presentation prints as an outline on one page.

5. Access the **Print** dialog box again.

6. In the *Print what* box, choose **Handouts**.

7. In the *Handouts* section, click the down arrow next to the *Slides per page* box and choose **9**.

8. Choose **Horizontal** as the order, if it is not already chosen.

9. Click **OK**. The presentation prints as a handout.

10. Leave the presentation open for the next Step-by-Step.

Hot Tip

You do not have to switch views to print a view different from the one you are currently using.

Closing a Presentation and Exiting PowerPoint

When you want to close a presentation, choose Close from the File menu or click the presentation's Close Window box. To exit PowerPoint, choose Exit from the File menu or click the PowerPoint Close box in the upper right corner of the screen. If there are any unsaved changes to a presentation you have been working on, you will be asked if you want to save them before exiting.

S TEP-BY-STEP ▷ 1.10

1. Choose **Close** from the **File** menu to close the presentation. Click **Yes** if prompted to save your changes.

2. Click the **Close** box in the upper right corner of the screen to exit PowerPoint.

Summary

In this lesson, you learned:

- PowerPoint is an Office 2000 application that can help you create a professional presentation. When you start PowerPoint, you have the choice of opening an existing presentation or creating a new one.

- PowerPoint has helpful features that come with the program that can make it much easier to create a presentation. You can use design templates to change the appearance of your slides. When you create a new slide or change the layout of an existing slide, there are 24 AutoLayouts to choose from. Clip art is available if you want to add pictures to your presentation.

- You can view your presentation five different ways: Normal view, Outline view, Slide view, Slide Sorter view, and Slide Show. Each view has its own advantages.

- Using the Print dialog box, you can print your presentation as slides using the Slide option, with notes using the Notes Pages option, or as an outline using the Outline View option. You can also choose to print handouts with two, three, four, six, or nine slides per page.

- To exit PowerPoint, choose Exit from the File menu.

LESSON 1 REVIEW QUESTIONS

MULTIPLE CHOICE

Select the best response for the following statements.

1. When an existing file you want to open is not shown in the PowerPoint dialog box, choose
   A. Open Another File
   B. Search
   C. More Files
   D. Browse

2. Which toolbar is *not* displayed by default in Normal view?
   A. Outlining
   B. Standard
   C. Formatting
   D. Drawing

3. Which is *not* one of the presentation views?
   A. Outline
   B. Notes
   C. Slide Show
   D. Slide

4. How many AutoLayouts are there to choose from in the Slide Layout dialog box?
   A. 22
   B. 18
   C. 20
   D. 24

5. Which option in the Print dialog box lets you choose whether the border of the slide appears when printed?
   A. Grayscale
   B. Print border
   C. Scale to fit
   D. Frame slides

FILL IN THE BLANKS

Complete the following sentences by writing the correct word or words in the blanks provided.

1. You can use a _Design Template_ to change the appearance of your slides without changing content.

2. A _placeholder_ reserves space in a presentation for the type of information you want.

3. You can add a slide to a presentation by clicking the _New Slide_ button on the toolbar.

4. _Slide Sorter_ view displays miniature versions of the slides on screen so that you can move and arrange slides easily by dragging.

5. In the Print dialog box you can choose to print your presentation with notes using the _Notes Page_ option.

LESSON 1 PROJECTS

PROJECT 1-1

1. Open **IP Project1-1** from the student data files.

2. Save the presentation as **Networking** followed by your initials.

3. On the title slide, replace *Student's Name* with your name.

4. Change the design template to **Network Blitz**.

5. Insert a new slide at the end of the presentation (slide 4) titled **Advantages** and key the following text in a bulleted list using normal view:

   - `A LAN allows people to share computer resources, such as printers, disk drives, software, and data.`

   - `By installing a LAN, your office can become more productive and more cost-efficient.`

6. Key this speaker's note on **slide 3**:

   `Explain backup system for each type of LAN.`
   `Allow time for questions.`

7. Save and leave the presentation open for the next project.

PROJECT 1-2

1. Change the layout of **slide 3** to **Text & Clip Art**.

2. Replace the clip art placeholder with a computer picture (key **computer** in the *Search for clips* box to see available choices).

3. Print **slide 3** using the **Notes Pages** option.

4. Switch to **Slide Sorter** view. Click **slide 3** and drag it so that it becomes the last slide of the presentation.

5. Print the presentation as audience handouts with all four slides on the page in horizontal order.

6. Run the presentation as a slide show.

7. Save and close the presentation.

CRITICAL THINKING

ACTIVITY 1-1

You are giving a presentation at a conference out of town and will be using a different computer that does not have PowerPoint installed. Use Help to find out what to do in order to be able to run your presentation.

ACTIVITY 1-2

It is helpful to plan a presentation before you actually create it on the computer. On paper sketch out ideas for a presentation that has at least four slides. Include a title slide and indicate where you would put clip art. Choose one of the following topics or make up your own.

- Motivate a sales force to achieve their quotas by offering incentives

- Encourage people to donate blood in the blood drive campaign next week

- Explain the procedure for some safety technique (doing CPR, fire prevention, how to baby-proof a house, performing first aid)

- Offer the opportunity to be involved in a community project or volunteer organization

- Introduce the grand opening of a new store

- Provide information about a new class that will be available in the fall

ENHANCING A POWERPOINT PRESENTATION

OBJECTIVES

Upon completion of this lesson, you should be able to:

- Create a new presentation.
- Delete slides.
- Add text to slides.
- Check spelling and style.
- Use the slide master.
- Change text appearance.
- Work with bullets.
- Use slide transitions.
- Insert animation.
- Work in Outline view.
- Utilize slide layout options.

⏱ **Estimated Time: 2 hours**

Creating a Presentation

From the PowerPoint dialog box that appears when you start PowerPoint, you have three choices for creating a presentation: AutoContent Wizard, Design Template, or Blank presentation. The ***AutoContent Wizard*** will guide you through a series of questions about the type of presentation, the output options, the presentation style, and the presentation options. The Wizard will then provide you with ideas and an organization for a new presentation based on your answers. If you decide to create a presentation using the Design Template option, you will be able to choose a design

 **Concept Builder**

Unless you have a particular reason for creating a presentation from a blank document, it is easier to use the Wizard or a design template to help you. You can always modify the presentation to suit your needs as you go along.

template that is right for the presentation you have planned. As you learned in Lesson 1, the design templates that come with PowerPoint are already designed and formatted with certain colors, fonts, and layouts. To start a presentation from scratch, choose the ***Blank presentation*** option. This allows you to create a presentation using whatever layout, format, colors, and style you prefer.

1. Start PowerPoint. With the PowerPoint dialog box on the screen, choose **AutoContent Wizard**.

2. Click **OK**. The AutoContent Wizard dialog box appears, as shown in Figure 2-1.

3. Read the screen and then click **Next >**.

4. Click the **All** or **General** button. Select **Generic** as the type of presentation you are going to give. Click **Next >**.

5. If it is not already selected, choose **On-screen presentation** in response to the question *What type of output will you use?* Click **Next >**.

6. In the *Presentation title:* box, key **Copier Purchase for Office**.

7. In the *Footer:* box, key **Mesa Foundation**.

8. Click the *Date last updated* box to remove the check. Click **Next >**.

9. Click **Finish**. Your presentation appears on the screen, similar to Figure 2-2.

10. Save the presentation as **Copier** followed by your initials, and leave it open for the next Step-by-Step.

FIGURE 2-1
The AutoContent Wizard helps you create a presentation quickly

FIGURE 2-2

The Wizard provides ideas and organization for your presentation

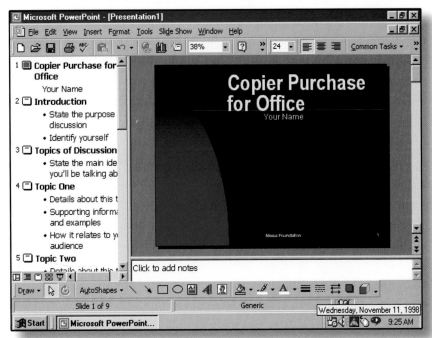

Deleting Slides

A presentation created using the AutoContent Wizard includes a predetermined number of slides based on the type of presentation you chose. If you decide that a slide does not fit your presentation, you can easily delete it. With that slide displayed, choose Delete Slide from the Edit menu. If you accidentally delete the wrong slide, immediately choose Undo Delete Slide from the Edit menu to restore the slide or use the Undo button on the toolbar.

S TEP-BY-STEP ▷ 2.2

1. Change the design template to *Capsules*.

2. Display **slide 2**, titled *Introduction*.

3. Choose **Delete Slide** from the **Edit** menu. The slide is deleted.

4. Display **slide 6**, titled *Real Life* and delete it.

5. Display **slide 6**, now titled *What This Means* and delete it.

6. Save the presentation and leave it open for the next Step-by-Step.

Adding Text to Slides

W hen the AutoContent Wizard helps you create a presentation, it creates placeholders on each slide that tell you what kind of information might go there. To replace a text placeholder, click on the text. A box appears around the text. You can then select the existing text and key your own text.

If you cannot see the text clearly, it is helpful to use the Zoom feature. Click the arrow next to the Zoom box on the toolbar. On the menu that appears there are preset percentages so that you can enlarge or reduce the size of the presentation on screen, or you can choose Fit to allow PowerPoint to display the slide at an optimal size.

 Concept Builder

To find and replace text, choose Replace from the Edit menu. Key the text you want to find and the text you want to replace it with. Click Find Next to find the next occurrence, Replace to replace the next occurrence, and Replace All to replace all occurrences.

 Concept Builder

You can add text to the top or bottom of a slide by inserting a header or footer. You can also add the slide number, date, or time in a header or footer. Choose Header and Footer from the View menu. Select the options and key the text you want. You will practice this later in the lesson, using the Slide Master.

S TEP-BY-STEP ▷ 2.3

1. Display **slide 2**. Click *Topics of Discussion*. A box appears around the text.

2. Click the down arrow next to the **Zoom** box on the toolbar. `38%`

3. Choose **50%** from the drop-down menu.

4. Select the existing text and then key **Office Copier Purchase**.

5. Click the bulleted text. Select the first bulleted item and then key the text as it appears in Figure 2-3. Press **Enter** and key the second bulleted item as shown.

 Hot Tip

Press Tab to demote a bullet one level.

6. Use this method to replace the existing text on the remaining slides to make them look similar to those in Figures 2-4.

 Extra Challenge

Change the bullets in your presentation to arrows, dots, stars, check marks, or some other character by choosing Bullets and Numbering from the Format menu.

7. If necessary, replace the subtitle on slide 1 with your name.

8. Choose **Fit** from the **Zoom** menu on the toolbar to return the slide to optimal size.

9. Save the presentation.

10. Display **slide 6**.

11. Enlarge the notes pane and then click where it says **Click to add notes**.

12. Key the text as shown in Figure 2-5.

13. Choose **Print** from the **File** menu. The Print dialog box appears.

14. In the *Print range* box, click **Current slide**.

15. In the *Print what* box, choose **Notes Pages**.

16. Click **OK**. Slide 6 prints with notes.

17. Access the Print dialog box again.

18. In the *Print range* box, click **All**.

19. Choose to print handouts 6 slides per page horizontally.

20. Click **OK**. The slides print on a single handout sheet.

21. Save and close the presentation.

FIGURE 2-3
Key the text to make your slide
look like this figure

FIGURE 2-4
Slides 3 through 6

Slide 3

Background
- Our present copier is slow and has few copying options.
- Money is currently available to purchase a new copier.

Slide 4

Key Issues
- We want to have the new copier in place by next month.
- We need to determine what copiers meet our needs for:
  - Speed
  - Size
  - Noise level
  - Optional features

Slide 5

Status
- A Copier Purchase Committee has been formed to oversee the purchase.
- We have gathered information about copiers in our price range.
- We will use the existing copier stand and the same location.

Slide 6

Next Steps
- We need input from all office members on copier requirements.
- Staff members should review available pamphlets/brochures.
- Committee members will collect and collate the suggestions.
- We will meet in two weeks to discuss and make a final decision.

(continued on next page)

FIGURE 2-5
Slide notes can help you remember
what to say during a presentation

Have Stephen talk briefly about information that has already been gathered.
List specific copier features that need to be agreed upon.
Hand out pamphlets and brochures that we currently have about new copiers.
See if Monday the 23rd at 2:00 will work for everyone.

Checking Spelling and Style

Automatic spell checking identifies misspellings and words that are not in PowerPoint's dictionary by underlining them with a wavy red line immediately after you key them. To correct a misspelled word that is underlined, position the pointer on the word and click with the right mouse button. A shortcut menu appears with a list of correctly spelled words. Click with the left mouse button on the suggestion that you want, and it replaces the misspelled word. The automatic spell checker can be turned on and off or adjusted by accessing the Spelling & Style tab of the Options dialog box through the Tools menu.

You can also check the spelling in a presentation after it is complete by clicking the Spelling button on the toolbar. The Spelling dialog box shown in Figure 2-6 contains options that allow you to ignore words, make changes, or add words to your own custom dictionary.

An effective presentation should be consistent, error-free, and visually appealing. PowerPoint helps you determine if your presentation conforms to the standards of good style. For instance, title text size should be at least 36 point and the number of bullets on a slide should not exceed six. A light bulb appears to alert you to problems with visual clarity such as appropriate font usage and legibility, and inconsistent capitalization and end punctuation. To make changes, click the light bulb and choose an option from the menu, as shown in Figure 2-7.

In the Style Options dialog box you can customize what are considered style errors or inconsistencies. Choose Options from the Tools menu and in the Spelling & Style tab, click the Style Options button to access the Style Options dialog box shown in Figure 2-8. Make any changes you want or click the Defaults button to restore the original settings.

FIGURE 2-6
Spelling dialog box

FIGURE 2-7
A light bulb alerts you to style
problems with a presentation

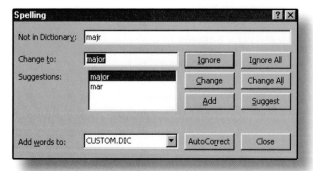

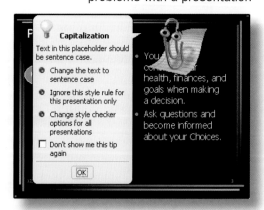

FIGURE 2-8
Style Options dialog box

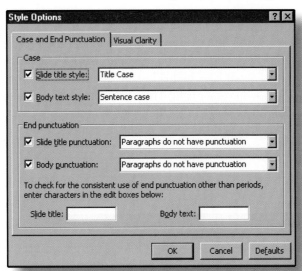

S TEP-BY-STEP ▷ 2.4

1. Open **IP Step2-4** from the student data files. Save the presentation as **Cypress**, followed by your initials.

2. Change the design template to *Nature*.

3. Click the **Spelling** button on the toolbar. The Spelling dialog box appears as shown in Figure 2-6. Make the spelling change as suggested.

4. When a message appears that the spelling check is complete, click **OK**.

5. Display **slide 3**. Click the light bulb and a menu appears as shown in Figure 2-7.

Hot Tip

If the light bulb is not visible choose **Show the Office Assistant** from the **Help** menu to display it.

6. Click *Change the text to sentence case*.

7. Display **slide 4**. Click the light bulb to display the menu and choose *Change text to be at least 36 point*.

8. Choose **Options** from the **Tools** menu.

9. Click the **Spelling & Style** tab.

10. Click the **Style Options** button. The Style Options dialog box appears as shown in Figure 2-8.

11. Click **Defaults** to make sure the original settings are chosen. Click **OK**, then Click **OK** again to close the Options dialog box.

12. Save the presentation and leave it open for the next Step-by-Step.

Changing Text Appearance

If you use a design template, the format of the text on your slides is predetermined so that the layout, color scheme, font, size, and style are consistent throughout the presentation. You can alter the format by making changes to individual slides. If you want the change to appear on all slides, you can use the slide master that you will learn about later in this lesson. You change the font, font style, size, effects, and color by choosing Font from the Format menu. The Font dialog box opens, as shown in Figure 2-9.

You can also use the toolbar as a shortcut to changing the font, font size, and font style, as shown in Figure 2-10. The Increase Font Size and Decrease Font Size buttons allow you to change the font size quickly in preset increments.

FIGURE 2-9
Font dialog box

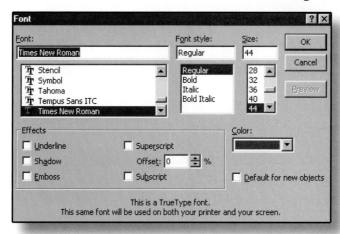

FIGURE 2-10
Formatting toolbar

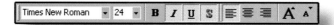

S TEP-BY-STEP ▷ 2.5

1. Display **slide 1** and select the title, *Cypress Village*.

2. Choose **Font** from the **Format** menu. The Font dialog box appears, as shown in Figure 2-9.

3. In the *Font* box, choose **Arial**.

4. In the *Effects* box, click **Shadow**.

5. In the *Size* box, choose **54**.

6. Click **OK**.

7. Select the subtitle, *Senior Living With Style*.

8. Choose **Font** from the **Format** menu. In the *Font Style* box, choose **Bold**.

9. In the *Size* box, choose **40**.

10. Click the down arrow in the *Color* box and choose the **green square** on the far right of the top row.

11. Click **OK**.

12. Display **slide 4** and select the title, *Cost Analysis*.

Changing Alignment, Spacing, Case, and Tabs

To change text alignment, click one of the alignment buttons on the toolbar. To change spacing, choose Line Spacing from the Format menu and make changes in the Line Spacing dialog box. To change the case of text, choose Change Case from the Format menu and then choose one of the five options in the Change Case dialog box. To set or clear tabs, display the ruler by choosing Ruler from the View menu. Set a tab by clicking the tab button at the left of the horizontal ruler. Clear a tab by dragging the tab marker off the ruler.

STEP-BY-STEP ▷ 2.6

1. Select the title, *Cost Analysis*, on **slide 4**.

2. Click the **Center** button on the toolbar.

3. Display **slide 3** and select the bulleted text.

4. Choose **Line Spacing** from the **Format** menu. The Line Spacing dialog box appears.

5. In the *Line Spacing* section, click the up arrow until it reads **1.2**.

6. Click **OK**.

13. Click the **Increase Font Size** button on the toolbar twice to increase the font size to 44.

14. Save and leave the presentation open for the next Step-by-Step.

7. Display **slide 4** and select the title of the table, *Prices as of January 1999*.

8. Choose **Change Case** from the **Format** menu. The Change Case dialog box appears.

9. Choose **UPPERCASE** and click **OK**.

10. Save the presentation and leave it open for the next Step-by-Step.

Working with Bullets

If bullets do not exist on a slide, you can add them by selecting the text or placeholder and clicking the Bullets button on the toolbar. You can customize a bulleted list after it has been created. You can change the appearance of the bullets, such as their shape, size, or color, and you can also adjust the distance between the bullets and the text. To change the appearance of the bullets throughout the presentation, make the changes on the slide master. You cannot select a bullet to make changes—you must select the associated text.

To change all the bullets in a bulleted list, select the entire list first. When you choose Bullets and Numbering from the Format menu, the Bullets and Numbering dialog box appears as shown in Figure 2-11. In the Bulleted tab, you can select a preset bullet or add a graphical bullet by clicking Picture or Character to choose a picture bullet or a different character. You can also change the color or the bullet size in relation to the text.

Concept Builder

If your list is numbered instead of bulleted, choose the Numbered tab in the Bullets and Numbering dialog box to customize the list.

FIGURE 2-11
Bulleted tab of the Bullets and Numbering dialog box

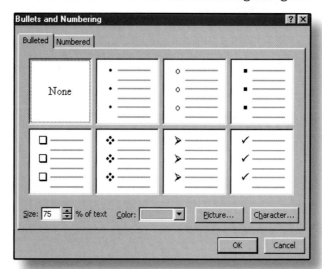

STEP-BY-STEP ▷ 2.7

1. Display **slide 2** and select the last four bulleted points.

2. Choose **Bullets and Numbering** from the **Format** menu.

3. Choose the **Bulleted** tab if it is not already selected, as shown in Figure 2-11.

4. Click the second bullet choice on the second row.

5. Click the up arrow in the *Size* box until it reads **90**.

6. Click the down arrow in the *Color* box and choose the **green color** on the far right of the second row.

7. Click **OK**.

8. Save and leave the presentation open for the next Step-by-Step.

Using the Slide Master

The **slide master** controls the formatting for all the slides in the presentation. You can use the slide master to change such items as the font, size, color, style, alignment, spacing, and background. Changing the slide master will affect the appearance of all of the slides and give them a consistent look. You can add headers and footers to slides. You can also place an object, such as a logo or graphic, on every slide by placing it on the slide master. To access the master title slide, shown in Figure 2-12, choose Master from the View menu, and then Slide Master from the submenu. When you have finished making changes to the slide master, click Close on the Master toolbar.

Concept Builder

You can override the format of the slide master by making changes directly to individual slides.

PowerPoint has other masters that work similarly to the slide master. The title master is used to format the first slide of your presentation. The handout master lets you add items that you want to appear on all your handouts, such as a logo, the date, the time, or page numbers. On the notes master, include any text or formatting that you want to appear on all your speaker notes. Choose Master from the View menu and then choose the master you want from the submenu.

Hot Tip

You can display a master by pressing Shift and clicking a view button.

FIGURE 2-12
Slide master

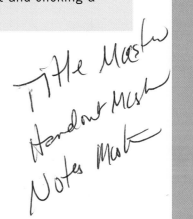

STEP-BY-STEP 2.8

1. Display **slide 5**. Notice that the appearance of this bulleted list did not change when you made changes to the bulleted list on **slide 2**.

2. Choose **Master** from the **View** menu and **Slide Master** from the submenu.

3. Select the text that says *Second level*.

4. Choose **Bullets and Numbering** from the **Format** menu and click the **Bulleted** tab.

5. Click the second bullet choice on the second row.

(continued on next page)

6. Click the up arrow in the *Size* box until it reads **90**.

7. Click the down arrow in the *Color* box and choose the **green color** on the far right of the second row.

8. Click **OK**.

9. Select *Click to edit Master title style*. (You might have to drag the Master toolbar out of the way first.)

10. Change the font to **Arial**.

11. Choose **Header and Footer** from the **View** menu. The Header and Footer dialog box appears.

12. Click the **Slide** tab, if necessary, and click the check boxes next to *Date and time* and *Slide number*.

13. Click **Apply to All**.

14. Click **Close** on the Master toolbar.

15. Scroll through the presentation to see that the appearance of all slide titles and bulleted lists have changed.

16. Print the presentation as handouts with 6 slides per page.

17. Save and leave the presentation open for the next Step-by-Step.

Using Slide Transitions

W hen running a presentation, ***slide transitions*** determine how one slide is removed from the screen and how the next one appears. You can set the transitions between slides by choosing Slide Transition from the Slide Show menu and making choices in the Slide Transition dialog box as shown in Figure 2-13.

In the *Effect* section you pick from a list of effects and select the speed at which it displays. In the *Advance* section you determine whether to advance the slides manually by clicking the mouse or set the timing to advance them automatically. To set slides to advance automatically, click *Automatically after* and enter the number of seconds you want the slide to be displayed on the screen. In the *Sound* section you can choose a sound effect that will play while the slide transition occurs. If you click Apply to All, the selections you made will affect all slides in the presentation. To add the transition choices only to the current slide, choose Apply.

FIGURE 2-13
Slide Transition dialog box

Extra Challenge

If you choose Random Transition in the Effect section, PowerPoint will randomly choose a transition effect for each slide when you run the presentation. Try it!

STEP-BY-STEP ▷ 2.9

1. Choose **Slide Transition** from the **Slide Show** menu. The Slide Transition dialog box appears as shown in Figure 2-13.

2. In the *Effect* section, click the arrow and choose **Checkerboard Across** from the menu. Choose **Medium** as the speed.

3. In the *Advance* section, **On mouse click** should be chosen and no sound should be selected in the *Sound* section.

4. Click **Apply to All**.

5. Display **slide 4** and access the Slide Transition dialog box.

6. In the *Sound* section, click the down arrow and choose **Cash Register**.

7. Choose **Apply**.

8. Display **slide 6** and access the Slide Transition dialog box.

9. In the *Sound* section, click the down arrow and choose **Applause**.

10. Display **slide 1** and choose **Slide Show** from the **View** menu.

11. Click the left mouse button to advance through the slides.

12. When the presentation is over save it and leave open for the next Step-by-Step.

Inserting Animation

To **animate** an object or text, you add a sound effect or special visual. Animation effects offer a way to enhance your presentation and increase audience interest. To select animation effects, choose Custom Animation from the Slide Show menu. The Custom Animation dialog box appears. In the Order & Timing tab, shown in Figure 2-14, you can select the objects you want to animate, arrange animation order, and determine whether to display the animation manually or automatically.

In the Effects tab of the Animation dialog box, shown in Figure 2-15, you can animate text to enter the screen in various ways. If desired, you can choose a sound to accompany it. You have the option of dimming the object after it has been animated. You can choose to have the text appear all at once, by the word, or by the letter. The Chart Effects tab allows you to determine how a chart will be animated. In the Multimedia Settings tab, you can select options for playing objects such as videos or sound clips.

Concept Builder

PowerPoint also offers a selection of preset animation effects that you can add by choosing Preset Animation from the Slide Show menu.

FIGURE 2-14
FIGURE 2-14

Order & Timing tab of the Custom Animation dialog box

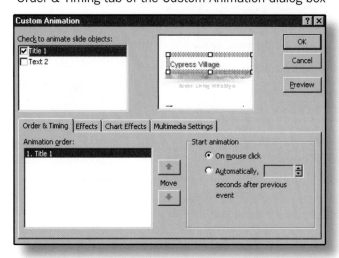

FIGURE 2-15

Effects tab of the Custom Animation dialog box

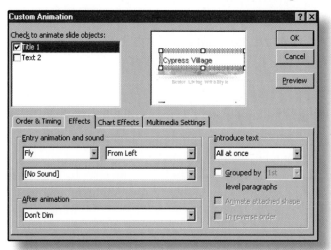

 STEP-BY-STEP ▷ 2.10

1. Display **slide 1** and choose **Custom Animation** from the **Slide Show** menu. The Custom Animation dialog box appears.

2. Click the **Order & Timing** tab.

3. In the *Check to animate slide objects* box, click to place a checkmark in the box next to **Title 1**. The Custom Animation dialog box should look like Figure 2-14.

4. Click the **Effects** tab. The Custom Animation dialog box now looks like Figure 2-15.

5. In the *Entry animation and sound* section, choose **Spiral** from the Animation menu and **Drum Roll** from the Sound menu.

6. Click the **Preview** button to see a preview of the animation.

INTRODUCTION TO MICROSOFT POWERPOINT

7. Click to place a checkmark in the box next to **Text 2**.

8. In the *Entry animation and sound* section, choose **Appear** from the Animation menu.

9. In the *Introduce text* box, choose **By Word**.

10. Click **Preview** to see a preview and then click **OK**.

11. Run the presentation. Click the left mouse button to start each animation.

12. Save the presentation and leave it open for the next Step-by-Step.

Extra Challenge

Animate the headings and text on the rest of the slides. Set the slides to advance automatically, choosing the number of seconds you want the slides to be displayed on the screen. Run the presentation to see the new effects.

Utilizing Slide Layouts

In Lesson 1, you learned how to change the layout of a slide by choosing one of the 24 Auto-Layouts in the Slide Layout dialog box. When creating a new slide you have the same layout options in the New Slide dialog box. Using various slide layouts can help keep your presentation interesting. This is an easy way to change text to 2-columns or insert media clips, organization charts, and tables.

S TEP-BY-STEP ▷ 2.11

1. Display **slide 6**.

2. Choose **Slide Layout** from the **Common Tasks** menu on the toolbar. The Slide Layout dialog box appears.

3. Choose the third layout on the first row, *2 Column Text*.

4. Click **Apply**. The layout changes to 2-column text.

5. Click the second column where it says *Click to add text* and key the following information:

```
Cypress Village
13 Forge Lane
Iuka, MS 38852
(601) 555-4279
```

6. Delete the bullet. Center and bold the information and change the font size to **36**.

7. Print the slide in Slides view.

8. Save and leave the presentation open for the next Step-by-Step.

Working in Outline View

Since Outline view shows slide titles and text in outline form, it is a good way to develop and organize your presentation. As you learned in the previous lesson, you can switch to Outline view by clicking the Outline view button or choosing Outline from the View menu. When working with an outline, it is helpful to use the Outlining toolbar that has buttons to help you rearrange the content of your presentation. (See Figure 2-16.) To display the Outlining toolbar, choose View, Toolbars, Outlining. You can also display the Outlining toolbar and use it to rearrange text when working in Slide view.

The Demote and Promote buttons move text one level to the left or right. The Move Up and Move Down buttons moves text up or down in the current order. The Collapse buttons display only the slide titles and the Expand buttons restore all the text. The Summary Slide button creates a new slide, called an agenda slide, with titles in a bulleted list. The Show Formatting button shows or hides character formatting.

To modify the slide sequence in Outline view, click the slide icon to the left of the slide title to select all the slide text. As you drag, a vertical line appears. Drag the line where you want to move the slide and release the mouse button.

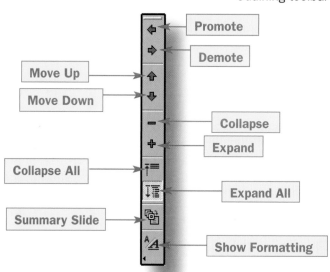

FIGURE 2-16
Outlining toolbar

STEP-BY-STEP ▷ 2.12

1. Switch to **Outline** view.

2. Display the Outlining toolbar by choosing **Toolbars** from the **View** menu and **Outlining** from the submenu.

3. On the **slide 3** title, select the word *Effectively* and change it to **Carefully**.

4. Click the **Collapse All** button to see only the titles, and then click the **Expand All** button to see all the titles and text.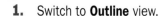

5. Place the insertion point after the second bullet on slide 3.

6. Click the **Demote** button.

7. Place the insertion point after the word *questions* and press **Enter** to create a new bullet.

8. For the bulleted item you just created, key **Become informed**.

9. On **slide 5** place the insertion point anywhere on the third bulleted item, *Weekly housekeeping*.

10. Click the **Move Up** button to make it the second bulleted item.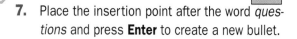

11. Switch to **Slide** view and display the Outlining toolbar.

12. Place the insertion point before the second bulleted item on **slide 6**.

13. Click the **Move up** button to make it the first bulleted item.

14. Click the **Move down** button to move it back to its original position.

15. Print the presentation in Outline view.

16. Save and close the presentation.

Summary

In this lesson, you learned:

■ There are three options for creating a presentation: the AutoContent Wizard, which provides you with ideas and an organization for a new presentation; design templates, which are already designed and formatted; and blank presentations, which allow you to create a presentation from scratch.

■ You can modify your presentation by deleting slides or adding text to slides. Check the spelling and style of a presentation to be sure it is consistent, error-free, and visually appealing.

■ The slide master controls the formatting for all the slides in a presentation. Other masters that help you create consistency are the title master, handout master, and the notes master.

■ To alter the format of text, access the Font dialog box. You can also make changes to the line spacing, alignment, and case, or customize a bulleted list.

■ Slide transitions and animation help maintain audience interest. Changing the slide layout can also make a presentation more interesting. The Outlining toolbar helps you develop and organize your presentation in Outline view.

LESSON 2 REVIEW QUESTIONS

MATCHING

Match the correct term in Column 2 to its description in Column 1.

Column 1	Column 2
D 1. Controls formatting for all slides in a presentation	A. AutoContent Wizard
A 2. Provides ideas and organization for a presentation based on given answers	B. slide transition
G 3. Adding sound effects or special visuals	C. blank presentation
B 4. Determines how one slide is removed from the screen and the next one appears	D. slide master
	E. design template

5. Good way to organize and develop the slide titles and text of a presentation

F. Outline view

G. animate

H. slide layout

WRITTEN QUESTIONS

Write a brief answer to the following questions.

1. What option would you use to create a presentation from scratch, using whatever layout, format, colors, and style you prefer?

2. Name three types of masters.

3. What are two examples of ways you can customize a bulleted list?

4. What button in the Slide Transition dialog box do you click to make your transition choices affect only the current slide?

5. How do you display the Outlining toolbar?

LESSON 2 PROJECTS

PROJECT 2-1

1. Start PowerPoint.

2. Open the presentation **Copier** that you last saved in Step-by-Step 2.3.

3. Save the presentation as **Copier Revised**, followed by your initials.

4. In **Slide** view on **slide 1**, change the slide layout to **Text & Clip Art**.

5. Replace the clip art placeholder with a light bulb picture.

6. Switch to **Slide Sorter** view. Move **slide 5** so that it appears between slide 2 and slide 3.

7. Switch to **Slide** view. Display **slide 1**. Animate the title so it swivels and is accompanied by a clapping sound.

8. Set the slide transition for all slides so the effect is **Box Out** and the speed is **Slow**.

9. Switch to **Slide Show** view and run the presentation on your computer.

10. Save the presentation and print it as handouts with all 6 slides on a page.

11. Leave the presentation open for the next project.

PROJECT 2-2

SCANS

1. Display the slide master and change the first level bullet to a checkmark whose size is 100% of the text.

2. Insert a new a slide with bulleted format between **slide 5** and **slide 6**.

3. Switch to **Outline** view.

4. On the new **slide 6**, key **Prices** as the title.

5. Research the prices of at least two copiers. Add the information to the new slide.

I P - 3 7

6. Add this speaker's note: **These prices are guaranteed for 2 weeks.**

7. Print **slide 6** in Notes Pages view.

8. Save and close the presentation.

PROJECT 2-3

1. Open the **Penumbra** presentation that you used in Lesson 1.

2. Save the presentation as **Penumbra Revised,** followed by your initials.

3. In **Slide** view, delete the slides with the titles *Goal and Objective, Today's Situation,* and *How Did We Get Here?* (currently **slides 3–5**).

4. Go to **slide 2** and change the title from **Vision Statement to Purpose**.

5. In **Normal** view, go to **slide 1** and key this text in the notes pane: **Be sure everyone has a handout.**

6. Print **slide 1** in **Notes Pages** view.

7. Display the slide master. Change the title font to **Comic Sans MS bold** and center it.

8. Save and print the entire presentation as a handout with 6 slides on a page.

9. Close the presentation and exit PowerPoint.

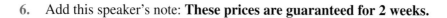

CRITICAL THINKING

ACTIVITY 2-1

SCANS

You work for Ambrosia Corporation. Your supervisor asks you to create a company handbook as a presentation so that it can be viewed online. Use the AutoContent Wizard, and the skills you learned in this lesson, to create and enhance a company handbook.

ACTIVITY 2-2

SCANS

Create a presentation using the ideas you organized in Critical Thinking Activity 1.1 in the last lesson. Choose a design template and clip art. Include slide transitions and animation. Run the presentation for your class.

WORKING WITH VISUAL ELEMENTS

OBJECTIVES

Upon completion of this lesson, you should be able to:

- Build and modify an organization chart.
- Build and modify charts.
- Create and modify tables within PowerPoint.
- Draw an object.
- Add shapes and apply formatting.
- Rotate and fill an object.
- Scale and size an object.
- Create a text box.

⏱ Estimated Time: 2 hours

Working with Organization Charts

O*rganization charts* are useful for showing the hierarchical structure and relationships within an organization. When you create an organization chart in PowerPoint, you are using a program called Microsoft Organization Chart. A separate window opens with menus, commands, and an icon bar designed specifically to help you build an organization chart.

Hot Tip

If the Microsoft Organization Chart program is not available, you will need to install it from the Office 2000 CD-ROM.

Building an Organization Chart

When including an organization chart on a slide, you can use the slide layout that has a placeholder for it. Double click the placeholder to open Microsoft Organization Chart, as shown in Figure 3-1. To fill in the chart, click in a box and key text. Use the box tools on the icon bar to add more boxes to the organization chart. Click the tool on the icon bar for the box you want to create and then click the box in the chart to which you want to attach it. Add a chart title by replacing the text placeholder. When you are ready to return to the presentation, click the Close box and choose to update the object when a message box appears.

FIGURE 3-1
Microsoft Organization Chart

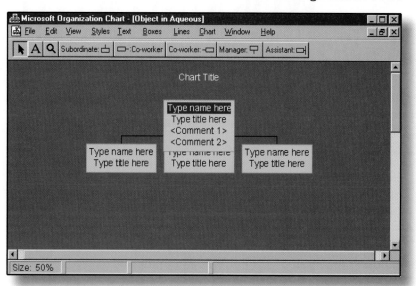

S **TEP-BY-STEP** ▷ 3.1

1. Open **IP Step3-1** from the student data files.

2. Save the presentation as **Aqueous** followed by your initials.

3. On **slide 1**, replace *Student's Name* with your name.

4. Display **slide 3** and click the **Common Tasks** button on the Formatting toolbar.

5. Choose **Slide Layout** from the menu. The Slide Layout dialog box appears.

6. Select the third layout in the second row (*Organization Chart*) and click **Apply**.

7. The slide is displayed with a placeholder for an organization chart. Double-click the placeholder.

8. Microsoft Organization Chart appears, as shown in Figure 3-1.

9. Highlight the words *Chart Title* at the top and replace with *Aqueous Organization Chart*.

10. Click in the top text box. Key

    Lucy Jordan
    CEO

11. Click in the left text box on the second row. Key

    Thomas Kent
    VP Operations

12. Click in the middle text box and key

    Jack Dawson
    District Manager

13. Click in the last text box and key

    June Oxford
    Public Relations

14. Click the **Subordinate** button on the toolbar. The insertion point turns to a box with a line on top.

INTRODUCTION TO MICROSOFT POWERPOINT

15. Click the *Jack Dawson* box. A subordinate box is added beneath.

16. In the box you just added, key

**Sam Mabry
Region Manager**

17. Click the **Assistant** button on the toolbar. Click the *Thomas Kent* box.

18. In the box you just added, key

**Diane Grey
Administration**

19. Choose **Close and Return to Aqueous** from the **File** menu.

20. An update message appears. Choose **Yes** to return to the presentation. The organization chart is displayed on the slide, as shown in Figure 3-2.

21. Save the presentation and leave it open for the next Step-by-Step.

FIGURE 3-2
Organization chart on slide

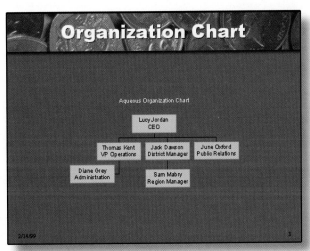

Modifying an Organization Chart

To modify an organization chart, double-click it to open the Microsoft Organization Chart program again. To reorganize the arrangement of boxes in the chart, select a box and drag it to where you want it. You can change the formatting of a box or text, such as the font, font style, font size, alignment, color, shadows, and borders, by selecting a box and choosing a command from the Text or Boxes menu. To change the background color of the chart, choose Background Color from the Chart menu. The Color dialog box appears, as shown in Figure 3-3, where you choose the background color.

Hot Tip

To make formatting changes to more than one box, click outside the boxes and draw a selection box around all the boxes you want to change.

FIGURE 3-3
Color dialog box

1. Double-click the organization chart to open Microsoft Organization Chart again.

2. Choose **Background Color** from the **Chart** menu. The Color dialog box opens, as shown in Figure 3-3.

3. Click the sixth box on the first row, and then click **OK**. The background color of the chart changes to gray.

4. Highlight the chart title. Choose **Font** from the **Text** menu. The Font dialog box appears.

5. In the *Font* box, choose **Impact**. In the *Font style* box, choose **Bold**. In the *Size* box, choose **24**.

6. Click **OK**. The formatting of the chart title changes.

7. Click the Diane Grey box and begin dragging it to the right. A dotted box appears.

8. Drag the dotted box to bottom of the June Oxford box until the insertion point turns into a white box with a T on top. Release the mouse button and the assistant box is now below the June Oxford box.

9. Select the Lucy Jordan box.

10. Choose **Color** from the **Boxes** menu. The Color dialog box appears.

11. Click the first color on the second row, and then click **OK**. The box changes to yellow.

12. Click outside and to the left of the Thomas Kent box and draw a selection box around the three middle boxes, as shown in Figure 3-4.

13. Change the color of the boxes to the fifth box on the first row of the Color dialog box. The selected boxes change to purple.

14. Change the Sam Mabry box to the fourth color on the first row. The organization chart should look similar to Figure 3-5.

15. Change the background color back to the original color.

16. Click the Microsoft Organization Chart Close box. When the update message appears, click **OK**.

17. Highlight the chart and click the square handles and drag to enlarge the chart on the slide.

18. Save the presentation and print **slide 3**.

19. Leave the presentation open for the next Step-by-Step.

FIGURE 3-4

Selecting more than one box in an organization chart

FIGURE 3-5
Modified organization chart

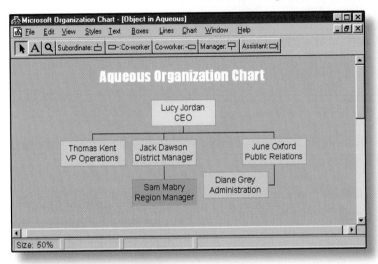

Working with Charts

C*harts*, also called *graphs*, provide a graphical way to display statistical data in a presentation. When you create a chart in PowerPoint, you are working in a program called Microsoft Graph. When you are building and modifying a chart, Microsoft Graph menus, commands, and toolbar buttons become available to help you.

Building a Chart

To include a chart in a presentation, choose one of the slide layouts that contains a placeholder for a chart. Double-click the placeholder to open Microsoft Graph and display a chart with sample data, as shown in Figure 3-6. Click the datasheet and replace the sample data with your own. The chart changes to reflect the new data. When you are ready to return to the presentation, click outside the chart on the PowerPoint slide.

FIGURE 3-6
Chart with sample data

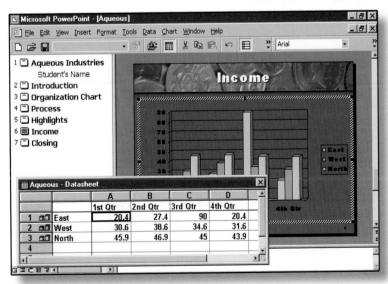

1. Display **slide 6** and access the **Slide Layout** dialog box.

2. Change the slide layout to the fourth style on the second row with a chart placeholder.

3. Double-click the placeholder. Microsoft Graph opens and your screen looks similar to Figure 3-6.

4. Delete row 3 by clicking the row number to select the entire row and choosing **Delete** from the **Edit** menu.

5. Select column D and delete it.

6. Change the sample data in the datasheet to look like Figure 3-7. (Key **Gross Profit** and **Net**

Income as your titles.) Notice that the chart in the background changes to reflect the new data.

7. Click outside the chart area on the slide to close Microsoft Graph and return to the presentation.

8. Save the presentation and leave it open for the next Step-by-Step.

FIGURE 3-7
Datasheet data for Step-by-Step 3.3

		A	B	C	D
		1999	2000	2001	
1	Gross Prof	1,218	3,168	4,995	
2	Net Incom	302	528	925	
3					
4					

Modifying a Chart

If you need to modify a chart, double-click it to open it. You can change the type of chart by choosing Chart Type from the Chart menu. The Chart Type dialog box appears, as shown in Figure 3-8. Choose a chart type and subtype. To see what the data will look like in a different type of chart, click and hold down the *Press and Hold to View Sample* button.

To add a chart or axis title, choose Chart Options from the Chart menu. Click the Titles tab in the Chart Options dialog box, as shown in Figure 3-9, and key a chart or axis title. To apply a texture or pattern, or to change color or border style, click the chart item you want to change. The Format dialog box appears for that item.

Concept Builder

You can animate a chart just as you did other slide objects. Choose Custom Animation from the Slide Show menu and click the Chart Effects tab. Choose how you want to introduce the chart elements and the entry animation and sound options.

FIGURE 3-8
Chart Type dialog box

FIGURE 3-9
Chart Options dialog box

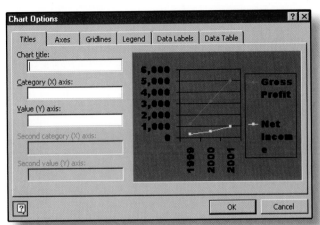

STEP-BY-STEP ▷ 3.4

1. Double-click the chart to open Microsoft Graph again.

2. If the datasheet is displayed, click the **View Datasheet** button on the toolbar to close it.

3. Choose **Chart Type** from the **Chart** menu. The Chart Type dialog box appears, as shown in Figure 3-8.

4. In the *Chart type* section, choose **Line**.

5. In the *Chart sub-type* section, choose the first type on the second row.

6. Click and hold the **Press and Hold to View Sample** button to see what the chart will look like.

7. Release the mouse button and then click **OK**. The chart changes to a line chart.

8. Choose **Chart Options** from the **Chart** menu. The Chart Options dialog box appears, as shown in Figure 3-9.

9. In the *Chart title* box, key **Aqueous**. The title is added to the sample chart as you key.

10. In the *Category (X) axis* box, key **year**.

11. In the *Value (Y) axis* box, key **in millions**.

12. Click **OK**.

13. Click outside the chart on the slide to close Microsoft Graph and return to the presentation.

14. Save the presentation and print **slide 6**.

15. Leave the presentation open for the next Step-by-Step.

Working with Tables

Tables are useful when data in a presentation is best displayed in tabular format. Information in rows and columns can be easier to read.

Creating Tables

When including a table on a slide, you can use the slide layout that has a placeholder for it. When you double-click the placeholder, the Insert Table dialog box appears, as shown in Figure 3-10. Choose the number of columns and rows you want and a table is inserted on your slide. Key text in the table. You can move between cells by pressing the Tab key.

Concept Builder

If you want to create a more complex table, use the Draw Table feature on the Tables and Borders toolbar.

FIGURE 3-10
Insert Table dialog box

S TEP-BY-STEP ▷ 3.5

1. Display **slide 5** and change the slide layout to the one with a table placeholder.

2. Double-click the placeholder. The Insert Table dialog box appears, as shown in Figure 3-10.

3. In the *Number of columns* box, choose **3**.

4. In the *Number of rows* box, choose **8**.

5. Click **OK**. A table with 3 columns and 8 rows is inserted on the slide.

6. Click in the first cell and key **(in millions)**. Press **Tab** to move to the next cell. Continue keying data as shown in Figure 3-11.

7. Save the presentation and leave open for the next Step-by-Step.

FIGURE 3-11
Data for the table in Step-by-Step 3.5

Highlights		
(in millions)	2000	2001
Net Revenues	$2,605	$3,864
Net Income	528	925
Earnings per share	1.23	1.99
Return		
Cash	$199	$264
Total Assets	7,920	10,875
Stockholder's equity	1,515	2,243

Modifying Tables

To modify the borders, fill, or text boxes in a table, choose Table from the Format menu. The Format Table dialog box appears, as shown in Figure 3-12.

When modifying tables, it is also helpful to display the Tables and Borders toolbar, shown in Figure 3-13, by right-clicking any toolbar and choosing Tables and Borders from the menu. Using the toolbar, you can insert columns and rows, merge or split cells, change the alignment and fill color, and format the borders.

To change the width of a column or row, click and drag a border. To insert or delete a column or row, click the Table button on the Tables and Borders toolbar and choose the command you want.

FIGURE 3-12
Format Table dialog box

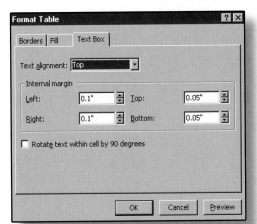

FIGURE 3-13
Tables and Borders toolbar

STEP-BY-STEP ▷ 3.6

1. Click and drag the column borders to enlarge the first column so all text fits on one line. Reduce the last two columns and size them equally.

2. Center the dates in the first row of the last two columns. Right align the rest of the data in the last two columns.

3. Place the insertion point in the cell with the word *Return*.

4. If it is not already showing, display the **Tables and Borders** toolbar, shown in Figure 3-13, by right-clicking any toolbar and choosing *Tables and Borders* from the menu.

5. Click the **Table** button on the toolbar and choose **Delete Rows** from the menu.

6. Click and drag the table to center it on the slide.

7. Save the presentation and print **slide 5**.

8. Leave the presentation open for the next Step-by-Step.

Creating Shapes and Objects

You can add shapes and other drawing objects to your presentation by using the AutoShapes and drawing tools on the Drawing toolbar. Shapes and objects can add interest to a slide.

Drawing an Object

The Drawing toolbar, shown in Figure 3-14, is displayed by default in PowerPoint. It contains buttons for drawing shapes and objects, such as lines, circles, arrows, and squares. Click the corresponding button to activate the tool. The Rectangle tool draws rectangles and squares. The Oval tool draws ovals and circles. To use, click and hold the mouse button, then drag to draw. To create a perfect circle or square, hold down the Shift key as you drag.

FIGURE 3-14
Drawing toolbar

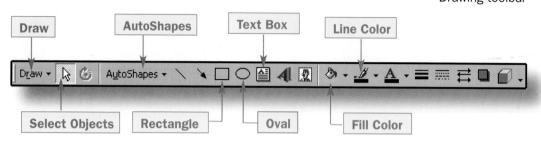

Adding a Shape

There are also a variety of other shapes you can add by clicking the AutoShapes tool on the Drawing toolbar. A menu appears that has lines, connectors, arrows, and other categories available to help draw the shape you want. Click the slide to insert the shape with a predefined size.

FIGURE 3-15
Selected object

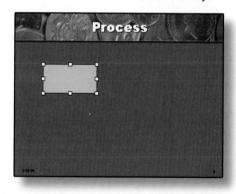

Selecting an Object

When you first draw an object, little squares appear at the edges of the graphic when you release the mouse button. (See Figure 3-15.) These small squares are called **handles**. They indicate that the object is selected, and they allow you to manipulate the selected object. When you choose another tool, the selection handles around an object disappear. You will learn more about selecting objects later in this lesson.

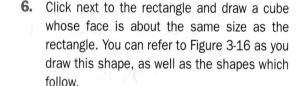

S TEP-BY-STEP ▷ 3.7

1. Display **slide 4**.

2. Click the **Rectangle** tool on the Drawing toolbar.

3. Click on the upper left corner of the slide and drag to draw a rectangle about 1 ¹/₂ " × 1". When you release the mouse button, handles appear on the object, as shown in Figure 3-15.

4. Click the **AutoShapes** button on the Drawing toolbar.   AutoShapes ▾

5. Choose **Basic Shapes** from the menu and click the **Cube** icon on the submenu.

6. Click next to the rectangle and draw a cube whose face is about the same size as the rectangle. You can refer to Figure 3-16 as you draw this shape, as well as the shapes which follow.

7. Click the **Oval** tool and draw an oval below the rectangle about the same size.

8. Click the **Rectangle** tool on the Drawing toolbar and draw a second rectangle below the cube, about the same size as the first.

9. Click the **AutoShapes** button and choose **Block Arrows** from the menu.

I P - 4 8

10. Click the **Right Arrow** icon on the submenu and draw a right arrow attached to the rectangle, as shown in Figure 3-16.

11. Click **AutoShapes**, **Block Arrows**, and click the **Right Arrow** icon.

12. Draw an arrow before the top rectangle. Your slide should look similar to Figure 3-16.

13. Save the presentation and leave open for the next Step-by-Step.

FIGURE 3-16
Slide with drawing objects

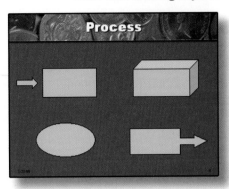

Manipulating Objects

Once you have created an object, there are many ways to manipulate it to achieve the final product. You can rotate, fill, scale, or size an object, as well as change its color or position.

Selecting an Object

As you learned earlier in the lesson, when you select an object, square handles surround it. To select an object, be sure the Select Objects (see Figure 3-14) tool is chosen on the toolbar, position the insertion point over the object, and click. The selection handles appear around the object, and you can then manipulate the object. A four-sided arrow appears with the arrow pointer. To deselect an object, click another object or anywhere in the window.

Hot Tip

To delete an object, select it and press Delete or Backspace.

Selecting More Than One Object

Sometimes you will want to select more than one object. PowerPoint gives you two ways to select more than one object. The first is called *Shift-clicking*. The second method is to draw a selection box around a group of objects.

SHIFT-CLICKING

To Shift-click, hold down Shift and click each of the objects you want to select. Use Shift-clicking when you need to select objects that are not close to each other or when the objects you need to select are near other objects you do not want to select. If you select an object by accident, click it again to deselect it.

DRAWING A SELECTION BOX

Using the Select Objects tool, you can drag a selection box around a group of objects. Objects included in the selection box will be selected. Use a selection box when all of the objects you want selected are near each other and can be surrounded with a box. Be sure your selection box is large enough to enclose all the selection handles of the various objects. If you miss a handle, that item will not be selected.

COMBINING METHODS

You can also combine these two methods. First, use the selection box, and then Shift-click to include objects that the selection box might have missed.

Grouping Objects

As your drawing becomes more complex, you will find it necessary to "glue" objects together into groups. *Grouping* allows you to work with several objects as though they were one object. To group objects, select the objects you want to group and choose Group from the Draw menu on the drawing toolbar. Objects can be ungrouped using the Ungroup command.

Rotating an Object

You can modify an object by rotating it. The three rotating commands include the Rotate Right command, the Rotate Left command, and the Free Rotate command. The Rotate Right command moves a graphic in 90-degree increments to the right. The Rotate Left command rotates the graphic in 90-degree increments to the left. The Free Rotate command lets you rotate a graphic to any angle. When you choose the Free Rotate command, the object becomes surrounded with green handles that you click and drag to rotate the object.

To rotate an object, select it, click Draw on the drawing toolbar, and choose Rotate or Flip from the menu. Choose the command you want from the submenu.

Concept Builder

You can flip an object by choosing the Flip Horizontal or Flip Vertical commands on the Rotate or Flip submenu.

STEP-BY-STEP ▷ 3.8

1. Draw a left arrow in the middle of the screen about twice as long as the ones you have already drawn.

2. With the arrow selected, click the **Free Rotate** button on the Drawing toolbar. Green circles surround the arrow.

3. Click one of the green circles and drag in a counterclockwise direction until the arrow points to the oval, as shown in Figure 3-17. If necessary, after rotating the arrow, move it so that it is not touching the oval.

4. Select the arrow before the rectangle.

5. Click the **Draw** button on the Drawing toolbar.

6. Choose **Rotate or Flip** from the menu and **Rotate Left** from the submenu. The arrow is now pointing up.

7. Click the **Draw** button, choose **Rotate or Flip** and then **Rotate Right**. The arrow points to the right again.

8. Save the presentation and leave it open for the next Step-by-Step.

FIGURE 3-17
Free rotating an object

Applying Formatting

The Drawing toolbar contains various ways to apply formatting to visual elements in a presentation. You can change the fill, line, or font color. You can also change the line, dash, or arrow style, and you can add shadows or make an object appear three-dimensional.

FILLING AN OBJECT

Filling an object can help add life to your drawing objects. Select the object you want to fill and click the Fill Color button on the Drawing toolbar. When you click the down arrow, a box appears, as shown in Figure 3-18.

FIGURE 3-18
Fill Color box

To change an object back to the default fill color, choose *Automatic*. To choose a color in the color scheme, click one of the eight choices below *Automatic*. Your selected object becomes filled with this color. To fill an object with a color not in the color scheme, click *More Fill Colors*. To fill an object with a gradient, texture, pattern, or picture, click *Fill Effects*. The Fill Effects dialog box appears, as shown in Figure 3-19.

CHANGING LINE COLOR

Another way to apply formatting to a drawing object is to change the line color. Click the arrow next to the Line Color button on the Drawing toolbar and choose an option in the Line Color box that appears. The Line Color box looks very similar to the Fill Color box.

FIGURE 3-19
Fill Effects dialog box

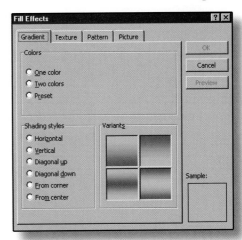

STEP-BY-STEP ▷ 3.9

1. Click the top rectangle to select it.

2. Click the arrow next to the **Fill Color** button on the Drawing toolbar. A box appears, as shown in Figure 3-18.

3. Click the last colored box on the first row. The rectangle changes to a gray color.

4. Select the cube. Click the down arrow next to the **Fill Color** button and then click **Fill Effects**. The Fill Effects dialog box appears, as shown in Figure 3-19.

5. Click the **Gradient** tab if necessary. In the *Shading styles* box, click **Diagonal up**. Click **OK**. The cube is filled with a gradient shading.

6. Select the oval. Access the Fill Effects dialog box and click the **Texture** tab.

7. Click the first texture in the first row (*Newsprint*), as shown in Figure 3-20.

8. Click **OK**. The oval is filled with a newsprint texture.

9. Hold down the **Shift** key and select both the bottom right arrow and rectangle. Access the Fill Effects dialog box and click the **Pattern** tab.

10. Click the second pattern on the last row (*90%*), as shown in Figure 3-21.

11. Click **OK**. Both objects are filled with a dotted pattern.

12. With the rectangle and arrow still selected, click the arrow next to the **Line Color** button on the Drawing toolbar.

13. Click the fourth box on the first row. The line around the rectangle changes to white.

14. Change the line around the cube, oval, and top rectangle to white also. Your slide should look similar to Figure 3-22.

15. Save the presentation and leave it open for the next Step-by-Step.

(continued on next page)

FIGURE 3-20
Texture tab of the Fill Effects dialog box

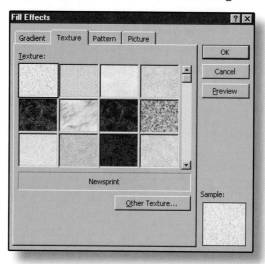

FIGURE 3-21
Pattern tab of the Fill Effects dialog box

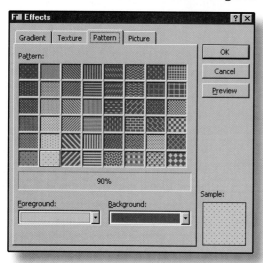

FIGURE 3-22
Your drawing should now look similar to this

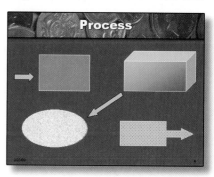

Scaling and Sizing an Object

Handles do more than indicate that an object is selected. They make it easy to resize an object that is too large or too small. Select the object to make the handles appear and then drag one of the handles inward or outward to make the object smaller or larger, as shown in Figure 3-23.

To scale an object, hold down Shift and drag a corner handle. This maintains an object's proportions. You scale and size ClipArt graphics just as you do objects. Many AutoShapes have a yellow diamond adjustment handle that you can drag to change the appearance of the object.

Concept Builder

You can size an object more precisely by choosing AutoShape from the Format menu. Click the Size tab and specify a height and width.

FIGURE 3-23
Sizing an object

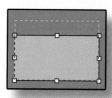

Copying or Moving an Object

To move an object, first select it and then drag it into place. You can cut, copy, and paste objects the same way you do text. The Cut and Copy commands place a copy of the selected image on the Office Clipboard. Pasting an object from the Office Clipboard places the object in your drawing. You can then move it into position.

STEP-BY-STEP ▷ 3.10

1. Select the top rectangle.

2. Move the pointer over the top middle handle until it becomes a two-headed vertical arrow.

3. Click and drag the handle up to enlarge the rectangle, as shown in Figure 3-23.

4. Select the cube.

5. Move the pointer over the top right corner handle until it becomes a two-headed diagonal arrow.

6. Hold down **Shift** as you click and drag upward to slightly enlarge the cube while maintaining the same proportions.

7. Slightly enlarge the oval while maintaining its proportions.

8. Select the bottom right arrow. One or more yellow diamond adjustment handles appear in addition to the regular handles.

9. If more than one appears, move the pointer to the top one. Click and drag to the right. The rectangle part of the object becomes longer, and the arrow becomes shorter, as shown in Figure 3-24. You can experiment with the others to see how the arrow is resized.

10. Select the arrow before the top rectangle. Choose **Copy** from the **Edit** menu. A copy of the arrow is pasted on the Office Clipboard.

11. Choose **Paste** from the **Edit** menu. The arrow is pasted from the Office Clipboard into the presentation.

12. Place the pointer over the arrow until it becomes a four-headed cross. Click and drag it to a new position in between the rectangle and the cube.

13. Paste another arrow in between the oval and the bottom rectangle.

14. Save the presentation, then display **slide 1**.

15. Choose **Picture** from the **Insert** menu and **From File** from the submenu.

16. Locate **water drop** in the student data files and click **Insert**.

17. The water drop graphic appears on your slide. Click and drag to position it on the top portion of the slide.

18. Click and drag the handles to size it approximately as shown in Figure 3-25.

19. Save the presentation and print **slide 1**.

20. Leave the presentation open for the next Step-by-Step.

Extra Challenge

Fill the arrows with a different color, gradient, or texture.

(continued on next page)

FIGURE 3-24
Modifying an object created
using AutoShape

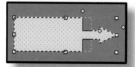

FIGURE 3-25
Your water drop should look similar to this

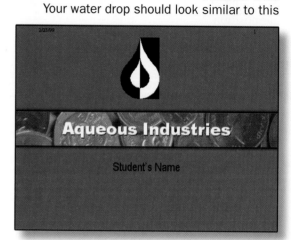

Creating a Text Box

If you want to add text on a slide that does not have a placeholder for it, you can create a text box. Click the Text Box tool on the Drawing toolbar. Click the left mouse button and drag to create a text box the size you want, as shown in Figure 3-26. To move the box, click and drag it to a new location. To resize the box, click and drag one of the handles. To insert text, click inside the text box and begin keying.

To place text inside a shape, simply create a text box on top of the shape. You can wrap text in a text box by choosing Text Box from the Format menu and then clicking the Text Box tab in the Format Text Box dialog box, as shown in Figure 3-27. The *Word wrap text in AutoShape* box should be checked.

FIGURE 3-26
Text box

FIGURE 3-27
Format Text Box dialog box showing the Text Box tab

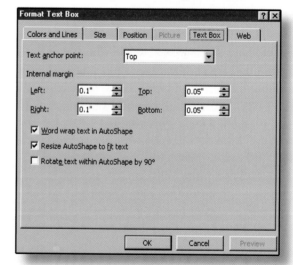

STEP-BY-STEP ▷ 3.11

1. Display **slide 4**.

2. Click the **Text Box** tool on the Drawing toolbar.

3. Click inside the top rectangle and drag to draw a text box that fits inside, as shown in Figure 3-26.

4. Choose **Text Box** from the Format menu and click the Text Box tab in the Format Text Box dialog box, as shown in Figure 3-27.

5. If necessary, click the *Word wrap text in AutoShape* check box. Click **OK**.

6. Key **Purification Center** inside the text box. Notice how the text wraps.

7. Select the text you just keyed in the text box and center and bold it. If necessary, select the text box and center it on the rectangle.

8. Create a text box on the face of the cube and key **Bottling Plant**. Bold and center the text. If necessary, select the text box and center it on the face of the cube.

9. Create a text box on the oval and key **Storage**. Bold and center the text. If necessary, select the text box and center it on the oval.

10. Create a text box on the bottom rectangle and key **Shipping**. Bold and center the text. If necessary, select the text box and center it on the rectangle. The slide should look similar to Figure 3-28.

11. Save the presentation and print **slide 4**.

12. Print the entire presentation as a handout with 6 slides per page and then close it.

FIGURE 3-28
Your slide should look similar to this

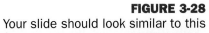
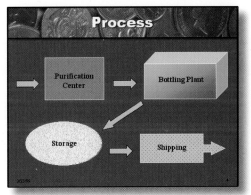

Summary

In this lesson, you learned:

- You can create and modify organization charts in a presentation using Microsoft Organization Chart.

- You can create and modify graphs in a presentation using Microsoft Graph. Replace the sample data with your own.

- Insert a table on a slide using the Insert Table dialog box and then modify it using the Tables and Borders toolbar.

- You can add shapes and objects to your presentation using the AutoShapes and drawing tools on the Drawing toolbar. You can rotate, fill, scale, or size an object as well as change its fill or line color.

- To add text on a slide or inside a shape, first create a text box. You can wrap text inside a text box.

TRUE/FALSE

Circle T if the statement is true or F if the statement is false.

T   F   1.   The background color of an organization chart must be the same as the color of the slide.

T   F   2.   When you double-click a table placeholder on a slide, the Insert Table dialog box appears.

T   F   3.   Using the Select Objects tool, you can drag a selection box around a group of objects.

T   F   4.   To change an object back to the default fill color, choose Default in the Fill Color box.

T   F   5.   To place text inside a shape, choose Insert Text from the Draw menu.

MULTIPLE CHOICE

Select the best response for the following statements.

1.   Pie, line, bar, and column are types of
    A.   Charts
    B.   Textures
    C.   Tables
    D.   Effects

2.   The small squares surrounding a selected graphic are called
    A.   Buttons
    B.   Tabs
    C.   Handles
    D.   Boxes

3.   To rotate a graphic to any angle, choose which of the following commands?
    A.   Rotate Left
    B.   Rotate Right
    C.   Free Rotate
    D.   None of the above

4.   You can fill an object with
    A.   Gradients
    B.   Texture
    C.   Patterns
    D.   All of the above

5.   To maintain an object's proportions when resizing, hold down which key while you drag a corner handle?
    A.   Ctrl
    B.   Shift
    C.   Alt
    D.   Tab

LESSON 3 PROJECTS

PROJECT 3-1

1. Open **IP Project3-1** from the student data files.

2. Save the presentation as **Ransom** followed by your initials.

3. Replace *Student's Name* on **slide 1** with your name.

4. Display **slide 2** and change the layout to include an organization chart placeholder.

5. Create an organization chart like the one shown in Figure 3-29. You may select the background color, font styles, and fill colors as shown here, or make your own selections.

6. Print **slide 2**.

7. Display **slide 3**. Use the Drawing toolbar and AutoShapes to help you create a layout like the one shown in Figure 3-30. Add fill colors to the shapes as shown here, or choose other colors or effects, as you wish.

8. Print **slide 3**.

9. Save the presentation and leave it open for the next project.

FIGURE 3-29	FIGURE 3-30
Key this text in your organization chart	Add these shapes to slide 3

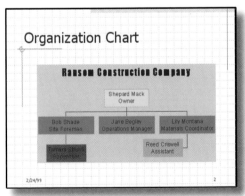

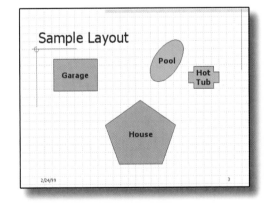

PROJECT 3-2

1. Display **slide 4** and change the layout to include a table placeholder.

2. Insert a table with 2 columns and 7 rows.

3. Key and format the text in the table, as shown in Figure 3-31.

4. Print **slide 4**.

5. Display **slide 5** and change the layout to **Chart**.

6. Replace the sample data in the chart datasheet with the data shown in Figure 3-32.

7. Add a title to the chart called **Room Options**.

8. Change the chart to a *Line graph with markers displayed at each data value.*

9. Print **slide 5**.

10. Save the presentation and print it as a handout with 6 slides per page.

11. Close the presentation.

FIGURE 3-31
Your text should look like this

Mortgage Analysis

Amount Financed	$185,000
Annual Interest	8.25%
Duration of loan (years)	30
Monthly payments	$1,389.84
Total number of payments	360
Finance Charges	$315,343
Total Cost	$500,343

2/24/99   4

FIGURE 3-32
Key this data

Ransom - Datasheet

		A	B	C	D	E
		2 Bdrm	3 Bdrm	4 Bdrm	5 Bdrm	
1	2 Bath	115,000	135,000	165,000	205,000	
2	3 Bath	n/a	185,000	225,000	260,000	
3	4 Bath	n/a	n/a	275,000	310,000	
4						

CRITICAL THINKING

ACTIVITY 3-1

SCANS

Use the Internet to do research about a company. Use the information you find to create a presentation about the company that includes an organization chart, a graph, a table, and drawing objects.

ACTIVITY 3-2

SCANS

You want to make some changes to some text boxes. Use the Help system to find out how to:

■ Change the shape of a text box to an AutoShape.

■ Display text vertically instead of horizontally in a text box.

■ Change the margins around the text in a text box.

EXPANDING ON THE BASICS OF POWERPOINT

OBJECTIVES

Upon completion of this lesson, you should be able to:

- Create a presentation from existing slides.

- Replace text fonts in an entire presentation.

- Use the Format Painter.

- Send a presentation via e-mail.

- Change the output format.

- Insert a hyperlink.

- Publish a presentation to the Web.

- Integrate PowerPoint and Word.

⊘ Estimated Time: 1.5 hours

Creating a Presentation from Existing Slides

Open the presentation upon which you want to base a new presentation. Make changes to the existing slides such as applying a different design template, adding or deleting slides, formatting text differently, or making changes to the slide master. When you are finished, choose Save As from the File menu, key a new name for the presentation, and click Save.

You can also add a slide to your new presentation by copying it from another presentation. Choose Slides from Files from the Insert menu. The Slide Finder dialog box appears, as shown in Figure 4-1. Click Browse, locate the presentation you want to copy a slide from, and click Display. Select the slide you want to copy and click Insert. If you want to insert the entire presentation, click Insert All. The slide(s) are inserted after the one displayed on the screen.

FIGURE 4-1
Slide Finder dialog box

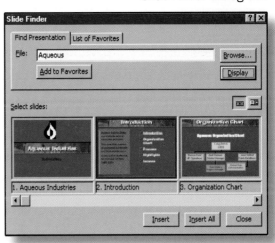

1. Open **IP Step4-1** from the student data files.

2. On **slide 1**, replace *Harris Clarke Securities* with **Dawson Sands Investments**.

3. Change the design template to **Straight Edge**.

4. Create a new slide with bulleted list layout at the end of the presentation and key the following text:

   Sands of Time

   • Our online magazine, Sands of Time, provides you with cutting edge information on current financial trends and timely ideas for short- and long-term planning.

   • An interactive section lets you post questions for our online analysts and get help making personal financial decisions.

5. Choose **Save As** from the **File** menu and save the file as **Online** followed by your initials.

6. Display **slide 1** on the screen.

7. Choose **Slides from Files** from the **Insert** menu. The Slide Finder dialog box appears.

8. Click **Browse** and locate the **Aqueous** file you last used in Step-by-Step 3.11.

9. Click **Display** to show the slides in the *Select slides* section.

10. Click **slide 2** so that it is outlined in blue as shown in Figure 4-1.

11. Click **Insert**. The slide is inserted after slide 1 in the **Online** presentation.

12. Click **Close** to close the Slide Finder dialog box.

13. Click the text box on the left of the slide and delete the shading and text.

14. Move the text box on the right and replace it with the slide titles for this presentation, as shown in Figure 4-2. Resize the text box, if necessary, to make all the text fit, as shown in the figure.

15. Save the presentation and leave it open for the next Step-by-Step.

FIGURE 4-2
Key text shown here

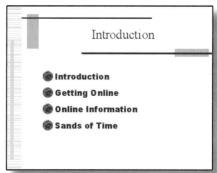

Formatting Text and Objects

In earlier lessons you learned the basics of formatting text and objects. PowerPoint has several helpful features to help you make formatting easier.

Replacing Text Fonts

You can change a font throughout your presentation by choosing Replace Fonts on the Format menu. The Replace Font dialog box appears, as shown in Figure 4-3. In the *Replace* box choose the font you want to replace. In the *With* box, choose the font you want to use as a replacement and then click Replace.

Using the Format Painter

If you format an object with certain attributes such as fill color and line color and then want to format another object the same way, use the Format Painter button on the toolbar. Select the object whose attributes you want to copy, click the Format Painter button, and then click the object you want to format. You can use the same process to copy text attributes such as font, size, color, or style to other text. To copy attributes to more than one object or section of text, double-click the Format Painter button, click the objects or text you want to format, and then click the Format Painter button when you are done.

FIGURE 4-3
Replace Font dialog box

Concept Builder

To apply the color scheme of one slide to another, switch to Slide Sorter view, select the slide with the color scheme you want to copy, click Format Painter, and then click the slide you want to apply the color scheme to.

S TEP-BY-STEP ▷ 4.2

1. Display **slide 1**. Choose **Replace Fonts** from the **Format** menu. The Replace Fonts dialog box appears.

2. In the *Replace* box, choose **Times New Roman** if necessary.

3. In the *With* box, choose **Papyrus** (or another font, if Papyrus is not an option), as shown in Figure 4-3.

4. Click **Replace**. All the text in New Times Roman font is replaced with the Papyrus font throughout the presentation.

5. Click **Close** to close the Replace Fonts dialog box.

6. Display **slide 2**. Select the first bulleted item, **Introduction**.

7. Change the font to **Papyrus** (or whatever font you used in step 3), 32-point, bold.

8. With **Introduction** still selected, click the **Format Painter** button.

9. The pointer changes to an I-beam with a paintbrush next to it. Click and drag it over the next bulleted item, **Getting Online**. The format changes to the same as *Introduction*.

10. Use the same process to format the remaining two bulleted items. Be sure to select **Introduction** each time.

11. Display **slide 3**.

(continued on next page)

12. Change the heading **Activate** to 32-point bold.

13. With **Activate** selected, double-click the **Format Painter** button.

14. Apply the format to the heading **Login** on the same slide and the headings **Accounts** and **Markets** on the next slide.

15. Click the **Format Painter** button again to de-activate it.

16. Use the Format Painter to apply the format from the title **Online Information** on **slide 4** to the title **Introduction** on **slide 2** and the title **Sands of Time** on **slide 5**.

17. Save the presentation and leave it open for the next Step-by-Step.

Delivering a Presentation

PowerPoint has many features to help make a presentation interesting and effective. There are several options for delivering a presentation. A presentation can be set up as a self-running presentation that can be viewed, for example, at a trade show booth. Or, an individual can view a presentation over a company intranet or on the Web. However, the most common method is to run a presentation with a speaker who directs the show.

Did You Know?

When using overheads or running a presentation, make the text at least 24 points so it can be easily read.

To start a presentation, click the Slide Show view button. You can start the slide show on any slide by displaying or selecting the slide you want to begin with before clicking the Slide Show view button. If you want a particular slide to be hidden when you run your presentation, select the slide in Slide Sorter view and choose Hide Slide from the Slide Show menu.

You can use on-screen navigation tools to control a presentation while delivering it. When you run the presentation, a triangle appears in the bottom left of the screen. Click the triangle and a menu is displayed with your options as shown in Figure 4-4.

When you click the left mouse button, the slides advance in order. You can choose Previous or Next from the menu to display the slide before or after the current one. To go to another slide, choose Go from the menu that is displayed and Slide Navigator from the submenu. The Slide Navigator dialog box appears, as shown in Figure 4-5. Choose the slide you want to display and click the Go To button. To exit the slide show, choose End Show from the menu.

Hot Tip

You display a hidden slide by choosing to go to it in the Slide Navigator dialog box. Parentheses around the slide number indicate that it is hidden.

When you move your mouse, an arrow appears so that you can point out parts of the slide. Choose Hidden from the Pointer Options menu to hide the pointer. Choosing Pen changes the mouse pointer to a pen so you can draw or write on the screen. To change the pen color, choose Pen Color and select a color. To erase what you have written, choose Screen, Erase Pen.

Concept Builder

To display your speaker notes, choose Speaker Notes. To blank the screen, choose Blank Screen from the Screen menu.

FIGURE 4-4
On-screen navigation tools

Click the triangle to display the menu

FIGURE 4-5
Slide Navigator dialog box

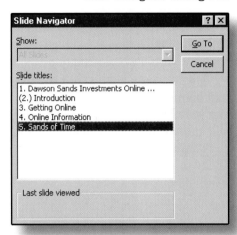

S TEP-BY-STEP ▷ 4.3

1. Switch to **Slide Sorter** view and select **slide 2**.

2. Choose **Hide Slide** from the **Slide Show** menu.

3. Select slide 5 and click the **Slide Show** view button. The presentation begins on slide 5.

4. Click the triangle on the bottom left of the screen. A menu appears, as shown in Figure 4-4.

5. Choose **Go** from the menu and **Slide Navigator** from the submenu. The Slide Navigator dialog box appears, as shown in Figure 4-5.

6. In the *Slide titles* box, select **(2.) Introduction.** Click the **Go To** button. **Slide 2** is displayed.

7. Click with the left mouse button to advance to the next slide.

8. Right-click and choose **Pointer Options** from the menu. Choose **Pen Color** from the submenu and **Magenta** from the next submenu.

9. Circle the words *Activate* and *Login*. Notice how difficult it is to draw a neat circle. Hold

the **Shift** key down and underline the words *Activate* and *Login*. Right-click and choose **Screen** from the menu and **Erase Pen** from the submenu.

10. Right-click and choose **Pointer Options** from the menu and **Automatic** from the submenu. The pen returns to a pointer.

11. Right-click and choose **Previous** from the menu to return to the previous slide.

12. Right-click and choose **End Show** from the menu to exit the slide show.

13. Leave the presentation on the screen for the next Step-by-Step.

Teamwork

Get in small groups and take turns running the slide presentation for the other members of your group.

Sending a Presentation via E-mail

There are several ways you can use e-mail in conjunction with PowerPoint. You can send a single slide as an e-mail message directly from PowerPoint, e-mail a copy of an entire presentation as an attachment, or route a presentation.

Open the presentation you want to send and click the e-mail button on the toolbar. The Office Assistant appears, as shown in Figure 4-6, asking whether you want to send the whole presentation as an attachment or send the current slide as an e-mail message. If you choose to send the slide as the body of an e-mail message, an e-mail header appears as shown in Figure 4-7.

Fill in the recipient information and click Send this Slide. A copy of the slide is e-mailed but the original stays open so you can continue working on it. The e-mail information is saved with the presentation and appears in the e-mail header the next time you send a copy of the slide.

If you choose to send the entire presentation as an attachment when prompted by the Office Assistant, an e-mail message window opens with the presentation attached, as shown in Figure 4-8. Fill in the recipient information, key a message, and click Send.

To *route* a presentation is to send it via e-mail for others to review. A routed presentation is sent as an e-mail attachment. First you must create a routing slip. Open the presentation you want to route, choose Send To on the File menu and Routing Recipient on the submenu. The Add Routing Slip dialog box opens, as shown in Figure 4-9.

Click Address to open your address book and choose recipients. Choose whether you want to route the presentation to recipients all at once or one after another. Key your message text and then click Route to route the presentation immediately. To route it later, click Add Slip and then when you are ready choose Send To on the File menu and Next Routing Recipient on the submenu.

Hot Tip

The e-mail message will be sent in HTML format and can be viewed by any e-mail program that can read HTML.

Concept Builder

To e-mail a presentation, you can also choose Send To on the File menu. To send a slide as a message, choose Mail Recipient on the submenu. To send the presentation as an attachment, choose Mail Recipient (as Attachment)... on the submenu.

Extra Challenge

Following the directions of your instructor, create a routing slip for a presentation and route it to two people in your class, one after another.

FIGURE 4-6
Office Assistant

FIGURE 4-7
Slide as an e-mail message

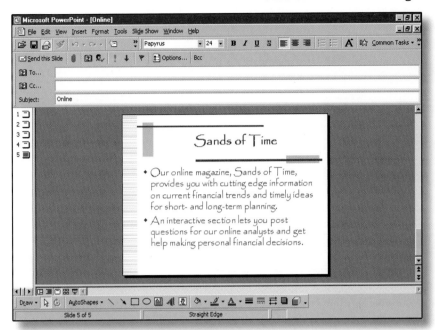

FIGURE 4-8
Presentation as an attachment

FIGURE 4-9
Add Routing Slip dialog box

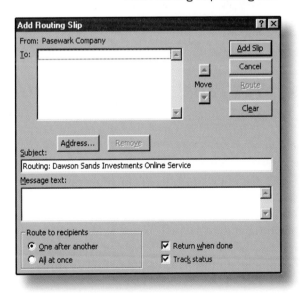

Creating Output

You can alter the output format of your presentation by choosing Page Setup from the File menu. The Page Setup dialog box appears, as shown in Figure 4-10. You can change the orientation of your slides or notes, handouts, and outline. You can choose the type of output from the menu in the *Slides sized for* box. For example, to print a slide as an overhead transparency, choose Overhead.

FIGURE 4-10
Page Setup dialog box

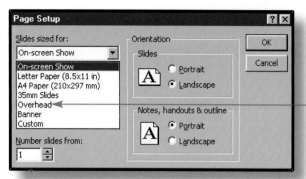

A slide can be printed as an overhead transparency.

STEP-BY-STEP ▷ 4.4

1. Choose **Page Setup** from the **File** menu. The Page Setup dialog box appears, as shown in Figure 4-10.

2. In the *Notes, handouts & outline* section, click **Landscape**.

3. Click **OK**.

4. Print the presentation as handouts with 6 slides per page.

5. Save the presentation and leave it open for the next Step-by-Step.

Inserting a Hyperlink

A hyperlink is used to jump to another location. For example, you can add a hyperlink to go to another slide within your presentation, a different presentation, another Office document, a Web site, or an e-mail address. To insert a hyperlink in a presentation, select the text you want to make a hyperlink and choose Hyperlink from the Insert menu. The Insert Hyperlink dialog box appears, as shown in Figure 4-11. In the *Link to* section, choose where you want the link to go. When you click OK a hyperlink is inserted in the document. The text you selected is displayed in blue with a blue underline; click it to go to the linked location.

Concept Builder

When you key an e-mail address on a slide, a hyperlink is automatically created.

FIGURE 4-11
Insert Hyperlink dialog box

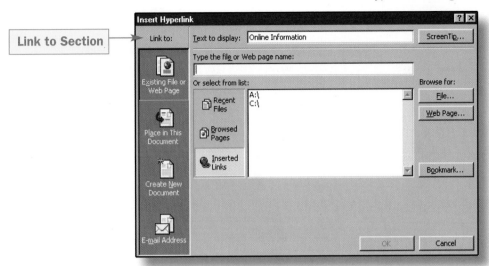

FIGURE 4-11
Insert Hyperlink dialog box

Link to Section

STEP-BY-STEP ▷ 4.5

1. Display **slide 2**.

2. Select the third bulleted item, *Online Information*.

3. Choose **Hyperlink** on the **Insert** menu. The Insert Hyperlink dialog box appears, as shown in Figure 4-11.

4. In the *Link to* section, click **Place in This Document**.

5. In the *Select a place in this document* box, click **4, Online Information**. The slide is displayed in the *Slide preview* box, as shown in Figure 4-12.

6. Click **OK**. The text is underlined in blue in the presentation.

7. Click the **Slide Show** view button. The slide show starts on **slide 2**.

8. Click the hyperlink, **Online Information**, on the screen. PowerPoint jumps to the linked location—slide 4.

9. Exit the slide show.

10. Save the presentation and leave it open for the next Step-by-Step.

(continued on next page)

FIGURE 4-12
Creating a hyperlink within a presentation

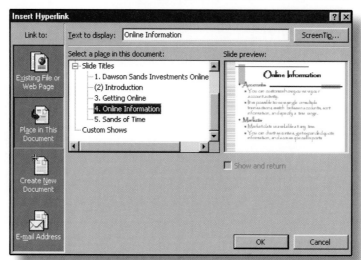

Publishing a Presentation to the Web

Similar to other Office 2000 applications, Power-Point also helps you create Web documents easily. You can create a new presentation or convert an existing presentation to a Web page so that a Web browser can view it. If you are creating a new presentation for the Web, you can use the AutoContent Wizard. If you are converting an existing presentation to a Web page, choose Save as Web Page from the File menu. The Save As dialog box appears, as shown in Figure 4-13.

Concept Builder

To make a presentation available on the Web is also known as "publishing a presentation."

FIGURE 4-13
Saving a presentation as a Web page

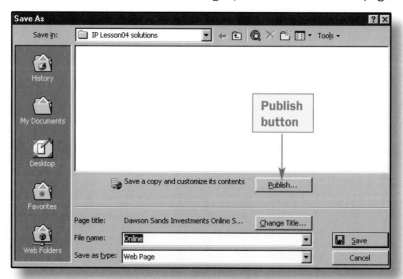

When you choose Publish in the Save As dialog box, the Publish as Web Page dialog box appears, as shown in Figure 4-14. To preview a presentation in your browser, choose Web Page Preview from the File menu. The browser opens and displays your presentation as a Web page.

FIGURE 4-14
Publish as Web Page dialog box

STEP-BY-STEP ▷ 4.6

1. Choose **Save as Web Page** from the **File** menu. The Save As dialog box appears, as shown in Figure 4-13.

2. Click the **Publish** button in the middle of the dialog box. The Publish as Web Page dialog box appears, as shown in Figure 4-14.

3. In the *Publish what?* box, choose **Complete Presentation** if it is not already selected.

4. Click **Publish**.

5. Choose **Web Page Preview** from the **File** menu. Your browser opens and the presentation is displayed as a web page. Your screen should appear similar to Figure 4-15.

6. Click the titles in the left-hand frame to go to each slide.

7. Click the **(X)** in the upper right-hand corner of the browser to close it.

8. Save and close the presentation.

(continued on next page)

FIGURE 4-15
Viewing your presentation in a browser

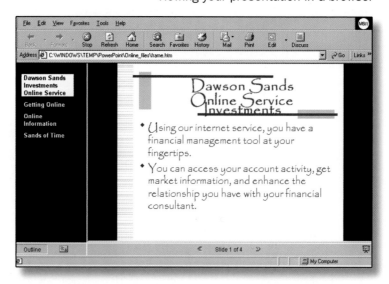

Integrating PowerPoint and Word

Importing Text from Word

You can import text from Word to create a new presentation or add slides to an existing presentation. A Word outline is the easiest kind of document to import because it is formatted with styles and each heading level is translated into a corresponding level of text in PowerPoint. For example, Heading 1 text is converted to slide titles. If the Word document does not have heading styles applied, PowerPoint uses the paragraph indentations to create an outline structure.

STEP-BY-STEP ⟩ 4.7

1. Open Word and open **IP Step4-7** from the student data files. Notice how the document is formatted as an outline.

2. Close the file and exit Word.

3. Open PowerPoint and choose **Open** from the **File** menu. The Open dialog box appears.

4. In the *Files of type* box at the bottom, choose **All Outlines**.

5. Locate **IP Step4-7** in the student data files and choose **Open**.

6. The Word document text is imported into a presentation and formatted as slides.

7. Save the presentation as **Recycling** followed by your initials.

8. Click the light bulb on each slide and choose to change the text to title case.

9. Create a new **slide 1** with a title slide layout. Key **Why Recycle?** as the title and your name as the subtitle.

10. Change the design template to **Sandstone**.

11. Save the presentation and print it as handouts, portrait orientation, with 4 slides per page.

12. Close the presentation.

Embedding Data

You have already learned that when you move data among applications by cutting or copying and pasting, Office changes the format of the information you are moving so that it may be used in the destination file. When it is easier to edit the information using the original application, you can *embed* the information as an object by accessing the Insert Object dialog box, shown in Figure 4-16.

The embedded information becomes part of the new file, but is a separate object that can be edited using the application that created it. For example, if you insert a table from a Word document into a PowerPoint presentation, you would edit it using Word instead of PowerPoint.

FIGURE 4-16
Insert Object dialog box

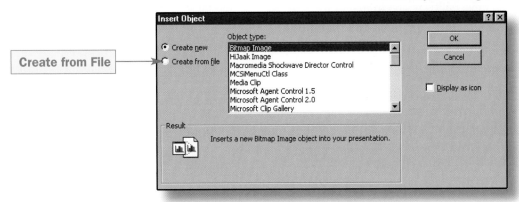

Create from File

STEP-BY-STEP ▷ 4.8

1. Open the **Copier Revised** presentation that you last saved in Project 2.1.

2. Save the presentation as **Copier Final** followed by your initials.

3. Switch to **Slide** view, if that is not the current view.

4. Display **slide 4**.

5. Delete the second bullet.

6. Select the words *has few copying options* on the first bulleted item.

7. Key **requires too much maintenance**. Click elsewhere on the slide to close the text box.

8. Change the slide layout to *Text over Object*.

9. Double click the object placeholder. The Insert Object dialog box appears, as shown in Figure 4-16.

10. Click **Create from file**.

11. Click the **Browse** button. The Browse dialog box appears.

12. Locate **Copy Table** in the student data files and click **OK**.

13. Click **OK** again and the table appears on the slide. Your slide should look similar to Figure 4-17.

14. Save and leave the presentation open for the next Step-by-Step.

FIGURE 4-17
Embedding a Word table

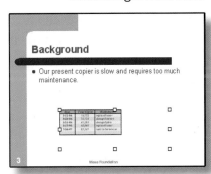

Editing Embedded Data

To make changes to the Word table embedded in the PowerPoint presentation, double-click on it. Word, the application in which the table was created, opens so that you can edit the table. When you finish and return to PowerPoint, the presentation includes the changes you made to the table.

STEP-BY-STEP ▷ 4.9

1. Click the bottom right handle and drag to enlarge the table until it is approximately the size shown in Figure 4-18. (You may need to repeat this step a few times.) Drag the table to position it as shown, if necessary.

2. Double-click the table to display the table in Word.

3. In the last (blank) row, key **10-3-99** in the Date column and key **97,153** in the Total Copies column and key **replaced master** in the Maintenance column.

4. Capitalize the first letter of the first word in each row of the Maintenance column.

5. Click somewhere on the slide other than on the table to exit Word.

6. Notice the changes you made are now part of the table in the presentation.

7. Save the presentation.

8. Print **slide 4** in Slides view.

9. Close the presentation. Exit PowerPoint and Word.

FIGURE 4-18
Enlarged embedded table

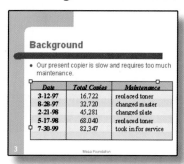

Summary

In this lesson, you learned:

- You can create a new presentation from existing slides and you can copy a slide from one presentation into another.

- To replace fonts throughout an entire presentation, choose Replace Fonts from the Format menu. You can change the formatting of an object or text with the Format Painter button.

- When delivering a presentation, you can start the slide show on any slide. To navigate through a presentation while it is running, click the triangle in the corner of the screen and choose from the menu.

- You can use your pointer as a pen to draw or write on a slide while running a presentation. To change the color of the pen, choose Pen Color from the Pointer Options menu and choose a color.

- You can send a single slide as an e-mail message directly from PowerPoint, e-mail a copy of an entire presentation as an attachment, or route a presentation for others to review.

- You can create a presentation for the Web using the AutoContent Wizard. To convert any presentation to a Web page, choose Save as Web Page from the File menu.

- You can import text from Word to create a new presentation or add slides. It is easiest for PowerPoint to convert the text to slides when the Word document is in outline form.

- Embedding is another way to integrate data between applications. Information is embedded as an object so that it can be edited using the original application.

- To make changes to an embedded object, double-click the object to open the application that created it. Changes made when editing will be reflected in the destination file.

LESSON 4 REVIEW QUESTIONS

FILL IN THE BLANKS

Complete the following sentences by writing the correct word or words in the blanks provided.

1. When running a presentation, click the _____ in the bottom left corner of the screen to display a menu of navigation tools.

2. A _____ is used to jump to another location.

3. When importing text from Word, an _____ is the easiest document for PowerPoint to convert.

4. To _____ a presentation is to send it to others for review.

5. To preview a published presentation in your browser, choose _____ on the File menu.

MATCHING

Match the correct term in Column 2 to its description in Column 1.

Column 1	Column 2
_D_ 1. Dialog box you use to copy a slide from another presentation	A. Format Painter
_G_ 2. View button you click to start a presentation	B. Insert Hyperlink
_C_ 3. Dialog box where you alter the output format of a presentation.	C. Page Setup
_A_ 4. Toolbar button you click to copy attributes of text or objects	D. Slide Finder
_E_ 5. Dialog box you access to embed information	E. Insert Object
	F. Slide Navigator
	G. Slide Show

PROJECT 4-1

1. Start PowerPoint and open the **Recycling** file that you last used in Step-by-Step 4.7.

2. Save the presentation as **Recycling 2** followed by your initials.

3. Replace the **Arial** font throughout the presentation with **Footlight MT Light**. (If that font is not available, choose another appropriate one.)

4. Select the title, **Why Recycle?** on **slide 1**.

5. Change the format to **Impact** font, **48** point. (If the Impact font is not available, choose another appropriate one.)

6. Use the **Format Painter** button to apply that title format to the rest of the titles in the presentation.

7. Publish the presentation as a Web page and preview it in a browser. Close the browser.

8. Change the output format so that the handouts will print landscape orientation.

9. Save, print the presentation as handouts with 4 slides per page, and close.

PROJECT 4-2

1. Open the **Ransom** presentation that you last used in Project 3.2.

2. Copy the last slide of the **Cypress** presentation that you last used in Step-by-Step 2.12 to make it the last slide of the **Ransom** presentation.

3. Save the presentation as **Ransom 2** followed by your initials.

4. Format **slide 6** to look like Figure 4-19. Change the address font size to **28** point. Resize and move the text boxes and replace information, as shown in the figure.

5. Display **slide 1**.

6. Select the title **Ransom Construction Company** and create a hyperlink to **slide 6**.

7. Click the **Slide Show** view button to run the presentation.

8. Click the hyperlink on **slide 1** to jump to **slide 6**.

9. Use the Slide Navigator to go to **slide 2**.

SCANS

SCANS

10. Advance to **slide 3**.

11. Use a green pen color to draw a driveway from the garage to the house and a tree on the right side of the house.

12. Erase the pen marks. Continue through the rest of the presentation.

13. Save the presentation and print it as handouts with 6 slides per page.

14. Close the presentation and exit PowerPoint.

FIGURE 4-19

CRITICAL THINKING

ACTIVITY 4-1

Your supervisor wants you to insert a chart into the presentation you are editing for him. You decide to use a Microsoft Excel chart that you have already created. Use the Help system to find out how to insert an Excel chart into a presentation.

ACTIVITY 4-2

Create an outline in Word using heading styles. Use at least three Heading 1 styles so your presentation will have at least three slides. Import the text into PowerPoint to create a new presentation. Convert the presentation into a Web page and view it with your browser.

COMMAND SUMMARY

FEATURE	MENU COMMAND	TOOLBAR BUTTON	LESSON
Align	Format, Alignment		2
Animation Effects			2
AutoShapes	Insert, Picture, AutoShapes	AutoShapes ▾	3
Black and White	View, Black and White		1
Bold	Format, Font	**B**	2
Bulleted List	Format, Bullets and Numbering, Bulleted		2
Case	Format, Change Case		2
Clip Art	Insert, Picture, Clip Art		1
Close	File, Close		1
Common Tasks		Common Tasks ▾	1
Copy	Edit, Copy		3
Create a New Presentation	File, New		2
Cut	Edit, Cut		3
Delete a Slide	Edit, Delete Slide		2
Demote			2
Expand All			2
Find	Edit, Find		2
Font	Format, Font	Times New Roman ▾	2
Font Color	Format, Font	A ▾	2
Font Size	Format, Font	44 ▾	2
Font Size, Decrease		A▾	2
Font Size, Increase		A	2

FEATURE	MENU COMMAND	TOOLBAR BUTTON	LESSON
Format Painter			4
Free Rotate			3
Header and Footer	View, Header and Footer		2
Hyperlink	Insert, Hyperlink		4
Italic	Format, Font		2
Line Color	Format, Colors and Lines		3
Move Up			2
New Slide	Insert, New Slide		1
Numbered List	Format, Bullets and Numbering, Numbered		2
Office Assistant	Help, Show the Office Assistant		1
Open Existing Document	File, Open		1
Paste	Edit, Paste		3
Print	File, Print		1
Replace	Edit, Replace		2
Replace Fonts	Format, Replace Fonts		4
Save	File, Save		1
Select Objects			3
Spell Check	Tools, Spelling		2
Tabs	Format, Tabs		2
Text Box	Insert, Text Box		3
Underline	Format, Font		2
Undo	Edit, Undo		2
View Datasheet	View, Datasheet		3
Views	View, desired view		1
Web Page	File, Save as Web Page		4
Web Page Preview	File, Web Page Preview		4
Zoom	View, Zoom	38%	2

TRUE/FALSE

Circle T if the statement is true or F if the statement is false.

T   F   1.   When you locate the presentation you want to open in the Open dialog box, a preview of the first slide displays.

T   F   2.   When you add a new slide, it is inserted into the presentation before the slide currently on the screen.

T   F   3.   Changing the slide master will affect the appearance of all the slides.

T   F   4.   To create a perfect circle with the Oval tool, hold down the Ctrl key as you click and drag.

T   F   5.   You can convert an existing presentation to a Web page by choosing Save as Web Page from the File menu.

MULTIPLE CHOICE

Select the best response for the following statements.

1.   Which of the following does the status bar *not* show?
   A.   A scroll box
   B.   A spell-check icon
   C.   Which slide is displayed
   D.   The design currently in use

2.   What reserves space in the presentation for the type of information you want?
   A.   Master
   B.   Object box
   C.   Template
   D.   Placeholder

3.   Which tab of the Animation dialog box would you access to choose to display the animation manually?
   A.   Multimedia
   B.   Chart
   C.   Order & Timing
   D.   Effects

4.   What is used to best show hierarchical structure and relationships in a company?
   A.   Table
   B.   Graph
   C.   Text box
   D.   Organization chart

5. A hyperlink is used in a presentation to:
   A. Connect together boxes in an organization chart
   B. Jump to another location
   C. Route a slide to a reviewer
   D. Import text from Word

 APPLICATIONS

APPLICATION 1

1. Use the AutoContent Wizard to create a Generic presentation (in the General category).

2. The type of output will be an on-screen presentation.

3. Key **Data Management** as the presentation title.

4. Include your name as the footer on each slide.

5. When the presentation has been created, save it as Computer Use followed by your initials.

6. Delete the subtitle on **slide 1**.

7. Change the design template to **Blends**.

8. Change the subtitle on **slide 1** to Responsible Computer Use.

9. Delete slides 9 (Next Steps), 8 (What This Means), 7 (Real Life), 3 (Topics of Discussion), and 2 (Introduction).

10. Switch to **Slide** view and key text on the remaining slides as shown in Figures 1-a through 1-c.

11. Insert a new **slide 5** and create objects to make it look like Figure 1-d.

12. Save and leave the presentation open for the next application.

FIGURE UR-1-A

Passwords

- Every morning you will log on to your computer with your user name and a 5-10 character password.
- Choose a password that is easy to remember but not easy for someone to figure out.
- Change your password periodically to keep it confidential.

3/1/99   Student's Name   2

FIGURE UR-1-B

Authorized Software Use

- The software installed on your computer is licensed under specific terms of agreement.
- Please do not delete, install, copy, or move any software without permission.

3/1/99   Student's Name   3

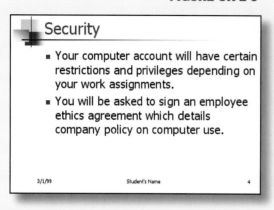

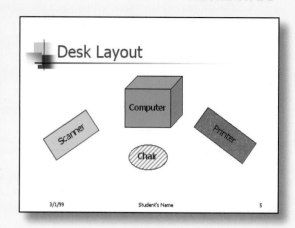

APPLICATION 2

1. Copy **slide 4** from the **Cypress** presentation you last used in Step-by-Step 2.12 so it becomes the last slide of the presentation. Modify it to look like Figure 1-e. (*Hint:* To delete the extra column, click the **Table** button on the **Tables and Borders** toolbar and choose **Delete Columns**.)

2. Change the layout of **slide 3** to **Text & Clip Art.**

3. Replace the clip art placeholder with a picture of a floppy disk. If a picture of a floppy disk is not available, make another computer related selection.

FIGURE UR-1-E

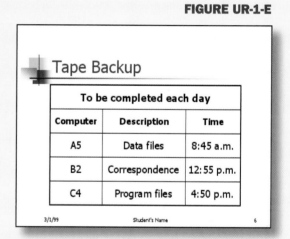

4. Add this speaker's note to **slide 4: Hand out employee ethics agreements. Be sure they are signed and returned by Friday.**

5. Print **slide 4** in **Notes Pages** view.

6. On **slide 1**, animate the title to **Zoom In** accompanied by an explosion sound.

7. Set the slide transitions for all slides to dissolve at medium speed.

8. Run the presentation as a slide show.

9. Change the output format so the handouts will print in landscape.

10. Print the presentation as audience handouts with 6 slides per page.

11. Save and close the presentation.

APPLICATION 3

1. Open **IP App3** from the student data files.

2. Save the presentation as **Hong Kong** followed by your initials.

3. Add a slide to the end of the presentation titled **Food**.

4. In **Outline** or **Normal** view, key the rest of the slide in bulleted list format:

   - **The basic food is rice and is often prepared with fish, pork, chicken, and vegetables.**
   - **Chopsticks are used with most meals.**
   - **When you eat, it is good manners to hold the rice bowl close to your mouth.**

5. Change the design template to **Sumi Painting**.

6. In Slide Sorter view, move **slide 4** so it becomes **slide 2**.

7. Replace the current font with **Tekton**, or another available font, throughout the presentation.

8. Change the title on **slide 2** to **Century Gothic**, **48** point, **bold**.

9. Use the **Format Painter** to copy the format to the title of **slides 3** and **4**.

10. Print the presentation in **Outline** view.

11. Save and leave the presentation open for the next application.

APPLICATION 4

1. In **Normal** view, display **slide 3**. Delete the words **Population and** from the title.

2. Delete the first bullet on the slide.

3. Change the slide layout to **Text & Clip Art**.

4. Insert a clip art picture with mountains.

5. Size the clip art and text boxes to make everything fit well on the slide.

6. On **slide 1** animate the title to crawl from the top and the subtitle to crawl from the bottom.

7. Apply a **Random Transition** set at slow speed to all slides and choose a **Slide Projector** sound to accompany the transitions.

8. Insert a hyperlink on the last slide using the words **Hong Kong** in the first bullet to jump to **slide 1**.

9. Start a slide show on the last slide.

10. Click the hyperlink to go to the first slide. Advance through the presentation to **slide 3**.

11. Use the red pen to underline *tropical climate*.

12. Exit the slide show.

13. Save and print the presentation as audience handouts with 2 slides per page.

14. Save the presentation as a Web page. Preview it in your browser. Close the browser.

15. Save and close the presentation. Exit PowerPoint.

ON-THE-JOB SIMULATION

Your manager asks you to create a presentation to show to all new members.

MARCH 20

1. Start PowerPoint and open **IP Job1** from the student data files.

2. Save the presentation as **Internet Basics** followed by your initials.

3. Change the layout of **slide 3** to **Text & Clip Art** and insert a clip art picture relevant to the slide.

4. Start Word and open **Table** from the student data files.

5. Save the document as **Computer Table** followed by your initials.

6. Center all headings in the table.

7. Close the table, exit Word, and switch to PowerPoint.

FIGURE UR-1-F

8. Insert a new slide after **slide 11** with the **Object** layout.

9. Key **Computer Equipment** as the title.

10. Embed **Computer Table** as the object.

11. Drag the bottom right selection handle to increase the size of the table until it is approximately the same size as shown in Figure 1-f.

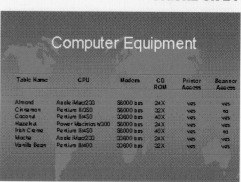

12. Double-click the table.

13. Change the **yes** to **no** in the first cell of the *Scanner Access* column.

14. Click the slide to return to the presentation.

Extra Challenge

Add animation and slide transitions and run the presentation.

15. Delete the three vocabulary slides (currently **slides 5–7**)

16. Save and print **Internet Basics** as handouts with 9 slides per page.

17. Close the presentation and exit PowerPoint.

UNIT

INTRODUCTION TO MICROSOFT® OUTLOOK

lesson 1   2 hrs.

Outlook Basics

lesson 2   1.5 hrs.

Outlook Today and E-mail

Estimated Time for Unit: 3.5 hours

OUTLOOK BASICS

OBJECTIVES

Upon completion of this lesson, you should be able to:

- Start Outlook.
- View the Calendar.
- Schedule and change appointments.
- Schedule and change events.
- Schedule a meeting.
- Print a daily, weekly, or monthly calendar.
- Create, view, manage, and print a task list.
- Record entries in the Journal.
- Create and view Notes.
- Exit Outlook.

🕐 **Estimated Time: 2 hours**

Introducing Outlook

Outlook is a desktop information manager that helps you organize information, communicate with others, and manage your time. You can use the various features of Outlook to send and receive e-mail, schedule events and meetings, record information about business and personal contacts, make to-do lists, record your work, and create reminders. You can organize all of this information into categories for viewing and printing. For example, you might group all the information on your most important customers into the *Key Customer* category. You can also create a new category for a specific group of information. For example, all of the information on your customers located in Texas could be grouped into the *Texas Customers* category.

Because Outlook is integrated, it can be used easily with all other Office 2000 programs. For example, you can send and receive e-mail messages in Outlook and you can move a name and address from a Word document into your Outlook contact list.

Starting Outlook

Outlook, like other Office 2000 applications, is started from the desktop screen in Windows 98. To start Outlook, click the Start button, select Programs, then choose Microsoft Outlook. The Inbox screen appears as shown in Figure 1-1. You will send and receive e-mail messages from the Inbox screen if your computer is set up for this.

FIGURE 1-1
Inbox screen

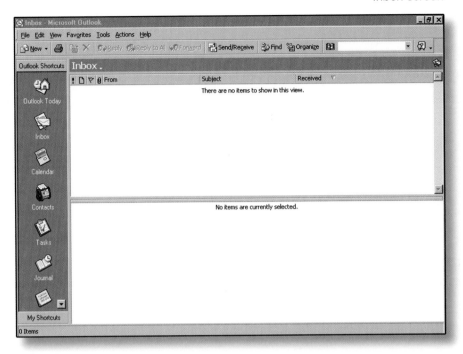

The **Outlook Bar** contains icons you can use to access many of the available features in Outlook, as shown in Table 1-1. The My Shortcuts button displays icons you can use to draft, send, receive, and organize e-mail messages. You will learn more about e-mail in Lesson 2. The Other Shortcuts button allows you to view the contents of any folder on your computer.

Concept Builder

You can customize the Outlook Bar by right-clicking on it and then making your choices from the menu that appears.

TABLE 1-1
Outlook Bar icons

ICON	NAME	DESCRIPTION
Outlook Today	Outlook Today	Lists today's activities from Calendar, Tasks, and Inbox and summarizes on one screen.
Inbox	Inbox	Contains e-mail messages you've received.
Calendar	Calendar	Schedules your appointments, meetings, and events.
Contacts	Contacts	Lists information about those you communicate with.

TABLE 1-1
(continued)

ICON	NAME	DESCRIPTION
Tasks	Tasks	Creates and manages your to-do lists.
Journal	Journal	Records entries to document your work.
Notes	Notes	Keeps track of anything you need to remember.
Deleted Items	Deleted Items	Stores files deleted from other folders.

STEP-BY-STEP ▷ 1.1

1. Chose **Start**, **Programs**, then **Microsoft Outlook**. If the Choose Profile dialog box appears, click OK. Your screen should appear similar to Figure 1-1.

2. Leave Outlook open for use in the next Step-by-Step.

Viewing the Calendar

The Calendar screen, shown in Figure 1-2, is where you enter your appointments, meetings, and events. You can display the Calendar screen by clicking the Calendar icon on the Outlook Bar.

You can view the Calendar in various ways. Choose the Current View option from the View menu to see a list of options. In Figure 1-2, the Calendar is displayed in Day/Week/Month view that shows tasks, appointments, and meetings scheduled for a given time frame. You can click buttons on the toolbar to see a daily, weekly, or monthly calendar, or to display the current day. If the buttons are not displayed on your toolbar, click the More Buttons icon on the toolbar to add them.

Use the **Date Navigator,** the monthly calendars at the top right, to change dates by clicking directly on the date you want to view. You can change months by clicking the arrows next to the month names. A boldface date on the Date Navigator means an activity is scheduled for that day.

> **Hot Tip**
>
> You can also change months by clicking the name of the month and choosing a month from the menu that appears.

The **Appointment book** displays appointments for the time frame you choose. The **TaskPad** on the Calendar screen displays the task list, which you will learn about later in the chapter.

FIGURE 1-2
Calendar screen

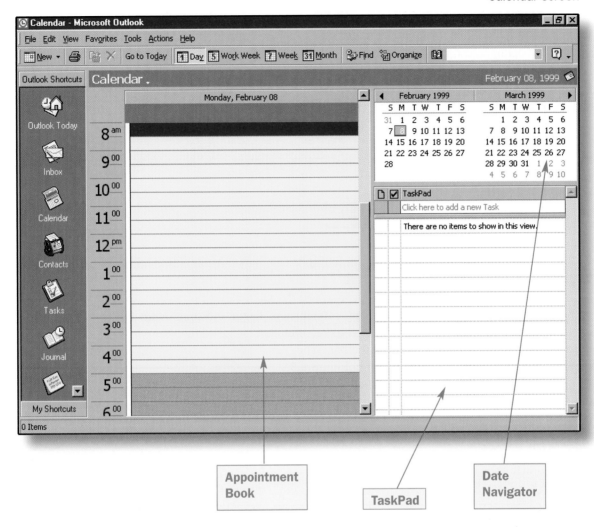

Appointment Book

TaskPad

Date Navigator

STEP-BY-STEP ▷ 1.2

1. Click the **Calendar** icon on the Outlook Bar. The Calendar appears, similar to Figure 1-2.

2. Using the **Date Navigator**, click tomorrow's date. Notice that the date automatically changes at the top of the Appointment book. If you had appointments scheduled, they would appear in the appointment area.

3. Click the **Week** button on the toolbar to display the current week's schedule.

4. Click the down arrow on the scroll bar to display next week's schedule.

Hot Tip

Like in the other Office 2000 programs, you can add or remove buttons from the toolbar. Click the More Buttons icon on the toolbar and choose the buttons.

(continued on next page)

5. Click the 20th of this month on the Date Navigator monthly calendar to display the schedule for the 20th.

6. Click the **Go to Today** button on the toolbar to move to today's date on the weekly schedule.

7. Click the **Month** button on the toolbar to display the current month's schedule.

8. Click the **Day** button on the toolbar to display the daily schedule once again.

9. Leave the Calendar on the screen for the next Step-by-Step.

Scheduling an Appointment

To add an appointment to your Calendar, use the Date Navigator to choose the date. In the Appointment book, click on the time the appointment will begin and drag down to the end time. Then choose New Appointment from the Actions menu or click the New Appointment icon on the toolbar. The Appointment dialog box appears, as shown in Figure 1-3.

Key the subject and location of the appointment in the appropriate boxes. Click the up or down arrows to change the *Start time* or *End time*, if necessary. Select the *All day event* option if the appointment is scheduled for the entire day. In the text box at the bottom, you can key any additional information about the appointment.

> **Hot Tip**
>
> You can type words such as "this Friday" or "midnight" in the date and time fields and Outlook's AutoDate feature will convert them for you.

FIGURE 1-3
Appointment dialog box

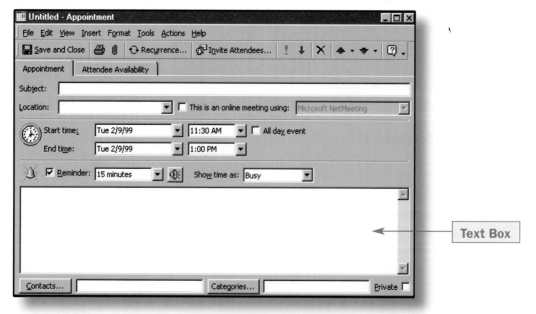

You can choose the *Reminder* option to have Outlook notify you a certain number of minutes, hours, or days before the appointment. A bell icon appears next to the appointment on the calendar indicating that a reminder is set. A dialog box displays when it is time for the reminder. At that time, you can dismiss the reminder, click the snooze button to be reminded again later, or open the appointment to remind yourself of the details.

The *Show time as* box lets you decide how to display the scheduled time on your calendar. The *Categories* box allows you to organize your appointments. The *Private* option prevents other users on an Intranet from viewing your appointment information. A key icon will appear next to the appointment on the calendar when the private option is in use.

When you have entered all the necessary information about the appointment, click *Save and Close* to return to the Calendar. You'll see the information in the appointment area next to the appointment time.

S TEP-BY-STEP ▷ 1.3

1. Click tomorrow's date in the Date Navigator.

2. Highlight the appointment time by clicking on 11:30 a.m. and dragging through to 1:00 p.m. as shown in Figure 1-4.

3. Click the **New Appointment** icon on the toolbar. The Appointment dialog box appears as shown in Figure 1-3.

4. In the *Subject* box, key **Lunch with Mark Anderson**.

5. In the *Location* box, key **Lakeview Cafe**.

6. Click the **Reminder** box to insert a check mark, if it isn't chosen already.

7. Click the down arrow in the *Reminder* box and choose **30 minutes** from the menu.

8. In the *Show time as* box, click the down arrow and choose **Out of Office**.

9. In the text box, key **Bring latest draft of proposal**.

10. Click the **Categories** box and choose **Key Customer**. Click **OK**. (*Note:* If the *Categories* and *Private* boxes are not shown, increase the screen size by clicking the maximize button in the top right-hand corner of the screen.)

11. Click the **Private** box.

12. Click **Save and Close** on the toolbar. The appointment information and icons appear in the appointment area. (*Note:* To view all of the information in the appointment area, place your pointer in the message area or click the border area.) The key icon indicates the appointment is private. The bell icon is your meeting reminder.

13. Leave the Calendar on the screen for the next Step-by-Step.

(continued on next page)

FIGURE 1-4

Highlight the appointment time

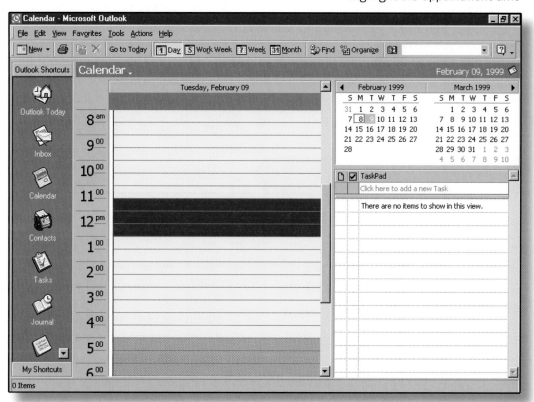

Changing an Appointment

To edit an appointment, double-click the appointment. The Appointment dialog box appears for you to make changes. To reschedule an appointment, click the border and drag the appointment to a new time, as shown in Figure 1-5. To delete an appointment, right-click the border and choose Delete.

Concept Builder

If the appointment occurs on a regular basis, you can choose New Recurring Appointment from the Actions menu. Key information in the dialog box and Outlook will schedule the appointment for you throughout your calendar.

FIGURE 1-5

Click and drag to reschedule

INTRODUCTION TO MICROSOFT OUTLOOK

S TEP-BY-STEP ▷ 1.4

1. Double-click the Mark Anderson appointment. The Appointment dialog box appears.

2. Change the location to **Trotsky's Deli**.

3. In the text box, add **Have Carolyn make reservations and call Mark about location change**.

4. Click **Categories** and the Categories dialog box appears.

5. In the *Available categories* box, click **Key Customer** to remove the check.

6. Click **Master Category List** at the bottom of the dialog box.

7. In the *New category* box, key **Anderson Consulting Co.** and click **Add**.

8. Click **OK** to return to the Categories dialog box.

9. Choose **Anderson Consulting Co.** as the new category and click **OK**. The Appointment dialog box appears.

10. Remove the check from the **Private** box.

11. Click **Save and Close**.

12. Reschedule the Mark Anderson appointment by clicking the border and dragging down until it appears between 12:00 and 1:30, as shown in Figure 1-5. (Your screen may show 13:30 and may show all of the appointment message.)

13. Leave the Calendar on the screen for the next Step-by-Step.

Extra Challenge

Add five more appointments to the Calendar for this month.

Scheduling an Event

An *event* is an activity that lasts at least 24 hours, such as a trade show. An ***annual event*** occurs every year on the same date, such as a birthday. A ***recurring event*** occurs every so many days, weeks, or months, such as a day-long stockholder's meeting scheduled every quarter (every three months). You can use your Calendar to schedule any type of event.

Use the Date Navigator to locate the date of the event, then choose New All Day Event from the Actions menu. The Event dialog box appears, as shown in Figure 1-6. Provide information about the event such as subject, location, and description. Choose the *Reminder* option if you would like to be reminded of the event. For example, you could set a two-day notice to buy a birthday card for someone. Select the *Private* option to prevent other users on an Intranet from viewing the event.

If it is an annual event, click the Recurrence button on the toolbar in the Event dialog box to bring up the Appointment Recurrence dialog box, shown in Figure 1-7. You can choose a recurrence pattern and your event will appear on the calendar every day, week, month, or year. Key a range of recurrence or a beginning and end date for how long the event should appear in the Calendar. Choose OK to return to the Event dialog box. Choose Save and Close when you are finished. The event information will be shown at the top of your daily schedule.

FIGURE 1-6
Event dialog box

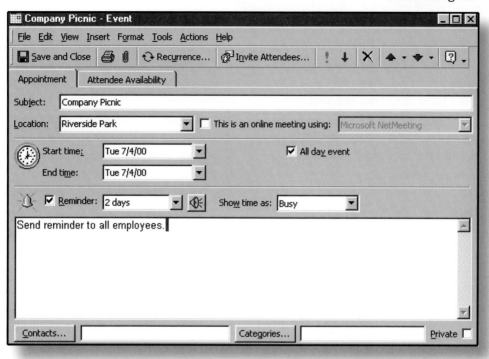

FIGURE 1-7
Appointment Recurrence dialog box

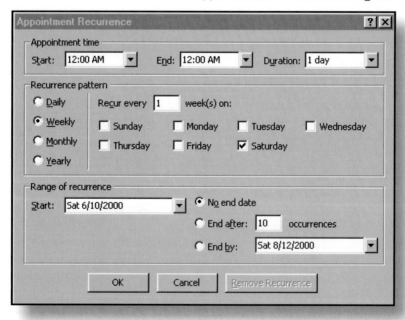

TEP-BY-STEP 1.5

1. Click July 4 of next year in the Date Navigator.

2. Choose **New All Day Event** from the **Actions** menu. The Event dialog box appears.

3. Key information to make the dialog box look like the one in Figure 1-6.

> ### Hot Tip
> You can use your Tab key to move around a dialog box.

4. Choose **Save and Close**.

5. Click June 10 of next year in the Date Navigator.

6. Choose **New All Day Event** from the **Actions** menu.

7. In the Event dialog box, key **Brittany's Birthday** in the *Subject* box.

8. Click the **Recurrence** button on the toolbar. The Appointment Recurrence dialog box appears, as shown in Figure 1-7.

9. Click **Yearly** in the *Recurrence pattern* box.

10. Click **OK**.

11. In the *Reminder* box, choose **1 day**.

12. Click **Save and Close**. The event appears at the top of the appointment area.

13. Leave the Calendar on the screen for the next Step-by-Step.

> ### Extra Challenge
> Add five more annual events to your Calendar, such as birthdays or anniversaries of family members and friends.

Changing an Event

To edit an event, double-click the event listed at the top of the calendar. The Open Recurring Item dialog box will appear as shown in Figure 1-8. Choose the option O*pen the series* to update every occurrence of the event. Choose the option *Open this occurrence* to open only a selected occurrence and not a series of recurring events. The Event dialog box appears for you to make changes. To delete an event, right-click the event at the top of the daily calendar and choose Delete from the menu.

FIGURE 1-8
Open Recurring Item dialog box

1. You realize that you confused Brittany's birthday with a co-worker's. Change the date of Brittany's birthday by double-clicking the event *Brittany's Birthday*. The Open Recurring Item dialog box appears as shown in Figure 1-8.

2. Click **Open the series**, then click **OK**. The Recurring Event dialog box appears.

3. Click the **Recurrence** button on the toolbar.

4. In the *Recurrence pattern* box, change the date to **Every May 22**. Click the down arrow next to the *Range of recurrence* box and change the date to **May 22**. Click **OK**. The Recurring Event

dialog box reappears with the new recurrence date in the middle of the box.

5. Click **Save and Close**.

6. Using the Date Navigator, click **May 22**. Brittany's Birthday should appear at the top of the calendar.

7. Click on the **Go To Today** button on the toolbar to go back to today's date.

8. Leave the Calendar on the screen for the next Step-by-Step.

Scheduling a Meeting

If you and your co-workers use Outlook and are connected by an Intranet, you can use your Calendar to schedule meetings with them. A ***meeting*** is an appointment to which you invite people and resources. ***Resources*** are any equipment needed in a meeting, such as a conference room, computer, or projector.

Use the Date Navigator to choose a date for the meeting. In the appointment area, choose the meeting time by clicking on the start time and dragging to the end time. Choose Plan a Meeting from the Actions menu and the Plan a Meeting dialog box appears, as shown in Figure 1-9.

FIGURE 1-9
Plan a Meeting dialog box

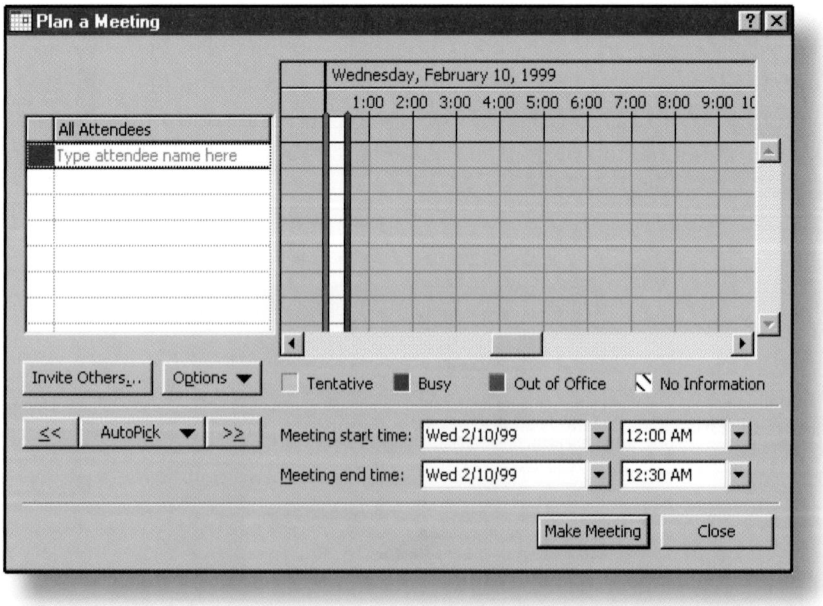

In the *All Attendees* list, key the names of people you want to attend the meeting. Set the date and make any necessary changes to the start and end times and then click Make Meeting. The Meeting dialog box appears, as shown in Figure 1-10. You can use this dialog box to include more details about the meeting, such as subject and location. Send invitations over the Intranet to the attendees by clicking the Send button.

Hot Tip

In the Plan a Meeting dialog box, click the Invite Others button to add the names of attendees from an address book or your Contacts list.

FIGURE 1-10
Meeting dialog box

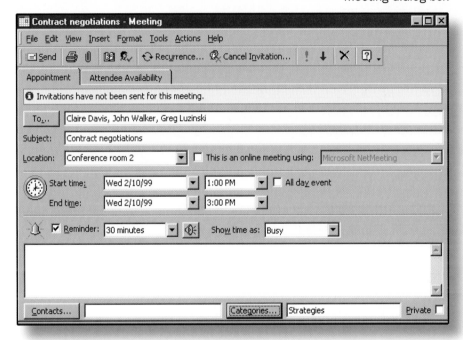

Printing a Calendar

You have several options for printing your Calendar. You can print a daily schedule, a weekly schedule, a monthly schedule, a tri-fold style, or a calendar details style that includes the daily calendar, task list, and weekly calendar. Choose Print from the File menu. The Print dialog box appears, as shown in Figure 1-11. Choose from the options in the *Print style* section and then click OK. You can print a more specific range of dates by choosing *Start* and *End* dates in the *Print range* section.

Extra Challenge

Choose a month and add some personal appointments, events, and a meeting. When finished, print a monthly schedule.

To preview a Calendar before printing, choose Print Preview from the File menu or click the Preview button in the Print dialog box. The mouse pointer changes to a magnifying glass that you can click to zoom in or out when previewing the page.

FIGURE 1-11
Print dialog box

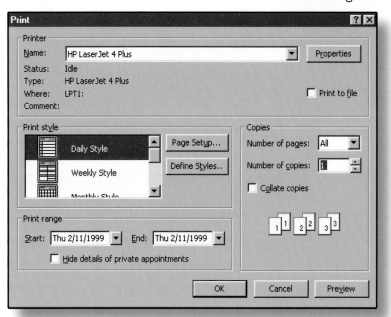

1. Using the Date Navigator, click the date with the Mark Anderson meeting. (In Step-by-Step 1.3, you added the Mark Anderson meeting to tomorrow's schedule.)

2. Choose **Print** from the **File** menu. The Print dialog box appears.

3. If necessary, click **Daily Style** in the *Print Style* box.

4. Click **OK**. A daily calendar will print.

5. Choose **Print** from the **File** menu. The Print dialog box appears.

6. Click **Weekly Style** in the *Print Style* box.

7. Click **OK**. A weekly calendar will print.

8. Choose **Print** from the **File** menu. The Print dialog box appears.

9. Click **Monthly Style** in the *Print Style* box.

10. Click **OK**. A monthly calendar will print.

11. Leave the Calendar on the screen for the next Step-by-Step.

Creating a Task List

You can use the Tasks screen in Outlook to create and manage your tasks. A **task** is any activity you want to perform and monitor to completion. You can assign tasks to categories, specify start and due dates, check the status of tasks, prioritize, and set reminders.

Click the Tasks icon on the Outlook Bar to display the Tasks screen. To add a task, click the New Task icon on the toolbar. The Task dialog box appears, as shown in Figure 1-12. When you are done creating the task, click Save and Close.

Concept Builder

If you and your co-workers are connected by an Intranet, you can assign a task to someone else by choosing New Task Request from the Actions menu. After keying the request click the Send button to e-mail it.

FIGURE 1-12
Task dialog box

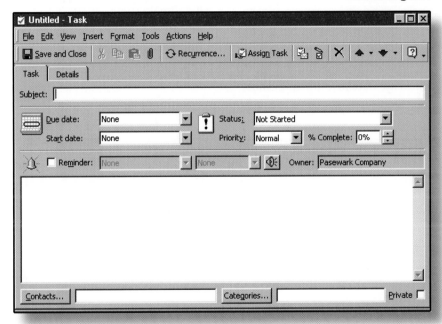

STEP-BY-STEP ▷ 1.8

1. Click the **Tasks** icon on the Outlook Bar. The Task screen appears. If necessary, delete the default *Welcome to Tasks!* by right-clicking the task and choosing **Delete** from the menu.

2. Click the **New Task** icon on the toolbar. The Task dialog box appears, as shown in Figure 1-12.

3. In the *Subject* box, key **Buy supplies**.

4. In the *Due date* section, click the down arrow and choose this Thursday from the calendar.

5. In the *Start* box, click the down arrow and choose last Friday from the calendar.

(continued on next page)

6. In the *Status* box, click the down arrow and choose **In Progress**.

7. In the *Priority* box, click the down arrow and choose **High**.

8. In the *% Complete* box, click the up arrow until **75%** appears. If necessary, enlarge the dialog box window to view the *% Complete* box.

9. Check the *Reminder* box if it is not already selected, then click the down arrow and choose this Wednesday from the calendar. Set the reminder time for 10:00 a.m.

10. In the text box key: **Purchase trees, bushes, ground cover, flowers, root starter, edging,** **and mulch. Already have shovels, spade, hoe, and wheelbarrow.**

11. Click the **Categories** button and click **Personal** in the *Available Categories* box. Click **OK**.

12. Click the **Private** button. Your Task dialog box should appear similar to Figure 1-13.

13. Click **Save and Close**.

14. Create three more tasks using the information shown in Figures 1-14, 1-15, and 1-16. (Key your own dates.)

15. Leave the Task screen open for the next Step-by-Step.

FIGURE 1-13
Create a task

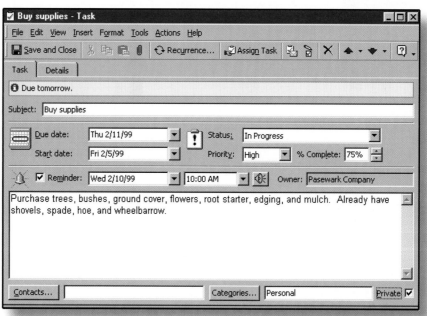

FIGURES 1-14, 1-15, AND 1-16
Create three more tasks

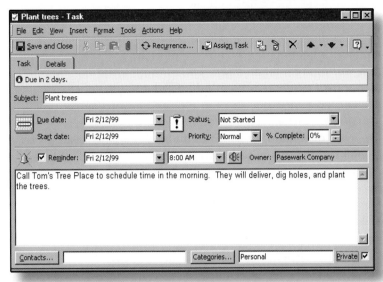

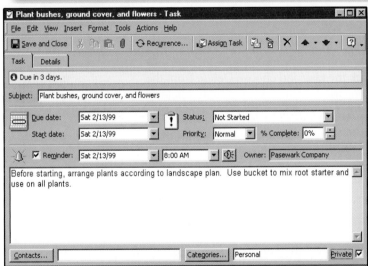

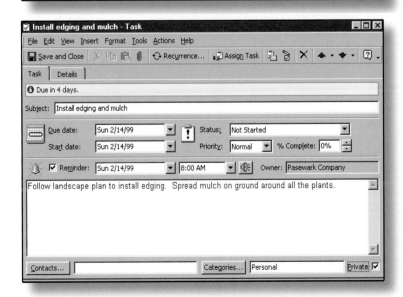

Managing Tasks

You can sort or group tasks, move tasks up and down the list, add or delete tasks, edit a task, or mark a task off when it is completed.

To sort or group tasks, choose Current View from the View menu, then click Customize Current View. The View Summary dialog box appears, as shown in Figure 1-17. Click the Sort button to display the Sort dialog box. In the *Sort Items By* box, click the down arrow and choose the fields to sort by. To group tasks, click the Group By button in the View Summary dialog box and follow the same steps. When finished, your task list should appear sorted and/or grouped according to your selections.

To move a task, be sure the Sort and Group By settings are cleared. Choose Current View from the View menu, then click Customize Current View. The View Summary dialog box appears, as shown in Figure 1-17. Click the Group By button and choose Clear All. Click OK to return to the View Summary dialog box. Follow the same steps to clear the Sort settings. When finished, highlight the task you want to move. Drag until the red arrows and line appear where you want the task, as shown in Figure 1-18, and release the mouse button.

To quickly add a new task, click the top of the list where it says *Click here to add...* and key the task. Click the *Due Date* box, then click the arrow and choose from the calendar to include a due date for the task.

You can mark a task as complete by clicking the completed task check box. A line appears through the task. To delete a task, right-click the task and choose Delete from the shortcut menu that appears. Edit a task by double-clicking the task. The Task dialog box appears where you make the changes and then choose Save and Close.

FIGURE 1-17
View Summary dialog box

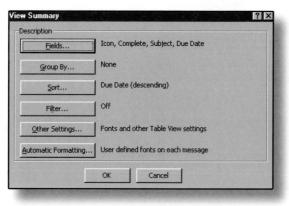

FIGURE 1-18
Move a task by clicking and dragging

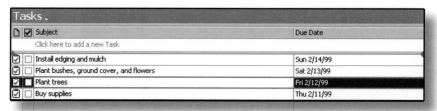

S TEP-BY-STEP **1.9**

1. Click the **Due Date** bar at the top of the task list to sort the list by due date.

   Due Date

   ### Concept Builder

   Clicking the Due Date bar once will sort the tasks by due date in descending order. To sort in ascending order, click the Due Date bar again.

2. Choose **Current View** from the **View** menu.

3. Choose **Customize Current View** from the submenu. The View Summary dialog box appears, as shown in Figure 1-17.

4. Click the **Sort** button and the Sort dialog box appears.

5. Click **Clear All** and then click **OK**. The View Summary dialog box returns.

6. Click **OK** to return to the task list.

7. Click the *Plant trees* task and drag up until the red arrows and line are at the top of the list, as shown in Figure 1-18.

8. Release the mouse button. *Plant trees* becomes the first task on the list.

9. Click the top row of the list where it says *Click here to add...* and key **Fertilize trees and plants**.

10. Click the due date box on the same line. Click the down arrow and choose next Monday's date from the calendar.

11. Click the **Sort by: Complete** check box next to the **Buy supplies** task to mark it as complete. A line appears through the task. (*Note:* If the *Sort by: Complete* check box is not in view on your screen, choose **Current View** from the **View** menu and click **Simple List**.)

   ### Hot Tip

   To mark a task completed, you can also right-click the task and select Mark Complete from the shortcut menu.

12. Double-click the *Plant bushes, ground cover, and flowers* task to open the Task dialog box for editing.

13. Remove the check mark from the *Reminder* box and click **Save and Close**.

14. Right-click the *Install edging and mulch* task. A shortcut menu appears.

15. Choose **Delete**. Your screen should appear similar to Figure 1-19.

16. Leave the Calendar on the screen for the next Step-by-Step.

   ### Extra Challenge

   Create a Task list that includes at least five things you need to do in the next week.

(continued on next page)

FIGURE 1-19
Task List

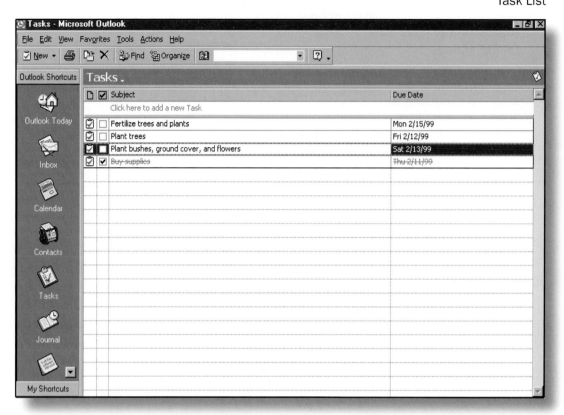

Viewing and Printing the Task List

To change how you view your tasks, choose Current View from the View menu. Choose from the list of view options. The view options are described in Table 1-2. Simple List is the default view.

To print your task list, choose Print from the File menu. The Print dialog box opens. The *Print style* box displays various options depending on what view you are using. You can choose to print your tasks in a Table or Memo Style.

 Concept Builder

By default, the current day's tasks will appear in the TaskPad when you are in Calendar view. To view all tasks on the TaskPad, click View, TaskPad View, All Tasks.

TABLE 1-2
View options for a task list

VIEW	DESCRIPTION
Simple List	Lists tasks, completed check box, and due date
Detailed List	Lists details about each task including priority and status
Active Tasks	Lists tasks that are still in progress
Next Seven Days	Lists tasks due in the next seven days
Overdue Tasks	Lists only overdue tasks
By Category	Lists tasks grouped by category and sorted by due date
Assignment	Lists tasks assigned to others
By Person Responsible	Lists tasks according to the person responsible for completing
Completed Tasks	Lists only completed tasks
Task Timeline	Tasks are displayed in chronological order according to start date

STEP-BY-STEP ▷ 1.10

1. Choose **Current View** from the **View** menu.

2. Choose **Detailed List** from the submenu. (*Note:* Adjust the columns so you can read your entries in the Subject, Status, Due Date, %Complete, and Categories columns.)

3. Choose **Print** from the **File** menu. The Print dialog box appears. Click the **Page Setup** button. The Page Setup: Table Style dialog box appears. Click the **Paper** tab. If it is not already selected, click the option button next to *Portrait.* Click **OK**.

4. In the *Print style* box, **Table Style** should already be highlighted. Click **OK**.

5. The task list will print in a table format, portrait orientation.

6. Leave Outlook open for the next Step-by-Step.

Using the Journal

You can use the Journal screen in Outlook to record entries and document your work. You can create journal entries manually to keep track of phone calls and other activities, or you can choose to automatically record e-mail, requests, and responses.

Click the Journal icon on the Outlook Bar to display the Journal screen. To add an entry manually, click the New Journal Entry icon on the toolbar. The Journal Entry dialog box appears, as shown in Figure 1-20. When you are finished making the journal entry, click Save and Close.

The default view is By Type which displays information as icons on a timeline, grouped by type. To change how you view your journal entries, choose Current View from the View menu. Choose from the list of view options. Choose Phone calls to display a list of phone calls recorded in your journal. Choose AutoPreview from the View menu to preview an entry.

Concept Builder

To automatically record entries, choose Options from the Tools menu and click the items and contacts you want to automatically record entries from in your Journal.

FIGURE 1-20
Journal Entry dialog box

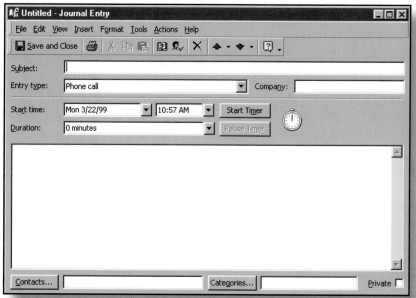

STEP-BY-STEP ▷ 1.11

1. Click the **Journal** icon on the Outlook Bar. If a message appears, click **No**. The Journal screen is displayed.

2. Click the **New Journal** icon on the toolbar. The Journal Entry dialog box  appears, as shown in Figure 1-20. (*Note:* The entries in your dialog box may not be the same as in the figure.)

3. In the *Subject* box, key **Decide topics and attendees for meeting on Tuesday**.

4. In the *Entry type* box, choose **Phone call**, if it is not already selected.

5. In the *Contacts* box, key **David Powell**.

6. In the *Duration* box, choose **15 minutes**.

Concept Builder

You can use the Start Timer and Pause Timer buttons like a stopwatch to record the actual time of your phone calls.

7. In the text box, key **He will fax finalized agenda and list of attendees on Monday**.

8. Click **Save and Close**.

9. Choose **Current View** from the **View** menu. If it is not already selected, choose **Phone Calls** from the submenu. Your screen should appear similar to Figure 1-21.

10. Leave Outlook open for use in the next Step-by-Step.

FIGURE 1-21
Preview a journal entry

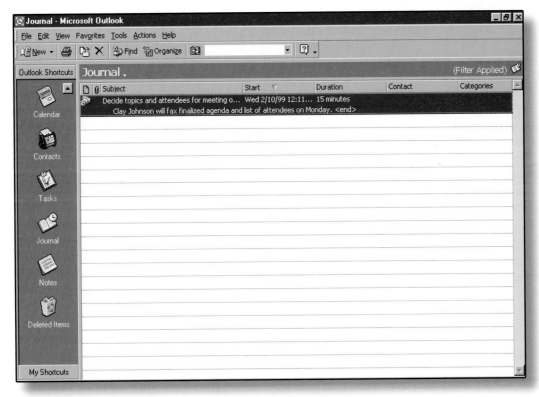

Using Notes

The Notes screen in Outlook is similar to using paper sticky notes as reminders. You can use Notes to key anything you need to remember, such as errands to run, birthday gift ideas, or a question to ask a co-worker.

Click the Notes icon on the Outlook Bar to display the Notes screen. To add a note, click the New Note icon on the toolbar. A blank note appears, as shown in Figure 1-22. The date and time are automatically added. Click the Close button (X) on the note to save and close it.

FIGURE 1-22
Use Notes to key important reminders

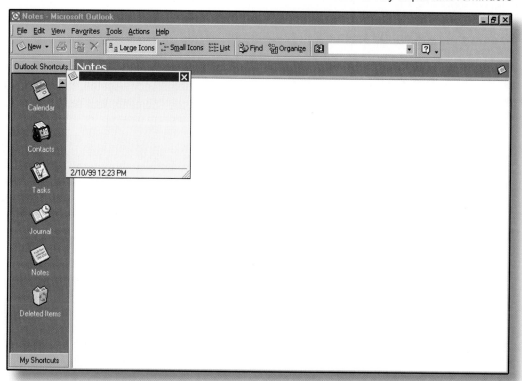

The default view on the Notes screen is Icons which displays each note with an icon. To change how you view your notes, choose Current View from the View menu. Choose from the list of view options.

Yellow is the default color of a note, but you can change it by clicking the note icon on an open note. Choose Color from the menu that appears and pick a color from the submenu, as shown in Figure 1-23. If you have different color notes, you can then display them according to color by choosing By Color from the *Current View* box.

Concept Builder

You can change the font, font style, size, and color of the text on your notes by choosing Options from the Tools menu and then clicking the Note Options button.

FIGURE 1-23
Changing the color of a note

STEP-BY-STEP ▷ 1.12

1. Click the **Notes** icon on the Outlook Bar. The Notes screen is displayed. If necessary, right-click the default note and choose Delete to remove it from your screen.

2. Click the **New Note** icon on the toolbar. Your screen should appear similar to Figure 1-22.

3. Key **Fax tax information to accountant.**

4. Click the **Note** icon in the upper-left corner of the note. A menu appears.

5. Choose **Color**. A submenu appears, as shown in Figure 1-23.

6. Click **Green.** The note color changes to green.

7. Click the **Close** button **X** to close the note. Notice that your note now appears on the Notes window.

8. Open a new note and key **Order supplies from OfficePro salesman.**

9. Change the color to pink and close the note.

10. Open a new note and key **Deposit payroll check into bank account.**

11. Change the color to green and close the note.

12. Open a new note and key **Call PrinterPlus about repair: 555-7822.** Close the note.

13. Choose **Current View** from the **View** menu.

14. Choose **By Color** from the submenu.

15. Click the plus sign (+) to the left of each *Color:* label to sort your notes by color. Your screen should appear similar to Figure 1-24.

16. Choose **Current View** from the **View** menu.

17. Choose **Icons** from the submenu to return to the default view.

18. Leave Outlook open for use in the next Step-by-Step.

(continued on next page)

FIGURE 1-24
Notes sorted by color

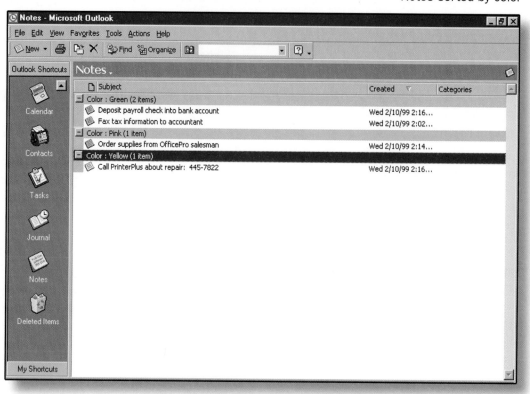

Exiting Outlook

You can exit Outlook by choosing Exit from the File menu. When Outlook exits, your screen will return to the Windows 98 desktop.

STEP-BY-STEP ⟹ 1.13

1. Choose **Exit** from the **File** menu. (If you are prompted to permanently delete items in the "Deleted Items" folder, choose **Yes**, unless instructed otherwise.)

2. The Outlook screen closes and the Microsoft Windows 98 desktop appears.

Summary

In this lesson, you learned:

■ Outlook is a desktop information manager that helps you organize information, communicate with others, and manage your time. The Outlook Bar contains icons you can use to access many of the available features in Outlook.

■ The Calendar is used to schedule appointments, meetings, and contacts. You can view the Calendar in daily, weekly, or monthly format. If you use the Reminder option, Outlook will notify you before the appointment. You can schedule a meeting and invite other people and reserve resources. You can also use the Calendar to schedule events. If the event occurs every year, use the Appointment Recurrence dialog box.

■ The Calendar information can be printed in a daily, weekly, or monthly schedule. It can also be printed in a tri-fold style, or calendar details style that includes the daily calendar, task list, and weekly calendar.

■ The Tasks screen is where you create and manage tasks. You can assign categories, specify start and end dates, check the status of tasks, prioritize, and set reminders. You can also move tasks up and down the list, sort by subject or due date, add or delete tasks, edit a task, or mark a task off when it is completed.

■ The Journal screen is used to record entries and document your work. You can have Outlook automatically record entries or use the Journal Entry dialog box to record entries manually.

■ The Notes screen is similar to using paper sticky notes as reminders. The date and time are automatically added. You can change the color of a note and view them according to color.

LESSON 1 REVIEW QUESTIONS

TRUE/FALSE

Circle T if the statement is true or F if the statement is false.

T F 1. The Outlook Bar contains the Calendar, Notes, and Tasks icons, among others.

T F 2. You can set the Alarm option to notify you before an appointment.

T F 3. An event is an activity that lasts at least 24 hours.

T F 4. Clicking the Due Date bar at the top of the task list will sort the tasks in alphabetical order.

T F 5. Using Notes in Outlook is similar to using sticky paper notes.

WRITTEN QUESTIONS

Write a brief answer to the following questions.

1. How do you start Outlook?

2. Which button do you click in the Date Navigator to return to today's date?

3. What does the Categories box allow you to do with the information added to Outlook?

4. What is the default view for your Task List?

5. What Outlook screen do you use to record entries and document your work?

LESSON 1 PROJECTS

PROJECT 1-1

1. Display the Calendar screen in Day view.

2. Use the Date Navigator to select tomorrow's date for a new appointment.

3. Highlight the appointment time from **9:00 a.m. to 11:00 a.m**.

4. Add an appointment with **Training Session with Staff** as the subject.

5. Add the location of the appointment, **Training Room 5**.

6. Set a reminder for 1 hour before the appointment.

7. In the text box, key **Request a TV and VCR**. Save and close the Appointment dialog box.

8. Add another appointment from **8:00 a.m. to 8:30 a.m.** with **Coffee with Greg** as the subject and **Daybreak Coffee Shop** as the location.

9. Don't set a reminder. Show the time as **Out of Office** and use the **Private** option.

10. In the text box, key **Ask him about tennis this weekend**. Save and close the Appointment dialog box.

11. Leave the Calendar open for the next project.

PROJECT 1-2

1. Move the time of the Training Session with Staff appointment to **10 a.m. to noon**.

2. Change the location to **Conference Room 3**.

3. In the text box, add **Make copies of new office policies**.

4. Add a new category called **Staff**.

5. Assign the Training Session with Staff appointment to the new category.

6. Use the Date Navigator to select this Sunday for an event.

7. Add **My Anniversary** as an annual event.

8. Set a reminder for 1 day before the event date. Save and close the Event dialog box.

9. Leave Outlook on the screen for the next project.

PROJECT 1-3

Tasks screen.

1.

2. Mark all existing tasks as complete.

3. Add a new task with **Paint bathroom** as the subject and due this Saturday.

4. Set a reminder at 5 p.m. on Friday.

5. In the text box, key **Get another drop cloth.** Save and close the Task dialog box.

6. Add another new task with **Pick up carpet samples** as the subject and due this Friday.

7. Set a reminder at 10 a.m. on Friday. Set the priority as **High**. Save and close the Task dialog box.

8. View the tasks in Detailed List view.

9. Sort the tasks by due date.

10. Leave Outlook open for the next project.

PROJECT 1-4

1. Display the Journal screen.

2. Create a new journal entry with **Phone interview** as the subject.

3. Use **Phone call** as the *Entry type*.

4. Key **Clay Sipowitz** as the Contact and **Rocky Mountain Journal** as the Company.

5. Choose a duration of **30 minutes**.

6. In the text box, key **Will send photographer Monday.**

7. Assign the journal entry to the category called **Phone Calls**. Save and close the Journal Entry dialog box.

8. Leave Outlook open for the next project.

PROJECT 1-5

1. Display the Notes screen.

2. Add a pink note that says **Order flowers for Aunt Mollie's birthday**.

3. Add a green note that says **Buy stamps**.

4. Add a yellow note that says **Call Tracey (555-2208) about summer trip**.

5. View the notes by color.

6. Exit Outlook.

CRITICAL THINKING

ACTIVITY 1-1

Pick a type of small business that you would like to own. Describe how you would use the Calendar, Tasks, and Journal features of Outlook to organize information, communicate with others, and manage time. Also, list four or more categories for grouping all of the information.

ACTIVITY 1-2

Your supervisor asks you to change the default settings for Journal tracking or the automatic recording of Outlook activities. Use the Help system and search for the steps to change the defaults.

OUTLOOK TODAY AND E-MAIL

OBJECTIVES

Upon completion of this lesson, you should be able to:

- Create, view, and print a Contacts list.

- Use Outlook Today.

- Send and receive e-mail.

- Create and use an Address Book.

⏱ Estimated Time: 1.5 hours

Creating a Contacts List

You can use the Contacts screen in Outlook to create and use your Contacts list. A ***contact*** is any person or company with whom you communicate. Your Contacts list contains mail, phone, and other information about your contacts.

Click the Contacts icon on the Outlook Bar to display the Contacts screen. It appears similar to Figure 2-1.

FIGURE 2-1
Contacts screen

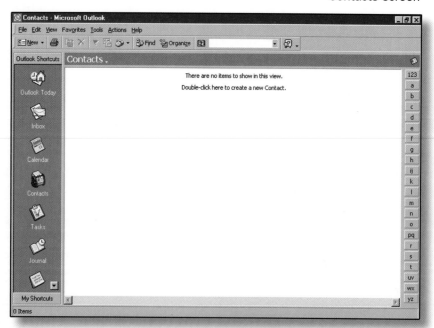

Adding a Contact

To add a contact, click the New Contact icon on the toolbar. The Contact dialog box appears, as shown in Figure 2-2. When you are done adding information about the contact, click Save and Close to return to the Contacts screen or click the Save and New button to add another contact.

Concept Builder

To edit information about a contact, double-click the contact's name in the Contact list.

Notice the five tabs at the top of the box. The General tab includes mailing, phone and other information, such as the contact's title and company name. The Details tab is where you can store additional information about a contact such as department, birthday, or nickname. The Activities tab is where you can track all journal entries related to a contact. You will learn more about the Journal later in this lesson. The Certificates tab allows you to send a secure message over the Internet. The All Fields tab allows the user to create custom fields.

FIGURE 2-2
Contact dialog box

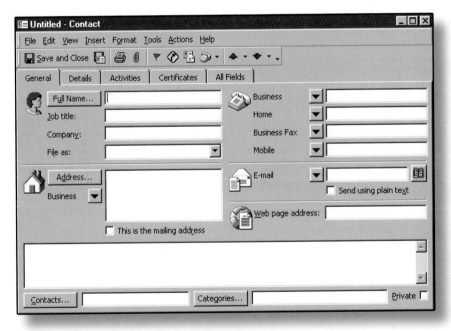

S TEP-BY-STEP ▷ 2.1

1. Click the **Contacts** icon on the Outlook Bar. The Contacts screen appears, similar to Figure 2-1.

2. Click the **New Contact** icon on the toolbar. The Contact dialog box appears as shown in Figure 2-2. Click the **General** tab, if it is not already chosen.

3. In the *Full Name* box, key **Mary Daly**.

4. Press **Tab**. The contact's name appears as *Daly, Mary* in the *File as* box.

(continued on next page)

5. In the *Job title* box, key **Sales Manager** and press **Tab**.

6. In the *Company* box, key **Northstar, Inc.** and press **Tab**.

7. For the remaining boxes, key the information as shown in Figure 2-3. If necessary, enlarge the Contact dialog box to see all your data entries.

8. After completing the information, click the **Save and New** button.

9. Add two more contacts using the information shown in Figure 2-4. When you are finished with the last contact, click **Save and Close** to return to the Contact screen.

10. Leave the Contacts list open for the next Step-by-Step.

 Extra Challenge

Add five more contacts, friends or family, to your Contacts list.

FIGURE 2-3
Your first contact

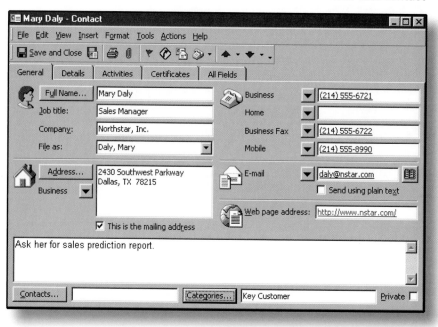

FIGURE 2-4
Add two more contacts

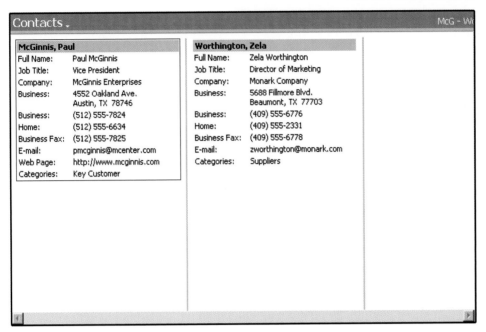

Viewing and Printing the Contact List

To change how you view your contacts, choose Current View from the View menu and then choose from the list of view options. The view options are described in Table 2-1. Address Cards is the default view.

To print your Contacts list, choose Print from the File menu. The Print dialog box opens. The *Print style* box provides different options depending on what view you are using. For example, you can choose to print your contacts as cards, booklets, or a phone list.

 Concept Builder

When using Address Cards view, you can click a letter on the bar on the right to quickly display contacts beginning with that letter.

TABLE 2-1
View options for contacts list

VIEW	DESCRIPTION
Address Cards	Default view displays general information on individual cards.
Detailed Address Cards	Displays detailed information about contacts on individual cards.
Phone List	Lists contacts in a table with all phone numbers included.
By Category	Groups contacts in a list according to category.
By Company	Groups contacts in a list according to company.
By Location	Groups contacts in a list according to country.
By Follow Up Flag	Groups contacts in a list according to follow-up dates.

1. With the Contacts screen displayed, choose **Current View** from the **View** menu.

2. Choose **Detailed Address Cards** from the pull-down menu. Your screen should appear similar to Figure 2-5.

3. Choose **Current View** from the **View** menu.

4. Choose **Phone List** from the pull-down menu.

5. Choose **Print** from the **File** menu. The Print dialog box appears.

6. In the *Print style* box, **Table Style** should already be highlighted. Click **OK**.

7. The Contacts list will print as a phone list.

8. Leave Outlook open for the next step-by-step.

Concept Builder

Creating a Contacts list makes it easy to communicate with others. To send an e-mail message to a contact, choose New Message to Contact from the Actions menu, key the message, then click Send. You will learn more about sending e-mail messages later in this lesson.

FIGURE 2-5
Contacts screen in Detailed Address Cards view

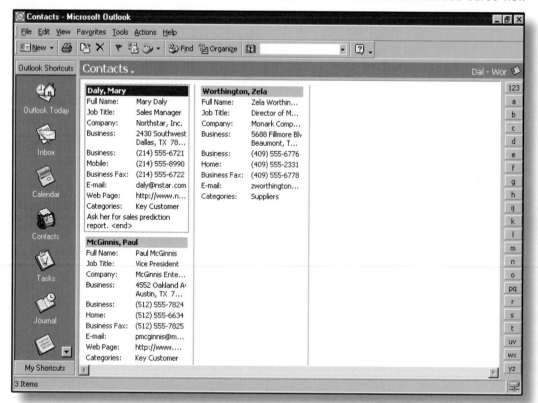

Using Outlook Today

Outlook Today gathers information about today's activities from Calendar, Tasks, and Mail and summarizes the information on one screen. You can display the Outlook Today screen, shown in Figure 2-6, by clicking the Outlook Today icon on the Outlook Bar.

FIGURE 2-6
Outlook Today screen

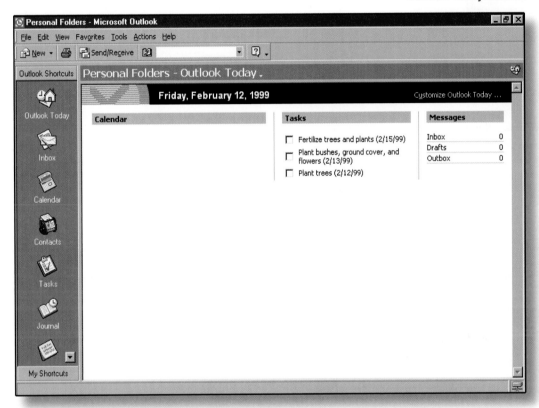

On the Outlook Today screen, the Calendar section displays the appointments for the day. The next appointment is flagged with an arrow and appointments earlier in the day display in a lighter type. The Messages section contains the number of unread messages. The Tasks section lists the previously entered tasks. When finished with a task, click the check box to add a check mark. The task displays with a strike through the text. To move around Outlook quickly, simply click on the icon or heading to each section.

To customize the Outlook Today screen, click *Customize Outlook Today* at the top of the screen. A list of options for customizing will display as shown in Figure 2-7. Click the check box next to *When starting, go directly to Outlook Today,* to automatically display the Outlook Today screen every time Outlook is started. You can also choose the message folders and how many days of your Calendar to display. In your task list you can sort and display all the tasks or only the tasks for the day. Different styles for the Outlook Today screen are also available.

FIGURE 2-7
Customizing the Outlook Today screen

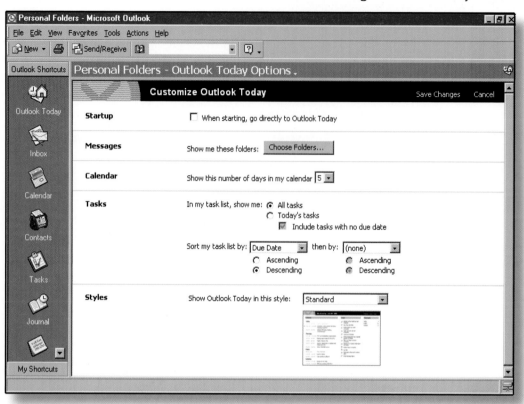

STEP-BY-STEP ▷ 2.3

1. Click the **Outlook Today** icon on the Outlook Bar. The Outlook Today screen appears, similar to Figure 2-6. (*Note:* Your screen will appear differently, depending upon items that you have deleted.)

2. Click **Customize Outlook Today** at the top of the screen. The Options screen for Outlook displays as shown in Figure 2-7.

3. Click to insert a check in the box next to **When starting, go directly to Outlook Today**. The Outlook Today screen will automatically appear every time Outlook is started.

4. Click **Save Changes** at the top of the screen to go back to the Outlook Today screen.

5. Click **Tasks** at the top of the screen to display the Tasks screen.

6. Click the **New Task** icon and create a task using today's date and the information shown in Figure 2-8.

7. When finished, click **Save and Close**. Click the **Outlook Today** icon on the Outlook Bar to return to the Outlook Today screen.

8. Click the **Calendar** icon to display the Calendar screen.

9. Create a new appointment using today's date and the information shown in Figure 2-9.

10. When finished, return to the Outlook Today screen. The new appointment displays in the Calendar section.

11. Leave Outlook open for the next Step-by-Step.

FIGURE 2-8
Add a task

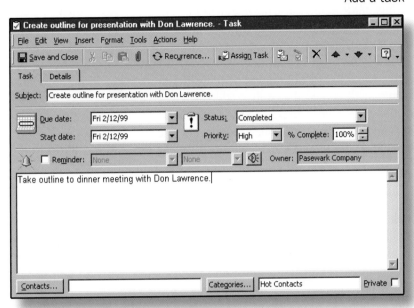

FIGURE 2-9
Add an appointment

Using E-mail

One of the most common and most useful services of the Internet is *electronic mail (e-mail),* the use of a computer network to send and receive messages. The value of e-mail is that it is faster than *snail mail* (the United States Postal Service method of delivering letters), less expensive, and more efficient, since it allows you to send a message to more than one person at the same time. E-mail is global and it is environment-friendly, since it does not require paper or fuel.

To use electronic mail, you need an e-mail address. The address includes your name; your host, server, or domain name; and an extension that tells whether the account is at a school, business, government location, or another country. No one has your unique e-mail address. E-mail addresses look like this:

> *dateline@abc.com*
> *president@whitehouse.gov*

Using Outlook 2000, you can send e-mail messages to others connected by your Intranet or if you have an Internet connection, to anyone around the world whom also has an Internet connection. E-mail has transformed business and personal communication to become an efficient and often preferred way to communicate with clients, co-workers, friends, and family. Your software will need to be configured with the appropriate profile and service settings to send and receive e-mail.

When you open Outlook, the Outlook Today screen should appear. Click the Inbox icon on the Outlook Bar to display the Inbox screen, as shown in Figure 2-10. Click the My Shortcuts button at the bottom of the Outlook bar to display a group of mail icons. Each icon represents a folder, such as the Drafts folder where unsent items are stored. The Outbox stores outgoing mail and Sent Items stores the e-mail messages you've sent. Click an icon to view its contents.

Double-click a message in the Inbox to open it. After reading a message, you can send a reply to the author of the message by clicking the Reply button on the toolbar. You can also print the message or click the Next Item button to read your next message.

To send e-mail, choose New Mail Message from the Actions menu or click the New Mail Message button on the toolbar. A blank e-mail message appears, like that shown in Figure 2-11. In the *To* box, key the e-mail address of the person to whom you are sending the message. You can send a copy of the message to someone by keying his or her e-mail address in the *Cc* box. Key the subject of your message in the *Subject* box and key your message in the message window.

Just as you did in other Office programs, you can use the buttons on the Formatting toolbar to change the font, size, color, style, and alignment of text in your message. You can also save and print the message or check its spelling. You can even attach a file to an e-mail message. When you're finished writing your message, you can send it by clicking the Send button on the toolbar.

FIGURE 2-10

Send and receive e-mail using Outlook

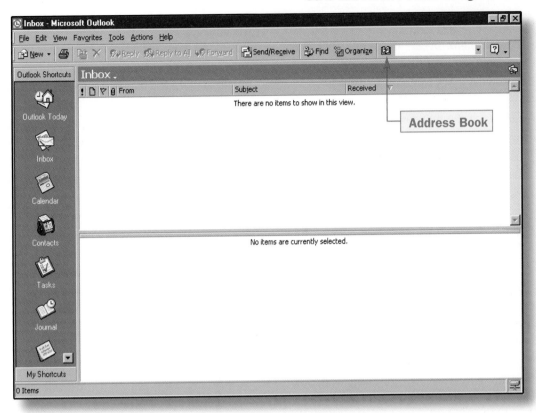

FIGURE 2-11

Blank e-mail message

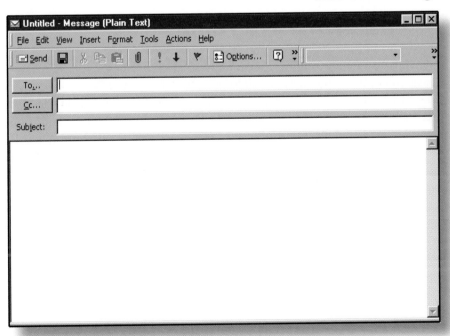

1. Click the **Inbox** button on the Outlook bar. Your screen should look similar to Figure 2-10, with the Inbox contents displayed.

2. Double-click the message from Microsoft, or another message, if you have one, in your Inbox. Scroll through and read the message. Notice all the formatting features used in the message.

3. Choose **Close** from the **File** menu. The message closes.

4. Click the **New Mail Message** button. A blank e-mail message form appears, as shown in Figure 2-11.

5. Key your e-mail address, or one provided by your instructor, in the *To* box.

6. Key **test** in the *Subject* box.

7. In the message window, key **This is a test**.

8. Click the **Send** button. Your mail is sent, and if Outlook is set up correctly for Intranet e-mail, you should receive the message in a few moments. (If you only have Internet e-mail, you'll need to choose **Remote Mail** from the **Tools** menu and **Connect** from the submenu.)

9. Click the **My Shortcuts** button on the Outlook Bar to display the mail icons.

10. Click the **Sent Items** icon on the Outlook Bar. The message you sent should be there. (*Note:* It may take a few minutes for your message to display.)

11. Click the **Outbox** icon on the Outlook bar. If the message you sent wasn't in your Sent Items folder, it is here.

12. Leave Outlook open for the next Step-by-Step.

Creating an Address Book

Most of the time you will be sending e-mail messages to the same people. To make sending an e-mail message easier, you can access names and addresses from an Address Book listing the ones that you use most often. The Address Book information is automatically created when you add a new contact to your contacts list. The Address Book includes the contact's name, e-mail address, and phone numbers.

To display the Address Book from the Inbox screen, choose Address Book from the Tools menu or click the Address Book button on the toolbar. The Address Book dialog box appears, as shown in Figure 2-12. To add a new contact click the New button and choose New Contact from the pull-down menu. The Properties dialog box appears, as shown in Figure 2-13. When you are done adding information about the contact, click OK to return to the Address Book dialog box. The new contact should display in the Address Book.

To display the more detailed information on a contact listed in the Address Book, click the contact's name and wait for a box to display with the information.

FIGURE 2-12
Address Book dialog box

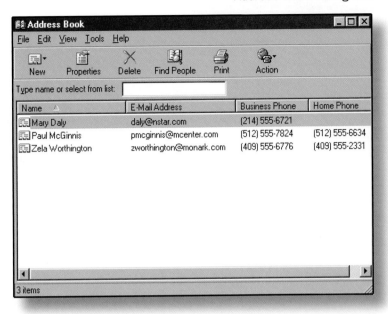

FIGURE 2-13
Properties dialog box

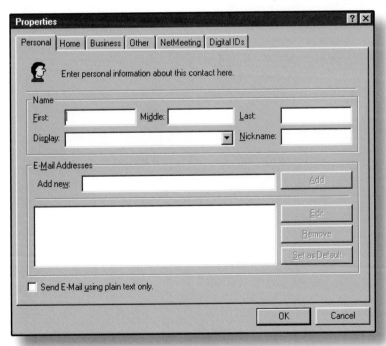

1. Click the **Inbox** button on the Outlook Bar to display the Inbox contents.

2. Display the Address Book by clicking the **Address Book** button on the toolbar. The Address Book dialog box displays as shown in Figure 2-12.

3. Click the **New** button and choose **New Contact** from the pull-down menu. The Properties dialog box displays as shown in Figure 2-13.

4. In the *First* box, key your **First Name**.

5. In the *Last* box, key your **Last Name**. The *Display* box should show your first and last names.

6. In the *Add new* box, key your e-mail address, or one provided by your instructor.

7. Click **OK**. The Address Book dialog box reappears with your name added to the list.

8. Click **Zela Worthington** and wait for a box to display the more detailed information added earlier to the Contact screen.

9. When finished viewing, choose **Close** from the **File** menu to return to the Inbox screen.

Using an Address Book

To display the Address Book from a blank e-mail message form, click Address Book from the Tools menu. The Select Names dialog box appears with names from your contacts list, as shown in Figure 2-14. Choose the contact to receive the message and click *To->*. The contact will appear in the *Message Recipients* box. Click OK and the contact's name appears in the *To...* box as the recipient of the e-mail message. When finished with your e-mail message, click the Send button on the toolbar.

FIGURE 2-14
Select Names dialog box

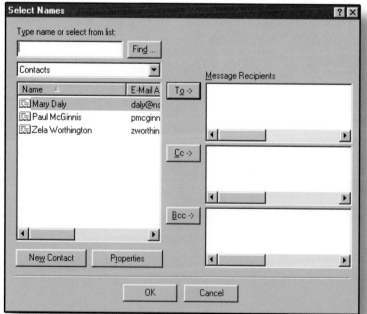

STEP-BY-STEP ⇨ 2.6

1. From the Inbox screen, create an e-mail message by clicking the **New Mail Message** button on the toolbar. A blank e-mail message form appears.

2. Choose **Address Book** from the **Tools** menu. The Select Names dialog box appears.

3. Highlight **Your Name** from the list of contacts and click the **To->** box. Your name will appear in the *Message Recipients* box.

4. Click **OK**. Your are the recipient of the e-mail message.

5. Key **Tomorrow's meeting** in the *Subject* box.

6. In the message window, key **Don't forget tomorrow's meeting at 1:30.**

7. Click the **Send** button.

8. Click the **My Shortcuts** button on the Outlook Bar to display the mail icons.

9. Click the **Sent Items** or the **Outbox** icon on the Outlook Bar to see the sent message.

10. Choose **Exit** from the **File** menu to close Outlook.

11. The Outlook screen closes and the Microsoft Windows 98 desktop appears.

Summary

In this lesson, you learned:

- You can create and use a Contacts list to store mail, phone, and other information about people and companies with whom you communicate. You can view or print your Contacts in several ways including as address cards or as a phone list.

- Outlook Today gathers information about today's activities from Calendar, Tasks, and Mail and summarizes the information on one screen. You can display the Outlook Today screen by clicking the Outlook Today icon on the Outlook Bar.

- The value of e-mail is that it is faster than snail mail, less expensive, and more efficient than snail mail, since it allows you to send a message to one or more persons. E-mail is global and it is environment-friendly, since it does not require paper or fuel.

- Using Outlook 2000, you can send e-mail messages to others connected to your network or if you have an Internet connection to anyone around the world who also has an Internet connection.

- Most of the time you will be sending e-mail messages to the same people. To make sending an e-mail message easier, you can use an Address Book listing the addresses that you use most often.

TRUE/FALSE

Circle T if the statement is true or F if the statement is false.

T F 1. The default view for Contacts is Phone List.

T F 2. In Outlook, the Inbox displays your new mail.

T F 3. The General tab on the Contacts dialog box is where you can store additional information about a contact such as department, birthday, or nickname.

T F 4. You can customize Outlook to automatically display the Outlook Today screen every time Outlook is started.

T F 5. The Address Book information is automatically created when you add a new contact to your contacts list.

WRITTEN QUESTIONS

Write a brief answer to the following questions.

1. What is a contact?

2. What are the advantages of e-mail over snail mail?

3. Name three types of contact information the General tab includes.

4. Outlook Today summarizes information about today's activities from what three areas of Outlook?

5. What information is contained in an Address Book?

LESSON 2 PROJECTS

PROJECT 2-1

You recently met two people to add to your contacts list.

1. Display the Contacts screen.

2. Add the two contacts using this information. Save and close when finished.

    Name: **Todd McKee**
    Job Title: **Associate Professor**
    Company: **Clark Junior College**
    Address: **1880 Holst-Grubbe Road**
    Berkshire, VT 53217
    Business Phone: **(420) 555-7642**
    Business Fax: **(420) 555-7644**
    E-mail: **t_mckee@cjc.edu**

    Name: **Claire Hunter**
    Job Title: **Head Pro**
    Company: **Litchfield Tennis Club**
    Address: **34 Segalla Lane**
    Litchfield, PA 60211
    Home Phone: **(709) 555-0901**
    E-mail: **hunter@spoloc.org**

3. View the Contacts list as Address Cards.

4. View the Contacts list as a Phone List.

5. Leave Outlook open for the next project.

PROJECT 2-2

Add the following tasks to prepare for a monthly staff meeting.

1. Display the Outlook Today screen.

2. Using the Tasks section, create a new task with today's date and with **Create agenda for staff meeting** as the subject.

3. Set the due date for today. Set the priority as **High**.

4. Do not set a reminder.

5. In the text box, key **Allow time for each staff member to give a project update**.

6. Add a new category called **Staff Meetings** to the *Categories* list.

7. Save and close the task.

8. Create another task with today's date and with **Send e-mail message** as the subject.

9. Set the due date for today.

10. Do not set a reminder.

11. In the text box, key **Meeting is today at 2:00 p.m. in Conference Room A**.

12. Assign the task to the category **Staff Meetings**.

13. Save and close the task.

14. When finished, go back to the Outlook Today screen and mark the tasks as completed.

15. Leave Outlook open for the next project.

PROJECT 2-3

Add the staff meeting to the calendar.

1. Display the Outlook Today screen.

2. Using the Calendar section, create a new appointment for today from **2:00** to **3:30 p.m.**

3. Key the subject **Staff Meeting** and the location **Conference Room A**.

4. Do not set a reminder.

5. In the text box, key **Take 15 copies of agenda**.

6. Assign the appointment to category **Staff Meeting**. Save and close the appointment.

7. When finished, go back to the Outlook Today screen and the new appointment should display in the Calendar section.

8. Leave Outlook open for the next project.

PROJECT 2-4

Create and send an e-mail message to your staff concerning today's meeting.

1. Display the Inbox screen.

2. Create a new mail message and key your e-mail address or the e-mail address of a classmate in the *To* box.

3. Key **Monthly Staff Meeting** as the subject.

4. In the message window, key **Meeting held in Conference Room A from 2:00 to 3:30 p.m. Be prepared to give an update on projects**.

5. Send the message.

6. Choose **Sent Items** or **Outbox** on the My Shortcuts bar. The message should be listed in either folder.

7. Open the message to read. When finished, close the message.

8. Leave Outlook open for the next project.

PROJECT 2-5

Create and send an e-mail message to yourself about the meeting next Tuesday.

1. Open the **Address Book** from the Inbox screen.

2. Create a new e-mail message and send it to yourself. Access your e-mail address from the Address Book.

3. Key **New Sales Promotion** as the subject.

4. In the message window, key **Meeting next Tuesday on the new sales promotion plan in Conference Room A, 2 – 3:00 p.m. Be prepared to discuss.**

5. Send the message.

6. Choose **Sent Items** or **Outbox** on the My Shortcuts bar to see the sent message.

7. Choose **Exit** from the **File** menu to close Outlook.

8. The Outlook screen closes and the Microsoft Windows 98 desktop appears.

CRITICAL THINKING

ACTIVITY 2-1

Design an Outlook Today screen for your supervisor using the customizing options. Explain in a short paragraph why you chose the particular options.

ACTIVITY 2-2

Use the Help system to find out how to drag and drop a name and address from a Word document into the Outlook contact list. Write down the basic steps.

Introduction to Microsoft Outlook

COMMAND SUMMARY

FEATURE	MENU COMMAND	TOOLBAR BUTTON	LESSON
Add a Contact	Actions, New Contact	New	2
Add a Journal Entry	Actions, New Journal Entry		1
Add a Meeting	Actions, Plan a Meeting		1
Add an All Day Event	Actions, New All Day Event		1
Add an Appointment	Actions, New Appointment		1
Add a Note	Actions, New Note		1
Add a Task	Actions, New Task		1
Add More Buttons			1
Address Book	Tools, Address Book		2
Change Views	View, Current View		1
Daily Calendar View	View, Day	Day	1
Delete an Appointment	Edit, Delete	X	1
Delete an Event	Edit, Delete	X	1
Exit Outlook	File, Exit		1
Go to Today		Go to Today	1
Group Tasks	View, Current View, Customize Current View, Group By		1
Monthly Calendar View	View, Month	Month	1
My Shortcuts		My Shortcuts	1
New Mail Message	Actions, New Mail Message	New	2
Print	File, Print		1
Print Preview	File, Print Preview		1

Recurring Appointment	Actions, New Recurring Appointment	↻ Recurrence	1
Save and Close	File, Save and Close	🖫 Save and Close	1
Sort Tasks	View, Current View, Customize Current View, Sort		1
Start Outlook	Start, Programs, Microsoft Outlook		1
Weekly Calendar View	View, Week	7 Week	1
Work Week Calendar View	View, Work Week	5 Work Week	1

REVIEW QUESTIONS

TRUE/FALSE

Circle T if the statement is true or F if the statement is false.

T F 1. A boldface date in the Date Navigator means an activity is scheduled for that day.

T F 2. Resources are people you invite to a meeting.

T F 3. Choose Current View from the View menu to change how you view your contacts.

T F 4. Use the Journal Entry dialog box to record entries manually.

T F 5. Exit Outlook by choosing Quit from the File menu.

WRITTEN QUESTIONS

Write a brief answer to the following questions.

1. What option do you use in the Appointment dialog box to prevent others from viewing the information?

2. How do you change an appointment?

3. What button on the Outlook bar do you click to display the mail icons?

4. How do you mark a task as complete?

5. How do you change the color of a note?

APPLICATIONS ▽

APPLICATION 1

Add the following tasks to prepare for an upcoming sales conference.

1. Display the **Tasks** screen.

2. Create a new task **Create agenda for sales conference in July** as the subject and due this Friday.

3. Set a reminder for **3:00 p.m**. on Friday. Set the priority as **High**.

4. In the text box, key **Call Dave Lowry for conference schedule and planned activities**. Save and close the Task dialog box.

5. Add a new category called **Sales Conference** and assign the task to it.

6. Create another task. Key **Write memo to send with the agenda.** as the subject. Make it due the following Monday.

7. Set a reminder for **1:00 p.m**. on Monday. Set the status as **In Progress**.

8. Set the percent complete as **50%**.

9. In the text box, key **Ask Molly to create labels from the sales mailing list**.

10. Assign the task to the category **Sales Conference**. Save and close the Task dialog box.

11. View the tasks in **Detailed List** view.

12. Leave Outlook open for the next application.

APPLICATION 2

You work for a local advertising agency during the day and attend classes at Southwest University in the evenings. Add an appointment with your advisor to discuss your classes for next semester. Also, add a friend's birthday so you don't forget it.

1. Display the **Calendar** screen.

2. Create a new appointment for tomorrow from **5:00 p.m**. to **5:30 p.m.**

3. In the subject box, key **Meet with advisor at school**.

4. In the location box, key **Business Education building, Room 2c**.

5. Set a reminder for **30 minutes** before the appointment.

6. Show the time as **Out of Office**.

7. In text box, key **Take class schedule for next semester**.

8. Assign the appointment to the **Personal** category. Save and close the Appointment dialog box.

9. Use the Date Navigator to select **September 12** of next year.

10. Create a new all day event and key **Sarah's birthday** in the subject box.

11. Choose a **yearly** recurrence pattern and set a reminder for **1 day** before the birthday.

12. Assign the event to the **Personal** category. Save and close the Event dialog box.

13. Leave Outlook open for the next application.

APPLICATION 3

After attending a sales convention in Austin, Texas, you have two new contacts to add to your Contacts list and Address Book.

1. Display the **Contacts** screen.

2. Add the two contacts using this information.

Name: **Brad Gatlin**
Job Title: **Sales Manager**
Company: **Software Specific, Inc.**
Address: **2190 Metric Blvd.**
  Austin, TX 78712
Business Phone: **(512) 555-9267**
Business Fax: **(512) 555-9269**
E-mail: **b_gatlin@softspec.com**

Name: **Rebecca McInturf**
Job Title: **Design Specialist**
Company: **Office Concepts**
Address: **610 W. Broadway**
  Lubbock, TX 79412
Business Phone: **(806) 555-8844**
Home Phone: **(806) 555-9241**
E-mail: **rmcinturf@offcon.com**

3. View the Contacts list as Address Cards.

4. View the Contacts list as a Phone List.

5. When finished, display the Address Book to view the contacts.

6. Leave Outlook open for the next application.

APPLICATION 4

1. Display the **Outlook Today** screen.

2. Click **Calendar** and add your birthday as a recurring event.

3. Click **Tasks** and add a task to today that you need to complete for school or for yourself.

4. When finished, go back to the Outlook Today screen and mark all tasks as completed.

5. Exit Outlook.

SCANS

You work at the Java Internet Café, which has been open a short time. The café serves coffee, other beverages, and pastries, and offers Internet access. Seven computers are set up on tables along the north side of the store. Customers can come in and have a cup of coffee and a Danish, and explore the World Wide Web.

Your manager asks you to write a letter to Mary Daly, a new contact recently added to the contact list. The message should include an invitation to the shop for a free specialty drink.

JOB 1

1. Open Outlook and display the Inbox screen. Click the **New Mail Message** button to open the Message dialog box.

2. In the *To* box, key Mary Daly's e-mail address. (*Hint:* Refer to your Contacts list for the address.)

3. In the Subject box, key **Java Internet Café**.

4. In the Text box, key the following:

    Mary,

    I enjoyed visiting with you at the last meeting of the Small Business Owners Association. Please let me know if I can be of any help in your new position as leader of the School Volunteer Project.

    Also, I am sending you an invitation to visit the Java Internet Café located at Highway 45 and Loop 210 in the Oakdale Shopping Center.

    The Java Internet Café is a coffee shop with a twist. While enjoying one of our specialty drinks such as a Café au lait and a danish, you can access the Internet and explore the World Wide Web on one of our seven high-speed computers.

    Visit us soon and bring a copy of this e-mail message with you for a free specialty drink. I hope you enjoy your visit at the Java Internet Café.

5. Do not send the message. Choose **Close** from the **File** menu. Click **No** when prompted to save your changes.

6. Exit Outlook.

UNIT

INTRODUCTION TO MICROSOFT® PUBLISHER & MICROSOFT® FRONTPAGE

lesson 1   1.5 hrs.

Publisher Basics

lesson 2   2 hrs.

FrontPage Basics

Estimated Time for Unit: 3.5 hours

PUBLISHER BASICS

OBJECTIVES

Upon completion of this lesson, you should be able to:

■ Start Publisher and create a project using the Wizard.

■ Identify parts of the Publisher screen.

■ Open and edit an existing Publisher project.

■ Create your own Publisher project. **⏱ Estimated Time: 1.5 hours**

Introduction to Publisher

Publisher is a desktop publishing program you can use to create a wide assortment of documents, such as business cards and restaurant menus. Publisher contains hundreds of pre-designed templates you can use as the basis for professional-looking projects. All you have to do is add your own custom touches.

Starting Publisher

To start Microsoft Publisher, click the Start button on the taskbar, click Programs, and then choose Microsoft Publisher. Publisher starts and the Catalog dialog box appears, as shown in Figure 1-1.

FIGURE 1-1
Microsoft Publisher Catalog dialog box

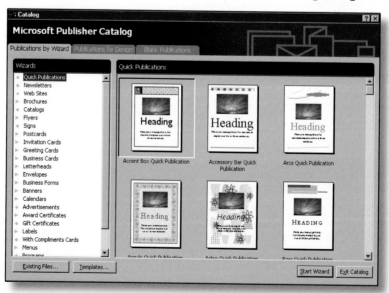

S TEP-BY-STEP ▷ 1.1

1. Click the **Start** button on the taskbar to open the Start menu.

2. Click **Programs** to open the Programs menu.

3. Click **Microsoft Publisher** to start the program. The Catalog dialog box appears, as shown in Figure 1-1. Leave the dialog box open for the next Step-by-Step.

Concept Builder

You can open the Catalog dialog box at any time by selecting **New** on the **File** menu.

Opening a Project

The Microsoft Publisher Catalog contains three tabs—*Publications by Wizard*, *Publications by Design*, and *Blank Publications*. Each is explained below.

PUBLICATIONS BY WIZARD

Wizards are predesigned templates of various types of publications. They provide the framework for the publication, and all you have to do is add your own custom touches. Publisher comes with more than 20 wizards. When you select a wizard from the *Wizards* list, the available designs for that type of publication are shown in the window on the right. In Figure 1-1, notice that there are diamonds or triangles next to some of the wizards. When you select a wizard with a triangle next to it, a list of subcategories appears. These subcategories represent more specific projects. Wizards with diamonds do not have additional subcategories.

PUBLICATIONS BY DESIGN

This option lets you create a series of documents (letterheads, business cards, envelopes, etc.) that incorporate the same design. This option also contains design sets that offer specific layouts for special events, holidays, and fundraising.

BLANK PUBLICATIONS

You can use this option to create your own publication from scratch using whatever format, colors, and designs you prefer.

Concept Builder

Click the **Existing Files** button in the Microsoft Publisher Catalog window to open any files you have previously saved.

S TEP-BY-STEP ▷ 1.2

1. With the Publications by Wizard tab displayed, click **Business Cards** in the Wizards list. A variety of designs appear on the right (see Figure 1-2). The **Accent Box Business Card** template should be selected as shown in Figure 1-2.

2. Click the **Start Wizard** button. An Introduction to the Business

Card Wizard appears on the left side of the screen. See Figure 1-3. The Accent Box template appears on the right side of the screen.

3. If a dialog box appears that prompts you to enter personal information, skip to steps 10–16, and then return to step 4.

(continued on next page)

P F - 3

4. Click the **Next** button at the bottom of the Business Card Wizard Introduction. The wizard prompts you to choose a color scheme. The Waterfall scheme should be selected. If it is not selected click on it, and then click **Next**.

5. The wizard prompts you to choose between portrait or landscape orientation. Click **Landscape**, and click **Next**.

6. The wizard asks if you want to include a placeholder for your logo on your card. Click **Yes** and click **Next**.

7. The Wizard asks how you want to print your business cards. Click **Several tiled on the page**, and then click the **Next** button.

8. You are prompted to select a personal information set for this project. Publisher comes with four personal information sets in which you enter data about yourself and your company. Click **Primary Business**, if necessary, and click the **Update** button. The Personal Information dialog box opens, as shown in Figure 1-4.

9. In the *Choose a personal information set to edit* box, select **Primary Business**, if necessary.

10. In the *Name* box, key **Mike Wytokay**.

11. In the *Address* box, key the following:

    10401 University Avenue
    Suite 4505
    Lubbock, TX 79494-4505

12. In the *Phone/fax/e-mail* box, key the following:

    Phone: 806-555-6100
    Fax: 806-555-6101
    E-mail: mwytokay@solutions.com

13. In the *Organization name* box, key **Computer Solutions**.

14. In the *Tag line or motto* box, key **Hardware & Software Solutions**.

15. In the *Job or position title* box, key **Technician**.

16. Click the **Update** button to close the Personal Information dialog box.

Hot Tip

You can use the **Back** button to make any corrections before finishing the wizard.

17. Click the **Finish** button at the bottom of the Wizard window to complete your business card. If a message box appears, asking you to save your work, click **Yes**. Your card should look like the one in Figure 1-5.

18. Save the file as **Card**, followed by your initials. Leave the file open for the next Step-by-Step.

FIGURE 1-2
Business Cards wizard

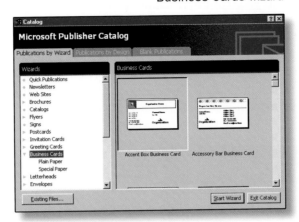

FIGURE 1-3
Business Card Wizard Introduction

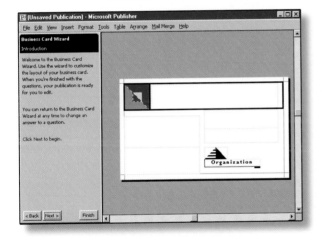

FIGURE 1-4
Personal Information dialog box

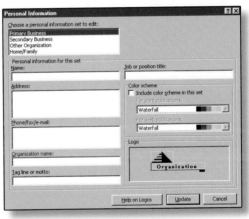

FIGURE 1-5
Finished business card

Adding a Logo

You can make changes to your card by clicking the name of the item you want to change in the Business Card Wizard list. You can also make changes by clicking on the item directly in the window. For example, if you wanted to change the title of Technician, you simply click on the item, and a blinking cursor appears, signaling that you can key a new title.

If you want to create a new logo for the card, you simply click on the existing logo. A Logo Creation Wizard icon appears. Click the icon to start the Logo Creation Wizard. Publisher lets you edit the current logo, add a Publisher-created logo, or add a logo of your own.

S TEP-BY-STEP ▷ 1.3

1. Click the logo portion of your business card to select it, as shown in Figure 1-6.

2. Click the **Logo Creation Wizard** icon. The Logo Creation Wizard dialog box appears, as shown in Figure 1-7.

3. Click **Design** in the upper pane. The lower pane lists the different types of designs available.

4. Click the **Foundation Bar** design. Notice that the logo design has changed. Click the Logo Creation Wizard close button. A message box appears asking if you want to save your document. Click **Yes**. Your business card should look similar to the one in Figure 1-8.

5. Select the word *Organization* in the logo part of your business card. The red box around the text indicates that you are able to edit it.

6. Key **Computer Solutions**. Click outside the red text box to close it.

7. Save the file by clicking the **Save** button on the toolbar. If a message appears asking if you want to save the modified logo, click **Yes**.

8. Choose **Print** on the **File** menu. In the print dialog box, click **OK** to print your business card.

9. Close the business card file by selecting **Close** on the **File** menu. Remain in the Publisher screen for the next Step-by-Step.

FIGURE 1-6
Editing the logo

FIGURE 1-7
Logo Creation Wizard dialog box

FIGURE 1-8
Modifying the logo design

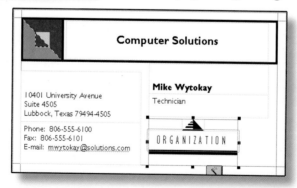

Publications by Design

The Publications by Design options let you apply the same design, information, and logo to an entire series of documents. This allows you to produce documents without changing the format for each document.

STEP-BY-STEP ▷ 1.4

1. Open the Catalog dialog box by selecting **New** on the **File** menu. Click the **Publications by Design** tab.

2. Click **Accent Box** in the *Design Sets* pane. The Accent Box templates appear on the right side of the screen.

3. Scroll down through the Accent Box templates, and click **Accent Box Special Offer Flyer**.

4. Click the **Start Wizard** button. The Flyer Wizard appears on the left side of the screen and a template of the flyer appears on the right side of the screen. The template display allows you to see the changes occur as you complete the wizard steps.

5. Read the introduction and click the **Next** button at the bottom of the Flyer Wizard. The wizard prompts you to choose a color scheme. The Waterfall scheme should be selected. If it is not selected, click it and then click **Next**.

6. The wizard asks if you want to include a placeholder for a graphic. Click **Yes** and click **Next**.

7. The wizard asks which elements you would like to add to your flyer. Choose **Coupon** and click **Next**.

8. The wizard asks if you would like to include a placeholder for your customer's address. Click **No**, and then click **Next**.

9. You are prompted to select a personal information set. Choose **Primary Business**, if nec-

essary, and click the **Update** button to display the Personal Information dialog box. If the data from Step-by-Step 1.2 is still in the Primary Business set, click **Cancel**, and skip to step 18.

10. In the *Choose a personal information set to edit* box, select **Primary Business**, if necessary.

11. In the *Name* box, key **Mike Wytokay**.

12. In the *Address* box, key this address:

```
10401 University Avenue
Suite 4505
Lubbock, Texas 79494-4505
```

13. In the *Phone/fax/e-mail* box, key the following:

```
Phone: 806-555-6100
Fax: 806-555-6101
E-mail: mwytokay@solutions.com
```

14. In the *Organization* name box, key **Computer Solutions**.

15. In the *Tag line or motto* box, key **Hardware & Software Solutions**.

16. In the *Job or position title* box, key **Technician**.

17. Click the **Update** button to close the Personal Information window.

18. Click the **Finish** button at the bottom of the wizard pane. Your flyer should look similar to Figure 1-9.

19. Save the file as **Flyer**, followed by your initials. Leave the publication on screen for the next Step-by-Step.

(continued on next page)

FIGURE 1-9
Completed flyer

You can make changes to the flyer using the same methods you applied to your business card.

STEP-BY-STEP ⇨ 1.5

1. Click the **Promotion Title** portion of the flyer, as shown in Figure 1-10. This allows you to edit the title.

2. Key **Spring Cleaning Sale**. Center the text by clicking the **Center** alignment button on the toolbar.

3. In the *Date of Sale* box, key in next Saturday's date. You may need to click the **Zoom In (+)** button on the toolbar to enlarge your edit area.

> Select Zoom on the View menu to change the view to one of the percentages listed on the submenu.

4. In the *Time of Sale* box, key **8:00 a.m. - 6:00 p.m.**

5. Click in the box that asks you to describe your location, and key **Located next to Willow Park Mall**.

6. Click on the **Free Offer** logo, and key **FREE Mouse Pad**.

7. With the logo still selected, click the **Wizard** icon. The Attention Getter Creation Wizard dialog box appears.

8. Click the **Shadowed Slant** design. Notice how the logo design changes. Click outside the dialog box to close it. Your flyer should look similar to the one in Figure 1-11.

9. Double-click on the picture in your flyer. The Insert Clip Art dialog box appears.

Concept Builder

You can also open the Insert Clip Art dialog box by choosing Picture on the Insert menu and Clip Art on the submenu.

10. In the *Search for Clips* box, key **Computer**, and press **Enter**.

11. Click a picture of a computer that you like.

12. A menu with four icons appears to the right of the picture. Click the first icon, **Insert clip**.

13. Close the Insert Clip Art dialog box. Notice that the picture on your flyer has changed.

14. Click in the box that contains the phone number, and key **806-555-6100**.

15. Click in the tag line box, and select **Hardware & Software Solutions**.

16. Change the font size of the tag line to **20**.

17. Click in the text box under the picture to select all the text. Key the following:

    We are putting everything that your computer needs on sale. From audio cards to disk drives we will meet your every computer need. We provide the latest technology, great pricing, and continuous service and support to keep your system running at its peak performance.

    With any purchase of hardware or software over $25, you will receive a free Computer Solutions mouse pad. Receive 15% off any purchase over $100 when you present the coupon below.

FIGURE 1-10
Editing the flyer

18. Click in the box that contains the text "List items here," and center the text by clicking the **Center** alignment button on the toolbar.

19. Key in the text below. Delete bullets if they appear automatically.

    Computers
    Printers
    Monitors
    Wide Selection of Software
    Service & Support

20. Click the **Name of Item or Service** text box on the coupon. Key **Any Purchase Over $100**.

21. Click the **00% OFF** text box. Key **15% OFF**.

22. Click in the box that asks you to describe your location, and key **Located next to Willow Park Mall**. You may need to click the **Zoom In** button to enlarge your edit area.

23. Click in the box that contains the phone number. Key **806-555-6100**.

24. Click in the box that contains the expiration date and key next Saturday's date.

25. Print your flyer. Then, save and close the file.

FIGURE 1-11
Flyer with Attention Getter

Summary

In this lesson, you learned:

■ Microsoft Publisher is a program that allows you to produce professional-looking documents in almost any format imaginable. Publisher makes this process even easier with the use of wizards.

■ Publisher wizards use a series of questions to direct you through the process of creating new documents. Your answers to the questions determine the outcome of your publication. You can also make changes to the publication once it has been created.

■ The Microsoft Publisher Catalog contains three options for creating publications: Publications by Wizard, Publications by Design, and Blank Publications. These options allow you to easily edit and create publications.

LESSON 1 REVIEW QUESTIONS

TRUE/FALSE

Circle T if the statement is true or F if the statement is false.

T F   1.   The Catalog dialog box automatically appears when you start Microsoft Publisher.

T F   2.   Publisher allows you to choose any color scheme that you want for your project.

T F   3.   You can open the Catalog at any time by choosing Catalog on the Open menu.

T F   4.   You cannot make any changes to your publication after you click the Finish button in a wizard.

T F   5.   A red box around text indicates that you are able to edit it.

WRITTEN QUESTIONS

Write a brief answer to the following questions.

1.   List the three options you have when you open the Publisher Catalog.

2. What does the Logo Creation Wizard let you do?

3. Which option in the Publisher Catalog allows you to create a series of documents (letterheads, business cards, and envelopes) with the same design?

4. What button in the Microsoft Publisher Catalog dialog box would you click to retrieve any files you have saved?

5. What does it mean when a Wizard category has a triangle next to it?

LESSON 1 PROJECTS

PROJECT 1-1

1. Start Publisher.

2. Click the **Existing Files** button in the Catalog dialog box to open the **Card** file.

3. Save the file as **Card1**, followed by your initials.

4. Use the Logo Creation Wizard to change the logo design from Foundation Bar to a **Crossed Corner** design.

5. Use the Logo Creation Wizard to add another line of text to the logo.

6. For the second line of text, key **Hardware & Software**.

7. Print the business cards.

8. Save the file and then close it.

PROJECT 1-2

1. Start Publisher, if necessary, and open the **Flyer** file.

2. Save the file as **Flyer1**, followed by your initials.

3. Use the Flyer Wizard to remove the coupon and add an order form.

4. Change the title of the order form to **Catalog Order Form**.

5. Print the flyer.

6. Save the file and then close it.

CRITICAL THINKING

ACTIVITY 1-1

SCANS

Use Publications by Wizard to create a business card that includes your name, a company or organization you are affiliated with, and colors of your choice. When you design your card, think about the impression you want the public to have about you and your organization.

ACTIVITY 1-2

SCANS

You are asked to add a picture frame to the picture inserted in the Flyer file you created in this lesson. Use the Help system to find information on picture frames and how to add them to existing documents. Write a brief essay that explains the procedure, and then add the frame to the Flyer document. Save the file as **Flyer with Frame**.

FRONTPAGE BASICS

OBJECTIVES

Upon completion of this lesson, you should be able to:

- Start FrontPage.

- Identify parts of the Page view screen.

- Create a Web page.

- Add pages to a Web and name them.

- Add a theme, banner, and navigation bars.

- Add text, a picture, and other formatting features.

- Add hyperlinks.

- View, print, and publish Web pages.

Estimated Time: 2 hours

Introduction to FrontPage

FrontPage is an Office 2000 application that can help you create professional-looking Web pages. A *Web page* combines text with audio, video, and animation in a graphical format that can be viewed on the Internet. Web pages are connected by *hyperlinks* that a user can click to jump from one Web page to another.

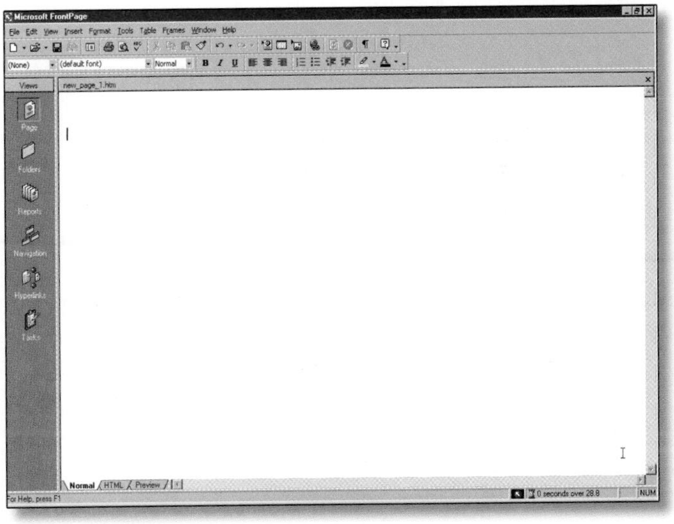

Starting FrontPage

FrontPage, like other Office 2000 applications, is started from the desktop screen in Windows 98. To start FrontPage, click the Start button, select Programs, and then choose Microsoft FrontPage. A screen displaying copyright information will appear briefly, followed by a blank page in Page view, as shown in Figure 2-1.

FIGURE 2-1
FrontPage opening screen

1. Click the **Start** button to open the Start menu.

2. Click **Programs**, then choose **Microsoft FrontPage**.

3. FrontPage starts and your screen appears in **Page** view.

4. Leave FrontPage on the screen for the next Step-by-Step.

> **Hot Tip**
>
> If your screen does not appear in Page view, click Page from the View menu.

Identifying Parts of the Page View Screen

When you start FrontPage, a blank page appears in *Page view* where you can edit Web pages. Buttons for other views are displayed in the *Views* bar on the left. To learn the purpose of each view, position the mouse pointer over its button and a screen tip appears with a description. To switch to another view, click its button. In this lesson, you will work in two views, Page and Navigation.

There are three tabs at the bottom of the Page view window. The Normal tab is what you will typically use to edit. The HTML (short for *HyperText Markup Language*) tab displays your page in HTML code so you can edit it directly. The Preview tab shows how your Web page will look when viewed by a Web browser. Click a tab to select it.

The Title bar, Menu bar, and Standard and Formatting toolbars are familiar parts of the screen that you have used in other Office 2000 applications. The Status bar across the bottom displays information and messages. For example, in Page view the Status bar gives an estimate of how long the page will take to download at a particular modem speed.

Creating a Web Page

To create a Web page, choose New from the File menu and Web from the submenu to display the New dialog box, as shown in Figure 2-2. Choose the template or wizard that you want to use from the group of displayed icons. The description of each is shown below the icon. You can specify a

> **Hot Tip**
>
> If the Folder List does not appear on your screen, click the Folder List button on the Standard toolbar.

location for the new Web page or click OK to accept the default. After you click OK, a Folder List appears on your screen, showing the folders and files FrontPage has created for your Web.

FIGURE 2-2
New dialog box

S TEP-BY-STEP ▷ 2.2

1. Choose **New** from the **File** menu and **Web** from the submenu to open the New dialog box.

2. If it is not already selected, click the **One Page Web** icon, then click **OK**. The Create New Web dialog box briefly appears while FrontPage is creating the Web page.

3. Click the **Navigation** button on the *Views* bar to switch to Navigation

view. Your screen should appear similar to Figure 2-3. (*Note:* If the Navigation toolbar is open on your screen, click the Title bar and drag the toolbar out of your way, or click the Close button (X) located in the upper right-hand corner.)

4. Leave the Web page open for the next Step-by-Step. You will add text to your Home page later in the lesson.

FIGURE 2-3
Navigation view

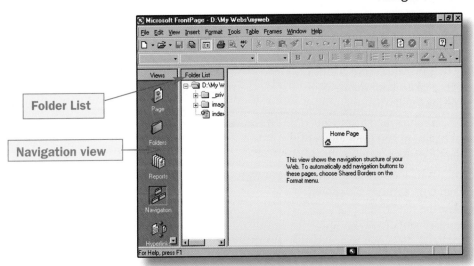

Adding Pages to a Web

After you create your Web page, you may want to add additional pages. The best place to do this is in *Navigation view*, so you can see the structure of your Web as you work. To add more pages, click the New Page button on the Standard toolbar.

Naming Pages

To name a page, click a page in Navigation view. The page color changes from yellow to blue to indicate it is selected. Click the text to select it and key a new name. You can also move from page to page by pressing the Tab key.

S TEP-BY-STEP ▷ 2.3

1. Click the **New Page** button on the Standard toolbar. A New Page 2 appears beneath the Home Page on your screen.

2. Click **New Page 2**, if it is not already highlighted in blue. Click inside the text box to highlight the text and key **Animals for Adoption.** Click **Home Page.**

(continued on next page)

3. Click the **New Page** toolbar button again. Click **New Page 2**, if it is not already highlighted in blue. Key **Volunteers/Donations** in the text box. Click **Home Page**.

4. Click the **New Page** toolbar button again. Click **New Page 2**, if it is not already highlighted in blue. Key **Links** in the text box. Your screen should now look similar to Figure 2-4.

5. Leave the Web on the screen for the next Step-by-Step.

FIGURE 2-4
Web in Navigation view

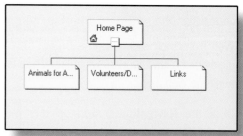

Adding a Theme to Your Web Page

FrontPage contains preset *themes* that allow you to apply designs and color schemes to either a single page or to your entire Web site. The Theme feature will also allow you to change the colors, graphics, and text to give your Web pages a consistent and professional appearance. To apply themes to your Web site, choose Theme from the Format menu. The Themes dialog box appears as shown in Figure 2-5. Choose the theme that you want to apply to your project and choose to apply it to *All pages* or *Selected page[s]*. You may also change the colors, graphics, and text by clicking the Modify button.

FIGURE 2-5
Themes dialog box

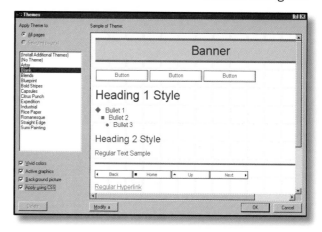

1. Choose **Theme** from the **Format** menu. The Themes dialog box appears, allowing you to select from a variety of themes for your Web page.

2. Choose **Blank**.

3. Click **All Pages** to apply the *Blank* theme to all of your Web pages.

4. If they are not already checked, click the check boxes next to **Vivid Colors**, **Active Graphics**, **Background Picture**, and **Apply using CSS**.

5. Click **OK**. Leave the Web on the screen for the next Step-by-Step.

Adding Banners, Navigation Bars, and Text to a Page

To begin building your Web pages you must switch to Page view. Most Web pages begin with a *banner*, which is a title or description of the content on the page. Display the page you want to construct and choose Page Banner from the Insert menu. The Page Banner Properties dialog box appears as shown in Figure 2-6.

If you want the banner to include the picture of the banner (not text only), click Picture and key the text in the *Page banner text* box, then click OK.

If your Web site contains more than one page, you will want your visitors to be able to go from one page to another. A ***navigation bar*** will allow the visitor to jump from page to page, using links. To add a navigation bar choose Navigation Bar from the Insert menu. The Navigation Bar Properties dialog box appears as shown in Figure 2-7. Select the hyperlink level that you want to add. Notice that the map next to the hyperlink levels changes to reflect exactly which pages you have selected. This dialog box will also allow you to display your navigation bar horizontally or vertically and as buttons or as text.

FIGURE 2-6
Page Banner Properties
dialog box

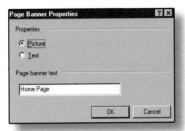

FIGURE 2-7
Navigation Bar Properties dialog box

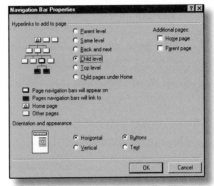

S TEP-BY-STEP ▷ 2.5

1. Double-click **Home Page** to select it.

2. Choose **Page Banner** from the Insert menu. The Page Banner Properties dialog box appears. If it is not already selected, click **Picture**, then key **Home Page** in the text box, if it is not already showing. Click **OK**. Click the **Center** button on the Formatting toolbar to center the banner, and then press **Enter**.

3. Click the **Style** button on the Formatting toolbar, then select **Heading 1**. Key the following text: **Plains Animal Welfare & Shelter**. If it is not already centered, center the heading, and then press **Enter**.

Hot Tip

If you can't see that your text is centered, you can maximize your screen by clicking the **Maximize** button at the top right corner of your screen or by dragging the boundary bar between the Folder List and your workspace to the left.

4. Key the following text:

   4908 Lincoln Road
   Abilene, Texas 79604
   (915) 555-0200

5. Highlight the text. Click the **Style** button on the Formatting toolbar, and then select

(continued on next page)

Heading 3. If the text is not already centered, center it, then click the line following the phone number.

6. Choose **Navigation Bar** from the **Insert** menu. The Navigation Bar Properties dialog box appears. If not already selected, click **Child Level, Horizontal,** and **Buttons**. Click **OK**. If it is not already centered, center the navigation bar and then press **Enter**. Your screen should look similar to Figure 2-8.

7. Click the **Font Size** button on the Formatting toolbar, then select **14 pt**, as shown in Figure 2-9. Click the **Bold, Underline** and **Align Left** buttons. Key **Shelter Hours** and then press **Enter**.

8. Click the **Font Size** button on the Formatting toolbar, select **Normal**, and then click the **Bold** and **Underline** buttons to deselect them. Key the following text, pressing **Enter** as indicated:

   ```
   Plains Animal Welfare & Shelter
   (PAWS) operating hours are: [Enter]
   8:00 a.m. - 6:00 p.m. Monday -
   Friday [Enter]
   9:00 a.m. - 5:00 p.m. Saturday
   [Enter]
   ```

9. Click the **Font Size** button on the Formatting toolbar, select **14 pt**, then click the **Bold** and **Underline** buttons.

10. To deselect them. Key the following text:

    ```
    From Interstate 20 & Treadaway
    Road [Enter]
    Go South on Treadaway for two
    miles. Turn left on Lincoln Road
    and go three blocks. We are
    located on the North side of
    Lincoln Road.[Enter]
    ```

11. Click the **Font Size** button on the Formatting toolbar, select **14 pt,** then click the **Bold** and **Underline** buttons. Key **Lost and Found** and press **Enter**.

12. Click the **Font Size** button on the Formatting toolbar, select **Normal**, then click the **Bold** and **Underline** buttons to deselect them. Key the following text:

    ```
    We maintain a Lost and Found list
    for animals in the Abilene area.
    If you lose or find an animal,
    please contact PAWS and provide
    information about your animal.
    Please remember that we receive
    new animals every day so you need
    to call daily to see if your pet
    has been located. [Enter]
    ```

13. Save the Web page, following your instructor's directions very carefully. Leave the page open for the next Step-by-Step.

FIGURE 2-8
Home page

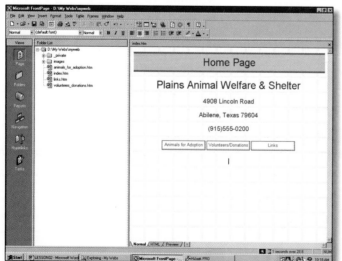

FIGURE 2-9
Font Size button on the Formatting toolbar

Adding a Picture to a Page

FIGURE 2-10
Picture dialog box

Pictures or *clip art* will help to liven up or further explain details on your Web site. To add a picture or clip art, choose Picture from the Insert menu. On the Picture submenu choose From File and the Picture dialog box appears as shown in Figure 2-10. You can choose to add pictures or clip art from a scanner, digital camera, video camera, the Internet, or from other sources such as your hard drive or a disk. Click the Select a file on your computer button. The Select File dialog box appears. Choose the location of the file that you want to insert, click the file, and then click OK. The picture will appear on your Web page.

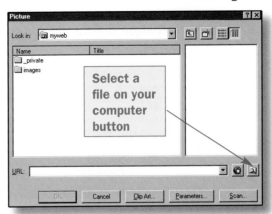

STEP-BY-STEP ▷ 2.6

1. Double-click **Animals_for_Adoption** in the *Folder List* to open the second Web page.

2. Choose **Page Banner** from the **Insert** menu. The Page Banner Properties dialog box appears. Select **Picture**, then click **OK**. Click the **Center** button on the Formatting toolbar to center the banner, and then press **Enter**.

3. Choose **Navigation Bar** from the **Insert** menu. The Navigation Bar Properties dialog box appears. If they are not already selected, click **Child pages under Home, Horizontal,** and **Buttons**. Click **OK**. If it is not already centered, center the navigation bar, and then press **Enter**.

4. Click the **Font Size** button on the Formatting toolbar, select **14 pt**, and then click the **Bold, Underline** and **Align Left** buttons. Key **Adoption Costs** and press **Enter**.

5. Click the **Font Size** button on the Formatting toolbar, select **Normal**, then click the **Bold** and **Underline** buttons to deselect them. Key the following text:

   All animals taken in by PAWS
   are given a thorough

examination. This includes all required vaccinations and being spayed or neutered. Cats are given a Feluk/FIV test. The fees are $55 for dogs and $40 for cats. **[Enter]**

6. Click the **Font Size** button on the Formatting toolbar, select **14 pt**, then click the **Bold** and **Underline** buttons. Key the following text: **Pet-of-the-Week** and press **Enter.**

7. Click the **Font Size** button on the Formatting toolbar, select **Normal**, then click the **Bold** and **Underline** buttons to deselect them.

8. Choose **Picture** from the **Insert** menu, then **From File** on the submenu. A Picture dialog box appears.

9. Click the **Select a file on your computer** button at the bottom right corner of the dialog box. A Select File dialog box appears.

10. Double-click **Ranger** from the student data files. Click the **Center** button on the Formatting toolbar to center the picture, as shown in Figure 2-11. Press **Enter**.

(continued on next page)

11. Click the **Left Align** button on the Formatting toolbar. Key the following text:

    ```
    Ranger is a three-year-old
    Brittany Spaniel/Border Collie
    mix. [Enter]
    ```

12. Choose **Navigation Bar** from the **Insert** menu. The Navigation Bar Properties dialog box appears. Click **Child Level**, **Home Page**, **Horizontal**, and **Buttons** to insert a link to your Home Page. Click **OK**. Click the **Center** button on the Formatting toolbar to center the navigation bar.

13. Save the page, following your instructor's directions.

14. Click **OK** when prompted to save the embedded file.

15. Leave the page open for the next Step-by-Step.

Concept Builder

If you use a file from an outside source such as the Internet or a disk, FrontPage will save or embed that file into your current Web page.

FIGURE 2-11
Picture centered on page

Adding Other Formatting Features to a Page

FrontPage contains many features that allow you to make your Web pages more exciting and easier to view. Adding moving text will draw a person's attention to an important piece of information. Position your cursor where you want to add moving text and choose Component from the Insert menu. On the submenu, choose Marquee. The Marquee Properties dialog box appears, as shown in Figure 2-12. Key the text that you want to move in the *Text* box. Select the direction that you want the text to move (*Left* or *Right*). Choose how long you want the text to delay before moving and how fast you want it to move in the *Speed* box. You can choose how the text moves in the *Behavior* box and where the text is aligned in the *Align with text* box. Choose how many times you want the text to move by selecting the number in the *Repeat* box or by clicking *Continuously*. You can select a different background for your text in the *Background color* box. Click OK to insert the marquee onto your Web page.

Adding a line to a Web page will visually separate two ideas on the same page. Position your cursor where you want to place a line and choose Horizontal Line from the Insert menu. The line will automatically appear on your Web page.

FIGURE 2-12
Marquee Properties dialog box

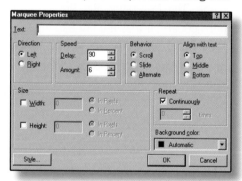

STEP-BY-STEP ▷ 2.7

1. In the Folder List double click **Volunteers_ Donations** to open your third page.

2. Choose **Page Banner** from the **Insert** menu. A Page Banner Properties dialog box appears. Select **Picture**, then click **OK.** If it is not already centered, center the banner, then press **Enter.**

3. Choose **Navigation Bar** from the **Insert** menu. A Navigation Bar Properties box appears. If they are not already selected, click **Child pages under Home, Horizontal**, and **Buttons**, and then click **OK**. If it is not already centered, center the navigation bar, and then press **Enter.**

4. Click the **Font Size** button on the Formatting toolbar, select **14 pt**, then click the **Bold, Underline** and **Align Left** buttons. Key **Volunteers** and press **Enter.**

5. Click the **Font Size** button on the Formatting toolbar, select **Normal**, then click the **Bold** and **Underline** buttons to deselect them. Key **We are in need of dedicated volunteers to:** and press **Enter.**

6. Click the **Bullets** button on the Formatting toolbar. Key the following text:

   ♦ Exercise and groom the animals at the shelter **[Enter]**
   ♦ Make presentations at special events **[Enter]**
   ♦ Operate display booths **[Enter]**
   ♦ Fundraising **[Enter]**
   ♦ Visit area nursing homes with animals **[Enter]**
   ♦ Maintain Web site **[Enter]**

7. Click the **Bullets** button on the Formatting toolbar to deselect it. Choose **Component** from the **Insert** menu and **Marquee** from the submenu. The Marquee Properties dialog box appears. In the **Text** box, key the following text:

   To volunteer, please contact us at (915) 555-0200.

8. If it is not already selected, click **Left** in the *Direction* box.

9. Set both the *Delay* and the *Amount* to **5** in the *Speed* box.

10. If it is not already selected, click **Scroll** in the *Behavior* box.

11. Click **Middle** in the *Align with text* box.

12. If it is not already selected, click **Continuously** in the *Repeat* box.

13. Set the background color to **white**, then click **OK**.

14. Press **Enter** to move to the next line. Choose **Horizontal Line** from the **Insert** menu. Press **Enter**.

15. Click the **Font Size** button on the Formatting toolbar, select **14 pt**, then click the **Bold** and **Underline** buttons**.** Key **Donations** and press **Enter**.

16. Click the **Font Size** button on the Formatting toolbar, select **Normal**, and then click the **Bold** and **Underline** buttons to deselect them. Key the following text:

    We are a non-profit organization that survives through the generous donations of organizations and individuals. In addition to financial donations, we are in need of the following items: **[Enter]**

17. Click the **Bullets** button on the Formatting toolbar. Key the following text:

    ♦ Leashes and collars **[Enter]**
    ♦ Pet toys **[Enter]**
    ♦ Stainless steel bowls **[Enter]**
    ♦ Cat and kitten food **[Enter]**
    ♦ Dog and puppy food **[Enter]**
    ♦ Cat litter **[Enter]**
    ♦ Newspapers **[Enter]**

(continued on next page)

18. Click the **Bullets** button on the Formatting toolbar to deselect it. Choose **Navigation Bar** from the **Insert** menu. The Navigation Bar Properties box appears. If they are not already selected, click the **Child Level**, **Home Page**, **Horizontal**, and **Buttons** options to insert a link to your Home Page, and then click **OK**. Click the **Center** button on the Formatting toolbar to center the navigation bar on the page.

19. Save the page, following your instructor's directions.

20. Leave the page open for the next Step-by-Step.

Adding Hyperlinks to Web Pages

A hyperlink allows you to "jump" from page to page within your Web site, or "jump" to another Web site. Choose Hyperlink from the Insert menu. The Create Hyperlink dialog box appears on your screen, as shown in Figure 2-13. This feature allows you to insert hyperlinks to connect to many different sources including pages on your Web site, pages on other Web sites on your computer or network, and pages on Web sites on the Internet. The current linkable pages are listed under the *Name* heading in the dialog box. You can link to any of these by highlighting the file and clicking OK. If you already know a page address you can key it into the *URL* text box or search for it on the Internet by clicking on the Web Browser button to the right of the *URL* text box.

FIGURE 2-13
Create Hyperlink dialog box

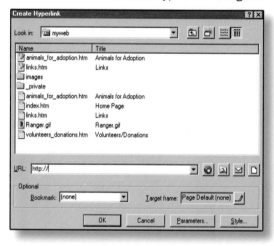

1. Double-click **Links** in the *Folder List* to open the fourth page.

2. Choose **Page Banner** from the **Insert** menu. The Page Banner Properties dialog box appears. Click **Picture** and then click **OK**. If it is not already centered, center the banner, then press **Enter**.

3. Choose **Navigation Bar** on the **Insert** menu. The Navigation Bar Properties dialog box appears. If they are not already selected, click the **Child pages under Home, Horizontal,** and **Buttons** options. Click **OK**. If it is not already centered, center the navigation bar, then press **Enter**.

4. Click **Font Size** on the Formatting toolbar, select **14 pt**, and then click the **Bold, Underline**, and **Align Left** buttons. Key **Links** and press **Enter**.

5. Click the **Font Size** button on the Formatting toolbar, select **Normal**, and then click the **Bold** and **Underline** buttons to deselect them. Key the following text:

```
Pet Finder [Enter]
American Veterinary Medical
Association [Enter]
Pet Care Tips [Enter]
```

6. Highlight **Pet Finder** and then choose **Hyperlink** from the **Insert** menu. The Create Hyperlink dialog box appears.

7. Click in the **URL** text box following the hypertext prefix http:// and key **www.petfinder.org/** and click **OK**.

Hot Tip

These are actual Web addresses; however, Web sites frequently change, and these may not be available when you publish your Web site.

8. Highlight **American Veterinary Medical Association**, then choose **Hyperlink** from the **Insert** menu. The Create Hyperlink dialog box appears.

9. Click in the **URL** text box following the hypertext prefix http:// and key **www.avma.org/care4pets/** and click **OK**.

10. Highlight **Pet Care Tips**, then choose **Hyperlink** from the **Insert** menu. The Create Hyperlink dialog box appears.

11. Click in the **URL** text box following the hypertext prefix http:// and key **www.creatures.com/** and click **OK**.

12. Press **Enter** to move to the next line. Choose **Navigation Bar** from the **Insert** menu . The Navigation Bar Properties box appears. If they are not already selected, select the **Child Level**, **Home Page**, **Horizontal**, and **Buttons** options to insert a link to your Home Page. Click **OK**. Click the **Center** button on the Formatting toolbar to center the navigation bar.

13. Save the page, following your instructor's directions.

Viewing, Printing, and Publishing Your Web Pages

T o view your completed Web page choose Preview in Browser from the File menu. The Preview in Browser dialog box will appear, as shown in Figure 2-14, and prompt you to choose a default browser. FrontPage will load your pages into the default browser on your computer which will allow you to see how your pages will look when they are published. To print a page, select it, then choose Print from the File menu in the browser. Continue this process for each page. To publish your pages to the Internet choose Publish Web from the File menu. The Publish Web dialog box appears and prompts you for the location to publish your Web pages.

FIGURE 2-14
Preview in Browser dialog box

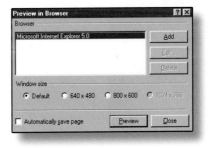

S TEP-BY-STEP ▷ 2.9

1. Your Web pages are ready to be published. To view your pages as they will appear on a browser, choose **Preview in Browser** from the **File** menu. The Preview in Browser dialog box appears. Click the **Preview** button.

2. View all the pages of your Web site by clicking the **Navigation Bar** buttons. Click the **Home** button to return to the home page. Click each

of the **Hyperlinks** you created on the Links page to view them.

3. Print each page by selecting it and then choosing **Print** from the **File** menu in your browser. The Print dialog box appears, as shown in Figure 2-15. Click the *Properties* button, then click the *Portrait* option in the *Ori-*

(continued on next page)

FIGURE 2-15
Print dialog box

entation box. Click **Apply**, then **OK**. Click **OK** in the Print dialog box.

4. You may, *following your instructor's directions*, publish your Web pages by choosing **Publish Web** from the **File** menu and specifying the address. Click **Publish** to save your pages to your Web site.

5. Choose **Close** from the **File** menu to close your browser. Choose **Close** from the **File** menu in FrontPage to close your Web pages. Choose **Exit** from the **File** menu in FrontPage to exit the program.

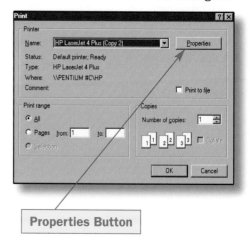

Properties Button

Summary

In this lesson, you learned:

■ FrontPage is an Office 2000 application that can help you create professional-looking Web pages. When you start FrontPage, a blank page appears in Page view.

■ In Page view you can edit Web pages. Navigation view shows you the structure of your Web.

■ To add pages to your Web, click the New Page button while in Navigation view. To name a page, select the page, click the text box, and key a new name. To add text, switch to Page view.

■ To add a theme to your Web pages, choose Theme from the Format menu. To add a banner or navigation bar to a Web page, choose Page Banner or Navigation Bar from the Insert menu.

■ You can add pictures or clip art to liven up or further explain details on your Web pages. To add a picture or clip art, choose Picture from the Insert menu. To add a horizontal line to separate data on a Web page, choose Horizontal Line from the Insert menu. To add moving text to a Web page, choose Component from the Insert menu.

■ Hyperlinks allow you to move around your Web site. To create hyperlinks, choose Hyperlinks from the Insert menu.

■ You can view your Web pages as they would look on the Internet by selecting Preview in Browser from the File menu.

■ To publish your Web pages to the Internet, select Publish Web from the File menu and key the address to publish to in the Publish Web dialog box.

LESSON 2 REVIEW QUESTIONS

TRUE/FALSE

Circle T if the statement is true or F if the statement is false.

T F 1. You can jump from one Web page to another by using hyperlinks.

T F 2. A page banner can be added by clicking on the Insert menu.

T F   3.   Page view allows you to view the hierarchy of your Web pages.

T F   4.   You can use the Tab key to move from page to page in Navigation view.

T F   5.   You can edit your Web page in the Preview mode.

WRITTEN QUESTIONS

Write a brief answer to the following questions.

1.   List the three ways to view your Web page in Page view.

2.   Describe how to apply themes to your Web pages.

3.   Which view shows the hierarchy or layout of your Web pages?

4.   Where can you find out how long it takes your page to download?

5.   How do you view your Web page in a browser?

PROJECT 2-1

1. Start FrontPage.

2. Open the **Plains Animal Welfare & Shelter** Web pages you saved in Lesson 2.

3. Switch to **Navigation view**. Add a new page to the Web site titled **Our Mission**. Add a banner and include the navigation bar. Add the following text, formatted as you wish:

   To offer medical care, nourishment, and refuge to animals in our community.

   To protect them from suffering because of cruelty, carelessness, neglect, or accidents through education, example, and enforcement.

   To encourage neutering and spaying to prevent overpopulation.

   To maximize community resources (financial contributions and volunteers) for the prevention of animal abuse.

4. Add the **Home** navigation bar at the bottom of the page.

5. Save, following your instructor's directions, and print the page from your Web browser.

6. Close the browser.

PROJECT 2-2

1. Change the theme on all the Plains Animal Welfare & Shelter pages to **Expedition**.

2. Add a horizontal line and create moving text on the **Our Mission** page you created in Project 2-1.

3. Spell check the **Our Mission** page. (*Hint:* Click the Spelling button on the Standard toolbar.)

4. Preview the changes from your Web browser.

5. Change the theme on all pages back to **Blank**.

6. Do not save your changes or print. Close all pages and exit FrontPage.

CRITICAL THINKING

ACTIVITY 2-1

SCANS

Create a Web page about yourself. Include your likes and dislikes, your favorite foods, or a list of books that you have read. Format the page as you wish, using at least two features presented in the lesson.

ACTIVITY 2-2

Use Microsoft FrontPage Help to change the colors of your theme.

Introduction to Microsoft Publisher and Microsoft FrontPage

COMMAND SUMMARY

PUBLISHER

FEATURE	MENU COMMAND	TOOLBAR BUTTON	LESSON
Center text		▤	1
Enlarge documents	View, Zoom	➕	1
Open existing files	File, Open	📂	1
Open Catalog dialog box	File, New		1
Print file	File, Print	🖨	1
Save file	File, Save	💾	1
Insert Clip Art	Insert, Picture, Clip Art	🖼	1

FRONTPAGE

FEATURE	MENU COMMAND	TOOLBAR BUTTON	LESSON
Add additional pages		🗋	2
Bullets		▤	2
Insert picture	Insert, Picture		2
Moving text	Insert, Component, Marquee		2
Horizontal Line	Insert, Horizontal Line		2
Align Left		▤	2
Apply theme	Format, Theme		2
Banners	Insert, Page Banner		2
Bold		**B**	2

Center text			2
Create a Web page	File, New, Web		2
Folder List	View, Folder List		2
Font Size	Format, Font, Size	Normal	2
Hyperlinks	Insert, Hyperlinks		2
Navigation Bar	Insert, Navigation Bar		2
Open existing Web pages	File, Open		2
Print Web pages	File, Print		2
Publish Web pages	File, Publish Web		2
Save Web pages	File, Save		2
Start FrontPage	Start, Programs, Microsoft FrontPage		2
Underline			2
View Web pages	File, Preview in Browser		2

REVIEW QUESTIONS

TRUE/FALSE

Circle T if the statement is true or F if the statement is false.

T F 1. To add a picture to a Publisher project, click the + key on the View menu.

T F 2. In Publisher, you should use the Publications by Design option to create a layout for special events such as holidays.

T F 3. Publisher's Publications by Wizard option allows you to create a series of documents that include the same design, information, and logo.

T F 4. Web pages are connected by hyperlinks that allow you to move around a Web site.

T F 5. In FrontPage, it is best to add new Web pages in Page view.

WRITTEN QUESTIONS

Write a brief answer to the following questions.

1. List at least three documents that you can create with Publisher.

2. What type of information can be updated in Publisher's Personal Information dialog box?

3. Describe how to add a banner to a FrontPage Web page.

4. Describe four ways FrontPage will display your navigation bar.

5. Describe how to add a hyperlink to a Web page.

APPLICATION 1

1. Start Microsoft Publisher and open the **PFP App1** Publisher file from the student data files. Save it as **Checkers Business Card**, followed by your initials.

2. Use the Business Card Wizard to change the design from Accent Box to **Checkers**.

3. Click on the items in the new business card and adjust the text layout to make the card easier to read.

4. Print the card and close the file.

APPLICATION 2

1. Create a thank you card for a new customer. Open Microsoft Publisher, and select the **Greeting Cards Wizard**.

2. Choose **Accent Box Thank You Card** from the Thank You Cards list box, and click the **Start Wizard** button.

3. The Greeting Card Wizard Introduction appears. Click **Next** to begin.

4. Choose the **Waterfall** color scheme if it is not already selected. Click **Next** to continue.

5. You can use the verse provided by Publisher, or choose another from a list of verses suggested by the Wizard. Click the **Browse** button and choose **Thanks for your business.** from the list of verses. Notice that the message will be applied to the front and an accompanying message will appear in the inside of your thank you card. Click **OK** and click **Next**.

6. You are prompted to select a personal information set for this project. Click **Primary Business**, if necessary, and click the **Update** button. You do not need to update the information for Computer Solutions. Click **Cancel**, and then click **Finish**.

7. Click the page **2/3** icons in the navigation buttons at the bottom of the screen.

8. Click the text frame under *Thank You* on page 2 to highlight it.

9. Click the **Center** button, and change the font size to **14**.

10. Key the following text:

    We appreciate your recent purchase from Computer Solutions. Remember that all of our sales and services are backed by a 100% guarantee. We are open from 8:00 a.m. to 6:00 p.m., Monday – Saturday, to serve you.

11. Click the page navigation buttons at the bottom of the screen to view your card.

12. Save the publication as **Thank You Card**, followed by your initials. Print the card and then close the file.

Your employer at Java Internet Café has created a Web page to advertise the store on the Internet. You are asked to create a postcard mailer for customers announcing the Web address.

JOB 1

1. Open Publisher, and click the **Postcards Wizard**.

2. Select **Informational**, and then choose **Marquee Informational Postcard**. Click the **Start Wizard** button.

3. The Postcard Wizard Introduction appears. Click **Next** to begin.

4. Choose the **Monarch** color scheme. Click **Next** to continue.

5. For the size of the postcard, choose **Quarter Page**, and click **Next** to continue.

6. The Wizard prompts you to choose the information that you want to include on the address side of your postcard. Choose **Only address**, and click **Next** to continue.

7. You are prompted to choose how you want your postcard printed. Choose **One in the center of the page**, and click **Next** to continue.

8. You are prompted to select a personal information set for this project. Click **Primary Business**, if necessary, and click the **Update** button. Key the following information in the appropriate text boxes. Delete any other data already keyed in the boxes.

   ```
   Java Internet Café
   2001 Zephyr
   Boulder, CO
   Phone: 303-555-JAVA
   E-mail: JavaCafe@Cybershop.com
   ```

9. Click **Update**, and then click **Finish**.

10. Save the publication as **Java Café Postcard**, followed by your initials.

11. Click in the box that contains *Product/Service Information* and key **Java Internet Café**.

FIGURE UR-1

12. Click the **Computer Solutions** logo to select it. Choose **Delete Object** on the **Edit** menu.

13. Double-click the picture of pears on your postcard. The Insert Clip Art dialog box appears. Key **Coffee** in the *Search for clips* text box, and press **Enter**. Insert any clip you want.

14. Adjust the company name, address, and phone number/e-mail address text boxes to get the best fit. Use Figure UR-1 as a guide.

15. Click in the text box underneath the coffee picture, and key the following text:

    Relax with friends, enjoy a great cup of coffee, and surf the net at the Java Internet Café. We now have seven new computers with high-speed Internet access.

    We are pleased to announce our new Web site. Check us out at: WWW.JavaCafe.Cybershop.com

16. Center the text you just keyed, and change the font and type size, if desired.

17. Print the card and close the file.

JOB 2

Your employer at Java Internet Café has asked you to add a page to the store's current Web site that includes the prices of the coffee served and the membership prices. Your boss also wants you to add a banner to the new page, and to link the two pages together.

1. Open FrontPage. From the **File** menu choose **Open**. Open the Web folder labeled **Job 2** from the student data files.

2. In **Navigation** view, highlight **Home Page**.

3. Add a new page named **Menu/Prices**.

4. Add the **Bold Stripes** theme to all pages.

5. Add a banner to the Menu/Prices page called **Java Internet Café Menu and Prices**.

6. Add a navigation bar that links to the Home Page. Center the bar.

7. Key the following text, formatting as you wish:

    Coffee Prices

House coffee	$1.00	Café breve	$2.25
Café au lait	$1.50	Café latte	$2.25
Cappuccino	$1.75	Con panna	$2.50
Espresso	$2.00	Espresso doppio	$2.75

    Membership Prices

    Membership fee – includes own account with personal ID, password, and e-mail address

    $10 per month

    Internet access (members) – includes World Wide Web, FTP, Telnet and IRC plus e-mail

    $4 per hour

    Internet access (non-members) – includes World Wide Web, FTP, Telnet and IRC plus e-mail

    $6 per hour

    Color Scanner – includes Internet access, use of software and the CD-ROM library

    $5 per $1/2$ hour

    Laser printer – inquire about copying capabilities

    $.15 per page

8. Save your pages, following the directions of your instructor. Print both pages and close the file.

Great Day Lawn Care Service

Estimated Time: 2 hrs.

Introduction

Throughout this book, you have learned to use Word, Excel, Access, PowerPoint, and Outlook. This unit is a simulation in which you will use each of these programs. The simulation, a business called Great Day Lawn Care Service, is operated by three friends.

You will use PowerPoint to modify a presentation. Then, you will use Word to create a form letter that will advertise Great Day Lawn Care's services. You will also create a calendar with Outlook. Microsoft Access will be used to maintain address and billing information for customers. Excel will be used to calculate and maintain data on earnings and expenses. You will integrate Access and Word to create a billing form and form letter that will be sent to customers. In addition, you will create a Web page.

BACKGROUND

You started Great Day Lawn Care Service last spring. You spent the warm months of the year (mid-May to mid-September) caring for ten lawns in the neighborhood. You offered the following services:

- Lawn mowing
- Edging
- Hedge clipping
- Watering

In September, several customers asked you about continuing your services the following year. In addition, a few neighbors of your current customers inquired about care for their lawns for the next year.

As the summer approaches, you are making plans to continue the lawn care business. You know that if you increase the number of lawns you mow and edge, you will need some extra help. In fact, with two more workers, you could finish each job faster. Since you own two mowers and one edger, all machines could be operated simultaneously and each job would be completed in approximately one-third the time.

MAY 1

You are thinking of asking two friends, Tracy and Jordan, to help you in your business. You have been working on a presentation in PowerPoint to show them.

1. Open PowerPoint and the **Presentation** file from the student data files.

2. Save the file as **GDPresentation**, followed by your initials.

3. Insert a new slide after slide 6 with the Bulleted List layout. Key the title and text as shown in Figure 1-1. (After keying the Advantages, press **Shift+Tab** to move text back one level.)

4. Change the title of slide 8 to **Option #3**.

5. Change the title of slide 6 to **Option #1**.

6. Display the first slide and then use Slide Show view to show the presentation.

7. Print the presentation as handouts with six slides per page.

8. Save, close, and exit PowerPoint.

Tracy and Jordan agree to join you in business. The three of you agree to work together and split the profits (giving you a greater share since everyone will be using your equipment). You begin a brainstorming session to solve the anticipated problems of the new business.

You all decide that Microsoft Office can help you generate business, bill customers, and monitor profits.

FIGURE 1-1

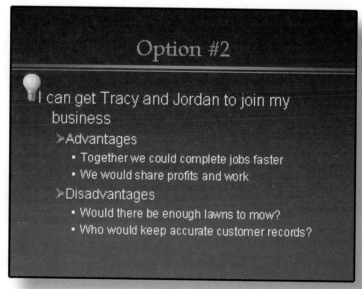

MAY 3

The three of you compile the addresses that appear in Figure 1-2. Names are available for some of the addresses because they were your customers the previous year. Other names are taken from mailboxes. If names are unavailable, the word "Resident" is used. All addresses are in the city of Smyrna, GA 30080.

Use these addresses to create a database that will supply addresses for the advertising letter and the billing form.

The three partners estimate a charge for their services based on the size of the lawn.

1. Create a new Access database named **Neighbors**. Create a new table using Design view. Define the following fields.

Field	Data type	Description
Title	Text	Title
Last Name	Text	Customer's Last Name
First Name	Text	Customer's First Name
Address	Text	Customer's Address
City, State, ZIP	Text	Customer's City, State, and ZIP
Fee	Currency	Amount to charge for this customer's lawn

2. Save and name the table **Potential Customers**. (No primary key is needed.)

3. Open the table in Datasheet view and enter the data shown in Figure 1-2. Adjust the widths of the fields appropriately. (*Hint*: You may use the Copy and Paste commands to enter Smyrna, GA 30080 in the City, State, ZIP field of each record.)

4. Save the table and the database file.

FIGURE 1-2

Title	Last Name	First Name	Address	City, State, ZIP	Fee
Mr.	Dye	Allen	200 Thistle	Smyrna, GA 30080	$15.00
Mr.	Dunsten	A.	201 Thistle	Smyrna, GA 30080	$20.00
Mr.	Mata	Ricardo	203 Thistle	Smyrna, GA 30080	$15.00
Mr.	Neman	John	204 Thistle	Smyrna, GA 30080	$22.00
Mr.	Rigby	Eddy	205 Thistle	Smyrna, GA 30080	$22.00
Mr.	Wolfe	James	206 Thistle	Smyrna, GA 30080	$22.00
Mr.	Carter	John	207 Thistle	Smyrna, GA 30080	$15.00
Ms.	Sanchez	Christina	208 Thistle	Smyrna, GA 30080	$15.00
Ms.	Marcus	Lois	209 Thistle	Smyrna, GA 30080	$20.00
Ms.	Lake	Jasmine	210 Thistle	Smyrna, GA 30080	$20.00
Mr.	Torres	Ruben	211 Thistle	Smyrna, GA 30080	$20.00
Ms.	Mueller	Anne	212 Thistle	Smyrna, GA 30080	$15.00
Resident			213 Thistle	Smyrna, GA 30080	$15.00
Mr.	Roberts	Chad	214 Thistle	Smyrna, GA 30080	$15.00
Ms.	Johnson	Virginia	215 Thistle	Smyrna, GA 30080	$15.00
Ms.	Novack	D. K.	216 Thistle	Smyrna, GA 30080	$15.00
Mr.	Keung	Y.	217 Thistle	Smyrna, GA 30080	$15.00
Mr.	Schultz	Jason	218 Thistle	Smyrna, GA 30080	$15.00
Mr.	Robinson	T.J.	219 Thistle	Smyrna, GA 30080	$15.00
Ms.	Estes	Jaunita	220 Thistle	Smyrna, GA 30080	$15.00

(continued on next page)

FIGURE 1-2

(continued)

Title	Last Name	First Name	Address	City, State, ZIP	Fee
Mr.	Reynolds	Clay	200 Kilt	Smyrna, GA 30080	$22.00
Ms.	Richards	Della	201 Kilt	Smyrna, GA 30080	$22.00
Mr.	Malcolm	R.J.	202 Kilt	Smyrna, GA 30080	$22.00
Ms.	Patel	Nina	203 Kilt	Smyrna, GA 30080	$22.00
Mr.	Cash	H. J.	204 Kilt	Smyrna, GA 30080	$22.00
Ms.	Phillips	Paula	205 Kilt	Smyrna, GA 30080	$22.00
Mr.	Moody	Mark	206 Kilt	Smyrna, GA 30080	$22.00
Mr.	Harper	G.H.	207 Kilt	Smyrna, GA 30080	$22.00
Mr.	Montoya	E. B.	208 Kilt	Smyrna, GA 30080	$22.00
Resident			209 Kilt	Smyrna, GA 30080	$22.00
Ms.	Strawser	L. T.	210 Kilt	Smyrna, GA 30080	$22.00
Mr.	Piper	Nate	211 Kilt	Smyrna, GA 30080	$20.00
Mr.	Williams	R. B.	212 Kilt	Smyrna, GA 30080	$20.00
Mr.	Hix	Jordan	213 Kilt	Smyrna, GA 30080	$20.00
Mr.	Guy	D. P.	214 Kilt	Smyrna, GA 30080	$20.00
Mr.	Carver	Alton	215 Kilt	Smyrna, GA 30080	$20.00
Ms.	Ellis	J. B.	216 Kilt	Smyrna, GA 30080	$20.00
Ms.	Liu	Lini	217 Kilt	Smyrna, GA 30080	$20.00
Mr.	Lauer	Corey	218 Kilt	Smyrna, GA 30080	$20.00
Mr.	Aslam	Ritu	219 Kilt	Smyrna, GA 30080	$20.00
Ms.	Gibb	H. T.	220 Kilt	Smyrna, GA 30080	$20.00
Mr.	Leon	Steven	200 Plaid	Smyrna, GA 30080	$15.00
Mr.	Gold	Richard	201 Plaid	Smyrna, GA 30080	$15.00
Mr.	Edge	A. V.	202 Plaid	Smyrna, GA 30080	$15.00
Mr.	Shell	Charles	203 Plaid	Smyrna, GA 30080	$15.00
Mr.	Valdez	Robert	204 Plaid	Smyrna, GA 30080	$20.00
Mr.	Yarbrough	Frank	205 Plaid	Smyrna, GA 30080	$20.00
Mr.	Sims	Trevor	206 Plaid	Smyrna, GA 30080	$20.00
Mr.	Terrell	Kevin	207 Plaid	Smyrna, GA 30080	$20.00
Resident			208 Plaid	Smyrna, GA 30080	$20.00
Ms.	Johnson	Veronica	209 Plaid	Smyrna, GA 30080	$20.00
Ms.	Levine	Heather	210 Plaid	Smyrna, GA 30080	$20.00
Mr.	Womack	David	211 Plaid	Smyrna, GA 30080	$15.00
Resident			213 Plaid	Smyrna, GA 30080	$15.00
Ms.	Yapp	B. J.	214 Plaid	Smyrna, GA 30080	$15.00
Ms.	Page	Misha	215 Plaid	Smyrna, GA 30080	$15.00
Ms.	Taylor	Vicky	216 Plaid	Smyrna, GA 30080	$15.00
Mr.	Sutton	Forrest	217 Plaid	Smyrna, GA 30080	$15.00
Mr.	Smith	Charles	218 Plaid	Smyrna, GA 30080	$15.00
Ms.	Ruff	Keesha	219 Plaid	Smyrna, GA 30080	$15.00

MAY 4

Tracy writes a form letter, shown in Figure 1-3, to advertise the services of Great Day Lawn Care Service. You design a letterhead template. The letter will be personalized by merging the names and addresses of potential customers in the database with the form letter.

1. Open Word.

2. Design a letterhead template for Great Day Lawn Care Service to be used with the letter in Figure 1-3. You can draw a graphic in Word or use clip art. Save it as a template in the Office 2000 templates folder (your program directory may be named something else) on your hard drive. Name it **Letterhead**. Close the file.

FIGURE 1-3

Great Day Lawn Care Service
221 Kilt Avenue
Smyrna, GA 30080
404-555-3894

May 4, ——

«Title» «First_Name» «Last_Name»
«Address»
«City_State_ZIP»

Dear «Title» «Last_Name»

Great Day Lawn Care Service is a partnership of friends. We would like to care for your lawn on a weekly basis and perform the following services:

Lawn Mowing
Edging
Hedge Clipping
Watering

We are prepared to offer these services to you at a cost of «Fee» per week, billed monthly. We are conscientious, guarantee all of our work, and will provide references in your neighborhood.

If you would like to employ our services or if you have any questions, please contact us at 555-3894.

Sincerely

Student's name   Tracy Ruthart   Jordan Perry

3. Open a new **Letterhead** file and key in the form letter. Do not key Great Day's address. This should be part of your letterhead template. Do not key the placeholders yet. Later you will put the placeholders in the form letter to pull data from the database file into the word processing file.

4. Save the file as **Form Letter** and leave it on the screen.

MAY 5

You need to print the form letters only for those for whom you don't have names so you can distribute them door-to-door.

1. Use Word's Mail Merge Helper to merge the form letters with the **Neighbors** database. Choose the Active window for the Main document and open the **Neighbors** database and the **Potential Customers** table as the data source. Insert placeholders as shown in Figure 1-3.

2. Use the Mail Merge Helper's Query Options to create a query to merge only those with **Resident** in the *Title* field to a new document. (There should be four records.)

3. Save the document as **Resident Letters** and print the four form letters.

4. Close **Resident Letters**.

5. Save the changes to **Form Letter** and close it.

MAY 6

Anticipating a response to the letters, Jordan suggests that the billing information for the month of May be set up.

Create a worksheet to figure and track billing. Columns will be created to show the amount owed by each customer for each week. For example, *3-May* will contain the amount owed for the third week in May. *May Bill* will contain the total amount owed by the customer for the month of May, and *May Paid* will contain the amount paid by the customer for the month of May.

1. Open a new Excel worksheet.

2. Save the worksheet as **Billing**, followed by your initials.

3. In **A1**, key **3-May**.

4. In **B1**, key **4-May**.

5. In **C1**, key **May Bill**.

6. In **D1**, key **May Paid**.

7. Enter a formula in **C2** to total the bill for May. It should contain the sum of the amounts in the 3-May and 4-May fields.

8. Copy the formula down to **C61**.

9. Save and close the document.

MAY 7

The three of you decide to create a Web page announcing your services. Use Front Page, the Web Page Wizard in Word, or create a Web presentation and save it as HTML. Use the logo and some of the text from the form letter on your page. Print and close the document.

MAY 8

The following people (mostly former customers) have notified you that they would like to employ the services of Great Day Lawn Care Service.

Carver, Alton	Phillips, Paula
Cash, H. J.	Piper, Nate
Guy, D. P.	Strawser, L. T.
Harper, G. H.	Williams, R. B.

In addition, the residents of 209 Kilt, Mr. Tom Alfreds, and 213 Thistle, Ms. Lillian Spears, have employed Great Day Lawn Care Service.

1. Switch to Access.

2. Insert the following new fields in the **Potential Customers** table of the **Neighbors** database.

Field	Data Type	Description
Cust	Yes/No	Is this a customer?
May Bill	Currency with 2 decimal places	Amount owed for May

3. The residents of 209 Kilt and 213 Thistle were not known when the database was created. Edit the Title, Last Name, and First Name fields to show their correct names.

4. Indicate the people who are now customers by clicking to insert a check mark in the **Cust** field box of your Access database. Since the database is large, you may want to use the Find command or sort the database alphabetically by last name to help you find customers.

5. Save the table.

MAY 9

In anticipation of billing new customers, Jordan drafts a billing form to be put in a word processing file. A copy of the draft is in Figure 1-4.

FIGURE 1-4

Great Day Lawn Care Service

221 Kilt Avenue
Smyrna, GA 30080
404-555-3894

June 2, ——

Charges for the Month of May

«Title» «First_Name» «Last_Name»
«Address»
«City_State_ZIP»

We have calculated your May bill based on our agreed amount of «Fee» per week. The total charge for May is «May_Bill».

Please make your check payable to "Great Day Lawn Care Service." Payment is due by June 10.

Thank you for your business.

1. Switch to Word.

2. Open the **Letterhead** file as a document and key the billing form from Figure 1-4 into the file. Do not insert the placeholders yet.

3. Save the file as **Bill form** and close.

MAY 10

Several more people have notified you that they would like to employ the services of Great Day Lawn Care Service for the summer:

Mata, Ricardo	Gold, Richard
Sanchez, Christina	Edge, A. V.
Lake, Jasmine	Valdez, Robert
Mueller, Anne	Yarbrough, Frank
Novack, D. K.	Johnson, Veronica
Robinson, T. J.	Yapp, B. J.
Lauer, Corey	Page, Misha

Switch to Access and indicate that these people are customers by inserting a check mark in the **Cust** field of the **Potential Customers** table.
Save the table.

MAY 11

For planning purposes, you decide to create a calendar.

1. Open Outlook.

2. Use the Date Navigator to go to **May 1999**.

3. View the entire month by choosing **Month** from the **View** menu.

4. Insert appointments on the days shown in Figure 1-5 by clicking on the day and keying the tasks.

FIGURE 1-5

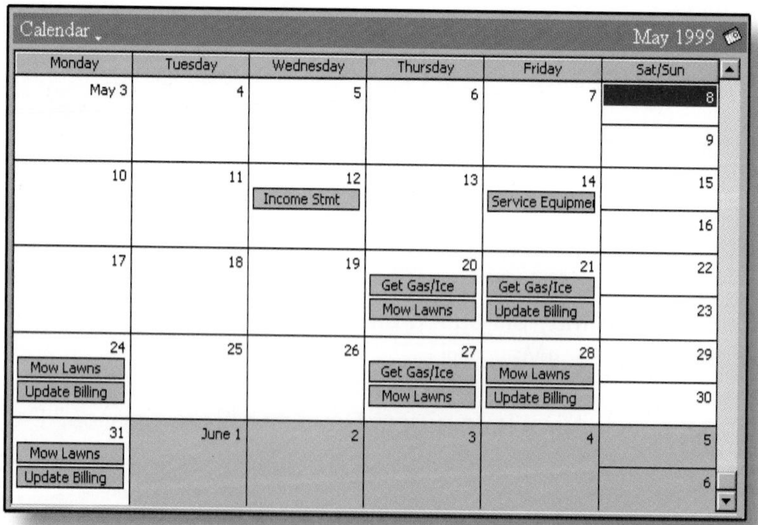

5. Print the monthly calendar. Be sure to choose the dates **5/1/99 to 5/31/99** in the print range.

6. Exit Outlook without saving.

MAY 12

An income statement will be prepared each month to report the profits of Great Day Lawn Care Service. Figure 1-6 is a draft of the income statement for the month of May. All three partners agree that the income statement will give them the information needed to evaluate the progress of their business venture.

1. Switch to Excel and set up an income statement, as shown in Figure 1-6, for the month of May.

2. Save the file as **Income Statement**. Computed fields and amounts will be added to the income statement later.

FIGURE 1-6

	A	B	C	D
1	**GREAT DAY LAWN CARE SERVICE**			
2	INCOME STATEMENT			
3	FOR THE MONTH ENDING MAY 31,——			
4				
5	REVENUES			
6				
7	Collected Lawn Care Revenues			
8	Uncollected Lawn Care Revenues			
9				
10	TOTAL REVENUES			
11				
12	EXPENSES			
13				
14	Gasoline			
15	Mower Repair and Maintenance			
16	Trailer Repair and Maintenance			
17	Refreshments and Ice			
18	Computer Supplies			
19	Misc. Expenses			
20				
21	TOTAL EXPENSES			
22				
23	NET INCOME			
24				

MAY 14

More residents have notified you that they want the services of Great Day Lawn Care for the summer:

Dye, Allen   Liu, Lini

Richards, Della   Gibb, H. T.

The residents of 208 Plaid, Mr. Reginald Hinkle, and 213 Plaid, Ms. Misty Lobo, have also employed the service.

1. Switch to Access.

2. The residents of 208 Plaid and 213 Plaid were not known when the database was originally created. Edit the fields to show their correct names.

3. Indicate that these people are customers by inserting a check mark in the **Cust** field of the **Potential Customers** table.

4. Save the table.

MAY 16

You want to be sure your equipment is in good shape before the summer begins. You take your lawn care equipment into the mower repair shop for servicing. The cost of servicing is $105.34. You also buy a new tire and brake light for the trailer. The total cost is $89.75.

1. Switch to Excel and the **Income Statement** file. Record the expense for Mower Repair and Maintenance in column **B**. Record the trailer costs as Trailer Repair and Maintenance.

2. Format column **B** for **currency** with **2** decimal places.

3. Save the file.

MAY 21

The lawns of the following customers have been serviced.

Dye	Gold
Mata	Edge
Sanchez	Valdez
Lake	Yarbrough
Mueller	Johnson
Novack	Yapp
Robinson	Page

1. Switch to Access and create a filter to show only those customers with a check mark in the *Cust* field. (*Hint*: Key **Yes** in the *Criteria* field. Do not use quotes.)

2. Sort the **Last Name** field in ascending order. Save the table.

3. Switch to Excel and open the **Billing** file. Insert three new columns to the left of column **A**.

4. Switch to Access and the **Potential Customers** table. Copy the **Last Name**, **Address**, and **Fee** columns from the filter to the three new columns in the **Billing** file in that order. (If you get the message: "Data on the Clipboard is not the same size and shape as the selected area, paste anyway?" click **OK**.)

5. Adjust field widths in the **Billing** file as needed.

6. In the **Billing** file, enter the amounts (listed in the **Fee** column) owed by the customers listed above in the **3-May** column. Format **C2:D31** for currency with **2** decimal places, if it is not already formatted.

7. In row **1**, center and boldface the headings and change the cell color to **None**. Remove the borders from **A1** through **C31**.

8. Save the file.

9. Switch to the **Income Statement** file and enter **$10.13** in column **B** for gasoline. Enter **$15.12** in column **B** for refreshments and ice.

10. Save the file.

MAY 24

The lawns of the following customers have been serviced.

Richards	Carver
Cash	Liu
Phillips	Lauer
Harper	Gibb
Strawser	Alfreds
Piper	Hinkle
Williams	Lobo
Guy	Spears

1. Switch to the **Billing** file and enter the amounts owed by each customer in the **3-May** field.

2. Save the file.

3. Switch to the **Income Statement** file and add **$6.33** to the existing amount in the Gasoline expense column. The $10.13 in the gasoline account should be replaced with the formula **=10.13+6.33**. Add **$6.56** to the existing amount in the Refreshments and Ice column. The $15.12 in the refreshments and ice account should be replaced with the formula **=15.12+6.56**.

4. Save the file.

MAY 28

The lawns of the following customers have been mowed and edged.

Dye	Sanchez
Mata	Lake
Richards	Mueller
Cash	Spears
Gold	Hinkle
Edge	Johnson
Valdez	Lobo
Yarbrough	Page

1. Switch to the **Billing** file and enter the amounts owed by the customers in the **4-May** column.

2. Format **E2:G31** for **currency** with **2** decimal places. Save the file.

3. Switch to the **Income Statement** file and add **$10.18** for gasoline, and **$6.78** for refreshments and ice to the previously recorded amounts in the expense column.

4. Save the file.

MAY 30

During May, $30.15 was spent on printer paper, and $20.51 of miscellaneous expenses were incurred.

1. Record the amount for computer supplies and miscellaneous expenses to the **Income Statement** file under the appropriate account names.

2. Save the file.

MAY 31

The lawns of the following customers have been serviced.

Novack   Liu
Robinson   Lauer
Phillips   Gibb
Harper   Yapp
Alfreds   Strawser
Piper   Williams
Guy   Carver

1. Switch to the **Billing** file and enter the amounts owed by the customers in the **4-May** column. Save the file.

2. Switch to the **Income Statement** file and add **$9.76** for gasoline and **$6.90** for refreshments and ice to the previously recorded amounts in the expenses column.

3. Save the file.

JUNE 2

The three partners decide to prepare the bills for the month of May. The bills are printed and distributed door-to-door.

1. Switch to Access and the **Neighbors** database.

2. With the Customers filter still in effect, sort by **Last Name** in ascending order if necessary.

3. Switch to Excel. Copy the amounts in the May Bill column (**F2** through **F31**) of the **Billing** file. Switch to Access. Click the **May Bill** field name of the **Potential Customers** table to highlight the entire field. Paste the data into the May Bill field. You will get the message: "You are about to paste 30 records. Are you sure you want to paste these records?" Click **Yes**.

4. Open **Bill form** in Word.

5. Use the Mail Merge Helper to merge with data from the **Potential Customers** database to a new document. Insert the placeholders as shown in Figure 1-4. Create a query in the Mail Merge Helper to merge only the billing forms for Spears and Novack.

6. Save the new document as **SNBills**.

7. Print the billing forms for Spears and Novack.

8. Close **SNBills**.

9. Save and close **Bill form**. Exit Word.

10. Close the database and exit Access.

JUNE 3

The following customers were at home when the bills were distributed and promptly paid the amounts due.

Dye	Guy
Mata	Lauer
Lake	Gold
Novack	Valdez
Robinson	Yarbrough
Cash	Hinkle
Alfreds	Lobo
Piper	Yapp
Williams	Page

Switch to Excel and record the collection of these amounts in the *May Paid* column of the **Billing** worksheet. Save the file.

JUNE 8

The following customers have delivered checks to Great Day Lawn Care Service.

Phillips	Harper
Strawser	Liu
Sanchez	Gibb
Spears	Johnson

1. Record the collection of these amounts in the **Billing** worksheet in the *May Paid* column.

2. Save the file.

JUNE 9

Tracy wonders about the unpaid bills. Calculate the amounts billed to the customers and the amounts actually received.

1. In the **Billing** file, clear **F32** through **F63**.

2. In **A33**, key **Totals**.

3. Enter a formula in **F33** to sum the *May Bill* column. Format the cell for **currency** with **2** decimal places if it is not already formatted.

4. Copy the formula to **G33**.

5. In **A35**, key **Uncollected**.

6. In **B35**, enter a formula to subtract the total *May Paid* from the total of *May Bill*. Format the cell for **currency** with **2** decimal places if it is not already formatted.

7. Boldface **A33**, **A35**, **B35**, **F33**, and **G33**.

8. Save, print, and close the file. (Print only **A1** through **G35**).

JUNE 10

Great Day Lawn Care Service has now compiled the data for the first month of operations. The partners want to know if they made a profit during May. They want copies of the May income statement to assess their progress.

1. Switch to the file **Income Statement**. This file already contains updated expenses for May.

2. In **B7**, key **960** and in **B8**, key **144**.

3. In **C10**, enter a formula to total the *Collected Lawn Care Revenues* and the *Uncollected Lawn Care Revenues*.

4. In **C21**, enter a formula to total all the expenses.

5. In **C23**, enter a formula to find the difference between the *Total Revenues* and *Total Expenses*.

6. Format column **C** for **currency** with **2** decimal places if it's not already formatted.

7. Save, print, and close the file. Exit Excel.

APPROVED COURSEWARE
EXPERT

APPENDIX A

THE MICROSOFT OFFICE
USER SPECIALIST PROGRAM

What Is Certification?

The logos on the cover of this book indicate that the book is officially certified by Microsoft Corporation at the **Core** user skill level for Office 2000 in Word, Excel, Access, and PowerPoint. This certification is part of the **Microsoft Office User Specialist (MOUS)** program that validates your skills as knowledgeable of Microsoft Office.

The following grids outline the various Core skills and where they are covered in this book.

MICROSOFT WORD 2000 CORE
TOTAL OBJECTIVES: 58

Standardized Coding Number	Activity	ICV Performance based?	Lesson #	Pages	Exercise #
W2000.1	**Working with text**				
W2000.1.1	Use the Undo, Redo, and Repeat commands	Yes	2	20-21	SBS2.3, P2-3
W2000.1.2	Apply font formats (Bold, Italic and Underline)	Yes	3	32, 33	SBS3.2, 3.4, P3-2
W2000.1.3	Use the SPELLING feature	Yes	5	68, 71	SBS5.5, 5.7, P5-1, 5-2
W2000.1.4	Use the THESAURUS feature	No	5	74-75	SBS5.10, P5-1, 5-2
W2000.1.5	Use the GRAMMAR feature	No	5	70, 71	SBS5.6, 5.7
W2000.1.6	Insert page breaks	Yes	8	121	SBS8.3, P8-1
W2000.1.7	Highlight text in document	Yes	3	35	SBS3.5
W2000.1.8	Insert and move text	Yes	2	22, 24	SBS2.3, 2.4, 2.6
W2000.1.9	Cut, Copy, Paste, and Paste Special using the Office Clipboard	Yes	2, 9	22-23, 161	SBS2.4, 2.5, 9.12, P2-1, 2-3
W2000.1.10	Copy formats using the Format Painter	Yes	3	40	SBS3.9, P3-1, 3-2
W2000.1.11	Select and change font and font size	Yes	3	31, 33	SBS3.1, 3.3, P3-1, 3-2
W2000.1.12	Find and replace text	Yes	5	76-78	SBS5.11, 5.12, P5-1, 5-2
W2000.1.13	Apply character effects (superscript, subscript, strikethrough, small caps and outline)	No	3	33-34	SBS3.4, P3

Standardized Coding Number	Activity	ICV Performance based?	Lesson #	Pages	Exercise #
W2000.1.14	Insert date and time	Yes	5	72	SBS5.8, P5-2
W2000.1.15	Insert symbols	No	5	74	
W2000.1.16	Create and apply frequently used text with AutoCorrect	No	5	64	SBS5.1, P5-1
W2000.2	**Working with paragraphs**				
W2000.2.1	Align text in paragraphs (Center, Left, Right and Justified)	Yes	3	36	SBS3.6, P3-1, 3-2
W2000.2.2	Add bullets and numbering	Yes	4	54, 57-59	SBS4.6, 4.8, P4-1, 4-3
W2000.2.3	Set character, line, and paragraph spacing options	Yes	4	47-48	SBS4.2, P4-1, 4-2, 4-3
W2000.2.4	Apply borders and shading to paragraphs	No	7	111-112	SBS7.6, P7-1, 7-2
W2000.2.5	Use indentation options (Left, Right, First Line and Hanging Indent)	Yes	4	44-46	SBS4.1, P4-2, 4-3
W2000.2.6	Use TABS command (Center, Decimal, Left and Right)	Yes	4	51-52	SBS4.4, P4-2
W2000.2.7	Create an outline style numbered list	No	4	55	SBS4.7
W2000.2.8	Set tabs with leaders	No	4	52	SBS4.4
W2000.3	**Working with documents**				
W2000.3.1	Print a document	Yes	1	11	SBS1.7, P1-1, 1-2
W2000.3.2	Use print preview	Yes	1	10	SBS1.6, P1-1
W2000.3.3	Use Web Page Preview	Yes	9	158	SBS9.11
W2000.3.4	Navigate through a document	Yes	1	6, 7	SBS1.3
W2000.3.5	Insert page numbers	Yes	8	127	P8-1
W2000.3.6	Set page orientation	Yes	1	12	SBS1.8, P1-1
W2000.3.7	Set margins	Yes	4	49	SBS4.3, P4-1
W2000.3.8	Use GoTo to locate specific elements in a document	No	8	123	SBS8.5
W2000.3.9	Create and modify page numbers	Yes	8	127	P8-1
W2000.3.10	Create and modify headers and footers	Yes	8	125	SBS8.6, P8-1, 8-2
W2000.3.11	Align text vertically	No	3	37	SBS3.7, P3-1
W2000.3.12	Create and use newspaper columns	Yes	6	83-84	SBS6.1, P7-1 7-2
W2000.3.13	Revise column structure	No	6	84	SBS6.1
W2000.3.14	Prepare and print envelopes and labels	Yes	9	152, 153	SBS9.8, 9.9, P9-1
W2000.3.15	Apply styles	Yes	8	131	SBS8.9, P8-2
W2000.3.16	Create sections with formatting that differs from other sections	No	8	129-130	SBS8.8, P8-1
W2000.3.17	Use click & type	Yes	3	38	SBS3.8

Standardized Coding Number	Activity	ICV Performance based?	Lesson #	Pages	Exercise #
W2000.4	**Managing files**				
W2000.4.1	Use save	Yes	1	8	**SBS1.4,**
W2000.4.2	Locate and open an existing document	Yes	1	9	**SBS1.5, P1-1**
W2000.4.3	Use Save As (different name, location or format)	Yes	1	8	**SBS1.8, P1-1**
W2000.4.4	Create a folder	No	1	8	SBS1.4
W2000.4.5	Create a new document using a Wizard	Yes	9	144	**SBS9.4**
W2000.4.6	Save as Web Page	Yes	9	158	**SBS9.11**
W2000.4.7	Use templates to create a new Word document	Yes	9	143	**SBS9.3, P9-1**
W2000.4.8	Create Hyperlinks	No	9	161	SBS9.12, P9-2
W2000.4.9	Use the Office Assistant	Yes	1	13	**SBS1.9**
W2000.4.10	Send a Word document via e-mail	No	9	160	
W2000.5	**Using tables**				
W2000.5.1	Create and format tables	Yes	9	**146, 148**	**SBS9.5, 9.7, P9-2**
W2000.5.2	Add borders and shading to tables	Yes	9	**148**	**SBS9.7**
W2000.5.3	Revise tables (insert & delete rows and columns, change cell formats)	Yes	9	**147**	**SBS9.6**
W2000.5.4	Modify table structure (merge cells, change height and width)	No	9	149	SBS9.7
W2000.5.5	Rotate text in a table	No	9	149	SBS9.7
W2000.6	**Working with pictures and charts**				
W2000.6.1	Use the drawing toolbar	Yes	6	**85-94**	**SBS6.3-6.8, P6-1, 6-2, 6-3**
W2000.6.2	Insert graphics into a document (WordArt, ClipArt, Images)	Yes	7	**100-101, 106-107**	**SBS7.1, 7.4, P7-1, 7-2**

MICROSOFT EXCEL 2000 CORE
TOTAL OBJECTIVES: 65

Standardized Coding Number	Activity	ICV Performance based?	Lesson #	Pages	Exercise #
XL2000.1	**Working with cells**				
XL2000.1.1	Use Undo and Redo	No	2, 3	27, 40	SBS2.9
XL2000.1.2	Clear cell content	Yes	1	9	**SBS1.6**
XL2000.1.3	Enter text, dates, and numbers	Yes	1, 5	7-8, 81	**SBS1.5, 5.4**
XL2000.1.4	Edit cell content	Yes	1	9	**SBS1.6**
XL2000.1.5	Go to a specific cell	Yes	1	5-6	**SBS1.3**
XL2000.1.6	Insert and delete selected cells	Yes	3	40	**SBS3.5**

Standardized Coding Number	Activity	ICV Performance based?	Lesson #	Pages	Exercise #
XL2000.1.7	Cut, copy, paste, paste special and move selected cells, use the Office Clipboard	Yes	3, 7	34-35, 38-39, 111-112	SBS3.1, 3.4, 7.3
XL2000.1.8	Use Find and Replace	No	1	5, 9	
XL2000.1.9	Clear cell formats	Yes	2	25-27	SBS2.9
XL2000.1.10	Work with series (AutoFill)	Yes	3	37-38	SBS3.3
XL2000.1.11	Create hyperlinks	No	6, 7	101, 122	ACT7-1
XL2000.2	**Working with files**				
XL2000.2.1	Use Save	Yes	1	14	P1-2
XL2000.2.2	Use Save As (different name, location, format)	Yes	1	10-11	SBS1.7
XL2000.2.3	Locate and open an existing workbook	Yes	1	4	SBS1.2
XL2000.2.4	Create a folder	No	1	10-Did You Know?	
XL2000.2.5	Use templates to create a new workbook	No	1	4-Did You Know?	
XL2000.2.6	Save a worksheet/workbook as a Web Page	Yes	7	116-117	SBS7.7
XL2000.2.7	Send a workbook via email	No	7	119	SBS7.9
XL2000.2.8	Use the Office Assistant	Yes	Intro-1, IE-1	10, 8	SBS1.8
XL2000.3	**Formatting worksheets**				
XL2000.3.1	Apply font styles (typeface, size, color and styles)	Yes	2	21-23	SBS2.6
XL2000.3.2	Apply number formats (currency, percent, dates, comma)	Yes	2	26-27	SBS2.9
XL2000.3.3	Modify size of rows and columns	Yes	2	16-18	SBS2.1, 2.2
XL2000.3.4	Modify alignment of cell content	Yes	2	20-21	SBS2.5
XL2000.3.5	Adjust the decimal place	Yes	2	32	P2-5
XL2000.3.6	Use the Format Painter	Yes	6	91-92	SBS6.3
XL2000.3.7	Apply autoformat	No	2	27, 33	ACT2-2
XL2000.3.8	Apply cell borders and shading	Yes	2	23-25	SBS2.7, 2.8
XL2000.3.9	Merging cells	Yes	2	20	SBS2.5
XL2000.3.10	Rotate text and change indents	No	2	19-20	SBS2.4, 2.5
XL2000.3.11	Define, apply, and remove a style	No	2	25-Hot Tip	
XL2000.4	**Page setup and printing**				
XL2000.4.1	Preview and print worksheets & workbooks	Yes	1, 3	11, 45-47	SBS1.8, 3.9
XL2000.4.2	Use Web Page Preview	No	7	116	SBS7.7
XL2000.4.3	Print a selection	No	3	43-46	SBS3.9

A - 4

Standardized Coding Number	Activity	ICV Performance based?	Lesson #	Pages	Exercise #
XL2000.4.4	Change page orientation and scaling	Yes	3	43-45	SBS3.8
XL2000.4.5	Set page margins and centering	Yes	3	43-45	SBS3.8
XL2000.4.6	Insert and remove a page break	No	3	44	
XL2000.4.7	Set print, and clear a print area	Yes	3	43-45	SBS3.8
XL2000.4.8	Set up headers and footers	Yes	3	43-45	SBS3.8
XL2000.4.9	Set print titles and options (gridlines, print quality, row & column headings)	No	3	43-45	SBS3.8
XL2000.5	**Working with worksheets & workbooks**				
XL2000.5.1	Insert and delete rows and columns	Yes	3	40	SBS3.5
XL2000.5.2	Hide and unhide rows and columns	No	6	95-Hot Tip	
XL2000.5.3 `	Freeze and unfreeze rows and columns	Yes	3	41-42	SBS3.6
XL2000.5.4	Change the zoom setting	Yes	1	10-11	SBS1.7
XL2000.5.5	Move between worksheets in a workbook	Yes	8	130	SBS8.3
XL2000.5.6	Check spelling	No	7	118	SBS7.8
XL2000.5.7	Rename a worksheet	Yes	8	131	SBS8.4
XL2000.5.8	Insert and Delete worksheets	Yes	6	97	SBS6.7
XL2000.5.9	Move and copy worksheets	No	1	9-Did You Know?	
XL2000.5.10	Link worksheets & consolidate data using 3D References	Yes	6	96-97	SBS6.7
XL2000.6	**Working with formulas & functions**				
XL2000.6.1	Enter a range within a formula by dragging	No	5	75	
XL2000.6.2	Enter formulas in a cell and using the formula bar	Yes	4	57-59	SBS4.1, 4.3
XL2000.6.3	Revise formulas	Yes	4	58-59	SBS4.4
XL2000.6.4	Use references (absolute and relative)	Yes	4	59-60	SBS4.4
XL2000.6.5	Use AutoSum	Yes	4	62-63	SBS4.6
XL2000.6.6	Use Paste Function to insert a function	No	5	74	SBS5.1
XL2000.6.7	Use basic functions (AVERAGE, SUM, COUNT, MIN, MAX)	Yes	5	75-78	SBS5.1, 5.2
XL2000.6.8	Enter functions using the formula palette	Yes	5	75-76	SBS5.1
XL2000.6.9	Use date functions (NOW and DATE)	Yes	5	81-82	SBS5.4

Standardized Coding Number	Activity	ICV Performance based?	Lesson #	Pages	Exercise #
XL2000.6.10	Use financial functions (FV and PMT)	**Yes**	**5**	**78-80**	**SBS5.3**
XL2000.6.11	Use logical functions (IF)	**Yes**	**5**	**82-83**	**SBS5.5**
XL2000.7	**Using charts and objects**				
XL2000.7.1	Preview and print charts	**Yes**	**8**	**131**	**SBS8.5**
XL2000.7.2	Use chart wizard to create a chart	**Yes**	**8**	**126-129**	**SBS8.1**
XL2000.7.3	Modify charts	**Yes**	**8**	**135-138**	**SBS8.9**
XL2000.7.4	Insert, move, and delete an object (picture)	**Yes**	**6**	**98-101**	**SBS6.8, 6.9**
XL2000.7.5	Create and modify lines and objects	No	7	113-114	SBS7.5

MICROSOFT ACCESS 2000
TOTAL OBJECTIVES: 48

Standardized Coding Number	Activity	ICV Performance based?	Lesson #	Pages	Exercise #
AC2000.1	**Planning and designing databases**				
AC2000.1.1	Determine appropriate data inputs for your database	No	1	4	
AC2000.1.2	Determine appropriate data outputs for your database	No	1	4-5	
AC2000.1.3	Create table structure	**Yes**	**1**	**11**	**SBS1.6**
AC2000.1.4	Establish table relationships	**Yes**	**4**	**73**	**SBS4.9**
AC2000.2	**Working with Access**				
AC2000.2.1	Use the Office Assistant	No	IN-1	10	
AC2000.2.2	Select an object using the Objects Bar	**Yes**	**1**	**6**	**SBS1.3**
AC2000.2.3	Print database objects (tables, forms, reports, queries)	**Yes**	**1, 3, 4, 5**	**18, 50, 65, 92**	**SBS1.10, 3.6, 4.3, 5.6**
AC2000.2.4	Navigate through records in a table, query, or form	**Yes**	**1, 3**	**16, 48**	**SBS1.9, 3.5**
AC2000.2.5	Create a database (using a Wizard or in Design View)	**Yes**	**1**	**8**	**SBS1.4**
AC2000.3	**Building and modifying tables**				
AC2000.3.1	Create tables by using the Table Wizard	**Yes**	**1**	**24**	**ACT1-1**
AC2000.3.2	Set primary keys	**Yes**	**4**	**72**	**SBS4.8**
AC2000.3.3	Modify field properties	No	2	35	SBS2.9
AC2000.3.4	Use multiple data types	**Yes**	**1**	**11**	**SBS1.6**
AC2000.3.5	Modify tables using Design View	**Yes**	**2**	**35**	**SBS2.9**
AC2000.3.6	Use the Lookup Wizard	No	1	11	
AC2000.3.7	Use the input mask wizard	No	2	35	

Standardized Coding Number	Activity	ICV Performance based?	Lesson #	Pages	Exercise #
AC2000.4	**Building and modifying forms**				
AC2000.4.1	Create a form with the Form Wizard	Yes	3	43	SBS3.1
AC2000.4.2	Use the Control Toolbox to add controls	Yes	3	50	SBS3.6
AC2000.4.3	Modify Format Properties (font, style, font size, color, caption, etc.) of controls	Yes	3	50	SBS3.6
AC2000.4.4	Use form sections (headers, footers, detail)	Yes	3	50	SBS3.6
AC2000.4.5	Use a Calculated Control on a form	Yes	3	54	SBS3.7
AC2000.5	**Viewing and organizing information**				
AC2000.5.1	Use the Office Clipboard	No	2	41	ACT2-2
AC2000.5.2	Switch between object Views	Yes	1	16	SBS1.9
AC2000.5.3	Enter records using a datasheet	No	1	15-16	
AC2000.5.4	Enter records using a form	Yes	3	48	SBS3.5
AC2000.5.5	Delete records from a table	Yes	2	29	SBS2.3
AC2000.5.6	Find a record	Yes	4	61	SBS4.1
AC2000.5.7	Sort records	Yes	4	69	SBS4.5
AC2000.5.8	Apply and remove filters (filter by form and filter by selection)	Yes	4	67	SBS4.4
AC2000.5.9	Specify criteria in a query	Yes	4	65	SBS4.3
AC2000.5.10	Display related records in a subdatasheet	No	4	76	SBS4.11
AC2000.5.11	Create a calculated field	Yes	4	65	SBS4.3
AC2000.5.12	Create and modify a multi-table select query	Yes	4	78	SBS4.12
AC2000.6	**Defining relationships**				
AC2000.6.1	Establish relationships	Yes	4	73	SBS4.9
AC2000.6.2	Enforce referential integrity	Yes	4	73	SBS4.9
AC2000.7	**Producing reports**				
AC2000.7.1	Create a report with the Report Wizard	Yes	5	85	SBS5.1
AC2000.7.2	Preview and print a report	Yes	5	92	SBS5.6
AC2000.7.3	Move and resize a control	No	5	94	SBS5.7
AC2000.7.4	Modify format properties (font, style, font size, color, caption, etc.)	Yes	5	94	SBS5.7
AC2000.7.5	Use the Control Toolbox to add controls	Yes	5	94	SBS5.7
AC2000.7.6	Use report sections (headers, footers, detail)	Yes	5	94	SBS5.7
AC2000.7.7	Use a Calculated Control in a report	Yes	5	94	SBS5.7

Standardized Coding Number	Activity	ICV Performance based?	Lesson #	Pages	Exercise #
AC2000.8	**Integrating with other application**				
AC2000.8.1	Import data to a new table	**Yes**	**6**	**106**	**SBS6.1**
AC2000.8.2	Save a table, query, form as a Web page	No	4	65-Did You Know?	
AC2000.8.3	Add Hyperlinks	No	6	118	ACT6-2
AC2000.9	**Using Access Tools**				
AC2000.9.1	Print Database Relationships	**Yes**	**4**	**75**	**SBS4.10**
AC2000.9.2	Backup and Restore a database	No	6	106-HOT TIP	
AC2000.9.3	Compact and Repair a database	No	3	55	

MICROSOFT POWERPOINT 2000
TOTAL OBJECTIVES: 50

Standardized Coding Number	Activity	ICV Performance based?	Lesson #	Pages	Exercise #
PP2000.1	**Creating a presentation**				
PP2000.1.1	Delete slides	**Yes**	**2, UR**	**21, 79, 82**	**SBS2.2, AP1, SIM**
PP2000.1.2	Create a specified type of slide	**Yes**	**1, UR**	**11, 80**	**SBS1.7, AP2**
PP2000.1.3	Create a presentation from a template and/or a Wizard	**Yes**	**2, UR**	**19-20, 79**	**SBS2.1, AP1**
PP2000.1.4	Navigate among different views (slide, outline, sorter, tri-pane)	**Yes**	**1**	**12-13**	**SBS1.8, P2-2**
PP2000.1.5	Create a new presentation from existing slides	**Yes**	**4, UR**	**59, 81**	**SBS4.1, AP3**
PP2000.1.6	Copy a slide from one presentation into another	No	4, UR	60, 74, 80	SBS4.1, P4-2, AP2
PP2000.1.7	Insert headers and footers	**Yes**	**2**	**22, 30**	**SBS2.8**
PP2000.1.8	Create a Blank presentation	No	2	19	
PP2000.1.9	Create a presentation using the AutoContent Wizard	**Yes**	**2, UR**	**19-20, 79**	**SBS2.1, AP1**
PP2000.1.10	Send a presentation via e-mail	No	4	64	
PP2000.2	**Modifying a presentation**				
PP2000.2.1	Change the order of slides using Slide Sorter view	**Yes**	**1**	**13-14, 18**	**SBS1.8, P1-2**
PP2000.2.2	Find and replace text	No	2	22	
PP2000.2.3	Change the layout for one or more slides	**Yes**	**1, UR**	**8-9, 18, 80, 81, 82**	**SBS1.5, P1-2, AP2, AP4, SIM**
PP2000.2.4	Change slide layout (Modify the Slide Master)	**Yes**	**2**	**29-30**	**SBS2.8, P2-3**
PP2000.2.5	Modify slide sequence in the outline-pane	No	2	33-34	SBS2.12

Standardized Coding Number	Activity	ICV Performance based?	Lesson #	Pages	Exercise #
PP2000.2.6	Apply a design template	Yes	1, UR	7-8, 17, 79, 81	SBS1.4, P1-1, AP1, AP3
PP2000.3	**Working with text**				
PP2000.3.1	Check spelling	No	2	24-25	SBS2.4
PP2000.3.2	Change and replace text fonts (individual slide and entire presentation)	Yes	4, UR	61, 81	SBS4.2, AP3
PP2000.3.3	Enter text in tri-pane view	Yes	1-2, UR	12, 17, 35, 81	SBS1.7, P1-1, P2-3, AP3, AP4
PP2000.3.4	Import Text from Word	Yes	4	70	SBS4.7
PP2000.3.5	Change the text alignment	Yes	2, UR	27, 82	SBS2.6, SIM
PP2000.3.6	Create a text box for entering text	Yes	3	54-55	SBS3.11
PP2000.3.7	Use the Wrap text in TextBox feature	No	3	54	
PP2000.3.8	Use the Office Clipboard	No	3	53	
PP2000.3.9	Use the Format Painter	Yes	4, UR	61, 81	SBS4.2, P4-1, AP3
PP2000.3.10	Promote and Demote text in slide & outline panes	Yes	2	33-34	SBS2.12
PP2000.4	**Working with visual elements**				
PP2000.4.1	Add a picture from the ClipArt Gallery	Yes	1, UR	9,11, 80, 81,82	SBS1.6, P2-1, AP2, AP4, SIM
PP2000.4.2	Add and group shapes using WordArt or the Drawing Toolbar	No	47,49, 3, UR	SBS3.7, 80	P3-1, AP1
PP2000.4.3	Apply formatting	Yes	3	47	SBS3.7, 3.8, 3.9
PP2000.4.4	Place text inside a shape using a text box	Yes	3, UR	54, 79	SBS3.11, AP1
PP2000.4.5	Scale and size an object including ClipArt	Yes	3, UR	52, 81, 82	SBS3.10, AP4, SIM
PP2000.4.6	Create tables within PowerPoint	Yes	3, UR	46, 57, 82	SBS3.5, P3-2, SIM
PP2000.4.7	Rotate and fill an object	No	3	50	SBS3.8
PP2000.5	**Customizing a presentation**				
PP2000.5.1	Add AutoNumber bullets	No	2	28	SBS2.7
PP2000.5.2	Add speaker notes	Yes	1-2	12, 17, 35	P1-1, P2-2
PP2000.5.3	Add graphical bullets	No	2	28	SBS2.7, P2-2
PP2000.5.4	Add slide transitions	Yes	2, UR	30-31, 80, 81	SBS2.9, P2-1, AP2, AP4
PP2000.5.5	Animate text and objects	Yes	2, UR	31-32, 80, 81	SBS2.10, AP2, AP4

Standardized Coding Number	Activity	ICV Performance based?	Lesson #	Pages	Exercise #
PP2000.6	**Creating output**				
PP2000.6.1	Preview presentation in black and white	No	1	15	
PP2000.6.2	Print slides in a variety of formats	**Yes**	**1-4, UR**	**14-15, 33, 57, 74, 80, 81**	**SBS1.9, 2.11, P1-2, 3-1, 4-1, 4-2, AP2, AP3**
PP2000.6.3	Print audience handouts	**Yes**	**1, UR**	**15, 82**	**SBS1.9, P1-2, AP4**
PP2000.6.4	Print speaker notes in a specified format	**Yes**	**1-2, UR**	**14, 18, 35, 80**	**P1-2, 2-2, AP2**
PP2000.7	**Delivering a presentation**				
PP2000.7.1	Start a slide show on any slide	**Yes**	**4, UR**	**62, 63, 81**	**SBS4.3, AP4**
PP2000.7.2	Use on screen navigation tools	**Yes**	**4**	**63**	**SBS4.3**
PP2000.7.3	Print a slide as an overhead transparency	No	4	65	
PP2000.7.4	Use the pen during a presentation	**Yes**	**4, UR**	**63, 67, 82**	**SBS4.3, P4-2, AP4**
PP2000.8	**Managing files**				
PP2000.8.1	Save changes to a presentation	**Yes**	**1**	**4-5**	**SBS1.2 (and at the end of most all other SBS)**
PP2000.8.2	Save as a new presentation	**Yes**	**1**	**4-5, 17**	**SBS1.2, P1-1 (and each time new data file is opened)**
PP2000.8.3	Publish a presentation to the Web	**Yes**	**4, UR**	**68-69, 82**	**SBS4.6, AP4**
PP2000.8.4	Use Office Assistant	No	1	2	
PP2000.8.5	Insert hyperlink	No	4, UR	66-67, 81	SBS4.5, P4-2, AP4

Key: SBS: Step-by-Step   P: Project   ACT: Critical Thinking Activity
       AP: Application   SIM: On-the-Job Simulation   UR: Unit Review

MICROSOFT WINDOWS 98 BASICS

This appendix is designed to familiarize you with the Windows 98 operating system. It provides you with the basic information you need to move around your desktop and manage the files, folders, and other resources you work with on a daily basics. It also covers the Windows 98 Help system.

Starting Windows 98

If Windows 98 is already installed, it should start automatically when you turn on the computer. If your computer is on a network, you may need some help from your instructor.

STEP-BY-STEP ▷ B.1

1. Turn on the computer.

2. After a few moments, Microsoft Windows 98 appears.

The Desktop

When Windows 98 starts up, the first window you see is the desktop. The **desktop** is the space where you access and work with programs and files. Figure B-1 illustrates a typical desktop screen. Your screen may vary slightly from the figure. For example, your screen may display icons that were installed with Windows 98 or shortcut icons you've created. You can customize and organize your desktop by creating files, folders, and shortcuts.

The main features of the desktop screen are labeled and numbered on the figure and discussed below:

1. The **Start** button brings up menus that give you a variety of options, such as starting a program, opening a document, finding help, or shutting down the computer.

2. The **Quick Launch** *toolbar t*o the right of the Start button contains icons so you can display the desktop or quickly start frequently used programs.

3. The **taskbar,** located at the bottom of the screen, tells you the names of all open programs. Figure B-1 shows that Microsoft Word is open.

4. **My Computer** is a program that allows you to see what files and folders are located on your computer.

5. **Internet Explorer** is a Web browser that allows you to surf the Internet, read e-mail, create a Web page, or download your favorite Web sites right to your desktop.

6. ***Network Neighborhood*** shows all the folders and printers that are available to you through the network connection, if you have one.

7. The ***Recycle Bin*** is a place to get rid of files or folders that are no longer needed.

8. Other ***icons,*** or small pictures, represent programs waiting to be opened.

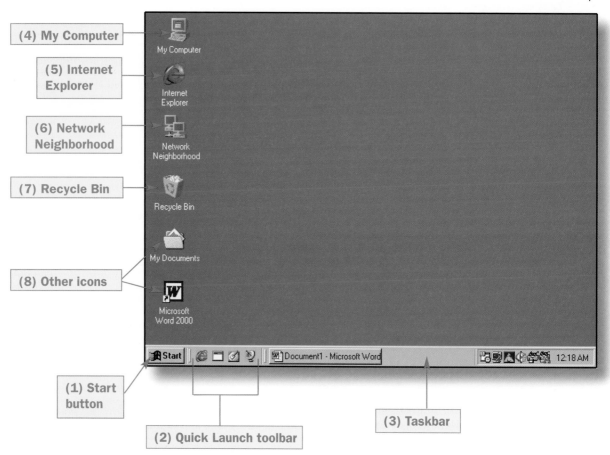

Windows 98 makes it easy to connect to the Internet. Just click the Launch Internet Explorer Browser button on the Quick Launch toolbar. The Quick Launch toolbar also has buttons so you can launch Outlook Express, view channels, and show the desktop.

With Windows 98 you can incorporate Web content into your work by using the Active Desktop, an interface that lets you put "active items" from the Internet on your desktop. You can use channels to customize the information delivered from the Internet to your computer. By displaying the Channel bar on your desktop you can add, subscribe to, or view channels.

1. Click the **Launch Internet Explorer Browser** button on the Quick Launch toolbar.

2. Click the **Show Desktop** button on the Quick Launch toolbar to display the Windows 98 desktop.

3. Click the **Internet Explorer** button on the taskbar to return to the browser window. (Your button may look a little different.)

4. Choose **Close** on the **File** menu to close Internet Explorer.

5. Point to the **Start** button.

6. Click the left mouse button. A menu of choices appears above the Start button as shown in Figure B-2.

7. Point to **Settings** without clicking. A submenu appears.

8. Click on **Control Panel**. A new window appears. The title bar at the top tells you that *Control Panel* is the name of the open window.

9. Leave this window on the screen for the next Step-by-Sep.

FIGURE B-2
Clicking the
Start button

Using Windows

Many of the windows you will work with have similar features. You can work more efficiently by familiarizing yourself with some of the common elements, as shown in Figure B-3, and explained below.

1. A *title bar* is at the top of every window and contains the name of the open program, window, document, or folder.

2. The *menu bar* lists available menus from which you can choose a variety of commands.

3. The *standard toolbar,* located directly below the menu bar, contains commands you can use by simply clicking the correct button.

4. The *Address bar* tells you which folder's contents are being displayed. You can also key a Web address in the Address bar without first opening your browser.

5. At the bottom of the window is the *status bar* that gives you directions on how to access menus and summarizes the actions of the commands that you choose.

- (1) Title bar
- (2) Menu bar
- (3) Standard toolbar
- (4) Address bar
- (5) Status bar

Moving and Resizing Windows

Sometimes you will have several windows open on the screen at the same time. To work more effectively, you may need to move or change the size of a window. To move a window, click the title bar and drag the window to another location. You can resize a window by dragging the window borders. When you position the pointer on a horizontal border, it changes to a vertical two-headed arrow. When you position the pointer on a vertical border, it changes to a horizontal two-headed arrow. You can then click and drag the border to change the width or height of the window. It is also possible to resize two sides of a window at the same time. When you move the pointer to a corner of the window's border, it becomes a two-headed arrow pointing diagonally. You can then click and drag to resize the window's height and width at the same time.

STEP-BY-STEP ▷ B.3

1. Move the **Control Panel** window by clicking on the title bar and holding the left mouse button down. Continue to hold the left mouse button down and drag the Control Panel until it appears to be centered on the screen. Release the mouse button.

2. Point anywhere on the border at the bottom of the Control Panel window. The pointer turns into a vertical two-headed arrow.

3. While the pointer is a two-headed arrow, drag the bottom border of the window down to enlarge the window.

4. Point to the border on the right side of the Control Panel window. The pointer turns into a horizontal two-headed arrow.

5. While the pointer is a two-headed arrow, drag the border of the window to the right to enlarge the window.

B - 4

6. Point to the lower right corner of the window border. The pointer becomes a two-headed arrow pointing diagonally.

7. Drag the border upward and to the left to resize both sides at the same time until the window is

about the same size as the one shown in Figure B-4.

8. Leave the window on the screen for the next Step-by-Step.

FIGURE B-4
Scroll bars, arrows, and boxes

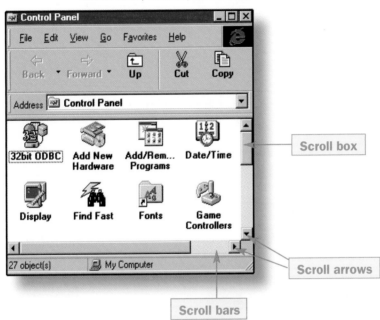

Scroll Bars

A *scroll bar* appears on the edges of windows any time there is more to be displayed than a window can show at its current size. See Figure B-4. A scroll bar can appear along the bottom edge (horizontal) and/or along the right side (vertical) of a window. Scroll bars appeared in the last step of the preceding Step-by-Step because the window was too small to show all the icons at once.

Scroll bars are a convenient way to bring another part of the window's contents into view. On the scroll bar is a sliding box called the *scroll box*. The scroll box indicates your position within the window. When the scroll box reaches the bottom of the scroll bar, you have reached the end of the window's contents. *Scroll arrows* are located at the ends of the scroll bar. Clicking on a scroll arrow moves the window in that direction one line at a time.

S TEP-BY-STEP ▷ B.4

1. On the horizontal scroll bar, click the scroll arrow that points to the right. The contents of the window shifts to the left.

2. Press and hold the mouse button on the same scroll arrow. The contents of the window scroll

(continued on next page)

quickly across the window. Notice that the scroll box moves to the right end of the scroll bar.

3. You can also scroll by dragging the scroll box. Drag the scroll box on the horizontal scroll bar to the left.

4. Drag the scroll box on the vertical scroll bar to the middle of the scroll bar.

5. The final way to scroll is to click on the scroll bar. Click the horizontal scroll bar to the right of the scroll box. The contents scroll left.

6. Click the horizontal scroll bar to the left of the scroll box. The contents scroll right.

7. Resize the Control Panel until the scroll bars disappear.

Other Window Controls

Three other important window controls, located on the right side of the title bar, are the *maximize button,* the *minimize button,* and the *Close button* (see Figure B-5). The maximize button enlarges a window to the full size of the screen. The minimize button shrinks a window to a button on the taskbar. The button on the taskbar is labeled and you can click it any time to redisplay the window. The Close button is used to close a window.

When a window is maximized, the maximize button is replaced by the restore button (see Figure B-6). The *restore button* returns the window to the size it was before the maximize button was clicked.

FIGURE B-5
Maximize, minimize, and Close buttons

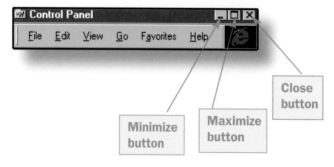

FIGURE B-6
Restore button

Restore button

S TEP-BY-STEP ⮕ B.5

1. Click the **maximize** button. The window enlarges to fill the screen.

2. Click the **restore** button on the Control Panel window (see Figure B-6).

3. Click the **minimize** button on the Control Panel window. The window is reduced to a button on the taskbar.

4. Click the **Control Panel** button on the taskbar to open the window again.

5. Click the **Close** button to close the window.

Menus and Dialog Boxes

To find out what a restaurant has to offer, you look at the menu. You can also look at a *menu* on the computer's screen to find out what a computer program has to offer. Menus in computer programs contain options for executing certain actions or tasks.

When you click the Start button, as you did earlier in this appendix, a menu is displayed with a list of options. If you choose a menu option with an arrow beside it, a submenu opens that lists additional options. A menu item followed by an ellipsis (...) indicates that a dialog box will appear when chosen. A *dialog box,* like the Shut Down Windows dialog box shown in Figure B-7, appears when more information is required before the command can be performed. You may have to key information, choose from a list of options, or simply confirm that you want the command to be performed. To back out of a dialog box without performing an action, press Esc, click the Close button, or choose Cancel (or No).

FIGURE B-7
Dialog box

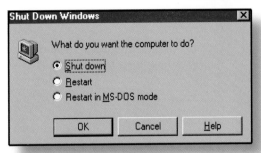

STEP-BY-STEP ▷ B.6

1. Click the **Start** button. A menu appears.

2. Click **Shut Down**. The Shut Down Windows dialog box appears, as shown in Figure B-7.

3. Click **Cancel** to back out of the dialog box without shutting down.

In a Windows application, menus are accessed from a menu bar (see Figure B-8). A menu bar appears beneath the title bar in each Windows program and consists of a row of menu names such as File and Edit. Each name in the menu bar represents a separate *pull-down menu*, containing related options. Pull-down menus are convenient to use because the commands are in front of you on the screen, as shown in Figure B-8. Like a menu in a restaurant, you can view a list of choices and pick the one you want.

You can give commands from pull-down menus using either the keyboard or the mouse. Each menu on the menu bar and each option on a menu is characterized by an underlined letter called a *mnemonic*. To open a menu on the menu bar using the keyboard, press Alt plus the mnemonic letter shown on the menu name. To display a menu using the mouse, simply place the pointer on the menu name and click the left button.

Just as with the Start menu, pull-down menus also have items with right-pointing arrows that open submenus, and ellipses that open dialog boxes. Choosing an item without an ellipsis or a right-pointing arrow executes the command. To close a menu without choosing a command, press Esc.

FIGURE B-8
Menu bar

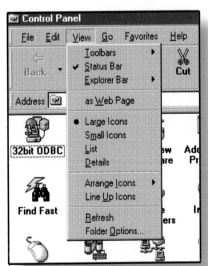

STEP-BY-STEP ▷ B.7

1. Open the Notepad accessory application by clicking **Start**, **Programs**, **Accessories**, and then **Notepad**. (See Figure B-9.)

2. Click **Edit** on the menu bar. The Edit menu appears.

3. Click **Time/Date** to display the current time and date.

4. Click **File** on the menu bar. The File menu appears (see Figure B-10).

5. Click **Exit**. A save prompt box appears.

6. Click **No**. The Notebook window disappears and you return to the desktop.

FIGURE B-9
Opening menus in an application

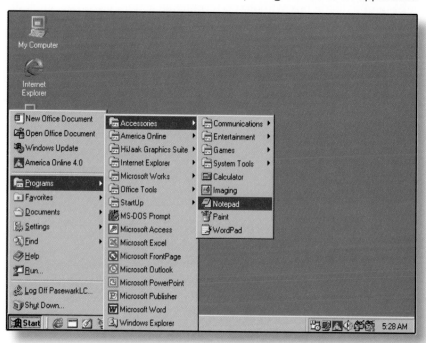

FIGURE B-10
Selecting the Exit command on the File menu

Windows 98 Help

This appendix has covered only a few of the many features of Windows 98. For additional information, Windows 98 has an easy-to-use help system. Use Help as a quick reference when you are unsure about a function. Windows 98 Help is accessed through the Help option on the Start menu. Then, from the Windows Help dialog box, you can choose to see a table of contents displaying general topics and subtopics, as shown in Figure B-11, or to search the help system using the Index or Search options. If you are working in a Windows 98 program, you can get more specific help about topics relating to that program by accessing help from the Help menu on the menu bar.

FIGURE B-11
Windows 98 Help program

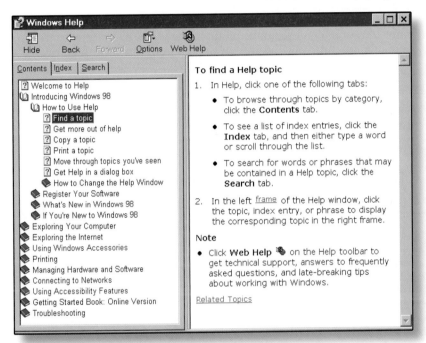

Many topics in the Help program are linked. A *link* is represented by colored, underlined text. By clicking a link, the user "jumps" to a linked document that contains additional information.

Using the buttons on the toolbar controls the display of information. The Hide button removes the left frame of the help window from view. The Show button will restore it. Back and Forward buttons allow you to move back and forth between previously displayed help entries. The Options button offers navigational choices, as well as options to customize, refresh, and print help topics.

The Contents tab is useful if you want to browse through the topics by category. Click a book icon to see additional help topics. Click a question mark to display detailed help information in the right frame of the help window.

STEP-BY-STEP ▷ B.8

1. Open the Windows 98 Help program by clicking the **Start** button, and then **Help**.

2. Click the **Hide** button on the toolbar to remove the left frame, if necessary.

(continued on next page)

3. Click the **Show** button to display it again, if necessary.

4. Click the **Contents** tab if it is not already selected.

5. Click **Introducing Windows 98** and then Click **How to Use Help**. Your screen should appear similar to Figure B-11.

6. Click **Find a topic**.

7. Read the help window and leave it open for the next Step-by-Step.

When you want to search for help on a particular topic, use the Index tab and key in a word. Windows will search alphabetically through the list of help topics to try to find an appropriate match, as shown in Figure B-12. Double-click a topic to see it explained in the right frame of the help window. Sometimes a Topics Found dialog box will appear that displays subtopics related to the item. Double-click the one on which you want more information.

FIGURE B-12
Index tab

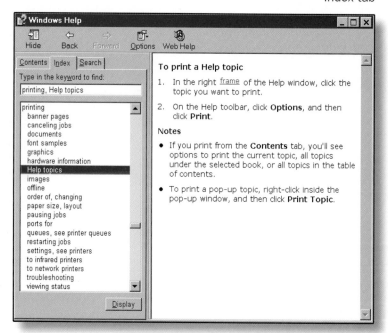

1. Click the **Index** tab.

2. Begin keying **printing** until *printing* is highlighted in the list of index entries.

3. Double-click the **Help topics** subtopic to display information in the right frame as shown in Figure B-12.

4. Read the help window, and then print the information by following the instructions you read.

5. Click **Back** to return to the previous help entry.

6. Click **Forward** to advance to the next help entry.

7. Close the Help program by clicking the Close button.

The Search tab is similar to the Index tab, but will perform a more thorough search of the words or phrases that you key. By using the Search option, you can display every occurrence of a particular word or phrase throughout the Windows 98 Help system. Double-click on the topic most similar to what you are looking for and information is displayed in the help window.

If you need assistance using the Windows 98 Help program, choose *Introducing Windows 98, How to Use Help* from the Contents tab.

If you are using an Office 2000 application, you can also get help by using the Office Assistant feature. These features are covered in the *Office 2000 Basics and the Internet* lesson.

Other Features

You need to know about several other features of Windows 98 before moving on, including My Computer, Windows Explorer, and the Recycle Bin. When open, these utilities display a standard toolbar like the one shown in Figure B-13.

FIGURE B-13
Standard toolbar

The Back and Forward buttons let you move back and forth between folder contents previously displayed in the window. The Up button moves you up one level in the hierarchy of folders. You can use the Cut, Copy, and Paste buttons to cut or copy an object and then paste it in another location. The Undo button allows you to reverse your most recent action. The Delete button sends the selected object to the Recycle Bin. The Properties button brings up a Properties dialog box with information about the selected object. The View button lists options for displaying the contents of the window.

My Computer

As you learned earlier, there is an icon on your desktop labeled My Computer. Double-clicking this icon opens the My Computer window, which looks similar to the one shown in Figure B-14. The My Computer program is helpful because it allows you to see what is on your computer. First double-click the icon for the drive you want to look at. That drive's name appears in the title bar and the window displays all the folders and files on that drive.

FIGURE B-14
My Computer window

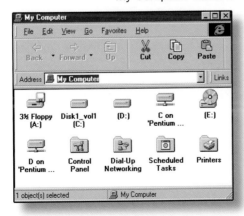

Because computer disks have such a large capacity, it is not unusual for a floppy disk to contain dozens of files or for a hard disk to contain hundreds or thousands of files. To organize files, a disk can be divided into folders. A *folder* is a place where files and other folders are stored. They help keep documents organized on a disk just the way folders would in a file cabinet. Folders group files that have something in common. You can also have folders within a folder. For example, you could create a folder to group all of the files you are working on in computer class. Within that folder, you could have several other folders that group files for each tool or each chapter.

When you double-click on a folder in My Computer, the contents of that folder are displayed—including program files and data files. Double-clicking on a program file icon will open that program. Double-clicking on a data file icon opens that document and the program that created it.

To create a new folder, double-click on a drive or folder in the My Computer window. Choose New on the File menu and then choose Folder on the submenu. A folder titled *New Folder* appears, as shown in Figure B-15. You can rename the folder by keying the name you want. Once you have created a folder, you can save or move files into it.

Hot Tip

You can change how folders and files are displayed by choosing **as Web Page**, **Large Icons**, **Small Icons**, **List**, or **Details** on the **View** menu.

FIGURE B-15
Creating a new folder in My Computer

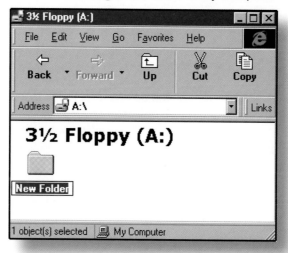

1. Double-click the **My Computer** icon on your desktop.

2. Double-click the drive where you want to create a new folder.

3. Choose **New** on the **File** menu and then choose **Folder** on the submenu. A folder titled *New Folder* appears, similar to Figure B-15.

4. Name the folder by keying **Time Records**. Press **Enter**.

5. Choose **Close** on the **File** menu to close the window.

Windows Explorer

Another way to view the folders and files on a disk is to use the Windows Explorer program. To open it, click Start, Programs, and then Windows Explorer. The Explorer window is split into two panes, as shown in Figure B-16. The left pane shows a hierarchical, or "tree" view of how the folders are organized on a disk; the right side, or Contents pane, shows the files and folders located in the folder that is currently selected in the tree pane.

The Explorer is a useful tool for organizing and managing the contents of a disk because you can create folders and rename them and easily delete, move, and copy files.

FIGURE B-16
Explorer window

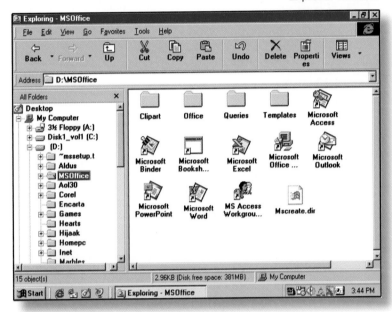

1. Open Windows Explorer by clicking **Start**, **Programs**, and then **Windows Explorer**.

2. In the tree pane, double-click the drive where the *Time Records* folder you just created is located.

3. Select the **Time Records** folder in the Contents pane of the Explorer window.

4. Choose **Rename** on the **File** menu.

5. Key **Finance**. Press **Enter**.

6. Leave Windows Explorer open for the next Step-by-Step.

Recycle Bin

Another icon on the desktop that you learned about earlier is the Recycle Bin. It looks like a wastebasket and is a place to get rid of files and folders that you no longer need. Until you empty the Recycle Bin, items that have been "thrown away" will remain there and can still be retrieved.

Recycle Bin

STEP-BY-STEP ▷ B.12

1. *Right*-click on the **Finance** folder.

2. Choose **Delete** on the shortcut menu. The Confirm Folder Delete dialog box appears, as shown in Figure B-17.

3. Click **Yes**. The folder is removed.

4. Choose **Close** on the **File** menu to close Windows Explorer.

FIGURE B-17
Confirm Folder Delete dialog box

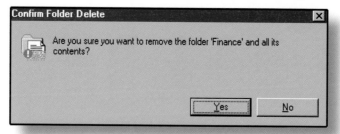

Summary

In this appendix, you learned:

■ The desktop organizes your work. Clicking the Start button displays options for opening programs and documents, and shutting down the computer. You can connect to the Internet using the Explorer browser and you can use the Active Desktop and channels to incorporate Web content into your work.

■ Windows can be moved, resized, opened, and closed. If all the contents of a window cannot be displayed in the window as it is currently sized, scroll bars appear to allow you to move to the part of the window that you want to view. Windows can be maximized to fill the screen or minimized to a button on the taskbar.

■ Menus allow you to choose commands to perform different actions. Menus are accessed from the Start button or from a program's menu bar near the top of the window. When you choose a menu command with an ellipsis (...), a dialog box appears that requires more information before performing the command. Choosing a menu option with an arrow opens a submenu.

- The Windows 98 Help program provides additional information about the many features of Windows 98. You can access the Help program from the Start button and use the Contents, Index, or Search tabs to get information. You can also get help from the Help menu within Windows programs.

- Folders group files that have something in common. To organize a disk, it can be divided into folders where files and other folders are stored. Other useful features of Windows 98 include: My Computer, which lets you see what is on your computer; Windows Explorer, which helps organize and manage your files; and the Recycle Bin for deleting unneeded files or folders.

APPENDIX REVIEW QUESTIONS

TRUE/FALSE

Circle T if the statement is true or F if the statement is false.

T F 1. The Quick Launch toolbar tells you the name of all the open programs.

T F 2. Channels allow you to customize the information delivered from the Internet to your computer.

T F 3. Scroll bars appear when all items in the window are visible.

T F 4. A menu item with an arrow indicates that a dialog box will appear when chosen.

T F 5. The Index tab is useful if you want to browse through help topics by category.

WRITTEN QUESTIONS

Write a brief answer to the following questions.

1. What is the interface that lets you put "active items" from the Internet on the desktop?

2. What button do you click to have the option of starting a program, opening a document, finding help, or shutting down the computer?

3. How do you move a window?

4. Where is the Close button located?

5. What is the purpose of the Recycle Bin?

APPENDIX C

COMPUTER CONCEPTS

What Is a Computer?

A computer is a mechanical device that is used to store, retrieve, and manipulate information (called data) electronically. You enter the data into the computer through a variety of input devices, process it, and output it in a number of ways. Computer software programs run the computer and let you manipulate the data.

Hardware

The physical components, or parts, of the computer are called hardware. The main parts are the central processing unit (CPU), the monitor, the keyboard, and the mouse. Peripherals are additional components like printers and scanners.

Input Devices. You enter information into a computer by typing on a keyboard or by using a mouse, a hand-held device, to move a pointer on the computer screen. Other input devices include a joystick, a device similar to the control stick of an airplane that moves a pointer or character on the screen, and a modem, which receives information via a telephone line. Other input devices include scanners, trackballs, and digital tracking. You can use scanners to "read" text or graphics into a computer from a printed page or to read bar codes (coded labels) to keep track of merchandise in a store or other inventory. Similar to a mouse, a trackball has a roller ball you turn to control a pointer on the screen. Digital tracking devices let you press a finger on a small electronic pad on the keyboard of a laptop to control the pointer on the screen, instead of using a trackball or a mouse.

Processing Devices. The central processing unit (CPU), is a silicon chip that processes data and carries out instructions given to the computer. The data bus includes the wiring and pathways by which the CPU communicates with the peripherals and components of the computer.

Storage Devices. The hard drive, is a device that reads and writes data to and from a round magnetic platter, or disk. The data is encoded on the disk much the same as sounds are encoded on magnetic tape. The hard drive is called hard because the disk is rigid, unlike a floppy disk drive, which reads and writes data to and from a removable non-rigid disk, similar to a round disk of magnetic tape. The floppy disk, is encased in a plastic sleeve to protect its data. The floppy disk's main advantage is portability. You can store data on a floppy disk and transport it to another computer to use the data there.

At one time, the largest hard drive was 10 MB, or 10,000,000 bytes of data. A byte stands for a single character of data. Currently, hard drives can be up to 14 gigabytes (GB). That's 14,000,000,000 bytes of data.

The most recent storage device is the CD, or compact disk, which is a form of optical storage. Information is encoded on the disk by a laser and read by a CD-ROM drive in the computer. These disks have a great advantage over floppies because they can hold vast quantities of information—the entire contents of a small library, for instance. However, most computers cannot write (or save) information to these disks; CD-ROMs are Read-Only Memory (ROM) devices. Drives are now available that write to CDs. Although these drives used to be very expensive and therefore were not used widely, they are becoming more affordable. The great advantage of CDs is their ability to hold graphic information—including moving pictures with the highest quality stereo sound. Similar to a CD, the digital video drive (DVD) can read high-quality cinema-type disks.

Another storage medium is magnetic tape. This medium is most commonly used for backing up, making a copy of files from a hard drive. Although it is relatively rare for a hard drive to crash (that is, to have the data or pointers to the data be partially or totally destroyed), it can and does happen. Therefore, most businesses and some individuals routinely back up files on tape. If you have a small hard drive, you can use floppy disks to back up your system.

Output Devices.   The monitor on which you view your work is an output device. It provides a visual representation of the information stored in or produced by your computer. The monitor for today's typical system is the SVGA (super video graphics array). It provides a very sharp picture because of the large number of tiny dots, called pixels, that make up the display as well as its ability to present the full spectrum of colors. Most laptop computers use a liquid crystal display (LCD) screen that is not as clear a display because it depends on the arrangement of tiny bits of crystal to present an image. However, the latest laptops use new technology that gives quality near or equal to that of a standard monitor.

Printers are another type of output device. They let you produce a paper printout of information contained in the computer. Today, most printers are of the laser type, using light to burn in an image as a copy machine does. Ink-jet printers use a spray of ink to print. Laser printers give the sharpest image. Ink jet printers provide nearly as sharp an image but the wet printouts can smear when they first come out. However, most color printers are ink jet; these printers let you print information in its full array of colors as you see it on your SVGA monitor. Laser color printers, are available but are more costly.

Modems are another output device, as well as an input device. They allow computers to communicate with each other by telephone lines. Modems convert information in bytes to sound media to send data and then convert it back to bytes after receiving data. Modems operate at various rates or speeds; typically today, a computer will have a modem that operates at 33,600 baud (a variable unit of data transmission) per second or better.

Laptops and Docking Stations.   A laptop computer is a small folding computer that literally fits in a person's lap. Within the fold-up case is the CPU, data bus, monitor (built into the lid), hard drive (sometimes removable), a 3.5-inch floppy drive, a CD-ROM drive, and a trackball or digital tracking device. The advantage of the laptop is its portability—you can work anywhere because you can use power either from an outlet or from the computer's internal, rechargeable batteries. The drawbacks are the smaller keyboard, liquid crystal monitor, smaller capacity, and higher price. The newer laptops offer full-sized keyboards and higher quality monitors. As technology allows, storage capacity on smaller devices is making it possible to offer laptops with as much power and storage as a full-sized computer. The docking station is a device into which you slide a closed laptop that becomes the desktop computer. Then you can plug in a full-sized monitor, keyboard, mouse, printer, and so on. Such a setup lets you use the laptop like a desktop computer while at your home or office.

Functioning

All of the input, processing, storage, and output devices function together to make the manipulation, storage, and distribution of data and information possible.

Data and Information Management.   Data is information entered into and manipulated in a computer. Manipulation includes computation, such as adding, subtracting, and dividing; analysis planning, such as sorting data; and reporting, such as presenting data for others in a chart. Data and information management runs software on computer hardware.

Memory.   There are two kinds of memory in a computer—RAM and ROM. RAM, or Random Access Memory, is a number of silicon chips inside a computer that hold information as long as the computer is turned on. RAM is what keeps the software programs up and running and keeps the visuals on your screen. RAM is where you work with data until you "save" it to a hard or floppy disk. Early computers had simple programs and did little with data, so they had very little RAM—possibly 4 or fewer megabytes. Today's computers run very complicated programs that "stay resident" (remain available to the user at the same time as other programs) and run graphics. Both of these tasks take a lot of memory; therefore, today's computers have at least 32 or more megabytes of RAM. ROM, or read-only memory, is the small bit of memory that stays in the computer when it is turned off. It is ROM that lets the computer "boot up," or get started. ROM holds the instructions that tell the computer how to begin to load its operating system software programs.

Speed.   The speed of a computer is measured by how fast the drives turn to reach information to be retrieved or to save data. The measurement is in megahertz (MHz). Early personal computers worked at 4.77 to 10 megahertz; today, machines run at 150 MHz or more. Another factor that affects the speed of a computer is how much RAM is available. Since RAM makes up the work area for all programs and holds all the information that you input until you save, the more RAM available, the quicker the machine will be able to operate.

One other area of speed must be considered, and that is how quickly the modem can send and receive information. As mentioned earlier, modem speed is measured in baud. The usual modem runs at 33,600 OR 56,000 baud per second or more.

Communications.   Computers have opened up the world of communications, first within offices via LANs (local area networks that link computers within a facility via wires) and, later, via the Internet. Using the Internet, people can communicate across the world instantly with e-mail and attach files that were once sent by mailing a floppy disk. Also, anyone with a modem and an access service can download information from or post information to thousands of bulletin boards.

Software

A program is a set of mathematical instructions to the computer. Software is the collection of programs and other data input that tells the computer how to operate its machinery, how to manipulate, store, and output information, and how to accept the input you give it. Software fits into two basic categories: systems software and applications software. A third category, network software, is really a type of application.

Systems Software.   Systems software refers to the operating system (OS) of the computer. The OS is a group of programs that is automatically copied in RAM every couple of seconds from the time the computer is turned on until the computer is turned off. Operating systems serve two functions: they control data flow among computer parts and they provide the platform on which application and network software work—in effect, they allow the "space" for software and translate its commands to the computer. The most popular operating systems in use today are the *Macintosh* operating system, and a version of Microsoft Windows, such as Windows 95 or Windows 98.

Macintosh has its own operating system that has evolved over the years since its introduction. From the beginning, Macintosh has used a graphical user interface (GUI) operating system—quite an innovation at its introduction in the mid-1970s. The OS is designed so users "click" with a mouse on pictures, called icons, or on text to give commands to the system. Data is available to you in WYSIWYG (what-you-see-is-what-you-get) form; that is, you can see on-screen what a document will look like when it is printed. Graphics and other kinds of data, such as spreadsheets, can be placed into text documents. However, GUIs take a great deal of RAM to keep all of the graphics and programs operating.

The OS for IBM and IBM-compatible computers (machines made by other companies that operate similarly) originally was DOS (disk operating system). It did not have a graphical interface. The GUI system, Windows™, was developed to make using the IBM/IBM-compatible computer more "friendly." Users no longer had to memorize written commands to make the computer carry out actions but could use a mouse to point and click on icons or words. Windows 3.1, however, was a translating system that operated on top of DOS—not on its own., and newer versions of Windows are continually being developed.

Windows 3.1 was a GUI system that operated on top of DOS; Windows 3.1 was *not* an operating system by itself. It allowed you to point and click on graphics and words that then translate to DOS commands for the computer. Data was available to you in WYSIWYG (what-you-see-is-what-you-get) form. Graphics and other kinds of data, such as spreadsheets, could be placed into text documents by Object

Linking and Embedding (OLE). However, Windows 3.1, because it was still using DOS as its base, was not really a stay-resident program. In other words, it did not keep more than one operation going at a time; it merely switched between operations quickly. Using several high-level programs at the same time, however, could cause problems, such as memory failure. Therefore, improvements were inevitable.

Windows 95 is its own operating system, unlike the original Windows 3.1, and is the replacement for Windows 3.1. Windows 95 has DOS built-in but does not operate on top of it—if you go to a DOS prompt from Windows 95, you will still be operating inside a Windows 95 system, not in traditional DOS. Windows 95 is the logical evolution of GUI for IBM and IBM-compatible machines. It is a stay-resident, point-and-click system that automatically configures hardware to work together. With all of its ability comes the need for more RAM or this system will operate slowly. Newer versions of Windows continue to be released.

Applications Software.   When you use a computer program to perform a data manipulation or processing task, you are using applications software. Word processors, databases, spreadsheets, desktop publishers, fax systems, and online access systems are all applications software.

Network Software.   Novell™ and Windows are two kinds of network software. A network is a group of computers that are hardwired (hooked together with cables) to communicate and operate together. One computer acts as the server, which controls the flow of data among the other computers, called nodes, on the network. Network software manages this flow of information. Networks have certain advantages over stand-alone computers. They allow communication among the computers; they allow smaller capacity nodes to access the larger capacity of the server; and they allow several computers to share peripherals, such as one printer, and they can make it possible for all computers on the network to have access to the Internet.

History of the Computer

Though various types of calculating machines were developed in the nineteenth century, the history of the modern computer begins about the middle of this century. The strides made in developing today's personal computer have been truly astounding.

Early Development

ENIAC, designed for military use in calculating ballistic trajectories, was the first electronic, digital computer to be developed in the United States. For its day, 1946, it was quite a marvel because it was able to accomplish a task in 20 seconds that took a human three days to do. However, it was an enormous machine that weighed more than 20 tons and contained thousands of vacuum tubes, which often failed. The tasks that it could accomplish were limited, as well.

From this awkward beginning, however, the seeds of an information revolution grew. Significant dates in the history of computer development are the first electronic stored program in 1948, the first junction transistor in 1951, the replacement of tubes with magnetic cores in 1953, the first high-level computer language in 1957, the first integrated circuit in 1961, the first minicomputer in 1965, the invention of the microprocessor (the silicon chip) and floppy disk in 1971, and the first personal computer in 1974 (made possible by the microprocessor). These last two inventions launched the fast-paced information revolution in which we now all live and participate.

The Personal Computer

The PC, or personal computer, was mass marketed by Apple, beginning in 1977, and by IBM, beginning in 1981. It is this desktop device with which people are so familiar and which, today, contains much more power and ability than did the original computer that took up an entire room. The PC is a small computer (desktop size or less) that uses a microprocessor to manipulate data. PCs may stand alone, be linked together in a network, or be attached to a large mainframe computer.

Computer Utilities and System Maintenance

Computer operating systems let you run certain utilities and perform system maintenance. When you add hardware or software, you might need to make changes in the way the system operates. Beginning with the Windows 95 version most configuration changes are done automatically; however, other operating systems might not, or you might want to customize the way the new software or hardware will interface (coordinate) with your system. Additionally, you can make alterations such as the speed at which your mouse clicks, how fast or slow keys repeat on the keyboard, and what color or pattern appears on the desktop or in GUI programs.

You need to perform certain maintenance regularly on computers. You should scan all new disks and any incoming information from online sources for viruses. Some systems do this automatically; others require you to install software to do it. From time to time, you should scan or check the hard drive to see that there are no bad sectors or tracks and to look for corrupted files. Optimizing or defragmenting the hard disk is another way to keep your computer running at its best. You can also check a floppy disk if it is not working properly. Programs for scanning a large hard drive could take up to half an hour to run; checking programs run on a small hard drive or disk might take only seconds or minutes. Scanning and checking programs often offer the option of "fixing" the bad areas or problems, although you should be aware that this could result in data loss.

Society and Computers

With the computer revolution have come many new questions and responsibilities. There are issues of responsibility and ethics, access control, and privacy and security.

Responsibility and Ethics

When you access information—whether online, in the workplace, or via purchased software—you have a responsibility to respect the rights of the creator of that information. You must treat electronic information in a copyrighted form the same way as you would a published book or article or a patented invention. For instance, you must give credit when you access information from a CD-ROM encyclopedia or a download from an online database. Also, information you transmit must be accurate and fair, like that printed in a book. When you use equipment that belongs to your school, a company for which you work, or others, the following ethical guidelines apply:

1. You must not damage computer hardware and must not add or remove equipment without permission.

2. You must not use an access code or equipment without permission.

3. You must not read others' electronic mail.

4. You must not alter data belonging to someone else without permission.

5. You must not use the computer for play during work hours or use it for personal profit.

6. You must not access the Internet for nonbusiness use during work hours.

7. You must not add to or take away from the software programs and must not make unauthorized copies of data or software.

8. You must not copy software programs to use at home or at another site in the company without multisite permission.

9. You must not copy company files or procedures for personal use.

10. You must not borrow computer hardware for personal use without asking permission.

Internet Access and Children

Children's access to the Internet is another matter to consider. Many of the online services allow parents or guardians to control what areas of the service users can access. Because there are some discussion topics and adult information that are inappropriate for younger computer users, it is wise to take advantage of this access-limiting capability. Families using direct Internet access can purchase software for this purpose. If this software is not available, the solution must be very careful monitoring of a child's computer use.

Privacy and Security

Not only are there issues of privacy in accessing work on another's computer, there are also issues that revolve around privacy in communicating on the Internet. Just as you would not open someone else's mail, you must respect the privacy of e-mail sent to others. When interacting with others online, you must keep confidential information confidential—such as the address of a new friend made online. You must think, too, about the information that you are providing. You do not want to endanger your privacy, safety, or financial security by giving out personal information to someone you do not know. A common scam (trick) on some online services is for someone to pretend to work for the service and ask for your access code or password, which controls your service account. *Never* give this out to anyone online because the person can use it and charge a great deal of costly time to your account. Also, just as you would not give a stranger your home address, telephone number, or credit card number if you were talking on the street, you should take those same precautions online.

Career Opportunities

In one way or another, all of our careers involve the computer. Whether you are a grocery checker using a scanner to read the prices, a busy executive writing a report on a laptop on an airplane, or a programmer creating new software—almost everyone uses computers in their jobs. And, everyone in a business processes information in some way. There are also specific careers available if you want to work primarily with computers.

Schools offer computer programming, repair, and design degrees. The most popular jobs are systems analysts, computer operators, and programmers. Analysts figure out ways to make computers work (or work better) for a particular business or type of business. Computer operators use the programs and devices to conduct business with computers. Programmers write the software for applications or new systems.

There are courses of study in using CAD (computer-aided design) and CAM (computer-aided manufacturing). Computer engineering and architectural design degrees are now available. Scientific research is done on computers today, and specialties are available in that area. There are positions available to instruct others in computer software use within companies and schools. Also, technical writers and editors must be available to write manuals on using computers and software. Computer-assisted instruction (CAI) is designing a system of teaching any given subject on the computer. The learner is provided with resources, such as an encyclopedia on CD-ROM, in addition to the specific learning program with which he or she interacts on the computer. Designing video games is another exciting and ever-growing field of computer work.

What Does the Future Hold?

The possibilities for computer development and application are endless. Things that were dreams or science fiction only 10 or 20 years ago are a reality today. New technologies are emerging. Some are replacing old ways of doing things; others are merging with those older devices. We are learning new ways to work and play because of the computer. It is definitely a device that has become part of our offices and our homes.

Emerging Technologies

The various technologies and systems are coming together to operate more efficiently. For instance, since their beginnings, Macintosh and IBM/IBM-compatible systems could not exchange information well. Today, you can install compatibility cards in the Power Macintosh and run Windows, DOS, and Mac OS on the same computer and switch between them. Macs (except for early models) can read from and write to MS-DOS and Windows disks. And you can easily network Macintosh computers with other types of computers running other operating systems. In addition, you can buy software for a PC to run the Mac OS and to read Macintosh disks. New technology in the works will allow you to incorporate both systems and exchange information even more easily.

Telephone communication is also being combined with computer e-mail so users can set a time to meet online and, with the addition of new voice technology, actually speak to each other. The present drawbacks are that users must e-mail and make an appointment to meet online rather than having a way just to call up each other, and speaking is delayed rather than in real-time. Although not perfected, this form of communication will certainly evolve into an often-used device that will broaden the use of both the spoken and written word.

Another emerging technology is the CUCME (see you, see me) visual system that allows computer users to use a small camera and microphone wired into the computer so, when they communicate via modem, the receiver can see and hear them. This technology is in its infancy—the pictures tend to be a bit fuzzy and blur with movement; however, improvements are being made so sharp pictures will result. For the hearing impaired, this form of communication can be more effective than writing alone since sign language and facial expression can be added to the interaction. CUCME is a logical next step from the image transfer files now so commonly used to transfer a static (nonmoving) picture.

A great deal of research and planning has gone into combining television and computers. The combined device has a CPU, television-as-monitor, keyboard, joystick, mouse, modem, and CUCME/quick-cam. Something like the multiple communications device that science fiction used to envision, this combined medium allows banking, work, entertainment, and communication to happen all through one piece of machinery—and all in the comfort of your home. There are already printers that function as a copier, fax machine, and scanner.

Trends

One emerging trend is for larger and faster hard drives. One- and two-gigabyte hard drives have virtually replaced the 540 megabyte drives, and 14.4 gigabyte drives are appearing on the scene. RAM today is increasing exponentially. The trend is to sell RAM in units of 8 or 16 megabytes to accommodate the greater purchases of 32, 64, and larger blocks of RAM. The 32-bit operating system is becoming the norm. All of these size increases are due to the expanding memory requirements of GUIs and new peripherals, such as CUCME devices and interfaces with other devices. Although the capacities are increasing, the actual size of the machines is decreasing. Technology is allowing more powerful components to fit into smaller devices—just as the $3\,^1/2$-inch floppy disk is smaller and holds more data than the obsolete $5\,^1/4$-inch floppy.

Another trend is the increased use of computers for personal use in homes. This trend is likely to continue in the future.

Home Offices.   More and more frequently, people are working out of their homes—whether they are employees who are linked to a place of business or individuals running their own businesses. Many companies allow certain workers to have a computer at home that is linked by modem to the office. Work is done at home and transferred to the office. Communication is by e-mail and telephone. Such an arrangement saves companies work space and, thus, money. Other employees use laptop computers to work both at home and on the road as they travel. These computers, in combination with a modem, allow an employee to work from virtually anywhere and still keep in constant contact with her or his employer and customers.

With downsizing (the reduction of the workforce by companies), many individuals have found themselves unemployed or underemployed (working less or for less money). These people have, in increasing numbers, begun their own businesses out of their homes. With a computer, modem, fax software, printer, and other peripherals, they can contract with many businesses or sell their own products or services. Many make use of the Internet and World Wide Web to advertise their services.

Home Use. As the economy has tightened, many people are trying to make their lives more time- and cost-efficient. The computer is one help in that search. Having banking records, managing household accounts, and using electronic banking on a computer saves time. The games and other computer interactions also offer a more reasonable way of spending leisure dollars than some outside entertainment. For instance, it might not be feasible to travel to Paris to see paintings in the Louvre Museum; however, it might be affordable to buy a CD-ROM that lets you take a tour of that famous facility from the comfort of your chair in front of your computer. This can be quite an educational experience for children and a more restful one for those who might tire on the trip but can easily turn off the computer and come back to it later. Young people can benefit enormously from this kind of education as well as using the computer to complete homework, do word processing, create art and graphics, and, of course, play games that sharpen their hand-to-eye coordination and thinking skills.

Purchasing a Computer

Once you decide to take the plunge and purchase a computer, the selection of a new computer system should be a careful and meticulous one to ensure that your needs are fulfilled. This section will help you evaluate what computer is best suited for you and help you select a new computer for purchase.

Choosing a Computer System

This is perhaps the most critical step in your quest for the ultimate computer system. It is generally best to buy a computer with an operating system and format you know. If you learned or are learning computers on a Macintosh, then you will most likely want to purchase a Macintosh system. It is also important to consider what kinds of tasks you wish to perform on your computer. IBM and IBM-compatibles have more available software and are more common in businesses, whereas Macintosh computers excel at desktop publishing and graphics. After you decide which type of computer you will buy, you must decide whether to buy a desktop or laptop. This will probably be decided for you by your pocketbook. Laptops generally cost more than desktop computers. If you need the portability a laptop has to offer and can afford the additional cost, then it might be the choice for you. Otherwise, desktops are very suitable for use in business, home, and school.

Outlining Your Needs

After you decide what kind of computer you will buy, it is time to confirm the details. When purchasing a computer, you should consider several specific components. The recommended *minimum* of a few of these are noted in Table C–1.

TABLE C-1

	IBM AND IBM-COMPATIBLES	MACINTOSH
Processor	Pentium	PowerPC 603e RISC processor
Speed	133 MHz	120 MHz
Memory (RAM)	32 MB	16 MB
Hard Drive	1.0 GB	1.0 GB
CD-ROM	8x (Eight-speed)	8x (Eight-speed)
Fax/Modem	33.6 kbps	28.8 kbps
Expansion Slots	5	3 to 6
Operating System	Windows 98	Mac OS 7.5 or higher

Depending on what you plan to do with your computer, you might need different components. For instance, if you plan to do a large amount of video and graphical analysis and manipulation, you probably want at least 64 MB of RAM, rather than 16 MB. High-powered gaming requires a faster video card with more RAM, as would any emerging technologies such as MPEG and virtual reality. If your office plans to do a large amount of online publishing and commerce via the Internet, a faster modem is a necessity.

Comparative Shopping

Next comes the most challenging task: finding your computer system. Perhaps the most effective way of doing this is to make a spreadsheet similar to the one in Table C–2. This lets you directly compare different systems from different companies while saving time. Using what you have learned in this book, you could even create charts to show how the different computer systems relate to each other graphically.

TABLE C-2

COMPUTER SYSTEM COMPARISON CHART

FEATURES	PREFERRED FEATURES	SYSTEM 1	SYSTEM 2	SYSTEM 3
Manufacturer	not applicable			
Model				
Processor	Pentium			
Speed	133 MHz			
Expansion slots	5			
3.5-inch drive	Yes (included)			
Price				
RAM	32 MB			
Price (if additional)				
Hard Drive	2.5 GB			
Price (if additional)				
Monitor	15″ SVGA			
Price (if additional)				
Video Card	2 MB RAM			
Price (if additional)				
Sound Card	16-bit			
Price (if additional)				
CD-ROM	8x			
Price (if additional)				
Fax/Modem	33.6 kbps			
Price (if additional)				
Printer	ink jet			
Price (if additional)				
Software	Windows 98			
Price (if additional)				
Subtotal				
Sales tax				
Shipping and Handling				
TOTAL PRICE				

Before you begin comparison shopping, it is important to be aware of hidden costs. For instance, many large chain stores offer computer packages that might not include a monitor. If a system does not include a monitor, you must add this cost. In addition to your system, you might need a printer or extra software. If your system will be mailed to you, then you must also consider shipping and handling costs. Sales tax, when applicable, is another hidden cost. On large purchases such as a computer, tax can rapidly add up, so it is important to figure this in before making the final decision.

Making the Final Decision

After you complete the chart, it is time to purchase your computer. Resist the temptation to buy the cheapest or most powerful system. The cheapest computer might be of lesser quality and might not have the features you desire. It is important to get a system powerful enough to last you at least three years but still be within your budget. The most powerful system might contain more features than you need, and could be too expensive. Also, remember that the most expensive does not necessarily guarantee superior quality. Sometimes the most expensive system contains "free" software or other extras that you do not need. It is good to consider the manufacturer's reputation when deciding where to purchase your system. Some good unbiased sources for this information include the Internet, where customers who have purchased computers often voice their opinions, and consumer magazines. Other points to consider include financing, warranty, available training, and technical support and service.

GLOSSARY

A

Absolute cell reference Cell reference that does not adjust to the new cell location when copied or moved.

Active cell Highlighted cell ready for data entry.

Alignment How text is positioned between the margins

And operator Used to find records that meet more than one criteria.

Animate Add a sound effect or special visual to an object or text.

Annual event Occurs every year on the same date, such as a birthday or anniversary.

Appointment book Located in the center of the Calendar screen, where dates and times of appointments, such as meetings and events, are displayed.

Argument Value, cell reference, range, or text that acts as an operand in a function formula.

Ascending sort Sort that arranges records from *A* to *Z* or smallest to largest.

AutoCorrect Wizard Option that provides you with ideas and an organization for a new presentation based on your answers to the series of questions it asks.

Axis Line that identifies the values in a chart; most charts have a horizontal (or X axis) and a vertical (or Y axis).

B

Banner Heading at the top of a Web page which gives the title or description of the content on the page.

Blank Presentation Option that lets you create a presentation from scratch using whatever layout, format, colors, and style you prefer.

Blank Publications Publication using the format, color, or design the user prefers.

C

Case Whether letters are capitalized or not; capital letters are uppercase, while others are lowercase.

Cell Intersection of a row and column in a worksheet or table.

Cell comment Message that provides information concerning data in a cell.

Cell reference Identifies a cell by the column letter and row number (for example, A1, B2, C4).

Chart Graphical representation of data contained in a worksheet.

Chart sheet Area separate from the Excel worksheet in which a chart is created and stored; the chart sheet is identified by a tab near the bottom of the screen.

Chart Wizard Four-step, on-screen guide that aids in preparing a chart from an Excel worksheet.

Clip art Graphics that are already drawn and available for use in documents.

Calculated control Control in a form or report that uses an expression to generate the data value for a field.

Clipboard A temporary storage place in memory.

Close button "X" on the right side of the title bar that closes a window

Close Removing a document or window from the screen.

Column chart Chart that uses rectangles of varying heights to illustrate values in a worksheet.

Columns Appear vertically in a worksheet and are identified by letters at the top of the worksheet window.

Conditional formatting Applies a font, border, or pattern to a worksheet cell when certain conditions exist in that cell.

Contact Any person or company with whom you communicate.

D

Database management system Any system for managing data.

Data labels Values depicted by the chart objects (such as columns or data points) that are printed directly on the chart.

Data series Group of related information in a column or row of a worksheet that is plotted on a worksheet chart.

Date Navigator The monthly calendars at the top right of the Calendar screen, used to select dates by clicking the requested date.

Database report A report that allows you to organize, summarize, and print all or a portion of the data in a database.

Datasheet view A form similar to a spreadsheet that allows records to be entered directly into a table.

Data source Contains the information that will vary in a form letter.

Data type Specification that tells Access what kind of information can be stored in a field.

Default Setting used unless another option is chosen.

Descending sort Sort that arranges records from Z to A or largest to smallest.

Design templates Presentations that come with PowerPoint that are already designed and formatted with certain colors, fonts, and layouts.

Design view Where you design and modify tables.

Desktop Space where you access and work with programs and files.

Desktop publishing The process of combining text and graphics, using a computer, to create attractive documents.

Destination File or application to which you are transferring data.

Destination file File you are moving data *to* when you are moving data between applications.

Detail Section in a form or report that displays the records.

Detail symbols Plus and minus signs that appear in the margins when a worksheet is in outline mode.

Dialog box A message box asking for further instructions before a command can be performed.

Double-clicking Pressing the left mouse button quickly two times in a row.

Drag and drop A quick method for copying and moving text a short distance.

E

Embed Place information in a file as a separate object that can be edited using the application that created it.

Embedded chart Chart created within the worksheet; an embedded chart may be viewed on the same screen as the data from which it is created.

Endnote Printed at the end of your document, it is used to document quotations, figures, summaries, or other text that you do not want to include in the body of your document.

End-of-file marker A horizontal line that shows the end of the document.

Entry The actual data entered into a field.

Event An activity that lasts at least 24 hours, such as a trade show.

F

Field name Name that identifies a field.

Field properties Specifications that allow you to customize a field beyond choosing a data type.

Field selectors Located at the top of a table, they contain the field name.

Fields Categories of data that make up records.

Filling Copies data into the cell(s) adjacent to the original.

Filter Simpler form of query that cannot be saved and displays all fields.

Financial functions Functions such as future value, present value, and payment are used to analyze loans and investments.

Folder A place where other files and folders are stored on a disk.

Font size Determined by measuring the height of characters in units called points.

Font style Certain changes in the appearance of a font, such as bold, italic, and underline.

Fonts Designs of type.

Footer Text that is printed at the bottom of the page.

Footnote Printed at the bottom of each page of your document, it is used to document quotations, figures, summaries, or other text that you do not want to include in the body of your document.

Form footer Section that displays information that remains the same for every record. Appears once at the end of the form.

Form header Section that displays information that remains the same for every record. Appears once at beginning of form.

Form letter A word processor document that uses information from a database in specified areas to personalize a document.

Format painting Copies the format of a worksheet cell without copying the contents of the cell.

Formatting toolbar Contains buttons for changing character and paragraph formatting.

Formula Equation that calculates a new value from values currently on a worksheet.

Formula bar Appears directly below the toolbar in the worksheet; displays a formula when the cell of a worksheet contains a calculated value.

Formula palette Specifies the elements to be included in the function formula of a worksheet.

Freezing Keeps row or column titles on the screen no matter where you scroll in the worksheet.

Function formula Special formulas that do not use operators to calculate a result.

G

Graphs *See* charts

Graphics Pictures that help illustrate the meaning of the text or that make the page more attractive or functional.

Gridlines Lines displayed through a chart that relate the objects (such as a columns or data points) in a chart to the axes.

Grouping Organizing records into parts or groups based on the contents of a field.

Grouping (Word) Working with several objects as though they were one object.

H

Handles Little squares that appear at the edges of a graphic that allow you to manipulate the selected object.

Hanging indents A type of indent in which the first line is a full line of text and the following lines are indented.

Header Text that is printed at the top of each page.

Highlight (Word) Change color to emphasize important text or graphics.

Highlight Entry point of a worksheet; a highlighted cell is indicated by a dark border.

Home page First page that appears when you start your browser.

Hyperlinks Links that allow user to jump from page to page within your website or jump to another Web site.

Hypertext Markup Language (HTML) The language or format for creating Web pages.

I

Icon Small pictures that represent an item or object, that also remind you of each button's function.

Image handles Small boxes that appear around an object when it is selected. You can drag the handles to resize the object.

Indent The space placed between text and a document's margins.

Indented text Moves the text several spaces to the right.

Indexing Feature of databases that allows a field to be more quickly searched.

Insertion point A blinking upright line that shows where text will appear when keyed.

Integrated software package Computer program that combines common tools into one program.

Integration Combining more than one Office application to complete a project.

Internet Vast network of computers linked to one another.

Internet Explorer Browser for navigating the Web.

Intranet A company's private Web.

L

Landscape orientation The orientation in which text runs left to right across the longer dimension of the paper.

Leader A line of periods or dashes that precedes a tab.

Legend List that identifies a pattern or symbol used in an Excel worksheet chart.

Line spacing The amount of space between lines of text.

Linking Placing a copy of an object or data in a destination file that will update when changes are made to the source file.

Line chart Chart that is similar to a column chart except columns are replaced by points connected by a line.

Link Colored, underlined text that "jumps" to a document containing additional information when clicked.

M

Macro Collection of one or more actions that Access can perform on a database.

Main document The information that stays the same in a form letter.

Margins Blank spaces around the top, bottom, and sides of a page.

Mathematical and trigonometric functions Functions that manipulate quantitative data in the worksheet using logarithms, factorials, sines, cosines, tangents, and absolute values.

Maximize button Button at the right side of the title bar that enlarges a window to its maximum size.

Meeting An appointment to which you invite people and resources.

Menu List of options from which to choose.

Menu bar A row of titles located at the top of the screen, each of which represents a separate pull-down menu.

Merge fields Fields in a main document where you want to print the information from a data source.

Mixed cell reference Cell reference containing both relative and absolute references.

Minimize button Button at the right side of the title bar that reduces a window to a button on the taskbar.

Mnemonic Underlined letter that is pressed in combination with the Alt key to access items in the menu bar, pull-down menus, and dialog boxes.

Multitable query Query that searches related tables.

My Computer Program to help you organize and manage your files.

N

Name box Area on the left side of the formula bar that identifies the cell reference of the active cell.

Navigation bars Buttons on Web page that allow user to jump from page to page using links

Navigation view View that allows the user to add additional pages and see the structure of the Web.

Network Neighborhood Shows all the folders and printers that are available to you through the network connection, if you have one.

O

One-to-many relationship A relationship in which a record in table A can have a number of matching records in table B, but a record in table B has only one matching record in table A.

Open Process of loading a file from a disk onto the screen.

Order of evaluation Sequence of calculation in a worksheet formula.

Operand Numbers or cell references used in calculations in the formulas of worksheets.

Operator Tells Excel what to do with operands in a formula.

Organization charts Show the hierarchical structure and relationship within an organization.

Or operator (Excel) Used to find records that meet one criteria or another.

Orphan The first line of a paragraph printed at the end of a page.

Outlines Worksheet outlines summarize large worksheets by (1) hiding data in rows or columns used to determine the formula results and (2) displaying cells with titles, headings, and formula results.

Outlook Bar Located on the left side of the Outlook screen, contains icons to access the features in Outlook.

Overtype mode Allows you to replace existing text with the new text that is keyed.

P

Page break Separates one page from the next.

Page view View that allows user to edit Web pages.

Pane An area of a split window that contains separate scroll bars to allow you to move through that part of the document.

Pie chart Chart that shows the relationship of a part to a whole.

Placeholder Space reserved in your presentation for information such as text, columns, clip art, and graphs.

Point-and-click method Constructs a cell formula in Excel by clicking on the cell you want to reference rather than keying the reference.

Points Unit for measuring type size, with 1 pt = $1/72^{nd}$ of an inch.

Primary key Field that contains a value which uniquely identifies each record.

Protecting Prevents accidental changes from being made to a worksheet; in a protected worksheet, data cannot be added, removed, or edited until the protection is removed.

Publications by Design Series of documents that incorporate the same design.

Publications by Wizard Predesigned templates that provide a framework for a publication.

Pull-down menu A list of commands that appears below each title in the menu bar.

Q

Query A search method that allows complex searches of a database.

Quick Launch toolbar Contains icons so you can display the desktop or quickly start frequently used programs.

R

Random access memory (RAM) Temporary storage in a computer; data and programs stored in RAM are lost when the computer is turned off.

Range Selected group of cells on a worksheet identified by the cell in the upper left corner and the cell in the lower right corner, separated by a colon (for example, A3:C5).

Read-only file File that can be viewed but not changed.

Record Complete set of database fields.

Record pointer The pointer that Access uses internally to keep track of the current record.

Record selectors Located to the left of a record's first field.

Recurring event Occurs every so many days, weeks, or months.

Recycle Bin Place to get rid of files or folders that are no longer needed.

Relationship Link between tables that have a common field, allowing you to create forms, queries and reports using fields from all tables in the relationship.

Relative cell reference Cell reference that adjusts to a new location when copied or moved.

Resources Any equipment needed in a meeting, such as a conference room, computer, or projector.

Restore button Button at the right side of the title bar that returns a maximized window to its previous size.

Rotated text Displays text at an angle within a cell of a worksheet.

Route Sending a presentation via e-mail for others to view.

Rows Appear horizontally in a worksheet and are identified by numbers on the left side of the worksheet window.

Ruler Allows you to quickly change indentions, tabs, and margins.

S

Sans serif A font that does not have serifs.

Save Process of storing a file on disk.

Scale Resizing a graphic so that its proportions are correct.

Scatter chart Chart that shows the relationship of two categories of data.

Scroll arrows Moves the window in that direction over the contents of the window when

Scroll bars Located at the bottom and right sides of the window, they allow you to move quickly to other areas of the document.

Scroll box Small box in the scroll bar that indicates your position within the contents of the window.

Search criteria In a query, it's the information for which you are searching.

Sections A part of a document that controls a column format.

Selecting Highlighting a block of text.

Serifs Small lines at the ends of the characters.

Shift-clicking Holding down the Shift key while clicking the mouse. Can be used to select more than one object.

Slide master Controls the formatting for all slides in a presentation.

Slide transitions Manner in which one slide is removed from the screen and the next one appears.

Sorting Arranges a list of words or numbers in ascending order (*a to z; smallest to largest*) or in descending order (*z to a; largest to smallest*).

Source File or application from which you transfer information to a destination file or application.

Source file File you are moving data *from* when moving data between applications.

Spreadsheet Grid of rows and columns containing numbers, text, and formulas; the purpose of a spreadsheet is to solve problems that involve numbers.

Standard toolbar Contains buttons used to perform common word processing tasks.

Start Button on the taskbar that brings up menus with a variety of options.

Statistical functions Functions used to describe large quantities of data such as the average, standard deviation, or variance of a range of data.

Status bar A bar located at the bottom of the editing screen that tells you what portion of the document is shown on the screen and the location of the insertion point, as well as displaying the status of certain Word features.

Style A predefined set of formatting options that have been named and saved.

Subdatasheet In tables that are related, you can show records from one table in the related record in the primary table.

T

Table An arrangement of data in rows and columns, similar to a spreadsheet.

Tabs Mark the place the insertion point will stop when the Tab key is pressed.

Task Any activity you want to perform and monitor to completion.

Taskbar A bar located at the bottom of the Windows 98 screens that shows the Start button, the Quick Launch toolbar and all open programs.

TaskPad Located on the Calendar screen, displays the task list.

Template A file that contains page and paragraph formatting and text that you can customize to create a new document similar to but slightly different from the original.

Theme Allows user to apply design and color themes to either a single page or to an entire Web site.

Thesaurus A useful feature for finding a synonym, or a word with a similar meaning, for a word in your document.

Title bar Bar at the top of every window that contains the name of the open program, window, document, or folder.

Triple-clicking Pressing the left mouse button three times in a row quickly.

U

Unbound control Control on a form or report that is not connected to a field in a table. Can contain text, like a title, or a graphic.

Uniform Resource Locators (URLs) Internet addresses that identify hypertext documents.

V

View buttons At the lower left corner of the document window, these buttons allow you to quickly change between Normal, Web Layout, Print Layout, and Outline view.

Web browser Software used to display Web pages on your computer monitor.

Web page Combines text with audio, video, and animation in a graphical format that can be viewed on the Internet.

Wizard Similar to a template, it asks you questions and creates a document based on your answers.

Word processing The use of a computer and software to produce written documents such as letters, memos, forms, and reports.

Word wrap A feature that automatically wraps words around to the next line when they will not fit on the current line.

Workbook Collection of related worksheets in Excel.

Worksheet Computerized spreadsheet in Excel; a grid of rows and columns containing numbers, text, and formulas.

World Wide Web System of computers that share information by means of hypertext links.

Wrapped text Begins a new line within the cell of a worksheet when the data exceeds the width of a column.

marquees, on Web pages, PF-23 to PF-24
masters
    displaying, IP-29
    editing, IP-29
    handout, IP-29
    notes, IP-29
    slide, IP-29
    title, IP-29
mathematical functions, IE-75, IE-158
    to IE-159
MAX function, IE-77
Meeting dialog box, IO-13
meetings
    resources, IO-12
    scheduling, IO-12 to IO-13
memory, RAM (random access
    memory), IW-8
menu bars
    Excel, IE-3
    Word, IW-3, IW-4
menus
    arrows on, IW-5
    choosing commands from, IW-5
    commands on, IN-7
    expanded, IW-5
    in PowerPoint, IP-6
    pull-down, IW-5
    in Word, IW-5
Merge dialog box, IW-158, IA-112
merge fields, IW-155, IA-108, IA-109
merging cells
    in Word tables, IW-149, IW-151
    in worksheets, IE-18
    See also mail merge
Microsoft Access. *See* Access
Microsoft Clip Gallery, IP-9, IP-10
Microsoft Excel. *See* Excel
Microsoft FrontPage. *See* FrontPage
Microsoft Graph, IP-43
Microsoft Office 2000. *See* Office 2000
Microsoft Organization Chart, IP-39
Microsoft Outlook. *See* Outlook
Microsoft PowerPoint. *See* PowerPoint
Microsoft Publisher. *See* Publisher
Microsoft Publisher Catalog dialog
    box, PF-2, PF-3
Microsoft Web site, IN-2
Microsoft Word. *See* Word
MIN function, IE-77
mixed cell references, IE-60
modifying. *See* changing; editing
modules, IA-5
More Buttons list, IW-5
mouse
    double-clicking, IW-18
    dragging and dropping, IW-24
    moving highlight in worksheets,
      IE-5
    navigating in tables, IA-15, IA-26
    selecting text, IW-18
    shift-clicking, IW-18, IW-93, IP-49
    triple-clicking, IW-18
    See also dragging and dropping
mouse pointer
    IN-beam, IW-4
    in presentations, IP-62

    in Word documents, IW-4
    in worksheets, IE-4
moving
    boxes in organization charts, IP-41
    clip art, IP-11
    data in worksheets, IE-38 to IE-39
    database entries, IA-29
    embedded charts, IE-132
    highlight in worksheets, IE-5
    insertion point in Word, IW-6 to
      IW-7
    objects, IP-53
    pictures in worksheets, IE-100
    tasks, IO-18
    text
      between Word documents,
        IW-120
      in Word documents, IW-22 to
        IW-23, IW-24
    Text Box controls, IA-95
    worksheets, IE-9
multilevel lists, IW-55 to IW-57
multiplication operator, IE-57
multitable queries, IA-77 to IA-78

N

Name box, IE-3, IE-4, IE-93, IE-94
names
    chart sheet, IE-125 to IE-126
    file, IN-6
    form, IA-46
    function, IE-73
    query, IA-64
    range, IE-93
    report, IA-92
    table, IA-12
    Web page, PF-18
    See also field names
The Nature Conservancy, IE-8
navigating
    in presentations, IP-5, IP-62
    tables
      buttons, IA-25 to IA-26
      in Datasheet view, IA-15
      forms, IA-47 to IA-48
Navigation Bar Properties dialog box,
    PF-20
navigation bars, on Web pages, PF-20
Navigation view, FrontPage, PF-17,
    PF-18
New dialog box
    Access, IA-7
    FrontPage, PF-17
    Word, IW-140, IW-141
New Folder dialog box, IW-8, IW-9
New Form dialog box, IA-43
New Office Document dialog box, IW-3
    General tab, IN-3
New Query dialog box, IA-62
New Record button, IA-25
New Report dialog box, IA-85
New Slide dialog box, IP-11
New Table dialog box, IA-9

Normal view
    of presentations, IP-5
      button, IP-12
      panes, IP-12
      toolbars, IP-6
    of Word documents, IW-3, IW-4
notes, in presentations. *See* speaker notes
notes masters, IP-29
Notes (Outlook), IO-23
    adding, IO-23
    closing, IO-23
    colors, IO-24
    displaying, IO-23
    fonts, IO-24
    saving, IO-23
    sorting, IO-24
    view options, IO-24
notes pane, IP-12
Notes screen, IO-23 to IO-24
NOW function, IE-81
Number data type, IA-10, IA-11
    decimal places, IA-35
    internal type, IA-34
number signs (#), in worksheet
    columns, IE-16
numbered lists, IW-54
    changing formats, IW-57, IW-58 to
      IW-59
    converting text into, IW-54
    creating, IW-54
    multilevel, IW-55 to IW-57
    on slides, IP-28
numbers, in worksheet cells
    formats, IE-25 to IE-26
    fractions, IE-26
    scientific format, IE-26

O

object placeholders, IP-71
objects
    database. *See* database objects
    in drawings on slides, IP-47 to IP-48
      colors, IP-50 to IP-51
      copying, IP-53
      deleting, IP-49
      flipping, IP-50
      Format Painter, IP-61
      grouping, IP-49 to IP-50
      handles, IP-48, IP-52
      moving, IP-53
      resizing, IP-52
      rotating, IP-50
      selecting, IP-48, IP-49
    in Word
      changing appearance of, IW-89
        to IW-90
      colors, IW-89 to IW-90
      copying, IW-88
      cutting and pasting, IW-88
      deleting, IW-88
      deselecting, IW-88
      drawing, IW-85 to IW-86
      flipping, IW-94